Suicide and the Body Politic ir

In early twentieth-century Russia, suicide became a public act and a social phenomenon of exceptional scale, a disquieting emblem of Russia's encounter with modernity. Drawing on an extensive range of sources, from judicial records to the popular press, this book examines the forms, meanings, and regulation of suicide from the seventeenth century to 1914, placing developments into a pan-European context. It argues against narratives of secularization that read the history of suicide as a trajectory from sin to insanity, crime to social problem, and instead focuses upon the cultural politics of self destruction. Suicide – the act, the body, the socio-medical problem – became the site on which diverse authorities were established and contested, not just the priest or the doctor but also the sovereign, the public, and the individual. This panoramic history of modern Russia, told through the prism of suicide, rethinks the interaction between cultural forms, individual agency, and systems of governance.

SUSAN K. MORRISSEY is Senior Lecturer at the School of Slavonic and East European Studies of University College London. She has written *Heralds of Revolution: Russian Students and the Mythologies of Radicalism* (1998) and published articles in *Past and Present*, *The Journal of Modern History*, and elsewhere. In 2004–5, she was a member of the Institute for Advanced Study, Princeton.

Cambridge Social and Cultural Histories

Series editors:

Margot C. Finn, *University of Warwick*
Colin Jones, *University of Warwick*
Keith Wrightson, *Yale University*

New cultural histories have recently expanded the parameters (and enriched the methodologies) of social history. Cambridge Social and Cultural Histories recognizes the plurality of current approaches to social and cultural history as distinctive points of entry into a common explanatory project. Open to innovative and interdisciplinary work, regardless of its chronological or geographical location, the series encompasses a broad range of histories of social relationships and of the cultures that inform them and lend them meaning. Historical anthropology, historical sociology, comparative history, gender history, and historicist literary studies – among other subjects – all fall within the remit of Cambridge Social and Cultural Histories.

Titles in the series include:

Suicide and the Body Politic in Imperial Russia

Susan K. Morrissey
University College London

CAMBRIDGE
UNIVERSITY PRESS

CAMBRIDGE UNIVERSITY PRESS
Cambridge, New York, Melbourne, Madrid, Cape Town,
Singapore, São Paulo, Delhi, Tokyo, Mexico City

Cambridge University Press
The Edinburgh Building, Cambridge CB2 8RU, UK

Published in the United States of America by Cambridge University Press, New York

www.cambridge.org
Information on this title: www.cambridge.org/9780521349581

First published 2006
First paperback edition 2011

A catalogue record for this publication is available from the British Library

ISBN 978-0-521-86545-6 Hardback
ISBN 978-0-521-34958-1 Paperback

Contents

Contents

Illustrations

Figures

Tables

Acknowledgments

I have accumulated many debts in writing this book, and it gives me great pleasure to acknowledge them here. The generous financial support of the International Research and Exchanges Board and the Deutsche Forschungsgemeinschaft made this project possible. Neither is responsible for the opinions or arguments herein expressed. A year at the Institute for Advanced Study in 2004–5 provided an idyllic environment in which to think and to write; my discussions there with faculty and fellow members greatly enriched this study. Here in London, David King has kindly allowed me to use images from his collection, including for the cover. I would also like to thank the staff at the libraries and archives where I conducted my research in Russia: the Central State Historical Archive, the Ethnographic Museum, the Institute for Russian Literature, the Russian National Library, the State Archive of the Russian Federation, the Central State Archive of Ancient Acts, the Russian State Library, and the State Archive of Nizhnii Novgorod Oblast. I would also like to express my appreciation to the staff at the following institutions: the Lehrstuhl für Osteuropäische Geschichte at the Friedrich-Alexander-Universität Erlangen-Nürnberg (especially Professor Helmut Altrichter); the Slavonic Library of the University of Helsinki; the Social Sciences and Historical Studies Library at the Institute for Advanced Study; the Princeton University Library; and the library at the School of Slavonic and East European Studies, University College London.

Some of my earlier efforts to conceptualize the history of suicide were published as journal articles. None of these are reproduced in this book, but pieces of them do appear, generally scattered across several chapters and in a changed form. I would like to acknowledge these articles and thank the presses for copyright permission: "Patriarchy on Trial: Suicide, Discipline, and Governance in Imperial Russia," *Journal of Modern History* 75:1 (2003) © by the University of Chicago, all rights reserved; "In the Name of Freedom: Autocracy, Serfdom, and Suicide in Russia," *Slavonic and East European Review* 82:2 (Apr. 2004); and "Drinking to Death: Vodka, Suicide, and Religious Burial in Russia," *Past and Present* 186:1 (Feb. 2005), by permission of the Past and Present Society.

Many people have added to this project by contributing references and discussing sundry issues, and I would like to thank them all collectively, especially my colleagues at SSEES. Thanks also go to my editors at Cambridge University Press, Michael Watson and Isabelle Dambricourt. My particular gratitude goes to the individuals who generously read and commented upon individual chapters or the entire manuscript at various stages of its revision: Caroline Arni, Roger Bartlett, Daniel Beer, Sergei Bogatyrev, Dan Diner, Tom Dodman, Christian Goeschel, Kinch Hoekstra, Geoffrey Hosking, Julian Graffy, Hubertus Jahn, Catriona Kelly, Thomas Laqueur, Stephen Lovell, Alex Oberländer, Irina Paperno, Steve Smith, and Faith Wigzell. Finally, I would like to thank all the members of my family, especially my daughter, Elisabeth, whose love and laughter have filled my life with magic.

The sudden death in 2004 of my doctoral advisor at Berkeley, Reginald E. Zelnik, came as a great shock to his many students and friends. Reggie encouraged this project from its earliest moments, and his careful scholarship and ethical engagement have long served as a personal model. I dedicate whatever merits this book may possess to his memory.

Note on transliteration, translations, and dates

I have used the Library of Congress system of transliteration and partially modified old-style orthography to conform to modern usage. In the main text, the names of rulers and well-known cultural figures have been rendered in the more familiar English versions – Nicholas (not Nikolai), Dostoevsky (not Dostoevskii), and place names written without the soft sign. All translations are my own, unless otherwise noted. Finally, dates are given according to the Julian calendar.

Abbreviations

ASMOG	*Arkhiv sudebnoi meditsiny i obshchestvennoi gigieny*
BE	*Entsiklopedicheskii slovar' Brokgaus i Efron*, 84 vols. (SPb, 1890–1907)
d.	delo (file)
EM	Etnograficheskii muzei
f.	fond (collection)
GANO	Gosudarstvennyi arkhiv Nizhegorodskoi oblasti
GARF	Gosudarstvennyi arkhiv Rossiiskoi federatsii
l., ll.	list, list'ia (folio, folios)
IRLI	Institut russkoi literatury (Pushkinskii dom)
op.	opis' (inventory)
OPNiEP	*Obozrenie psikhiatrii, nevrologii, i eksperimental'noi psikhologii*
PSS	*Polnoe sobranie sochinenii*
PSZ	*Polnoe sobranie zakonov*
RAPKMB	*Russkii arkhiv patologii, klinicheskoi meditsiny i bakteriologii*
RGADA	Rossiiskii gosudarstvennyi arkhiv drevnykh aktov
RGB	Rossiiskaia gosudarstvennaia biblioteka: Rukopisnyi otdel
RGIA	Rossiiskii gosudarstvennyi istoricheskii arkhiv
RP	*Russkie pisateli 1800–1917: biograficheskii slovar'*, 4 vols. to date (Moscow, 1989–99).
SPb	St. Petersburg
SSSM	*Sbornik sochinenii po sudebnoi meditsine, sudebnoi psikhiatrii, meditsinskoi politsii, obshchestvennoi gigiene, epidemiologii, meditsinskoi geografii i meditsinskoi statistike*
SZ	*Svod zakonov*
TS	Vladimir Dal', *Tolkovyi slovar' zhivogo velikorusskogo iazyka*, 4 vols. (reprint: Moscow, 1994)
TsGIA SPb	Tsentral'nyi gosudarstvennyi istoricheskii arkhiv, g. S.-Peterburga
VKSPN	*Vestnik klinicheskoi i sudebnoi psikhiatrii i nevropatologii*
VNPM	*Voprosy nervno-psikhicheskoi meditsiny*

VOGSPM	*Vestnik obshchestvennoi gigieny, sudebnoi i prakticheskoi meditsiny*
VPKAG	*Vestnik psikhologii, kriminal'noi antropologii i gipnotezii*
VSMOG	*Vestnik sudebnoi meditsiny i obshchestvennoi gigieny*
ZhMVD	*Zhurnal Ministerstva vnutrennykh del*
ZhMNP	*Zhurnal Ministerstva narodnogo prosveshcheniia*
ZhROONZ	*Zhurnal Russkogo Obshchestva okhraneniia narodnogo zdraviia*

Introduction

> [T]he general is not thought about with passion but with a comfortable superficiality. The exception, on the other hand, thinks the general with intense passion.
>
> Søren Kierkegaard, *Repetition*, 1843

> Sovereign is he who decides on the exception.
>
> Carl Schmitt, *Political Theology*, 1922

> [T]he "state of exception" in which we live is not the exception but the rule.
>
> Walter Benjamin, *Theses on the Philosophy of History*, 1940

Suicide is an exception. Only a small minority of people actively seek death. This fact renders suicide unusual and particular. Yet its particularity rests not on the numbers of such deaths. Throughout European history, self-killing has also been regarded as a special – and usually a terrible – way to die. It has formed not just a deviation from normalcy but also an assault upon it. Modern Western societies now tend to see suicide as the consequence of a mental illness or depression that has undermined the "natural instinct" to preserve life. While many suicides may indeed be related to illness, this approach renders the decision to die intrinsically pathological, even trivial, because it disputes the potential of ethical choice and reflexivity. Another feature of recent times, in contrast, is the contentious debate about the "right to die," a right that is typically circumscribed to those instances when disease or incapacity has already destroyed the "quality" of life. This exception (to the exception) confirms the tautological norm prevalent today: healthy people would not choose to take their own lives, unless they were not healthy. Life thereby becomes the ultimate value, the right to reject it denied. The historian Lisa Lieberman argues that modern, medical concepts take the defiance out of suicide by excluding the act from the bounds of the normal.[1]

To claim defiance as a quality of suicide is not to read all suicides as political or even willful acts. Only a small number are explicitly defiant. Among the most famous cases is that of Jan Palach, who, in January 1969, set himself

---

[1] Lisa Lieberman, *Leaving You: The Cultural Meaning of Suicide* (New York, 2003). Compare the different approach of psychiatrist Kay Redfield Jamison, *Night Falls Fast: Understanding Suicide* (New York, 1999).

on fire in Prague's Wenceslas Square as a demonstration against the invasion of Czechoslovakia by Warsaw Pact troops. Yet Palach was himself concerned that his act should be viewed not as a suicide but as a protest, an archetypical distinction predicated here upon the opposition of the personal and pathological to the political and conscious.[2] Agency and ethics were thereby excluded from the category of suicide but attributed to the heroic feat of political action. In contrast to Palach's case, the defiance in suicide is usually only implicit: to reject life is to challenge its meaning and its order. This challenge has historically demanded a response. In medieval and early-modern Christianity, roughly since the era of St. Augustine, both life and death were considered prerogatives of the sovereign, that is, of God who determined the duration of man's worldly existence. Within the sphere of earthly affairs, the divinely constituted sovereign power likewise claimed a monopoly upon the right to take or to give life: to declare war, to execute criminals, or to bestow the gift of clemency.[3] Intentional suicide was consequently conceived as a mortal sin and a heinous crime, an act of insubordination against God's dominion that was often linked to demonic forces. Its consequence was eternal perdition. In a noteworthy distinction to contemporary times, the defiance of self-murder was fully acknowledged, for this framed the rituals of exclusion. The bodies of suicides were not buried in the consecrated ground of the church cemetery but interred profanely, without commemoration, and sometimes desecrated. The symbolic erasure of these lives reaffirmed the rightful order and authority.[4]

On the eve of the modern era, attitudes first hardened, and the enforcement of the legal prohibitions grew more severe; but then they slowly softened, and these rituals began a long process of decline. Philosophers condemned superstition, writers penned sympathetic portraits of suicidal heroes and heroines, and newspapers reported incidents within the context of everyday social and economic life. By the mid-nineteenth century, criminal statutes across Europe had usually been liberalized and often eliminated altogether. Simultaneously, suicide was becoming the object of two new scientific disciplines, moral statistics and psychiatry, both of which disputed the agency of the act. By locating its causes in the social environment or human physiology (and later the psyche), they cast suicide as a social problem and a medical pathology, either way as an abnormality requiring expert intervention.

Self-killing did not fully lose its defiance, however, despite these many transformations. In analogy with changing notions of political sovereignty, it was

---

[2] See the following website (consulted July 19, 2005) that likewise includes information on several other suicides inspired by Palach: http://archiv.radio.cz/palach99/eng/.

[3] See Michel Foucault's brief discussion of death, sovereignty, and bio-politics in his *The History of Sexuality*, vol. 1, trans. Robert Hurley (New York, 1990), 139–45.

[4] See the masterly studies by Alexander Murray, *Suicide in the Middle Ages*, 2 vols. (Oxford, 1998, 2000).

no longer situated within the primary domain of divine authority but instead inserted into the space between individual (moral) autonomy and social duty. The public debates drew upon the categories of ancient philosophy, natural law, and the social contract to produce arguments both for and against suicide. When life becomes a burden due to illness or infirmity, it was claimed, for example, then we have the right to relinquish it. More recently, the political philosopher Giorgio Agamben has noted the parallel between suicide and the sovereign decision on the state of exception, that is, the most fundamental act of sovereignty that lies in the very suspension of law.[5] Such a notion of suicide as the decisive expression of man's autonomy has underpinned some of the greatest literary and philosophical works of the nineteenth and twentieth centuries. In his exploration of the consequences of a God-less world, Fedor Dostoevsky provided perhaps the paradigmatic account in his anti-hero, Kirillov, for whom shooting himself represented "the fullest point of his self-will," even his transfiguration into God.[6] Later existentialists would define suicide as a problem integral to human freedom and the assertion of meaning, a conceptual frame that has also shaped some well-known suicides among writers and artists.[7] The concepts governing suicide have thus changed dramatically over the last centuries.

The history of suicide now forms a large field in its own right. The first studies generally concentrated on intellectual debates, literary representations, and law.[8] More recent works have broadened their scope in an attempt to grapple with the complex character and dynamics of change itself. This narrative – so briefly and schematically sketched above – fits easily into the conventional periodization of European history, and it has often been told as the story of modernity. "From Sin to Insanity" is the title of a recent collection of articles on suicide in early-modern Europe, when "modern" suicide, "suicide as we know it – decriminalized, secularized, and medicalized – [took] hold among

---

[5] Giorgio Agamben, *Homo Sacer: Sovereign Power and Bare Life*, trans. Daniel Heller Roazen (Stanford, 1998), 136.

[6] Dostoevsky frequently returned to the theme of suicide, especially in his novel, *The Demons*. The best analysis of his views is Irina Paperno, *Suicide as a Cultural Institution in Dostoevsky's Russia* (Ithaca, N.Y., 1997).

[7] The now classic work is Albert Camus, *The Myth of Sisyphus*, trans. Justin O'Brien (London, 1955). See also the essays of Jean Améry, who conceived suicide as an act defining our humanity and who ultimately died by his own hand: *On Suicide: A Discourse on Voluntary Death*, trans. John D. Barlow (Bloomington, Ind., 1999).

[8] Among the most important early works are A. Bayet, *Le Suicide et la morale* (Paris, 1922); Henry Romilly Fedden, *Suicide: A Social and Historical Study* (London, 1938); A. Alvarez, *The Savage God: A Study of Suicide* (London, 1971); and John McManners, *Death and the Enlightenment: Changing Attitudes toward Death among Christians and Unbelievers in the Eighteenth Century* (Oxford, 1981). For recent bibliographies (and discussions), see the following websites (consulted July 19, 2005): http://plato.stanford.edu/entries/suicide/#Bib and http://home.olemiss.edu/~hswatt/biblsuic.html.

Europeans."[9] This general paradigm has also been called the "secularization of
suicide," a term that seeks to describe the shift away from a primarily religious
view of self-murder, the growing lenience in its judicial prosecution (leading
ultimately to its decriminalization), and the development of social and medical
explanations for the act. That suicide continued to be viewed as a sin was noted
only in passing for the primary interest lay in conceptualizing the dynamic
progression toward the secular and modern.[10] Among the many virtues of this
approach has been its approach to suicide as culturally and historically variable. Attention has focused upon its meanings and representations, its religious
and judicial regulation, and how these have evolved over time. Furthermore,
it has placed suicide in the center of the historical process, shaped within the
complex interplay of religious, political, legal, social, scientific, and cultural
developments.

A second strand of historiography has focused more on the modern period,
especially the nineteenth century. Many of these works have continued to follow – implicitly or explicitly – the narrative of secularization, examining, for
example, the displacement of religious views with the rise of sociological and
medical-psychiatric paradigms.[11] Other studies have instead applied the methods of statistical sociology, most importantly the theories of Emile Durkheim
and his followers. These works have refined the sociological model, sometimes
even undermining long-held assumptions.[12] But they also rely upon statistics,
which are unreliable in light of variations in the compilation of data (including

[9] The articles in this collection range widely over the European continent (though not Russia). See
the editor's introduction, Jeffrey R. Watt, ed., *From Sin to Insanity: Suicide in Early Modern
Europe* (Ithaca, N.Y., 2004), 8. See also Jeffrey R. Watt, *Choosing Death: Suicide and Calvinism
in Early Modern Geneva* (Kirksville, Miss., 2001). For other works on the early-modern period,
see: Markus Schär, *Seelennöte der Untertanen: Selbstmord, Melancholie und Religion in Alten
Zürich* (Geneva, 1975); George Minois, *Histoire du suicide: La Société occidentale face à la mort
volontaire* (Paris, 1995); Gabriela Signori, ed., *Trauer, Verzweiflung, und Anfechtung: Selbstmord
und Selbstmordversuche in mittelalterlichen und frühneuzeitlichen Gesellschaften* (Tübingen,
1994); Vera Lind, *Selbstmord in der Frühen Neuzeit: Diskurs, Lebenswelt und kultureller Wandel
am Beispiel der Herzogtümer Schleswig und Holstein* (Göttingen, 1999); and Julia Schreiner,
*Jenseits vom Glück: Suizid, Melancholie und Hypochondrie in deutschsprachigen Texten des
späten 18. Jahrhunderts* (Munich, 2003).
[10] The "secularization of suicide" was the thesis of a widely praised and debated book, that has
justifiably become a model in the field, including for this study. See Michael MacDonald and
Terence Murphy, *Sleepless Souls: Suicide in Early Modern England* (Oxford, 1990), 6. For
critical discussion, see Thomas Kselman, "Funeral Conflicts in Nineteenth-Century France,"
Comparative Studies in Society and History 30 (1988), 314, 319–20, 328–30; and "Debate: The
Secularization of Suicide in England 1660–1800," *Past and Present* 119 (May 1988).
[11] For a literary and cultural approach, see Barbara T. Gates, *Victorian Suicide: Mad Crimes and
Sad Histories* (Princeton 1988). For a study of discourses, see Ursula Baumann, *Vom Recht auf
den eigenen Tod: Geschichte des Suizids vom 18. bis zum 20. Jahrhundert* (Weimar, 2001).
[12] In an influential study, Olive Anderson analyzed contemporary statistics (despite acknowledging
their shortcomings) and rejected, for example, the long-accepted tenet that suicide was more
frequent in large industrial cities. See her *Suicide in Victorian and Edwardian England* (Oxford,
1987).

the identification of suicide) as well as a tendency to cover up incidents due to both the legal consequences and the social stigma.[13] More fundamentally, the social explanation of suicide occurred within the idiom of modernity: Durkheim's *Le Suicide* (1897) was itself a founding manifesto of sociology, an eloquent assertion of the primacy of society in shaping the human being. The point is not to reject the relevance of social factors to suicide but to recognize that this approach is part and parcel of a specific historical configuration. A cultural history of suicide in the twentieth century has not been written, which is a striking lacuna. The making of modern suicide has apparently presented a more straightforward historical problem than the ambiguous faces of modern suicide itself, which have been shaped by the paradigms advanced by Durkheim, Freud, Camus, and others.[14]

Whilst acknowledging many debts to the existing historiography, this book will not tell the well-known story from the perspective of yet another geographical entity. Though focused on the Russian case, it seeks to rethink the grand narrative, which first requires a closer examination of its key terms. In its most basic sense, secularization describes the fundamental shift in the social and political status of religion that has occurred in Western societies over the last three centuries. From the center of politics, culture, and selfhood, religion was pushed to the margins and became a matter of personal choice. This model has been justifiably criticized on numerous grounds, from its top-down model of historical change to its institutional definition of religion that neglects the more nebulous issue of belief.[15] Most problematic is its definition of a (secular, rational) modernity in opposition to (religious) tradition. While organized religion has lost its once leading role in most Western societies, such normative narratives impose a model of displacement upon historical developments. The religious and the secular are not opposing, however, but mutually complicit and highly political categories. Modern states continue to delimit the public domain of religion in a variety of ways; and secular powers have sacralized

---

[13] For the now standard critique of statistics, see Jack D. Douglas, *The Social Meanings of Suicide* (Princeton, 1967). Victor Bailey has instead argued that the study of suicide must be grounded in a complete and informative source lest it suffer from impressionistic and speculative arguments. Unfortunately, his method is hardly adaptable to other times and places. Recognizing the problems in official statistics, he analyzed some 700 suicides culled from a complete run of coroners' papers in Kingston-upon-Hull – a source base that has apparently not been duplicated in England, much less in other countries that lack the institution of the coroner's court. On this basis, Bailey concludes that social isolation provides the best explanation for suicide. See his *This Rash Act: Suicide across the Life Cycle in the Victorian City* (Stanford, 1998).

[14] Studies have tended to focus more on the prominent cases of well-known public and cultural figures. One scholar who is confronting this issue has fruitfully combined an analysis of discourse, statistics, and case studies. See Christian Goeschel, "Suicide at the End of the Third Reich," *Journal of Contemporary History* (Jan. 2006); and "Suicides of German Jews in the Third Reich," *German History* (forthcoming).

[15] For an overview, see Steve Bruce, ed., *Religion and Modernization: Sociologists and Historians Debate the Secularization Thesis* (Oxford, 1992).

certain principles, such as the nation and the inviolable rights of the individual.[16] Historians have also returned religion to modern history, including the Enlightenment, not just as the object of reason's ridicule, but as an integral part of its intellectual, social, and political world. But its intellectual integration into the conceptualization of the modern era remains ambiguous.[17]

Just as secularism shadows modernity, so too does its veiled counterpart. A different expression of secularization theory has been to read modern institutions and ideas – the revolution, the work ethic, progress, nationalism – as secularized theological concepts. Hidden within the modern and secular, it is argued, is a religious core.[18] Such assertions have become common, if often too literal, and their explanatory value remains unclear. Is secularization a description of a process or an actual argument about its motive forces or trajectory?[19] What does the "unveiling" of the religious within the secular accomplish? If religion should be read as a cultural system, how does religion differ from culture?[20] Has modernity disenchanted the world or spun new forms of enchantment? Despite such enduring questions, these approaches allow a distinction to be drawn between religion and the habitus. Concepts initially delimited within religion can continue to shape cognition, behaviors, and institutions, though they also acquire new meanings, roles, and functions. Indeed, the modern world has not lost its interest in questions of redemption, transcendence, or immortality. Despite (or perhaps because of) its frequent reduction to physiological processes, death often retains a kind of supernatural mystery, which makes suicide even more of an enigma.

To discard the term secularization is impossible. Not only does the history of religion, belief, and theology still need to be further explored. The term itself forms an integral part of the historical landscape.[21] By the late nineteenth century, many Europeans believed that secularization – however defined – was a very real part of their lives. They also considered it a primary cause of suicide, which was often understood to be a socio-medical problem of unprecedented magnitude produced by both the declining authority of tradition and

---

[16] See especially the two books by Talal Asad, *Genealogies of Religion: Discipline and Reasons of Power in Christianity and Islam* (Baltimore, 1993); and his *Formations of the Secular: Christianity, Islam, Modernity* (Stanford, 2003).

[17] My analysis has been influenced by the review article by Jonathan Sheehan, "Enlightenment, Religion, and the Enigma of Secularization," *American Historical Review* no. 4 (2003). Among the most influential works on the nineteenth century was David Blackbourn, *Marpingen: Apparitions of the Virgin Mary in Bismarkian Germany* (Oxford, 1993).

[18] The classic examples are Max Weber's theory of the Protestant work ethic and Karl Löwith's analysis of progress in his *Meaning in History: The Theological Implications of the Philosophy of History* (Chicago, 1949).

[19] See Hans Blumenberg, *The Legitimacy of the Modern Age*, trans. Robert M. Wallace (Cambridge, Mass., 1985).

[20] Cf. Clifford Geertz, "Religion as a Cultural System," in his *The Interpretation of Cultures* (New York, 1973).

[21] This point is emphasized by Sheehan, "Enlightenment."

the concomitant rise of egoistic individualism and anomie. Its terrain was the metropolis.[22] Yet ideas about the causes and nature of suicide have been closely intertwined with ideas about secularization and modernity since at least the eighteenth century.[23] To write the history of suicide as either an exemplar or a result of secularization is consequently to inscribe normative frameworks upon it.

Rather than reading the grand narrative, therefore, this study probes its history and historical functions, investigates its omissions and ambiguities, and explores alternative narrations. The point is not to argue that the religious status of suicide remained unchanged. In both Russia and the West, the condemnation of self-killing as a terrible sin has faded (though not disappeared),[24] a process shaped in part by new cultural and scientific paradigms, which, in turn, created new contexts for suicide. But metaphors of sequence and displacement fail to capture the shifting configurations of the secular and the religious, the political and the personal, the social and the individual. Organized churches continued to regulate (and condemn) suicide in the nineteenth and twentieth centuries, though their aspirations and practices also changed as they were forced to grapple with the competing claims of other authorities. Especially important to the modern history of suicide were also qualities once defined and regulated within a broadly spiritual sphere. Despite the influence of sociological and psychiatric models, the act of suicide continued to raise issues of both governance and morality, including virtue and vice, character and conduct. But these issues interacted, in turn, with various medical, social, and political regimes to produce new systems of moral regulation for both individuals and populations. The modern era has thus been characterized by the conflict and dialogue between competing authorities and paradigms.[25] One result has been the creation of hybrid meanings for suicide with new regulatory practices. At the turn of the twentieth century, for example, it was defined as a conjoined vice and disease of the social body (a population), which then allowed for the elaboration of a range of therapeutic and prophylactic measures, from the religious, moral, and physical education of youth to the prohibition of alcohol. A different confluence of factors informed the contemporaneous phenomenon of political suicide, which combined sacred narratives with modern ideologies. Such processes – the migration of concepts between the spheres of religion, medicine, and sociology, between theology

[22] Cf. Emile Durkheim, *Suicide: A Study in Sociology*, trans. John A. Spaulding and George Simpson (New York, 1951). The original was published in 1897.

[23] See Howard I. Kushner, "Suicide, Gender, and the Fear of Modernity in Nineteenth-Century Medical and Social Thought," *Journal of Social History* (Spring 1993).

[24] Despite the authority of social and medical explanations, killing oneself has remained a shameful act in the Western world; it is a painful topic often addressed only with silence. This stigma can be dismissed as some sort of meaningless vestige of sin, but it is nonetheless present.

[25] Heidi Rimke and Alan Hunt, "From Sinners to Degenerates: The Medicalization of Morality in the 19th Century," *History of the Human Sciences* no. 1 (2002).

and politics – require metaphors of conversion and translation, metaphors that evoke affinities within transformations.[26]

In taking the perspective of the *longue durée*, this study does not present a comprehensive review of all suicide in Russia, and some famous cases will be passed over in silence. It seeks neither to elucidate suicide's objective causes nor, following Durkheim, to compile statistics in order to read their social significance. The goal, in sum, is not to establish why particular individuals took their own lives or which social groups were more or less prone to killing themselves. Instead, this study tells a specific story of suicide that centers upon its complex nexus with sovereignty. At its core, therefore, are questions about the making of modern subjectivity. The affirmation of the rational, autonomous subject, who possesses innate human dignity, has been central to modern ideas about citizenship and rights, including the right to choose death.[27] Yet this liberal self has also been challenged and fragmented by other notions of the personality: physiological man determined by biology or heredity; psychological man driven by irrational drives and desires; and alienated man cut off from his essential self by capitalism (or some other external source). Politics is also integral to this story. Indeed, this study contends that suicide itself – the act, the physical and symbolic body, the life story, the final words, the burial, the social and medical problem – formed the site on which diverse authorities were established and contested, not just the priest or the doctor, but also the sovereign, the public, the nation, the individual. The term "body politic" is used in this sense: not as a direct analogy between the human body and the polity, but as a metaphor for the simultaneously political and material character of suicide, its fusion of symbolic representation into social action. A worldly yet transcendent act, suicide embodies both the profane and the sacred, a quality potentially so disturbing that most cultures have attempted to divide the two, to distinguish self-murder from martyrdom. The history of suicide over the last centuries helps to map the contested terrain upon which the modern self and the modern world were erected.

Suicide in imperial Russia

Russia, too, forms a kind of exception. Located on the fringes of Europe, it possesses a distinctive faith (Russian Orthodoxy), large religious and ethnic minorities, a different legal tradition (untouched by Roman law and the Napoleonic Codes), and different historical epochs (the "Mongol yoke," the absence of a Renaissance and Reformation). Only under Peter the Great at the turn of the

[26] Cf. the concept of "secondary conversion" in Dan Diner, "Editorial," *Jahrbuch des Simon-Dubnow-Instituts* III (Göttingen, 2004).
[27] Charles Taylor, *Sources of the Self: The Making of Modern Identity* (Cambridge, 1989).

eighteenth century did Russia self-consciously turn its face to Europe and sub-sequently become a full and active participant in its political, cultural, and social life. Yet the view from the margins can be illuminating. Despite the specificity of Russia's historical development, the history of suicide there reveals numer-ous parallels and intriguing differences. One reason may be a kind of cultural reflexivity. Often convinced of their own backwardness, Russians constantly looked to Europe in order to interpret past and present experiences and to antic-ipate future developments. Another reason may be the particular trajectory in Russia of pan-European currents in politics, culture, and science. Both make the Russian case historically relevant to scholars of Europe, and both benefit from the perspective of the *longue durée*.[28]

The history of suicide in imperial Russia has largely been the domain of literary scholars.[29] The most important work to date is Irina Paperno's study of suicide in Dostoevsky's Russia. Although she provides an overview of law, folklore, science, and public opinion, her book is fundamentally concerned with illuminating Dostoevsky's influential approach to the problem. Paperno employs an interpretative method that privileges the play of metaphor and rep-resentation. She thus argues that suicide is a practice associated with patterns of symbolic meaning that are specific to particular societies and cultures yet that also draw upon meta-historical paradigms (such as the deaths of Socrates and Christ). This definition usefully highlights the contextualized meaningful-ness of the act, but Paperno privileges the cultural construction of meaning as a sphere autonomous from either actual suicides or regulatory systems. This focus on meaning detached from practice fails to account for historical change and effectively renders suicide a discourse, divorced from both its physical violence and its everyday world.[30]

---

[28] Most historians of Russia have preferred to work within established periods, whether the long eighteenth century or the late imperial era (1856 to 1917). Important exceptions to this gen-eralization include Richard Wortman, *Scenarios of Power: Myth and Ceremony in Russian Monarchy*, 2 vols. (Princeton, 1995, 2000); Catriona Kelly, *Refining Russia: Advice Litera-ture, Polite Culture, and Gender from Catherine to Yeltsin* (Oxford, 2002); and Stephen Lovell, *Summerfolk: A History of the Dacha, 1710–2000* (Ithaca, N.Y., 2003).

[29] See N. N. Schneidman, *Dostoevsky and Suicide* (Oakville, Ont., 1984); and Grigorii Chkhar-tishvili, *Pisatel' i samoubiistvo* (Moscow, 1999). For the history of death more generally, see Thomas Trice, "The 'Body Politic': Russian Funerals and the Politics of Representations, 1841–1921" (Ph.D. Dissertation, University of Illinois, 1998); and Catherine Merridale, *Night of Stone: Death and Memory in Russia* (London, 2000). On suicide in the Soviet period, see Kenneth Pin-now, "Making Suicide Soviet: Medicine, Moral Statistics, and the Politics of Social Science in Bolshevik Russia, 1920–1930" (Ph.D. Dissertation, Columbia University, 1998).

[30] By tracing "conversions" and "transferences" of meaning through various texts (scientific treatises, newspaper articles, literary works), Paperno emphasizes the hermeneutic paradoxes of suicide. While her analysis is often inspired, aspects of her arguments are not convincing, as I will occasionally point out below. The themes, arguments, and sources found in this book differ considerably from those found in hers, in part because I have engaged in extensive archival research. I have also deliberately neglected the ideas of Dostoevsky in light of her concentration on them. See Paperno, *Suicide*, 2–3, 11, 17, 204–5.

Suicide is, therefore, a meaningful act that is constituted at the intersection between power and subjectivity. Its history occurs in the mutual interplay of ideologies with practices, disciplining strategies with individual tactical appropriations.[31] This dynamic is exemplified in the peculiar dialogue that often surrounds cases of self-killing. The individual act can form an attempt to author a death and thereby to finalize a life's meaning. Authorial control passes with death, however, when external authorities – priests, judges, doctors, communities – pass judgment and thereby inscribe their own meanings, often literally, upon the body. Yet the last word is not the final word.[32] Although both sides of this dialogue are delimited within the existing discursive categories and practices of the culture, both can also be productive of new meanings and practices. This small dialogue around the individual case thereby contributes to a much larger dialogue across time and space, history and culture.

The book has been organized into three roughly chronological sections. These three periods do not reflect "the sensibility of an age" (Philippe Ariès), nor are they propelled by epistemic breaks. Rather, they constitute distinctive contexts in which particular meanings for suicide were negotiated and within which particular practices and forms of intervention predominated. The shifts in these representations and practices depended upon both broader social and political conditions as well as internal dynamics within the phenomenon of suicide. The first section, "Public Order and its Malcontents," covers the longest period and comprises six chapters. It opens with a chapter on suicide in Muscovite Orthodoxy that concludes with its conversion into criminal law and a secular jurisdiction under Peter the Great. The dawn of the modern era in Russia during the seventeenth century proved a formative moment for the phenomenon of suicide. Defined within a conjoined religious and political idiom, the act of self-killing dwelled in the interstices between submission and willfulness, martyrdom and treason, faith and unbelief. The subsequent five chapters then cover the years until about 1860, when the meanings and regulation of suicide continued to develop in tandem with notions of public order and disorder.

Since the early eighteenth century, Russia's rulers had aspired not only to establish and maintain Russia as a European power but also to organize and shape her population. The myriad prescriptive regulations enacted by Peter the Great are well known: they ranged from the shaving of beards and instructions on dress to the mandatory use of new technologies in manufacture and industry. While the overt coercion and brutality of Peter's reign distinguished

---

[31] One inspiration for this study has been Michel de Certeau, who endeavored to create a space for individual interventions with his theory of cultural consumption. See his *The Practice of Everyday Life*, trans. Steven Rendall (Berkeley, 1984).

[32] A second inspiration has been the work of Mikhail Bakhtin on utterance, genre, and dialogue, though I include an analysis of practices as well as texts. See especially his "Discourse in the Novel," in *The Dialogical Imagination*, ed. Michael Holquist, trans. Caryl Emerson and Michael Holquist (Austin, Tex., 1981).

it from both his model of the German *Policeystaat* and the methods of most of his successors, Russian absolutism continued to be legitimized and celebrated through images of a dynamic and modernizing autocrat acting upon an often recalcitrant population. The specific myths of the tsars – their "scenarios of power" – would vary, but they nonetheless claimed to represent civility and civilization, technical advancement and the rationalization of administration. Consequently, autocratic power remained personal, coercive, and arbitrary. In many respects, this model reached its apogee under Nicholas I (1825–55), but the image of autocracy as a dynamic and modernizing force was by then losing its resonance.[33]

Central to the self-representation and legitimacy of autocracy was the maintenance of public order (*obshchestvennoe blagoustroistvo, blagochinie*), a term that connoted the moral and political goals of the well-ordered *Policeystaat*, the hierarchies of absolutist authority, including its delegation within social institutions (the family, serfdom), and the norms of proper conduct. At the pinnacle of this system was the tsar, whose unlimited power was legitimized through a paternal metaphor – he was father to his subjects. An analogous principle structured numerous other relationships: the landlord and his serfs; the father and his household; the officer and his soldiers. As in many parts of early-modern Europe, the exercise of power was conceived to embody a paternalist ethos of reciprocity; deference, service, and obedience were to be exchanged for protection and care.[34] In fact, of course, reciprocity was often minimal, for the tsar, the serf owner, and the husband *cum* father possessed almost absolute authority over their subordinates, whose obligation to submit was likewise almost unlimited. In practice, however, the ethos of paternalism structured complex forms of social and political interaction, not a unilateral exercise of domination. But public order and social stability nonetheless rested upon the visible submission of individuals to hierarchies and norms defined by such categories as rank, estate, age and seniority, and gender.[35] Proper conduct in public and personal spaces was to be maintained by compulsion and tutelage as well as education. As only the (male) elites were deemed fully capable of self-regulation, they were in turn to act as the exemplars and guardians of virtue with their subordinates.[36] The

---

[33] In addition to Wortman, *Scenarios of Power*, the best general treatments of the "ideology" of autocracy are Marc Raeff, *The Well-Ordered Police State: Social and Institutional Change through Law in the Germanies and Russia, 1600–1800* (New Haven, 1983); and J. P. LeDonne, *Absolutism and Ruling Class: The Formation of the Russian Political Order, 1700–1825* (New York, 1991).

[34] This was a patriarchal system in the sense discussed by Pavla Miller, *The Transformations of Patriarchy in the West, 1500–1900* (Bloomington, Ind., 1998).

[35] It should be noted, however, that some movement between social estates was possible. See Elise Kimerling Wirtschafter, *Social Identity in Imperial Russia* (De Kalb, Ill., 1997).

[36] For further discussion of these and related issues, see Kelly, *Refining Russia*, esp. introduction, chs. 1, 2. See also Norbert Elias, *The Civilizing Process*, 2 vols. (New York, 1982).

military parade – a beloved exercise, even obsession, of Russia's tsars – formed the epitome of the well-ordered polity.

Suicide resonated as an issue of public order – the act was a violation, an affront to it. Consequently, it existed at the intersection between the ideology of absolutism and its everyday practices.[37] The first obvious signs of controversy date to the 1790s, when a handful of individuals, drawing upon the Enlightenment cults of reason, nature, and sensibility, crafted their suicides as public claims to self-sovereignty. Recognizing the defiance in these acts, Russia's emergent public – its small educated elite that included writers and publicists as well as civil servants and officials – developed discursive techniques to denounce suicide and thereby to affirm religious, social, and political order. At this time, the phenomenon was first interpreted as possessing national, social, and historical qualities, which began to shape a causal nexus between suicide, secularism, and modernity. Chapter 2 sketches these developments, paying particular attention to the role of cultural Westernization and the emergence of new concepts of the self and the public.

By the closing decades of the eighteenth century, the government was also displaying more interest in the crime of self-murder, and Chapter 3 examines the development of two regulatory contexts: administration and law. As suicide became an object of everyday policing, it was written up into official reports, which, in turn, became the source of a new governmental project designed to produce statistical information about population. Though intended to provide the information necessary to proper governance, statistics began to mold suicide into a social problem and, inadvertently, to challenge official representations of public order. The chapter also considers the changing legal status of suicide and the patterns of its judicial prosecution, both of which illuminate important shifts in official attitudes. The micro-historical world of regulation forms the topic of Chapters 4 and 5, which together analyze how actual cases of suicide were policed, prosecuted, judged, and punished. These chapters explore both the modalities of personal, paternalist authority, especially the interaction between the powerful and the powerless, and the emergence of alternative modalities of authority around the principles of science, expert knowledge, and the rule of law. Finally, Chapter 6 analyzes suicide notes and their re-readings by officials, arguing that these composed a kind of dialogue, sometimes a contentious one, about the relationship between the individual and the polity. By this time, the implicit defiance within suicide was colliding with the political ethos of custodial tutelage.

---

[37] Few historians have examined the relationship between ideology and practice on the local level. Among these exceptions are Daniel Field, *Rebels in the Name of the Tsar* (Boston, 1989); Steven Hoch, *Serfdom and Social Control: Petrovskoe, a Village in Tambov* (Chicago, 1986); and Elise Kimerling Wirtschafter, *From Serf to Russian Soldier* (Princeton, 1990).

The death of Nicholas I and defeat in the Crimean War inaugurated a new epoch in Russia. Under Tsar Alexander II (1855–81) a series of major social and administrative reforms took place. Most important was the emancipation of the serfs in 1861, which liberated peasants from the personal authority of the serf owner but also enmeshed them into a new administrative and fiscal system. Rather than actively integrating peasants into Russian society, therefore, the emancipation even perpetuated their isolation. The impulse to restructure affected many other spheres, and specific measures included the liberalization of laws governing censorship and the universities, the introduction of local self-government (the *zemstvo*), and a reform of the judiciary. Despite subsequent periods of conservative reaction, above all following the assassination of Alexander II in 1881, the Great Reforms formed a watershed in Russia's nineteenth century.[38]

Russian society and culture changed radically after the 1860s, especially in the cities. As new professional opportunities emerged in law, medicine, science, journalism, and teaching, both secondary and higher education expanded to meet (and further feed) the demand. An educated public took shape, and many of the new professionals – whether public health doctors or defense attorneys – were increasingly autonomous from direct state control. The press also experienced unprecedented growth. With the easing of legal restrictions, numerous "thick" journals fed the thirst for information, and their ambit ranged from scientific papers and reviews of the latest European scholarship to fiction, literary criticism, and commentary on current affairs. Professional publications likewise proliferated, including journals aimed specifically at doctors, jurists, ethnographers, and priests. Finally, commercial newspapers were established in both the capital and provincial cites, and their number, range, and readership rapidly expanded.[39] As the new journals and newspapers competed for the public eye, science and openness became catchwords of the era, a means to illuminate and thereby to transform everyday life. Part II, "Disease of the Century," explores the place of suicide in this new world inaugurated by the Great Reforms.

In comparison to the first half of the century, when it was usually shrouded in bureaucratic darkness and rarely reached the public world of print, suicide became a highly visible and contentious issue during and after the 1860s. Its environment and referent was now society. Because it was reported almost daily in newspaper columns on urban life and crime as well as the occasional feuilleton, its many faces and stories were woven into the fabric of everyday life in the modern city. Central to its prominence was its translation into the languages

---

[38] For an overview of recent scholarship on the reforms, see Ben Eklof, John Bushnell, and Larissa Zakharova, eds., *Russia's Great Reforms, 1855–1881* (Bloomington, Ind., 1994). On the era more generally, see Wortman, *Scenarios of Power*, vol. 2.

[39] On the new world of print, see Louise McReynolds, *The News under Russia's Old Regime* (Princeton, 1991).

of science, which forms the topic of Chapter 7. The new science of statistics suggested that suicide rates had been rising steadily in the most developed parts of Europe, a trend that was often linked to secularization and civilization. By the 1870s, Russia, too, seemed to be following this pattern. When suicide was mapped upon numerical grids, therefore, the resultant charts did not represent the well-ordered polity but raised questions of historical and comparative development: What did the Great Reforms augur for Russia's movement into the (European) future? How was the social and gender order changing? Initially, statistics seemed to provide a basis for political critique and the potential for expert intervention. But answers to these questions became increasingly ambivalent, even pessimistic, especially by the 1880s and 1890s. While its etiology as a social problem was never seriously called into question, its assimilation into theories of degeneration, neurophysiology, and Social Darwinism were producing disturbing new metaphors of suicide that joined individuals, populations, and history. Though long understood as a disease of civilization, suicide gained additional layers of meaning: it could now evidence socio-biological processes – including both progress and decline.

Suicide thereby acquired symbolic significance within the various struggles in this period to reconfigure the public order, whether to secularize the law, to spread science and enlightenment, to transform the patriarchal family, or to liberate the personality – male and female. Chapter 8 explores the disputes between legal, medical, and religious authorities about the causes, judgment, and burial of suicides. At issue was first the definition of suicide, whether it constituted a crime, disease, or sin. From this arose the problem of regulation, whether courts, doctors, or the church should possess jurisdiction over the mind and body of the suicide – and, implicitly, over the mental, physical, and spiritual health of the social body more generally. Chapter 9 then traces the broader resonances of suicide through Russian society. It argues that one of the central issues in the public imagination was the relationship between suicide and despotism. Whether in the family, the secondary school, or society at large, the act of suicide came to articulate the conflict between individual dignity and its social and political suppression. Probing the implications of its earlier association with disorder and its contemporary medicalization, this debate articulated a new set of questions about selfhood and autonomy, violence and power, and the challenge of human agency.

These questions form the heart of Part III, "Political Theology and Moral Epidemics," which focuses on the few years between the turn of the twentieth century and the outbreak of World War I in 1914. At this time, a massive industrialization campaign was rapidly transforming Russia's major cities, thereby demonstrating Russia's irrevocable commitment to a meta-narrative of European modernity. Faced with the triumphal rise of capitalism, a term that became increasingly influential after 1900, Russia's progressives initially placed their faith in its heralded companion, democratization. The revolutionary events of 1904–7 seemed at first to fulfill such expectations. Widespread social and political unrest forced Nicholas II to concede important reforms in October 1905, including the pledge of civil liberties and an elected parliament. Nevertheless, the revolution's achievements proved more fragile than many had hoped. Despite the damage to his legitimacy, the tsar continued to regard himself as an autocrat, and his government reasserted many of its prerogatives over the next years. Nevertheless, a vibrant, new public sphere had opened up, and the government proved unable to contain, much less suppress it.[40]

The revolution of 1904–7 was not only a political event but also a cultural watershed. While it should not be regarded as an epistemic break in the history of suicide, it did act as a catalyst, helping to rearrange its extant medical, political, and theological potentialities to create two parallel and mutually sustaining public spectacles: heroic suicide and epidemic suicide. In its conjoined aspect as an individual feat and a social phenomenon, suicide garnered unprecedented publicity as well as the sustained attention of governmental bodies and the medical profession. The two chapters in this section seek to explain this conjunction and resonance.

During the late nineteenth and early twentieth centuries, a new tradition of political martyrdom coalesced in Russia that would subsequently shape the narratives and practices of revolutionary struggle more broadly. Chapter 10 thus explores how the act of suicide became an explicitly public and political gesture. The narratives of revolutionary transformation and the practices of political violence, including suicide and terrorism, were often expressed in a sacred idiom. Images of suffering, transcendence, redemption, and martyrdom proliferated, whether in revolutionary propaganda, memoirs, or suicide notes. This chapter argues that the evocation of the sacred into the world of politics transformed the meaning and function of violence: killing the self became a means in and of itself to act politically. Indeed, by converting their bodies into weapons of struggle, revolutionaries explicitly exploited the nexus between symbolic representation and social action inherent in the act of suicide. Partly in response to such events and images, suicide also provided a rival metaphor for Russia's revolutionary experience: the radical intelligentsia was seeking death, some critics asserted, not creating life. Revolution was itself a form of mass suicide.

Violence escalated over these years, spurred as well by the brutal force of political reaction and martial law, which resulted in the perfunctory execution of hundreds of people, especially in 1906 and 1907 but also afterwards. This violent assault of the autocracy upon the nation, many doctors and psychiatrists

---

[40] For an overview, see Abraham Ascher, *The Revolution of 1905*, 2 vols. (Stanford, 1988, 1992); Wortman, *Scenarios of Power*, vol. 2, chs. 12–14.

asserted, had traumatized the entire population, and one of its manifestations was an "epidemic of traumas," including mass violence against the self. Superimposed upon the various political narratives, therefore, was also a sociomedical reading, which undercut the presumption of agency within heroic suicide. This epidemic forms the topic of Chapter 11. It opens with an analysis of statistics, their production and interpretation, and then turns to the most disturbing and controversial aspect: the skyrocketing rates among the young, especially teenagers. The most striking aspect of this phenomenon was not just its overt politicization – the blame frequently heaped upon both the government (which controlled the school system) and the modern city (which seduced, estranged, and weakened youth). Instead it was the persistence of heroic suicide. Though the motives and motifs varied, the acts shared a disturbing quality: young people were inscribing politics upon their own bodies, killing themselves as a means to act politically.

By the early twentieth century, therefore, suicide had moved from the margins and peripheries of Russian society to its very center. This was not simply a byproduct of the massive, simply unprecedented publicity the problem received. Nor was it just due to either its politicization or its apparently epidemic proliferation. Instead, the exception had defined the rule; it had engulfed the norm. This book explores how and why this happened.

Part I

Public order and its malcontents

Those who kill themselves, bestially and swinishly, [are] demonic; but those who suffer lawfully, valiantly and gloriously, are pleasing to God.

Evfrosin, Untitled [Treatise against Suicidal Death], 1691

Following his instructions, his remaining moneys were distributed to beggars, and the priests got nothing. Consequently, the beggars tearfully accompanied his dust to its place of interment, and the priests cursed his name.

Mikhail Sushkov, *The Russian Werther*, 1801

Forgive me that I write this to your Excellency without the proper courtesy: the dead do not know respect for rank.

From the suicide note of Fedor Moskal'tsov, 1856

1   Victims of their own will

If we have died with him, we shall also live with him.

2 Timothy 2: 11

At some point during the sixteenth century, the intact corpse of a man was found and a miracle proclaimed. The remains were thought to belong to the steward Kirill Vel'skii, who, fearing the anger of the Novgorod governor (*namestnik*), had jumped into a river and drowned. His body had then been buried without commemoration by the river, where it was later found. Local residents built a chapel on the spot to hold the relics and celebrated the cult annually in June. When the chapel burned down, however, the cult died out.[1] According to historian Eve Levin, a significant number of mystery cults arose following the discovery of preserved remains, even when their identity was never established, and the popular belief in the miraculous properties of these relics sometimes even allowed the recasting of suspicious deaths.[2] Such a process apparently occurred in Kirill Vel'skii's case: the polluted body of a suicide had briefly become a holy relic. Nevertheless, the disappearance of the cult following the fire suggests that the local population (and possibly the church) remained ambivalent about this suicide cum saint; the signification had again been inverted, the sanctified revealed as sacrilege.

Unfortunately the evocative case of Kirill Vel'skii is a rarity. Sources on suicide in medieval and early-modern Russia are scattered and elliptical.[3] Those that do exist include normative texts (church rules) and more literary ones

---

[1] For the brief summary, see *Polnyi pravoslavnyi bogoslovskii entsiklopedicheskii slovar'* (reprint: Moscow, 1992), 1303.

[2] The preservation of the physical body was understood as a sign of holiness in Orthodoxy. Although she does not mention any suicides, one case involved the body of a boy struck by lightning, typically a suspicious death, who had been buried in unconsecrated ground. See Eve Levin, "From Corpse to Cult in Early Modern Russia," in Valerie A. Kivelson and Robert H. Greene, eds, *Orthodox Russia: Belief and Practice under the Tsars* (University Park, Penn., 2003), esp. 87, 94. See also Alexander Pantschenko, "Unverweste Reliquien und nackte Gebeine. Der Tod in der russischen Kultur," *Der Tod in den Weltkulturen und Weltreligionen*, ed. Constantin von Barloewen (Munich, 1996). On miracle cults more generally, see Paul Bushkovitch, *Religion and Society in Russia: The Sixteenth and Seventeenth Centuries* (New York, 1992), chs. 4, 5.

[3] The historiography of death in Russia is likewise in its early stages. See Daniel Kaiser, *Death and Dying in Early Modern Russia*, Occasional Paper of the Kennan Institute for Advanced Russian

(chronicles, miracle tales, didactic literature). While such documents confirm suicide's religious prohibition and illuminate formal norms, they provide neither a theological elucidation of suicide as a sin nor a picture of social practices or attitudes. As a result, little is known about who committed suicide and for what reasons, its repercussions for the family or community, the rituals of burial, or the consequences of an unsuccessful suicide attempt. The relative dearth of sources is compounded by the absence of suicide from secular law. It did not appear in the medieval *Russkaia pravda* nor the Muscovite legal codes (*sudebniki*) or the Law Code of 1649. Instead, it first became a crime in the jurisdiction of secular courts during the reign of Peter the Great in the early eighteenth century.

This same period also witnessed the emergence of the modern Russian words for suicide: the composites of self and murder in *samoubiistvo* (the act) and *samoubiitsa* (the actor). The earlier practice, which persisted well into the eighteenth and even nineteenth centuries, was to designate the act by its method (to hang, to drown, to stab oneself), or by such general phrases as "to die by one's own hand." This shift in terminology coincided with a movement of religious dissent that included numerous incidents of mass self-immolation. Not only did this constellation – especially the vigorous intervention of the state against the dissenters – politicize the act of voluntary death; it also helped to shape a long-term nexus between martyrdom and suicide. As the case of Kirill Vel'skii suggests, however, this duality had been present even earlier. By the seventeenth century, self-murder was configured within systems of meaning that derived from the norms and practices of both religious and worldly governance. Central to its conceptualization was its willfulness, which was understood as the inverse of pious submission. And pious submission could also provide a basis to celebrate a voluntary death as virtuous. The religious and later the secular regulation of suicide was predicated, therefore, upon notions of morality, moral conduct, and adherence to religious and communal norms.

Church regulations: means, intention, and morality

Despite the later intensity of its prohibition, suicide was not an especially significant issue in the first centuries of Christianity. Neither the Old nor the New Testament explicitly censures suicide as such, and the currents of extreme asceticism and martyrdom among the early Christians hardly point to a prevalent hostility toward voluntary death.[4] Only in the fourth century would the first major Christian thinker confront the issue. Denouncing suicide as both a crime – a

---

Studies, no. 228 (Washington, D.C., 1988); and esp. Ludwig Steindorff, *Memoria in Altruβland: Untersuchungen zu den Formen christlicher Totensorge* (Wiesbaden, 1994).

[4] Even Christ's voluntary sacrifice for humanity has sometimes been seen as a kind of suicide, but it – crucially – formed part of a divine plan rather than a self-willed death. See Irina Paperno,

kind of murder – and a sin in his *City of God*, St. Augustine condemned such Roman heroes as Cato and Lucretia, rejecting their claims to honor. Only suicide under the direct command of God could be justified, he allowed, for Samson's act (and especially its unambiguous celebration) would otherwise be difficult to explain. By the fifth century and partly in response to the mass martyrdoms, the church likewise began to address the issue, and the prohibition would become canonical at the Council of Braga in 561. Those who killed themselves – without any noted exception – were henceforth to be denied religious commemoration and burial and thereby expelled from the Christian community. Despite its absolute status, the Braga canon slowly evolved over the next centuries, and a concept not originally present in the text penetrated religious teachings – suicidal intent. The notion of intention built upon the premise that a person, possessing the capacity to choose between good and evil, chooses to do evil. In principle, if not always in practice, only people who had deliberately taken their lives were to suffer the consequences.[5]

At first glance, the prohibition of suicide in Eastern Orthodoxy shows marked differences to the Latin tradition. It drew instead upon a fourth-century pronouncement of Timotheos of Alexandria that gained canonical status at the Sixth Ecumenical Council in 691.[6] In contrast to the Braga canon, intention was at the core of the problem: "If someone who is not in his right mind lays hands upon himself or throws himself down from a height: should an offering be made for him or not?" The canonical answer (translated from a modern Russian edition) reads:

About such [cases] the priest must determine whether he really did this while not in his right mind. For very often those close to the victim, wanting to secure him an offering and prayer, will tell an untruth and claim that he had not been in his right mind. But it could be that he did this from human insults [*obidy chelovecheskie*] or in some other case from faint-heartedness [*malodushie*]: and for him no offering should be made, for he is a suicide. Therefore the priest must without fail and with every care put [each case] to the test, so that he not fall under condemnation.[7]

The framing of both the question and answer suggests that the prohibition of offerings and prayers for suicides was well known; at issue was whether it was

Suicide as a Cultural Institution in Dostoevsky's Russia (Ithaca, N.Y., 1997), 7–8, 210–11. On images of Christ's death and the problem of martyrdom more broadly, see Arthur J. Droge and James D. Tabor, *A Noble Death: Suicide and Martyrdom among Christians and Jews in Antiquity* (San Francisco, 1992).

[5] The best survey of suicide in medieval Europe is Alexander Murray, *Suicide in the Middle Ages*, 2 vols, vol. 2: *The Curse on Self-Murder* (Oxford, 2000), here esp. ch. 3.

[6] On the Byzantine origins, see O. I. Levitskii, "Starinnye vozzreniia na samoubiistvo i otgolosok ikh v narodnykh obychaiakh iuzhnoi-Rusi," *Kievskaia starina* 35 (Dec. 1891); and N. S. Tagantsev, *O prestupleniiakh protiv zhizni po russkomu pravu*, 2 vols. (SPb, 1871), here vol. 2, 407–9. See also Murray, *The Curse on Self-Murder*, 100–1.

[7] Rule 14 of Timotheos of Alexandria (and rule 178 of the *Nomokanon*). See *Pravila Pravoslavnoi tserkvi s tolkovaniiami Nikodima*, 2 vols. (SPb, 1911–12), vol. 1, 486–87.

necessary to determine intent.[8] Despite this specific reference to the motive and
mental state of the person, however, church regulations from Muscovite Russia
typically ignored such issues. In this respect, regulatory precepts were similar to
those identified in Latin Christianity. In addressing suicide, churchmen focused
upon the circumstances of death and, increasingly, the moral conduct of the
person.

Christianity was not unknown in Rus' before the official conversion in 988,
but the process of Christianization would take many centuries, just as it did in
other parts of Europe. Not only was it necessary to build churches and develop
an institutional infrastructure; priests also needed to be trained and given guidance in the pastoral care of their flocks. The canon on suicide was included in the
Kormchaia kniga, collections of canon law drawn from Byzantine ecclesiastical
sources and a range of other materials, including chronicle accounts and texts of
South Slavic and Russian origin.[9] Especially important for the everyday needs
of parish priests were also canonical questions and answers designed to guide
them in the procedures to be followed in everyday life. The most important of
these in the early period was the twelfth-century "Questions of Kirik," which
contained advice on a wide range of issues – confession, marriage, baptism,
sexuality, drunkenness, as well as death and commemoration. Suicide was not
addressed, but the text did stress the importance of avoiding death in a state
of sin. It instructed priests to hear confession and grant the final sacrament,
even if a person had turned to the priest at the last moment.[10] This emphasis
underlines the fundamental importance of salvation in the medieval world, a
concern that also underlay the prohibition of suicide: life was a gift from God,
a gift that only God could give or take away. Because the conferral of Christian
burial was a sacrament in Eastern Orthodoxy, as in Latin Christianity, it ide-
ally formed the culmination of a Christian death: a confession on the deathbed
followed by Holy Communion. Funeral rites, prayers, and other commemoration both accompanied the deceased along his last journey and beseeched God

[8] A second canonical reference to suicide without mention of intent occurs in the 22nd Apostolic
Rule in an apparent allusion to ascetics and martyrs. See Levitskii, "Starinnye vozzreniia,"
351.
[9] Unfortunately, these manuscript collections have not been published or systematically analyzed. For a preliminary study, see Ivan Žužek, *Kormčaja kniga: Studies on the Chief Code of
Russian Canon Law* (Rome, 1964). The first published version, the *Iosifskaia Kormchaia* of
1650, did include the canon on suicide, as did later compilations of canon law sponsored by
the Russian Orthodox Church in the nineteenth century. See *Kniga pravil sviatykh apostolov,
sviatykh soborov vselenskikh i pomestnykh i sviatykh ottsov* (SPb, 1839); and A. Pavlov, ed.,
Nomokanon pri Bol'shom trebnike (Odessa, 1872), 156. This summary version of the canon
reads: "If a man kills himself, then do not sing over him or pray for him unless he had been
taken strange, that is, was out of his mind."
[10] Steindorff, *Memoria in Altruβland*, 85–86. For the original text, "Voprosy Kirika," *Russkaia
istoricheskaia biblioteka*, vol. 6: *Pamiatniki drevne-russkogo kanonicheskogo prava* (SPb,
1908), no. 2.

for mercy. Burial occurred in the consecrated ground of the church cemetery, which was both a holy and a communal site, an extension of the Christian community.[11]

Generally a sign of salvation, the conferral of Christian burial required an important spiritual decision, and not everyone merited it, as church regulations attempted to explain. An early text dated to the late fifteenth century but containing language reminiscent of the twelfth century thus states: "If a man drowns or hangs himself, should such ones be accompanied? They should be laid in the earth away from God's church, and do not sing for them, for [he] is a victim of his own will and not God's."[12] A sixteenth-century variation adds an additional method – stabbing oneself (*pokoletsia sam*) – but it likewise avoids an abstract formula for the intentional taking of one's life.[13] How should these brief texts be understood? First, the listing of methods suggests that the physical cause of death was itself a relevant consideration, and the verb for drowning could designate both an accidental and a deliberate act.[14] Second, the intentionality of a suicide was not at the forefront of concern: in contrast to the canon, both rules neglected any reference to motives, circumstances, or mental states. Instead, the first text describes these acts as "self-willed," which is an interesting term that will be discussed later in this chapter. The second text emphasizes the action of the individual with the insertion of the word *sam* (oneself), but it provides no further guidance regarding a need to assess motive or intention.[15]

These two hypotheses are corroborated by the 1416 Charter of Metropolitan Fotii, the head of the Russian church, to the Pskov clergy on various matters of church discipline. In a paragraph on death and commemoration, Fotii responded to a question about those who have died wrongly (*naprasno*) and in sin (*po grekhu*) – probably a reference to accidental or sudden death without the final sacrament. In his answer, he explicitly distinguishes these cases, for whom a proper burial and commemoration should be accorded, from those who have taken their own lives:

[11] On commemoration, see Steindorff, *Memoria in Altruβland*. On "good" death, see Daniel E. Collins, "Early Russian Topoi of Deathbed and Testament," *Medieval Russian Culture II* (Berkeley, 1994).

[12] I do not comment on disputes about attribution or dating in this or other sources, for neither is crucial to my argument. See "Voprosy i otvety o raznykh sluchaev pastyrskoi praktiki," *Pamiatniki*, 861.

[13] Ibid., 861 n. 2.

[14] References to drowning could indicate either an accidental or a deliberate act. Furthermore, according to Levitskii ("Starinnye vozzreniia," 356), such references to hanging were also ambiguous and could refer to either execution or suicide. The word emphasizes strangulation. For another example, perhaps from the twelfth century, see "Letopis' Avraamki," *Polnoe sobranie russkikh letopisei*, vol. 16 (SPb, 1889), 301.

[15] A twelfth-century text attributed to Metropolitan Georgii forms an exception for it refers generally to taking one's life and alludes to intention with a reference to diabolic possession. See S. I. Smirnov, ed., *Materialy dlia istorii drevne-russkoi pokaiannoi distsipliny (teksty i zametki)* (Moscow, 1912), 122.

But he who perishes by his own hand, hangs himself or cuts himself with a knife, or plunges himself into water: in this case, according to Holy Rules, they should not be buried by a church; do not sing over them, or pray for them, but put them in an empty place, in a pit, [and] bury them; the Lord will care for their souls as He Himself determines, according to their unspeakable fate, for the Holy Fathers name them victims of their own will, bestowed not unto God.[16]

This instruction also focuses on the physical causes of death (hanging, cutting), though it does add a general formulation ("perishes by his own hand") that frames all of the methods listed. Its main purpose was to distinguish sudden or accidental death from self-willed death. This suggests, in turn, that the differences were not always clear to contemporaries and that the linkage was perceived as a problem. Fotii did not address the motive or mental state of the victim, however, but merely generalized them as self-willed deaths. Once again, intention was not a primary interest.

In the seventeenth century, ecclesiastical regulations on suicide increased in number and length, a trend that likely reflects institutional and cultural changes in the church. In a broad endeavor to centralize power and judgment in the clerical hierarchy, church leaders attempted to assert control over local priests through the standardization of appointments and the supervision of behavior. Local autonomy, which was traditionally quite extensive, was somewhat curtailed. Anxious as well about both popular culture and popular piety – evidence suggests that church attendance was low and that the sacramental rituals of Christian life were often not observed – the church hierarchy actively sought to categorize sin, to propagate the norms of proper Christian behavior, and to combat religious dissent, though its actual success was minimal. By the early eighteenth century, mandatory annual confession had been decreed (some 500 years after the Latin Church) and both parish registers and confession books began to come into active usage.[17]

In 1619, Patriarch Filaret provided detailed new instructions on the conferral of Christian burial. At first glance it seems that he was following the principle laid down by Fotii, for he elaborated two categories of death: accidental and self-willed. The first group – people who die an early death but merit a Christian burial – include those who choke to death (*kusom podavitsia*), get cut by a knife, fall from a tree, drown after having been swimming (*utonet iskupaiuchisia*), or die from poison, though not when they poison themselves. The second category – those who do not merit the ministrations of the church – does not

---

[16] *Pamiatniki*, 379.

[17] On the transformation of the church in the seventeenth century, see Bushkovitch, *Religion and Society*; Georg Michels, *At War with the Church: Religious Dissent in Seventeenth-Century Russia* (Stanford, 1999); Max Okenfuss, *The Rise and Fall of Latin Humanism in Early-Modern Russia: Pagan Authors, Ukrainians, and the Resiliency of Muscovy* (Leiden and New York, 1995); and Kivelson and Greene, *Orthodox Russia*, esp. 5–10.

quite follow the same pattern: "For the man who drinks himself to death [*vina op'etsia*], or hangs himself, or stabs himself, or falls from a swing, or drowns while swimming [*kupaiuchis' utonet*], or poisons himself, or does something else bad to himself [*ili kakoe durno nad soboiu uchinit*], – do not bury them next to God's church or give them a funeral service, but take them and put them in *ubogie doma* [wretched houses]."[18] Noteworthy is the parallel construction of the two lists: choking versus hanging oneself, falling from a tree versus falling from a swing, and so forth. This suggests that Filaret, like Fotii, was addressing a tendency (among priests or populace) to focus upon the physical cause of death. At issue, he stressed, was not death by suffocation but its context: choking is different from hanging oneself. Yet the parallel reference to drowning points to the difficulty Filaret faced in defining this distinction: the first reference contains a perfective verb, implying that the person has finished swimming before drowning, whereas the second verb is imperfective. Furthermore, the lack of an explicit phrase on dying "by one's own hand" (such as Fotii provided) is striking, especially in light of Filaret's apparent attempt to distinguish accidental from self-willed death. Indeed, his reference to doing evil to oneself is unusual, but precisely this logic governs the subsequent list. It combines several examples of deliberate self-killing (hanging, stabbing, poisoning) with various forms of dying, which, while not suicidal in a modern, intentional sense, are the consequences of willful sin, including drunkenness and impiety (swings were fairground amusements).[19] In other words, the instruction first distinguishes accidents from suicides but then combines other forms of death with suicide into a broad category of what might be termed immoral and willful behavior.

A similar pattern occurs in other documents. A 1658 charter detailed the procedure to be followed in cases of sudden death: a diligent investigation by the priest was to determine "whether he drank himself to death, or whether he hanged himself, or whether he stabbed himself?" In such instances when "he committed such a murder upon himself," he was to be taken to the *ubogii dom*.[20] In this document, drinking to death is explicitly equated with murdering the self. Sharing this spirit, at least in part, was the prayer book (*trebnik*) of

[18] I will discuss the *ubogii dom* further below. This text is quoted in I. M. Snegirev, *Pokrovskii monastyr', chto na ubogikh domakh v Moskve* (Moscow, 1872), 8, 16. Unfortunately, I do not have the original, and the two quotations in this volume vary slightly. I wish to thank Natasha Kurashova for her help with interpreting this text.
[19] Swings were a standard feature at the Russian fairground and carnival, and churchmen frequently condemned such forums of entertainment. See Catriona Kelly, *Petrushka: The Russian Carnival Puppet Theater* (Cambridge, 1990), 24; and G. P. Fedotov, *The Russian Religious Mind*, 2 vols. (Cambridge, 1966), vol. 2, 102–5.
[20] "Zakaznaia gramota Markella, Arkhiepiskopa Vologodskogo i Belozerskogo, na Beloozero, sobornomu protopopu Avraamiiu o sbore venechnykh i pokhoronnykh poshlin" (1658), *Akty sobrannye v bibliotekakh i arkhivakh Rossiiskoi Imperii Arkheograficheskoiu ekspeditsieiu Imp. Akademii nauk*, 4 vols. (SPb, 1836), vol. 4, 146.

Petr Mogila, Metropolitan of Kiev, which stated that Christian burial should be denied not only to those who "killed themselves out of disappointment or anger, unless they displayed signs of repentance before death," but also to those who had died from drink or illegal combat (*poedinok*). The placement of suicide, drinking to death, and combat under one rubric is suggestive, for the nature of intent varies between these phenomena. Nevertheless, Mogila did, for the first time, specify mental states associated with suicide. This is likely due, however, to his interest in Latin Christianity; this rule was apparently appropriated from a Roman prayer book that had recently been translated into Slavonic.[21]

The most elaborate statement on burial was issued by Patriarch Adrian in 1697. This instruction would subsequently be cited by religious and secular authorities throughout the nineteenth century and included in the Complete Collection of Law of the Russian Empire (1830). Like his predecessors, Adrian sought to distinguish between accidental and willful death, and he too linked willfulness with immorality. In contrast to Filaret, he more clearly distinguished blameless from blameworthy drowning by referring explicitly to demeanor. Furthermore, he stressed the importance of investigating personal morality, even in cases of accidental death:

20. If it appears that the deceased drowned while swimming but not playing and not boasting, or falls from a tree, or died an early death without his spiritual father, and not from other hands, and if someone asks humbly for his funeral commemoration, such people should be diligently investigated about whether he had been to confession with his spiritual father that year; and if he had, then bury him by God's church, and perform a service for him as for other Christians [. . .]

21. But if a man gives himself to the devil [*obesitsia*], or stabs himself, or drowns while bathing and boasting and playing [in the water], or drinks to death, or falls down from a swing, or causes his own death in some other way with his own hands, or is killed while robbing or thieving: do not bury these dead bodies by God's church, and do not conduct funeral services, but take them and put them in the forest or in a field, but not in a cemetery or *ubogii dom*.[22]

Disparate categories were again grouped together: demonic possession, self-killing, drinking to death, certain kinds of accidents, and dying in the course of committing a serious crime. At the core of church rules at the end of the seventeenth century, therefore, was less a condemnation of suicide narrowly defined through deliberate intention than a flexible rubric of sinful and self-willed death.

[21] Cited in Tagantsev, *O prestupleniiakh*, 408–9 n. 10. On its origins, see Makarii, *Istoriia russkoi tserkvi*, 12 vols. (SPb, 1882), vol. 11, 608, 608 n. 485. In a 1410 instruction, Fotii also condemned to profane burial those who died in an illegal combat (which is not to be confused with the Western chivalric tradition of the duel). *Pamiatniki*, 276.

[22] "Instruktsiia Starostam popovskim, ili Blagochinnym Smotriteliam ot Sviateishego Patriarkha Moskovskogo Adriana," *PSZ*, vol. 3, decree no. 1612, 417.

Historians have offered various explanations for the association of accidental with suicidal death, which occurred in both Eastern and Western Christianity. According to Philippe Ariès, sudden death seemed a "vile and ugly death" in the medieval West because it "destroyed the order of the world in which everyone believed; it became the absurd instrument of chance, which was sometimes disguised as the wrath of God." In other words, God had struck down a sinner, rendering the body unclean and hence unsuited for Christian burial. Ariès finds that the church fought such beliefs halfheartedly and sometimes emphasized the demeanor and activity of the individual at the time of death.[23] Similar beliefs and fears can likewise be found in Rus' and Muscovy.[24] The scholar of Orthodoxy G. P. Fedotov instead explains the phenomenon with reference to Christian rituals. He links the fear of sudden death to the belief that dying without repentance and absolution increases the chances of damnation.[25] Building on the pioneering work of ethnographer Dmitrii Zelenin, Ludwig Steindorff has further explored the role of pagan beliefs in shaping church practices in the medieval period.[26] Zelenin himself was interested in the belief systems of East Slavic peasants in the nineteenth century, who possessed an elastic notion of unnatural death, a category that included accidents and suicides.[27] Although each of these explanations raises important and valid points, none provides a fully satisfactory explanation.

Alexander Murray's research on the medieval West offers new insights, in part by focusing more on suicide than accidents. Highlighting what he calls the "method-mindedness" of most regulations (especially hanging and stabbing),[28] he asks why they failed to provide an abstract definition of suicide and only occasionally appended some phrase on perishing "by one's own hand." Even this last formula, Murray notes, is a material description of the act rather than an abstract definition. References to the motive, intention, or mental state of the individual were likewise frequently absent, and many suicides – even in cases where insanity was documented – did not receive a Christian burial. Murray

[23] Philippe Ariès, *The Hour of our Death*, trans. Helen Weaver (New York, 1981), 10–13.

[24] See the discussion below of the sermons of Serapion of Vladimir as well as the long discourse on God's punishments of the sinful in *The Domostroi: Rules for Russian Households in the Time of Ivan the Terrible*, ed. and trans. Carolyn Johnston Pouncy (Ithaca, N.Y., 1994), 113.

[25] Fedotov, *Russian Religious Mind*, vol. 2, 89–92.

[26] Steindorff, *Memoria in Altrußland*, 70. See also Paperno, *Suicide*, 52.

[27] His rich material should not be taken as direct evidence of pre-modern belief systems, however. See D. K. Zelenin, *Izbrannye trudy*, vol. 2, *Ocherki russkoi mifologii: Umershie neestestvennoiu smert'iu i rusalki* (1916; reprint: Moscow, 1995).

[28] While Russian texts share this method-mindedness, drowning was more prominent in Russia than in Western Europe. One reason for this may be the importance of the *rusalka* in Eastern Slavic folk belief. These supernatural creatures inhabiting water were generally thought to be women who had died an unnatural death, typically drowning, though some regions also included un-baptized infants in this category. The best overview is Zelenin, *Ocherki russkoi mifologii*, 141–233.

then argues that method (e.g. suffocation) was itself important, and that contemporaries projected a notion of pollution onto these corpses. Superimposed upon these beliefs was a second system that privileged Christian issues of morality, guilt, and intention. Murray charts a slow shift in regulatory emphasis from the physical act of self-killing to the moral intention underlying it, but he stresses the complex interaction between these two approaches and traces the roots of the former into ancient popular beliefs.[29]

Such an explanation also illuminates the Russian case, where regulations were likewise "method-minded," and where a formal shift in emphasis toward moral issues had occurred by the seventeenth century. One of the very few records of an actual suicide (from 1691) points as well to parallel dynamics of judgment (though the lack of additional corroborating evidence must be emphasized): a peasant woman had suffered from illness and hanged herself in an unguarded moment, but the archbishop ordered that she be buried on the site of her suicide.[30] Finally, as historian Eve Levin has shown, notions of pollution were crucial in medieval Orthodoxy, where churchmen often conflated impurity and sin in the sphere of sexuality. The imperative to purify oneself after menstruation or childbirth provides perhaps the best illustration of this, for neither involves any direct transgression or sin.[31]

Yet the Russian case is also particular, not simply a belated adherence to a set pattern. What Murray describes as "moral intention" seems different from the categories and concepts used by Orthodox churchmen. In the West, intention usually denoted the deliberate choice of the individual to commit suicide, which, in turn, implied some sort of mental process (as the legal term for not-guilty implies: *non compos mentis* or not of sound mind). Muscovite regulations, in contrast, tended to distinguish blameless accidental deaths from blameworthy deaths, a category that included suicide but was not limited to it. In other words, deliberate intention or mental state was conflated into morality, both moral character in general and moral conduct in particular. Issues of morality and conduct were often relevant to the judgment of suicides in Western Europe, of course, for a pattern of sin and vice could constitute evidence of criminal intent, but the regulatory emphasis was increasingly placed on intention. The Muscovite emphasis on moral conduct probably reflects the central place of

[29] This is a simplified summary of a complex argument. See Murray, *The Curse on Self-Murder*, esp. chs. 13, 14. Ancient Greek possessed dozens of phrases to describe self-killing but not a single term that would encompass the many specific cases. Instead, suicides were placed in various categories, such as the violently killed (*biaiothanatos*), which could also include accidental deaths and murders. On the hundreds of Greek phrases denoting suicide and the absence of a completely hostile use, see Anton J. L. van Hoof, *From Autothanasia to Suicide: Self-Killing in Classical Antiquity* (London, 1990), 136–41.

[30] Nada Boškovska, *Die russische Frau im 17. Jahrhundert* (Cologne, 1998), 72.

[31] Though childbirth is a consequence of fornication, of course. Eve Levin, *Sex and Society in the World of the Orthodox Slavs, 900–1700* (Ithaca, N.Y., 1989), 46.

honor in regulating social life as well as the absence of suicide from criminal law. An additional factor is the comparatively late appearance of the concerns for interiority that arose in the late-medieval and early-modern West and that would become especially prominent in certain forms of Protestantism. Even as concepts of individualism and inwardness began increasingly to shape religious and secular culture in seventeenth-century Russia, a process that would accelerate after 1700, the ambiguous intersection of means, morality, and intention would continue to frame legal, religious, and popular responses to suicide well into the nineteenth century.[32]

The wretched house

As communities throughout Europe developed their own ritual approaches to the disposal of suicides, these practices were embedded in local criminal and customary law. In England, suicides were typically buried at a crossroads with a stake driven through the body. In continental Europe, the procedure varied: corpses were dragged through the streets and strung up to rot, decapitated and buried with the head between the legs, buried under rocks, buried at boundaries, and set afloat on rivers – souls doomed to endless wandering. Intended to hinder the harmful activity of the suicide among the living, such traditions of profane burial point to widespread popular fear of supernatural danger.[33]

While comparable local traditions existed in Russia as well, they were either not recorded or have been lost to the written record.[34] Ecclesiastical regulations usually specified that suicides be buried away from the church; both Fotii, with a reference to "pits," and Adrian, to fields or forests, provided only slightly more detail. Yet three of the seventeenth-century texts directly contradict each other and draw attention to an intriguing tradition of semi-profane burial. Patriarch Filaret and Archbishop Markell both ordered that suicides be buried without rites in an *ubogii dom*. Literally "wretched house," this term referred to large pits located outside of towns, sometimes covered by "chapels for prayer" (*molitvennye khramy*), usually a wooden shack. Initially makeshift rather than permanent constructions, they would be moved when full.[35] In contrast, Patriarch Adrian specifically directed that suicides not be buried in either the cemetery or the *ubogii dom*. It is thus possible that he conceived the latter

---

[32] Most scholars agree that the seventeenth century witnessed major changes in the meaning of the individual, as illustrated in the appearance then of secular portrait painting and new literary forms. See D. S. Likhachev, *Chelovek v literature drevnei Rusi* (Moscow, 1970). On honor more generally, see Nancy Shields Kollmann, *By Honor Bound: State and Society in Early Modern Russia* (Ithaca, N.Y., 1999).

[33] Murray, *The Curse on Self-Murder*, ch. 1 and *passim*.

[34] Nineteenth-century ethnography points to vibrant local beliefs and practices.

[35] Snegirev, *Pokrovskii monastyr'*, esp. 5–22. Disposal in carrion pits was also practiced in parts of Europe. See Murray, *The Curse on Self-Murder*, 45–46.

as a kind of intermediate burial place: those who had been killed during the commission of a robbery or thievery or executed could be granted burial in these pits, provided they had confessed before dying.

The first references to the *ubogii dom* (*skudel'nitsa*) date to the thirteenth century and designated mass graves around Novgorod during a time of famine. Their existence has subsequently been documented in Moscow, Novgorod, Arzamas, Vologda, Kostroma, Smolensk, Suzdal, Iaroslavl, and other localities. Certain kinds of dead bodies were thrown into the pit without ceremony and without covering them with earth. The list varied geographically and could include suicides, strangers, beggars, un-baptized infants, victims of accidents or other sudden deaths, those who had been executed, and, beginning in the era of Peter the Great, autopsied remains. This practice confirms from a different perspective the association of suicide with accidental and sinful death.[36]

A commemoration for the dead occurred annually at *Semik*, the seventh Thursday after Easter. Initially an unofficial or popular ritual, the church came to accept it, which likely helped to transform the *ubogii dom* from a temporary into a permanent structure.[37] The local priest would conduct a funeral service (*panikhida*) there, and the bodies would then apparently be covered with earth. Over time, the practice became so accepted that even the patriarch and tsar attended the *Semik* services in seventeenth-century Moscow. Indeed, the growing popularity of *Semik* is one plausible reason why Patriarch Adrian expelled suicides from them in 1697. Catherine the Great would finally ban them in 1771. Whether her reasons lay in her own revulsion upon visiting one out of curiosity, as an apocryphal tale has it, or hygienic concerns arising due to a plague epidemic, must remain unclear. Thereafter, however, they did slowly disappear.[38] Only *Semik* remained. In the late nineteenth century, a service was still held at the cemetery of Moscow's Peter and Paul parish.[39]

Though the origins of the *ubogii dom* are disputed, Zelenin has argued that the church elite created them as a compromise measure to mollify popular resistance to the burial of those who had died an unnatural death. In his view, the traditional practice – building on pagan reverence for mother earth – had

---

[36] The church historian E. Golubinskii was so struck at the mixing of suicides and accidental deaths, that he improbably attributed it to the presence of strangers, thrown into the pit so that relatives could later identify and bury them. See his *Istoriia russkoi tserkvi*, 2 vols. (Moscow, 1901–11), vol. 1, 460–61.

[37] Snegirov cites a 1548 decree sanctioning the performance of a general prayer during *Semik* for all who had died a sudden death and interprets this an expression of the church's spirit of mercy. See his *Pokrovskii monastyr'*, 9–10. Steindorff further shows that prayers for suicides in particular were sometimes allowed. See his *Memoria in Altruβland*, 71.

[38] Zelenin, *Ocherki russkoi mifologii*, 94–100, 136–37; and Steindorff, *Memoria in Altruβland*, 71–78.

[39] Grigorii Georgievskii, "Zelenye sviatki: Semik i semitskaia nedelia," *Moskovskie vedomosti* (June 1, 1894), 3.

been to throw such bodies unburied in a deserted place, such as a swamp.[40] Although Zelenin's argument cannot be definitively proven, two pieces of evidence do point to tensions between church and populace regarding burial. The first is a thirteenth-century sermon of Serapion, Bishop of Vladimir. Famous for their depiction of the horrors of the Tatar invasion, which was represented as an expression of God's wrath, his sermons are stern and eloquent summons to repentance. In one case, he specifically admonished his flock for digging up the corpses of those who had died from drowning or strangulation in the belief that the burial of these bodies provokes the wrath of God in the form of natural disasters. As in his other sermons, he blames the sins of the living for God's punishments and demands repentance. A second source dates to the sixteenth century, when Maksim Grek condemned this same response to the burial of individuals who, in this case, had drowned or been killed. He too explicitly rejected the idea that God punishes these burials in the form of natural disasters and again pointed to the sins of the living. Neither Serapion nor Maksim Grek explicitly mentioned suicide as such but rather the unnatural cause of the death in question – drowning and strangulation can occur through suicide, accident, murder, or (in the latter case) execution. Though condemning the actions of the populace as unchristian, they remained silent regarding the character of the original burials.[41] Nevertheless, these texts once again reinforce the same broad patterns: the importance of the material cause of death; the association of suicide with other forms of unnatural death; and the view of the corpse as polluted.

Drinking to death

In the seventeenth century, church leaders explicitly associated "drinking to death" with suicide. The conflation of these two phenomena persisted for over two centuries and provides one of the best illustrations of how intention came to be associated with moral conduct. It even acquired its own specific expression – *vina op'etsia* – that combines the noun for wine (alcohol) with a reflexive verb possessing the root "to drink." By the nineteenth century, the expression would often be shortened to a verb (*opit'sia*) and include a noun designating the person (*opoitsa*).[42] One historian has translated this term as death from

---

[40] Zelenin, *Ocherki russkoi mifologii*, 94–100.
[41] For long excerpts from and analysis of these texts, see A. Kotliarevskii, *O pogrebal'nykh obychaiakh iazycheskikh Slavian* (Moscow, 1868), 34–35; Evgenii Petukhov, *Serapion Vladimirskii, russkii propovednik XIII veka* (SPb, 1888), 167–77; and Zelenin, *Ocherki russkoi mifologii*, 92–95.
[42] According to the nineteenth-century linguist and ethnographer, Vladimir Dal', *opivat'sia/opit'sia* had the following key definitions: to drink excessively (*pit' lishnee*), to drink hard (*p'ianstvovat'*), to die from drink or from excessive drinking (*umirat' ot opoiu, c perepoiu*); and to poison oneself with drink (*otravit'sia iadovitym poilom*). An *opoitsa* was someone who had died from drink (*opilsia vina, pomer c opoiu*). See *TS*, vol. 2, 1757, 1764.

alcohol poisoning, but such a translation is too modern and clinical as well as misleading.[43] Not only does it emphasize the physiological cause of death (itself of dubious relevance in the early-modern period) over the act of drinking, it also neglects the moral dimensions of dying in or due to drunkenness.

Although one explanation for the appearance of the *opoitsa* in seventeenth-century regulations on burial is the better availability of sources, two other factors may also have contributed to its sudden prominence. First was the rapid spread of grain alcohol in Muscovy after the 1590s, when new distilling techniques facilitated the production of more potent libations and may have prompted church leaders to reinforce teachings on drunkenness.[44] Even more important, however, were the broader changes in the seventeenth-century church, especially the growing regulatory impulse within the church hierarchy. Still, the roots of the *opoitsa* are much deeper and more interesting, though they can only be summarized briefly here.

Church leaders had long condemned drunkenness, but not moderate drinking, for they saw it as both a cause and an expression of sin.[45] Some of the earliest texts of Kievan Rus' thus included admonitions to "Drink mead sparingly; to the degree that you curtail it, it will bring you benefit and make you sober." And further: "One must renounce drunkenness, for after sobering up one groans and repents over it."[46] According to Levin, churchmen often associated drunkenness with illicit sexual activity.[47] A parallel association seems to have existed between drunkenness and suicide. One sixteenth-century source describes drunkenness as a "door to the passions" in a reference to fornication, but it also links it to other sins typically associated with suicide, including hopelessness (*beznadezhia*) and despair (*otchaianie*). Not only are drunkards enemies of Christ, it is warned, but drunkenness destroys the soul with the body.[48]

[43] This is the translation used by Christine Worobec in her otherwise excellent article, "Death Ritual among Russian and Ukrainian Peasants: Linkages between the Living and the Dead," in *Cultures in Flux: Lower-Class Values, Practices, and Resistance in Late Imperial Russia*, ed. Stephen P. Frank and Mark D. Steinberg (Princeton, 1994), 30 n. 82.

[44] On the spread of vodka and the state monopoly, see David Christian, *"Living Water": Vodka and Russian Society on the Eve of Emancipation* (Oxford, 1990), 26–31; and I. G. Pryzhov, *Istoriia kabakov v Rossii v sviazi s istoriei russkogo naroda* (1868; reprint: Moscow, 1991).

[45] On the general condemnation of drunkenness, see Fedotov, *Russian Religious Mind*, vol. 2, 100–3.

[46] "The *Izbornik* of 1076," *The Edificatory Prose of Kievan Rus'*, trans. W. R. Veder (Cambridge, Mass., 1994), 25, 28. See also the reference to drunks in "Letopis' Avraamki," 301.

[47] Levin, *Sex and Society*, 57.

[48] *Smolenskaia "nakaznaia" gramota Vserossiiskogo Mitropolita Makariia (Iz istorii Stoglava)* (Moscow, 1996), 186–87. An important though largely unexplored topic is the meaning of despair in the cosmology of medieval Russia. As Murray has documented (*The Curse on Self-Murder*, chs. 10–11), the sin of despair connoted an absence of faith and this, in turn, was seen as a cause of suicide. The embodiment of this principle was Judas, whose damnation depended less

This last point recurred repeatedly not just in regulatory texts but also in devotional literature. At issue was not the moderate consumption of alcohol, but habitual drunkenness, which was sometimes likened to an illness, curable by prayer.[49] The fate of unrepentant drunkards was sealed, however, for they destroyed themselves in body and soul. According to a passage from the *Izmaragd*, an anthology of readings intended to instruct a general audience in the norms of virtue, drunkards would be judged with heathens (*s poganymi*) and idol-worshippers (*s kumirosluzhebniki*).[50] The sixteenth-century household manual, the *Domostroi*, likewise provided a series of warnings about the dire consequences of unrestrained drunkenness: shame, ridicule, violence, loss of property, and even death – for many drunkards freeze to death on the road. "Intoxication with wine brings death to soul and body and loss of property. Drunkards waste both earthly goods and heavenly ones. For they do not live for God but for alcohol. The Devil alone rejoices in them, and their fate lies with him unless they repent."[51] Like suicides, therefore, drunkards willfully harmed their bodies and ultimately destroyed their souls. The potential for repentance and redemption existed, however, at least until death.

Willfulness and submission, suicide and martyrdom

Churchmen often condemned suicide because it was "self-willed" – such a willful death was contrary to God's plan. Yet not all forms of voluntary death constituted suicide. The most prominent examples are Boris and Gleb, the first canonized saints in the Russian Church whose hagiographies appeared in numerous versions over many centuries.[52] In the Primary Chronicle, Boris and Gleb are celebrated as martyrs and imitators of Christ. The story is well known. The scheming Sviatopolk organizes the murders of his brothers Boris and Gleb, neither of whom offers resistance. Modeling his sacrifice on the Passion of Christ, Boris prepares himself with prayer and offers his death as atonement for the sins of man (and his brother). Murdered several weeks later, Gleb prefers

on his betrayal of Christ than on his subsequent despair – his belief that God could not forgive his treason. In contrast, references to Judas in Russian sources usually evoke his betrayal (and sometimes his avarice) rather than his despair. I wish to thank David Goldfrank for sharing his knowledge of medieval texts in two email communications from March 23, 2000. For examples, see *Sermons and Rhetoric of Kievan Rus'*, trans. and intro. Simon Franklin (Cambridge, Mass., 1991), 65; and "The Izbornik of 1076," 32.

[49] See Eve Lewin, "Miracles of Drunkenness: The Culture of Alcohol in Muscovite Hagiography and Miracle Tales." Paper presented at the 1997 conference of the AAASS in Seattle. I thank the author for allowing me to read her text.

[50] Numerous extant versions date from the fifteenth to the seventeenth century. See "Iz 'Izmaragda,'" *Pamiatniki literatury drevnei Rusi: seredina XVI veka* (Moscow, 1985), 62–65.

[51] *Domostroi*, ed. Pouncy, 81–83.

[52] For an analysis of the cult more generally, see Gail Lenhoff, *The Martyred Princes Boris and Gleb: A Socio-Cultural Study of the Cult and the Texts* (Columbus, Oh., 1989).

a virtuous death with Boris to life in a deceitful world.[53] The point is not to claim that Boris and Gleb were suicides but rather to highlight an ambivalence. With the material world depicted as transient and full of temptation, medieval Christian teachings portrayed death as a reward for virtue, a punishment for vice. However, the notion of welcoming death could sometimes veer in the direction of seeking death. Note the language in this example of edificatory prose from the eleventh century: "Blessed is he who hastens to the things to come, for he considers the things that are now as perishable and in his mind is joyously drawn toward death."[54] This is not a reference to suicide, of course, but contains interpretative potential for the vibrant traditions in Russia of asceticism.

Martyrdom could also encompass more active forms of self-willed death. Medieval chronicles and tales thus contain positive examples of women choosing to die. The Fourth Novgorod Chronicle from the year 1372 recounts the plundering of the city, during which "good wives and girls" (*dobrya zheny i devitsa*) threw themselves "from shame and grief" (*ot sramoty i bedy*) into the river and drowned rather than submit to their violation.[55] Mentioned in passing, amidst the violent deaths of other inhabitants, this account contains no censure but only implicit praise for the virtue of these "good" women.[56]

Rendered in a more emotional and dramatic language was the tragic fate of Princess Evpraksia of Riazan, which composes one segment of "The Tale of the Destruction of Riazan by Batu." This famous tale is a fictionalized and composite account of the Mongol invasion dating to the thirteenth century but only existing in altered manuscripts from the sixteenth and seventeenth centuries. The segment about Evpraksia was probably a later addition. The tale begins with the invasion of Batu, who sends envoys to Riazan demanding the payment of tributes. In response, Grand Prince Iurii dispatches his son Fedor to plead with Batu, but upon hearing of the beauty of Fedor's wife, Evpraksia, Batu demands that she be brought to him. When Fedor refuses, he is killed. A servant escapes, buries the body secretly, and returns to Evpraksia. Standing in the tower with her son Ivan in her arms, the princess learns of her husband's fate, and, "filled with grief [*i goresti ispolneny*]," she throws herself from the window to their deaths. The tale then returns to the conquest of Riazan, the bloody battles and epic heroes. That Evpraksia's act was truly virtuous is underlined at the conclusion of the tale. In a long section on the efforts of Prince Ingvar to find and

[53] "Lavrent'evskaia letopis'," *Polnoe sobranie russkikh letopisei* (reprint: Moscow, 1962), vol. 1, 132–41.

[54] "The Izbornik of 1076," 29–30.

[55] "Novgorodskaia chetvertaia letopis'," *Polnoe sobranie russkikh letopisei* (Petrograd, 1915), vol. 4, 299.

[56] B. N. Putilov mentions that the very occasional examples of voluntary death in medieval texts were typically configured as martyrdoms to faith, virtue, or the Russian land. See his "K voprosu o sostave Riazanskogo pesennogo tsikla," in *Trudy otdela drevnerusskoi literatury* 16 (Moscow, 1960), 233–34.

bury the dead, the faithful princess is again evoked in a wholly positive manner: the bodies of Fedor, Evpraksia, and their son are buried together, stone crosses placed over their grave.[57] The resonance of this tale was especially striking. According to legend, the Church of St. Nikolai Zarazskii was located on the site of Evpraksia's suicide.[58] Moreover, Prince Nikita Grigor'evich Gagarin placed three new crosses on the presumed site of the grave in 1665.[59]

In contrast to the good women of Novgorod, Evpraksia is not immediately faced with violence and danger. Instead, her suicide is framed with reference to her grief, or in a variant text, to her love for her husband. This is a remarkable and unusual narrative precisely because the motive – whether grief or love – seems worldly and personal. The episode does not conform to an epic martyrdom, as B. N. Putilov shows, but possesses important parallels to a female image found in lyric songs – the wife awaiting her husband, learning of his death, affirming her love in laments, and, very rarely, dying when unable to accept his death.[60] Paradoxically, therefore, Evpraksia's despairing death nonetheless embodied a kind of feminine submission – that of the good wife. In this sense, her death, like those of the women of Novgorod, was not an act of impious self-will but of virtuous submission and wifely love for her husband.

Willfulness constituted a rather different quality, as historian Valerie Kivelson has argued: "Together with the descriptor 'insubordinate' (*neposlushnyi*), the adjective 'free' or 'at-will' (*vol'nyi*) signified disorder and disturbance, disruptive willfulness." As she points out, the concept of liberty or freedom (*volia*) possessed largely negative connotations in Muscovy, not because Muscovites were servile and passive, but because individual will was associated with "disruptive, selfish passions." In other words, it was opposed to the higher good of social cohesion and the common welfare, both of which were served by norms of piety, morality, and submission.[61]

Precisely this range of meanings informed the representation of suicide in regulatory texts as an act of self-will, an act that effectively elevated the self above God the sovereign. Indeed, the one reference to suicide in the *Domostroi* occurred within the framework of insubordination. A general discussion of the

[57] "Povest' o razorenii Riazani Batyem," *Pamiatniki literatury drevnei Rusi: XIII vek* (Moscow, 1981), 186–87, 198–99.

[58] See the introduction to the (partial) English translation in Serge A. Zenkovsky, ed. and trans., "Tale of the Destruction of Riazan by Batu," *Medieval Russia's Epics, Chronicles and Tales* (New York, 1974), 198; for a variant explanation, see Putilov, "K voprosu," 235.

[59] See the annotations in *Pamiatniki literatury drevnei Rusi: XIII vek*, 554.

[60] Putilov, "K voprosu," 230–36. For further analysis of the tale, see John Fennell and Antony Stokes, *Early Russian Literature* (London, 1974), 88–97.

[61] Kivelson, along with other historians whom she cites in this article, has convincingly dismantled the stereotype of Muscovy as a primitive despotism composed of an all-powerful tsar ruling over an abject population and puts in its place a complex model of political culture built upon the concept of "enfranchised subjecthood." Valerie Kivelson, "Muscovite 'Citizenship': Rights without Freedom," *Journal of Modern History* 74 (Sept. 2002), 484–86.

management of domestic servants includes a passage about the female servant who has been tempted into evil, a process that leads to thievery, drunkenness, consorting with young men, running away, and, at last, suicide by drowning.[62] In this serial logic, suicide was both an expression and a result of vice, crime, and passions. Similar patterns can be found in seventeenth-century literature, when the average person first became a hero and personal life a set topic of literary representation. In "The Tale of Woe and Misfortune," which dates to the latter part of the century, the son of a merchant fails to submit to his parents' will, pursues a life of vice and debauchery, and is consequently pursued by woe and misfortune. Driven to the brink of suicide, he is ultimately saved by entering a monastery.[63] The tale still associated suicide with immorality, but gave despair a human face.

The notion of suicide as an act of self-will also occurred in a passage in the *Izmaragd*, which construes suicide and martyrdom as mutually constitutive binary oppositions. Among chapters addressed to vices, including drunkenness, greed, and miserliness, is also one devoted to the drowned. The text opens with a definition of the problem – a man drowns while swimming across a river. At the outset, the exposition presents two possible interpretations of this event only to reject them. First, the notion that "he received his just reward" cannot account for the accident, it is stressed, because we would then all perish in torment for our sins. In other words, the text rejects the idea that accidents occur as God's punishment for sin by stressing man's inherent state of sinfulness. The second rejected argument touched upon the role of demonic intervention. While the devil can tempt us to our death, the text notes, the final decision – the choice to do evil – rests with the person. This is, of course, an affirmation of free will. The chapter then explicates the "correct" interpretation of sudden death:

If someone leaves his house in winter in bitter cold and dies from the frost on the way, – they die a self-willed death [*samovolnoiu smertiiu umiraiut takovii*]. But if he leaves his house in good weather and is met by misfortune [bad weather] and cannot find shelter, then they die a martyr's death. And more: if someone comes to a river and sees turbulent waves in which nobody could swim but he, confident in crossing by his own daring, sets off and falling into trouble dies, then he is not worthy of offerings in church: he is a murderer of himself [*sam bo ubiitsa sebe est'*]. And if someone, having heard of brigands [active] along a road and as if courageously takes this way and is killed, then he is also a murderer of himself. [. . .] But if someone experiences sudden misfortune, or drowns, or is murdered, or something unforeseen happens, they die a martyr's death.[64]

---

[62] *Domostroi*, ed. Pouncy, 107–8.

[63] Reprinted in I. P. Eremin, *Russkaia povest' XVII veka* (Moscow, 1954). For further discussion, see Likhachev, *Chelovek*, 154–57; and Stokes and Fennel, *Early Russian Literature*, 253–56.

[64] See "Iz 'Izmaragda,'" ch. 82 ("Slovo Blazhennogo Evseviia-Arkhiepiskopa ob utopaiu-shchikh"), 64–65.

Although the categories of this passage recall those of regulatory texts, its aim
was devotional and didactic. Consequently, it sought less to provide specific
rules of judgment than to explicate the norms of moral behavior and to encourage their contemplation.[65] An accidental death could thus constitute either martyrdom or suicide, depending on the moral or immoral conduct of the individual
beforehand. The terms used in this second context are familiar references to
suicide: to die a self-willed death and to murder oneself.[66] The point, therefore,
was to illuminate the moral dangers of foolhardiness, imprudence, arrogance,
and pride, all of which constituted aspects of willfulness and egoism.

Scattered sources also indicate a relationship between suicide and domestic
violence, which raises the issue of submission from another angle. According to
historian Nada Boškovska, women were often driven to suicide by their abusive
husbands (though she only cites two cases as evidence). In the first, a black-
smith's wife hanged herself, and her husband was subsequently interrogated
about the conditions of their marriage; he denied severe beatings but did confess to drinking bouts which had led to various conflicts and incidents. In the
second case, a man formally reported his daughter-in-law for constantly running
away and threatening to kill herself. (She claimed, apparently, that she could
not live with her husband.) By informing local authorities, he hoped to prevent
himself or his son from being blamed should she one day be found drowned,
hanged, or frozen.[67] That many suicides – and not just of women – occurred
within the context of domestic abuse is plausible, though a direct causality can
not be demonstrated.[68] Equally important is that contemporaries perceived a
causal relationship. Some people were clearly concerned that they could be held
legally or socially responsible for the suicide of dependents. Notable in the first
case is that the body of the victim was taken down from her noose to be washed,
a conventional procedure in a natural death. Was the woman regarded more as
a victim than an agent? Though this question cannot be answered in this case,
the plot of a miracle tale is suggestive of broader attitudes. It recounts how two
saints saved a young woman who had cut her throat in fear of her husband's
beatings. In restoring her to life, they erased her wounds, thereby erasing marks
of the event.[69] The woman is clearly represented as a victim, who is saved from
the dire fate of suicide, but suicide itself remains an absolute evil.

Fear and violence were important techniques in the maintenance of social
order in Muscovite Russia. The *Domostroi* has traditionally been cited as an

[65] I would like to thank Caroline Bynum for pointing this out.
[66] Fedotov (*Russian Religious Mind*, vol. 2, 91) actually translates them as suicide.
[67] Boškovska, *Die russische Frau*, 71.
[68] This is not to minimize the abuse suffered but rather to admit the enigma of suicide. Why does
one person chose suicide in this context and another not?
[69] Summarized in Isolde Thyrêt, "Women and the Orthodox Faith in Muscovite Russia: Spiritual
Experience and Practice," in Kivelson and Greene, *Orthodox Russia*, 172.

example of the harsh ethos of despotism, beatings, and enforced submission
that ruled in the household and, by extension, in society as a whole. In this
framework, the political and social order relied upon coercion and passivity.
Yet equally striking, even in the *Domostroi*, is the concomitant emphasis on
both social cohesion (the obligations of being a good father, wife, parent, household manager, neighbor) and social reputation (the maintenance of personal and
familial honor).[70] Historians have likewise argued that the stereotype of despotic
Muscovy needs revision, that the political and social order also encouraged various forms of participation, including the active defense of status rights, honor,
and obligations.[71] Although further research is necessary, available evidence
suggests that the configuration of suicide built upon an underlying dichotomy
of submission to willfulness, martyrdom to suicide. It further operated within a
paternalist moral economy as both a willful act of insubordination and a possible
result of an abuse of authority.[72]

Mass martyrdom and the invention of suicide

Under the leadership of Patriarch Nikon, various changes in sacred texts and
rituals were instituted during the 1650s and 1660s, including textual correc-
tions (primarily of a linguistic nature) as well as the substitution of a three-
fingered sign of the cross for a two-fingered one. Violence subsequently rent the
Russian Orthodox Church. Though provoked by the seemingly minor reforms,
the schism grew upon a fertile soil of social tensions, vibrant traditions of popular religiosity, and the centralizing ambitions of both the church and the state.
Over the next decades, spiritual authorities began to categorize and combat various forms of religious expression as the product of a schism, and segments of
the populace likewise came to articulate their piety in parallel terms, a process
that would shape the movement of Old Believers by the end of the century.[73]

---

[70] See e.g. the following passages in the *Domostroi*, ed. Pouncy, 95–100, 103–4, 120–22, 143–44.

[71] In addition to Kivelson, "Muscovite 'Citizenship,'" see esp. Kollmann, *By Honor Bound.*

[72] For a reference to suicide in the context of contracting marriage, see the twelfth-century Statute
of Iaroslav. In the early versions, parents can be penalized for forcing children to marry or for
preventing a desired marriage, but later versions weaken the provision, a trend that points to the
growing strength of the patriarchal family. This underlines the association of suicide with both
insubordination and an abuse of authority. See "Ustav Kniazia Iaroslava. Kratkaia redaktsiia,"
Rossiiskoe zakonodatel'stvo X–XX vekov, 9 vols. (Moscow, 1984), vol. 1, 168–70 (arts. 24, 33).
See also art. 29 of the "Prostrannaia redaktsiia," 191. For a later version, see *Polnoe sobranie
russkikh letopisei* (Moscow and Leningrad, 1925), vol. 5, 120–22. For further analysis, see Ia.
N. Shchapov, *Kniazheskie ustavy i tserkov' v drevnei Rusi, XI–XIV vv.* (Moscow, 1972), 216–18,
238, 295–96.

[73] The emergence of Old Belief has been linked to the reforms but also to the social, religious,
and political world of seventeenth-century Russia – the hardening of serfdom, the rise of absolutism, and the character of popular piety and religious dissent. See Michels, *At War with the
Church*; for an excellent overview, Robert O. Crummey, *The Old Believers and the World of the*

The government also employed increasingly draconian measures to persecute the heresy. Building upon the full legal establishment of political crimes in the Law Code of 1649, a 1684 decree declared adherence to the schism a crime of state. Those who refused to renounce their faith under torture faced execution by fire.[74] With the struggle now explicitly politicized, one method of resistance was active self-sacrifice. Small groups had already discovered martyrdom through fire in the 1660s, but persecution encouraged the movement. Rather than surrender to the forces surrounding their settlements, groups of dissenters – numbering in the thousands on occasion – would shut themselves in their church (sometimes using force to compel local peasants or family members to join them), and set it alight. Many of these incidents were deliberately provoked by people actively seeking martyrdom, for the presence of armed troops facilitated their self-representation as victims of persecution. Cases of group suicide have also been linked to the influence of hermits as well as itinerant monks and nuns. While the dominant technique was self-immolation, some incidents involved peasants who buried themselves alive or shut themselves in their huts without food or drink until they died. The individual motivations driving such acts remain elusive, of course, but the religious framework of eschatology was certainly essential. With the apocalypse often believed to be imminent – indeed, with the Antichrist embodied in the Russian sovereign – salvation required a withdrawal from the corrupt world. Self-immolation was one such means of withdrawal: it promised to purify sin and to open a direct path to paradise. Another means was active political resistance to the government and its agents, including tax collectors and census takers. As the government demonstrated a limited resolve to accommodate the movement and the number of radicals inevitably declined, the most extreme practices became increasingly rare over the eighteenth century, and the Old Believers turned more to building their own separate communities.[75]

The disturbing spectacle of mass self-immolation occurred roughly simultaneously with the emergence of the modern terms for suicide and the introduction of suicide into criminal law. This confluence lent long-lasting political meanings to suicide. The first known text in which the problem of suicide was explicitly

Antichrist: The Vyg Community and the Russian State, 1694–1855 (Madison, Wisc., 1970); for an interpretation emphasizing the semiotic basis, see Boris Uspensky, "The Schism and Cultural Conflict in the Seventeenth Century," in *Seeking God: The Recovery of Religious Identity in Orthodox Russia, Ukraine, and Georgia*, ed. Stephen K. Batalden (De Kalb, Ill., 1993).
[74] *PSZ*, vol. 2, no. 1102.
[75] See Crummey, *The Old Believers*, 26–57, 187–93; Michels, *At War with the Church*, 154–55, 206–9; and, on the political basis of the conflict, Michael Cherniavsky, "The Old Believers and the New Religion," in Cherniavsky, ed., *The Structure of Russian History: Interpretative Essays* (New York, 1970). A useful overview is also found in D. I. Sapozhnikov, *Samosozhzhenie v russkom raskole (so vtoroi poloviny XVII veka do kontsa XVIII): Istoricheskii ocherk po arkhivnym dokumentam* (Moscow, 1891).

analyzed was thus a long manuscript from 1691 written by the Old Believer Evfrosin, who was critical of the apocalyptic mentality.[76] Using both archaic and modern terms for suicide, including *samoubiistvo* (the act), *samoubiitsa* (the actor), and *samoubiistvennyi* (the adjective), Evfrosin polemicized against the mass martyrdoms. Self-immolation (and other forms of voluntary death) did not constitute a genuine or a valid (*zakonnyi*) martyrdom, he argued, but rather suicide. True Christians would flee persecution and, if caught, endure torture. Would not God give them the strength to remain faithful until death? The model was Christ, who had suffered on the cross until the very end and thereby submitted to divine will. Early martyrs, he further stressed, had been tormented to their deaths by others; they had not killed themselves. In contrast, those who perished in suicidal deaths (*samoubiistvennye smerti*) – he used the abstract term – suffered eternal torments, and Evfrosin further emphasized the possibly diabolic temptation of voluntary death.[77]

Though motivated by the perceived need to combat self-immolation among his fellow Old Believers, Evfrosin thus elaborated the only known discourse from the Muscovite period on suicide. The influence of this text was probably limited, but its polemics nonetheless illuminate a broader conceptual logic: suicide was again constituted as the inverse of martyrdom. Rather than signifying true faith and submission to divine will, self-immolation demonstrated doubt and despair, disobedience and audacity (*derzost'*). Having defined these voluntary martyrdoms as a form of suicide, Evfrosin used the concluding pages of the manuscript to emphasize the consistent and universal Christian condemnation of suicide and its inevitable consequence – eternal perdition. Two interlocked points were repeatedly stressed: the act was "unlawful," contrary to God's plan; and it was audacious, that is, self-willed.[78]

The binary opposition of martyrdom to suicide was not unique to Evfrosin's text, as the following tale – reported by opponents of the schism – illustrates: Having gathered in a barn and taken communion, a group of peasants set the fire. As the flames spread, however, two demons were seen flying over the building, celebrating and singing, "Ours, they are ours." Seeing the apparitions and understanding their error, the peasants escaped and ran to the nearest priest, to whom they confessed and recanted.[79] Such narratives illustrate the tremendous disquiet inspired by self-immolation, which could signify the two extremes of

---

[76] Little is known about Evfrosin. For a brief discussion, see Crummey, *The Old Believers*, 56–57. See also the introduction to its published version, "Otrazitel'noe pisanie o novoizobretennom puti samoubiistvennykh smertei: Vnov' naidennyi staroobriadcheskii traktat protiv samosozhzheniia, 1691 goda," in Kh. Loparev, ed. *Pamiatniki drevnei pis'mennosti* 108 (SPb, 1895), pp. 01–071. The manuscript has 117 printed pages.

[77] In addition to such generalized reference to suicidal deaths, Evfrosin also sometimes listed methods. See "Otrazitel'noe pisanie," 46–49, 79–81, 86–88, and *passim*.

[78] See "Otrazitel'noe pisanie," 108–17, which includes quotations from church regulations.

[79] As recounted by Dmitrii Rostovskii, summarized in Sapozhnikov, *Samosozhzhenie*, 18.

sacred purification and demonic temptation. These attitudes may help to explain Patriarch Adrian's 1697 directive on burial: the first category to be denied rites were those possessed by the devil.[80] Indeed, as one historian has recently noted, the spread of voluntary martyrdom was causing church leaders to regard suicide itself as a possible sign and expression of heresy.[81]

One of the tactics adopted by the government in its struggle against the schism also built upon this same logic: to de-sacralize voluntary martyrdom with the label of suicide. On April 28, 1722, Peter the Great directed the Holy Synod to formulate, publish, and distribute a statement about those, who, whether out of "ignorance" or "extreme malice," harm or kill themselves.[82] Two days later, the Synod issued its exhortation on the "deterrence of willful suffering and the taking of life," that, it ordered, was to be read monthly at Sunday services, as well as during seigniorial holidays, "at fairs, where there are large crowds, and in front of churches as a liturgy for the multitudes of people so that all can hear." The exhortation combined spiritual with political exegesis. In distinguishing between worthy and unworthy (including "unlawful") suffering, it stressed that suffering for its own sake was not spiritually cleansing. Self-inflicted suffering and death did not lead to the gates of heaven, it repeatedly admonished, but to the eternal torments of hell. The modern noun for "suicide" is used only once and in this context: these self-proclaimed martyrs are really nothing other than regular suicides (*samoubiitsy*). It is further noteworthy that the exhortation depicted self-inflicted suffering and death in an unambiguously political light: it was a form of insurgence against God and the tsar, God's chosen representative on earth. Hardly out of context, therefore, was a reference to Bulavin, the leader of a mass rebellion in 1707–8, in which Old Believers had played a visible role.[83] The criminalization of suicide shortly before this edict would draw on the same motifs: suicide was a sin against God and a crime against the tsar.

Absolutism and self-killing

In some parts of Western Europe, self-killing became a secular crime under the jurisdiction of criminal courts as early as the late Middle Ages, and the state took

---

[80] See n. 22.   [81] Michels, *At War with the Church*, 119.
[82] For the synodic decree, *PSZ*, vol. 6, no. 4053, 742–46; for the version which includes a preface relating the tsar's order and the admonition to read it monthly (repeated in closing), see *Polnoe sobranie postanovlenii i rasporiazhenii po vedomstvu pravoslavnogo ispovedaniia Rossiiskoi Imperii: Tsarstvovanie gos. imp. Petra I*, vol. 2, no. 588, 232–35. Later decrees also equated these kinds of martyrdom to suicide. See *Polnoe sobranie postanovlenii i rasporiazhenii po vedomstvu pravoslavnogo ispovedaniia Rossiiskoi Imperii*, 1st series, 10 vols.; 2nd series, 4 vols. (SPb, 1872–1905), 2nd series, vol. 1, no. 618 (June 22, 1771); vol. 2, no. 1163 (Mar. 18, 1784).
[83] On the Bulavin rebellion, see Paul Avrich, *Russian Rebels, 1600–1800* (New York, 1972), 132–77.

an increasing interest in the problem over the next centuries. Partly due to its categorization within criminal law, the question of intent was integral to its legal judgment. In England, for example, coroners' juries were to decide whether a suicide was *felo de se* (a felony of himself) or *non compos mentis* (not of sound mind). By the twelfth century, some kingdoms, including France, promulgated laws on the confiscation of property, a practice that built on Roman precedents. Similar practices are found in English common law, and royal interest in the financial benefits was apparent by the thirteenth and fourteenth centuries. Some German principalities followed by the sixteenth century, though practices there varied widely. An increase in severity, both in law and in judgment, accompanied the counter-reformation and the rise of the absolutist state.[84] With monarchies attempting to limit local autonomy by standardizing their legal codes, many new statutes on suicide were also devised. France's ordinance of 1670, for example, declared suicide a crime against God and king, punishable by the confiscation of property, desecration, and profane burial. Similar laws date to the early eighteenth century in Bavaria and Prussia.[85]

As the influence of Roman Law did not extend as far east as Muscovy, a financial motive for the criminalization of suicide did not exist; instead, the political dynamics of the Petrine era were crucial. Two statutes from 1716 and 1720 transformed suicide into a crime under the jurisdiction of the criminal courts. The new laws differed from ecclesiastical regulations in four main respects. They provided an abstract definition of suicide as the murder of the self, placed intention at the heart of judgment, legally prescribed the desecration of the body, and introduced attempted suicide as a capital offense. Article 164 of the Military Regulations thus stated: "If someone kills himself, then the executioner is to drag his body away to a dishonorable place and bury it there, having dragged it beforehand along the streets or the army camp." The criteria for judging intention were complex. For suicides committed while of unsound mind (*bespamiatstvo*, literally, "without memory"), illness (*bolezn'*), or melancholy (*melankholiia*), the body was to be buried in a special but not dishonorable place. The penalty for attempted suicides was death, but mitigating circumstances included torment (*muchenie*), disappointment (*dosada*), madness (*bespamiatstvo*), and shame (*styd*): in these cases, the offender was to be thrown out of the regiment but not executed.[86] Article 117 of the Naval Regulations was slightly different: it specified that the body of a suicide be strung up by its feet, and that attempted suicides be executed by hanging. The criteria of judgment also varied: in cases of unintentional suicide, committed due to

---

[84] See e.g. Michael MacDonald and Terence R. Murphy, *Sleepless Souls: Suicide in Early Modern England* (Oxford, 1990).

[85] For an overview of the legal history of suicide, see R. Weichbrodt, *Der Selbstmord* (Basel, 1937), 76–82.

[86] *PSZ*, vol. 5, 370.

torment or an unbearable burden (*nesnosnaia naloga*), or in the madness of a feverish or melancholic illness, then the specified punishments were not to be employed, and the consequences were not further specified.[87] While these regulations had initially been formulated for the army and navy, their sections on criminal offenses were also given a civil jurisdiction, and they would officially remain in force until the 1830s (though without the death penalty).[88]

The specific reasons for introducing suicide into criminal law remain obscure, but one important context was certainly the continuing struggle with Old Believers together with the specter of the mass martyrdoms. Yet these statutes should also be placed in a pan-European context. Western contacts and influences had already been expanding during the seventeenth century, and the process culminated under Peter the Great, who made Westernization into a concerted policy. His vigorous effort to forge a modern European state and military transformed almost all aspects of governance and elite life, and both the Military and Naval Regulations were modeled on Western prototypes.[89] The criminalization of suicide in Russia in this period was not atypical, therefore, though it possessed its own particular dynamics.

An important conceptual frame was the new imperial state, which drew upon both Byzantine and Western sources. Peter was the first tsar to elevate the defense of the state to an absolute priority, and one of the central tenets of his system was universal service: each individual – from tsar to noble to serf – was embedded into a hierarchical pyramid of command and submission. Though he did not use the expression, Peter saw himself as the first servant of the state, and this principle governed his own efforts at modernization. With governmental service obligatory for the elite, a Table of Ranks accorded social status, political power, and the opportunity for personal advancement. While this system did not fully displace other forms of precedence, especially those based on family, it did superimpose a rival principle with a formal structure. The concurrent reinforcement of serfdom likewise occurred within the idiom of obligatory service, duty, and submission to constituted authorities. To sanction this system, Peter employed a new kind of paternalist metaphor. As one religious primer from 1720 emphasized, the Fifth Commandment required men to honor not just their fathers and mothers, but all those who exercised paternal authority. "The first order of such persons" was the tsar, and his subjects, "like good sons," must honor him.[90] Not only was the tsar honored as the "father of the fatherland,"

---

[87] *PSZ*, vol. 6, 77.
[88] On the formation and jurisdiction of the Military and Naval Regulations, see Christoph Schmidt, *Sozialkontrolle in Moskau: Justiz, Kriminalität und Leibeigenschaft 1649–1785* (Stuttgart, 1996), 137–43. For a discussion of these statutes, see Tagantsev, *O prestupleniiakh*, vol. 2, 409–10. On the abolition of the death penalty under Elizabeth I, see N. S. Tagantsev, *Russkoe ugolovnoe pravo*, 2 vols. (reprint: Moscow, 1994), here vol. 2, 103–10.
[89] On Peter's reign, see Lindsey Hughes, *Russia in the Age of Peter the Great* (New Haven, 1998).
[90] See ibid., 92–100, esp. 94.

his image was sacralized as the "earthly god," that is, as the law-giver and creator, who had brought modern Russia into existence. Not incidentally, Peter proclaimed himself Emperor Peter I, a title that ignored his own paternity (as in Tsar Peter Alekseevich, son of Alexis).[91] Accordingly, the new statutes on suicide built upon the established association with willfulness and disobedience but also conferred a now explicit political and worldly signification: the act of self-killing effectively denied the sovereignty not only of God, but of the tsar.[92] Absolute paternal authority – together with its duty of custodial care – was likewise vested in other figures, ranging from civilian officials, military officers, and priests to serf owners, husbands, and fathers. This new political rhetoric would subsequently be mediated and negotiated by institutions and individuals.

By transforming the sin of suicide into a crime and empowering secular authorities to rule on the question of intention, Peter was also asserting the primacy of secular over ecclesiastical authority. An additional context for the criminalization of suicide was the changing balance of power between church and state, which had traditionally been conceived in Byzantium as a kind of symphony. The shift toward worldly power pre-dated Peter's reign, but the new dominance of the state now received an institutional expression. When Patriarch Adrian died in 1700, Peter left the position unfilled and ultimately replaced the patriarchy with a Most Holy Governing Synod in 1721. Not only was the Synod subordinated to the tsar and placed within the governmental administration; beginning the following year, it was also led by an appointed layman, the over-procurator. In some respects, the church profited from the new arrangements. It received primary jurisdiction over important spheres of social life, most notably, marriage and divorce. For the next two centuries, the church would defend both the sanctity of the family and the authority of fathers and husbands. For its part, the state used its resources to uphold the church's authority against various threats, especially Old Belief and sectarianism more broadly. Conceiving religion and morality as integral to the maintenance of social order, moreover, Peter (and his successors) actively sought to uphold religious observance by legislating on a wide variety of religious issues, whether mandatory confession or the observance of church holidays.[93]

---

[91] On the representations of monarchical power, see ibid., 92–100; and Richard Wortman, *Scenarios of Power: Myth and Ceremony in Russian Monarchy* (Princeton, 1995), vol. 1, esp. 42–78. Cherniavsky ("The Old Believers," 170–78) likewise shows how this new political symbolism inflamed religious dissidence and encouraged the branding of Peter as the Antichrist; the interests of the state were now seen as a good in themselves, not subordinated to the spiritual imperatives of salvation.

[92] On the tendency to equate crime with both heresy and political disloyalty, see J. P. LeDonne, *Absolutism and Ruling Class: The Formation of the Russian Political Order, 1700–1825* (New York, 1991), 202.

[93] On the reforms, see James Cracraft, *The Church Reforms of Peter the Great* (Stanford, 1971); on the relationship of the church to the state, G. Freeze, "Handmaiden of the State? The Church in Imperial Russia Reconsidered," *Journal of Ecclesiastical History* 36 (1985).

The promulgation of a new law does not mean that the law was immediately enforced. A recent study of Moscow's criminal courts between 1649 and 1785 found numerous cases of murder, theft, robbery, and rape, but not suicide or attempted suicide.[94] This absence is likely due to both institutional and cultural factors. Russia's judicial and administrative apparatus was undeveloped in comparison to many Western European states, and the huge territorial expanses exacerbated the problem.[95] One of the ways in which the state handled the proverbial under-governance of the provinces was also to empower the local elites. With the provinces ruled more by local traditions and loyalties than a centralized bureaucracy, the criminalization of suicide need not have led to the law's routine enforcement. It is probable that responses and procedures differed widely, even from case to case, depending on local conditions, customary practices, and the attitudes of officials and priests.[96] Indeed, the scholar Boris Gasparov has emphasized the "implicitness" of Eastern Orthodoxy, which relied more upon local traditions and community consensus than abstract rules and regulations.[97] This quality likely underscored the regulation of suicide. The religious and criminal dimensions of suicide were not yet at odds; church, state, and community probably acted in tandem.[98]

The cultural meanings of suicide in medieval and early-modern Russia refracted ideas about death and dying in general, the good and the bad life, faith and despair, morality and vice, submission and willfulness, and the relationship of the individual to the polity. Just as some forms of voluntary death were categorized as martyrdom (hence heroic or virtuous), some forms of sudden and drunken death became relatives of suicide. This duality was embodied quite literally in Kirill Vel'skii, the suicide whose preserved remains were briefly

---

[94] Secular authorities were charged with assessing the intention of a suicide, which was necessary to determine the rituals of burial. See Schmidt, *Sozialkontrolle*, pt. 2. I confirmed this absence in a conversation with the author.

[95] LeDonne, *Absolutism and Ruling Class*, 121–235; Marc Raeff, *The Well-Ordered Police State: Social and Institutional Change through Law in the Germanies and Russia, 1600–1800* (New Haven, 1983), 181–250.

[96] Noteworthy in this regard is a 1721 Instruction to Petersburg clergy from Archimandrite Trifillii that directs local clergy to investigate suspicious deaths and deny rites to certain categories reminiscent of earlier church decrees rather than the new criminal statutes. Excerpted by Iv. Pavlovskii, "Zakon o trekhdnevnom sroke dlia pogrebeniia i vopros ob usypal'nitsakh," *Tserkovnyi vestnik* no. 43 (1878), 5 n. 4.

[97] As quoted and with additional discussion in Kivelson and Greene, *Orthodox Russia*, 14–15.

[98] Passing references to suicide in various charters dating from the fifteenth to the seventeenth centuries likewise suggest a pre-existing consensus. Cases were to be properly investigated, but the determination of burial procedures were left to the church. See "Belozerskaia ustavnaia gramota" (1488), *The Laws of Rus': Tenth to Fifteenth Century* (Salt Lake City, Ut., 1992), ed. and trans. Daniel H. Kaiser, 125; "Zhalovannaia [. . .] gramota Ivana IV Igumenu Iosifo-volokolamskogo monastyria" (1539), *Pamiatniki russkogo prava* (Moscow, 1956), vol. 4, 113; "Zhalovannaia [. . .] gramota ts. Mikhaila Fedorovicha [. . .] na monastyrskie votchiny [. . .]" (1613), *Russkii diplomatarii: arkhivnye materialy po istorii Moskvy* (Moscow, 1997), 67.

venerated. By the late seventeenth century, a complex pattern of correspondences and affinities was crystallizing, a process that was embodied within the spectacle of mass death among Old Believers. The many acts of self-immolation documented the power of martyrdom as a model, but they were also stigmatized – both within the movement and outside it – as forms of suicide. This process thereby conferred particular meanings upon voluntary death more generally: it could enact either a pious submission to or a willful rejection of God's dominion. The criminalization of suicide under Peter the Great made the political implications explicit. Suicide was henceforth configured within worldly forms of authority as well. The history of suicide should not be understood, therefore, as a linear progression from material (pagan) through moral-religious (Christian) to criminal (secular) and ultimately social or medical (scientific) models. Instead, the layering of cultural systems occurred through conversions and accommodations, in which pre-existing symbolic configurations were adapted into new contexts. The next important influence lay in the process of cultural Westernization during the eighteenth century.

2 Virtue and vice in an age of Enlightenment

> I can only say that Cato is of course greater than the convict who chooses to suffer and live, and that I am free to throw off the burden [of life] even if I can't pick it up again, especially as we are destined to drop it sooner or later anyway.
>
> Mikhail Sushkov, Suicide Note, 1792

> This is the consequence of unbelief and debauchery! This is the fruit of the lack of restraint [*neobuzdannost'*] and of delusion!
>
> I. Zavalishin, Letter to the Publishers of *New Monthly Compositions*, 1794

When Mikhail Sushkov killed himself in the summer of 1792, he authored his death as a public statement: "My position has burdened me already for a long time," he wrote, "but it has burdened me as a philosopher." His act built upon three primary models. He acknowledged Goethe's notorious hero but denied too close a resemblance: "Perhaps even Werther helped me in part, but for God's sake, don't consider me an ape of Werther, still less insane." He then cited a verse from his (then unpublished) epistolary tale, *The Russian Werther*, thereby linking himself to his own fictional hero. His second model was a materialist credo: even Voltaire, he ironically noted, had been unable to convince him of the immortality of the soul. Finally, because he did not have reason beyond the principle itself, Sushkov constructed his suicide as a rational and, as such, heroic act. Citing Cato's feat, he asserted his own sovereignty over life and the consequent right to choose the time of his death. With his eclectic references to German, French, and Roman culture, Sushkov was a typical product of Russia's Enlightenment. But his explicit rendering of suicide as a kind of public self-fashioning was new and disturbing: his four suicide notes are among the earliest extant in Russia; and the news of his voluntary death was so sensational that it quickly reached the highest levels of government.[1]

---

[1] The most complete analysis of Sushkov is the well-researched article by M. G. Fraan'e [Fraanje], "Proshchal'nye pis'ma M. V. Sushkova. (O probleme samoubiistva v russkoi kul'ture kontsa XVIII veka)," *XVIII vek: sbornik 19* (SPb, 1995). It reproduces the full texts of the suicide notes and other archival documents. Fraanje stresses Sushkov's emulation of Cato over the other allusions; despite differences in emphasis, I agree with Irina Paperno that the suicide was an

In the decades since Peter the Great had first made Westernization into an official policy, Russian society had fundamentally changed. As Western culture streamed into Russia during the eighteenth century, the elites encountered the great literary works of Western Europe, its modern philosophy, and the Greek and Roman heritage (often mediated through German, English, and French writers).[2] This celebration of Western culture had its center at the imperial court but soon spread across the empire, though it left the vast majority of the population – the peasantry – largely untouched. By the closing decades of the century, both men and women of the elite had become avid readers, often proficient in several European languages, and a new world of print was supplying hundreds of titles annually.[3] Though more limited than in Western Europe, many of the institutions and social spaces of a public sphere now existed; these included salons, clubs, theatres, parks, masonic lodges, and, after 1783, private presses and journals. Shaped within the discursive context of the new print culture as well as new social spaces, the public was both an object of absolutist regulation and a cultural presence in its own right.[4]

Suicide was a common theme in moral, philosophical, and literary texts of this period.[5] Among the most influential foreign treatments were works of fiction, which were read in the original languages or in translations: Montesquieu's *Persian Letters*, Voltaire's Roman tragedies, Goethe's *Sorrows of Young Werther*, and Rousseau's *The New Héloïse*.[6] Yet Russia's reading public did not simply internalize the perspectives propagated in print. As in pre-revolutionary France, the act of reading was also desacralized in Russia, though for different reasons.[7]

"amalgamation of paradigms." See her *Suicide as a Cultural Institution in Dostoevsky's Russia* (Ithaca, N.Y., 1998), 13–14. This case will be discussed further below.

[2] See Mark Raeff, "The Enlightenment in Russia and Russian Thought in the Enlightenment," in *The Eighteenth Century in Russia*, ed. J. G. Garrard (Oxford, 1973).

[3] Isabel de Madariaga, *Russia in the Age of Catherine the Great* (New Haven, 1981), chs. 21, 33, 34; Gary Marker, *Publishing, Printing, and the Origins of Intellectual Life in Russia, 1700–1800* (Princeton, 1985); and Marc Raeff, *Origins of the Russian Intelligentsia: The Eighteenth-Century Nobility* (New York, 1966).

[4] While the notion of a public sphere has become a commonplace in studies of eighteenth-century Europe, historians of Russia have traditionally emphasized the primacy of the state and, accordingly, the absence of a civil society. For an argument that Russia did possess a civil society, see Douglas Smith, *Working the Rough Stone: Freemasonry and Society in Eighteenth-Century Russia* (DeKalb, Ill., 1999). For a recent attempt to rethink the public sphere in Western and Central Europe, see T. C. W. Blanning, *The Culture of Power and the Power of Culture: Old Regime Europe 1880–1789* (Oxford, 2002).

[5] References to suicide seem rare, but this is deceptive. Only ten entries appear in the standard bibliographies: A. N. Neustroev, *Ukazatel' k russkim povremennym izdaniiam i sbornikam, 1703–1802* (SPb, 1898); and V. S. Sopikov, *Opyt rossiiskoi bibliografii* (SPb, 1904).

[6] In this period, *Werther* appeared in two complete translations: in 1781 (reprinted 1794, 1796) and 1798 (reprinted 1816). See V. Zhirmunskii, *Gete v russkoi literature* (Leningrad, 1937), 46–47. Most of Rousseau's works (except *Social Contract*) and Voltaire's Roman tragedies were likewise translated. See de Madariaga, *Russia in the Age*, 330, 338–39, 626 n. 14, 537.

[7] Roger Chartier, *The Cultural Origins of the French Revolution*, trans. Lydia G. Cochrane (Durham, N.C., 1991), esp. 17–19, 89–91.

Cultural Westernization had forced the elite to adopt new forms of conduct and behavior but also to see these as "foreign," and readers maintained a similarly external relation to the printed word.[8] This position was further encouraged by the juxtaposition of diverse and often contradictory texts within Russia's Enlightenment journals. Textual references to suicide do not form transparent sources on beliefs or practices, therefore, but contributions to cultural dialogues. They shaped both models of virtue linked to the art of dying as well as discursive categories for denouncing suicide as a vice and crime. The diffusion of ideas entailed a creative process of appropriation and transformation. Drawing on diverse concepts and images from the world of print, some individuals – primarily young men of the elite – crafted their suicides as public acts of self-expression; and the public reveled in its role as spectator, actively assessing and creatively reworking the authorial intention.

The history of suicide in this period illuminates two broader developments. The first was the shaping of new notions of the autonomous self. While Russian culture already possessed some positive images of voluntary death, these had generally reproduced the virtues of piety and submission. By the turn of the nineteenth century, however, the cults of honor and sensibility were providing alternative models of virtue and virtuous action. In contrast to the Muscovite emphasis upon collective and familial honor, an individualized form of honor had evolved among elites over the eighteenth century, a process encouraged by the state and shaped by Western cultural imports. The suicide of honor would consequently become a recognized genre, often associated with the defense of dignity, rights, and self-sovereignty, sometimes within the context of despotism.[9] It was situated within a rational, autonomous subject. The culture of sentiment, in contrast, focused more upon the inner self, the emotions, and the cultivation of a natural moral essence. Narratives of sentimental suicide were more ambivalent; the act was impulsive and mad, yet also noble and venerable. It was situated in the conflict between the individual and social duty. The second innovation was the crafting of a strategy to combat the socio-political threat symbolized by suicide, including its particular challenge to the authority of church and state as well as to the patriarchal family and social hierarchy more generally. The public thus constituted itself as a force of moderation, morality, and order alongside, not opposing the monarchy.[10] Affirmations of autonomy

---

[8] On Russianness and "foreignness," see Iurii Lotman, "The Poetics of Everyday Behavior in Eighteenth-Century Russian Culture," in *The Semiotics of Russian Cultural History*, ed. A. D. and A. S. Nakhimovsky (Ithaca, N.Y., 1985).

[9] Muscovite forms of honor did not disappear, and all social groups continued to possess honor and to litigate in its defense. For further discussion, see Nancy Shields Kollman, *By Honor Bound: State and Society in Early Modern Russia* (Ithaca, N.Y., 1999), esp. 233–47.

[10] Elise Kimerling Wirtschafter has argued that Russia possessed a "civic" society that strived to institutionalize civic engagement within the existing social and political framework. The public

and self-sovereignty were countered by assertions of religious faith, social norms, and political stability. Consequently, both actual and literary suicides became a potent forum to contest and affirm the nature of political and social power, especially their claims upon the individual.

Passionate reason

Suicide was not a central element in Enlightenment thought, but it was addressed by most philosophers during the eighteenth century. Although many attacked what they considered the barbaric punishments and the superstitions propagated by the church, few actually defended an absolute right to suicide. In his article in the *Encyclopédie*, Denis Diderot condemned suicide, not as contrary to divine law, but as unnatural and anti-social, that is, as an affront to nature and society. Such affronts were apparently rare, however, for he maintained that most suicides occurred in insanity. Voltaire was more tolerant, if also more mocking. Dismissing romantic motives as pitiful, he advised prospective suicides to seek diversion in activity. Nevertheless, he insisted that each act be judged according to its individual circumstances and acknowledged the right to end one's life when life became unreasonable. For Voltaire, as for Montesquieu, the essential issue was individual self-determination, a right that was founded on man's faculty of reason. The two philosophers likewise shared a fundamental irony about man's self-importance, for both stressed his relative insignificance within the enormity of the universe: God would not even notice should the soldier desert his post. Because individuals possessed the right to terminate the social contract should society no longer offer sufficient advantage, only reason should dictate the time of departure.[11] As historians have documented, the primacy accorded human reason had important consequences for modern notions of the self. Most importantly, it invested man with a new moral autonomy (that many argued was God-given) and thereby permitted the scrutiny of traditional authorities, both divine and worldly.[12]

In Russia, the discourse of reason provided a potent means to challenge the prohibition of suicide as an offense against God and tsar. Sushkov insisted that his act was fundamentally rational. Anticipating and rejecting both medical and religious explanations for his suicide, he maintained that it was neither the

---

reaction to suicide largely supports this finding. For further discussion, see Elise Kimerling Wirtschafter, *Social Identity in Imperial Russia* (De Kalb, Ill., 1997), 96–99; and especially her *The Play of Ideas in Russian Enlightenment Theater* (DeKalb, Ill., 2003).

[11] On debates over suicide in the eighteenth century, see John McManners, *Death and the Enlightenment: Changing Attitudes to Death among Christians and Unbelievers in Eighteenth-Century France* (Oxford, 1981), ch. 12. On the Enlightenment more generally, see Jonathan Israel, *Radical Enlightenment: Philosophy and the Making of Modernity 1650–1750* (Oxford, 2001).

[12] Charles Taylor, *Sources of the Self: The Making of Modern Identity* (Cambridge, 1989).

consequence of "English spleen"[13] nor, as "some fanatics will say," the work of the devil. Instead, it followed a principled assessment of his own and the human condition. With a certain sardonic humor, he mused: "For the good [of my siblings] I wish that they would begin to reason later than I did: life would poison them with [its] afflictions or compel them all to shoot themselves. That thought is rather amusing, is it not? Nine people come into being only all to shoot themselves. Still, are not millions of people born only to die in all sorts of ways?"[14] Maintaining that the inevitability of death made its actual timing irrelevant, Sushkov asserted his right to kill himself. Especially striking was his choice of method. Although the pistol – like the dagger in antiquity – was associated with nobility and honor, Sushkov chose the noose, which was usually regarded as an ignominious and shameful death.[15] One explanation, though speculative, is that Sushkov deliberately played with these associations: to hang himself under the banner of personal autonomy constituted an additional assault upon social convention.

A further illustration of Sushkov's subversive playfulness can be found in his story, *The Russian Werther*, published posthumously in 1801. In the author's introduction, which forms a kind of frame, Sushkov encouraged readers to read the story as autobiography: "Here is presented a young man, who possesses an ardent nature [and] a sensitive heart [*chuvstvitel'naia serdtsa*], and who began perhaps too early to nourish his reason with philosophy – in a word, such a man who is close to my morals and manners." Like many of his contemporaries, Sushkov perceived no necessary contradiction between sensibility and reason. Nevertheless, the evocation of reason was crucial to the originality of his Werther, who, like Goethe's hero is involved in a love triangle, but, in contrast to him, is an avowed materialist and atheist. Fusing Werther with Voltaire, this hero then evoked Cato's heroic act. In the room where his body was found – also in a noose – was a volume of Joseph Addison's *Cato* opened to the final scene. In both the fictional work and his actual suicide, Sushkov merged the three models, though in slightly different ways.

Finally, in a separate introduction to the volume, which formed a second frame, the publisher promoted a literal and didactic reading: "My intention with the publication of these letters [the story] is to show society a strange

---

[13] Compare the 1798 French Academy definition of spleen as "ennui de toutes choses, maladie hypocondriaque propre aux Anglais," as cited in Wolf Lepenies, *Melancholy and Society*, trans. J. Gaines and D. Jones (Cambridge, 1992), 69, 219 n. 41.

[14] As cited in Fraan'e [Fraanje] , "Proshchal'nye pis'ma," 155.

[15] Hanging was associated with capital punishment, and the method was often reserved for the lower estates as well as the most despicable criminals. On honorable and dishonorable forms of punishment, see Richard J. Evans, *Rituals of Retribution: Capital Punishment in Germany, 1600–1987* (London, 1996), 53–56. In France, the introduction of the guillotine was seen as a social equalizer; see Dorinda Outram, *The Body and the French Revolution: Sex, Class, and Political Culture* (New Haven, 1989), 106–10.

young man, who describes with a cold-bloodedness – incomprehensible to me – his own character, almost all the circumstances of his life, and finally [his] death. Each [person] who reads these lines will consider them the author's fancy, but alas, he has turned to dust for already eight years, having freely taken his own life at the age of 17 and in exactly the same way as he described the end of the imaginary Werther."[16] Sushkov's tale was not in fact autobiographical, but the preface illustrates the contemporary proclivity to erase the boundary between actual and literary suicides – and to search both for their moral lessons.

Sushkov was not the only one to link suicide to reason. In 1793, the year after Sushkov's death, a young nobleman from Iaroslavl province, Ivan Opochinin, also killed himself, and he too claimed a rational basis for his act. Following an introductory paragraph modeled along a last testament, the explanatory note opens with a materialist credo: "Death is nothing other than the transition from being to complete annihilation." Asserting that he had no particular reason for killing himself other than his "loathing for our Russian life," Opochinin depicted suicide as the logical consequence of reason: "If only all wretches possessed the courage to use their sound reason, despising the superstition that blinds all weak-minded people, and would imagine their death for what it really is – they would likely see that it is just as easy to refuse life as to change one's clothes, the color of which no longer please. I find myself precisely in such a situation. [. . .] In a little while, several particles of gunpowder will destroy this moving machine which my proud and superstitious contemporaries call the immortal soul." Proclaiming his freedom from God and the law, Opochinin celebrated his death as an "act of self-will" – a term previously used to condemn suicide. Like Sushkov, moreover, he linked himself (explicitly) to Voltaire and (implicitly) to Cato: his death, too, was an exemplar of heroic virtue to be emulated by those who possessed the courage to live according to their reason.[17]

Sushkov and Opochinin are the only two known examples of reasoned suicides in this period. At the core of their motives was not a particular doctrine absorbed from foreign texts but rather an affirmation of personal autonomy: the rational self, not the external truths of church and state, was the source of authority. While the linkage between suicide and self-sovereignty depended on the new status accorded reason in eighteenth-century thought, it also drew upon less abstract images. In Russia, as in Western Europe, the heroes of antiquity

---

[16] See *Rossiiskii Verter, pospravedlivaia povest', original'noe sochinenie M. S. molodogo, chuvstvitel'nogo cheloveka, neschastnym obrazom samoizvol'no prekrativshego svoiu zhizn'iu* (SPb, 1801), i, iii, 85–86. The novel has consequently been described as a "full confession" of the author. See *BE*, vol. 38, 214.

[17] For his suicide note, see L. N. Trefolev, ed., "Predsmertnoe zaveshchanie russkogo ateista," *Istoricheskii vestnik* no. 1 (1883), 224–26. According to Fraanje ("Proshchal'nye pis'ma," 153), the letters of Opochinin and Sushkov were included in a manuscript literary collection that circulated in the early nineteenth century.

populated both print culture and the public imagination.[18] By the 1760s,
Russia's journals were recounting the stories of Socrates, Cato, Lucretia,
Seneca, Brutus, and so forth, and such tales became increasingly common by
the 1780s, when they also began to shape norms of behavior.[19] Russian readers
were not especially well informed about the intricacies of Greek or Roman philosophy (or its subsequent interpretation), but this was not the point. The many
scenes of heroic death instead offered evocative models of the autonomous self.
Translations often lingered on the self-mastery and personal virtue of classical heroes: "I decided to die," insisted Socrates, drinking the hemlock, and he
remained "self-possessed" ("*vsegda obladaiushchii samim soboiu*") during his
final hours.[20] Whether the death of Socrates even constituted a suicide has long
been debated, for he had in fact been sentenced to death.[21] Nevertheless, such
texts focused upon his self-discipline and self-sovereignty: he was not subject
to the will of others but freely chose to die.[22]

Most influential in Russia, as in Western Europe, was the cult surrounding Cato of Utica, who disemboweled himself rather than submit to tyranny
under Caesar. Historical rewritings through the centuries have linked Cato's act
to individual liberty, the republican struggle against despotism, and personal
dignity.[23] These themes all appear in the Russian readings of his feat, but it is
worth separating three strands of influence. The first strand is best exemplified
by Sushkov, for he emulated Cato's heroism but did not have a Caesar. In other
words, the model did not require him to follow the original story line. Instead, he
evoked the long-standing nexus between Cato's act and the debates on immortality. Before his death, Cato was supposed to have read Plato's *Phaedo*, the
text in which Socrates affirms the immortality of the soul before dying. Accent-
ing this juxtaposition in his famous theatrical rewriting of Cato's feat, Joseph

[18] On the cult of antiquity more generally, see Andrew Kahn, "Readings of Imperial Rome from Lomonosov to Pushkin," *Slavic Review* no. 4 (1993).

[19] These included both brief and lengthy excerpts from both ancient and modern sources. In his index of periodicals, Neustroev (*Ukazatel'*) has three entries under Lucretia, sixteen for Cato and an entire column for Socrates.

[20] "O Sokratovoi smerti," *Novye ezhemesiachnye sochineniia*, pt. 71 (1792), esp. 58–59, 64. For other examples, see "Sokrat (Perevod iz Anakharsisa)," *Panteon inostrannoi slovesnosti*, bk. 2 (1792; reprint: 1818), 299; and "O smerti Sokratovoi," *Sochineniia i perevody, k pol'ze i uveseleniiu sluzhashchiia* (Apr. 1760), 362–67.

[21] For further discussion, including citation of scholarly literature, see Paperno, *Suicide*, 6–8, 209–10.

[22] Alternative readings were also possible: had not the tyranny of the republic murdered Socrates? See "Smert' Sokrata," *Rastushchii vinograd* (July 1786), 36.

[23] See Paul Plass, *The Game of Death in Ancient Rome: Arena Sport and Political Suicide* (Madison, Wisc., 1995); M. Rist, *Stoic Philosophy* (Cambridge, 1969), ch. 13; and M. Griffin, "Philosophy, Cato, and Roman Suicide," *Greece and Rome* 33 (1986). For later readings: Alexander Murray, *Suicide in the Middle Ages*, vol. 2: *The Curse on Self-Murder* (Oxford, 2000), 116–17, 140–42; Michael MacDonald and Terence R. Murphy, *Sleepless Souls: Suicide in Early Modern England* (Oxford, 1990), 179–83; Paperno, *Suicide*, 9–11; and Outram, *The Body*, chs. 5, 6.

Addison lingered on Cato's ruminations and ultimately affirmed his belief in immortality. For his part, Sushkov reconfigured Addison's terms: it is the fact of human finitude that confers true heroism on Cato.[24]

A quite different and more common interpretation associated Cato's feat with personal dignity and honor. "I will die but not humiliate myself," the young officer Sergei Glinka purportedly declared in 1793, when he refused to apologize for a minor misunderstanding with another officer. Although Glinka did not act on this impulse, he recalled in his memoirs how Cato's image filled his imagination, making suicide seem the only honorable course of action.[25] This association was encouraged by other translations that were appearing in contemporary journals, especially Cato's speech refusing counsel at the Oracle of Ammon. These excerpts from Lucan focus on Cato's personal dignity, his desire to die well. "Do I prefer death to humiliation?" he muses, answering, of course, in the affirmative.[26]

This complex of meanings is best understood by exploring a parallel later drawn by the poet Aleksandr Pushkin. In notes made upon his reading of Tacitus (in a French translation), he remarked that suicide had been as frequent in ancient Rome as the duel was in contemporary Russia.[27] For Pushkin, the juxtaposition of these distinctive acts seemed natural for both could enact and defend honor. As Iurii Lotman and Irina Reyfman have shown, the concept was relatively new, for Russia did not possess a tradition of chivalric honor among the nobility. The great popularity of the duel – which arrived in Russia in the eighteenth century and would reach its high point in the first third of the nineteenth century, counting Pushkin among its victims – was a completely new phenomenon tied to the changing self-consciousness of the nobility.[28] In the eighteenth century, the government actively encouraged the development of noble self-consciousness, especially after the elimination in 1762 of obligatory state service. The Charter

---

24 Although Plato's Socrates argues that death was ultimately desirable in light of the immortality of the soul, this did not equate to a free defense of suicide as such, for Plato saw life as a divine gift: man must wait his appointed time. See Murray, *The Curse*, 123–24. For a detailed analysis of Sushkov's (mis)reading of Addison, see Fraan'e, "Proshchal'nye pis'ma," 161–62. For translations, see "Monolog. Iz tragedii Katon, sochinennoi g. Adissonom [*sic*]," *Novye ezhemesiachnye sochineniia*, pt. 25 (July 1788), 74–76; "Smert' Katona, ili rozhdenie rimskogo edinonachaliia," *Ippokrena*, pt. 8 (1801), 90–229; and *Katon, tragediia Adissonom [sic]*, trans. Aleksei Kolmakov (SPb, 1804).

25 *Zapiski Sergeia Nikolaevicha Glinki* (SPb, 1895), 102–3, 61–63.

26 "Katon v Livii. Perevod iz Lukanovoi Farsalii," *Panteon inostrannoi slovesnosti*, pt. 1 (1789), 79–92 (reprinted 1802, 1803, 1818); (untitled translation from Lucan), *S.- Peterburgskii Merkurii*, pt. 3 (1793), 35–37; "Iz IX. knigi Farsalii Marka Anneia Lukana," *Trudoliubivaia pchela* (Nov. 1759), 674–76.

27 A. Pushkin, *Sobranie sochinenii v desiati tomakh*, 10 vols. (Moscow, 1962), vol. 7, 235.

28 See Irina Reyfman, *Ritualized Violence Russian Style: The Duel in Russian Culture and Literature* (Stanford, 1999); and Iurii Lotman, *Besedy o russkoi kul'ture: Byt i traditsii russkogo dvorianstva (XVIII–nachalo XIX veka)* (SPb, 1994), 164–79. On the duel in Germany, see Ute Frevert, *Ehrenmänner: Das Duell in der bürgerlichen Gesellschaft* (Munich, 1991); and Kevin McAleer, *Dueling: The Cult of Honor in Fin-de-Siècle Germany* (Princeton, 1994).

of the Nobility (1785) rewarded nobles with an official recognition of their special status and innate honor. Yet the nobility was also defining itself in opposition to the common people, or "dark masses," as they were sometimes called. Not just birth and family but culture and civilization – articulated through complex rules of behavior – came to be important markers of status.[29] The rituals of the duel thus allowed nobles to claim honor as the innate characteristics of their estate, both in relation to political power and social hierarchy.

Suicide was certainly less common than the duel, but it could sometimes – in a similarly ritualistic way – function as an ersatz. The most famous such case occurred in 1816, when five Polish officers shot themselves in Warsaw following a perceived insult by the Grand Duke Constantine. As a member of the royal family, he could not be challenged to a duel. Similarly, Pushkin considered suicide while in internal exile in 1822, for he was physically unable to challenge his opponent to a duel.[30] The cult of honor extended the principle of self-sovereignty into a variety of spheres, from personal reputation to bodily inviolability. Yet honor and dignity can also be very political commodities for they place an implicit limit on the absolute power of the monarch.

Cato's suicide was, of course, a political act of resistance against Caesar, but its imitation could be selective: neither Sushkov nor Glinka articulated an explicitly political target. Nevertheless, the literary construction of suicide as a political act was well established by this period. The earliest treatments in the Russian literary canon date to the mid-eighteenth century, when A. P. Sumarokov wrote numerous plays on the theme of tyranny, in which the occasional tragic suicide enacted heroic resistance. Most of these plays were performed at court, where they were not perceived as subversive: their attack on despotic power vilified the despot but also elevated the enlightened ruler.[31] Indeed, the self-representation of Catherine II, especially in the first two decades of her reign, propagated precisely such images of the enlightened ruler, who had vanquished the despot, that is, her deposed husband.[32] The theatrical plot remained common into the 1780s. A typical play from the era recounted the tragic fate of a heroine who preferred poison to submission to Rome.[33]

---

[29] On cultured behavior, see Catriona Kelly, *Refining Russia: Advice Literature, Polite Culture, and Gender from Catherine to Yeltsin* (Oxford, 2002), ch. 1.

[30] On the overlap between the duel and some suicides, see Reyfman, *Ritualized Violence*, 16–17, 126; and A. V. Vostrikov, "Ubiistvo i samoubiistvo v dele chesti," *Smert' kak fenomen kul'tury* (Syktyvkar, 1994), 23–34.

[31] These plays, which also explored the conflict between love and duty, are discussed in some detail in Wirtschafter, *The Play of Ideas*, 57–60, 148–56, 222 n. 14.

[32] Richard Wortman, *Scenarios of Power: Myth and Ceremony in Russian Monarchy*, 2 vols. (Princeton, 1995, 2000), vol. 1, 110–46.

[33] Ia. B. Kniazhnin, "Sofinisba: Tragediia v piati deistviiakh," in *Rossiiskii featr ili polnoe sobranie vsekh rossiiskikh teatral'nykh sochinenii*, 43 vols. (SPb, 1786–94), vol. 34, 109–204. See also "Epigramma na smert' Liukretsii," *Novye ezhemesiachnye sochineniia*, pt. 2 (Aug. 1786), 64. On the myth of Lucretia, see Ian Donaldson, *The Rapes of Lucretia: A Myth and its Transformations* (Oxford, 1982).

By the 1790s, however, the subversive potential of such themes had become apparent, and the fate of Iakov Kniazhnin's tragedy, *Vadim of Novgorod*, is illustrative. Adapting the fall of the Roman republic to a mythical account of Russian history, Kniazhnin explored the dramatic victory of the imperial state – embodied by the virtuous and just ruler Riurik – over the republicanism of Novgorod, led by Vadim. The final moments of the play are replete with pathos and republican patriotism. Ramida, the passionate but dutiful daughter of Vadim, loves Riurik but stabs herself at her father's behest. "Watch," she proclaims to him, "Am I worthy of being your daughter?" Vadim's reply celebrates her dutifulness: "O joy! Everything I am vanishes from this land! O beloved daughter! Your blood is truly heroic!" He then turns to Riurik and proclaims (before stabbing himself): "Amidst your victorious troops, / Crowned might beholding everything at your feet, / What are you against him who dares to die?"[34] Finished in 1789 and published in 1793, two years after Kniazhnin's death, the play had the misfortune of appearing at the height of the French Revolution, a coincidence that sealed its fate. Because it was "full of audacious and pernicious pronouncements against the legal autocratic power," Catherine the Great ordered it to be burned.[35] As this response illustrates, "to dare to die" was perceived as a form of resistance, an affirmation of human freedom. According to Elise Kimerling Wirtschafter, Kniazhnin's offense was less the tragic suicide (which was a literary commonplace), but Vadim's refusal to submit to a just and enlightened monarch.[36] By implication, therefore, any monarchy could be configured as tyranny.

The phenomenon of heroic, political suicide was also finding expression in a contemporary Russian setting. In 1790, Russia's first well-known radical (and later most famous suicide of this era), Aleksandr Radishchev, published his most important work, *A Journey from St. Petersburg to Moscow*, for which he was exiled to Siberia. Believing that the world – particularly in Russia – had fallen into abject slavery, a condition that contradicted the nature of man, he argued that the task of the enlightened philosopher was not just to proclaim the truths of freedom and citizenship but to translate them into life. To effect the transition from slavery to freedom it was necessary to awaken the people to their enslavement and their ability to grasp man's inherent liberty. This was perhaps his primary goal in this book, which contains passionate and evocative

---

[34] V. Savodnik, ed., *Vadim Novgorodskii: Tragediia Ia. Kniazhnina* (Moscow, 1914), 63.

[35] Kniazhnin may not have intended his work to be read in this way. He enjoyed good relations with Catherine, voluntarily withdrew the play from production, and fashioned Riurik (not Vadim) as the most positive character – sensible, just, and merciful. The enlightened ruler as a force of progress was, after all, an image cultivated by Catherine and many *philosophes*. For the quotation, see V. Ia. Stoiunin, "Kniazhnin-pisatel'," *Istoricheskii vestnik* nos. 7, 8 (1881), esp. no. 8, 754–57. In Catherine the Great's own version of the myth, Vadim becomes Riurik's loyal subject. See de Madariaga, *Russia in the Age*, 536, 545–46.

[36] Wirtschafter, *The Play of Ideas*, 167–69.

scenes on the evils of serfdom. Yet one chapter also defended a form of heroic suicide as the last preserve of human dignity, as the expression of freedom amidst despotism: "If your virtue can no longer find any earthly shelter," a father counsels his sons, "if you have reached your ultimate limit, if nothing more protects you from oppression, then remember that you are a man . . . Die. As my bequest, I leave you the words of the dying Cato."[37] Radishchev depicted suicide as the right – even the obligation – of the individual in defense against tyranny. "To know how to die" was proof that one was not a slave but a man, possessing true nobility of character.[38] This linkage between suicide and resistance to slavery recurred in other sources, though it was typically situated in antiquity. Journals thus published this excerpt from Cato's final missive: "So Caesar, Rome is already a slave; the world bows; [but] Cato is not a slave – he despises you and your world." Self-sovereignty becomes a political act: "Death is an invincible, sacred right," Cato proclaims, "I can dispose of my own life."[39]

According to the publicist D. I. Fonvizin, however, the cult of the heroic deed was fundamentally superficial. Russia's Catos were daring in their criticism of flattery and talk of courage and fortitude. Yet as soon as they crossed the threshold of the palace, they underwent a complete transformation, becoming everything they claimed to despise.[40] Fonvizin was perhaps right, and Glinka's fleeting impulse supports this conclusion. Yet he may have been looking in the wrong place. In his memoirs, which he based on personal journals, Aleksandr Nikitenko described his perilous youth as a gifted and morally oppressed young serf at the turn of the nineteenth century. Very well read in philosophy and literature, ancient and modern, he experienced moments of despair when it seemed he would never escape his state of slavery.

No, no one can and nothing can convey the moral struggle a strong and courageous 16-year-old went through to consider suicide and find relief in the idea itself. A shaft of light, it made an indelible impression and raised my spirits. I realized that letting myself

[37] Because Radishchev's ideas have been well documented, I will not discuss them further. I remain unconvinced, however, by Lotman's assertion that Radishchev enacted his principles in his own suicide, which was rushed and lacking a clear motivation or note. For the quotation, see Aleksandr Radishchev, *PSS*, 3 vols. (Moscow, 1938–41), vol. 1, 295. On his writings and suicide, see Lotman "The Poetics of Everyday Behavior," 87–94; and his *Besedy o russkoi kul'ture: Byt i traditsii russkogo dvorianstva (XVIII–nachalo XIX veka)* (SPb, 1994), 258–69; Paperno, *Suicide*, 15–16; Allen McConnell, *A Russian Philosophe: Alexander Radishchev, 1749–1802* (The Hague, 1964), 85–86, 189–92. On the philosophical basis for his moral stance, see Raeff, "The Enlightenment in Russia," 43–44.
[38] See Radishchev, *PSS*, vol. 1, 351.
[39] "Poslanie Katona k Iuliiu Kesariu," *Trudy obshchestva liubitelei rossiiskoi slovesnosti*, pt. 3 (Moscow, 1812), 27, 31. Notably, the translator, F. F. Ivanov, was the author of *Marfa Posadnitsa*, a tragedy with the theme of heroic suicide. See also "Pis'mo Katona k Iuliiu Tsesariu," *Sobesednik liubitelei rossiiskogo slova*, pt. 8 (1783), 35.
[40] D. I. Fonvizin, *Sobranie sochinenii v dvukh tomakh*, 2 vols. (Moscow, 1959), vol. 2, 48–49.

wallow in despair would solve nothing. "No," I told myself, "this self-pity won't do. So what if I'm not my own master; so what if I'm nothing in the eyes of society and its laws! Still, I have one right that no one can take away from me! The right to die." [. . .] For some reason, I preferred to die by the gun. I acquired a pistol, powder, and two bullets, and from that instant on I felt better. A new sense of daring took root in me. [. . .] I became proud and independent.[41]

Most striking is the sense of inner freedom conferred by the weapon, the symbol of the ability to choose suicide. While Nikitenko came close to acting several times, he was able to secure his freedom and, ironically, became a censor under Nicholas I.

Some two decades later, however, another serf would fashion his death as an exemplar of heroic protest. Trained as a neoclassical artist in a private art school in the provincial town of Arzamas, Grigorii Miasnikov had been offered a place at the Imperial Academy of Art – contingent on a generous offer to purchase his freedom.[42] When his master refused, Miasnikov designed his exit within the neoclassical tradition: he shot himself in the school's Gallery of Antiquity, and his note included the following lines: "Do not reproach me for my act – I am showing you [my friends] how to oppose the superciliousness of ambitious men. [. . .] Write on my tomb that I died for freedom."[43] With the careful staging and evocation of freedom, this serf had translated the noble refusal of slavery into the context of serfdom and thereby violated the fundamental rules of social order in Russia. The brisance of the case led to its investigation on the highest levels of government where his claim to honor was firmly rejected. In his final report penned early in 1829, the head of the secret police, Count Benckendorff, wrote: "This incident was clear evidence of the harmful consequences of half-education, especially for people from the lower estates, who, in acquiring knowledge without moral guidance, grumble about their fate, [who], considering themselves higher than their condition, do not willingly obey their elders, [and who], spreading false notions, often become the cause of calamitous adventures."[44] To acknowledge a serf's claim to dignity

[41] Aleksandr Nikolenko, *Up from Serfdom: My Childhood and Youth in Russia, 1804–1824*, trans. Helen Saltz Jacobson (New Haven, 2001), 129–30, 155, 189.

[42] On the school, see P. Kornilov, *Arzamasskaia shkola zhivopisi: pervoi poloviny XIX veka* (Moscow, 1947). For further discussion of this case, see my "In the Name of Freedom: Suicide, Serfdom, and Autocracy in Russia," *Slavonic and East European Review* (Spring 2004).

[43] The account of the Arzamas sheriff (GANO, f. 5, 1828g., op. 45, d. 202, ll. 2–3) states only that Miasnikov's body had been found in a room located in a wing of the school, but a memoir written by a fellow student recalls that Miasnikov's body was found in the Gallery of Antiquity (which was located in this wing). See I. K. Zaitsev, "Vospominaniia starogo uchitelia I. K. Zaitseva, 1805–1887," *Russkaia starina* no. 6 (1887), 669.

[44] RGIA, f. 1167, op. XVIm – 1826, d. 183, ll. 1–5. For other reports on the case, see GANO, f. 5, 1828g., op. 45, d. 202; and f. 180, op. 640, 1828, d. 5; and GARF, f. 109 IV, 1828g., op. 168, d. 139.

and self-sovereignty was too disruptive of both cultural norms and the entire system of social distinction.

One reason for the high-level reaction to Miasnikov's case was its timing just three years after the Decembrist revolt in 1825, when groups of army officers, united already for several years in conspiratorial networks, attempted to oppose the accession of Nicholas I to the throne.[45] These officers had likewise brought the various elements of heroic suicide together into a coherent political narrative and public spectacle. Unlike Sushkov or Glinka, who had both extracted useful elements from Cato's legend, the Decembrists were interested in the story as a whole. As Lotman has shown, the Decembrists modeled themselves as romantic heroes, as men of action for whom the virtues of honor, dignity, and courage possessed absolute value. Constantly pondering death, they plotted their life stories as tragedies.[46] The glory of self-sacrifice in the name of the people and nation thus formed a central theme in Decembrist writings and rhetoric. The poet Kondratii Ryleev, who enjoyed tremendous popularity among his comrades and was later to be executed, elevated martyrdom to one of life's primary tasks. In his poem "The Citizen," he designated a heroic death in the name of freedom as the only goal for honorable men. At a meeting held the evening before the uprising, Ryleev likewise spoke of the patriotic duties of the citizen and the certain death awaiting them all. In his enthusiasm, Prince Aleksandr Odoevskii supposedly shouted that they were all to die, to die gloriously.[47] For the Decembrists, suicide was conceived as a performance on the stage of History. It merged personal honor and dignity with political principle.

While the revolt itself can be interpreted as a symbolic martyrdom – the officers who gathered on Senate Square seemed to expect defeat and death – several Decembrists also took their own lives in the weeks after the uprising. These suicides affirmed allegiance to the cause and subsequently became part of the Decembrist mythology, glorified as heroic feats. Just one day after the revolt, Captain Ivan Bogdanovich shot himself because, it was reputed, he had missed the chance to join his comrades on Senate Square and thought he had done too little for the cause.[48] Believing that he had missed an opportunity to shoot

[45] For an overview of the groups, leaders, and programs, see A. Mazour, *The First Russian Revolution, 1825: The Decembrist Movement, its Origins, Development, and Significance* (Berkeley, 1937).

[46] See Lotman, "Poetics of Everyday Behavior," 86–87; and his, "The Decembrist in Daily Life (Everyday Behavior as a Historical-Psychological Category)," in Nakhimovsky and Nakhimovsky, *The Semiotics*, 112.

[47] Mazour, *First Russian Revolution*, 164. Ryleev likewise explored the legend of Vadim/Cato as the defender of the republic against the empire, and Nikita Murav'ev recalled being "obsessed with the limitless love of Cicero, Cato, and others for the fatherland." See Hans Lemberg, *Die nationale Gedankenwelt der Dekabristen* (Cologne and Graz, 1963), 95–98, 100.

[48] M. V. Nechkina, *Dvizhenie dekabristov*, 2 vols. (Moscow, 1955), vol. 2, 266. See also A. E. Rozen, "Iz zapisok dekabristov," *Pisateli-dekabristy v vospominaniiakh sovremennikov*, 2 vols. (Moscow, 1980), vol. 1, 155.

Nicholas I, Ryleev's school friend Colonel Bulatov smashed his head against his cell wall in the Peter and Paul Fortress.[49] Both Bogdanovich and Bulatov construed suicide as a means to restore their besmirched honor. Ryleev's poetic appeal likewise echoed among some of the exiled Decembrists. For his role in the revolt, Ivan Sukhinov was sentenced to forced labor in Siberia, where he attempted to organize a rebellion. Not a member of the nobility and hence not exempted from corporal punishment, Sukhinov was condemned to knouting, branding, and hanging. Unaware that his sentence had been commuted to an honorable death by firing squad, Sukhinov resolved to escape humiliation: his third attempt at suicide proved successful.[50] His act linked personal honor with freedom and resistance to imperial power. Russia had at last produced its own mythic Catos.

Sukhinov's fate is particularly illuminating, because his aspiration to personal honor conflicted with the government's attempt to administer it. As the sole possession of the elites, most importantly the nobility since 1785 but also a handful of other select groups (which often lobbied for precisely this recognition), honor became a method of governance during the first half of the nineteenth century, integral to the maintenance of social hierarchy and serfdom. In her history of corporal punishment in imperial Russia, Abby Schrader has shown how the elites were expected to behave according to an internalized sense of honor, whereas commoners were to be intimidated with the threat and spectacle of bodily punishment.[51] Sukhinov's self-image was clearly that of an officer, but his social status denied him the privileged exclusion from corporal punishment. Although overtly political suicide would largely disappear from Russia in the decades following the Decembrist revolt, honor would remain an important and sometimes contested commodity. Aware perhaps of its potential dangers, Nicholas I attempted to become the ultimate arbiter of honor by encouraging (what he considered) proper forms of patriotism and norms of elite behavior. Yet honor would continue to shape individual motives for suicide and sometimes come into conflict with the ethos promoted by the state.

Reasoned sensibility

The Enlightenment is often seen as an era characterized by the rise of science and rationality, when philosophers debated the social contract and the natural rights

---

[49] Nechkina, *Dvizhenie dekabristov*, vol. 2, 285, 398.

[50] Soviet hagiography celebrates him as Russia's first revolutionary from the *raznochintsy*. See Nechkina, *Dvizhenie dekabristov*, vol. 2, 435–36; Sergei Gessen, *Zagovor dekabrista Sukhinova* (Moscow, 1930), 46–48; and the memoir accounts of M. A. Bestuzhev and A. E. Rozen, reprinted in *Pisateli-dekabristy*, vol. 1, 119, 155, 189, 395.

[51] Abby M. Schrader, *Languages of the Lash: Corporal Punishment and Identity in Imperial Russia* (DeKalb, Ill., 2002).

of man. This is true, of course, but one-sided. Intersecting the cult of reason was a new interest in the inner self, especially the emotions, and this interest found expression in sentimental literature. Often termed "tearful drama," this genre explored the intimate realm of feeling within the everyday lives of regular people – not the epic feats of heroes. Its central concept in Russia – *chuvstvitel'nost'* or sensibility – was defined in the *Academy Dictionary* (1794) as "the quality of a person who is moved by the unhappiness of another," and it conceived the depth and purity of emotion as evidence of virtue.[52] Sentimental texts built upon the notion that a moral sensibility was integral to natural man and, further, that the cultivation of this inborn essence formed the basis of moral judgment.[53] In an important sense, therefore, they propounded man's moral autonomy, especially in the sphere of personal life, just as the notion of inborn reason had encouraged claims to self-sovereignty. These two currents were distinct but not necessarily at odds.

Alongside Goethe's *Werther*, the most influential sentimental novel was probably Rousseau's *The New Héloïse*, which recounts the story of Saint Preux and Julie, whose marriage is forbidden due to their social inequality. Despite her enduring love for Saint Preux, Julie ultimately does her duty by marrying Wolmar and remains true to her vows unto death. The novel also contained the most important discourse on suicide in this era. It took the form of two letters, the first by Saint Preux recapitulating the arguments for suicide, and the second, by his friend, Lord Bomston, arguing against it. Whereas the first letter highlighted the freedom of the individual to choose suicide when one is tired of or unhappy with life, the response countered with the individual's duty to give life its meaning through good works. (An exception was allowed when pain and disability impede a productive life.) While the form of this debate as well as its function within the literary text prevent a neat extrapolation of Rousseau's own views, it is significant that Saint Preux chooses the path of duty at the end of the novel. In many respects, this can be seen as a conservative outcome: in society, unlike the state of nature, man must suppress the unruly passions in the name of social harmony. The right to moral autonomy required the proper education and disciplining of the self to internalize the broader good of civil society.[54]

A complete translation of the book appeared in Russia, and journals published excerpts from the passages on suicide in 1780, 1785, 1794, and

---

[52] This quotation is taken from *The Handbook of Russian Literature*, ed. Victor Terras (New Haven, 1985), 395. See also V. V. Sipovskii, "Ocherki iz istorii russkogo romana," in *Zapiski Istoriko-filologicheskogo fakul'teta Imp. S.-Peterburgskogo Universiteta* 98 (SPb, 1910); and Zhirmunskii, *Gete*, ch. 2.

[53] On sentimentalism and sensibility, see William Reddy, *The Navigation of Feeling: A Framework for the History of Emotions* (Cambridge, 2001), esp. 164.

[54] My interpretation has been influenced by Lisa Lieberman, *Leaving You: The Cultural Meaning of Suicide* (Chicago, 2003), 44–54.

1800.[55] Once again, translation and selection shaped meanings. Only one of the four periodicals even included the first letter, and it presented the second letter as the correct response to the error of the first.[56] The other three texts drew exclusively from the second letter, even skipping the sections on suicide's limited admissibility. Ambiguity was thereby excised in favor of an absolute condemnation: we were put on earth to fulfill our duty to our fellow man; suicide was consequently the act of a weak and corrupted character.

Appearing four times in twenty years, Rousseau's defense of life clearly resonated in Russia.[57] These translations should be understood as contributions to a broader public interest in the cultivation of the self, the virtuous life, and the threat posed by a corruption of morals.[58] The same journal which contained an excerpt from Rousseau included two meditations on related themes. The first, suggestively entitled "To Life," vilifies well-known vices as harmful to the individual and social good.[59] The second piece addressed the theme of "unhappiness" and adopted a variant of Rousseau's solution: "The time of unhappiness is the time of virtue, duty, hope, strength of mind, and the sensibility of the soul."[60] Meaningful juxtapositions also occurred in the freemason Nikolai Novikov's journal. Whereas the excerpt from Rousseau depicts suicide as a "violent and shameful death," "an effrontery committed against humanity," adjacent texts ruminate on the "Soul after Death" and (in a more ironic tone) "Solitude," which recapitulated the debate about whether virtue required active engagement in or withdrawal from society.[61]

The significance of these ruminations lies less in their originality than in their conventionality: countless such pieces filled Russia's journals in this period. Constantly offered models of virtue and warnings against vice, the reading public was invited to better itself, to mold its manners and morals according to such principles as moderation, duty, good works, charity, and service. Yet the cultivation of the self also raised difficult questions: what was the proper relationship between individual desires and social norms, freedom and duty,

---

[55] "Pis'mo: O samoproizvol'noi smerti," and "Otvet na predydushchee pis'mo," trans. Moisei Smirnov, *Akademicheskie izvestiia* (Feb. 4, 1780), 244–84; "Samoubivstvo [*sic*]," *Pokoiashchiisia trudoliubets*, pt. 4 (1785), 193–95; "O samoubiistve," *Priiatnoe i poleznoe preprovozhdenie vremeni*, pt. 2 (1794), 117–21; "Samoubiistvo," *Chto nibud' ot bezdel'ia na dosuge* (1800), 257–62.

[56] Thomas Barran, *Russia Reads Rousseau, 1762–1825* (Evanston, Ill., 2002), 222–23.

[57] The appeal to perform good works as an antidote to suicide was likewise popular in Europe. See McManners, *Death and the Enlightenment*, 423–24.

[58] Cf. Prince M. M. Shcherbatov, *On the Corruption of Morals in Russia*, trans. and ed. A. Lentin (Cambridge, 1969).

[59] "K zhizni," *Priiatnoe i poleznoe preprovozhdenie vremeni*, pt. 2 (1794), 3–5. It also published a story with a sentimental suicide: Pavel L'vov, "Sofiia," 303–27.

[60] N. Kh. "Neschastie," *Priiatnoe i poleznoe preprovozhdenie vremeni*, pt. 2 (1794), 78–80.

[61] See "Dusha po smerti," and "Uedinenie," *Pokoiashchiisia trudoliubets*, pt. 4 (1785), 121–22, 196. The parallels with masonic teachings are many. See Smith, *Rough Stone*, esp. 44–52 and de Madariaga, *Russia in the Age*, ch. 33.

autonomy and discipline? Precisely these questions were often addressed in literature. Though Rousseau may have come down on the side of discipline and duty, the moral status of suicide in sentimental tales remained deeply ambiguous, in Russia as in Europe. Often neither defending nor condemning the act, stories tested its moral essence by placing it within an everyday social world. In encouraging readers to judge – and empathize – for themselves, this very approach was subversive of church teachings, which did not admit debate. Was morality universal and absolute? Or could it stem from man's nature and sensibility?

The most important text shaping the sentimental suicide in Russia was Nikolai Karamzin's famous tale, *Poor Liza* (1792). The story opens and closes with the ruminations of the narrator, who converses with the reader *cum* public and forms an exemplar of dignified *chuvstvitel'nost'*: "Ah, I love those topics which move my heart and compel me to shed tears of tender sorrow," he sighs, as he commences the tale of the beautiful and kind Liza.[62] The basic plot is simple: Liza meets Erast, and they fall in love, but the social difference is too great for a formal match: Liza is a peasant, Erast a nobleman. Their love remains chaste until Erast is overcome by sensual passion and consummates the relationship. Erast ultimately leaves Liza, and she drowns herself after discovering that he is to marry another. The inversion of conventional social roles made the story radical for its time. Whereas the illiterate peasant girl possesses a noble soul, the nobleman is weak, forced by his debts to choose money over love. This theme plays into a second dichotomy: the association of nature (Liza) with sensibility and virtue in contrast to the association of the city (high society, Erast) with artifice and vice. While the link between sensibility and nature evokes *Werther* and the ideal of natural man, the negative judgment of the city reflected mounting concern in Europe about urban modernity. The valuation of suicide in this tale is ambiguous. Karamzin emphasized its impulsive, even mad character, but he never questioned Liza's virtue, despite her fall. Indeed, her grave functioned not as a profane but as a sacred site: "There I often sit in contemplation (*zadumchivost'*), leaning on the receptacle of Liza's dust," recounts the narrator. "Before my eyes flows the pond, above me rustle the leaves."[63] Furthermore, Erast's vice does not go unpunished: upon learning of Liza's death, he suffers and leads an unhappy life.[64]

The theme of love thwarted by social difference proved popular in Russia, as it had in Western Europe. In Pavel L'vov's *Dasha, The Village Girl*, for

[62] N. Karamzin, "Bednaia Liza," *Moskovskii zhurnal*, pt. 6 (2nd edn: 1802), 229.

[63] Ibid., 263.

[64] My interpretation draws on V. Sipovskii, "Vliianie 'Vertera' na russkii roman XVIII veka," *ZhMNP* no. 1 (1906), 61–63; Maarten Fraanje, "Nikolai Karamzin and Christian Heinrich Spiess: Poor Liza in the Context of the 18th Century German Suicide Story," *Study Group on Eighteenth-Century Russia: Newsletter*, no. 27 (Nov. 1999), 15–17.

example, the narrator ruminates about Dasha's sad fate: "Had she received an upbringing equal to her kindness [*liubeznost'*], then, perhaps, she would have been compared to Julie as described by the sage from Geneva [i.e. Rousseau], or to Richardson's Pamela. But the lovely Dasha had to wither like a flower in the desert simply because she was a peasant daughter."[65] Such tales challenged the social order by implying that inner virtue was more important than the status conferred by birth. Sentimental representations of peasants in particular played an important role in conferring humanity on the "dark masses."

A similarly unjust fate awaited Aleksandr Klushin's *Unfortunate M-v*, an outstanding young man possessing both reason and heart, who had been born a commoner. This social fact proves more important than all of M-v's noble qualities. Employed as a tutor, M-v meets the virtuous Sofiia, and the young people fall in love only to be separated by Sofiia's father. Here the tale diverges from Rousseau's: wrongly believing that Sofiia had deceived him, M-v shoots himself. The error is then punished: Sofiia devotes her life to M-v's memory, and her father comes to regret and suffer for his pride. "Everyone who knew M-v pitied him," the narrator concludes, venerating their sorrows, "everyone shed tears – as did I – and these minutes were the sweetest in my life."[66] The tale challenged both the principles of social hierarchy and the core ethos of the patriarchal family: the duty of children to obey their parents. Not only did it oppose the father, who defends social status, to the children, who assert their right to marry for love, it depicted the parent's values as false.[67] This story was rumored to be based on the actual case of a certain Maslov, which only increased its sensation.[68]

As this literary theme echoed through Russian society during the 1790s, its socio-political implications were understood and debated. "Meanwhile our city has been occupied with a discussion of two young people, who died in Petersburg," the director of the Moscow Archive of the Collegium of Foreign Affairs Nikolai Bantysh-Kamenskii thus wrote in a personal letter to a friend on January 29, 1791. Only the second of the two deaths involved suicide, but they possessed a common theme: the conflict between love and filial duty. For his part, Bantysh-Kamenskii took the perspective of the father and defended social hierarchy. A certain Mr. L., an Armenian who had achieved gentry status and tremendous wealth, had high hopes for his son's successful marriage. Unknown to his father, however, the son had fallen in love with the daughter of

---

[65] See, P. Iu. L'vov, "Dasha, derevenskaia devushka," *Russkaia sentimental'naia povest'*, ed. P. A. Orlov (Moscow, 1979), 68.

[66] A. Klushin, "Neschastnyi M-v. Povest'," *S.-Peterburgskii Merkurii*, pt. 1 (1793), esp. 225–26.

[67] Not all parents were negative characters. Compare L'vov, "Sofiia."

[68] Zhirmunskii, *Gete*, 65. For another supposedly real case, this time of a reputed "Russian Werther," see Vladimir Izmailov, *Puteshestviia v poludennuiu Rossiiu* (1802) as summarized in Zhirmunskii, *Gete*, 75.

an army doctor (*lekar'*), promised to marry her, and made her pregnant. Upon learning of the affair, Mr. L. forbade the marriage, causing the doctor and his daughter "to go mad," and the doctor ultimately to die. Though the son obeyed his father and deserted the young woman, he found his pleasures elsewhere, came down with a disease (presumably syphilis), and, as Bantysh-Kamenskii cursorily summarized, "lost his nose and finally his life." The second anecdote shared the theme of inappropriate romance. The son of Aristarkh Kashkin had fallen in love with a German-Russian girl, the daughter of a lieutenant-colonel. This time, when the father forbade the match, the son shot himself.[69] With the sentimental narrative seemingly turning up in real life, Bantysh-Kamenskii linked it to the corruption of morals in good society, extreme luxury, and an "enlightened" education, which was leading children away from religion and God. A kind of secularization had resulted in two major transgressions – filial disobedience and the inability to govern one's passions – and thence to suicide.

Bantysh-Kamenskii's critical appraisal was not exceptional, for sentimental representations of suicide often relied upon paradox. Most tales did associate vice with the negative characters (Erast, Sofiia's father), and virtue with the heroes and heroines, who remain true to their beloved, united with nature, and die tragically. However, the act of suicide was an impulsive action, often accompanied by emotional frenzy and even madness. Situated on the boundary between pure emotions and violent passions, suicide could pose a warning to readers, a warning sometimes made explicit. On one (fictional) grave was written: "Passer-by! Look at the dust of Sofiia; sigh about her – and fear your passions."[70] Similarly, an anonymous composition from 1792 briefly recounted the "audacious courage" of a virtuous young man faced with unrequited love, but his heroism was qualified with a warning: "Oh youth! Learn from this story, which may elicit tears from your eyes, what bitter fruits love for beauties yields."[71] The cult of sensibility did not celebrate all emotional experience, therefore, but privileged certain spheres and, moreover, called for the disciplining of the passions.[72] This mastery of emotional life, and especially the passions, presents an important parallel to the cult of rational self-sovereignty. In many senses, therefore, the narrators of sentimental prose form the real role models of the genre, for they are able to combine reason and self-control with

---

[69] In his correspondence from 1791–92, Bantysh-Kamenskii would mention seven cases of suicide, all involving members of the elite. See N. N. Bantysh-Kamenskii, "Moskovskie pis'ma v poslednie gody Ekaterinskogo tsarstvovaniia," *Russkii arkhiv* no. 11 (1876), here 258–59.

[70] L'vov, "Sofiia," 326.

[71] "Samoubiistvo," *Delo ot bezdel'ia ili priiatnaia zabava*, pt. 3 (1792), 136.

[72] On the concern in this period to curb the passions, see Smith, *Rough Stone*, 39–44. Note also the Russian translations of Christian Spiess, which identified the passions as a cause of suicide: *Samoubiitsy, ili uzhasnye sledstviia strastei, istinnye povesti, sobrannie g. Spisom* (Moscow, 1808); see also *Samoubiitsy ot liubvi: Trogatel'nye povesti soch. G. Spisa* (Moscow, 1812).

the most tender of emotions. Understood in this way, the sentimental tale was to stimulate feelings within the reader, especially pity, empathy, and benevolence, which in turn formed the universal basis of moral judgment (virtue) and fortified one against unruly and disruptive passions.

Some texts built explicitly on Rousseau's model, countering the selfishness of suicide with the selflessness of duty. "We will try to live," affirmed one hero, whose despair was interrupted by the sound of women weeping, "until it is possible to save another."[73] The hero of another tale likewise contemplates suicide but is saved by the wisdom of his faithful servant (paraphrasing Rousseau): "We will live so long as we can be useful on earth – if only to one person."[74] Furthermore, suicide could have a negative valuation. In Karamzin's story *Sierra-Morena*, the three characters in an inadvertent love triangle each choose different paths: one kills himself, but as a form of vengeance; the second joins a strict convent (and later dies of natural causes); and the third – the narrator – withdraws from the world into a life of solitude.[75]

Alternatives to suicide were thus available. Indeed, the sensibility of many heroes and heroines was so great that they simply died of their sorrows, which suggests a distinction between willing one's death and actively causing it.[76] This theme, along with the explicit representation of suicide as a shameful and debasing act, is particularly well developed in D. P. Gorchakov's *Plamir and Raida*. Following the early death of his wife, the handsome and noble Plamir rejects high society and decides to raise his son in a provincial town, where he meets the lovely, modest, and *chuvstvitel'naia* Raida, the daughter of a rich nobleman. As they read *Werther* together, their love grows, but Raida is ultimately forced to marry a man she does not love (quite literally in a shotgun wedding). In despair, believing that Raida had deceived him, Plamir devotes himself to his son, who soon dies. "Suicide seemed to his mind the only refuge, but the rules with which he had been raised repulsed this idea. However, to live was impossible; all the bonds that had tied him to life had been torn asunder." Inverting the logic of heroic suicide, Plamir decides to die "not like a base slave, furtively running from his master," but with honor, "being useful to somebody." He goes off to fight in France and dies courageously in battle: the fatal bullet passes through Raida's portrait which he had kept next to his heart as he had vowed. In an implicit reference to the dishonorable burial of suicides, the narrator stresses that Plamir's body was given to the earth with full military

[73] "Filon," *Muza*, pts. 1–4 (1796), pt. 1, 155.
[74] V. Izmailov, "Rostovskoe ozero," *Priiatnoe i poleznoe preprovozhdenie vremeni*, pt. 5 (1795), 316.
[75] N. M. Karamzin, "Sierra-Morena," *Izbrannye sochineniia*, 2 vols. (Moscow and Leningrad, 1964), vol. 1, 674–79.
[76] See L'vov, "Dasha." See also A. E. Izmailov, "Bednaia Masha: Rossiiskaia, otchasti spravedli-vaia povest'," also in *Russkaia sentimental'naia povest'*, ed. Orlov.

honors. For her part, already weakened by despair and consumption, Raida dies upon learning of Plamir's fate.[77]

In testing the moral essence of suicide, sentimental prose explored the conflict between freedom and duty but did not arrive at a uniform position. Some tales presented suicide as the tragic outcome of injustice, and they criticized – explicitly or implicitly – the social order and the patriarchal family as hindrances to the moral autonomy of the individual. Others, warning of the dangers of the passions, called for self-discipline and dedication to the social good. Sentimental texts also engaged in a dialogue with other models. Is not Plamir's decision to die in service to a just cause a judgment on Cato's reasoning?

As in other parts of Europe, sentimentalism did not remain within the literary text but pervaded people's personal lives, where it provided a language for understanding both the self and the other.[78] In 1803, Mikhail Sushkov's brother published a collection of Mikhail's poetry. The introduction lays bare the sensibility of the inner self and the path to virtuous action:

The unfortunate composer of most of these verses has not existed for a long time; the tears of brotherly affection have irrigated his cold grave for more than nine years. He died at the age of 17, and I am publishing his compositions in the hope that every feeling man will heave a sigh that the abilities of this unfortunate were cut off at the very beginning of their flower. At the composer's death, I was too young to sort out his papers. [. . .] Now that I have entered the age in which it is possible to feel, I believe that the publication of the remaining compositions of a beloved brother will in some sense pay the last honors of familial tenderness.[79]

Such tender feelings seem to contradict the harsh legal and religious penalties for suicide. Did the act necessitate the punishment of profane burial or was absolution possible? In his private papers written decades later, one of Sushkov's other brothers, Nikolai, eloquently advocated the latter view. Still hoping for God's forgiveness, Nikolai prayed for Mikhail's soul, despite the church's prohibition.[80]

---

[77] D. P. Gorchakov, "Plamir i Raida, Rossiiskaia povest'," *Sochineniia Kniazia D. P. Gorchakova* (Moscow, 1890), 135, 137 and *passim*. Compare the suicide of the tender Mariia, who stabs herself following her betrayal by Evgenii. "Vice triumphed over innocence," the narrator remarks, and Mariia depicts herself as accursed and criminal in her suicide note. See N. Mamyshev, "Zloschastnyi: Istinnoe proisshestvie," *Russkaia sentimental'naia povest'*, ed. Orlov, 281.

[78] For examples of the sentimental mood in letters and diaries of the era, see Sipovskii, "Ocherki," 620–25. See also E. N. Marasinova, *Psikhologiia elity rossiiskogo dvorianstva poslednei treti XVIII veka* (Moscow, 1999).

[79] *Pamiat' bratu, ili sobranie sochinenii i perevodov Mikhaila Sushkova, naidennykh posle ego smerti* (Moscow, 1803). For another commemoration of Sushkov's suicide in a sentimental manner, see Grigorii Khovanskov, *Zhertva muzam ili sobranie raznykh sochinenii, podrazhenii i perevodov v stikhakh* (Moscow, 1795), 95.

[80] He also collected the suicide notes as well as many texts from the public debate in his own private tribute. See RO RGB, f. 297, k. 4, d. 6, ll. 10–16; for his analysis of Christian views on suicide, see 16–30.

This example serves as a reminder that suicide was a very real and disturbing event and that textual allusions did not exist in isolation. By evoking the public as a discursive object, Russia's new print culture actively encouraged readers to engage in a dialogue with the printed word.[81] It provided new categories with which to contemplate suicide – to probe its moral essence and to reflect on its social and political meanings. One response was the compassion of the sentimental voice, which would resurface in the coming decades. In a display of their benevolence and pity, the tsar's elite servitors would regularly intervene on behalf of suicides and attempted suicides, particularly among the peasantry, depicting them less as criminals than as victims. The era of sentimentalism had passed, but its legacy remained. Alongside this current, however, was also a powerful swell of denunciation, which emerged in the 1790s and persisted in modified form into the twentieth century.

The politics of denunciation

"I have become bored with being in the public performance," Opochinin wrote in his suicide note, "the curtain has closed for me."[82] Comparing life to a stage, he made his death into a spectacle. As Lotman has persuasively argued, a sense of theatricality permeated elite identity by the turn of the nineteenth century, when, following the conventions of Romanticism, life began to imitate art: "the entire world, having become a theatrical world, is transformed according to the laws of theatrical space, [where] things become signs of things." Despite his suggestive metaphor, Lotman's analysis focused almost entirely on the actors and their performance.[83] Yet the spectacular nature of (literary and actual) suicides in this period created not just actors, but also spectators, even a discursive space in which a public opinion could form. Indeed, the public claimed a collective right of judgment.

That the modern genre of suicide notes first emerged in this era is significant. To write a final message, people must not only be literate but also believe that their death has a broader meaning. As an artifact, therefore, the note articulates in some way a sense of individual selfhood and an intended audience. Suicide letters appeared in England rarely before 1700, and their ultimately mass popularity depended in large part on the spread of the daily newspaper, which reported suicides and printed suicide notes.[84] In Russia, where censorship remained strong and newspapers were poorly developed, the intended and actual

---

[81] This was a frequent motif both within fictional works (especially in the narrator's voice) but also more generally. Note the translator's introduction to "Katon v Livii," 79.

[82] Trefolev, "Predsmertnoe zaveshchanie," 224–26.

[83] See Iu. Lotman, "Teatr i teatral'nost' v stroe kul'tury nachala XIX veka," *Izbrannye stat'i*, 3 vols. (Tallinn, 1992), vol. 1, 269. Outram (*The Body*, 79–80) makes a similar observation.

[84] MacDonald and Murphy, *Sleepless Souls*, 228, 324–34.

audience for many notes was nonetheless the public, and it was fascinated by them. Bantysh-Kamenskii had not only read Sushkov's letter but recommended that his correspondent do the same. Similarly, Karamzin had also read a copy and offered to send it on to a friend.[85] When the son of Count Apraksin, an ensign in the Izmailovskii Regiment, shot himself in 1793, the governor acted quickly to prevent the circulation of the letter.[86] Concerned that suicide – especially the suicide note – could become a model, the high-ranking officer (and occasional publicist), Irinarkh Zavalishin published a two-part didactic article in 1794 entitled "The Letter of a Suicide."[87] The circulation of suicide notes was apparently so widespread, that the journalist and critic Nikolai Strakhov would ironically propose that it be legally prohibited to circulate letters of suicide victims, for they "fly around the city like an arrow and in the end strike the first weak heart."[88]

The proliferation of rumors further illustrates both the informal networks of social communication and the theatricality of public space. When two sons of Senator Vyrubov shot themselves within several months of each other, public interest was so great that Moscow's Governor General, Prince A. A. Prozorovskii, pursued the matter personally and presented his findings in a special report to the empress. Having questioned the commander of the second brother in private, he finally obtained what he considered reliable information; notably, this was the talk of the town. Whereas the first son had reputedly been unloved by his father and melancholic by disposition, the second had been his father's favorite and hence compelled to serve in an artillery division close to home rather than allowed to go into active service, as he preferred.[89] While the explanations were not sensational, they nonetheless echoed contemporary concerns about personal autonomy and filial duty. Rumors likewise spread through private correspondence. After a woman poisoned herself following her husband's discovery of a love affair, a letter provided intimate details, emphasizing her sense of social shame.[90] Bantysh-Kamenskii recounted seven suicides in

---

[85] Bantysh-Kamenskii, "Moskovskie pis'ma," 274; and Ia. Grot and P. Pekarskii, eds. *Pis'ma N. M. Karamzina k I. I. Dmitrievu*, (SPb, 1866), vol. 1, 30.

[86] Unfortunately, it is not included in the report. See RGADA, f. 16, d. 526, ch. 7, l. 319.

[87] The article combined excerpts from the suicide note with Zavalishin's running commentary on them. I. Z. [I. Zavalishin], "Pis'mo k Izdateliam Novykh ezhemesiachnykh sochinenii," *Novye ezhemesiachnye sochineniia*, pt. 101 (1794), 5–6. Followed by "Pis'mo samoubiitsy," 6–33; continued in pt. 102 (1794), 18–60. Zavalishin was a major general, the commander of the Astrakhan garrison regiment, and finally, the General Inspector of transport. See *RP*, vol. 2, 297.

[88] Nikolai Strakhov, *Moi peterburgskie sumerki* (SPb, 1810), 53.

[89] RGADA, f. 16, d. 582, ch. 3, ll. 78–9, 146.

[90] This is the only female suicide from the elite that I have found in this period, the daughter of Princess Shakhovskaia. See "Vesti iz Rossii v Angliiu 1796 goda. Pis'ma grafa F. V. Rostopchina k grafu S. R. Vorontsovu," *Russkii arkhiv* no. 4 (1876), 413. Compare the laconic memoirs of her lover (which do not mention the suicide), "Iz zapisok grafa E. F. Komarovskogo," in *Osmnadtsatyi vek. Istoricheskii sbornik*, bk. 1 (Moscow, 1868), 341–42.

his letters, and his information was clearly drawn from hearsay – he discussed financial improprieties, an unhappy love affair, and a familial cover-up. Altogether, he pictures a rather rumor-hungry public with a worldly understanding of suicide.[91]

These spectators to the drama of suicide were not passive. Instead, they developed discursive strategies to denounce the act of suicide – to deny the claim to virtue or heroism and thereby to defuse its more radical social and political implications. Exemplary in this regard was the public reaction to the most controversial case of the era, that of Mikhail Sushkov. In part because his uncle was Catherine's personal secretary, Sushkov's audience included the court. In a special report to the empress (not unlike his later one on the Vyrubov brothers), Prozorovskii summarized the facts of the case, enclosed copies of the letters, and offered his own commentary: "Observe, if you please, the image of debauched judgment and lawlessness; it is evident that he was raised [*vospitan*] as a debauched Frenchman, for the forthright principles of a man were not established in him."[92] Influenced perhaps by this formulation, Catherine was said to have exclaimed, "What an upbringing! Christian law was not inculcated [in him]."[93] Sushkov's uncle later reported another comment from Catherine: "I pity the father and mother who lost such a son. But I pity him even more. If he had remained alive, we would have soon forgotten about Voltaire."[94] In September 1792, a month after the overthrow of the French monarchy, Bantysh-Kamenskii also commented on the case: "What is going on in France? Is it possible that enlightenment can lead man into such darkness and delusion! [It is all] villainy to perfection. This example will serve everyone rejecting faith and authority. Speaking about foreigners, I will say a word about our own monstrosity [*urod*] Sushkov, who embraced [*oblobyzal*] the fate of Judas. Read his letter: how much cursing of the Creator! How much arrogance and vanity! Such is a large part of our youth, intellectually fervent and guided neither by the law nor their faith."[95] Finally, writing several decades later, Nikolai Sushkov depicted his brother's suicide as the direct result of atheism arising from the "fatal study" of philosophy.[96]

These responses share three primary motifs. First, suicide was somehow foreign, imported into Russia along with cultural Westernization. Second, atheism and unbelief were its primary causes, and these, in turn, were the results of

[91] Bantysh-Kamenskii, "Moskovskie pis'ma," 271, 280, 282, 284.
[92] For complete transcripts, see Fraan'e [Fraanje], "Proshchal'nye pis'ma," 156–57. I also consulted the original report in RGADA, f. 16, d. 582, ch. 3, l. 132. Copies of the letter follow.
[93] For complete transcripts, see Fraan'e [Fraanje], "Proshchal'nye pis'ma," 157. For the original source, see N. Barsukov, ed., *Dnevnik A. V. Khrapovitskogo s 18 ianvaria 1782 po 17 sentiabria 1793 goda* (Moscow, 1901), 237.
[94] As cited in Fraan'e [Fraanje], "Proshchal'nye pis'ma," 158.
[95] Bantysh-Kamenskii, "Moskovskie pis'ma," 274.
[96] See RO RGB, f. 297, k. 4, d. 6, ll. 10–16.

(an enlightened) education and the reading of philosophy. Another outcome of such an upbringing, though only implicit in Prozorovskii's language, was libertinism, depravity, and vice. Finally, suicide was an assault on religious and secular authority, on God and the law. The logical development in Bantysh-Kamenskii's account is particularly striking, for it was his fury about events in France that prompted him to mention Sushkov, whom he calls a foreigner, a monstrosity, and a Judas.

The cultural geography of suicide in Russia placed its origins in Europe. That Sushkov's case had been linked three times to France was hardly surprising. The French Revolution had shattered the faith of Europe's governing elites in the natural perpetuity of both absolutism and social hierarchy, and the over-throw of the monarchy seemed ample confirmation of the radical threat within much Enlightenment philosophy. The perceived context of his suicide was not a familial drama but a socio-historical one: the treachery of the revolution, the treachery of Judas, and the treachery of free-thinking youth in general. Yet not only France, but also a damp and gloomy England was linked to suicide. Both the English and continental Europeans had often commented upon this association, and the cause of the "English malady" (or spleen, as Sushkov had called it) was usually ascribed to climate, unbelief, or a melancholic disposition.[97] In reporting interesting cases from Western Europe, Russia's journals sometimes built on the stereotype with such catchy titles as "A New Kind of Suicide in England."[98] The metaphor also appeared in Bantysh-Kamenskii's correspondence, this time with reference to the Vyrubov brothers. "Did I write to you that yet another young man, the son of Senator Vyrubov, placed a pistol in his mouth and took his life? This occurred, it seems, at the beginning of the month [of September]: the fruits of our acquaintance with the English people. We only borrow the bad from everyone." A month later, he added: "What an unhappy father Senator Vyrubov must be. Yesterday his other son, an artillery officer, shot himself. In two months, two sons ended their lives so shamefully. There is a danger that this English disease will come into fashion with us."[99] Drawing on the connotation of England as the everyday home of suicide, Bantysh-Kamenskii likened these deaths to Western fads and maladies. Indeed, to render suicide foreign – whether French and political or English and everyday – was to idealize an abstract Russian landscape, where sons had submitted to fathers, faith was unquestioned, and suicide had been a rarity.

The mapping of suicide onto France and England was not just a result of national stereotypes or its alleged prevalence there. It also reproduced another

---

[97] A more convincing explanation lies in the rise of a periodical press in England which reported and publicized suicide. On that and the "English disease" more generally, see MacDonald and Murphy, *Sleepless Souls*, chs. 5, 9.

[98] "Novogo rodu samoubiistvo v Anglii," *Vestnik Evropy*, pt. 2, no. 8 (1802), 351–54.

[99] Bantysh-Kamenskii, "Moskovskie pis'ma," 276, 277–78.

perceived divergence between Russia and the West: the level of civilization. For the first time, it was thought that aspects of modern civilization, especially its secularism, actually encouraged people to kill themselves, and this linkage would persist for the next century. One of the earliest empirical scholars of suicide was Voltaire, who, citing both historical accounts and contemporary newspaper reports, found that suicide was more common in the city – the great site and symbol of modernity.[100] While he explained this pattern by the greater leisure of city dwellers, it also played into another stereotype: the association of the city with vice, debauchery, and unbelief (and the parallel association of the countryside with tradition and stability). Encouraged by the sentimental idealization of nature, this association had become so common that it was parodied.[101] In many respects, the linkage of suicide to the vices of modernity built upon its religious associations with immorality but placed the familiar religious condemnation into a new geographical and social context. Yet these assumptions also had two results: the perception that suicide was a disease of the city and its educated elites; and, by the 1830s, the contention that Russia's backwardness – the persistence of patriarchy and tradition – could confer immunity.

One of the best expositions of this general approach can be found in Nikolai Strakhov's book, *My Petersburg Twilight* (1810). Alongside chapters on Nevskii Prospect, shopping, and drunkenness was one devoted to suicide – this very fact an illustration of the importance of suicide and its perceived link to urban life.[102] Beginning with a "bad upbringing" and concluding with unbelief, suicide's causes read like a catalogue of vices. Indeed, this "terrible villainy" was a logical outcome of immorality, whether the premature entrance into mixed society or the triad of luxury, extravagance, and idleness that ultimately rendered life a burden.[103] Despite Strakhov's concern to situate suicide into the modern, Westernized city (and urban elites), his serial logic also possessed parallels with some pre-Petrine texts, especially the tendency to represent suicide as the logical result of a pattern of immoral conduct.

The other key cause of suicide was literature, Strakhov asserted, echoing a preoccupation that had spread throughout Europe in the eighteenth century. Comparing libraries to pharmacies, he pointedly noted that they contained both

---

[100] Voltaire's findings were accepted for the next century but have since been discredited. See Jacques Choron, *Suicide* (New York, 1972), 125; and Howard I. Kushner, "Suicide, Gender, and the Fear of Modernity in Nineteenth-Century Medical and Social Thought," *Journal of Social History* (Spring 1993), 461–90. Similarly, Rousseau had associated urban life with corruption, See Outram, *The Body*, 72.

[101] In one Russian story, for example, the virtuous Sofiia responds to the evil Evgenii's proposal: "Go to [Moscow]? Ah, no, I am afraid. Grandpa has told me of many evils about [cities]. It is said that ogres live there." G. Kamenev, "Sofiia," *Muza*, pt. 1 (Mar. 1796), 212–13.

[102] Strakhov, *Moi peterburgskie sumerki*, 44–54.

[103] Compare the causal structure in these anecdotes from Western Europe. "Samoubiitsa. Anekdot," *Moskovskii zhurnal*, pt. 1 (1791), here 2nd edn (1803), 60–66; G. Kamenev, "Ramier ili samoubiitsa," *Ippokrena*, pt. 6 (1800), 411–16.

strong medicines and lethal poisons. Like many of his contemporaries, he cited *The New Héloïse* and *The Sorrows of Young Werther* as particularly dangerous, with the latter alone – in his view – having already caused several hundred suicides. Indeed, sentimental tragedies had wreaked destruction on the level of an "epidemic disease."[104] Fearing literature was a source of moral infection, Strakhov chose a medical metaphor, and he was not the only one. The notion that suicide was infectious – and that literature was a source of contagion spreading the disease of unbelief – would persist for many decades. To combat this evil, Strakhov advocated the strengthening of morality and religious education (apparently as a kind of inoculation). He thereby joined the growing swell of voices throughout Europe that feared modernity – secularization and urbanization – as a threat to traditional values and social stability.

These conjoined metaphors provided a key weapon in the public's attack on suicide. In Zavalishin's published response to a supposed suicide letter, he entered into a dialogue with those "young people" who defended the "ungodly act [*bogoprotivnyi postupok*]." His apparent goal was to mold public opinion by making the supposed role model into an object of pity and derision. The article is dialogical: quoted excerpts from a suicide letter are accompanied by a running commentary about an improper upbringing, the vices of pride and luxury, the virtues of self-restraint and moderation, and so forth. The excerpted suicide letter bears some similarities to Sushkov's, indicating that Zavalishin had probably read a copy, but it is fundamentally different, suggesting that he had perhaps edited the text to suit his own needs. This suicide is still a believer – he desperately begs God for forgiveness of his sin, cites his despondency, and seems unstable.[105] As most members of Russia's public would have only heard rumors and not read Sushkov's actual notes, Zavalishin's technique denied the act nobility. He is instead dissolute, debauched, and a bit pathetic. Denunciation was thus a means to affirm society's core values: duty, self-discipline, and faith.

Almost a decade later, Karamzin pursued a similar tactic by publishing a translated article on suicide in his influential journal *Herald of Europe*.[106] Its timing was not insignificant: it closely followed both Radishchev's suicide

---

[104] Strakhov, *Moi peterburgskie sumerki*, 46.

[105] Fraanje ("Proshchal'nye pis'ma," 159) reads this text as a comment on Sushkov's suicide. While he does show some textual similarities, these are minor in comparison to the major differences. In addition to those cited, these include the age of this suicide (25, not Sushkov's 17), and his initials (P. S.). Notably, a certain Petr Sievers had shot himself several years earlier, but the report does not mention any kind of note. See I. Z. "Pis'mo," 6–10, 26. On Sievers, RGADA, f. 16, d. 526, ch. 2, l. 189.

[106] "O samoubiistve," *Vestnik Evropy*, pt. 5, no. 19 (1802): 207–9. According to Fraanje ("Proshchal'nye pis'ma," 160), this was a translation of S. F. Genlis, "Entretiens sur le suicide, ou Courage philosophique, opposé au courage religieux / Par Marie-Nicolas-Silvestre Guillon," *Nouvelle bibliothque des romans* (Paris, 1802), vol. 15, 194–97. Such arguments have a long tradition. St. Augustine had thus depicted Cato as a coward, suicide as a dishonor. See Murray, *The Curse*, 116–17.

and the posthumous publication of Sushkov's *Russian Werther*.[107] In a three-pronged assault, the review maintained that suicide was not heroic, virtuous, or patriotic. The great heroes of antiquity had really killed themselves in despair, wanton pride, and cowardice, and "wise contemporaries" had condemned their acts as disastrous for the fatherland. Furthermore, both ancient and modern suicides were almost all scoundrels, either debauched persons or youth weakened by passion and influenced by false models, especially literature. Suicide was rendered a vice in both a moral and a civic sense: it was depraved and unpatriotic, the absolute antithesis to virtue.

Perhaps the most evocative example of the emerging techniques of denunciation was the appearance in Russia of a social "type," the Voltairian (*Vol'ter'ianets*). As Victoria Frede has shown, this stereotype of the free-thinker linked reading Voltaire to unbelief and from thence to numerous calamitous consequences: folly, immorality, debauchery and dissipation, disobedience, and suicide.[108] This paradigm was found in contemporary writings and persisted in later autobiographies. In the memoir of A. D. Galakhov, for example, the narrator ironically summarized his grandfather's encounter with Voltaire's essays with a medical metaphor: "He was infected [*zarazilsia*] with religious unbelief and became, as his neighbors called it, one of the 'godless' [*bezbozhnik*]." The result was an "enlightened" education for the son (the narrator's uncle) that, in a causal chain, led to his suicide. An army officer quartered in a provincial city and leading a life of dissipation and debauchery, the uncle had argued with a fellow officer but a duel was averted through reconciliation. A late and drunken night followed:

On the way back to their apartments, uncle stopped and said: "How absurd life is! Mornings we argue, evenings we reconcile; tomorrow we will again argue, the day after again reconcile. I don't want to live anymore; I'll shoot myself." "Don't talk nonsense," his comrades objected, "you won't shoot yourself; you're only talking like this because you're drunk." – "Really, I swear to God, I'll shoot myself!" – "You won't shoot yourself." Uncle fell silent, but as soon as he entered his apartment, he took his pistol and shot himself. And so ended the life of a gifted and good man ruined by a strange upbringing.[109]

Though Galakhov had not been present at this scene, he accounted for his uncle's death with the stage image of the grandfather as a Voltairian: the act of

---

[107] Lotman ("Poetics of Everyday Behavior," 93) emphasizes the first, and Fraanje ("Proshchal'nye pis'ma," 160) the second.

[108] In contradistinction, it should be noted, to Voltaire's deism and ambivalent view of suicide. See Victoria Frede, "The Rise of Unbelief in the Late Imperial Period" (Ph.D. Dissertation, University of California, Berkeley, 2002), 21–38. On the broader reception of Voltaire in Russia, see P. R. Zaborov, *Russkaia literatura i Vol'ter XVIII–pervaia tret' XIX veka* (Leningrad, 1978).

[109] Sto odin [A. D. Galakhov], "Ded moi pomeshchik Serbin. Iz zapisok cheloveka," *Russkii vestnik* no. 11 (1875), 70, 79–80; for further examples, see also Sipovskii, "Ocherki iz istorii," 625–27.

reading had led to unbelief, a godless education, and a life of meaningless vice that logically ended in suicide. Though a fiction, this pattern possessed a core of accuracy: both the diverse texts streaming into Russia combined with new ways of reading had helped to shape modes of self-fashioning, up to and including the extreme act of self-destruction. Yet the serial logic of condemnation also denied moral autonomy to the actor. In this theatrical space, suicide had become a sign of unbelief and vice. It could also be a bit pathetic and even comical.

At first glance, the categories of public debate around suicide had been completely transformed between the seventeenth and the late eighteenth centuries, when Westernization shaped new models of statecraft, social life, and personal virtue. Russia's elites – both public and officialdom – possessed a seemingly secular attitude toward suicide. Not only were church teachings or prohibitions hardly mentioned, but the reported causes of self-killing were typically everyday events and experiences. Yet the rhetoric of condemnation echoes earlier texts. Suicide remained a fundamentally moral issue, explained with reference to unbelief and insubordination, vice and depravity. Its cure lay in voluntary submission and religious faith. When it condemned suicide, Russia's public was thereby defending the socio-political order – which was precisely what the "self-will" of the individual seemed to threaten. And therein was a significant innovation. In contrast to the earlier era, positive images of suicide as an affirmation of self were now established, whether embedded in rational self-sovereignty, civic patriotism, honor and dignity, or personal moral autonomy. "To know how to die" was a new kind of political statement, and its claim to worldly self-sovereignty undercut a central principle of absolutist governance: the voluntary submission of the individual to the guardianship of divinely constituted political and social authorities.

Even as they evoked religious norms and traditions, these debates also began to situate the act of suicide within new social and national geographies. They first shaped the politics of social distinction. Though sentimental narratives had often challenged the equation of birth with virtue, the public was only interested in its own suicides. True sensibility and the rational mastery of the self were achievements apparently presumed impossible for actual, uneducated peasants.[110] The debates also shaped a narrative of moral and political danger, in which various phenomena – luxury, idleness, immorality, disobedience, free-thinking, atheism, treason – were conflated into one powerful sign. This

---

[110] The only exception is a fragment of the prolific memoirist Andrei Bolotov, in which he recounted a conversation he overheard between two serfs complaining about their lot and debating the merits of suicide. The point of the text, however, was to demonstrate the ignorance and superstition of the simple folk, who did not understand the Christian doctrine of the immortality of the soul, even when Bolotov tried to explain it to them. See "Iz neizdannogo literaturnogo naslediia Bolotova," *Literaturnoe nasledstvo* no. 9/10 (1933), 179–80.

narrative contained both national and social elements, for suicide was associated with the secular ideas and materialistic principles imported from the West. Could "enlightenment" – knowledge, education, and Westernization – lead to the erosion of belief and thence to numerous calamitous events: Insubordination and filial disobedience? Immorality and debauchery? The rejection of the sovereignty of God and tsar – that is, of law and social order more generally? Even as they politicized the act of suicide, these associations also helped to disarm its most disruptive implications. To represent suicide as a vice, a kind of debauchery, was to shift the meaning from an abstract political or ideological level back to a concrete, personal one: the moral failings of the individual had led to the sin and crime of suicide. Although Russia's public as a whole defined itself through its Western culture and civility, an ambivalence lingered about the nature and costs of this civilization.

3 The regulation of suicide

> He who is convicted of the intention to take his life [. . .] shall be punished
> [. . .] as for attempted murder.
>
> *Digest of Laws*, 1835

> We dare to think that this regulation is both unjust and awkward in [its] imple-
> mentation.
>
> Commentary to the Penal Code of 1845

The criminal regulation of suicide reached its highpoint in imperial Russia
during the first half of the nineteenth century. Local authorities began to investigate suicides as a matter of routine, and reports flowed into the central bureaucracy in St. Petersburg, where they would ultimately form the basis of the first
statistical studies in Russia of crime and mortality. The legal prosecution of suicide and attempted suicide likewise became a standard practice, and the rubric
appeared in the annual statistical reports on judicial activity that began to be
published in 1834. Both of these developments were encouraged by legal codification. After almost two centuries of failed projects, a digest of criminal laws
was enacted in 1835 followed by a revised penal code in 1845. Though suicide was not formally decriminalized, its legal status and punishment changed
fundamentally. The 1845 code no longer defined suicide as a form of murder,
and it was henceforth to be punished with a combination of civil and religious
penalties. At this time, the legal prosecution of suicide began a slow process of
decline.

In some respects, these developments parallel the pattern found in Western
and Central Europe. By the 1820s and 1830s, specialists there had turned their
attention to suicide, and both medical and statistical studies would proliferate
over the next decades. Many European countries were also following the lead of
revolutionary France, which had abolished the criminal prosecution of suicide
in 1791. This process was uneven, however, and suicide remained a criminal offense in parts of Europe into the second half of the nineteenth century.
In England, where suicide was fully decriminalized only in 1961, such harsh
penalties as dishonorable burial, the forfeiture of property, and imprisonment
with hard labor (for unsuccessful attempts) were only repealed in the 1870s and

1880s. The application of penalties depended, however, upon an increasingly rare verdict of mental competence.[1] With the progressive elimination of criminal sanctions, therefore, suicide was increasingly consigned to the competing jurisdictions of religion, science, and public culture.

Despite the various parallels, the criminal regulation of suicide in Russia possessed important particularities. The translation of suicide into the languages of science did begin in this period, but political conditions – including censorship and restrictions on travel and education – hindered the development of an active scientific community. Furthermore, formal decriminalization did not actually occur until after the collapse of the monarchy in 1917. Most distinctive, however, was the ongoing resonance of suicide as a threat to the social and political order. This occurred in the routine administration of suicide but became especially prominent during the reign of Nicholas I (1825–55), who possessed a radical vision of a unitary state and society, with each person embedded into relations of authority and subordination. Precisely this vision would confer sometimes contradictory meanings upon the act of self-killing.

Crime reports

By the late eighteenth century, suicide was appearing in documents produced by the growing state bureaucracy. In his official weekly digests on events in St. Petersburg province compiled for Catherine the Great between 1785 and 1793, civil governor Petr Konovnitsyn reported on food prices, the weather, crime, and 113 cases of suicide and attempted suicide.[2] While this was not the first time that suicide had been mentioned in a digest sent to the empress, its regular inclusion – especially routine cases – was still not typical in this period.[3] Although the elites did not pay them particular attention in their personal papers or letters, these reports document that suicides were happening in the palaces and on the estates of Russia's most illustrious families – the Orlovs, Potemkins, Razumovskiis, Golovkins.

---

[1] On suicide in England, see Olive Anderson, *Suicide in Victorian and Edwardian England* (Oxford, 1987); and Barbara T. Gates, *Victorian Suicide: Mad Crimes and Sad Histories* (Princeton, 1988). On the French case, see Lisa Lieberman, "Romanticism and the Culture of Suicide in Nineteenth-Century France," *Comparative Studies in Society and History* 33: 3 (July 1991). On Germany, see Ursula Baumann, *Vom Recht auf den eigenen Tod: Geschichte des Suizids vom 18. bis zum 20. Jahrhundert* (Weimar, 2001).

[2] See "Doneseniia gubernatora Petra Konovnitsyna po upravleniiu Peterburgskoi gubernii," RGADA, f. 16, d. 526, ch. 1–7.

[3] I have found two other earlier cases in Petersburg: a French merchant, who cut his throat; and an unidentified peasant boy, who threw himself into the Neva. See f. 16, d. 481, ch. 6, ll. 54–5 (report of the police chief Nikolai Chicherin, Oct. 16, 1776); f. 16, d. 500, ll. 147–48 (report of Governor General Aleksandr Golitsyn, June 10–24, 1783). In a random examination of administrative reports from other provinces during Catherine's reign, I also found material on several high-profile scandals from Moscow in the 1790s.

The fact that these cases were reported at all points to important changes in local administration, changes which were more advanced in the capital.[4] By the 1780s, Catherine the Great had already done more than any of her predecessors to rationalize and streamline local government. The 1775 Statute for the Administration of the Provinces of the Russian Empire had established the basic framework of administration and justice that would survive until the Great Reforms of the 1860s. By 1785, existing provinces had been reorganized into forty-one smaller units, roughly based on population, and each of these new provinces was being subdivided into more or less standard-sized districts (*uezd*) with local capitals sometimes founded just for administrative purposes. An appointed governor or governor general was charged with the oversight of both the administration of the province and the welfare and interests of all its inhabitants. As the personal representative of the empress, he possessed the right to correspond directly with her.[5] The police ordinance of 1782 regulated the policing of cities and placed this sphere under the authority of the governor as well. St. Petersburg itself was divided into ten districts (*chast'*) staffed by district police officers, and subdivided, in turn, into a total of forty-two quarters each with police inspectors. For every crime committed against a person, police officers were directed to file a report identifying the victim and perpetrator, the method or weapon, the time and place, and the context, including whether the crime had been premeditated. Crowning this system was a central organ, charged with oversight of the police and compiling monthly reports on crime, noteworthy incidents, bread prices, and so forth.[6] The 113 cases reported by Konovnitsyn traveled up to his office through these bureaucratic channels. Table 3.1. presents an overview of them.

Administrative records should not be read as an accurate gauge of the real number of suicides or attempted suicides. As scholars have shown, the identification of suicide is historically contingent, for the official determination of cause of death in cases of drowning, shooting, and poisoning – all of which can plausibly be accidental – was influenced by local factors.[7] It can reflect the staffing levels, attitudes, and receptivity to bribery of local officials. Given the legal penalties and social shame associated with suicide, moreover, families have also tried to cover it up. Leaving aside the question of numbers, these

[4] On the character and evolution of the bureaucracy, see George L. Yaney, *The Systemization of Russian Government: Social Evolution in the Domestic Administration of Imperial Russia, 1711–1905* (Urbana, Ill., 1973).

[5] Isabel de Madariaga, *Russia in the Age of Catherine the Great* (New Haven, 1981), chs. 1, 3, 18, 19.

[6] *PSZ*, vol. 21, no. 15379, esp. art. 33, 105. On the situation in St. Petersburg, *Ocherki istorii Leningrada*, 7 vols. (Moscow and Leningrad, 1955), vol. 1, 363–64.

[7] The cultural contingency of statistics was first discussed in detail by Jack D. Douglas, *The Social Meanings of Suicide* (Princeton, 1967). It has since become a commonplace in the historical literature on suicide.

Table 3.1 *Reported Suicides in St. Petersburg Province, 1785–93*

Sex	Reported cases	Location	Reported cases
Male	106	St. Petersburg	60
Female	7	Province	53
Social Identity	*Reported cases*	*Method*	*Reported cases*
Peasants	54	Hanging/Strangulation	68
Soldiers/Sailors	12	Drowning	17
Urban Orders	18	Cutting/Stabbing	14
Aristocrats/Officers	8	Shooting	12
Others*	21	Other	2

Source: RGADA, f. 16, d. 526, ch. 1–7.
*These include nine foreigners, several unidentified individuals, and a varied mix of people difficult to place in official categories: a retired medical officer (*lekar'*), minor officials, a colonist, a palace cook, etc.

records demonstrate that self-killing was being investigated as a crime by the local police, sometimes accompanied by medical personnel. Their formulaic content likewise points to the standardization of investigatory procedures generally along the lines specified in the 1782 police ordinance. The bureaucratization of policing was thus leading to the creation of a new kind of document – the crime report – that would in turn become the basis for a new governmental project in the nineteenth century: statistics.

Given the brevity and standardized format of crime reports – they were often as short as four or five lines – it is necessary to tease out the underlying patterns of meaning. On the whole, they succinctly presented the material evidence: the discovery and location of the body, the method of death, and the social identity (though not always the name) of the victim. In addition, a large majority referred to some sort of broader context – a cause, motive, or circumstance, presumably extracted from the reports of local officials, who, in turn, obtained their information from witnesses (family members, neighbors, serf owners) and medical personnel. These elliptical comments are important. At issue is not their accuracy, for that cannot be determined in any case, but the associations and perspectives they construct. First, the crime of suicide was reported and thereby shaped within social relationships of power, including paternal authority. Second, the crime was overlaid with both moral and medical significance. Indeed, they point to important parallels with the techniques of denunciation employed in the more sensational cases discussed in the previous chapter.

Social hierarchy played an important role in the attribution of cause. For suicides involving members of the elite, the will to judge was strikingly weak. In many instances, no motive or cause was found. This even included the case of Lieutenant Kashkin, who, according to the detailed account supplied by Bantysh-Kamenskii, had shot himself when his father forbade an inappropriate marriage.[8] The only ascribed motive in other cases was financial, either debt or the misuse of public funds, and the dispassionate language of the reports suggests that such motives were readily comprehensible.[9] Finally, reference was also made to the conjoined medical and spiritual condition of melancholy and the related illness of hypochondria, both of which were fashionable foreign terms popularized in Russia's journals.[10] Rather than describing the actual behavior or symptoms, however, the accounts were usually laconic: "the retired ensign Karl Norden, while melancholic [*buduchi v melankholii*], cut his throat in the middle of the night at two o'clock and died."[11] In sum, these reports are noteworthy for their restraint. One reason may have been the low social status of police who were not accorded full cooperation by influential and powerful families.

In reports on suicides among the middle and lower orders, the language is more colorful, and some form of explanation is almost universal. For middle orders, such as merchants, the ascribed context included financial affairs, disease, and drunkenness.[12] A similar range of circumstances occurred in cases involving peasants, though the material causes were more modest – a peasant binge-drinking the entire proceeds of a journey to market, for example.[13] Striking for their absence were references to unhappiness in love, illegitimate pregnancy, or familial conflicts.

The most common practice was to ascribe suicide to a pattern of improper or immoral behavior. This motif was especially noteworthy in cases involving serfs. When an unnamed serf belonging to Baroness Natal'ia Stroganova hanged herself, for example, the police investigation revealed that she had generally conducted herself indecently (*byla ne poriadochnogo povedeniia*) and had acted in drunkenness.[14] Similarly, another (unnamed) serf hanged himself because, it was established, "his behavior was intemperate; for this reason, his master intended to put him into the army."[15] As this last case implies but does

---

[8] The report included the time, place, and method of the suicide (a bullet into the right temple), and concluded that his motives had not been uncovered. RGADA, f. 16, d. 526, ch. 6, l. 97.

[9] RGADA, f. 16, d. 526, ch. 4, ll. 159, 188; ch. 6, ll. 425–27, ch. 7, l. 12.

[10] See e.g. "Prosti," *Moskovskii zhurnal*, pt. 8 (2nd edn: 1803), 172–73; F. K. "Skuka," *S.-Peterburgskii vestnik* no. 6 (Sept. 1780), 199; "Melankholiia," *Vestnik Evropy*, pt. 1, no. 1 (1802), 53–54. For further analysis, see Julia Schreiner, *Jenseits vom Glück: Suizid, Melancholie und Hypochondrie in deutschsprachigen Texten des späten 18. Jahrhunderts* (Munich, 2003).

[11] RGADA, f. 16, d. 526, ch. 7, l. 3. See also ch. 4, l. 275 (a foreigner); ch. 4, l. 279 (a merchant); and ch. 5, l. 186 (a Baltic German).

[12] See e.g. RGADA, f. 16, d. 526, ch. 1, ll. 222, 255, 263.

[13] For cases involving money, see RGADA, f. 16, d. 526, ch. 1, l. 141; ch. 3, ll. 108, 268 (a son who stole money from his father).

[14] RGADA, f. 16, d. 526, ch. 7, l. 23.   [15] RGADA, f. 16, d. 526, ch. 5, l. 178.

not explicitly state, a broader context was the fear of punishment. This is hardly surprising for serfs in particular suffered under an almost complete dependency on their owners, who possessed extensive rights to employ physical discipline, though not to kill or maim.[16] Still, the causal nexus in these documents was suicide and vice: with the punishment presumably justified, attention remained focused on the immorality of the serf, not on the dynamics of discipline. Fearing punishment for drinking and misbehavior, a certain Leont'ev hanged himself.[17] State Secretary Tatishchev intended to send his serf to a house of correction for trying to run away, but Agaf'ia Petrova instead slashed herself with a razor.[18] The servant Filipov ruined an article of his master's clothing and threw himself into a canal to escape punishment.[19] This last case was unusual: the reasons why a serf feared punishment were usually unreported, as they were irrelevant. The authoritative interpreter of these suicides was the paternal authority, typically the serf owner, who had likely uttered such phrases as "intemperate behavior" and "indecent conduct." Construed as the ultimate disobedience, self-killing constituted a criminal refusal to submit to divinely sanctioned social authority. To disparage the suicide's moral character was then to affirm social order.

The most frequently cited factor overall was drunkenness, which was a criminal offence, a breach of public decorum, and a sign of moral corruption.[20] Drinking is explicitly mentioned in forty-one cases, over one-third of the total. They involved state peasants, household serfs, soldiers and sailors, craftsmen, as well as two merchants and two foreigners but no officers or aristocrats. Details on the drinking habits of suicides are abundant. Numerous reports state that the deceased had been drinking (often for a specified number of days) beforehand or was drunk at the time. Others state that the offender was always or often drunk. Such information apparently provided sufficient explanation of the suicide, for no further attention was devoted to the issue of cause, motive, or intention. The very first case cited in these digests is thus typical: "From the 15th to the 16th [of July, 1785] in the Liteinyi district, resident in the building of the St. Petersburg Arsenal canon-maker apprentice Nikolai Moiseev took a rope to the storeroom and hanged himself during the night. The investigation revealed that he was always getting drunk [*on obrashchalsia vsegda v p'ianstve*]."[21]

---

[16] But, as one historian has ironically noted, if a serf died after a prolonged whipping, then the landlord was hardly to blame for such an accident. See Jerome Blum, *Lord and Peasant in Russia* (Princeton, 1961), 441. I will return to this issue in Chapters 4 and 5.

[17] RGADA, f. 16, d. 526, ch. 6, l. 270.   [18] RGADA, f. 16, d. 526, ch. 4, l. 148.

[19] RGADA, f. 16, d. 526, ch. 4, l. 181.

[20] The 1782 Police Ordinance punished crimes committed by drunkards or in drunkenness with particular harshness (yet, paradoxically, also stipulated lenience in cases of an unintentional or unpremeditated crime committed in drunkenness but not habitual drunkenness). *PSZ*, vol. 21, no. 15379, art. 256.

[21] RGADA, f. 16, d. 526, ch. 1, l. 5.

Similarly, the peasant Osipov was found hanged on September 11, 1789, and the investigation revealed that he had been in a drunken stupor since August 28.[22] The nexus between drinking and suicide evokes the tradition of the *opoitsa*, though this term is not used. Consistent with this tradition, these reports construed suicidal intent in terms of moral behavior rather than mental competence. The reason for investigating the drinking habits of suicides was thus based on a parallel construction of causality: those who drank too much demonstrated the immoral and depraved character of a suicide. It was as much to show that the individual was capable of committing suicide as to find a reason for the crime.[23] The slippage between morality, motive, and cause is particularly well illustrated by the language in one case that made drinking into the direct cause of death: "According to the evidence of the staff medical officer, the merchant Ermolin hanged himself out of drunkenness [*ot p'ianstva*]."[24] Drinking was presented as evidence on two questions: moral accountability and causality.

Illness was also regarded as a major factor in suicidal death. Fourteen reports contain terms listed in the criminal statutes, and details were occasionally provided. A diamond-cutter's apprentice was reported to have acted in madness (*v sumasshestvii*). According to witnesses, he had been in a "tremendous pensiveness" (*v velikoi zadumchivosti*) the day before and had appeared somehow "agitated and disordered" (*bespokoen i besporiadochen*).[25] In this case, witnesses had tried to describe a sudden change in behavior, a shift in normality that they later linked to the suicide. An additional eleven cases cite pensiveness (*zadumchivost'*) or anguish (*toska*), terms not found in the statutes but nonetheless designating a kind of malady.[26] In a merchant's suicide, a police officer established with unusual detail that the deceased had been pensive (*v zadumchivosti*), a condition not ameliorated by bloodletting, and had then committed suicide in his anguish (*v toske*).[27] In seven cases, a fever (*goriachka*) is mentioned thereby indicating some kind of sickness. If all of these cases are calculated together, then we have a tentative total of thirty-two such judgments, or just under 30 percent.[28]

---

[22] RGADA, f. 16, d. 526, ch. 4, l. 231.

[23] Michael MacDonald also finds that moral behavior (including drunkenness) was a central factor in the judgment of suicidal intent in eighteenth-century England. See his reply in "Debate: The Secularization of Suicide in England 1660–1800," *Past and Present* 119 (May 1988), 169–70.

[24] RGADA, f. 16, d. 526, ch. 1, l. 263.   [25] RGADA, f. 16, d. 526, ch. 5, l. 207.

[26] My assessment is also based on the governor's reports on hospitals and mad houses (*doma sumasshedshikh*), in which the number of patients are listed under categories of disease including those suffering from both madness and pensiveness (*zadumchivost'*). For examples, see RGADA, f. 16, d. 526, ch. 7, ll. 22, 134–36.

[27] RGADA, f. 16, d. 526, ch. 7, l. 23.

[28] Although this sample is too small to allow firm conclusions, a disproportionately small number of these cases involved peasants (13) thereby indicating some correlation between social identity and judgment.

Moral and medical categories did not just coexist, however, they also over-lapped.[29] In several instances, drinking was combined with disease. Whether the drinking was the cause or the result appears to vary. A lackey was said to have been drinking for a week from persistent anguish (*ot posledovavshei toski*) before his suicide, yet no reason for the anguish was given.[30] An unnamed peasant, "possessed by disease and delirious" (*oderzhimyi bolezn'iu v bespamiatstve*), had stabbed himself and then jumped into a river. Subsequent investigation revealed that "he had been drinking beforehand and from that had taken ill."[31] The term *bespamiatstvo* designated a diseased condition of mind and hence a mitigating factor for the crime of self-murder. Yet if this state had been caused by drinking, had this peasant really just drunk himself to death? How had he been judged, and where was he buried? The text is silent on these questions.

None of the reports indicates the formal judgment rendered; nor do they refer to the kind of burial. It is possible to explain this as an oversight, but administrative records through the mid-nineteenth century also tend to neglect these details that, to the modern eye, seem central to the entire criminal status of suicide.[32] One possibility is that the police may have investigated suicides but nonetheless allowed clergymen to make the determination of burial. Another is that suicide continued to be understood in material and moral terms: perhaps the question of intention was secondary to both the material fact of self-killing and the moral character of the criminal/victim. Indeed, the law was ambiguous on the judgment of suicide. According to the Military Regulations (and a subsequent draft revision), suicides judged "not of sound mind" were not to suffer desecration and profane burial, but they were nonetheless to be buried in a special, though not dishonorable place. In other words, these bodies still posed a problem – just as they had in medieval Russia and Europe.[33] Furthermore, Russian courts possessed a tripartite system of verdicts that would have reinforced the notion of an intermediate category: guilty, not guilty, and – when neither could be established – under suspicion.[34] Seen in this light, the occasional blending of illness and immorality may not have posed a perceived contradiction.

---

[29] See the 1793 case of Captain Koch, who shot himself in Moscow. The reason, according to the medic, was the "agonizing pain" of gout combined with the "intemperance of his manners." RGADA, f. 16, d. 580, l. 71.

[30] RGADA, f. 16, d. 526, ch. 1, l. 202.   [31] Ibid., l. 225.

[32] English records almost always refer to a verdict of the coroner's court. See Michael MacDonald and Terence R. Murphy, *Sleepless Souls: Suicide in Early Modern England* (Oxford, 1990), 360–66.

[33] In contrast, another draft revision, from a 1766 project, eliminated this intermediate category, even specifying Christian rites for those acquitted of self-murder. *PSZ*, vol. 5, p. 370, For the draft revisions, see A. A. Vostokov, ed., *Proekty ugolovnogo ulozheniia 1754–1766 godov* (SPb, 1882), 101–2.

[34] For further discussion, see I. V. Gessen, *Sudebnaia reforma* (SPb, 1905), 7.

When an administrative report sketched a suicide, it always identified the social status of the individual but did not always provide a name. Whereas the method of self-killing was important, a motive was secondary. Often a characterization of (moral) behavior was sufficient. Out of the wealth of available information, therefore, particular details were selected for inclusion and a judgment passed. While this process was always subjective, it was socially unequal. The voices of the elite were strong and authoritative, those of their subordinates, especially serfs, often elusive. Eclipsed by the dismissive words of their owners, these suicides were categorized as a form of misbehavior and disobedience – a consequence of the serfs' immorality, depravity, and insubordination. The regulatory meanings of suicide were thus intertwined with the norms of conduct and public order.

Measuring morality

Europe's rulers had first realized the usefulness of numbers in the exploitation of human, natural, and economic resources as early as the sixteenth and seventeenth centuries. By the late eighteenth and early nineteenth centuries, the methods of acquiring and analyzing numbers had grown much more refined, resulting in the emergence of both an academic discipline and governmental projects throughout Europe.[35] One of these disciplines was "moral statistics," which was primarily concerned with the analysis of society. As statisticians discovered regularities, which they likened to positive social laws, statistics became a key forum for debates over free will and determinism. Suicide was the decisive case in point: was it not the most individual and hence arbitrary of acts? Arranged according to age, sex, ethnicity, religion, social class, education, time of year, climate, and method, statistics seemed to provide evidence to the contrary. Rates show a remarkable consistency over time and within populations; men commit suicide in greater numbers than women; numbers rise in the spring and fall in the winter.[36] Statistics thus offered a new way to conceive and explain human behavior.

In the early nineteenth century, the Russian government also began to organize the collection of data about population. As information from the provinces began to flow more regularly into the center, a new statistical agency was founded in 1811 to analyze governors' reports, particularly with regard to local economy and demography. In the 1830s, the Ministry of Internal Affairs set up a statistical section and began to publish statistics in a wide range of areas,

---

[35] In the mid-eighteenth century, Johann Peter Süssmilch was the first to discover such regularities, which he interpreted as an expression of the divine order. On the history of statistics, see Ian Hacking, *The Taming of Chance* (Cambridge, 1990), here 20–21.

[36] On the history of suicide statistics, see Hacking, *The Taming of Chance*, 64–80, 115–32, 170–79.

including mortality rates, crime, and suicide.[37] The first published reference to suicide as a statistical phenomenon appeared in 1820.[38] The following decade witnessed several attempts to use statistics in the analysis of suicide, and many of these were informed by the categories of Western social science. Consequently, these studies reproduced the cultural norms embedded in their original sources (governors' reports) yet also reworked them into the new scientific genre. On the one hand, they sanctioned common assumptions about suicide and its causes and thereby affirmed religious and political authority. On the other hand, they exposed an underbelly to public orderliness and thereby challenged the self-representation of absolutism as a well-ordered and benevolent patriarchy.

The first scientific analysis of suicide in Russia was conducted by Karl Herrmann, "the founder of the science of statistics in Russia."[39] Born in Danzig in 1767, Herrmann had studied with August-Ludwig von Schlözer at Göttingen University before coming to Russia in 1795. In 1805, he affiliated with the Academy of Sciences and, the following year, assumed the chair in statistics at the St. Petersburg Pedagogical Institute (which became St. Petersburg University in 1819). As a proponent of *Staatskunde* (or *Staatswissenschaft*), as it was formulated by the Göttingen school, Herrmann regarded statistics as an autonomous science dedicated to the analysis of those factors necessary to proper governance – territory, population, production, and finances.[40] In the early 1820s, he began a new project on crime: using governors' reports, he attempted to calculate murder and suicide rates. In his first article, he correlated rates with population for eight regions in the years 1819 and 1820.[41] Intrigued by some of the contradictions within his findings, he focused his second study

---

[37] The centralization of statistical reporting led to the founding in 1857 of the Central Statistical Committee, empowered to coordinate, collect, and assess all statistical information necessary to the state. For an overview of the institutional basis of statistics in Russia, see I. Miklashevskii, "Statistika," *BE*, 497–504.

[38] To the best of my knowledge, the first mention (in Russia) of suicide in a statistical context was by Genrikh Liudvig fon Attengofer in his *Mediko-topograficheskoe opisanie Sanktpeterburga* (SPb, 1820), 142. In his data on sudden death in St. Petersburg for the years 1808–11, he included suicides, drowning, and death from drinking.

[39] This attribution is from A. I. Somov's short biography of Herrmann in *BE*, vol. 8, 532. See also A. Nikitenko, "Vospominaniia o Karle Fedoroviche Germane," *Severnaia pchela* no. 213 (1839), 831–35.

[40] His major works included theoretical studies and the first comprehensive analysis of population in Russia. See his *Kratkoe rukovodstvo k vseobshchei istorii statistiki* (SPb, 1808); *Vseobshchaia teoriia statistiki* (SPb, 1809); *Statisticheskoe opisanie Iaroslavskoi gubernii* (SPb, 1808); and *Statisticheskie issledovanniia otnositel'no Rossiiskoi Imperii*, pt. 1: *O narodonaselenii* (SPb, 1819).

[41] The regions were: Original Russia (Smolensk, Tver, Pskov), North, Baltic, Central Russia, Volga Plateau, White Russia, Ukraine, Steppes and Caucauses, and Siberia. See Ch.-Th. Herrmann, "Recherches sur le nombre des suicides et des homicides commis en Russie pendant les années 1819 et 1820," *Mémoires de l'Académie impériale des sciences de St.-Petersbourg*, series 6, vol. 1 (SPb, 1832), 3.

exclusively on Russia's central provinces (where the population was mostly
ethnic Russian), for the years 1821 and 1822. This time he also attempted to
analyze the role of social identity.[42] Herrmann was a pioneer in his field inter-
nationally, for the statistical study of suicide was just beginning in Western
Europe in the 1820s. Indeed, he even described his work as "an essay in moral
statistics," a term which first appeared in France in 1833.[43]

Like most statisticians, Herrmann admitted shortcomings in his data but
nonetheless believed that they revealed underlying patterns.[44] He introduced
his study in the following evocative terms: "As the principle causes of these
crimes are typically located in extremes, in the barbarism of custom or in the
refinement of civility that degenerates into egoism, in irreligion or in fanaticism,
in anarchy or in oppression, in extreme poverty or in extraordinary opulence,
the picture of these crimes committed over many years reveals at least in part
the moral and political state of a nation."[45] The metaphor of extremity built
on existing notions linking suicide to the diseases of civilization, especially
its egoism and irreligion. Yet Herrmann further claimed that crime statistics
functioned as an index for the health (or sickness) of the nation. His metaphors
and statistical methods would ultimately help to shape new notions of suicide
not as an immoral act of free will but as a deviation from the norms of social
health.

Herrmann interpreted his data with reference to socio-economic and geographical factors and generally found what he had expected. Regions possessing
culture and material wealth experienced more suicide, whereas poorer, agricul-
tural regions experienced less. He drew a moral lesson from this observation:
where simple, traditional values were strongest, the suicide rates were lowest.
Indeed, the suicide rate was highest "in the extremities of European Russia,"
stressing the extremity not just of suicide but of Russia itself, located on the
edges of Europe and not fully sharing in its modern culture.[46] The contradictions
in his results – industrial development did not always lead to higher rates of

---

[42] Ch.-Th. Herrmann, "Recherches sur le nombre des suicides et des homicides commis en
Russie pendant les années 1821 et 1822," *Mémoires de l'Académie impériale des sciences de
St.-Petersbourg*, series 6, vol. 2 (SPb, 1934).

[43] According to Irina Paperno (*Suicide as a Cultural Institution in Dostoevsky's Russia* (Ithaca,
N.Y., 1997), 216 n. 22), the first use of the term was by A. M. Guerry, *La Statistique morale
de la France* (Paris, 1833). Herrmann ("Recherches," 1834, 257) probably used it in July 1832,
when this article was first given as a lecture.

[44] He believed that his figures were incomplete, that there were errors in record keeping, and
that longer time periods should be studied. As a pioneer in the field of statistics and a child
of the Enlightenment, Herrmann could not have recognized the role of cultural factors in the
identification of suicide. See his "Recherches" (1832), 4 and *passim*.

[45] Ibid., 3.

[46] Ibid., esp. 11, 19. These findings should not be accepted uncritically though they would continue
to characterize the cultural geography of suicide into the early twentieth century. I compared
rates of reported suicide, accidental death, and drowning in selected years and found a striking
pattern: those regions with a high suicide rate (especially the western borderlands) possessed

suicide – only prompted him to continue his investigation, this time by excluding ethnic and religious variation and concentrating on one region.

The second set of data conformed more closely to his expectations: the highest rates of suicide occurred in Moscow, city and province, followed by Iaroslavl and Vladimir, which were both characterized by above-average industrial development. He found a much higher rate among men than women, and among soldiers and nobility (although the highest number of cases occurred among peasants, the largest population group). Whereas the "traditional values" of country life were thus the best "police," Moscow's population was in "an astonishing motion, a veritable ebb and flow of society" (*un mouvement étonnant, c'est un véritable flux et reflux de monde*). A parallel set of metaphors explained gender differences. Men often found themselves in extreme situations, but women were protected from extreme emotions and conditions by the protective system of "patriarchal customs." They married young, had large families to keep them busy, and retained the Christian values of subordination and obedience. "The condition of women is happy and untroubled," Herrmann concluded, "and the suicides of women are consequently very rare."[47] Men were thus described with the same metaphors of vigor and development used in reference to cities and industrialized regions. In their passivity and fidelity to traditional values, women duplicated the characteristics of the backward, protected peasantry.

In Herrmann's framework, patriarchy and custom were the single most important factors in the establishment of the suicide rate. Indeed, tradition and civilization were located on two poles, with most suicides caused by a disruption of traditional values. Herrmann thus belonged squarely in the European tradition and likewise constructed his analysis around a series of binary oppositions: modern–traditional, urban–rural, male–female, individualized elites–peasantry. Despite the quantification, however, he did not associate the causes of suicide with social problems but with individual vices: ruined health, despair, delirium, and unhappy circumstances, whether physical or moral.[48] His work thus contained an internal tension between two conceptions of suicide: as a social phenomenon and as an individual act.

The second major statistical study of suicide in Russia was published in 1847 by the government official, K. S. Veselovskii. Aware of the latest trends and studies published in Western Europe, Veselovskii situated himself within the field of moral statistics, which, he believed, revealed the "recesses of the human soul."[49] Though he did not elaborate on this suggestive comment, he did

proportionally lower rates of accidental death and drowning; those regions with low suicide rates (the Russian heartland) had proportionally higher levels of accidental death and drowning. This suggests a strong cultural factor in the identification of suicide and death by accident or drowning.

[47] Herrmann, "Recherches" (1834), 264–65, 270.   [48] Ibid., 260.

[49] He tentatively raised the issue of laws regulating moral life and the consequent problem of free will. See K. S. Veselovskii, *Opyty nravstvennoi statistiki Rossii* (SPb, 1847), 1, 55.

acknowledge and accept the social determinism implied by statistical patterns and regularities. His study further illustrates how the categories of analysis shaped the interpretation of data. When he failed to find a clear causal nexus between urban living and the incidence of suicide, for example, he argued that many Russian towns were in reality just big villages.[50] He thus reworked the data so that it would fit the model, this time linking the incidence of suicide in the two capitals and western provinces to higher levels of industry and population density.[51] His analysis of gender differences built upon a similar tactic: the lower rates among women and the higher rates among men were associated with such "natural" qualities as feeling, harmony, and silent suffering, on the one hand, and reason, action, and will, on the other. The unexpectedly high rates of attempted suicide among women were explained through women's indecision, her lack of energy and strength.[52] Veselovskii did not let this suggestive data on suicidal behavior undermine his cultural assumptions about gender.

Although Herrmann and Veselovskii published the only scholarly studies devoted to the statistics of suicide before the reform era, public interest in both suicide and statistics was much greater.[53] This period witnessed the establishment of a new genre of popular-scientific work that combined (in varying proportions) history, travel guide, literary sketch, and statistics into an entertaining and informative portrait of a city. In many respects, these works can be seen as forerunners of the better-known "physiological sketch" of the naturalist school, for despite some differences in style, they shared a fundamental interest in the "scientific" observation of the truth or actuality of life itself. This interest likewise extended beyond the boundaries of official Russia into the hidden corners of the city, the world of poverty, disease, vice, and crime.[54] Moral statistics and literary naturalism were allies in the creation of a new vision of the urban environment and human behavior.

In many respects, these studies presented a well-established view of suicide as the act of an immoral person. The causal explanations reproduced the original categories of the reports, which, in turn, reflected local power dynamics, particularly the influence of serf owners and other elites. According to *Statistical Information about St. Petersburg* (1836), which was based on 148 administrative reports from 1831 to 1833, the most common cause of suicide was misbehavior and drunkenness (53 cases) followed by disease and insanity (29) and then fear of punishment (13). (An additional 39 cases remained without explanation,

---

[50] Danial Brower remarks that this was a common strategy in this period, usually as a means of criticizing Russian backwardness. See his *The Russian City between Tradition and Modernity, 1850–1900* (Berkeley, 1990), 14, 28–29.

[51] Veselovskii, *Opyty*, 29.   [52] Ibid., 39–42.

[53] Note the extensive summary of Veselovskii's pamphlet in "Smes'," *Sovremennik* no. 3 (1847), 251–58.

[54] The key work of the naturalists was *Fiziologiia Peterburga* (1846).

and the remaining 14 cases fell into such rubrics as poverty, family, love, and anger.) The language was often sweeping in its generalization. Its anonymous author, Andrei Zablotskii-Desiatkovskii, thus summarized: Of the twenty-nine peasants who had hanged themselves, "all were drunkards except for five who hanged themselves out of pensiveness."[55] Despite the quantification, drunkenness and debauchery were not conceived as social problems. Instead, the individuals were portrayed as morally responsible (and hence legally culpable) for their misbehavior. Similarly, poverty – which would become an object of statistical analysis and a "social problem" in the 1860s – was presented as the result of individual failings rather than extra-individual economic or social causes. The association of suicide with the fear of punishment also did not provoke general observations about serfdom or patriarchal discipline.[56] Indeed, one case described as "remarkable" received significantly more attention: a serf had been able to explain his act before dying from his wounds. When living with his master, he recounted, he had been content with everything and provided for in all respects, but when he had gone out to work on his own (*khodit' po pasportu*), he had often failed to find a place. Consequently, he had begun to suffer from pensiveness. The suicide of this serf was depicted as the result of too much freedom, and serfdom as a benevolent patriarchy.[57]

Yet this pattern was not unchallenged. Alongside sweeping generalizations about drunkenness and dissipation in this volume were also scenes of personal tragedy, including four suicides due to grief at the death of loved ones and one case involving the homesickness (*toska po rodine*) of a well-behaved serf boy taken away from his village by his owner. Similarly, some cases seem to have evoked sympathy on the part of the investigator, such as the "well-behaved merchant's wife with five children and on top of that pregnant, who became melancholic after her husband was taken to prison for gambling, and who was pondering the fate of her children."[58] As these examples imply, the determination of motive points to an underlying tension: suicide could be depraved and criminal or sad and pitiful, meriting either condemnation or compassion. Whereas some motives constructed suicide as a violation of social norms and relationships, others focused instead upon inner emotional dynamics. A review

---

[55] *Statisticheskie svedeniia o Sanktpeterburge* (SPb, 1836),192. This was published anonymously by the Interior Ministry. On the authorship of Zablotskii-Desiatkovskii, see *RP*, vol. 2, 295–97.

[56] In contrast, literature published abroad or after 1861 did identify a direct causal relationship between serfdom and suicide. See L. Léouzon Le Duc, *La Russie contemporaine* (Paris, 1853), 299–301; I. I. Ignatovich, *Pomeshchich'i krest'iane nakanune osvobozhdeniia* (Moscow, 1910), 228–36; and A. Povalishin, *Riazanskie pomeshchiki i ikh krepostnye: Ocherki iz istorii krepostnogo prava v Rossii v Riazanskoi gubernii v XIX stoletii* (Riazan, 1903), 301–3.

[57] *Statisticheskie svedeniia*, 193. For examples of suicide linked to fear of punishment, see *Statisticheskie svedeniia*, 191–98; V. Androssov, *Statisticheskaia zapiska o Moskve* (Moscow, 1832), 87–88; and E. Karnovich, *Sanktpeterburg v statisticheskom otnoshenii* (SPb, 1860), 123–24.

[58] *Statisticheskie svedeniia*, 191–99.

of this study in the journal *The Contemporary* contained this alternative reading. Without even mentioning the majority of depraved suicides, it highlighted the five cases involving grief and homesickness as especially thought-provoking for the "philanthropist-philosopher" – evidence that common people could kill themselves from the most "worthy" reasons.[59] This reviewer thus challenged the assumptions underpinning social hierarchy in a manner reminiscent of sentimentalism: virtuous suffering need not correspond to social status.

Although the equation of immorality with criminality was a long-established convention, the attempt to represent morality with numbers had more radical implications. In *Panorama of St. Petersburg* (1834), Aleksandr Bashutskii framed his entire investigation with a rhetorical question: "Is it possible to determine the level of moral depravity (*stepen' razvrata nravov*) by the numbers of actions and crimes?" He placed suicide alongside drunkenness, vagrancy, and murder, which were all offenses against morality.[60] *The Survey of Governmental Regulation of Public Order for 1831*, a publication of the interior ministry, likewise equated public order (*obshchestvennoe blagoustroistvo*) with public morality. Its statistical charts on crime, population, and so forth were thought to illuminate "the state of popular morality" (*sostoianie narodnoi nravstvennosti*) in various parts of the empire.[61] By using statistics as a window into the moral condition of the nation, these works began to project an autonomous social sphere. The statistical approach implicitly undermined the individualized explanation of crime.

It also invited comparison, and the initial conclusions pointed to Russia's relative health. The incidence of suicide was seemingly much lower in Russia than in Western Europe; though rates were higher in St. Petersburg and Moscow than elsewhere in the empire, they too remained well behind Paris or London.[62] These accounts explained this divergence in terms of levels of civilization. In concluding his study on suicide in Moscow, Vasilii Androssov noted the rarity in Russia of those sorrowful causes – family arguments, disease, poverty – which were reputedly so common in the West. Traditional religious values had retained their force in Russia, he believed. Those who had committed suicide were mostly young people torn from their families, lured to their destruction by an unstable life and debauchery (*uvlechennye v gibel' buinnoiu zhizn'iu i rasputstvom*).[63] Zablotskii-Desiatkovskii came to a similar conclusion and

---

[59] "Razbor knigi: Statisticheskie svedeniia o S.-Peterburge," *Sovremennik* no. 7 (1837), 356–57.

[60] Aleksandr Bashutskii, *Panorama Sanktpeterburga* (SPb, 1834), 89–92.

[61] *Obozrenie gosudarstvennogo upravleniia po chasti obshchestvennogo blagoustroistva v 1831 godu* (SPb, 1834), 3.

[62] Veselovskii (*Opyty*) was the first to attempt to compile a national suicide rate, and he used a variety of administrative and judicial sources. Although the extremely uneven and incomplete nature of the data make any comparison meaningless, contemporaries took it as a given that Russia's suicide rate was amongst the lowest in Europe.

[63] Androssov, *Statisticheskaia zapiska*, 90.

employed almost the exact same wording: the majority of suicides occurred among the simple folk; a tempestuous and dissolute life (*buinaia i rasputnaia zhizn'*) had led them to disappointment. Unlike in the West, it was concluded, extreme poverty (*nishcheta*) was still a rarity, passions were hardly developed, and religious faith remained firm.[64] Only Bashutskii was less sure of Russia's immunity to Western influence, though he located the problem exclusively in the "luxury" of the city – the long-standing symbol of Western civilization. He concluded: "Divine Providence still protects the common morals [*nravy obshchie*], the morals of the masses, from that frightful disease, which humanity has few means to heal. Their minds are still pure, and the impartial observer remarks with joy that the vice [*porok*] is here the consequence of foolishness and weakness, and not the fruit of unbelief, the deep depravity of the heart, and the intentionally directed will."[65] Though recalling eighteenth-century paradigms that linked suicide to luxury and unbelief, Bashutskii now conceptualized the problem explicitly in terms of social and geographical categories.

While the results of these studies were reassuring, even Russia's comparatively low rates needed explanation, and these early works offered several. On the one hand, they duplicated contemporary norms and assumptions: suicide was the result of either illness or immorality. The many references to dissipation and debauchery constructed suicide as a criminal act of free will, the result of individual moral failings. On the other hand, these studies also outlined a social context for suicide. By correlating rates with social estate, gender, geography, climate, and so forth, statisticians undermined the significance of (individual) morality in favor of moral levels within populations. Furthermore, statistics constructed the narrator *cum* scientist as "impartial observer," the numbers as "facts." Consequently, they could raise some unsettling, if implicit questions. How were the levels of debauchery and drunkenness to be explained? Was serfdom really safeguarding public morality?

Precisely these kinds of considerations propelled a simmering controversy about the political implications of statistics. Although Herrmann had conducted his studies in the 1820s, publication had been delayed for a decade due to the opposition of the Minister of Education, A. S. Shishkov, who considered such inquiries to be pointless, frivolous, and even dangerous. "It is advantageous to inform people about good deeds," Shishkov concluded, "but deeds like murder and suicide ought to be plunged into eternal oblivion."[66] A victim of the growing conservatism late in the reign of Alexander I, Herrmann even lost his university position in 1824 amidst accusations of propagating atheism and materialism – accusations that were linked to his specialization in statistics.[67] Such concerns

---

[64] *Statisticheskie svedeniia*, 196.   [65] Bashutskii, *Panorama*, 92–93.

[66] For Shishkov's response, see Paperno, *Suicide*, 70–71.

[67] Herrmann retained his position at the Academy of Sciences and continued his research until his death in 1838. On his dismissal from the University, see *Materialy dlia istorii obrazovaniia*

were not without cause. Though the concept of social problems – and the potential they created for intervention into the social sphere – would only emerge in the 1860s, the projection of suicide onto a social plane undermined official representations of the well-regulated polity. Androssov's *Statistical Description of Moscow* (1832) likewise provoked a heated reaction, even accusations of anti-Russian views and opinions.[68] Two models of statecraft had come into conflict in these works: the need to compile the information necessary for good governance; and the imperative to project a positive image of a well-ordered society and nation.

Legal codification

Despite the tremendous administrative and legal transformations of the eighteenth century that rendered the Law Code of 1649 obsolete, attempts to codify the law repeatedly failed. Whether conceived primarily as the systemization of existing laws or as the drafting of a new code based on laws or legal principles imported from the West, codification had stumbled against a defining principle of governance in Russia – the primacy of personal, paternalist authority, exemplified on the highest level by the absolutist power of the autocrat. An ideal of custodial justice rather than impersonal procedure characterized Russia's legal and political culture; consequently, administrative and not judicial reform had received precedence. Only in the nineteenth century would the requirements of centralized administration, the growing institutional power of the Ministry of Justice, and the obligations of national prestige finally produce results.[69]

The most radical attempt to draft new criminal and civil codes occurred during the reign of Alexander I.[70] Developed under the direction of Mikhail Speranskii

---

v *Rossii v tsarstvovanii Imp. Aleksandra I*, pt. 2 (SPb, 1886), 82–97. On the political context, see S. V. Rozhdestvenskii, ed., *S.-Peterburgskii universitet v pervoe stoletie ego deiatel'nosti 1819–1912*, vol. 1, *1819–1835: Materialy po istorii S.-Peterburgskogo universiteta* (Petrograd, 1919), 173 and *passim*.

[68] His patriotism was impugned. On Androssov and the reaction to his publication, see *RP*, vol. 1, 73. Although many of the authors of these studies were employed at some point by the interior ministry, most did move in progressive circles, and some were outspoken opponents of serfdom.

[69] See Marc Raeff, *The Well-Ordered Police State: Social and Institutional Change through Law in the Germanies and Russia, 1600–1800* (New Haven, 1983), 181–250; and Richard Wortman, *The Development of a Russian Legal Consciousness* (Chicago, 1976). See also Laura Engelstein, *The Keys to Happiness: Sex and the Search for Modernity in Fin-de-Siècle Russia* (Ithaca, N.Y., 1992), 17–127.

[70] See also the two draft revisions of the criminal code – the first from 1754 and the second from 1766. While suicide was categorized as a serious criminal offense in both drafts, the prescribed penalties grew more lenient. According to the 1754 text, the bodies of self-murderers were to be desecrated as specified in the original statutes, and stringing them up by their feet was explicitly conceived as a form of deterrence: "so that others would not dare to perpetrate such lawlessness upon themselves." In contrast, the 1766 version no longer mentioned desecration and instead simply directed that bodies be taken to the wretched house. The proposed statutes were reprinted in Vostokov, *Proekty ugolovnogo ulozheniia*, 101–2.

until his fall from favor in 1812, a wholly new criminal code was formulated and presented to the State Council in 1813 and again in 1824. Disturbed both times by external events – the war with Napoleon and the death of Alexander I – consideration of the proposal was never brought to a conclusion.[71] Hostile to abstract principles and jealous of his prerogatives, the new tsar rejected this attempt to develop a modern code and instead insisted upon historicist and national principles. Nicholas I appointed (a rehabilitated) Speranskii to head a commission charged first with the compilation of all laws enacted since the last code of 1649 and then with the development of a digest. The forty-five-volume *Complete Collection of Laws of the Russian Empire* appeared in 1830, followed by the fifteen-volume *Digest of Laws*, which was constituted as the primary source of law in Russia in 1835.[72] The digest suffered from numerous deficiencies, not the least of which were substantive gaps, internal contradictions and inconsistencies, and an overall imprecision especially on such central questions as scales of punishment. These shortcomings resulted from its haphazard character and failure to formulate general principles or legal norms: it was an amalgamation of earlier decrees, broken up and distributed into classifications drawn from Western criminal codes. In light of these problems, Nicholas I sponsored a revision. However, the resulting penal code of 1845 suffered from many of the same flaws as its predecessor, especially a scorn for abstractions and a distinct preference for police mechanisms.[73] It would nevertheless remain the foundation of criminal law until 1917.[74]

A comparison of the laws on suicide proposed in 1813 with those implemented in 1835 illustrates the repercussions of the historicist approach to codification. Following the example of many Western European codes, the 1813 project treated suicide as an act with primarily medical and religious significance. Designating those who had attempted suicide "mentally disturbed" (*pomeshavshegosia v razume*), article 392 prescribed a penalty of medical treatment in a hospital and then church penance. Burial was likewise to be regulated by church rules and police procedures, by which was presumably meant

---

[71] For the proposal, see "Proekt ugolovnogo ulozheniia" (SPb, 1913), in *Arkhiv Gosudarstvennogo Soveta*, vol. 4 (SPb, 1874). For general background, see Marc Raeff, *Mikhail Speransky: Statesman of Imperial Russia* (The Hague, 1961).

[72] See *Polnoe sobranie zakonov Rossiiskoi Imperii* (SPb, 1830), and *Svod zakonov Rossiiskoi Imperii* (SPb, 1835). The criminal code appeared in vol. 15 of the *Svod Zakonov* under the title *Zakony ugolovnye*, henceforth *ZU*. I have used the edition published in 1836.

[73] Though revised editions appeared in 1857, 1866, and 1885, the 1845 code was never substantively modified. See *Ulozhenie o nakazaniiakh ugolovnykh i ispravitel'nykh* (SPb, 1846). On the shortcomings of the *Digest* and penal code, see N. S. Tagantsev, *Russkoe ugolovnoe pravo. Lektsii*, 2 vols. (Moscow, repr. 1994), vol. 1, 103–7.

[74] Subsequent legal debates and draft revisions will be discussed in Chapter 8. For a useful overview of suicide's legal history in Russia, see N. S. Tagantsev, *O prestupleniiakh protiv zhizni po russkomu pravu*, 2 vols. (SPb, 1870–71), here vol. 2, 401–46.

conformity with both canon law and sanitary and forensic standards.[75] The historicist digest, in contrast, built on the precedent of Peter the Great's statutes and categorized self-killing as a felony offense. Suicide attempted while in sound mind was to be punished according to the same principles as attempted murder, that is, with penalties ranging from forced labor and Siberian exile on the one extreme, to corporal punishment and church penance on the other. The body of a premeditated suicide was to be denied Christian burial.[76] The two paradigms took contrary approaches. Whereas the 1813 project advocated decriminalization and therapeutic measures, the 1835 digest affirmed suicide's status as a crime akin to murder.[77]

Shortly before the enactment of the digest though after its initial publication, a question of legal procedure traveled up the bureaucratic ladder to St. Petersburg. The internal discussions suggest that some governmental officials did not share the principles articulated in the digest. In 1834, the acting civil governor of Kazan province formally requested clarification on the procedures to be followed with individuals who had attempted suicide during an "attack of insanity." Though such people were routinely (*neredko*) being taken to the local mental hospital, no existing regulation actually outlined the proper procedure. The acting governor thus inquired whether the same principle applied for attempted suicides as for attempted murderers. He cited a possible precedent – an 1827 decree stipulating that murderers who had acted in insanity were to be confined in mental institutions until they had displayed no signs of illness for a period of five years.[78] Russia's highest administrative body, the State Council, considered the inquiry, consulted with the Medical Council of the interior ministry, and then made its determination.

In its initial consideration, the State Council questioned whether the regulations governing murder could apply for attempted suicide and provided three lines of argumentation. Murder, it was first reasoned, drawing on contemporary European legal notions, was a social act: it was a crime committed against another, and the confinement of the murderer was thereby necessary not just to punish the criminal but also to protect society. In contrast, attempted suicide

---

[75] *Proekt ugolovnogo ulozheniia*, arts. 392, 395. A therapeutic response was likewise present in an earlier draft statute. Those who had made attempts on their lives while suffering from disease or melancholy were to be confined and supervised until cured. Compare Vostokov, *Proekty ugolovnogo ulozheniia*, 101–2.

[76] Articles 347 and 348 in *ZU*; compare the articles on murder and attempted crimes (332–46, 115–17).

[77] Confinement of attempted suicides in mental hospitals increased over the eighteenth century in Western Europe. See Anderson, *Suicide*, ch. 11; and the article by Christina Vanja, in *Trauer, Verzweiflung und Anfechtung: Selbstmord und Selbstmordversuche in mittelalterlichen und frühneuzeitlichen Gesellschaften*, ed. Gabriela Signori (Tübingen, 1994), 210–32. Whether forced confinement marked "progress" in care is disputed. See Michel Foucault, *Madness and Civilization*, trans. Richard Howard (New York, 1965).

[78] RGIA, f. 1149, op. 2 (1834), d. 9, ll. 2–5.

was a crime of a different order: it was neither completed nor directed against society. The second argument concerned the role of insanity in suicide. "As is well known, [people] sometimes make an attempt on their own lives, not during an attack of insanity but during a disease, which quickly passes." In these cases, it was noted, five years' confinement was simply too long. The final point built on this last assumption. Because confinement would seem to be a form of punishment akin to imprisonment, it would not ameliorate but rather worsen the mental condition. Taken together, these arguments forcefully distinguished suicide from murder; it did not conform to a social definition of crime and required therapeutic measures rather than retributive penalties. The State Council thus contested the equation of suicide with murder.[79]

When the question was sent to the Medical Council for its evaluation, however, the opposite conclusion was drawn: the same procedures should be used for both murderers and attempted suicides. If the attempt had occurred during an attack of insanity, it was reasoned, the object could just as easily have been someone else as the self. These specialists saw no significant difference in the character of murder and suicide committed in insanity because the central factor was the insanity, not its object. Their rationalization was consistent: in those cases of murder and attempted suicide judged to have occurred during a temporary disease rather than "real" insanity, the period of observation was reduced to six weeks. In an 1835 decree, the State Council adopted this approach, and the new procedures in cases of murder and attempted suicide were adopted.[80] Although the difference of opinion had been resolved, the conflict revealed divergent approaches. Defining crime as a social act, the State Council had distinguished suicide from murder on this basis. As judged from the tone of the report, its authors had automatically – even instinctively – rejected the equation of suicide with self-murder. In contrast, citing contemporary medical knowledge, the Medical Council had drawn the opposite conclusion.

In certain respects, the new statutes on suicide in the 1845 penal code represented an extension of the debate in the State Council. Although suicide and attempted suicide both remained criminal offenses, the murder of the self was no longer equated with the murder of another. While an early draft of the penal code had proposed punishing attempted suicide with imprisonment for a period of six to twelve months, the editors had rejected this proposal. Their reasoning was unequivocal: suicide could not be compared to any form or degree of murder, and such a punishment might actually lead to a repeat attempt.[81]

---

[79] RGIA, f. 1149, op. 2 (1834), d. 9, ll. 7–11.

[80] For the report from the Interior Ministry, RGIA, f. 1149, op. 2 (1834), d. 105, ll. 2–19, esp. 17–18; for the final decision of the State Council, ll. 21–23. For the decree, no. 7872, *PSZ*, series 2, vol. 10, no. 1.

[81] See arts. 1943 and 1944 in the *Ulozhenie*. (In the 1866 revised version, these articles appear as nos. 1472–73.) For the proposal with commentary, *Proekt ulozheniia o nakazaniiakh ugolovnykh*

Concerned less with retribution and punishment, the new statutes focused more on deterrence and correction. Yet this shift reflected less a medical than a moral therapeutics. Harking back to a draft statute from 1766, the new penalty for attempted suicide was a penance to be assigned by the local religious consistory. This conception of suicide as an act of moral free will also shaped a new civil penalty introduced in cases of intentional suicide. In addition to the denial of Christian burial, which continued to be the main legal punishment for suicide, the new code also called for the invalidation of last wills and testaments. In their commentary, the authors argued that the fear of depriving loved ones of financial support would perhaps dissuade potential suicides, even those in a most melancholic mood. Whether this "wise and useful" measure ever deterred a suicide attempt is unknown; it did, however, introduce a major contradiction into statutory law. Whereas existing civil law stipulated the invalidation of testaments in cases of suicide associated with insanity, criminal law stipulated the same penalty but in cases of suicide when competence could be established.[82]

The 1845 code thus retained mental competence as the central factor in the determination of guilt. Penalties applied only when courts determined that a suicide or attempted suicide had been "intentional" (*s namereniem*), that is, not committed in madness or temporary insanity (*bespamiatstvo*) caused by a disease.[83] Notably absent from the 1845 code was the list of mitigating circumstances enumerated in the Military and Naval Charters and reiterated in the *Digest of Laws*: unbearable burden or oppression, torment, disappointment, and shame. As a justification, the editors of the code legitimately cited the imprecision of these concepts, but they also rationalized that the punishment for attempted suicide was minimal in any case.

By eliminating specific criteria for clemency, the editors of the penal code defined the crime of suicide according to the legal categories of intention and (mental) competence. Yet they persisted in judging suicide as a question of personal morality. A statute new to the 1845 code even enhanced the importance of moral character in the evaluation of suicide: it introduced two exclusions based on motive. If an individual should risk life or even choose death "for the preservation of government secrets and in other similar cases," then this patriotic suicide was not to be considered under any criminal provisions. The

---

i ispravitel'nykh, vnesennykh v 1844 godu v Gosudarstvennyi Sovet, s podrobnym oznacheniem osnovanii kazhdogo iz vnesennykh v sei proekt postanovlenii (SPb, 1871), 622–24.

[82] Art. 1944, *Ulozhenie*. For the commentary, *Proekt ulozheniia*. For the civil legislation, *PSZ*, no. 4844 (1831), vol. 6, series 2; *SZ*, arts. 1016–17, vol. 10. See also Tagantsev, *O prestupleniiakh*, 417, 434–35.

[83] According to the Regulations of the Medical Police, which stipulated procedures governing burial in general, the bodies of deliberate suicides were to be turned over to the executioner for burial in a dishonorable place. A direct citation from Peter the Great's Military Regulations, this measure contradicted the intention of the 1845 code but remained in force. See "Ustav meditsinskoi politsii," *SZ*, vol. 13, arts. 370 (subsequently 923) and 368.

equivalent act for a woman – self sacrifice in the name of virtue – was likewise exempted from punishment.[84] According to this logic, the supreme values of patriotism and chastity outweighed the criminal and moral transgression of suicide. This covert reference to Cato and Lucretia should not, however, be understood as an endorsement of these myths. Instead, they comprised part of a broader effort under Nicholas I to transform the state into an arbiter of honor: not self-sovereignty but submission to tsar and husband lay at the heart of this statute.

Finally, the 1845 code introduced two completely new provisions, which both associated suicide with murder and greatly expanded the purview of investigation. In the first statute, an accessory to suicide – whether passively through encouragement or actively through the procurement of a means – was to be prosecuted as an accessory to murder. "Although the murderer and the victim are united in one figure," the editors explained, "[the accessory] is without doubt an accessory to murder, even an accessory to premeditated murder, especially as neither unhappiness nor passion can serve as an excuse." According to the second provision, parents, guardians, or other individuals vested with authority, found to have driven a dependent to commit suicide through a manifest abuse of power that included cruelty, could be subject to a wide range of punishment, including the forfeiture of rights, church penance, and imprisonment.[85] This second provision, which was unusual in a European context and will be discussed in some detail in Chapter 5, was an explicit attempt to regulate the paternalist ethos, especially within the context of serfdom but also within the army and the family.

The evolution of the laws on suicide between 1835 and 1845 reflected contradictory impulses. On the one hand, the digest and the penal code both rejected the predominantly medical approach articulated in the 1813 project and defined suicide in terms of a binary model of crime/sin or disease. Furthermore, the 1845 code categorized suicide – alongside murder and assault – under the heading of crimes against the life, health, freedom, and honor of private persons. On the other hand, signs of change were apparent. The 1845 code explicitly rejected the equation of attempted suicide with attempted murder and reduced the applicable penalties to civil and religious measures – the invalidation of last testaments, the denial of Christian burial, and, in cases of attempted suicide, penance. Although Russia had not formally decriminalized suicide, following the example of much of Western Europe, the new laws did replace criminal sanctions with measures designed to reinforce and inculcate Christian morality. By introducing the exclusions of patriotism and chastity, the code further undermined the criminal status of suicide: certain motives could transform this

---

[84] Arts. 1943–45/1472–74, *Ulozhenie o nakazaniiakh* (1846/66). See also *Proekt ulozheniia*; and Tagantsev, *O prestupleniiakh*, 422.

[85] Arts. 1946–47/1475–76, *Ulozhenie o nakazaniiakh* (1846/66). See also *Proekt ulozheniia*; and Tagantsev, *O prestupleniiakh*, 439.

crime into a praiseworthy, even heroic act. Other measures countered this movement toward decriminalization: a new civil penalty for suicide, a reduction of the number of mitigating factors, and the introduction of two new crimes. By officially extending the jurisdiction of investigation into the sphere of personal and social relations, the laws governing the abetting and instigation of suicide actually increased the state regulation of suicide overall. Liberalization was thus counteracted by the expansion of administrative authority.

The scales of justice

Beginning in the 1830s, the Ministry of Justice began to publish annual reports on the prosecution of crime. They categorized suicide – alongside murder and brigandage – as a most notable and serious crime (*zamechatel'neishoe prestu-plenie*). The reports specified the number of new cases initiated each year, an overview of decisions reached and punishments meted out, and the gender of both the defendants and those found guilty. This information was broken down according to three levels of courts: the Governing Senate, which was the high court in both criminal and civil matters; the provincial-level criminal chambers, which were appellate courts charged as well with the mandatory review of a wide range of criminal cases (for which lower courts were allowed to issue opinions but not decisions); and the courts of conscience, which possessed jurisdiction in criminal cases involving juveniles and the mentally or physically incompetent.[86] Judicial statistics can form an important source on the history of crime but not because they necessarily provide a reliable gauge of actual crime rates. Instead, they are shaped by numerous contingent factors, including the modification of court jurisdictions and laws, shifts in governmental policy, and changing attitudes among police officers, judges and the general public. Precisely such influences make judicial statistics into a kind of barometer: they show fluctuations in the definition, investigation, and prosecution of crime.[87]

Table 3.2 shows the prosecution of suicide in the Senate, criminal chambers, and courts of conscience in two-year intervals for the period between 1834 and 1868. The table indicates the number of new cases, the total number of defendants, and the sex of defendants.

A strong trend cuts across all judicial instances: the steady rise of new cases, which reached a peak in 1846, followed by a subsequent decline.[88] Despite

---

[86] The following discussion is based on the annual *Otchet Ministerstva iustitsii* (1834–68) examined in alternate (even) years only.

[87] For a persuasive analysis of Russian judicial statistics from this perspective, see Stephen P. Frank, "Narratives within Numbers: Women, Crime, and Judicial Statistics in Imperial Russia, 1834–1913," *Russian Review* no. 4 (1996).

[88] It is also striking that the number of defendants varied from the number of new cases. While this could be explained by the death of the defendant in cases of suicide, the number of defendants before the Senate actually exceeded the total number of cases, suggesting that these appeals also involved instigators, who were often individuals belonging to privileged groups and hence more likely to appeal.

Table 3.2 *The Prosecution of Suicide, 1834–68*

Year	Governing Senate New Cases	Defendants Total	Male	Fem	Criminal Chambers New Cases	Defendants Total	Male	Fem	Courts of Conscience New Cases	Defendants Total	Male	Fem	Total New Cases
1834	6	11	6	5	431	377	279	98	23	24	14	10	460
1836	9	9	7	2	427	365	274	91	27	28	22	6	463
1838	13	22	16	6	479	363	245	118	54	54	36	18	546
1840	13	13	8	5	608	507	356	151	74	79	53	26	695
1842	22	23	12	11	612	419	294	125	66	66	47	19	700
1844	17	18	16	2	597	428	283	145	93	91	72	19	707
1846	21	26	21	5	916	563	392	171	122	133	98	35	1059
1848	6	6	3	3	574	356	278	78	106	109	77	32	686
1850	5	7	6	1	580	277	200	77	99	106	68	38	684
1852	7	10	4	6	516	306	227	79	40	38	24	14	563
1854	8	8	4	4	558	332	239	93	38	37	29	8	604
1856	10	13	10	3	565	320	230	90	21	18	13	5	596
1858	4	6	6	0	507	421	321	100	13	10	8	2	524
1860	2	NA	NA	NA	457	NA	NA	NA	13	NA	NA	NA	472
1862	2	NA	NA	NA	350	NA	NA	NA	12	NA	NA	NA	364
1864	2	NA	NA	NA	353	NA	NA	NA	5	NA	NA	NA	360
1866	9	NA	NA	NA	445	NA	NA	NA	1	NA	NA	NA	455
1868	4	NA	NA	NA	206	NA	NA	NA	1	NA	NA	NA	211
Total	160	172	119	53	9,181	5,999	4,298	1,701	808	793	561	232	10,149

Source: Otchet Ministerstva iustitsii (1834–68)

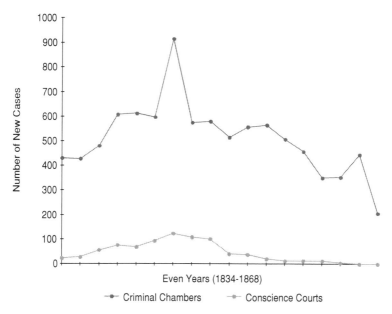

Fig. 3.1 The prosecution of suicide

population growth, an expanding court system, and increasing administrative efficiency, the number of recorded cases fell by 1868 to under half the level of 1834. Figure 3.1 plots these patterns.

The reason for the initial rise in prosecution rates is likely connected to the publication of the 1835 digest and the 1845 penal code.[89] Whatever their shortcomings, these authoritative sources on criminal law encouraged a more systematic approach to the prosecution of crime and especially to its categorization. The decline in the number of cases likewise has an institutional component: by the mid-1860s, established court structures were being radically reorganized, a process reflected, for example, in the growing disuse of the courts of conscience.

An examination of verdicts over this same period suggests that changing attitudes toward suicide also played a significant role in the declining number of new cases. Table 3.3 shows the number of cases decided by decade (calculating even years only), the total number of defendants, the number of defendants left under suspicion, and the number and percentage of defendants found guilty

---

[89] The extreme jump of 1846 was an aberration, for the number of new cases in the criminal chambers was 581 in 1845 and 654 in 1847, figures more consistent with the rest of the decade. See *Otchet Ministerstva iustitsii za 1845* and *za 1847*.

Table 3.3 *Suicide Verdicts, 1834–68 (even years only)*

Year	Cases decided	No. of defend	Under suspicion	Not guilty		Guilty			
				Total	Percent	Total	Percent	Male	Female
The Governing Senate									
1834–40	41	58	4	15	25.9	30	51.7	NA	NA
1842–50	71	80	11	24	30.0	33	41.3	26	7
1852–58	29	37	7	10	27.0	11	29.7	8	3
The Criminal Chambers									
1834–40	1,987	1,666	104	663	39.8	762	45.7	NA	NA
1842–50	3,281	2,083*	124	859	41.2	666	32.0	442	224
1852–58	2,124	1,310*	73	654	49.9	266	20.3	169	97
The Courts of Conscience									
1834–40	180	182	2	98	53.8	44	24.2	NA	NA
1842–50	524	523	10	263	50.3	107	20.4	74	33
1852–58	114	106	1	60	56.6	16	15.1	15	1
All Courts									
1860–68	NA	2,385*	171	989	41.5	633	26.5	472	161

Source: *Otchet Ministerstva iustitsii* (1834–68)
*Also includes individuals freed by imperial manifesto.

and not guilty.[90] Two points of information: the absolute figures should be interpreted in proportional relation because the number of years included in each decade varied; and data for the 1860s were published in aggregate form and are thus presented separately.

These data point to an increasing lenience in the judgment of suicide. Even when prosecution rates rose in the 1830s and 1840s, between 25 and 50 percent of defendants were found not guilty. Furthermore, as Figure 3.2 illustrates, the percentage of guilty verdicts fell dramatically in all three venues between 1834 and 1858.

A parallel rise in the percentage of not-guilty verdicts was less dramatic and occurred primarily in the criminal chambers. The slack was taken up by a rise in the number of cases returned to the lower courts and, in the Senate, by verdicts of suspicion. Overall the Senate was the most prone to issue a verdict of guilty, the courts of conscience the least. As the latter judged cases in which competence was already at issue, the higher rate of not-guilty verdicts – itself

---

[90] When evidence was deemed insufficient to justify either conviction or acquittal, a defendant could be "left under suspicion," that is, neither guilty nor innocent. According to one estimate, this pernicious verdict was issued in over 87 percent of decisions after 1832, a much higher rate than shown by the figures above. See Gessen, *Sudebnaia reforma*, 7. The chart excludes cases returned to the lower courts without action, for the original decision in these cases is unknown.

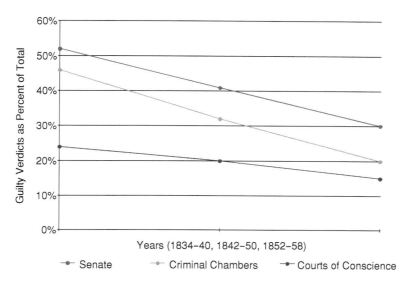

Years (1834–40, 1842–50, 1852–58)

-●- Senate   -◌- Criminal Chambers   -●- Courts of Conscience

Fig. 3.2 Verdicts of guilty, 1834–58

a judgment of incompetence – is to be expected.[91] Although the aggregate data hinder comparative analysis, these trends apparently slowed in the 1860s. Still, this brief increase in judicial activity may very well have reflected the idealistic concern of the era with legality and due process. Substantive public discussion of suicide (and critique of its legal status) would begin late in the decade.

Taken together, judicial statistics point to a growing reluctance to reach a guilty verdict and hence an increasing lenience in the judgment of suicide overall.[92] The rise in new cases in the 1840s was accompanied by a clear drop in the percentage of guilty verdicts, a trend which continued in the 1850s when the number of new cases also began to fall. The rising prosecution rates in the 1830s and 1840s should therefore be interpreted in relation to institutional and legal changes. Most fundamentally, of course, legal codification allowed criminal prosecution to proceed on the basis of a recognized standard. In addition, the centralization of administrative control in the ministries facilitated the flow of

[91] The patterns of judgment also suggest a role for gender with women found guilty disproportionately often in the criminal chambers. For the period 1842–50, 29 percent of defendants and 34 percent of those convicted were female. This discrepancy increased in the period 1852–58, when only 26 percent of defendants but 36 percent of convicts were female. In contrast, women composed 25 percent of those convicted in the 1860s.

[92] This generalization does not hold for the military courts. For the years 1860–63, guilty verdicts were reached in 70 to 81 percent of cases, and not-guilty verdicts ranged from 8 to 23 percent. Indeed, only 3 of 40 defendants were found not guilty in 1863. These figures underline the cultural specificity of judging suicide. See *Statisticheskii vremennik Rossiiskoi Imperii* (SPb, 1866), 4–11.

information to the center as well as the systemization of provincial justice. On the local level as well, administration was centralized and streamlined from the governor down to district police agencies. Though a bureaucratization of policing and justice initially helped to stimulate a rise in prosecution rates, signs of change were apparent by mid-century. It is hardly coincidental that the annual reports of the justice ministry dropped suicide from the list of most notable and serious crimes after 1854.[93] By the turn of the twentieth century, and despite a doubling of the population in the meantime, the number of prosecuted suicides would remain at the approximate level established in 1834.[94]

In 1860, the jurist Mikhail Bul'mering cited the suffering of family members to argue that the denial of Christian burial was cruel and outmoded. Were not all suicides in some way insane? At the same time, however, he asserted that suicide was a crime because it transgressed society's moral standards; on this basis he supported the invalidation of the suicide's last will and testament.[95] Only a few years later, many legal scholars would reject this premise, arguing that law should be divorced from morality. Though Bul'mering did not share this approach, his language points to important changes in the emotional valuation of suicide that underpinned the shifts in its legal and moral status during the first half of the nineteenth century. His contradictory words were telling: suicide seemed both pitiful and criminal, mad and immoral.

The statutes on suicide formulated in the 1830s and 1840s did not distinguish between the criminal and moral dimensions of the act. Self-murder was both a crime and a sin, and its combined penalties reinforced this dualism. With law perceived and exercised as an instrument of rule, the legal regulation of social values and morality had never been questioned for that was indeed one of its objects. In this framework, suicide was punished as a moral transgression against God and as a criminal transgression against secular authority without contradiction. Nevertheless, the legal status of suicide was not undisputed. Even in the 1830s, some governmental officials resisted the equation of suicide with murder, and this viewpoint emerged victorious in the 1845 penal code. Judicial statistics likewise point to significant changes in the legal response to suicide in the decades leading up to the Great Reforms. The rise and subsequent fall in prosecution rates as well as the fall in conviction rates point to a shift in attitude, which set the stage for the debates and jurisdictional conflicts of subsequent decades.

---

[93] *Otchet Ministerstva iustitsii za 1854*, 6.

[94] In 1899, 474 cases were initiated in European Russia, including Poland and the Caucasus (total pop. approx. 113,000,000); in 1904, 415 cases. See *Sbornik statisticheskikh svedenii Ministerstva iustitsii* here vol. 15 (za 1899), pt. 1 (SPb, 1901), 123–27; and vol. 20 (za 1904), pt. 1 (SPb, 1906), 142–43.

[95] Mikhail Bul'mering, "O samoubiistve," *Iuridicheskii vestnik* no. 5 (1860), esp. 41, 44–45.

To characterize this attitude is more difficult. Although the act of suicide continued to be condemned, it was no longer placed within the same category of transgression as murder or brigandage. In addition, punishment for attempted suicide began to be conceived – at least among top officials – more in terms of correction and moral instruction than retribution. At the core of this attitude were two subtle shifts in emphasis both of which built upon a combined sentimental and paternalist idiom. First, a modern and tautological presumption was emerging that a morally upright person could not kill himself unless (temporarily) insane. If suicide was thereby the act of a madman, then the person could be perceived more as a victim than as a fully competent perpetrator. In this light, the retributive punishments could suddenly seem unduly harsh. Second, the need to condemn the suicide with a public ritual began to compete with another concern, which was also articulated by the editors of the 1845 penal code: the need to take the sensibility of the family into consideration. In other words, the outrage provoked by suicide competed with the empathy felt for those left behind. Such a response was emotional, though the editors would probably not have seen it that way, and it points to the lasting influence of sentimental representations: one need not approve suicide to feel pity.

Despite these shifts in emphasis, suicide continued to resonate as a threat to public order, and the parallels with the techniques of denunciation developed by Russia's public at the turn of the nineteenth century are numerous. The large numbers of suicide among the lower orders attributed to depravity and drunkenness point to the explanations provided by serf owners and local elites more generally. These acts were constituted as a sign and consequence of misbehavior and disobedience – a failure to conduct oneself properly or to submit to one's place in the social hierarchy. Furthermore, statistics were beginning to confer a scientific validity upon an explanatory framework which linked low rates of suicide to patriarchy and tradition, and high rates to vice and civilization. Yet despite their seeming endorsement of social conventions, these studies exposed a hidden world behind the public façade of orderliness, and this exposure caused some anxiety. Did not Divine Law, autocratic legitimacy, and social order require the celebration of patriarchal authority? Should not negative phenomena be cast into oblivion?

4 Punishing the body, cleansing the conscience

> Kurochkina is hereby sentenced to five lashes, to be carried out at the police precinct by one of its lower subordinates, and then, for the cleansing of the conscience, to church penance, as determined by the spiritual authority.
>
> Opinion of the Nizhnii Novgorod District Court in the case of Agrafena Kurochkina, accused of fornication and attempting to hang herself, 1829–30

It all began, according to Agrafena Kurochkina, the daughter of a soldier living in the city of Nizhnii Novgorod, when the soldier Stepan Fedotov beat her up in a fit of jealousy.[1] On that fateful day in November 1829, he hit her in the head, pulled her across the floor by her hair and kicked her; later that same day, he hit her so hard that she lost consciousness. Consequently, she could not remember going into the courtyard much less that she "supposedly wanted to hang herself" there. In claiming to have acted, literally, "without memory" (*bespamiatstvo*), Kurochkina was pleading innocent to the charge of attempting suicide by reason of what might be called temporary insanity.[2] We cannot know whether she was telling the truth, or, equally interesting, whether she understood the legal importance of intention in the prosecution of a felony, but the latter is a plausible explanation for the language in the court protocol. Steadfastly denying the charges, Kurochkina herself apparently used the term *bespamiatstvo*. Unfortunately for Kurochkina, the police did not believe her story. The investigation established that she was living in an illegal cohabitation with Fedotov, who admitted the sexual relation but denied beating up Kurochkina that day. Because of her "depraved behavior," moreover, he had actually decided to break off the relationship. His story was partially confirmed by witnesses, the landlady and several other women, who all testified that they had not seen any beating. Again, it cannot be established who was telling the truth, for tensions within the house may have influenced the statements of Kurochkina's neighbors. More important to understanding the prosecution of

---

[1] The discussion below is based on two archival files: GANO, f. 176, op. 94, 1829, d. 8; and f. 570, op. 557, 1830, d. 153.

[2] This term is defined as a condition of man deprived of memory, that is, of feelings and consciousness; not remembering oneself; faint, stupor, loss of memory or consciousness. See *TS*, vol. 1, 171–72.

suicide in the early nineteenth century is rather the evidential importance of behavior. By uncovering the additional crime of fornication, the investigation had besmirched Kurochkina's character.[3]

While her case was being investigated, Kurochkina was waiting in prison, and her trial was conducted with unusual speed, about one month after her arrest in November 1829. In its verdict, the court cited the testimony of the witnesses as the decisive factor. Her claim to have acted in temporary insanity was judged – in the words of the police report – "completely false," and, in addition to attempted suicide, she was convicted of fornication. The criminal chamber gave its stamp of approval to the ruling in January 1830, and Kurochkina was lashed. Her file was then sent to the local spiritual consistory, which ruled that she perform one year of penance at the Nikolaevskii Convent in Arzamas, followed by an additional thirty months under the supervision of her parish priest. This sentence was lenient – in light of the corporal punishment, her penitence time had been cut in half. Nevertheless, its terms were strict: in addition to performing set duties, Kurochkina was to attend every service, prostrating herself twenty-five times before an icon. Obliged to confess though not granted absolution, she could receive communion only upon the completion of penance or upon her deathbed. The case was ordinary until this point for Kurochkina refused to submit and twice ran away, the second time successfully. Her fate is unknown.[4]

As suicide and attempted suicide became the object of judicial and administrative regard during the nineteenth century, official records were produced in significant numbers. Not only do they serve as a vivid reminder that individuals such as Kurochkina make up the data of statistics; they also offer a micro-historical perspective on the regulation of suicide. Yet police and judicial documents from this period present historians with many challenges. Until the 1864 reform, criminal prosecution relied upon an inquisitorial procedure and closed trials. Verdicts were reached upon an examination of a written summary of the case, in which testimony was paraphrased rather than recorded. As Russia lacked an adversarial tradition, the confession was deemed the highest form of evidence, and neither defendants nor witnesses were usually called to testify in person. Such practices contained the potential for arbitrariness at all stages:

---

[3] On the crime of fornication, see Laura Engelstein, *The Keys to Happiness: Sex and the Search for Modernity in Fin-de-Siècle Russia* (Ithaca, N.Y., 1992), 51–55.

[4] In October 1830, she escaped from the convent but was arrested several months later and sentenced to two weeks in a workhouse for running away. Three years later, the search for Kurochkina began once again. Initially intending to close the case, correspondence between the Nizhnii Novgorod police, district court, spiritual consistory, and Nikolaevskii Convent instead found that Kurochkina had disappeared somewhere between the workhouse and the convent. Her file would nonetheless be closed in 1839. Because the term of the penitence had ended in 1833, and her current residence was unknown, the religious consistory marked Kurochkina's case "resolved" and sent it to the archive. GANO, f. 176, op. 94, 1829, d. 8; and f. 570, op. 557, 1830, d. 153.

police authorities collected and presented the evidence without oversight; a clerk compiled an official summary; and judges were typically members of the local gentry rather than fully trained professionals. Not surprisingly, bribery, duress, and related forms of persuasion were rampant.[5]

Despite their obvious limitations, judicial and police records are rich and complex sources that provide a micro-historical perspective on the regulation of suicide. From the perspective of case studies, two main factors combined to propel the statistical trend toward lenience in judgment. First was an increasing effort among courts to apply legal standards and medical opinion, an effort that points to a spreading ethos of professionalization among both government officials and doctors. Second was a shift in the moral conceptualization of suicide. While an assessment of character and conduct would remain central to legal judgments throughout this period, the official response to both suicide and attempted suicide increasingly reflected an attitude of pity rather than simple condemnation. Archival documents further illuminate a wide range of social attitudes and responses toward suicide. As Kurochkina's case demonstrates, the powerless were not passive. Not only did she run away, which was more unusual, she also claimed the right to speak for herself and consistently refused to submit to her accusers. She was not alone. In their interactions with the institutions and rhetoric of state power, individuals articulated their views and attempted to advance their goals. They, too, negotiated the complex legal, medical, and moral terrain on which the regulation of suicide occurred.

The burial of suicides: morality and medicine

In their commentary, the editors of the 1845 penal code recommended that the law stipulating the profane burial of suicides should not be followed in all cases. "When it is known that the suicide was not only honorable and not debauched but also, submitting himself to the teachings of Faith and Church, distinguished himself with Christian virtues and may have only taken his life in a moment of juridically undocumented insanity," they proposed, "it seems more convenient and proper to leave it to the spiritual authority to decide in each particular case whether or not the suicide should be denied a Christian burial."[6] Although this proposal was not implemented, it highlights both the ambiguous jurisdiction of suicide and the primacy given moral character (rather than motive or mental state). Indeed, the editors had effectively suggested that the regulation of suicide

---

[5] The most evocative description of pre-reform legal procedure is I. V. Gessen, *Sudebnaia reforma* (SPb, 1905), 1–30. See also John LeDonne, "Criminal Investigations before the Great Reforms," *Russian History* no. 2 (1974), 101–18, and Richard Wortman, *The Development of a Russian Legal Consciousness* (Chicago, 1976).

[6] *Proekt ulozheniia o nakazaniiakh ugolovnykh i ispravitel'nykh, vnesennykh v 1844 godu v Gosudarstvennyi Sovet, s podrobnym oznacheniem osnovanii kazhdogo iz vnesennykh v sei proekt postanovlenii* (SPb, 1871), 622.

be shared with religious authorities: should doctors fail to establish a medical cause for the act, it was implied, then priests should be empowered to judge the person on the basis of moral criteria, including both qualities of character and patterns of conduct. This proposal evokes the regulatory formulas of the pre-Petrine era, though, in contrast to them, seems more directed toward leniency. With their tautological reasoning rendering suicide an intrinsically insane or immoral act, the implication was that healthy and decent people do not kill themselves.

This logic was especially prominent in a sensational case from 1792: Moisei, Bishop of Feodosia and Mariupol was found in his apartment with his throat cut. A fragmentary note indicated that he had acted upon his own volition, and civil authorities soon ruled out foul play. In the report sent to the Most Holy Synod in St. Petersburg, the apprehension was palpable: how could a bishop possibly kill himself? The explanation was twofold. It first cited a pattern of illness (head pain and signs of a fever) to hypothesize that Moisei must have been feverishly delirious (*goriachka v bespamiatstve*), when he laid hands on himself. Simultaneously, it left open the possibility (wholly discounted by civil authorities) that he might really have been murdered after all. Repeating this either/or formulation several times, the report justified the decision to grant a Christian burial as the proper application of church rules for both possible scenarios. This reasoning points to an inability to comprehend suicide and hence its representation as inherently insane: the bishop could not have been fully lucid when he killed himself, for otherwise he would never have done so in the first place. Yet the need to excuse the act was clearly tied to the person of the bishop: it was perhaps personal – the result of friendship or sympathy with the deceased – or political – the symbolism of burying a bishop of the church as a plain suicide.[7]

A more contested example of this problem occurred in 1840 when the civil governor of Vitebsk province, Petr L'vov, shot himself. A flurry of correspondence with detailed reports soon flooded St. Petersburg. The immediate context was personal: his wife was apparently threatening to leave him, and, more controversially, to initiate divorce proceedings on the basis of his physical inability to consummate their marriage.[8] Even beyond the shame of such an event, L'vov apparently loved his wife passionately and tried to convince her to stay with him. Late one night at home, after several fraught encounters with family, servants, and his wife's doctor, he then shot himself. Subsequently at issue was less

---

[7] For the reports, see RGIA, f. 796, op. 205, d. 118, ll. 2–5. See also the discussion in N. N. Bantysh-Kamenskii, "Moskovskie pis'ma v poslednie gody Ekaterinskogo tsarstvovaniia," *Russkii arkhiv* no. 11 (1876), 280–83.

[8] Divorce was extremely difficult to obtain but one recognized basis was failure to consummate the relationship. Judging from a medical report, it seems probable that L'vov's testicles had never descended into his scrotum.

the private drama, than the public one. L'vov had been appointed to his position due to local tensions between Polish Catholics (nobles) and Eastern Orthodox (peasants) as well as reports of corruption on the highest levels of the provincial administration. Consequently, he had made many powerful enemies, and these men avenged themselves upon his corpse. Immediately judged to have acted in full reason, he was formally denied a religious burial. Rumors then began to fly. Had L'vov really been murdered? What had happened at the burial?[9]

A special investigation was initiated, and the gendarme officer discounted the rumors of murder but uncovered the following rituals of burial:

The corpse of L'vov, naked, covered only with a sheet, was left in that state for three days in the Governor's residence and was the object of universal curiosity, rather like a desecration. Everyone, without regard for station, was freely admitted to its inspection. Then, at midnight, the corpse was placed on a knocked-together board, taken out of the house through a window by low-ranking policemen, and was driven out of the city on a Jew's dray cart [na lomovoi zhidovskoi podvode] and given to the earth.[10]

The family had begged for permission to put some clothes on the body, even old ones, but in vain. This "inhuman burial," as the investigating officer called it, had caused an uproar among the "lower orders," that is the Orthodox peasants, who had seen L'vov as a kind of defender. Similarly, the Jewish community and some Catholics had also apparently responded with dismay, feeling – in the words of the official report – "compassion" and "common humanity" with the former governor. But L'vov's enemies chortled, asserting that the law – Peter the Great's version – had simply been followed. Apparently, some Catholics even gave thanks to heaven for rescuing them from a strong and evil enemy. At issue, of course, was the political fallout: L'vov had been the representative of the tsar, and the ritual desecration could consequently be understood as a figurative assault upon imperial power.[11] The controversy illustrates both the growing discomfort with the "archaic" rituals of a bygone era, and the political potential within such rituals. The interment of a suicide had been converted into a public and political act.

Though this case was certainly unusual, the desire for a dignified and religious ritual remained common among all social groups. Scattered sources suggest that some elite families were able to influence the judgment and burial of their loved ones.[12] In his private correspondence from 1791 to 1792, Nikolai

---

[9] For the account written by one of the officials who orchestrated the burial, see GARF, f. 109 IV, op. 180, (1840), d. 98, ll. 8–14. For the letter of Baron Aleksandr Rozen, who happened to be in Vitebsk on business and was shocked by what had happened, see l. 22. On the rumors of murder, see l. 21.

[10] GARF, f. 109 IV, op. 180 (1840), d. 98, l. 31.   [11] Ibid., l. 32.

[12] For a probable example, see the case of Vera Andreeva, the 18-year-old daughter of a state counsellor, who shot herself in August 1858. The verdict was accidental death, and the evidence relied on the family's description of her character. Not only had she had no reason to kill herself,

Bantysh-Kamenskii described two such instances. A certain Viktor Samarin had slashed himself with a razor – because his mistress had left him, according to Bantysh-Kamenskii. A doctor nonetheless certified that he had acted in unsound mind (*v lishenii uma*), thereby securing a Christian burial. Similarly, the retired brigadier Aleksandr Protasov cut his throat, and Bantysh-Kamenskii supplied a wealth of information about the circumstances. Before dying, Protasov had apparently told a priest, who had been quickly called, that he could not remember what he had done. Though the family cited the fashionable disease of hypochondria, Bantysh-Kamenskii glibly discounted this explanation and reported the gossip – a financial affair involving the loss of property held in guardianship. Protasov was buried in Moscow's Donskoi Monastery, but without a service in the parish. "While this is contrary to all church regulations," Bantysh-Kamenskii concluded, "this leniency (*sniskhozhdenie*) is apparently used for the family and relatives."[13] These comments suggest rather mixed attitudes: alongside the presumption of worldly motives was both censure of the act and pity for the family.

In the judgment of less prominent cases, moral and medical factors often coexisted, for an assessment of character and conduct was integral to the judgment of motives, mental states, and hence criminal intent. Among the earliest sources is a fragmentary report from local authorities in Arzamas. In two cases from 1802, the behavior of the deceased formed crucial pieces of evidence.[14] Fedosiia Stepanova, a peasant woman, was found to have hanged herself in insanity and granted a Christian burial in the local church cemetery. According to her husband, her behavior had become erratic over a year earlier. For their part, neighbors simply described Stepanova as a good woman, who had lived honestly and decently (*zhila ona dobroporiadochno*).[15] A second case involved a peasant named Kireev, who had been found dead in a noose, a clear suicide. No specific reasons were found for the act, but the investigation established that he had committed fornication with a woman working for him. The decision went against Kireev: he had been in his right mind (*v polnom razume*) when he committed suicide.[16] The assessment of moral character was double-edged: it could help either to acquit or to convict.

Later police investigations likewise focused as much on patterns of conduct as upon the circumstances of an incident. In the 1828 case of Private Vasilii Rubasov, who had shot himself while guarding public monies in Vilna, the final

she been cheerful during the preceding days and possessed a "quiet and modest disposition." See the report of the St. Petersburg governor general, GARF, f. 109 IV, op. 198 (1858), d. 208, l. 3.

[13] See Bantysh-Kamenskii, "Moskovskie pis'ma," 271, 284.

[14] GANO, f. 101, op. 1, d. 19. These materials are in poor shape, and the next surviving reports date to 1806 (d. 102) and then the 1830s and 1840s (d. 351, 517, 561, and 612).

[15] GANO, f. 101, op. 1, d. 19, 6–8.   [16] Ibid., 9–11.

report emphasized that all avenues of investigation had been pursued: "Rubasov was of sound mind and good behavior; in service he was never corrected for any vice; there were no penalties or punishments; he did not have any grounds for grumbling; the public monies [he guarded] were always complete and correct; in his free time, he occupied himself with making boots, and he always conversed with his comrades in the guard as was appropriate. His motives for suicide are unknown, and nobody anticipated that he had such intentions."[17] Precisely because suicide had long been understood as the result of vice and disobedience, Rubasov's unblemished record made his case especially confusing.[18]

Yet evidence of disease and incapacity did not necessarily constitute grounds for leniency, and scattered cases suggest instead that the denial of Christian burial was common practice. When the herbalist Ivan Solovtsev was found dead in a noose in 1829, he was immediately buried as a suicide though the investigation had not yet been completed. Indeed, his wife had not been informed, and she subsequently lodged a protest. The inquiry revealed that Solovtsev was sober and well behaved but had been suffering from headaches and general weakness for some time. Moreover, witnesses noted his pensiveness (*zadum-chivost'*) in the days before his death. While sympathy to the wife's "tender virtues" was explicit, the official reports cited the lack of evidence to overturn the original judgment.[19]

This pattern recurred in other instances. Like Solovtsev's wife, witnesses themselves sometimes linked the suicide to physical disease and consequent mental states, clearly implying a causal dynamic. The structure of the formal reports tended, however, to emphasize the ambiguous status of physical and mental health. When Cavalry Captain Kmit shot himself in 1831, his physical condition was not considered sufficient explanation or motive. Although he suffered from numerous ailments, including hypochondria and (what appears to be) advanced-stage syphilis, it concludes that the motives for his act were still being investigated.[20] In the 1827 case of retired Captain Svechin, who shot himself in front of his wife and daughter, no motive was found, it was stressed, except for his "despairing condition" (*otchaiannoe polozhenie*) caused by an old wound to his thigh. At times, the suffering had driven him to a frenzy (*dovodit' ego do isstupleniia*). An official medical diagnosis is not mentioned, however, nor is a verdict.[21]

[17] GARF, f. 109 IV, op. 168 (1828), d. 175, ll. 1, 3, 4.

[18] Compare the case of a Moscow student whose behavior was likewise irreproachable: GARF, f. 109 IV, op. 176 (1836), d. 72, l. 1.

[19] GARF, f. 109 IV, op. 169 (1829), d. 114, ll. 1, 4–7. Though he suffered from attacks of melancholy and had a record of good behavior, the surveyor Pavel Prizhimov was also buried as a suicide. See GARF, f. 109 IV, op. 192 (1852), d. 128, ll. 1, 10.

[20] GARF, f. 109 IV, op. 171 (1831), d. 141, l. 1.

[21] GARF, f. 109 IV, op. 167 (1827), d. 95, l. 2. For another case involving physical illness combined with hypochondria, see GARF, f. 109 IV, op. 171 (1831), d. 141.

Unfortunately the process of judgment is particularly difficult to assess because many investigatory and judicial records failed to specify a verdict or place of burial. Although medical practitioners often examined corpses, their primary concern was the establishment of the physical cause of death – the identification of suicide, murder, or accident – rather than of the accompanying mental state.[22] Furthermore, many judicial files contained a formulaic statement relegating the fate of the suicide to the judgment of God (*predat' sudu Bozhiiu*), a formula that was not defined but may have referred to the role of priests in making a determination. The point here is not to suggest that attitudes toward suicide were uniformly severe in this period or that some suicides did not receive Christian burials.[23] Indeed, both investigating officials and witnesses often agreed that moral character and signs of disease were highly relevant to an investigation. Nevertheless, the material fact of suicide constituted a serious transgression that needed explanation, if not always exculpation.

By mid-century, the role of doctors in assessing the mental and physical condition of suicides had grown in significance, a function the Senate was encouraging with its relatively consistent recognition of medical evidence.[24] This trend reflects important changes in the education and position of doctors. Peter the Great had founded Russia's first surgical school in 1706, but foreign doctors had dominated the profession in the eighteenth century with Russian-trained practitioners generally possessing a rudimentary knowledge and little social status. The scale and scope of medical education increased dramatically in the nineteenth century. By the 1830s and 1840s, qualifications had been standardized for medical practice and a higher social status accorded to physicians.[25]

At this time, doctors began to assert themselves more confidently as forensic experts and to offer an assessment of mental and physical states. In the 1857 case of Katerina Darmorisova, a 15-year-old serf who hanged herself following a punishment, a doctor cited "the moroseness [*ugriumost'*] of her character" caused by "the derangement of the liver."[26] This diagnosis drew on long-established medical concepts: the association of melancholy with an imbalance of black gall (and hence the liver) dates back to Hippocratic writings. Other cases did not cite autopsy results but instead treated mental disorder as

---

[22] In one case of suicide attributed to insanity, a peasant had been found insane several years earlier, after he had murdered his daughter, and subsequently been confined in a monastery. See GARF, f. 109 IV, op. 168 (1828), d. 162.

[23] Irina Paperno cites one case from mid-century in which Metropolitan Filaret reversed a judgment and allowed a Christian burial. See her *Suicide as a Cultural Institution in Dostoevsky's Russia* (Ithaca, N.Y., 1997), 52.

[24] For an example, see the 1839–41 case of Aleksei Mitiurev. RGIA, f. 1345, op. 113, d. 271, esp. ll. 1–8, 116–18, 123.

[25] On the history of the medical profession in Russia, see Nancy Mandelker Frieden, *Russian Physicians in an Era of Reform and Revolution, 1856–1905* (Princeton, 1981).

[26] GARF, f. 109 IV, op. 197 (1857), d. 229, l. 7.

a symptom of physical disease. Such was the diagnosis in the 1858 suicide of Ul'iana Stankevich, who suffered from consumption. As the report concluded: "this sick condition was accompanied by pensiveness, prolonged insomnia, and the absence of healthy reason. This is likely the cause of the suicide." Yet a parallel moral explanation simultaneously embedded the act into family life. Though a virtuous and loving wife, Stankevich was quite plain – in contrast to her "rather handsome" husband – and was, consequently, prone to extreme jealousy.[27] The moral and the medical here coexisted.

Incapacity was also a factor in the suicide of men, but it was typically configured more in terms of their public or economic life. When Major Selivanov shot himself in 1860 after a long military career, for example, he was found to have acted while "deranged in mind" and granted a Christian burial. The underlying reason in this case was less private morality than public honor. His father, it seems, had squandered his heritage and then disinherited him in favor of an illegitimate son. Poverty and the prospect of losing the final legal battle for the property had brought him to the breaking point. Equally important was his long record of exemplary military service: his character was not besmirched.[28]

Although the establishment of deliberate intention had long been integral to the legal status of suicide, many investigations instead conflated intention with morality and hence judged the person rather than the state of mind accompanying the act. By the 1850s, however, doctors and investigators were explicitly discussing suicidal intention in terms of physiological conditions and mental capacities. Yet morality remained relevant to the judgment of suicide, for character and conduct could themselves be factors in the medical diagnosis. By the end of the nineteenth century, a new scientific paradigm would build upon this long-standing nexus between the moral and the medical.

Attempted suicide: the politics of punishment

According to the *Digest of Laws*, attempted suicide was to be punished as for attempted murder, but the determination of punishment depended upon the social estate of the convict. For the lower orders, whose moral fiber was deemed intrinsically weak, power was exercised through bodily discipline. Corporal punishment thus inscribed the state's judgment – quite literally – on the criminal's body. A birching was seen as particularly mild, a favored method employed in domestic spheres. More serious infractions – as determined by the courts, serf owners, parents, or other similar authorities – could also result

---

[27] Although this diagnosis was made by the gendarme official writing the report, the language suggests that he had obtained this information from a doctor. See GARF, f. 109 IV, op. 198 (1858), d. 221, ll. 2, 11.

[28] GARF, f. 109 IV, op. 200 (1860), d. 200, esp. 1. 19. See also the case of Kazan university student Ivan Sibiriakov, who suffered from poverty and pensiveness. While the forensic examination concentrated solely on the physical cause of death, the landlord (a deacon) stressed his melancholy. See GARF, f. 109 IV, op. 197 (1857), d. 232, ll. 1–4.

in a specified number of lashes (with a whip, birch branches, or other implements) administered in private at the local police precinct. The most serious penalty in Russian law (as the death penalty was formally abolished and very rarely applied) was the knout until its abolition in 1845. Knouting, which was performed in public by the executioner, enacted the civil death of the criminal, who was subsequently consigned to Siberian exile or hard labor. Though many officials had become concerned about the subversive potential of the public spectacle, the ritual was meant to display the power of the state, to deter crime, and thereby to enforce social order. Members of the upper orders were exempt from corporal punishment, for their supposed attributes included personal honor and moral self-discipline. With criminal behavior consequently perceived as evidence of dishonor, the state designed its punishment accordingly: convicted criminals could lose the rights and privileges accorded their social status, that is, to take an example from the language of the era, their noble dignity (*dvorianskoe dostoinstvo*). Only then could they be exiled to resettlement or hard labor in Siberia. More common, especially for minor offenses, were reprimands from the appropriate corporate body, such as the local assembly of the nobility.[29]

The punishment of commoners for attempted suicide typically combined some form of corporal punishment with a church penance. Retribution thus coexisted with correction: the body was to be punished for the crime, the soul cleansed of the sin. Kurochkina's sentence was not unusual. In 1829, the serf Ivan Sakulin was sentenced to twenty lashes and church penance for his attempted suicide. His character had been sullied by accusations of drunkenness and debauchery, and his owner was to be informed of his poor behavior.[30] Justice ministry data confirm this general trend. Before 1845, the criminal chambers routinely sentenced people to corporal punishment at the police precinct, including 67 people (of 149 convicted) in 1842, 90 (of 201) in 1844, and 71 (of 177) in 1845.[31] This practice changed after 1845 when the new penal code specified penance as the sole penalty for attempted suicide, and the cases of individuals found guilty were subsequently referred to diocesan authorities.[32] Nevertheless, corporal punishment continued to occur

---

[29] These general issues and the policy debates have been carefully analyzed by Abby M. Schrader, *Languages of the Lash: Corporal Punishment and Identity in Imperial Russia* (De Kalb, Ill., 2002).

[30] GANO, f. 176, op. 94, 1829, d. 33, 2–12.

[31] Unfortunately, the original data (*Otchet Ministerstva iustitsii*) is inconsistently organized and hence difficult to interpret. In the 1830s, corporal punishment was included under "light" or "other" punishments as was, apparently, confinement in workhouses and prisons (eighteen cases in these three years). It should also be noted that these figures do not include the verdicts of lower courts that were reviewed and left unchanged.

[32] Most received five years, sometimes including a year at a monastery or convent. For such cases, see GANO, f. 570, op. 558 (1850), d. 132; f. 133, op. 121a (1847), d. 193. See also the case of the *meshchanin* Petr Krasil'nikov, who received a nine-year term in 1865–66 (GANO, f. 570, op. 558 (1866), d. 460, l. 2, 7–8) and five cases from the 1880s, GANO, f. 570, op. 559 (1888), d. 48–52.

in part because it belonged to the everyday maintenance of order. In 1846, a serf woman received a penance for attempting to hang herself and eight strokes with birch branches for misdemeanors related to her attempt, including twice absenting herself without permission.[33] Discipline also remained harsh in the military: in 1846, a soldier ran a gauntlet of 500 fellow soldiers, but his penance was consequently reduced from five to two years.[34]

The prosecution and punishment of elites for attempted suicide is more difficult to assess due to the paucity of sources. After 1845, the legal consequences were likely restricted to penance, though criminal convictions for nobles were also reported to local corporate institutions.[35] Furthermore, the small number of cases reviewed by the Senate before and after 1845 suggests that elites were not normally given severe penalties. The loss of rank or status rights was grounds for appeal, and the tsar reviewed all instances involving the forfeiture of nobility.[36] Such cases that reached the State Council (the highest governmental body) generally involved multiple offenses, that is, attempted suicide in addition to other serious crimes. In 1845, for example, Anton Patsunskii was caught in the act of stealing sheep and, as he initially admitted but later denied, attempted to cut his throat due to fear of punishment. Further weakening his case were the reports on his character made by six noblemen and two peasants that described him as lazy and prone to drunkenness. Rejecting his claims to innocence and citing expert medical testimony, the Senate and State Council revoked the rights and advantages of his station and sentenced him to resettlement in Vologda province, where he was to serve nine months in prison before beginning his penance.[37] Because such prosecutions involved more than one crime, the relative significance of the attempted suicide is unclear.[38] Still, a moral character besmirched by criminal activity undermined any claim to innocence.

Before 1845, most cases of attempted suicide were likely punished with a mixture of penance and corporal punishment or other "light" penalties, but some verdicts were more severe. Between 1834 and 1844 (even years only), 39 people were sentenced to penal servitude, and an additional 93 people received sentences of exile to resettlement in Siberia or conscription into military service. The most extreme year was 1834 with 51 such sentences (30 for hard labor

---

[33] GANO, f. 133, op. 121a (1846), d. 162, l. 15.

[34] GANO, f. 570, op. 557 (1846), d. 204, ll. 1, 3–4.

[35] See the 1856 case of the civil servant Petr Strunin, GANO, f. 570, op. 558 (1856), d. 313, esp. 9, 18–19, 25.

[36] See *SZ*, arts. 1317–18.   [37] RGIA, f. 1151, op. 3 (1846), d. 102, ll. 3–7, 13.

[38] See also the following cases: Petr Ianishevskii, who was convicted of theft and attempted suicide in 1863, lost his nobility and was resettled in Perm province, where he performed penance. RGIA, f. 1151, op. 6 (1863), d. 270, ll. 1–8; Petr Terent'ev, accused of theft, debauchery, and attempted suicide, f. 1151, op. 2 (1838), d. 60; and that of an under-age nobleman convicted of murder and attempted suicide and sentenced to penal servitude, f. 1151, op. 4 (1851), d. 17.

alone), and the typical range was 14 to 18 cases.[39] While these figures may not be large overall, they nonetheless highlight the fact that attempted suicide was often considered a serious crime, despite the statistical trend toward leniency in judgment.

Noble and serf

Two case studies, the one involving a nobleman and the other a serf, illuminate the dynamics of the legal process. The first began in 1833, when the nobleman Erazm Veliobitskii reported to local authorities that he had been attacked by bandits, who had stolen his money and papers and then slashed his throat. Upon interrogation a different account emerged. Dismissed from military service for poor behavior, the cadet had gone to St. Petersburg, where he had tried unsuccessfully to enter the civil service. While there, his brother had refused to help, and the police had ultimately expelled him, marking in his passport a prohibition of residence in either capital. While on the road, considering his limited options, he had then met his former comrades, which only underscored his miserable situation: "Finally, in a fit of unbearable frustration and strong despair [*v poryve nesterpimoi dosady i sil'noi skuki*], he tore up his passport and wounded himself, but reported the attack of bandits because he was beside himself, his mental faculties deranged [*nakhodilsia togda v bespamiatstve i rasstroistve rassudka*]." Citing the articles on attempted suicide in Peter the Great's Military and Naval Regulations, the district court ruled that Veliobitskii was to forfeit his rank and nobility. In light of his motive – shame (*styd*) and pensiveness (*zadumchivost'*) – the court decided to conscript him into military service rather than send him into penal servitude, which was the surrogate for the death penalty specified in the statute. Probably in response to the severity of this sentence, Veliobitskii returned to his original story about bandits, claiming that he had signed the confession without knowing its contents. Nevertheless, the Novgorod Criminal Chambers, the Senate, and the State Council endorsed the verdict, agreeing that his motive – "disappointment (*dosada*) about his unfortunate situation leading to *bespamiatstvo*" – constituted a mitigating factor.[40]

Although the courts recognized that Veliobitskii had acted under duress, in a mental state they described as *bespamiatstvo*, he nonetheless lost his noble status and was conscripted into military service. This ruling points to a significant gray area in the judgment of suicide. Veliobitskii's mental state mitigated against

[39] On some of the problems with these statistics, see n. 31. For further consideration of the numbers exiled to Siberia for attempted suicide, though with some inconsistencies, see S. Maksimov, *Sibir' i katorga*, 2 vols. (SPb, 1871), vol. 2, 74–75, 335, 350.

[40] A slightly different version of events appears in the summary of the case for the Senate. See RGIA, f. 1151, op. 2 (1834), d. 60, ll. 1–3, 26–30. The terms *styd*, *dosada*, and *bespamiatstvo* all appear in articles 347 and 348 of the *Digest of Laws*.

full punishment yet did not constitute grounds to acquit him of the crime. One reason for the severity may have been Veliobitskii's other transgressions: the unspecified misbehavior that had resulted first in his expulsion from the army and then from the capital followed by the destruction of his official papers. Nevertheless, a voice of dissent was raised. In light of Veliobitskii's age – 20 years – and in the hope that he would correct his ways, the Novgorod civil governor suggested that he enter military service but not lose his nobility.[41] According to this view, which advocated a corrective rather than retributive notion of punishment, Veliobitskii should have the opportunity to redeem himself. Furthermore, he implied that youth itself constituted a mitigating factor, one that had affected Veliobitskii's capacity to handle setbacks and control himself. Under Catherine the Great, age had first been formally accorded legal status as a mitigating factor in criminal offenses, and this principle would be affirmed in the *Digest of Laws* and penal code, but Veliobitskii was well over the age of minority. Both arguments, which would become common over the next decades, were shaped by a combination of cultural and legal factors. Changing views of suicide, especially a more sentimental idiom of pity, were intersecting with an effort to apply both legal norms and cultural-scientific principles, including ideas about the physiology of youth.[42]

The second case study likewise illuminates the range of factors contributing to the judgment of attempted suicide in this period. In contrast to the near unanimity of Veliobitskii's judges, this case reveals discord and disagreement at all levels of government. The official summary provided the following facts: In February 1842, Danil Parfenev, age 17, lived as a serf in Mogilev province. Due to various pranks (*shalosti*), his owner had ordered him taken to the local police precinct for punishment. On the way, he tried to run away but, when caught, hit himself with a rock in an attempt either to maim or to kill himself. Later, while locked in his cell, he hit himself in the face with a brick, breaking his nose and front teeth. The owner then requested that Parfenev's behavior be investigated as an attempted suicide. Likewise on his prompting (for the master clearly wished to rid himself of this serf), Parfenev indicated his willingness to join the military (*cantonisty*). The court summary elaborated in three main areas. First, it recounted the prank. The previous week Parfenev had been mistakenly given a silver ruble instead of a 5-kopeck coin to buy some beer. Rather than pointing out the error, he had purchased the beer, pocketed the change, and subsequently denied ever having received the extra money. Though he ultimately confessed his guilt, he had already spent the money. Second, it sketched Parfenev's moral character. Describing his behavior as bad (*khudoi*), his fellow serfs (including

[41] RGIA, f. 1151, op. 2 (1834), d. 60, l. 28.
[42] For further discussion of the legal and cultural status of age, see below and Schrader, *Languages of the Lash*, 114.

family members) mentioned drinking, card playing, and a penchant to thievery. Even Parfenev's mother had apparently conceded her son's poor behavior and clear suicidal intent. Finally, the inquiry revealed another attempted suicide which had occurred two months earlier. Hoping (again) to escape punishment for losing the boots of his landlord's son, he had thrown himself into a vat of water (used in distilling), but had been fished out. Faced with a caning for this attempt to drown himself, he had then grabbed a knife and tried to cut his throat but had again been restrained. He was subsequently birched at the precinct for twice intending to take his life – a detail that suggests, incidentally, that one reason for the officially low rates of attempted suicide in Russia was that it was punished on the local level as a form of insubordination.[43]

Having reviewed the case and interrogated Parfenev, the Bykhovskii district court ruled that he should be subject to the most extreme form of punishment allowed under Russian law: eleven strokes of the knout – a public spectacle symbolizing his death – followed by exile to hard labor in Siberia. In support of its decision, the court cited a medical opinion certifying Parfenev's physically robust constitution. Milder forms of punishment would apparently be insufficient.[44] While the proposed number of strokes was not excessive, it is nonetheless striking that this decision occurred in a case involving no additional serious offenses and just three years before the knout was abolished. The *Digest of Laws* did specify that attempted suicide should be punished as for attempted murder, but such severe sentences were not the norm.

The subsequent disputes about Parfenev's punishment touched upon notions of character and competence, retribution and correction. In its decision, the Mogilev Criminal Chambers ruled:

The defendant, the peasant Danil Parfenev, freely admitted his attempted suicide, but it is apparent from his case and testimony that he had acted due to fear of punishment [. . .] and besides at 17 years of age and not out of considered intent [*ne po obdumannomu zamyslu*] but, as it is possible to suppose, out of foolishness and stupidity [*po nerazumiiu i gluposti*]. In such an instance, the attempted suicide should not be punished according to art. 348, vol. 15, *Digest of Laws*, according to which it should be punished as for attempted murder.[45]

Citing article 126, which specified a reduction of punishment for minors, the criminal chambers reduced the sentence to twenty-five lashes, to be administered privately at the police precinct, followed by penance, the length and location of which was to be determined by diocesan authorities. Whereas the corporal punishment possessed a retributive function, the penance was explicitly correctional: it was "to instill fear and aversion for the thought of suicide."

---

[43] Parfenev claimed that someone had inadvertently taken the wrong boots and that he had been blamed. There are also minor discrepancies, including whether the landlord's son had birched or caned him. RGIA, f. 1345, op. 117, d. 538, ll. 40–8.

[44] RGIA, f. 1345, op. 117, d. 538, l. 49.   [45] Ibid., ll. 50–51.

Finally, Parfenev was to be returned to his place of residence unless his owner wished him to be banished.

However, the procurator requested that the criminal chambers reconsider its opinion. Arguing that the punishment was still too harsh, he emphasized Parfenev's youth, motive (fear of punishment), and level of understanding, specifically citing his stupidity, simplicity (*prostota*), and thoughtlessness (*legkomyslie*).[46] The chambers disagreed. Seeing the repeated attempts as evidence of his bitterness (*ozhestochenie*) and malice (*zlost'*) and citing his strong and healthy physical build (medically certified at the district level), the court argued that "the reduction of punishment could serve – both for the criminal himself and for other despairing and cowardly [individuals] – as a temptation and harmful example, especially as the attempts at suicide had occurred so frequently." At this point, the governor also intervened, but on the side of retribution: he called for twenty lashes plus Parfenev's conscription into the army or a convict labor gang (*arestantskie roty*).[47]

Although Parfenev's case had inspired four different proposals for his punishment, some issues were not disputed. While the district court's sentence had clearly ignored the legal status of minors, all other parties agreed that youth should indeed be a mitigating factor, and they filled the concept with cultural meaning. As the many references to foolishness and thoughtlessness imply, his age was sometimes linked to his (apparently) immature understanding. At the same time, the documents also constructed two contradictory images of Parfenev as either bitter and malicious or simple and foolish. These correspond to the Janus-faced stereotypes of peasants as embodiments of primitive violence on the one hand and childlike naïveté on the other hand. They also legitimized punishment differently, with the first constructing it as retributive, the second as correctional. Indeed, the two representations coexisted not only in this case but in the dichotomy between punishing the body and cleansing the conscience cited in many judgments on attempted suicide. The testimonial to Parfenev's robust build provides an additional piece of the puzzle. The district court and criminal chambers used this medical opinion to justify arguments for severe punishment, which was, in turn, seen as a necessary deterrent.

In defending their positions, the various parties in this case also articulated ideas about the mentality of suicide. For both the district court and the criminal chambers, the central issue was that Parfenev was a repeat offender.[48] As

---

[46] These three terms are drawn directly from article 129 of the *Digest of Laws*, which allowed a reduction in the level of punishment due to the level of understanding of the defendant.

[47] RGIA, f. 1345, op. 117, d. 538, ll. 50–56.

[48] In contrast, suicide threatened but not actually attempted was ruled not to constitute a crime. Accused of various financial crimes, governor's secretary Dobrynin threatened suicide but did not actually attempt it. While the Senate found him guilty of attempted suicide, the State Council overturned the decision in 1847, ruling that a threat did not constitute an actual attempt. See the summary in *Zhurnal Ministerstva iustitsii* no. 3 (1861), 640–42.

birching had already failed to deter him from this criminal misbehavior, more severe methods were advocated. Their arguments reflected the conviction not only that suicide was a crime but that recurring attempts demonstrated premeditation and criminal intent. Though quite different from modern Western attitudes that generally assume a psychological basis (depression or mental illness) for multiple attempts, this same perspective has also been found in early-modern England, particularly before 1700.[49] In contrast, the acting procurator saw attempted suicide as a crime meriting corporal punishment, but he advanced a different, more psychological explanation for the repeat offenses. In each instance, he pointed out, the attempt had occurred because Parfenev had feared punishment. The procurator thus maintained that fear had clouded his reason and thereby constituted a mitigating factor. The Senate agreed. Though guilty of attempting such a "serious crime," Parfenev was sentenced to ten lashes and church penance. A report from January 1844 confirmed that the verdict had been carried out; Parfenev had returned to his village and was completing his penance under the guidance of his parish priest.[50]

Mitigating circumstances

As the experiences of Veliobitskii and Parfenev illustrate, the prosecution, judgment, and punishment of attempted suicide depended upon a wide range of factors, including status considerations but also medical principles and cultural beliefs. As officials became more aware of the human body as a physical organism in the late eighteenth and nineteenth centuries, they inscribed physiology with new cultural meanings. Standardized into penal law under Nicholas I, the idea that certain bodies were more or less able to withstand corporal punishment drew on medical, legal, and philosophical notions of health, body type, age, and gender.[51] These factors were not always mutually consistent, as Parfenev's powerful physique and young age illustrate. Notions not just of the body but also of the mind shaped legal practices, and these too were inscribed with cultural meaning. To judge suicide and attempted suicide, it was necessary to assess intention, and one customary tactic was to subsume it under the broader category of moral character. Yet other tactics were also possible, and officials were striving to apply now standardized, if not always precise, legal norms. More fundamentally, they were beginning to conceptualize a psychology of suicide that associated the act with particular emotional

---

[49] In these cases, previous attempts at suicide constituted evidence of premeditation when coroners were examining cases of completed suicide. Attempted suicide only became the routine object of prosecution in the nineteenth century. See Michael McDonald and Terence Murphy, *Sleepless Souls: Suicide in Early Modern England* (Oxford, 1990), 229–30, 350–51.

[50] RGIA, f. 1345, op. 117, d. 538, ll. 64–76, 84.

[51] This study confirms many of the arguments in Schrader, *Languages of the Lash*, 112–43.

states, most importantly youth and the fear of punishment but also old age and drunkenness.

An interest in the psychology of suicide, especially youthful suicide, was apparent in the various statistical studies from the 1830s and 1840s. In his analysis of suicide in St. Petersburg, Andrei Zablotskii-Desiatkovskii had naturalized the higher levels of suicide among young men (contextually, in this case, from the nobility) in the following terms: "The time of youth is the time for the development of the passions; it is naturally the age at which man has more reasons and resolution to take his own life."[52] Seeing age as determining "the level of development of concepts and passions," the statistician K. S. Veselovskii had likewise coupled suicide with passion, even articulating a brief philosophy of the life cycle from the boiling blood of youth through the cold indifference of old age.[53] By this time, cases involving the very young (and a handful involving the very old)[54] were being regularly announced in the miscellany section of the *Journal of the Ministry of Internal Affairs*. While these accounts usually only provided the most basic facts, they often remarked on "this strange psychological phenomenon," and even sorrowed for these "victims of lamentable unreason." Indeed, the sensibility aroused by such events built upon a notion not only of childhood but also of suicide, which was clearly distinguished from murder. One report thus opened with a reference to a previous item on a boy who had murdered his little brother: "The preceding case provokes consternation and horror; but [with suicide] one can only pity these unfortunate victims − needless to say − of weak-mindedness [*slaboumie*]."[55] In sum, youthful suicide was associated with emotional and mental immaturity as well as a lack of self-control. Such associations may well have informed the attempt of the Novgorod civil governor to help Veliobitskii, who was 20 years old − no longer a minor but still unable to govern his emotions. They also shaped the intervention of high-ranking officials into seemingly trifling cases involving the weakest members of society, both the very young and the very old.

In 1839, for example, the governor of Kursk province petitioned the Senate in support of the serf Semen Udaloi, who faced a lashing and Siberian resettlement for his attempted suicide.[56] Only 16 years old and apprenticed with a weaver,

---

[52] [Andrei Zablotskii-Desiatkovskii], *Statisticheskie svedeniia o Sanktpeterburge* (SPb, 1836), 198. Referring to the young officers and noblemen who had shot themselves, V. Androssov used almost the exact same wording. See his *Statisticheskaia zapiska o Moskve* (Moscow, 1832), 89–90.

[53] K. S. Veselovskii, *Opyty nravstvennoi statistiki Rossii* (SPb, 1847), 42–46.

[54] See also the accounts in *ZhMVD* (1846), pt. 13, 468; pt. 15, 175.

[55] I found twenty-eight cases involving children reported between 1845 and 1848. For these examples, see *ZhMVD* (1846), pt. 14, 520; pt. 15, 175; pt. 16, 185.

[56] The following discussion is based on RGIA, f. 1345, op. 113 (1939), d. 147, esp. ll. 1a, 40–41, 43.

Semen testified that he had feared punishment – a birching – for his dogged wish to go home to his parents and a general antipathy toward life (*opostylost' k zhizni*). As Semen's behavior was certified as good (if sometimes coarse) by twenty-four witnesses, the governor cited his age and motive in a bid for clemency. The first factor was grounded in the *Digest of Laws* but disputed in this case due to uncertainty about Udaloi's actual year of birth. The problem of age, which could connote either physical or psychological development, had also propelled the dispute about Parfenev's punishment. Whereas the district court had cited his mature physical development, the criminal chambers had emphasized his immature understanding. Similar disagreements also occurred in this case. In response to the governor's petition, the Senate ordered a strict application of the law and consequently demanded that Udaloi's age be formally established as a prerequisite to the determination of punishment. The lower court then responded with an estimate – based on his appearance – of 23 years, which would have made him 19 at the time of his attempted suicide and thus over the age of majority. This estimate was three years higher than that of the governor, who, not incidentally, advocated lenience.

The second factor cited by the governor was Udaloi's fear of punishment, which was not specifically mentioned in the statute on attempted suicide (though it did include the emotional states of torment, an unbearable burden, and shame).[57] Instead, this commonly cited motive had become a mitigating circumstance largely due to the dynamics of official intervention. While serfs were indeed subject to the often arbitrary and cruel punishments of their masters and may very well have chosen suicide for such reasons, the act of intervention framed these cases within the language of paternal guardianship. The fear of punishment was thus constructed as an irrational fear, an expression of a youthful lack of control and emotional immaturity. The aim of intervention was less to call into question the legitimacy of corporal punishment (though this did occur in other cases which will be discussed in the next chapter). Instead, it constituted an expression of pity, a display of imperial power, and an act of clemency.[58] In Udaloi's case, the Senate sided with the governor and quashed the lower court's sentence of Siberian exile. After some two years in prison awaiting a verdict, the young man was given ten lashes and sent back to his village.

Like youth, old age also became a mitigating factor. In these cases, the appeal for clemency tended to associate age with infirmity. In one case from the 1850s, a doctor examined the defendant and found no diseases – excepting his age,

[57] Art. 348, *SZ*.
[58] Compare the brief report entitled "Suicide from fear of a deserved punishment" in *ZhMVD* (1847), pt. 18, 320.

which was approximately 62.[59] In another case, the acting civil governor of
Minsk intervened on behalf of the serf Andrei Tomkevich, who had attempted
to hang himself while drunk. Citing both age and intoxication, the district
court had sentenced him to three weeks incarceration followed by penance, but
the criminal chambers had rejected this reasoning, instead stipulating twenty
lashes and Siberian resettlement. Finding this sentence incommensurate with
Tomkevich's years, the governor had initiated a review. According to article 127
of the *Digest of Laws*, convicts over 70 years old should be freed from corporal
punishment, though not exile. In fact, however, the governor's intervention was
based less on law than on his own sense of paternal obligation: Tomkevich was
only 67. While the Senate agreed on the question of punishment (ruling that
Tomkevich should remain one more month in prison – where he had already
been for four months – and then perform penance), it did not cite age but
rather drunkenness as the key factor. Following article 113, the punishment for
crimes committed in drunkenness could be increased or decreased depending
on whether the crime had been premeditated.[60] Once again, the Senate was
most concerned with the precise application of the law.

As this case illustrates, another mitigating factor could be drunkenness. The
Senate thus ruled that Tomkevich's behavior was best explained by the foolhardiness (*bezrassudstvo*, literally, the absence of reason or sense) peculiar
to the drunken condition.[61] In his own version of events, Tomkevich stressed
this psychology: he had returned home drunk from a wedding, argued with
his wife, and then gone to the barn not really to hang himself but to frighten
his family. Blaming his behavior on his drunkenness, he denied any suicidal
intent.[62]

Yet this ruling was a rarity. The more common pattern of judgment in these
cases built instead on notions of moral character: drunkenness constituted evidence of immorality and hence criminal intent. Aleksei Nefedkin was found
guilty of attempting suicide in 1852 "not in madness or an attack of insanity
but in fact from drunkenness [*sobstvenno ot p'ianstva*]."[63] Like Tomkevich, he
claimed it was the passive consequence of intoxication. When Nefedkin woke
up and found himself under arrest, he testified that he had gone out drinking and

[59] See the case of Kiril Podoprigorenko, RGIA, f. 1151, op. 5 (1857), d. 90, esp. l. 3. Such was
also the implication of Mikhail Bezsonov's statement on the suicide of one of his elderly serfs.
See GANO, f. 101, op. 1, d. 102, l. 2.

[60] RGIA, f. 1345, op. 240 (1842), d. 700, esp. ll. 1, 7–9, 26–27.

[61] In the definition of *bespamiatstvo*, Dal' cites *odurenie* (stupefaction, torpor) as a synonym and
provides the following example of its use: *s odnogo stakana odurmanilo* (stupefied from one
glass). See *TS*, vol. 3, 1687.

[62] RGIA, f. 1345, op. 240 (1842), d. 700, ll. 7–8, 26–27.

[63] GANO, f. 570, op. 558 (1852), d. 232, l. 7. Compare the case of Second Lieutenant Ozh'e,
who shot himself while under detention for drunkenness. GARF, f. 109 IV, op. 175 (1835),
d. 72.

had no memory of trying to hang himself. Likewise blaming the alcohol, he was nevertheless content with his punishment of penance.[64] That Nefedkin could not even remember trying to kill himself yet nonetheless performed a penance illustrates how the confluence of dissolute with criminal behavior could eclipse the issue of reasoned intent.

The punishment of attempted suicide involved numerous other judgments. Russian law specified some of the factors to be considered, including age, drunkenness, and mental competence, but ideas about morality and immorality, retribution and deterrence, physiology and psychology, also shaped the legal process. Witnesses, governmental officials, and doctors had to weigh their relative significance in each instance. Individuals from all social groups repeatedly explained cases of suicide and attempted suicide with reference to patterns of moral behavior and the moral character of the victim/perpetrator. This concern with moral responsibility demonstrates the ongoing resonance of Christian categories of sin. Yet morality was increasingly infused with physiological, social, and psychological concepts as well. The view of youthful suicides as people not yet fully competent to make moral judgments shows how it was associated with evolving ideas about life stages. Similarly, drunkenness and fear of punishment could constitute mental states impairing judgment.

Though their form was particular to the Russian context, these developments occurred in a pan-European environment. Medical approaches to disease but also to crime and deviance were building on broader scientific, cultural, and political trends. Just as ideas about natural law helped to shape liberal political thought during the eighteenth and early nineteenth centuries, doctors, scientists, and philosophers began to locate gender and ethnic hierarchies in the body. Casting physical differences as "natural" and hence immutable, the new sciences of the body legitimized social and political structures, especially gender roles and the ideologies of empire. Over the course of the nineteenth century, many human behaviors – including suicide – would be embedded within physiological models.[65] Yet medical categories did not displace the interest in moral character but were often superimposed upon them, ultimately rooting morality and conduct in physiology.

Though uneven and inconsistent, two trends are apparent by the middle of the nineteenth century. First, the equation of suicide with murder, attempted suicide with attempted murder, was losing ground, especially in the Senate but also in many provincial-level judicial instances. With the act often provoking feelings

---

[64] GANO, f. 570, op. 558 (1852), d. 232, l. 3–4. Compare the case of Kiril Podoprigorenko, RGIA, f. 1151, op. 5 (1857), d. 90.

[65] This theme recurs through many articles in Catherine Gallagher and Thomas Laqueur, eds., *The Making of the Modern Body: Sexuality and Society in the Nineteenth Century* (Berkeley, 1987).

of pity rather than condemnation, the set punishments – especially for attempted suicide – could seem harsh and inappropriate. Second, regulatory practices were themselves evolving. The rationalization of administration, which occurred in tandem with rising professional standards, reinforced the authority of specialized knowledge, especially jurisprudence and medicine. The attempt to apply this knowledge in the judicial process clearly shaped the various mitigating factors in cases of attempted suicide. In other words, legal norms and medical principles were helping to recast the place of intention in the etiology of suicide.

The timing of these changes is striking. Intuitively, one would expect to find them not under the repressive reign of Nicholas I but after his death, in the reform era, when major administrative and social changes took place. Furthermore, historians of England have linked the rise of lenience there to the growth of a commercial press, which, in reporting suicide, situated it into everyday contexts and narratives.[66] Yet the public reporting of suicide was quite rare in Russia until the late 1860s. Rather than reflecting changes in public life, therefore, these trends depended more on the changing culture of Russia's officialdom. Most fundamentally, the education of servitors was constantly improving, and many were well acquainted with contemporary currents of literature, philosophy, and scholarship, perhaps including the debates about suicide. These developments confirm the practical importance of the new professional ethos among Russia's so-called "enlightened bureaucrats," those servitors who would play a central role in many of the reforms of the 1860s.[67]

While most officials seemed to regard suicide as a serious transgression, if not generally on par with murder, their visions of how to defend and promote public order sometimes diverged, leading on occasion to overt conflict. The complex of meanings associated with the "fear of punishment" is illustrative. Fear itself was an accepted method of rule in Russia. In the belief that the lower estates (as well as some women and national minorities) did not possess the basis of moral self-regulation, many officials argued that physical forms of discipline – that inspired feelings of fear – were essential to the maintenance of law and public order. Fear was therefore construed as a reactive and primal emotion, unmediated by mind and lacking considered intent. When fear of punishment became a recognized motive for suicide, therefore, it was primarily ascribed to people from the lower estates. It was met with significantly less favor among elites (including Veliobitskii and Patsunskii), for these men were deemed capable by their social status of moral control. Yet the notion that fear should be regarded as a mitigating factor in a crime suggests some ambivalence

---

[66] See Michael McDonald, "Suicide and the Rise of the Popular Press in England," and the response of Reginald E. Zelnik, *Representations* no. 2 (1988).

[67] The literature is extensive but the most important study of this process within the sphere of law is Wortman, *Russian Legal Consciousness*, pts. I, II, esp. chs. 2, 8.

about its role in the maintenance of public order more broadly. If fear could motivate immoral and criminal behavior, such as suicide, then perhaps it was not suitable as a method of rule. It was hardly coincidental, therefore, as the next chapter will explore, that the government was attempting to develop alternative methods of paternal rule. The ideology of autocracy built upon images not just of discipline and fear but also of custodial care and supervision.

5   Policing and paternalism

> In the records of occurrences in Tambov Province, it was incidentally stated that the landowner of Kirsanov district Zaitsov – while drunk – cruelly punished his serf Savel'ev [. . .] due to which the named peasant hanged himself. Next to this report, located in the extracts of May 9, 1831, His Highness deigned to write: "Find out what is happening with the landowner."
>
> From the file of the Third Section of His Majesty's Own Chancellery entitled "On the landowner Zaitsov, who cruelly punished his peasant"

The principle of personal governance had long stood at the heart of Russia's political system, and it was especially important during the reign of Nicholas I. Jealously preserving his role as autocrat, he regarded law as an instrument of rule, preferred administrative solutions, and often bypassed established institutions of state, particularly in his use of informal committees. Recognizing the rampant corruption in the bureaucracy, he sought to combat abuses through acts of intervention, police surveillance, and the appointment of upstanding servitors. He consequently strengthened the supervisory powers of governors, who formed an extension of his personal authority in the provinces, and established His Majesty's Own Chancellery, which soon became a powerful new administrative apparatus. At the heart of Nicholas's system was the Third Section of his chancellery, the secret police or gendarmerie. Though chiefly concerned with sedition, the Third Section possessed a wide sphere of competence, including matters relating to sectarianism, foreigners, counterfeiting, statistical information pertinent to policing, and "reports about all occurrences without exception."[1] As the historian Richard Wortman summarizes, it was "to oversee the enforcement of the law and the virtue of the citizenry. The supreme power became a 'social conscience,' whose righteous imperatives would inspire proper conduct, just as personal conscience inspired individual morality."[2]

[1] Nicholas V. Riasanovsky, *Nicholas I and Official Nationality in Russia, 1825–1855* (Berkeley, 1959), 220–21.

[2] Richard Wortman, *The Development of a Russian Legal Consciousness* (Chicago, 1976), 240. On the Third Section, including its ethos of paternalism, see also Riasanovsky, *Nicholas I*, 191, 219–21; Sidney Monas, *The Third Section: Police and Society in Russia under Nicholas I* (Cambridge, Mass., 1961); and P. S. Squire, *The Third Department: The Establishment and Practices of the Political Police in the Russia of Nicholas I* (Cambridge, 1968).

Yet this idealized model of personal, paternal justice contained an intrinsic contradiction. On the one hand, it formed the guiding principle that underpinned the well-ordered and orderly society that, according to official rhetoric, really existed. This was the vision of Russia as represented in the military parade, the vision that required such negative phenomena as crime statistics to be cast into eternal oblivion. In this framework, the purpose of government was to administer the well-ordered state, not to change it. On the other hand, however, this surveillance also constituted a transformative project. Its goal was not just to correct particular abuses but also to promote a paternal ethos (virtue) as the glue necessary to hold the socio-political system together and to make it work. These two visions of public order – of that which was and that which should be – formed a particular expression of a larger paradox within Nicholas's reign: the conservative politics of reaction combined with a modernizing agenda, whether in legal codification, the expansion and rationalization of bureaucracy, or the positive intervention in the behavior of individuals.

The custodial ethos and practices of autocratic power were plainly visible in the definition of the fear of punishment not only as a recognized motive for suicide but also – and largely through the formal act of intervention on the part of high-level officials – as a mitigating factor in the decision on punishment. They were even more important in the elaboration of the crime of instigated suicide, which entailed the prosecution of those vested with paternal power for abusing their power and thereby driving a subordinate to commit suicide. Official paternalism shaped particular meanings for suicide, therefore, but it was not simply a method of rule. Rather than elaborating an ideology of domination with a subaltern discourse of resistance, categories that raise difficult issues of agency and too often simplify relations of power, this chapter explores how power was negotiated.[3] The interactions and dialogues between officials and populace point to a complex system of governance predicated in part upon the principles of paternal obligation. While it has proven difficult to reconstruct the voices of non-elites, sources suggest that many categories, including moral character and paternal justice, transcended social divisions. Nevertheless, witnesses and defendants sometimes invoked these categories in quite distinctive ways. They were not passive objects of the state, therefore, but active, if not equal participants in the legal process.

---

[3] According to James C. Scott, official documents contain a hidden transcript that articulates the attitudes and experiences of those who could not leave written records. See his *Domination and the Arts of Resistance: Hidden Transcripts* (New Haven, 1990), esp. chs. 1–2. To articulate these responses as resistance, however, often creates an oppositional structure between the official and the popular. For critical considerations of resistance, see Sherry Ortner, "Resistance and the Problem of Ethnographic Refusal," *Comparative Studies in Society and History* no. 1 (1995); and Martha Kaplan and John D. Kelly, "Rethinking Resistance: Dialogics of 'Disaffection' in Colonial Fiji," *American Ethnologist* no. 1 (1994), esp. 125–30.

The ethos of surveillance

The visionary intention of the Third Section was once articulated by its long-time head, Alexander von Benckendorff, in an instruction to one of his gendarme officers:

Your own characteristic sentiments of nobility and righteousness will undoubtedly arouse the respect of all classes; and then your title, fortified by the people's confidence, will achieve its purpose and bring great benefit to the state. All will see in you an official who can carry the voice of suffering humanity through me up to the throne of the tsar and quickly bring the defenseless and voiceless citizen under the supreme protection of the tsar emperor. So many [. . .] illegal and unending disputes you can bring to an end; so many men with evil intentions [. . .] will become afraid.[4]

In theory, therefore, the Third Section formed a bureaucratized extension of the tsar's role as paterfamilias. Just as the tsar was the symbolic embodiment of personal, familial, and national virtue, the gendarme officer was to become a model of virtue on the local level, and, on this basis, to inspire public confidence. In this role, he was to mediate between society and the tsar, channeling deserving cases and correcting abuses. In practice, of course, the Third Section was much feared and resented, and it would fail in its mission to correct either the rampant corruption or the arbitrary exercise of power.

Over the course of more than fifty years, the Third Section reviewed numerous cases of suicide.[5] Many investigations were initiated by officials, and these were part of the Third Section's broader task of policing public morality. Because of the very unusualness (*po neobyknovennosti*) of the incident, one gendarme officer thus reported the mysterious suicide of the 22-year-old wife of an army major, who had shot herself without any warning or explanation after an evening playing cards.[6] In other instances, suicides were investigated because they implicated additional crimes. A civil governor informed the tsar of the suicide of a school director, who had confessed to gambling away public money in letters written to the governor, among others, before his death. An investigation of local gambling was underway.[7] Many files likewise concerned the instigation of suicide, particularly on the manor estate; the investigation of the circumstances was to determine whether an abuse of power had occurred.[8]

More striking is the fact that Nicholas I frequently intervened on his own initiative. While reviewing the official chronicle of events in the empire compiled for him, he would request information on any incident that caught his

---

[4] Cited in George L. Yaney, *The Systemization of Russian Government: Social Evolution in the Domestic Administration of Imperial Russia, 1711–1905* (Urbana, Ill., 1973), 224.

[5] Altogether thirty-five files dating to the reign of Nicholas I survive in the archive. A further twenty-five date to the reign of his son, Alexander II.

[6] GARF, f. 109 IV, op. 190 (1850), d. 163.

[7] GARF, f. 109 IV, op. 167 (1827), d. 167, ll. 1, 4.

[8] These will be discussed separately below.

eye, thereby triggering an investigation. At times his goal was apparently to encourage proper attention to detail and form among his subordinates. In other words, he reminded them of his constant oversight. In one instance, the tsar noted that the chronicle from Iaroslavl province had neglected to include the rank of an officer who had shot himself. The local gendarme officer zealously investigated the matter as directed, and the tsar ordered that the governor be told of his error.[9] In other instances, the motive was apparently plain curiosity. When an unknown man cut his throat in Moscow, the tsar noted, "Inform me of what is uncovered."[10] Of most interest to Nicholas I, however, were incidents of suicide among army officers as well as of the alleged instigation of suicide. Attention to such seemingly trivial matters demonstrated the omnipresence and unlimited personal authority of the sovereign, but it also embodied a more utopian goal: the unification of public and private life under the ethos of paternalism. To penetrate everyday life was also to propagate the principles of conduct within the social and political hierarchy.

The investigation of the 1840 suicide of a Moscow student, Ivan Mezentsov, illustrates particularly well how surveillance occupied the boundary between public and personal life. An initial gendarme report outlined the circumstances, indicated that no reasons for the suicide had been uncovered, and provided a possible medical explanation ("an attack of *delirium tremens*"). However, the tsar ordered further investigation, probably due to the prominence of the family. In response, Mezentsov's uncle, a high ranking civil servant, requested that all inquiries be halted "for the tranquility [*spokoistvie*] of the family." Precisely this request reinforced interest in the case, and orders were issued to continue the investigation. Ultimately, the uncle presented a private confession to Moscow's governor general: "Knowing the exalted virtue and compassion of Your Eminence," he wrote, "I consider it my sacred duty to reveal our family secret to you." Appealing to the traditional, exclusive, and (above all) discreet relationship that bound individuals to the tsar and his servitors, he explained the situation: Mezentsov had shot himself due to unrequited love for his first cousin (the uncle's daughter). Having discovered some references to the affair among his nephew's papers, the uncle had destroyed them in an attempt to protect his family. Public exposure would have created a social scandal and thereby damaged the reputation of the innocent girl. He begged for forgiveness: "I hope that this impulsive act of a heart so cruelly startled will be forgiven by people who know the extent of this distressing circumstance."[11] The story of the suicide thereby metamorphosed into a story of family honor, a sentiment that tapped into official ideology – the celebration of familial tranquility as the core of a

---

[9] GARF, f. 109 IV, op. 168 (1828), d. 213, esp. ll. 1, 4. For another example, see op. 179 (1839), d. 126.

[10] GARF, f. 109 IV, op. 167 (1827), d. 171.

[11] GARF, f. 109 IV, op. 180 (1840), d. 176, esp. ll. 2–3, 6–7, 9.

harmonious social order.[12] By ruling that the matter be immediately closed, the tsar then affirmed the principle and acted to safeguard the public honor of the Mezentsev family. Both the character of supplication and the response to it illustrate how Nicholas cultivated his paternalistic authority. Though he had rejected the initial request for privacy, the "family secret" remained confidential, the tsar – its guardian. As in pre-revolutionary France, this discretion was integral to the maintenance of public order.[13] Yet the policing of society was also understood as a creative force. Not only did it enact the ethos of paternal care within absolutism. It also constructed a kind of parallelism between the (official) norms of public life and the conduct of personal life.

In the early years of his reign, Nicholas's successor, Alexander II, continued many of his father's practices. Despite important differences in style and policy, both tsars shared a faith in autocracy. Paternal intervention and surveillance consequently remained central to the exercise of autocratic power. Occasionally, Alexander II requested additional information and petty details on cases of suicide mentioned in the official chronicles of events. The first time this occurred was just two months after his ascension to the throne. Informed of the suicide of the landowner and retired private Pushchin, Alexander first wanted to know "which Pushchin" (i.e. his full name) and then, in a subsequent directive, why a nobleman had retired at such a lowly rank.[14] Suicides associated either with an abuse of power (instigation) or the misappropriation of public funds likewise received attention.[15] In contrast to Nicholas I, who had been the stern paterfamilias, Alexander II cultivated what Wortman has called the scenario of love. As tsar, he was an the exemplar of sympathy, who worked in the interests of his people and thereby received their gratitude and love. Though maintaining the hierarchical distance between tsar and people, the scenario evoked more the benevolence of the tsar-father.[16]

While the direct influence of the new scenario should not be overstated, Alexander's paternalism – as mediated through the Third Section – often assumed a benevolent form. In 1856, Alexander was informed of the case of a low-ranking civil servant who had been fired for having reported various abuses of his supervisor and then failed to find redress with the local governor.

---

[12] Richard Wortman, "The Russian Imperial Family as Symbol," in *Imperial Russia: New Histories for the Empire*, ed. Jane Burbank and David L. Ransel (Bloomington, Ind., 1998), esp. 64–68, 71. I will discuss this issue further below.

[13] Cf. Roger Chartier, *The Cultural Origins of the French Revolution* (Durham, N.C., 1991), 35.

[14] He received detailed information on the promotions and demotions of a rather disorderly individual. GARF, f. 109 IV, op. 195 (1855), d. 131, l. 3. For other examples, f. 109 IV, op. 196 (1856), d. 129; and op. 199 (1859), d. 175.

[15] For cases involving instigation, see, GARF, f. 109 IV, op. 197 (1857), d. 229; op. 198 (1858), d. 257; op. 199 (1859), d. 147. For cases involving gambling and misappropriation of public funds, see op. 208 (1868), d. 107; and d. 194.

[16] Richard Wortman, *Scenarios of Power: Myth and Ceremony in Russian Monarchy*, 2 vols. (Princeton, 1995, 2000), vol. 2, ch. 1.

In response, Alexander directed that the widow be given 100 silver rubles.[17] Individuals also petitioned for formal redress in more traditional ways. In 1858, Nikolai Kutlubitskii wrote to the head of the Third Section, with a request for intervention: he wanted to know the true reasons for his sister's suicide several months earlier, but his inquiries had always been met with the bland statement that the investigation was continuing.[18] A similar hope structured the following appeal from 1863: "The widow of Collegial Registrar Kuznetsov, not finding justice anywhere and as a last resort, dares [osmelivaetsia] to inconvenience the chief of the Corps of Gendarmes with a request about the review in St. Petersburg of a matter that happened in Irkutsk, the suicide of her husband, which occurred due to his oppression [pritesnenie] by his boss." The request was acted upon, and a detailed report on the circumstances was sent from Irkutsk to St. Petersburg.[19] Petition-writing was a common practice in Russia, before and after 1855 (and 1917), and it suggests that the principle of personal intervention resonated within the general population. Kuznetsov in particular was not a member of the elite but a postal sorter at the very lowest level of service, and his wife's appeal reflected her own sense of place in the social hierarchy.

The surveillance of public order resulted in the accumulation of information about people's personal lives and allowed the tsars to exercise their power either to discipline errors or to redress wrongs.[20] Rather than generalizing problems and potential solutions, however, surveillance tended instead to ascribe crime and misbehavior to individual free will. Its transformative goals were not designed to alter the traditional institutions of the social order but to infuse them with virtue. This paradigm would soon end in an impasse. Widows could be given pensions, but individual paternal intervention could not always lead to satisfactory answers. By the late 1860s and 1870s, moreover, the emergence of a new social sphere would help to challenge the personal basis of autocratic politics. At this time, when the reign of Alexander II had lost its early dynamism and the revolutionary movement was gathering steam, almost all investigations

---

[17] GARF, f. 109 IV, op. 196 (1856), d. 235, esp. ll. 1, 5, 7–8. For further discussion, see Chapter 6.

[18] Having gathered information from the local gendarme and the Ministry of War (as she was the wife of an officer), Dolgorukii informed Kutlubitskii that the suicide lacked a clear cause but may have been related to illness. GARF, f. 109 IV, op. 198 (1858), d. 221, esp. 1, 14–15.

[19] Kuznetsov had been fired from his job as letter sorter in the postal service, but the courts had rejected his wife's argument that this constituted "oppression." While the loss of his job and overall poverty were the likely cause of the suicide, the courts reasoned, suicide was not the inevitable consequence of being fired, nor had the postmaster acted illegally. Kuznetsov had been buried as a suicide, and no further action was taken. GARF, f. 109 IV, op. 203 (1863), d. 179, ll. 1, 13–16.

[20] On other forms of surveillance, see Oleg Kharkhordin, *The Collective and the Individual in Russia* (Berkeley, 1999); and Peter Holquist, "'Information is the Alpha and Omega of Our Work': Bolshevik Surveillance in Its Pan-European Context," *Journal of Modern History* 69 (Sept. 1997).

of suicide by the Third Section involved revolutionary politics.[21] Not public
virtue, therefore, but sedition and, increasingly, the safety of the tsar were at
issue.[22] In the end, having lost its visionary character, the Third Section was
disbanded in 1880, its gendarmes absorbed into the Department of Police of
the Ministry of Internal Affairs.[23]

Discipline, cruelty, and the politics of social order

The Penal Code of 1845 contained an unusual new crime.[24] It criminalized the
abuse of power within the patriarchal relationship, but only in very specific
contexts:

Parents, guardians, and other individuals possessing some sort of power [*vlast'*], who,
through the manifest abuse of this power combined with cruelty, drive [*pobudiat*][25] a
subordinate or someone entrusted to their guardianship to commit suicide, are [subject to
the following penalties]: the loss of certain rights [. . .] and privileges and incarceration in
a house of correction for a term lasting from eight months to one year and four months; in
addition, if they are Christians, they are to be assigned a church penance, as determined
by their spiritual authority.[26]

Although the instigation of suicide was not a common offense in imperial
Russia, neither was it a curiosity limited to a few exceptional incidents. Scores
of references and cases date from as early as the 1820s and persist through the
end of the imperial period.[27] Indeed, the existence of cases from the 1820s and
1830s indicates that the 1845 statute was more a response to existing practices
than an innovation imposed from above.

The emergence of this crime, and especially its focus on cruelty, was part of a
broader shift during the early nineteenth century. Despite Catherine the Great's

[21] On the reign of Alexander II and particularly his loss of conviction after an assassination attempt
in 1866 and the death of his son, see Wortman, *Scenarios of Power*, vol. 2, chs. 3, 4.
[22] An 1879 suicide was investigated only because it was thought – erroneously – to relate to
assassination attempts on the tsar. GARF, f. 109 III, 1879, d. 220. For other examples see f.
109 III, 1879, d. 611; f. 109 III, 1880, d. 794; and f. 109, op. 3, d. 3054. For one earlier case
involving the Polish rebellion, see f. 109 IV, op. 204 (1864), d. 97.
[23] For further discussion, see Jonathan Daly, *Autocracy under Seige: Security Police and Opposition
in Russia, 1866–1905* (DeKalb, Ill., 1998).
[24] This statute was unusual in an international context but apparently not unique. According to
the jurist N. S. Tagantsev similar statutes did exist in several German codes, and he cites one
from Braunschweig, which criminalized the abuse of authority leading to suicide, infanticide,
abortion, child abandonment, and the concealment of a birth. See his *O prestupleniiakh protiv
zhizni po russkomu pravu*, 2 vols. (SPb, 1871), vol. 2, 442 n. 27.
[25] I use the terms "instigation" or instigating suicide as synonyms for "driving someone to commit
suicide" which is probably the best translation of the Russian *pobudit'* but often difficult to use
for stylistic reasons.
[26] Article 1476, *Ulozhenie o nakazaniiakh ugolovnykh i ispravitel'nykh* (SPb, 1846).
[27] Unfortunately, it is impossible to calculate the number of prosecutions because judicial statistics
did not distinguish this particular offense.

enthusiasm for Enlightenment philosophy, she had rarely concerned herself with the inner workings of Russia's "delegated absolutism"[28] in the family, the serf estate, the military, the workshop, and so forth. Instead, the right – even the duty – to employ physical discipline was fully accepted, and its function varied: to punish disobedience, misbehavior, or minor crime; to act as an example and deterrent; and to instill a proper respect for authority, that is, an ethos of submission and obedience. In the case of serfs, the judicial system only handled major crimes and relegated general police and judicial powers to serf owners, who were supposed both to protect and to discipline their charges. Until the nineteenth century, however, few restrictions short of a nominal ban on maiming and outright killing limited their right to punish their serfs as they pleased, and the use of corporal punishment as a means of social control was very common.[29] Similar autonomy governed the family, for the husband and father possessed the right to control residence and employment as well as to use corporal forms of correction.[30] During the early nineteenth century, however, the legitimacy of punishment was explicitly called into question with the notion of (illegitimate) cruelty.[31] This occurred primarily within the institution of serfdom, but the army and family were affected as well. Under Alexander I and Nicholas I, restrictions on the forms of legal punishment of serfs steadily became more severe, and the number of prosecutions for maltreatment rose significantly.[32] While these measures wholly failed to correct the abuses of serfdom, they demonstrate the state's real concern about the problem.

Fears of social unrest and humanitarianism have been identified as reasons for this concern. The importance of the first factor can hardly be overstated. For decades after its suppression, the Pugachev rebellion continued to haunt Russia's elites, and its specter shaped the perception of the usually minor disorders in the countryside, which were in fact becoming more frequent. Though less substantial, examples of discontent and even mutiny in the military also gave cause for unease. The role of humanitarianism is more difficult to assess.[33] Interest in charity and philanthropy had grown in Russia, particularly after 1812,

---

[28] From Laura Engelstein, *The Keys to Happiness: Sex and the Search for Modernity in Fin-de-Siècle Russia* (Ithaca, N.Y., 1992), 26.

[29] Steven Hoch, *Serfdom and Social Control: Petrovskoe, a Village in Tambov* (Chicago, 1986), esp. ch. 5.

[30] On the role of patriarchy in Russian civil and criminal law, particularly as it related to family structures, see William Wagner, *Marriage, Property, and the Law in Late Imperial Russia* (Oxford, 1994), *passim*; and Engelstein, *Keys to Happiness*, esp. pt. 1.

[31] On legitimacy and violence, see Susan Dwyer Amussen, "Punishment, Discipline, and Power: The Social Meanings of Violence in Early Modern England," *Journal of British Studies* 34 (Jan. 1995), 1–34.

[32] For an overview of the judicial and police powers of the serf owner, see Jerome Blum, *Lord and Peasant in Russia from the Ninth to the Nineteenth Century* (Princeton, 1961), 428–41.

[33] For further discussion, see Abby M. Schrader, *Languages of the Lash: Corporal Punishment and Identity in Imperial Russia* (De Kalb, Ill., 2002).

and these currents may have shaped policy decisions.[34] An additional factor, however, was the way in which power was exercised, in particular the ethos of paternal guardianship that theoretically underpinned the system of social and political hierarchy as a whole. As Elise Kimerling Wirtschafter has demonstrated, paternalist principles were crucial in the everyday regulation of the army. Though they failed to shield subordinates from abuse, they shaped a culture of interaction between officers and soldiers. Officers could thereby justify the strict use of discipline as a corrective measure yet also exhibit a fatherly concern for welfare. For their part, the soldiers sometimes made claims for (paternal) justice and exploited their (reputed) childish naïveté.[35] Similarly, recent studies of the peasantry have emphasized the system of mutual obligation which bound serf owners and serfs.[36] Under Nicholas I, paternalism would become more interventionalist as the state actively sought to monitor and organize the conduct of both public life and private virtue, that is to infuse a paternalist ethos into the institutions of "delegated absolutism." Following Nicholas's own example, officials exercised their right to order and administer the affairs of their charges.

In the late 1830s, a seemingly minor matter traveled up the judicial ladder to the Senate in St. Petersburg, because the governor of Poltava province had decided to intervene on what he apparently considered a miscarriage of justice. The case began on February 6, 1837, when collegial registrar Il'ia Doroshenko appeared at the Lokhvitskii district court to report that his serf, Petr Kovtun had cut his throat and died.[37] Explaining that Kovtun had possessed a passion for alcohol, Doroshenko stressed how the serf had been drunk at the time. Upon investigation, fellow peasants confirmed that Kovtun was in fact more often drunk than sober and that he had indeed been drunk on February 4 when Doroshenko had had him taken to the manor house to sober him up. Upon Doroshenko's order, Kovtun had been undressed and chained to a column in the courtyard, where he had been left until evening. Concerned about "the clouding of [his] mental faculties" (*pomrachenie rassudka*), Doroshenko then ordered that Kovtun be brought to the kitchen and chained to a table. The next morning, however, he was found there dead, his throat slit with a kitchen knife. In addition to confirming the suicide, the investigation revealed the following facts: according to Kovtun's wife, Doroshenko had struck Kovtun for shirking his work before taking him from his hut to the manor house for punishment; other

---

[34] On charity more generally, see Adele Lindenmeyr, *Poverty is not a Vice: Charity, Society, and the State in Imperial Russia* (Princeton, 1996).

[35] See Elise Kimerling Wirtschafter, *From Serf to Russian Soldier* (Princeton, 1990). Wirtshafter notes that the position of soldiers was better than serfs in one respect: they did possess the right to petition for the redress of grievances.

[36] See David Moon, *The Russian Peasantry 1600–1930: The World the Peasants Made* (London, 1999), ch. 3; Hoch, *Serfdom, passim.*

[37] For the entire case, RGIA, f. 1345, op. 236, d. 759, esp. ll. 21–24.

witnesses – gentry-born and common – reported that Doroshenko's behavior was above reproach, and that he treated his peasants well.

Despite arrest and prosecution, the serf owner continued to possess significant influence. Throughout the prosecution of this case, Doroshenko remained ensconced in his home, surrounded by his servants, who were also the primary witnesses. His interaction with the local gentry (the judges) was likewise unaffected. More fundamentally, his authoritative voice framed events within the generally recognized categories of paternalism: the moral weakness of the serf had required the use of discipline. By stressing Kovtun's drunkenness and laziness, he tapped into established stereotypes of serf (mis)behavior, legitimized his use of corporal punishment, and explained the suicide all at once. Nevertheless, the investigation of Kovtun's death also gave a voice to Kovtun's wife and fellow serfs. Although they confirmed the story of Kovtun's drinking and Doroshenko's intent to punish it, they were less passive than first appears. The serfs who had placed Kovtun in chains explicitly denied Doroshenko's suggestion that they had acted without his full knowledge. Although they did not make any direct accusation, their testimony on specific points undermined Doroshenko's own version.

In his routine review of the verdicts passed by the criminal chambers, the civil governor chose to intervene in this case. Seemingly motivated by humanitarian concerns, he indignantly pointed out that the incident had occurred in February, which was the coldest month of the year. In his view, to chain a serf outside without proper clothing constituted cruelty. The Senate agreed. Doroshenko received six weeks' imprisonment and was admonished to use only legal forms of punishment in the future.[38] It is important to stress, however, that the governor did not perceive any affront to Kovtun's personal dignity – something serfs were not generally thought to possess. His intervention was not prompted by ideas about Kovtun's rights or a sense of a shared humanity, though it did enact the governor's own humanity. Instead it constituted an effort to enforce social order by disciplining the erring serf owner. Consequently, Kovtun's suicide was not understood as a kind of active protest: agency lay instead in Doroshenko's cruelty. The act of paternal intervention thus constructed the suicide as a passive victim.

The prosecution of nobles for driving serfs to commit suicide both reinforced political structures and called them into question. In almost all cases, the intervention of high-ranking civil servants – usually the governor but occasionally the provincial procurator, a gendarme official, and even the tsar – spurred a more vigorous prosecution. Using their authority to correct erring subordinates, these powerful figures displayed their own superior sensibility and upheld the system as a whole. However, intervention could also raise unsettling questions about

---

[38] RGIA, f. 1345, op. 236, d. 759, esp. ll. 1–2, 21–34.

the relationship between official ideology and everyday practices. If serf owners were not guided by a paternalist ethos, how then could serfdom be justified as a benevolent and protective system of governance? Could intervention (which was itself fully random) rectify cruelty and abuse? As some tsarist officials were well aware, they could only intervene on a tiny minority of cases and their intervention would be limited to the particular case and not address the broader problem.[39] The predicament was similar to the one prompted by crime statistics: the very act of intervention was an admission that the system had failed to function properly, that cruelty and abuse were significant problems.

In fact, the chances of a serf owner being called to account were minimal if the serf survived the punishment. Only the presence of a dead body could really force an investigation of the causes of death and hence the character of household discipline. In other words, the body was the key piece of evidence, and this fact likely shaped the emergence of a particular crime linking abuse and suicide. Yet bodies do not recount unambiguous tales but must themselves be interpreted. Forensic evidence consequently came to play a crucial role in many cases involving suspected instigation, and this very fact sometimes encouraged attempts at concealment. In one case that provoked the particular wrath of the tsar, Nikolai Zavitaev actually dug up and moved the body of a serf to prevent a forensic examination that could have implicated his wife in a cruel beating.[40] This was a blatant example, however, for serf owners could simply fail to report a suicide promptly, thereby "accidentally" destroying the physical evidence.[41] Several of the most controversial cases in this period also involved maltreated serfs whose deaths could have been either suicide or murder.[42] Still, forensic evidence was used in most instances to assess the truthfulness of testimony. In 1842, for example, Titular Counsellor Mostovskii and his bailiff admitted punishing the serf Grigorii Afanas'ev for his "vulgarity" and "disobedience" shortly before Afanas'ev hanged himself. However, the forensic examination revealed that the marks on Afanas'ev's body could not have been inflicted with the small whip identified by Mostovskii. In other words, Mostovskii had lied, an act the Senate deemed unbefitting a nobleman.[43] This last consideration

---

[39] See the well-known letter of Prince M. Vorontsov to Count Benckendorff from 1831, extensively quoted in I. I. Ignatovich, *Pomeshchich'i krest'iane nakanune osvobozhdeniia* (Moscow, 1910), 42–43.

[40] GARF, f. 109 IV, op. 167 (1827), d. 156. For another attempt to hide the body, see op. 199 (1859), d. 147.

[41] For examples, see Ignatovich, *Pomeshchich'i krest'iane*, 39, 228, 230–32, 236.

[42] See the case of Irina Pavlova, RGIA, f. 1151, op. 3, d. 90.

[43] Although some senators called for a more severe penalty, the Senate ruled that the bailiff receive five days' imprisonment, perform a penance, and, for reports of frequent violence with serfs, lose his job. Mostovskii received a fine of 50 silver rubles (plus court costs), penance, and, for lying about the whip, a citation with the local assembly of the nobility for behavior unbefitting a nobleman. RGIA, f. 1345, op. 117, d. 474, ll. 4–39 (court records), and ll. 67–80 (the opinions of senators and the ober-prokuror as well as the final decree).

was crucial not only to this particular case but also to the growing number of prosecutions for seigneurial abuse in general. The goal was to correct the injustices of serfdom by inculcating honor in the serf owner, that is, a sense of paternal duty, self-restraint, and judiciousness.

While many serf owners were found guilty of cruelty and hence instigating suicide, many others were exonerated. Cruelty against serfs was to be punished, but the right and duty of the serf owner to discipline and instruct them was considered legitimate. When the body of a serf was discovered in 1842, the forensic examination established that he had died from hanging, but it also revealed abrasions on his back. The investigation subsequently found that he had hanged himself following a punishment for drunkenness. However, the district court, the criminal chambers, and the Senate all found the serf owner and her steward to be fully innocent of any wrongdoing. The punishment could not have been the cause, the courts ruled, because the five or six lashes had been completely legal, and the doctor had confirmed the mildness of the punishment. The case likewise conformed to cultural expectations: the reputation of the serf owner was above reproach, and the serf had been known to be a habitual drunkard. The cause of his suicide, it was concluded in passing, remained unknown.[44]

Discipline that did not degenerate into cruelty was consequently a legitimate part of the patriarchal relation. This dynamic is illustrated by another, more unusual case in which the civil governor of St. Petersburg intervened on behalf of the serf owners. Facing a birching for theft and running away, the serf had twice attempted to kill himself and then defended himself by accusing his owners of cruelty. The civil governor indignantly intervened at the ruling of the criminal chambers. To sentence the serf to twenty lashes for attempting suicide was perfectly appropriate, he argued, but to admonish the serf owners was "a travesty of justice" (*sovershenno protivno vsiakoi spravedlivosti*). Asserting that the threatened birching would have been the proper response to the serf's misbehavior, the governor maintained that the serf owners had done nothing wrong and should not receive a formal caution from the court. The Senate agreed: there was no evidence that the serf owners had violated the law, and they were fully exonerated.[45]

That this last case involved an attempted rather than completed suicide is significant. Serf owners were regularly found guilty of abuse and cruelty, but not when the serf survived. One important reason for this involved the role of social hierarchy in the legal process. Both the notion of driving a subordinate to suicide and the subsequent act of paternal intervention depended upon the representation of the suicide as a passive victim. However, this representation

---

[44] RGIA, f. 1345, op. 240, d. 667, *passim*.
[45] This is the only case I have found in which intervention occurred for the serf owner. See RGIA, f. 1345, op. 112, d. 129, esp. ll. 1–4, 71–72.

was much easier to maintain with a dead body than a live witness. Not only was the testimony of serfs weighted lower than that of their masters, but their experience of state power was also mediated by fear and inexperience.

The 1842 case against Anna Kostiukovicheva provides a good example of this dynamic. It began when her owner, Collegial Assessor Strumilo, brought her to the police explaining that she had been fished out of Petersburg's Obvodnyi Canal. Kostiukovicheva initially testified that she had attempted to drown herself due to fear of punishment. Because she had given some milk to a poor woman without permission, Strumilo had threatened to birch her daily, to put her on a diet of bread and water, and to cast her seven-week-old daughter – she named Strumilo as the father – to the devil. Not surprisingly, Strumilo denied everything, accusing Anna of debauchery, theft, and misbehavior. The problem was that Anna was terrified of prison (where she remained, awaiting the resolution of her case) and twice changed her story. During the second interrogation, she testified that Strumilo had not threatened her directly – she had overheard him – and that she had not really intended to kill herself but only to scare her master. She further withdrew the identification of him as the father of her child. Finally, when called to testify before the court, she returned to the first story, identifying Strumilo as the father of her child (and the other primary witness against her – a serf woman – as his lover). When asked why she had changed her story, she testified that a police officer had persuaded her by saying how she was bringing shame upon her master. She had not actually been threatened, however, and could present no proof. In contrast to Anna, whose attempts to maneuver undermined her account, Strumilo successfully manipulated the situation. Accusing the police of insulting him with their accusations, he affirmed his honor by dragging Anna's reputation through the mud. Indeed, he would never have "debased" himself with this "debauched peasant." Though found innocent of attempting suicide – the court had believed her testimony that she had just wanted to frighten her master in order to keep her baby, she received a prison sentence and church penance for the crime of fornication. She was then returned to Strumilo, and her subsequent fate is unknown.[46]

The focus on cruelty thus led to a paradox. A merited punishment or a "light" beating could not instigate a suicide because it was not illegal. At issue, therefore, was less the suicide than the exercise of paternal power. Consequently, little attention was devoted to what could be called a psychology of punishment. This was not because there was no interest in psychology, as the case of Katerina Darmorisova illustrates. Only 15 years old and known for her good behavior and diligence, she had been taken from her family to serve her mistress who had moved away. For three weeks, her behavior deteriorated – she became lazy and disobeyed orders – until she was birched. The following day she was

[46] RGIA, f. 1345, op. 117, 1842, d. 138, esp. ll. 42–44, 48, 55.

found dead in a noose. While the investigation found that Darmorisova had misbehaved in an effort to get sent back home, it concluded that the beating could not have caused the suicide because it had been mild and appropriate to Darmorisova's behavior. In other words, psychology – missing her parents – was recognized as the cause of the misconduct, but no psychological dynamics were acknowledged in the suicide because it was perfectly legal for serf owners to take serf children away with them and to birch them for disobedience. For their part, Katerina's parents attempted to change the categorization of their daughter's suicide. They formally accused their mistress of cruelty, but – with paternal benevolence – the authorities excused their unfounded accusations as the expression of grief.[47]

In addition to cruelty, the other key issue in these cases was the reputation of the serf owner, and reputation comprised two major components: personal conduct and the proper administration of the estate. Investigations always inquired after prior criminal offenses, behavior (especially drunkenness and illicit sexual activities), the general treatment of peasants, and the financial condition of the estate. Occasionally, the investigation of a suspicious suicide led to an investigation of estate management and ultimately to calls that the estate be sequestered. Though such drastic measures were in fact seldom taken, the breadth of investigation is significant. At issue was not just a particular instance of maltreatment but a general pattern of behavior. In one such case (not coincidentally from 1859, just two years before the abolition of serfdom), the broader investigation was in fact initiated because two peasants had seized the opportunity to lodge a complaint with the governor against their owners just as the investigation of the suicide was beginning. Not fear of punishment, they stressed, but an abuse of power lay at the root of the problem. Further complicating the case was the attempt of the mistress of the estate first to hide the fact of suicide and then to delay informing the authorities so that the body would not be available for forensic examination. While she succeeded in destroying the physical evidence of her beatings, the peasants testified with noteworthy enthusiasm: not only did they blame her for provoking the suicide, they also reported cruel treatment in general as well as an overall worsening of their economic situation, including an increased corvée, restrictions on land use, and so forth.[48]

In other court decisions, in which serf owners were either found guilty or left under suspicion, moral character and behavior often formed the key evidence. A stained reputation could have very real consequences. In one 1831 case from Tambov province, a district court ruled that the nobleman Ensign Zaitsev should lose his rank and noble status and be returned to military service. The case was

---

[47] GARF, f. 109 IV, op. 197 (1857), d. 229.

[48] GARF, f. 109 IV, op. 199 (1859), d. 147. In another case, the landowner was cleared of any wrongdoing, but also instructed to correct various irregularities in the administration of the estate. See GARF, f. 109 IV, op. 197 (1857), d. 229, esp. 1. 6.

appealed, and the ultimate verdict is unfortunately unknown. Nevertheless, the evidence used against Zaitsev is suggestive of the broader criteria of judgment in such cases. While drunk, Zaitsev had cruelly punished his serf for taking insufficient care in his duties, and the serf had then hanged himself. Although additional details on this event are not given, the serf's suicide cast attention on Zaitsev himself. The investigation uncovered two prior offenses. In the first, the details of which were not mentioned, Zaitsev had been freed by imperial manifesto, but in the second, he had been found guilty of insulting superiors, using improper language, and debauched behavior. For these offenses, he had been sentenced to two months' imprisonment and a reprimand by the local assembly of the nobility. As the vice-governor noted in conclusion to his report, "all these measures were insufficient to instruct or convince Zaitsev to correct his behavior, for the general inquiry into his behavior has revealed that he [has continued to] indulge in drunkenness, disorderly conduct, and the cruel treatment of his servants."[49] The critical evidence in this case was less the bruised body of the serf than the character of the serf owner. The maltreatment of serfs thus directly raised the question of the behavior befitting the nobility.

This issue more than any other shaped the crime of instigated suicide under Nicholas I. Following the example of European monarchs and similarly concerned with combating ideas of popular sovereignty, Nicholas propagated new images of autocracy, in which the private, familial virtue embodied and celebrated in the imperial family (as opposed to the public virtue of the civil servant) came to represent "the attitudes towards authority and modalities of conduct, both official and private, that should prevail in the macrocosm of the empire." As Wortman has convincingly demonstrated, the sentimental idyll of the imperial family – with its display of probity, moderation, self-restraint, and religious faith – thereby became the exemplar of autocracy, and Nicholas himself was the "stern and righteous paterfamilias."[50] In this broad endeavor to strengthen the institutions of Russian society (and not just the state), it was necessary to punish vice among the nobility and hence to promote a standard of conduct befitting a nobleman. Based on the concept of patriarchal honor, this ideal of nobility was, in turn, to be expressed in a stern if benevolent paternalism with subordinates, especially serfs, but also wives and children. Fearing the social instability arising from the abolition of serfdom, Nicholas instead sought to reform it through intervention and the dissemination of paternalism as a model and practice.

Though policing the relationship between lord and serf was a clear priority for the government, similar examples of intervention also occurred in other institutions. In her examination of pre-reform military justice, Wirtschafter

[49] GARF, f. 109 IV, op. 171 (1831), d. 194, ll. 1–5.
[50] Wortman, "The Russian Imperial Family," esp. 64–68, 71.

finds very similar phenomena: "cruelty" was prosecuted as a way to shape the sense of honor among officers, to correct abuses, and to preserve social order. Wirtschafter also describes cases from as early as 1820, in which suicide and attempted suicides among subordinates led to the investigation and punishment of superior officers for cruelty and abuses of authority (that is, for driving a subordinate to such a desperate and illegal act).[51] While additional research in military archives would be needed to evaluate the extent of this phenomenon, police records from the 1850s confirm Wirtschafter's evidence. While dying from a self-inflicted gunshot wound, for example, a sergeant-major named the oppression (*pritesnenie*) of his superior officer as his motive but then withdrew his accusation. The accused was nonetheless fully investigated and ultimately exonerated as a good and energetic officer.[52]

That the crime of instigated suicide existed at all in Russia was due not to the imposition of laws from above but to practices that coalesced during the first third of the nineteenth century. Its genealogy drew on several factors, including fears about the potentially explosive dangers of serfdom, changing understandings of honor among the nobility, and a more interventionalist style of governance. As concern grew about the character and limits of patriarchal discipline, especially within serfdom, the absolutism of the manor was increasingly subjected to the regulation and sometimes – such as following the report of a suicide – the scrutiny of the government. An association of suicide with "cruelty" likely evolved in this environment, for punishment often left signs on the body, which formed the primary evidence (along with recent behavior) in a case of suspicious death. Yet this explanation alone is insufficient. It was also necessary to conceive suicide as an act that can be caused or instigated by cruelty. Possible antecedents include the eighteenth-century statutes that listed "oppression" and "torment" as mitigating factors in the judgment of suicide. Speculation aside, the key legal issue in its prosecution was initially the establishment of cruelty, which was defined as a violation of the laws on punishment, and little attention was devoted to the mechanism linking punishment to suicide. Based on a paternalistic concept of authority, the law presumed that the suicide of a subordinate could be directly attributed to the actions of a superior, and it sought to discipline the superior in order to inculcate virtue and uphold public order more generally.

The prosecution of instigated suicide consistently constructed the victim as passive, for it was precisely this representation that allowed the active intervention of the tsar and his officials. By denying agency to the suicide, prosecution produced a gendered representation of patriarchal justice with clear distinctions drawn between passive victims and their active protectors. Yet a

---

[51] Wirtschafter, *From Serf*, chs. 5–6, esp. 126–37, 196 n. 77.
[52] GARF, f. 109 IV, op. 198 (1858), d. 257. For another case, f. 109 IV, op. 190 (1850), d. 215.

disproportionate number of cases involved accusations against women, which may reflect the attitudes of male elites as well as the willingness of peasants and servants to testify against their mistresses. The image of the cruel serf owner was often female: Dar'ia Saltykova is the archetype from the eighteenth century – the case always cited to prove both the extremes of abuse (she had tortured serfs to death before her detention) as well as the general failure of the government to intervene. Similarly, the most famous portraits of serf abuse from nineteenth-century literature also single out female landowners: Ivan Turgenev's "Mumu" and Lev Tolstoy's "Polikushka." Nevertheless, these and other literary works were in fact concerned with a fundamentally different issue – the annihilation of dignity, autonomy, and the self. In the 1860s and after, benevolent patriarchy was to be exposed as arbitrary rule.

Violence in the family

Although cruelty and abuse were certainly common within the family, the frequency of both police investigations and judicial prosecutions was low in this period, especially in comparison to serfdom. Isolated examples do exist. For cruelty leading to the suicide of her daughter-in-law, for example, a local court in Nizhnii Novgorod province sentenced a peasant woman to five lashes and five years of church penance, including one year at a convent.[53] Another case involved the suicide of a peasant woman whose husband was accused of having beaten her beforehand.[54] When a young peasant tried to kill himself in 1859 "due to the oppression of his mother" (*ot pritesnenii svoei materi*), he was sentenced to the standard five-year term of penance, and the records do not indicate any penalty for his mother. Even in the context of abuse, an attempted suicide apparently required the cleansing experience of penance.[55] In another case, a young peasant had tried to kill both herself and her infant daughter, but she survived and was tried for murder and attempted suicide. Upon judicial review, her harsh sentence of seventy lashes followed by eighteen years of hard labor was commuted by imperial decree to thirty lashes, Siberian exile, and a penance. The decisive factors were the sincerity of the confession, her otherwise upstanding moral character, and the maltreatment she had suffered at the hands of her mother-in-law. By representing her as a passive victim, the state once again legitimized its act of clemency.[56]

The reasons why the family was comparatively neglected as an object of paternal intervention in this period were several. Most fundamentally, the government

[53] GANO, f. 570, op. 557, 1830, d. 156.
[54] The criminal chambers left him under suspicion and assigned him a penance. See RGIA, f. 1345, op. 236, d. 743.
[55] GANO, f. 570, op. 558, 1859, d. 159.
[56] The incident occurred in 1850. *Zhurnal Ministerstva iustitsii* no. 12 (1861), 537–39.

perceived less of a threat to social stability in abusive familial relations than it did in serfdom or the army. Unlike serfdom, moreover, the moral legitimacy of the strict patriarchal family was not yet questioned within mainstream society. Only in the 1860s would the family emerge as a familiar environment for suicide and hence as a site for intervention. This shift drew in part upon the mechanisms of governance established under Nicholas I, both its failures and its successes.

In 1866, the Third Section investigated a case of attempted suicide that clearly raised the issue of physical abuse. Despite the late date (for the familial order was very much in the public eye by this time), this investigation largely conformed to the principles established under Nicholas I and illustrates their limitations. Rather than generalizing problems and potential solutions, this form of policing constructed crime and immorality as facts of an individual character. Although the investigation was wide-ranging, the file was closed without resolution, thereby exemplifying the broader failure of this transformative policing. The case was straightforward. Using the borrowed passport of her sister, Antonina Zhmakina had taken her young daughter and fled from her husband, who was a retired second-lieutenant and landowner in Perm province. When caught, she poisoned herself but was revived. On the one hand, the investigation uncovered marginal indications of sedition that could potentially explain her (immoral) decisions to leave her husband and to attempt suicide. (The school where she had been educated was associated with atheist currents.) On the other hand, however, it also revealed that Zhmakin possessed a bad character (*durnyi kharakter*), though he was not a drunkard. Consequently, married life had been marred by constant arguments and beatings, which had reputedly reduced Antonina to despair. Local rumors, a gendarme officer reported, portrayed Antonina herself as responsible for this, for she had allegedly not been a virgin when she married and other reasons for her husband's behavior could not be found. Still, neighbors admitted that her subsequent behavior had been decorous in all respects.[57] In sum, both the abuse and the attempted suicide were explained by references to individual characters but not to the structure of family relations. The file ends without even a statement on the current status and location of Zhmakina. The case had been investigated and closed. Zhmakin possessed the right to beat his wife and to compel her to stay with him. Surveillance had failed to rectify the problems uncovered because that was not in fact its primary function.

In contrast to policing, the law proved to be a more promising means of social intervention. A landmark decision from 1854 reflected a new impetus to regulate the conduct of family life. It all began because rumors had reached Moscow's military governor general that Ekaterina Leont'eva had been cruel to

---

[57] GARF, f. 109 IV, op. 206 (1866), d. 123.

her 9-year-old son Fedor. Indeed, the case proved so sensational that the Senate referred it to the State Council. The facts were sobering. Leont'eva was accused of beating Fedor with a rod, feeding him poorly, tying his hands and feet, and locking him in a small wardrobe as well as an unheated larder. In her defense, she followed established convention by arguing that such measures had been necessary to punish him for misbehavior and (more originally) to cure him of his masturbation. However, expert testimony – and not just forensic data – was now included as evidence: the Medical Council ruled that such punishment, far from curing him, could even worsen his behavior. Furthermore, a daughter testified that two other brothers had also been beaten and poorly fed before their untimely deaths. The indignation of the judges was almost palpable, but they were faced with a legal quandary: no specific law regulated child abuse, and Fedor had not actually attempted suicide. Nevertheless, Leont'eva was convicted under the instigation statute due to her "manifest abuse of power combined with cruelty." Rather than being sent to prison as specified therein, she was instead sentenced to a convent for three years at which time she was to be released if she had truly repented her "unnatural" behavior. Interestingly, the court linked the abuse of her son to previous instances of serf abuse, for which she had already lost the right to administer her estate and serfs.[58]

This fascinating case built upon established modes of exercising administrative power. Not only had it originated with the offended sensibility and paternal intervention of the governor general. The State Council had also reinforced the arbitrary character of governmental regulation by applying a law that was not applicable. Yet this case also foreshadowed coming developments. The State Council had now rendered the family a site of intervention, and during the next decades, the prosecution of instigated suicide would most often contend an abuse of power within the family. Furthermore, the conduct of this case demonstrates the growing importance of expert testimony within the judicial process. Though medical opinion had been acknowledged since the eighteenth century, the status accorded such expert evidence had been steadily increasing since the 1830s. The reasons for this development include both the professionalization of medicine and the influence of Russia's "enlightened bureaucrats," those well-educated and idealistic servitors who believed that transparent norms of regulated professional conduct should replace the practices of arbitrary administrative power. Alongside these progressive shifts was a related development: a growing interest in the biology of the self, especially a naturalized female identity and a notion of childhood. In describing the behavior of Leont'eva as "unnatural," the judges thus predicated their verdict upon her violation of a natural maternal instinct. Similarly, their condemnation of her cruelty presumed particular norms of discipline for children. Paradoxically, therefore, the various

---

[58] RGIA, f. 1151, op. 4 (1854), d. 149, esp. ll. 2, 114–16, 119–23.

attempts under Nicholas I to create the well-ordered police state were helping to shape new mechanisms of governance that would undermine the personalized foundations of political and social power and produce new meanings for suicide.

At the core of the government's concern for "cruelty" was an effort to maintain the existing social system. This regulation of delegated paternal authority constituted a combined effort to prevent abuse from undermining the public order and to promote the norms of behavior among serf owners that would uphold it. The intercession of the tsar and his servitors on behalf of the most lowly members of society thus enforced social and political hierarchies within a paternalist idiom. The representation of some suicides as unfortunate victims – itself a sentimental trope – allowed a formal display of pity and condescension on the part of the official. After all, the object of sentimental literature had been to evoke these virtuous emotions within the reader, not to glorify suicide as such. Yet agency was restricted to the intercessor, and the suicide itself was cast as a passive act. Not only did this structure reproduce conventional social norms, it subverted and denied any element of protest or accusation – which may have sometimes been present – by rendering suicide a kind of victimization.

Yet paternalism was not a unitary ideology but a combination of sometimes conflicting attitudes and practices.[59] As an ethos of mutual obligation (at least in principle), paternalism also shaped the practices and language of many less-powerful members of society. Attempts to eliminate and punish abuse thus coexisted with popular expectations that this was possible. Despite their formulaic and inquisitorial character, official records demonstrate the complexity of power relations within the social and political hierarchy. In numerous cases involving an alleged instigation, peasants played key roles in drawing the attention of authorities to the incident; and their testimony regularly incriminated serf owners – more often indirectly but sometimes directly, especially by the late 1850s when the future of serfdom was openly debated. In using laws and legal structures to bypass local power hierarchies, their goals likely varied: to protect themselves against abuses; to attain just redress; or simply to get their owners in trouble. Evidence does not suggest that serfs saw suicide as an act of resistance, though they may have interpreted it as a kind of accusation. While they used established explanatory categories, including immorality, the fear of punishment, or abuse, they also interpreted them. In numerous cases, therefore, they attempted to transform legitimate discipline into illegitimate cruelty,

---

[59] I therefore disagree with Peter Kolchin, who argues that Russia's nobility did not have a paternalistic ethos and cites the lack of elaborate written defenses of serfdom on the basis of paternalism, such as what one finds in the American South. See his *Unfree Labor: American Slavery and Russian Serfdom* (Cambridge, Mass., 1987). For an opposing view, see Moon, *The Russian Peasantry*, 88–89.

victimization into accusation. The charges levied by Katerina Darmorisova's parents provide a good example. In their eyes, the decision to take their young daughter away from her home constituted an abuse of power, but, as court officials were well aware, the serf owner was well within her rights. Beginning in the 1860s, the paternal basis of autocracy would be openly challenged in Russian society, and one forum would coalesce around the body of the suicide. Despite the many innovations of the later periods, however, the nexus between suicide and an abuse of power had already been established within the social world of serfdom.

6   Arbiters of the self: the suicide note

You be Don Quixote but I've had enough.

Lieutenant Kvitsynskii, From his suicide note, 1852

Motives for suicide often seem inadequate to the outside observer, and many scholars have bemoaned the inadequacy of suicide notes in particular. Rather than illuminating the causes, the experience, or the drama of the act, they tend instead to be "steeped in the mundane."[1] Indeed, notes are often replete with awkward turns of phrase, hackneyed images, bad poetry, and detailed directions on quite mundane issues, such as the disposal of personal belongings. To seek a sublime meaning or a credible cause in the suicide note leads, almost inevitably, to disappointment. The very conventionality of notes makes them interesting for the historian, however. When approached as documents, these texts can shed light on both the culturally specific motives for suicide and the dynamics of their reception.

By the 1830s, investigatory files regularly included suicide notes. Despite their increasing frequency, however, they remained primarily a showcase for educated men who wished to stake a public claim with their voluntary deaths. They do not, therefore, illustrate the range of motives within Russian society as a whole. Most people from the lower social orders did not leave written records, and the causes of their suicides were much more likely to be categorized within the rubrics discussed in previous chapters: vice and disobedience; illness; fear of punishment; and external abuse and cruelty. Yet even among members of the educated elites, the suicide note remained exceptional, a gesture that many people chose not to make.

Before the rise of a mass-circulation press later in the century, the intended audience of suicide notes in Russia included both the private world of friends and family and the semi-public world of officialdom, sometimes including the tsar himself. By writing a note, people were attempting to shape the reception of their act. Some hoped to elicit a specific emotion – whether pity, anger, or admiration. Others aimed to provoke a particular chain of reactions – an

---

[1] Irina Paperno, *Suicide as a Cultural Institution in Dostoevsky's Russia* (Ithaca, N.Y., 1997), ch. 5, esp. pp. 110–11.

investigation of the circumstances, the punishment of villains, or the redress of perceived wrongs. Officials, in turn, assessed the motives, rejecting some but accepting others and occasionally interceding on this basis. Because they are inherently dialogical, having at their core an intention to shape particular meanings for a voluntary death, these notes illuminate modes of self-fashioning as well as points of (perceived or actual) conflict between the individual and the social order. Furthermore, their inclusion in investigative reports created hybrid texts and hence a second kind of dialogue. Despite the religious and criminal prohibitions, the act of suicide was not inherently radical or subversive in this period. To the contrary, some final notes affirmed the norms of the social and political order, even as they sought to explain (and thereby to justify) the decision to depart from life. Others, in contrast, explicitly framed the act of suicide as a means to affirm personal autonomy and self-sovereignty against external authorities. Similarly, the fact that officials actively assessed the legitimacy of motives indicates that the condemnation of suicide was far from absolute.

Two broad genres of motive echoed through suicide notes by the mid-nineteenth century. The first, which can be categorized under the rubric of honor, evolved out of paradigms established before 1825 and constituted a dominant and easily recognized motif. The second, in contrast, was more exceptional, and it was typically met by a silence that signified incomprehension. This motive built upon the poetics of boredom and would become more common later in the century. In the Russia of Nicholas I, however, both honor and boredom were configured – by the authors of suicide notes as well as their readers – within the ideology of autocratic paternalism.

The politics of honor

All estate groups possessed notions of honor in Russia, and the concepts of character and reputation consequently played an important role in social, legal, and political life.[2] Police and court records include numerous suicides of honor, almost all of which involved men of the elite. Some reasons for this bias are circumstantial. Such men were more likely to be literate and thus able to leave a note. Similarly, their deaths were deemed more important, hence worthy of being reported to superiors. Although the relevance of such factors cannot be denied, the conceptualization of honor itself also contributed to this bias. Though peasants and townspeople possessed ideas about dignity, reputation, and shame, official documents rarely recognized such sentiments, at least not in the language of honor.[3] Instead, honor was fundamentally an attribute of

---

[2] Nancy Shields Kollman, *By Honor Bound: State and Society in Early Modern Russia* (Ithaca, N.Y., 1999).

[3] Note the "remarkable" case of a 14-year-old sailor's daughter who was conscience stricken at the sight of a man from whom she had stolen two kerchiefs. *Statisticheskie svedeniia o Sankt-peterburge* (SPb, 1836), 195–96.

rank; only one who already possessed honor could suffer dishonor. Despite continuities with earlier periods, therefore, honor became an especially contested commodity after 1825. The Decembrists had grounded their claims to political authority – and myths of honorable death – with reference both to their personal, aristocratic dignity and to their civic patriotism. Partly in response to their insurrection, Nicholas I forcefully reasserted the government's prerogative to govern the meanings and expressions of honor in Russian society.

According to the lexicographer Vladimir Dal', the Russian word for honor (*chest'*) had four main definitions. The first refers to innate character: "the inner moral dignity of man, valor, integrity, the nobility of the soul and a pure conscience." For the Decembrists, of course, this interiority was the supposed referent of both their conduct and their politics, and the importance of conduct as evidence of (innate) honor continued to resonate after their exile. The second definition, in contrast, refers to external reputation: "conventional, worldly, everyday nobility, often false and imaginary." The dichotomy here is important for these two definitions contrast absolute inner qualities with fleeting and superficial social ones. This raises a practical and epistemological problem: how should internal honor be recognized if not for everyday conduct and reputation? It is likewise noteworthy that the examples provided for the second definition include a reference to the illegal practice of dueling. The third and fourth definitions are interconnected: "a high title, order, rank, or position" could thus serve as "external evidence of excellence," respect, and recognition.[4] None of these meanings are peculiar to the Russian language, for both English and French contain the distinction between honor as an innate quality or virtue and honors connoting external recognition and social status.[5]

Nevertheless, the configuration of honor in Russia under Nicholas I depended upon several particular dynamics. On the one hand, the tsar claimed to be the ultimate arbiter of honor. Not only could he confer the honor of nobility as well as the honors of rank and decoration, he could also ritually dishonor a servitor by withdrawing recognition of his dignity (and legally expelling him from his estate).[6] Similarly, the policing of society as well as attempts to inculcate a paternalist ethos in the nobility both constituted efforts to make personal honor an object of governance. And finally, the elimination in 1845 of penalties for suicides committed in defense of state secrets or feminine virtue explicitly conferred honor upon specific forms of voluntary death. On the other hand, however, honor remained integral to the fashioning of corporate identity, particularly for the nobility. Its negotiation thus occurred within the rituals of the dual, which reached its peak of elite popularity in this period, despite

[4] *TS*, vol. 4, 1328.
[5] William M. Reddy, *The Invisible Code: Honor and Sentiment in Postrevolutionary France, 1814–1848* (Berkeley, 1997), 7–16.
[6] On the legal regulation of honor, see Abby M. Schrader, *Languages of the Lash: Corporal Punishment and Identity in Imperial Russia* (De Kalb, Ill., 2002), *passim*.

(or perhaps because of) the disapproval of the state.[7] Equally important was its configuration within the rhetoric of civility and status, hence in opposition to the presumed ignorance and backwardness of the "dark masses."[8] Not just a function of corporate identity, honor also adhered to the ideal of the rational, autonomous individual, which was itself a primarily masculine and elite concept in this era. The notion of honor thus infused a wide range of legal, political, and social practices.[9]

These sometimes contradictory meanings shaped both the act of suicide and its reception, thereby illuminating both the norms of the honor code and the ways in which they were adapted to life situations. When retired Staff Cavalry Captain Astaf'ev shot himself in 1841, the high-ranking gendarme officer quoted from the note – "he who wants to avoid dishonor must die" (*tot kto khochet izbavit'sia ot beschest'ia dolzhen umeret'*) – as evidence for his conclusion: Astaf'ev had killed himself to evade the shame of arrest for his failure to repay a debt of 1,700 silver rubles.[10] He thus rejected the claim to honor by casting the suicide as a cowardly response to impending social disgrace. In many respects, shame is a necessary counterpart to honor: the avoidance of shame is integral to its maintenance, especially its concern for reputation and external recognition. However, the gendarme officer's emphasis on shame was also a means to undermine the claim to honor, understood as inner dignity and integrity. This kind of honor is likely what Astaf'ev hoped to demonstrate with his death. In an attempt to wash away dishonor, he had sought to pay his debt with blood. In this sense, suicide – like the duel – could be construed as a means to restore one's honor.[11]

Literary works from this period reinforced both perspectives. An 1837 poem by the minor romantic poet Dmitrii Struiskii entitled "The Suicide" (*Samoubiitsa*) explored neither motive nor cause but focused solely on the material fact and moral transgression of suicide. The bloody body stands here as evidence of shame and sacrilege.

He averted death with death / The earth gave shelter to the takings, / But not in the family of native graves / Did his grave rise black. / I saw his pale body in the corner, / His hand frozen with the dagger, / And blood like a crimson veil / Impressed itself upon the floor. / The bloody face of the suicide / Like God's wrath was fearful to me, / As a warrior who

---

[7] See Irina Reyfman, *Ritualized Violence Russian Style: The Duel in Russian Culture and Literature* (Stanford, 1999), esp. 35–62.

[8] On honor and civility, see Catriona Kelly, *Refining Russia: Advice Literature, Polite Culture, and Gender from Catherine to Yeltsin* (Oxford, 2002), ch. 1.

[9] The Russian word for "nobility" (as in "the nobility of the soul") translates literally as well-born (*blagorodstvo*). For further discussion see, Reyfman, *Ritualized Violence*, pp. 204–7.

[10] GARF, f. 109 IV, op. 181 (1841), d. 123, l. 1.

[11] Similarly, Captain Kublitskii apparently saw suicide as an honorable response to (financial?) ruin. His note was succinct: "[I] fell in love, ruined myself, shot myself. Kublitskii." See GARF, f. 109 IV, op. 168 (1828), d. 97, l. 1.

surrendered without glory / Despised in his native land. / His disgraced body was not accorded a funeral, / But was taken exactly at midnight, / And the sad cross stands / Reproachfully upon the mound of earth.[12]

With its military and national metaphors, the message of this poem was unambiguous. There was no honor in self-killing; to the contrary, profane burial appears as the sad but fitting response to a shameful act of cowardice.

During this same period, however, one of the most popular writers in Russia was the disgraced Decembrist Aleksandr Bestuzhev, who published many stories about honor, including honorable death, under the pseudonym Marlinskii. Following a period of Siberian exile he was allowed to serve in the army and was stationed mostly in the Caucasus during the 1830s. Like the better-known Mikhail Lermontov, he was fascinated by the Romantic hero, and his tales of the region were full of great deeds and duels.[13] His 1833 story, *Frigate Hope*, also contained a kind of suicide.[14] The tale is convoluted, but suffice it to say that Previn, the hero and the captain of the frigate, conducts a love affair with the young wife of an elderly man, and they are ultimately discovered. At the same time, Previn's impulsive actions lead indirectly to the death of some of his sailors and his own serious injury. Tortured by his conscience yet fully indifferent to possible punishments, he declares himself unable to outlive his honor; he ultimately tears off his bandages and bleeds to death. As the literary scholar Irina Reyfman summarizes: "Since Previn's dishonor has been caused by his own actions, he is his own 'opponent' in this affair of honor. Suicide is therefore his only recourse. By killing himself, he wins his last duel, washes away dishonor with blood, and makes peace with himself."[15] Despite Previn's significant transgressions, he remains a positive character for whom honor – here configured as duty and integrity – was primary. In many respects, therefore, Bestuzhev-Marlinskii remained true to his Decembrist roots, depicting honor as an innate quality of character that could be evidenced in a noble and tragic death. When juxtaposed, the divergent approaches of Bestuzhev-Marlinskii and Struiskii evoke the longstanding debates over Cato's feat – was it a heroic and patriotic deed or a craven and treacherous capitulation?

A social sphere in which noble honor played a crucial role was the world of gambling. As several studies have recently noted, the problem was so widespread that it led to the impoverishment of entire noble families as well as the ineffectual efforts of the state to legislate against it. One reason for this failure was the close nexus between gambling and the norms of the honor code.

[12] D. Struiskii, "Samoubiitsa," *Sovremennik* no. 7 (1837), 180.
[13] See Lewis Bagby, *Alexander Bestuzhev-Marlinsky and Russian Byronism* (University Park, Penn., 1995).
[14] Serialized in *Syn otechestva* nos. 9–17 (1833); reprinted in A. A. Bestuzhev (Marlinskii), *Ispytanie: Povesti i rasskazy* (Moscow, 1991).
[15] I am indebted to Reyfman's interpretation. See her *Ritualized Violence*, 184–87, here 187.

Like the military battle or the duel, high-stakes gambling was often configured as a grand confrontation with fate, a measure of character, fortitude, and self-possession. Though many of the rituals and myths were often manipulated in practice, occasionally prompting accusations of (dishonorable) cheating, the payment of debts (at least to fellow noblemen) was considered an obligation of honor, not a mere monetary transaction.[16] It is hardly surprising, therefore, that suicide likewise became a constituent part of both gambling mythologies and their extensions into life.[17] Unable to pay off his huge gambling debts, the son and heir of Count I. S. Laval' shot himself in 1825 rather than face social dishonor.[18]

Literary and didactic narratives linking gambling to suicide abounded, particularly within the context of sentimentalism. As Ian Helfant has demonstrated, these texts often treated the victims of gambling as objects of pity, who, in their youth and naïveté, struggle with the vices of the city and are sometimes driven to attempt suicide. Yet these talented young men are also complicit in their misfortunes, for they have succumbed to their own elemental "passions" and "delusions," which lead them to despair and suicide.[19] The moral implications were drawn particularly well by the writer and critic Nikolai Strakhov. In his characteristic serial logic, gambling destroyed virtue, thus paving the way toward the ultimate calamity of suicide: "The idle rich man, playing to pass the time, unexpectedly loses his entire fortune. The poor man, ravaged by luxury and extravagance, rushes to the gaming houses like a vessel directing its path toward an abyss or an underwater rock. In these tombs of despairing people, they first lose their money, and then their conscience. First they learn to hate virtue, and then life itself."[20]

The 1827 suicide of school director Aleksandr Koiandr, who had gambled away some 20,000 rubles of school funds and was facing imminent discovery, offers a different perspective into the nexus between suicide, honor, and gambling. Not only did the circumstances catch the eye of the tsar resulting in a detailed investigation, he also left several long and fascinating notes. In a formal declaration to the civil governor of Kaluga province, Koiandr first made a full confession. "In order not to impose a sin upon my soul nor to allow the imposition of a penalty upon my senior teachers for my own squandering of

[16] My discussion draws on the studies of Ian Helfant, *The High Stakes of Identity: Gambling in the Life and Literature of Nineteenth-Century Russia* (Evanston, Ill., 2002); and Iu. M. Lotman, *Besedy o russkoi kul'ture: Byt i traditsii russkogo dvorianstva (XVIII–nachalo XIX veka)* (SPb, 1994), 136–63.

[17] On gambling and suicide in England, see Michael MacDonald and Terence R. Murphy, *Sleepless Souls: Suicide in Early Modern England* (Oxford, 1990), 278–81.

[18] Helfant, *High Stakes*, 15.

[19] In addition to the texts discussed by Helfant (*High Stakes*, pp. xvii–xxi), see G. Kamenev, "Ramier ili samoubiitsa," *Ippokrena ili utekhi liubosloviia*, pt. 6 (1800), 411–16.

[20] Nikolai Strakhov, *Moi peterburgskie sumerki* (SPb, 1810), 48.

the money, I consider myself obligated to leave a list of those culpable for my misfortune," and he then named his fellow gamblers and the amounts he had lost to them. Noting that his hand was shaking "from the strong agitation of his spirit," he documented his authorship by stamping his letter with the official seal of the school. Finally, he informed the governor that he had sent a duplicate letter to the minister of education, apparently to prevent any cover-up. The care he took in exposing the world of illegal gambling, documenting his identity, and thwarting concealment all suggests that he saw his letter as a kind of atonement, a last chance to demonstrate his sense of duty and honor as a civil servant. In his report, the governor recognized yet rejected Koiandr's claim to honor. He was not some naïve youth, the governor stressed in an implicit reference to the sentimental model, but an experienced man of fifty years with a wife and seven children. The very notion that he was involved in illegal gambling had consequently never occurred to him. Tapping instead into the stereotype of the suicide as morally corrupt, the governor curtly summarized: "The unfortunate decided upon such an illegal act, as is possible to conclude from his notes, from a false understanding of honor and weak principles in religion."[21]

Koiandr adopted a very different tone in his separate letter to his wife. It opened in the language of sentimentalism: "At this moment I have just left your bedside, having long gazed upon you. You are sleeping quietly – a sweet dream, and your features express the tranquility of your soul, your pure innocence! You don't sense the threat that has gathered over your head prepared by me and ready to burst [. . .]. I who love you with all my soul and all my heart. Thank you for your love [. . .]." Turning then to his motivation, Koiandr evoked a slightly different form of honor than he had in his declaration, construing his death as the sole means to pay his debt and thus to cleanse himself of shame. "I am so embroiled in my misfortune that I do not see any means for salvation. 20,000 rubles – how can I pay it except with my life?" Yet his resolve was not absolute: "I am shuddering at the thought of it, but there is nothing to be done. [. . .] I do not have the strength to endure the disgrace – merited of course by my thoughtlessness – nor the [. . .] terrible punishment." He then returns to his feelings of love and anguish, begging his wife to forgive him, to remember him, and to pray for God's mercy. He mourned that his very public misfortune was about to destroy the purity, serenity, and (financial) security of his family.

In sum, this letter constructs honor as a masculine and public attribute.[22] Most importantly, Koiandr represented the public world of power, success, and gambling as the antithesis to the domestic idyll of innocence and virtue. His

---

[21] Koiandr's concern about a cover-up seems justified: the governor provided excellent character references for most of the persons listed. GARF, f. 109 IV, op. 167 (1827), d. 167, ll. 1–8. For another case involving social shame and the misuse of public funds, see GARF, f. 109 IV, op. 170 (1830), d. 170.

[22] See Lotman (*Besedy*, 136–63) for further discussion of the gendered nature of gambling.

misdeeds were now about to explode the private sanctity of his family – even his elder daughters were now faced with going into service as governesses. Interestingly, he evokes the language of chance in this context: "But against implacable fate I am weak, unable to resist." Which fate did he mean – the fate of the cards? At the conclusion of his note, Koiandr again taps into a sentimental narrative but in a different way. His final words do not allude to his misdeeds but to his victimization and exploitation, implying that his gambling losses were due to the failure of his fellow gamblers to adhere to the honor code: "I perish from my weaknesses, from [my] excess of good nature and from excess trust in people who did not merit it."[23] Yet this repeated emphasis on his own weakness undermines his claim to honor, that is, valor and integrity. At least in his private letter to his wife, Koiandr fears that his conduct, including his suicide, has revealed not the fortitude, courage and self-possession of his character, but their opposites.

Dishonor could occur not only through the disclosure of misdeeds but also through complex social mechanisms. As Gogol's stories and plays illustrate most evocatively, social status within the elite was both extremely important and extremely fluid. Because status often depended on a variety of factors, including wealth, family, rank, and personal cultivation, the negotiation of position (and recognition) within the social hierarchy had become extremely complex. Many nobles thus needed their salaries to fund their standard of living, the display of which was crucial to their social status more generally. When the various elements constituting social status began to conflict, social insecurity – dishonor and shame – could result.

These dynamics shaped one 1843 case. Having been exiled to service in Riazan province for possession of illegal poetry, the Polish aristocrat Iul'ian Bokshanskii designed an elaborate plan for his suicide. At his request, a gendarme officer, the vice-governor, and the police chief accompanied him to his apartment, where he gave his visitors some papers and went into the next room. Having seen that the top paper was (once again) a formal "declaration" signed by the suicide Bokshanskii, the police chief was able to rush into the other room and wrest the pistol out of Bokshanskii's hands, who was then taken away under guard. Among the papers were letters to the tsar, the governor, his supervisor, and several relatives. The main explanation focused upon Bokshanskii's sense of wounded dignity. Given a lowly post as scribe upon arriving in Riazan six months earlier, he had waited in vain for a better position and found himself unable to live on his humble salary of 10 rubles per month. He had consequently amassed debts totaling several hundred rubles. Dishonor had taken the form of humiliation, a double assault on his sense of personal dignity. First, he blamed the governor for always promising but never actually giving him an

---

[23] For the (copied) note to his wife, see GARF, f. 109 IV, op. 167 (1827), d. 167, ll. 9–10.

appointment (with proper recompense) suitable for an aristocrat. Second, he had suffered indignities and mortifications from his social inferiors, especially his landlord to whom he owed money. Fashioning himself as a blameless victim of circumstances (and the governor), unable to pay off his debts and lacking any future, he affirmed suicide as the only means to maintain his honor and to protest his dishonorable treatment. Listing his debts and asking that his meager possessions be sold to offset them, he expressed his hope that the emperor, in his mercy, would satisfy the amount outstanding. In an important sense, therefore, Bokshanskii was also requesting the intervention of the tsar as the arbiter of honor. By inviting the three witnesses he had intended to prevent a cover-up: his goal was to have the circumstances of his case heard by the tsar and his character vindicated.[24]

Such an appeal to the tsar was not exceptional, for the personal nature of autocratic power (often combined with the corruption and intrigues of the bureaucracy) invited individual and direct petition. This motif likewise occurred in the case of Fedor Moskal'tsov. Fired for reporting the corruption of his superiors, he sought redress with the governor, who initially helped him but then withdrew his patronage, preferring an alliance with Moskal'tsov's old boss. Left penniless and with powerful enemies, unable to feed his wife and infant son, he shot himself. In his first letter, addressed to the governor, Moskal'tsov lambasted the governor's dishonorable behavior and called for atonement. Appealing to his sense of "human conscience" (by which he meant shame), Moskal'tsov requested one-time financial aid for his penniless wife and child. Evoking the contrasting meanings of honor, he implied that the governor's high title was not matched by his inner virtue: "Forgive me that I write this to your Excellency without the proper courtesy: the dead do not know respect for rank." His second letter was a deathbed confession addressed to the archbishop. In it, he explained how he had always sought to act honorably. In reporting on his boss, he had followed his sacred oath of service to the tsar. Furthermore, with his suicide, he would now save the lives of two innocent people. After all, a widow and orphan – but not a nobleman – could ask for charity without dishonor. "Who is guilty of my violent death?" he asked the archbishop to decide. Should he have violated his oath to the tsar, compromised his conscience, acted dishonorably – and thereby kept his job? Or was his suicide really murder? Both letters were forwarded to Alexander II, who, in an implicit answer to these questions, gave the widow 100 silver rubles.[25]

[24] He implied that the tsar should make those responsible for his position (the governor) pay them. His concerns about a cover-up were not unfounded as letters he had written earlier to the Third Section had not apparently been delivered. The outcome of this case is not indicated, but Bokshanskii requested to be sent into military service. See GARF, f. 109 IV, op. 183 (1843), d. 149.

[25] GARF, f. 109 IV, op. 196 (1856), d. 235. For another case that met with imperial pity, see the report on Major Selivanov, GARF, f. 109 IV, op. 200 (1860), d. 200, ll. 1–4, 6.

Non-nobles did occasionally leave final notes, including two medical students, both the sons of priests. Neither explicitly claimed honor, but they did cite its usually implicit counterpart – shame. In 1836, a young man named Pavlov, who was a student at Moscow University, left a note to his father in which he claimed to be unworthy of his forgiveness or the condescension of (university?) authorities. As Pavlov's conduct and studies were both excellent, the official reporting the case confessed himself unable to uncover any crime or misdemeanor.[26] A case from 1827 shows parallel dynamics. Recording his final words in the margins of a letter to him from his father, Aleksandr Rudinskii wrote: "I am ready to say before the entire world that there is not a more virtuous father [than my own] nor a more debauched son; I am worthy of death, I [will] die. Inspector Goranskii is a murderer."[27] Both Pavlov and Rudinskii had addressed their notes to their fathers, and both had implied their own lack of worthiness, not as autonomous individuals or as members of a particular social group but as sons.[28] While honor and shame were configured within the familial relationship, it is nonetheless significant that these two students wrote notes at all and thereby claimed authorship over the meanings of their deaths. In Rudinskii's case, this claim was especially strong, for he chose to kill himself with a razor in a public place. Moreover, he accused someone of a (figurative) murder. This authoring of suicide as accusation even garnered the attention of the tsar, prompting a thorough police investigation. Rudinskii, it was established, had recently been expelled from the Medical-Surgical Academy because Goranskii, an inspector at the Academy, had informed academic authorities of some unspecified misbehavior. Consequently, the accusation was described as groundless, a product of malice (*zloba*). This information was sufficient to close the investigation. With Rudinskii's character thus sullied, his suicide was easily relegated into conventional categories: his shameful death embodied his own immorality.

One final example underlines the nexus between honor and social status but also points to its democratization. In 1868, a postman drowned himself because he had gambled away 130 rubles of public funds. To expiate his shame, he named his fellow gambler in a brief note. Though he did not use the word, he had in fact claimed honor in the very form of his voluntary death.[29]

Not just social identity but also masculinity was integral to the notion of honor. Many of these cases, most explicitly those of Koiandr and Moskal'tsov,

---

[26] GARF, fond 109 IV, op. 176 (1836), d. 72, l. 1.

[27] GARF, fond 109 IV, op. 167 (1827), d. 171, ll. 1–4.

[28] Another example dates to 1864, but the student in this case claimed an incipient mental illness as a motive and apologized to his father both for his failure to live up to his expectations and for the shamefulness of his death. In addition, he left a second note for the police in which he emphasized his voluntary decision to kill himself. See GARF, f. 109 IV, op. 204 (1864), d. 98, ll. 1–8.

[29] See GARF, f. 109 IV, op. 208 (1868), d. 107.

had built upon an opposition of public and masculine virtues to private and feminine ones. In principle of course, women possessed their own version of honor: suicide in defense of chastity was not illegal under the 1845 penal code (though I have not found a single such case). Similarly, the literary image of female suicide evoked the feminine principles of passivity and erasure of self; their deaths provide a space on which men could inscribe their own identities.[30] Yet such gender distinctions were not absolute, as exemplified in an 1869 case involving a noblewoman, Grasil'da Banevich, whose suicide alluded to but also transgressed these established norms. The previous year, she had married and subsequently given birth to a child. Already trying to pay off considerable family debts, she and her husband had then received a large tax bill and faced financial ruin. Accusation rather than entreaty characterizes her suicide note; it suggests how an aristocratic woman could claim honor, even seeking to pay a debt with blood:

Let the Sovereign know that I am paying his percentages with the lives of myself and my child. I am leaving a most honorable and good man – my husband. I can not bear the [prospect] that he will be denied the means to feed himself in his old age. Please God, let the Sovereign and His children endure that which I am [enduring] at this moment! My unfortunate husband – he is working in the fields and does not anticipate what I am preparing him. Nobody is to blame for my death; I myself, not strong enough to work and from love for my husband, have decided upon this terrible deed.

The officials handling the case failed to acknowledge Banevich's claim to honor, though pity rather than condemnation was the dominant tone. Both the civil governor and the governor general agreed that it would be improper to let this case follow the usual procedure, especially as the child had been saved. "Not used to hardship and seeing the hopeless position of her husband and family," the governor general summarized, Banevich "decided upon suicide, of course in an attack if not of insanity then of nervous irritation after having given birth." With imperial mercy, all investigations were duly halted and penalties voided.[31] While Banevich's suicide had inspired compassion, her act was also rewritten into a more suitable domestic and medical idiom: childbirth and nervous illness – not accusation or honor – had led to her death.

A generic suicide of honor did not exist in Russia during the period between the Decembrist revolt and the Great Reforms. The motifs of these cases varied widely, for the safeguarding of honor depended upon complex notions of

---

[30] I am referring to A. S. Pushkin's famous narrative poem, "The Prisoner of the Caucasus," in which the Circassian maiden sacrifices herself to the Russian captive, helps him escape, and ultimately drowns herself. See Stephanie Sandler, *Distant Pleasures: Alexander Pushkin and the Writing of Exile* (Stanford, 1989); and Joe Andrew, *Narrative and Desire in Russian Literature, 1822–49: The Feminine and the Masculine* (Houndmills, Basingstoke, and London, 1993).
[31] GARF, f. 109 IV, op. 209 (1869), d. 191, esp. ll. 1, 3, 6.

publicity and privacy, external conduct and internal character. Some notes fashioned suicide as a heroic feat that would wash away a stain on one's honor and thereby demonstrate one's truly honorable character. Others construed a relationship between honor and public duty, citing a principle especially prized by Nicholas I. A third pattern transformed suicide into a kind of accusation, a defense of one's personal honor against social humiliation or some other kind of (external) injury. Finally, some notes expressed a sense less of honor than of dishonor, and their authors often perceived the inherent shamefulness of their suicides as well. This diversity only underscores the central place of honor in Russian society. While its meanings and expressions were contested, its importance as a standard of social regulation was not. In this sense, most suicides of honor were fundamentally conservative because they reflected some effort to conform to social norms or to remonstrate against their violation. Particularly striking, moreover, is the vibrancy of the dialogue. In claiming honor, almost all the authors of these notes appealed to (and sometimes argued with) an intended readership, not just implicitly but often explicitly. While some looked to their families or their social milieu, most appealed to external authorities for approval or absolution. The actual readers – especially Russia's officialdom, including the tsar – likewise responded to the claims made, at times endorsing them (if not necessarily the act of suicide) and at times rejecting them.[32] In other words, the motive mattered; it had the potential to legitimize or delegitimize the act. The dialogic quality inherent to the suicide of honor thus embodied a complex arbitration over the moral governance of the self.

Boredom and bureaucracy

Boredom with life (*skuka zhizni*) has a long history in the annals of suicide motives, and the modern English word does not catch its full range of meanings. More than just a feeling of tedium, dullness, and monotony, boredom can also denote a metaphysical world-weariness that is better expressed by the French word ennui (which was itself imported into English during the seventeenth century). Similarly, the Latin expression, *taedium vitae*, refers to the mental or emotional state of being weary with life itself, hence the connection with suicide.[33] The Russian word for boredom is *skuka*, and while it can also refer to the

---

[32] Unfortunately, I cannot assess the readings of friends and family members.

[33] As Patricia Meyer Spacks has shown, the word "boredom" dates from the nineteenth century, the verb "to bore" from the eighteenth. The emergence of these terms, she suggests, points to the invention of a concept distinct from earlier notions of ennui, and she analyzes the interplay between the "trivial" and "profound" significations. See her *Boredom: The Literary History of a State of Mind* (Chicago, 1995). For further discussion of ennui (excluding the "trivial" boredom) and acedia from antiquity to the present, see Reinhard Kuhn, *The Demon of Noontide: Ennui in Western Literature* (Princeton, 1976).

range of ordinary feelings, it possesses more deep-seated connotations. Its primary definitions refer to this complex of meanings: "a burdensome feeling from an inert, idle, inactive condition of the soul; the lassitude of inaction; anguish (*toska*), dejection (*grust'*), the lassitude of grief." Notable here is especially the reference to the soul, that is, to the essential spiritual being of a person rather than to a mere mood or attitude. Furthermore, the definitions suggest a very powerful and all-encompassing emotion, not the almost trivial connotations of the English translation. The examples of usage likewise point first to a linkage with vice ("boredom loves idleness" and "to drive away boredom set yourself to work"), and then with death and suicide ("boredom is deadly, frenzied," "I will hang myself from boredom," and "to perish from boredom").[34]

As in the Western European tradition, therefore, the notion of *skuka* was built upon a religious basis. The vice of acedia (*prazdnost'*) blended idleness and inactivity into a spiritual malaise, that was, however, a sin and a kind of test: it could be combated through faith and effort. While this concept framed at least some manifestations of spiritual torpor in medieval Europe and Russia, its resonance continued in subsequent periods.[35] In eighteenth-century Russia, didactic literature repeatedly condemned the vice of idleness. One popular journal, for example, published in 1794 a moralizing text entitled "To Life." In vilifying well-known vices, it also warned its elite readers against boredom: "He does not live, who, weakened by idleness and luxury, flies from amusement to amusement and is bored [*skuchaet*] with everything; [...] Live for the wellbeing of yourselves and others."[36] This implied solution to idleness and boredom brings one of the most famous texts of the era to mind, Rousseau's letters from *The New Héloïse*, in which good works and charity were posited as antidotes to the suicidal impulse. Such connections between luxury, idleness, and suicide remained standard fare in the early nineteenth century, well exemplified in Nikolai Strakhov's analysis of the causes of suicide: "Idleness is the inseparable friend of luxury and city life, [it] compels [us] to search for harmful distraction, and this leads us sooner or later first to a dislike and then to a loathing for life." This was most dangerous for children, Strakhov stressed, who become accustomed to a life eased by handouts. "The luster and noise of luxury is the seed of future suffering, moans, despair, and suicide."[37] A parallel juxtaposition occurs in Aleksandr Bashutskii's *Panorama of St. Petersburg*, which termed luxury the "pernicious inhabitant of the capitals" and linked it to a wide range of misfortunes and vices that sometimes culminated in suicide.[38] Bashutskii

[34] *TS*, vol. 4, 212–13.
[35] The sin of acedia has a long history into antiquity and cannot be treated here. For further discussion, see Kuhn, *The Demon of Noontide*, esp. 39–66.
[36] "K zhizni," *Priiatnoe i poleznoe preprovozhdenie vremeni*, pt. 2 (1794), 3–5.
[37] Strakhov, *Moi peterburgskie sumerki*, 46–47.
[38] Aleksandr Bashutskii, *Panorama Sanktpeterburga* (SPb, 1834), 92–93.

did not explicitly mention luxury's partner – boredom. This absence is itself significant, for *skuka* would not become a fully recognized motive for suicide in Russia until later in the century. Nevertheless, the craving for amusement (which is at the heart of the vices of luxury and idleness) implies the unnamed presence of an emptiness, of time needing to be filled, and, therefore, of boredom.[39] Strakhov did make this connection, though he also located this problem far away from Russia's borders:

Many frivolous people consider the frequency of English suicides to be a sign of their talent [*darovanie*] and philosophy. [. . .] But when we recall [the case of] that Englishman, who, [despite] possessing a solid fortune threw himself into the Thames solely in order to convince an acquaintance that a happy person could also be bored living in this world, then we sense that neither the talent nor the philosophy of Englishmen were the reasons for his suicide, but rather a laziness of spirit, a boredom born of immoderation in amusements and insufficiencies in virtues.[40]

Russian literature of the Romantic era presents the reverse pattern: much ennui and few suicides. As in Western Europe, poems often lingered on feelings of metaphysical despair, loneliness, and alienation, but, more uniquely, neither poetry nor prose contained many specific references to suicide.[41] Russia's great Romantic poet, Mikhail Lermontov, repeatedly evoked this imagery, for example, describing the anguish and suffering of man's spiritual isolation, the "fetters of life" that make us celebrate death.[42] One of his most famous poems explicitly placed boredom at the heart of an intense spiritual crisis. Its opening lines have become among the most oft-cited in Russian poetry: "I am bored and sad [*I skuchno i grustno*], and there is no one to whom I can give my hand in the moment of my spiritual adversity." The poem then describes the inexorable passage of time and the transience of love, happiness, suffering, and passion. Its final lines highlight the disjunction between the inner self and the outer world: "And life, if you look round with cold attention, is such a hollow and stupid joke."[43] Rather than seek to probe the complexities of Lermontov's imagery (much less Russian Romanticism), the point here is more modest. In the context of broader currents in literature and philosophy, especially an intensive

---

[39] Spacks (*Boredom*) argues that modern notions of boredom have also been conditioned by new attitudes and practices regarding both work and leisure. On the rise of leisure opportunity in Russia, see Stephen Lovell, *Summerfolk: The History of the Dacha, 1710–2000* (Ithaca, N.Y., 2003).

[40] Strakhov, *Moi peterburgskie sumerki*, 48–50.

[41] On the importance of suicide to Western Romanticism, see Barbara T. Gates, *Victorian Suicide: Mad Crimes and Sad Histories* (Princeton, 1988); and Lisa Lieberman, "Romanticism and the Culture of Suicide in Nineteenth-Century France," *Comparative Studies in Society and History* 33: 3 (1991).

[42] See e.g. his 1830 poem, "Odinochestvo," in M. Iu. Lermontov, *Sobranie sochinenii v trekh tomakh* (Moscow, 1996), vol. 1, 371.

[43] Lermontov, *Sobranie sochinenii*, vol 3, 342.

encounter with German idealism, many Russian writers and intellectuals were exploring (and thereby creating) a new sense of personal inwardness. Yet this exploration also set up a fundamental disjunction – the longing of the self for perfection and infinitude conflicted with the imperfect and transient external world. This disjunction helped to engender both a preoccupation with self-reflection and representations of the world as absurd. In an important sense, reality existed within the self, and the world was but a projection.[44] Following in this broad framework, *skuka* can be understood as a condition of intense spiritual suffering, an existential alienation from the world, and, simultaneously, a mark of genius. Consequently, it also embodied danger and the potential of temptation. Pushkin's rewriting of the Faust legend thus began with the words, "I am bored, devil," to which Mephistopheles replies, "What is to be done, Faust?"[45]

A third and related sphere of meaning concerns the nexus between boredom and melancholy.[46] Since antiquity, the two phenomena have been so closely intertwined that they often cannot be distinguished. According to the highly influential theory of humors, the differing proportions between four bodily fluids – blood, phlegm, yellow bile, and black bile – determined the character and disposition of man as well as his bodily and mental health. Within this framework, a preponderance of black bile shapes the melancholic personality. From the very beginning of this concept's long history, melancholy was considered to be both a malady and a quality of genius. It could also trigger acts of violence, especially against the self. As Renaissance Europe rediscovered the ancients, including the various discussions of melancholy and ennui – from Aristotle to Seneca – a modern history of the concepts began (one that included an ongoing and complex interaction with the Christian vice of acedia). The single most influential work was Robert Burton's 1621 *magnum opus, Anatomy of Melancholy*, which went into innumerable editions over subsequent centuries.[47] Arguing that melancholy was a disease particularly affecting those who live a life of the mind, he acknowledged its physiological basis in a preponderance of black bile but also pointed to environmental causes and a range of therapies, including, for him, the act of writing, but, more generally, various guidelines for everyday conduct and diet. One of its most important symptoms, incidentally, was *taedium vitae*.

---

[44] On the era, the ideas, and leading intellectual figures, see Martin Malia, *Alexander Herzen and the Birth of Russian Socialism* (New York, 1961); and Aileen M. Kelly, *Toward Another Shore: Russian Thinkers Between Necessity and Chance* (New Haven, 1998).

[45] I have taken this observation from Pamela Davidson. See her "Russian Views of Art as Demonic," in Pamela Davidson, ed., *Russian Literature and its Demons* (New York, 2000), 161 n. 75. For further discussion of ennui and romanticism, see her "Russian Literature and its Demons," *ibid*, esp. 13–15.

[46] The following discussion draws on Kuhn, *Demon of Noontide*; and Wolf Lepenies, *Melancholy and Society*, trans. J. Gaines and D. Jones (Cambridge, 1992).

[47] For a recent edition, see Robert Burton, *The Anatomy of Melancholy* (New York, 2001).

The processes of cultural Westernization in Russia included the importation of melancholy, which was adapted into the Russian *melankholiia*. The term thus appeared among the mitigating factors listed in Peter the Great's original statutes criminalizing suicide. Later in the century, it showed up in crime reports, where it coexisted with many Russian terms designating similar kinds of maladies, including *toska, grust'*, and *zadumchivost'*. Other common designations included "spleen" and the "English malady." In the nineteenth century, it was defined as a pensive anguish (*zadumchivaia toska*), despair (*unyn'e*), a silent despair (*tikhoe otchaianie*) without apparent cause, and a dark view of the world; it also cited the related disease of hypochondria.[48] Altogether, then, it was a conjoined malady, psychic state, and temperament. Though an explicit link to boredom was not made, the two terms clearly overlap with boredom possessing perhaps more a connotation of lassitude.[49] Indeed, Pushkin linked the sources of poetic inspiration – that is, of writing – to a state of mind shaped by *skuka*, idleness, and gloom (cf. Burton's therapy against melancholy).[50] Over the course of the nineteenth century, however, *skuka* would gain in relative prominence, a process that was propelled in part by the displacement of the archaic malady of melancholy by new medical concepts. Modern approaches to human physiology had undermined the theory of the four humors, thus denying melancholy its once firm medical basis.[51] In the twentieth century, the expression, *mne skuchno*, could also sometimes mean "I am depressed."

Yet many of the underlying patterns persisted. A doctor diagnosed the 1857 suicide of a serf as the consequence of the moroseness of her temperament caused by a malady of the liver, which was, not incidentally, associated with the production of black bile.[52] Similarly, the secret police report on the suicide in 1852 of newly graduated surveyor Pavel Prizhimov stated that he possessed a melancholic disposition and regularly suffered "attacks" of melancholy (though he would nonetheless be buried as a suicide). This information then framed his note, which, in an accusatory tone, situates his motive as a rejection of a passive, albeit figurative death in favour of an active one (suicide): "The reason for my suicide is the Director of the Land-Survey Office, Anan'ev: he appoints all graduates of the Marinskii Land-Survey School to district surveyors in places where the raven does not lay its bones, and there they end their lives. Those

[48] *TS*, vol. 2, 823.
[49] Even this distinction might not hold. In the case of Veliobitskii, discussed in Chapter 4, he cited his disappointment and "strong tedium" (*sil'naia skuka*) as immediate causes for his impulsive decision to slash his neck. See RGIA, f. 1151, op. 2 (1834), d. 60, ll. 1–3, 26–30.
[50] For discussion and analysis, see Davidson, "Russian Views," 148–51.
[51] See the entry under *melankholiia* in *BE*. It has been subsumed into the modern medical discourse of mental alienation and illness.
[52] This was, of course, a humane judgment that probably facilitated a Christian burial. GARF, f. 109 IV, op. 197 (1857), d. 229, l. 7.

were his actual words. In this case, I would rather end my life in the capital than somewhere in the thick woods or in a provincial town. I would write a bit more but it's time to pull the trigger."[53] Prizhimov did not actually cite *skuka*, but it was his dismay at being sent away from Moscow to "die" in a provincial backwater that prompted him to shoot himself. He thus claimed the right to author his death – a quick bullet was preferred to a slow stagnation. This interpretation was not shared by the investigating officer. Despite mentioning the malady of melancholy, he failed to pursue this line of enquiry but rather confirmed Prizhimov's provincial assignment, his (otherwise) upstanding character, and the lack of any apparent explanation for the suicide. Perhaps Prizhimov's logic did not make sense to him, though the absence of any moralizing comments – regarding the obvious disregard of duty, for example – is also striking.

A handful of other suicide notes evoked the various meanings of *skuka* much more explicitly. As a motive, however, it was typically met by outsiders with a palpable degree of bewilderment. Zablotskii-Desiatkovskii's review of suicide in St. Petersburg included two such cases. First was a foreigner who killed himself "from nothing to do" (*ot nechego delat'*). Additional information was not provided, and this phrase, likely from the suicide note, was included literally as an entire rubric in a statistical chart. In other words, it was not subsumed under a more general category (such as *skuka*).[54] This is all the more noteworthy because the author of this study commented on an analogous incident and even quoted the note:

Occasionally suicides are possessed by some sort of strange, inexplicable humor at the moment of their crime; such was the case of a civil servant who shot himself and in whose pocket the following note was found: "Report to the ** Department, from Collegial Secretary **: I have become bored with living in this world, for which reason I intend to set off for the next world. About this [fact] I have the honor to inform the ** Department."[55]

What was the "strange, inexplicable humor" – the form of the note as an administrative report or its reference to boredom? Indeed, the two aspects were not mutually exclusive. This civil servant had crafted his suicide note as a parody of officialdom: in announcing his boredom with his world, he followed bureaucratic procedures and employed the language of deference and subordination. With his note, he thereby sought to transform his boredom into a mark of genius and his suicide into a public feat of personal rebellion. Though contemporaries were fascinated by this case, they perceived it as an enigma; the act

[53] GARF, f. 109 IV, op. 192 (1852), d. 128.
[54] *Statisticheskie svedeniia*, 194. It is perhaps worth mentioning that only one case was listed under this rubric in the tables.
[55] *Statisticheskie svedeniia*, 196 n.

of communication had apparently failed.[56] The concept of *skuka* as a motive for suicide did not quite make sense.

A case investigated by the Third Section displays similar dynamics. In 1852, Lieutenant Kvitsynskii cited the absurdity of life before shooting himself twice, once in the chest and then in the jaw. His note alluded to the consequences of boredom but, like the civil servant, he represented his voluntary death as rebellion, as an extravagant refusal to conform to senseless social norms: "It is time to end the stupid drama with laughter – Farewell public and actors, down with the stage sets of the worldly circus, you be Don Quixote but I've had enough [*donkikhotstvuite vy a s menia dovol'no*]." Staging his suicide as a theatrical exit, Kvitsynskii likened his world to the tragicomic landscape of Don Quixote, which was a popular work in Russia. The idea of the world as a stage dates back to antiquity, of course, and it was especially popular in the European Baroque when Cervantes was writing. It was also a defining characteristic of early Russian Romanticism, though high tragedy (rather than comedy) was the dominant genre of the Decembrists' generation.[57] By the 1830s and 1840s, however, both Gogol and Dostoevsky were exploring the absurdity (and the tragic sensibility) of the "little man," especially the petty bureaucrat who suffered within the regimented hierarchy of social norms and bureaucratic ranks. A self-conscious theatricality along with parodies of bureaucratism were thereby woven into the cultural fabric of the era.[58] This broader context informed Kvitsynskii's gesture. Like the civil servant before him, Kvitsynskii proclaimed the absurdity of life – including his own death. Such self-conscious suicides were consequently fashioned as feats of genius, of individual willfulness in the face of social conformity. Although Kvitsynskii lambasted his world by calling it a circus, his point did not apparently resonate. The official report on his suicide dryly summarized the facts, stated that the motives were unknown, and quoted the note without commentary.[59] Absurdity was met by silence.

A different representation of boredom informed the 1827 suicide of Aleksei Iakovlev. After spending the day as a guest at his neighbor's house, a (female) landowner, Iakovlev had returned home, ordered his servant to leave him, and shot himself. He had already burned his papers but left a note in a sealed envelope for the local police, and this formality was acknowledged in official reports which described it as a declaration (*ob"iavlenie*) rather than the more typical "note" (*zapiska*). This information, including a transcript of the note, had

---

[56] The case was described as "strange" and quoted in full without comment in a book review. See "Razbor knigi: Statisticheskie svedeniia o S.-Peterburge," *Sovremennik* no. 7 (1837), 357.

[57] Gavriel Shapiro, *Nikolai Gogol and the Baroque Cultural Heritage* (University Park, Penn., 1993), esp. 130–39. Iurii Lotman, "Teatr i teatral'nost'" v stroe kul'tury nachala XIX veka," *Izbrannye stat'i*, 3 vols. (Tallinn, 1992), vol. 1.

[58] Iurii Lotman, "Concerning Khlestakov," *The Semiotics of Russian Cultural History*, ed. A. D. and A. S. Nakhimovsky (Ithaca, N.Y., 1985), 150–87.

[59] GARF, f. 109 IV, op. 192 (1852), d. 115, l. 3.

then been passed from the local police to the governor and thence to the Third
Section. "I am leaving this boring, sad world forever [*Ia skuchnyi, grustnyi
mir na veki ostavliaiu*]," the note began, with a peculiar echo of Lermontov's
later poem, "and for eternity [will] gaze at the other world; the police sleeps,
Iakovlev ends the sad century . . . You . . . sleep and he breathes for the last
time; when you hear . . . see, that he is no longer in this world . . . that he could
no longer bear the burden of Fate . . . but now I go into the eternal night. By
the way, the world will forget me, and I will forget it. I have already distributed
my things. [signed] Former Karachevskii landowner, retired lieutenant of the
Aleksandriiskii Hussar Regiment, Aleksei Petrov son Iakovlev."[60] Although
the peculiarity of this suicide meant that the Third Section and the tsar were
informed, the response to this "declaration" was, once again, silence. There
was no further investigation, and the identity of the imagined reader of the note
(the neighbor?) was not clarified. This note, with all its awkward language,
illuminates a different nexus between *skuka* and suicide than the cases discussed
above. Rather than an act affirming genius or autonomy, Iakovlev's departure
appears as a form of self-annihilation – even memory is to be erased. Boredom
had here led to weakness, inertia, and the passivity of death.

In his study of the modern history of melancholy, Wolf Lepenies distinguishes
two archetypes that can offer some insight into these dynamics of intention and
reception. First is a melancholy of disorder, in which melancholy is represented
as a deviation from (social, bodily, political) order and hence a kind of deviance.
Second is a melancholy of order which arises from a surfeit of order.[61] These
two poles help to illuminate the meanings of *skuka* in the world of Nicholas I.
On the one hand, *skuka* did not fit into the utopian vision of an ordered society
modeled upon the military parade, the imperial family, and the principles of
hierarchy, duty, and submission. For this reason, perhaps, the official reactions
to the suicide of boredom in particular were strikingly uniform: silent perplexity.
Boredom simply did not make sense. Still, this silence was uneasy. Why did
officials chose not to employ the language of moral denunciation (as they did
with many suicides of honor)? It would have been quite possible to condemn
boredom as a vice and as a violation of one's duty to God and tsar. Yet they
remained silent. On the other hand, this same punctilious regulation of public
life and personal conduct may actually have encouraged a melancholy of order.
The resultant environment of *poshlost'* – a term that connotes banality and
vulgarity – could become the object of parody not just in literature but also in
life. A few people thus fashioned suicides in the name of *skuka* as a form of
revolt, an affirmation of the inner self against the outer world. Equally striking

---

[60] GARF, f. 109 IV, op. 167 (1827), d. 135, l. 3.
[61] For a rather different application of these ideas, see Lepenies, *Melancholy and Society*, chs. 1,
    2.

is the humor in two of these cases, a quality that highlights their carnivalesque quality. After all, laughter and mirth have long functioned as subversive forces, particularly in societies possessing a closed, governing ideology.

Yet even at the height of Romanticism, with its cult of genius and the personality, the motif of romantic suicide was negligible in both literature and life, which marks a major contrast with Western Europe. Available evidence does not suggest that the motive of boredom was widespread. Nevertheless, these malcontents provide a fascinating perspective into changing ideas about the relationship between the individual and the polity, including the right of the individual to self-determination. They also point to a new configuration of suicide as an almost existential act embodying the contradiction between the inner self and the outer world, a configuration that would become increasingly influential in both Russia and the West.

Still, the relative dearth of public suicides persisted with the emergence of literary realism in the 1840s and 1850s. One reason for this, paradoxically, may have been the extreme popularity of boredom – with its companions inertia and powerlessness – within the ordered façade of Nicholas I's Russia. While many literary characters (and some writers) thought about suicide, they simply did not have the energy or will to do it.[62] This mentality would be immortalized in Goncharov's Oblomov. The "superfluous man," disenchanted with his world yet unable to act upon it, was an established type of the era. Only in the 1870s would the nexus between boredom and suicide be reconstituted into a significant social and cultural phenomenon.

Nevskii Prospect

To understand motives for suicide, both contemporary observers and later scholars have often turned to literature.[63] Indeed, literary works frequently informed the specific meanings of suicide and the various states of mind associated with it, whether Lermontov's romantic pessimism or Bestuzhev-Marlinskii's cult of honor. In contrast to the often awkward prose and narrow focus of suicide notes and investigatory files, moreover, the artistic text can explore suicide from multiple perspectives; its tone and generic emplotment can likewise suggest broader attitudes. One important literary work of Russia's Romantic era did in

---

[62] See e.g. a parody of the Werther theme which ends without suicide. [A. V. Druzhinin], "Samoubiistvo," *Sovremennik* no. 12 (1848), 85–108.

[63] This was the strategy of the later populist thinker, N. K. Mikhailovskii, who lamented the particular inability of Russian suicides to articulate the motives for their acts. See his "Zhiteiskie i khudozhestvennye dramy," reprinted in *Sochineniia N. K. Mikhailovskogo* (SPb, 1897), vol. 4. Similarly, as I will discuss in the next chapter, doctors and psychiatrists often drew on literary case studies. Finally, Paperno (*Suicide*, ch. 4 and *passim*) emphasizes the unresolved epistemological problem posed by suicide and consequently privileges the authority of the literary voice more generally.

fact focus on the problem of suicide: Nikolai Gogol's masterpiece from 1835, "Nevskii Prospect."[64] Although it did not evoke the poetics of boredom, it did parody romantic suicide, which it placed within an environment of social artifice, including the quest for honor and status. Consequently, this canonical text contributed to the dialogical meanings of suicide in the Russia of Nicholas I.[65]

The tale opens with a wonderfully sardonic description of the social space of Nevskii Prospect, St. Petersburg's main artery, from early in the morning till late in the evening. Against this lively exhibition of humanity's follies unfolds the tragicomic fate of two young men, the sensitive artist Piskarev and the proud Lieutenant Pirogov, who are out one evening for a stroll. Mistaking a prostitute for a virtuous girl, Piskarev follows her home and discovers her corruption. Even a subsequent proposal of marriage does not tempt the degenerate young woman. Unable to reconcile the squalidness of reality with his vision of beauty and purity, he falls into a despair verging on madness, turns to opium, and ultimately takes his own life. For his part, the self-important Pirogov mistakes the respectable wife of a German artisan for a lady of ill repute and ultimately receives his just comeuppance from her husband. Humiliated and indignant, Pirogov intends to report his mishandling but his anger soon dissipates in the diversions offered by the city. He is last seen dancing a mazurka, basking in (self) admiration (Illus. 1). The entire affair is a parody of the cult of honor. Concerned solely with his outward image and social reputation, Pirogov possesses a clear conscience, despite insulting a respectable woman. Equally important, he promptly forgets his dishonor at the hands of social inferiors; it certainly does not form a reason for some kind of protest, much less suicide. Because he embodies the artifice of Nevskii Prospect, he flourishes there.

Although Piskarev perishes, his demise fails to articulate any genius or talent. Instead, the tale systematically parodies the romantic cult of interiority and beautiful death. Like Pirogov, Piskarev is solely concerned with attaining social recognition and status, thereby overcoming his stereotypical poverty and obscurity. Similarly, his identity as a Petersburg artist is fatally undermined; both his artistic ideals and his specific fantasies of saving the fallen woman are clichéd. Not the incongruity of beauty and corruption, the ideal and the real, frame his death, therefore, but the opposite: Piskarev embodies the values of his society too completely. He is just as banal as Pirogov. The representation of the suicide itself completes this portrait. Having failed in his attempt to convince his beloved to renounce her life of vice and become his wife, he

---

[64] It is reprinted in N. V. Gogol, *Sobranie sochinenii v semi tomakh* (Moscow, 1984), vol. 3. For a new translation, see *The Collected Tales of Nikolai Gogol*, trans. Richard Pevear and Larissa Volokhonsky (New York, 1998).

[65] I wish to thank Julian Graffy, whose penetrating critique of an earlier version of this section inspired a fundamental revision. The strengths of this interpretation are to his credit, the weaknesses to mine.

Illus. 1 Lieutenant Pirogov dancing the mazurka, from D. Kardovskii,
"*Nevskii Prospekt*: Poruchik Pirogov na vechere u pravitelia kollegii" (1904).

wanders the streets and ultimately shuts himself up in his rooms. A week later
his body is found with the throat cut, but Piskarev has botched his penultimate
artistic scene: "From his convulsively outstretched arms and from the horribly
contorted expression, it was possible to conclude that his hand had been untrue,
and that he had suffered a long time before his sinful soul departed his body"
(Illus. 2). Furthermore, he is not permitted to author his own death. A suicide
note was not found, a fact which underlines the meaninglessness of the suicide –
both Pisarev's failure to articulate a meaning and the narrator's disinterest in
finding one. This lack of meaning is further underlined in the indifferent
response to the death. Pirogov could not be bothered with it, and the narrator highlights its banality by neglecting to mention it for the rest of the tale. The
last reference occurs when the funeral passes unnoticed:

Thus perished the victim of a mad passion, poor Piskarev, quiet, timid, modest, childishly
ingenuous, who possessed a spark of talent [*iskra talanta*] which might in time have
blazed up widely and brightly. No one wept over him; no one could be seen by his soulless

Illus. 2 The contorted body of the suicide, the artist Piskarev, from D. Kardovskii, *"Nevskii Prospekt*: Konets khudozhnika Piskareva" (1904). Especially striking is what appears to be a suicide note – though Piskarev did not leave one. By the twentieth century, when this print was made, the suicide note would be so common that such a scene could hardly be imagined without one.

body except the ordinary figure of a district inspector and the indifferent countenance of a city doctor [*lekar'*]. His coffin was quietly taken – even without religious ceremonies – to Okhta [an outlying district in St. Petersburg]; behind it wept a soldier-sentry, and that because he had drunk an extra bottle [*shtof*] of vodka.[66]

That Gogol parodied Piskarev's fate, locating it amidst the banal philistinism of the capital city, suggests that the image of the romantic suicide was quite familiar. Educated Russians were well acquainted, of course, with contemporary European Romanticism, but the objects of parody were also closer to home. One was the sentimental suicide, including Karamzin's "Poor Liza," whose death had likewise been the result of a "mad passion." In this case, the representation

---

[66] Gogol, *Sobranie sochinenii*, 28.

of virtue and vice had lacked irony and parody. Instead, the characters were consistent with their material worlds, with the virtuous Liza a product of nature, and the weak Erast a product of the city. The tragedy occurs in part because Erast gambles away his fortune, thereby necessitating his marriage to a rich widow. While an external betrayal thus drives Liza to her death, self-deception provokes Piskarev's act. Another object of parody was the slightly different association of suicide with the modern city, which was propagated in both didactic literature and the emergent genre of naturalist city portraits. These presumed a nexus between suicide and the vices of artifice, luxury, and idleness. Yet Gogol also transformed these well-known paradigms. In contrast to gambling narratives, the vices of the city do not kill Piskarev by infecting him and undermining his moral character. Rather, Piskarev has internalized the values of his social environment too well; he is ambitious, vulgar, and superficial. Later in the century, the metropolis – epitomized by St. Petersburg – would become an important site for suicide, both literary and actual, and Gogol's imagery would prove prescient, though his parodic voice would often be lost in more earnest representations of prostitutes successfully redeemed and virtuous heroes and heroines suffering morally amidst the poverty and vice of the city.[67]

Gogol also introduced a new factor into the literary representation of both suicide and its social environment, one that did not resonate in suicide notes of the era. Drawing upon both religious and folkloric motifs, he represented St. Petersburg itself as a diabolical force; its instability, chaos, and especially deception were thus demonic in origin.[68] "Oh, do not believe this Nevskii Prospect," the narrator concludes the tale. "Along with the street lamps everything breathes deceit. It lies all the time, this Nevskii Prospect, but most of all at the time when night lies its condensed mass upon it [. . .], and when a demon himself lights the lamps only to show everything not in its real form."[69] While Piskarev's suicide is in part the result of things shown in an unreal form (for the unrepentant prostitute appears to him as a virtuous woman), a more fundamental point is that the romantic suicide is revealed to be mundane and pathetic, certainly not beautiful or noble.

[67] For an overview of literary representations, see Ian Lilly, "Imperial Petersburg, Suicide, and Russian Literature," *Slavonic and East European Review* no. 3 (1995), 401–23. I disagree, however, with his attempt to distinguish the psychological and philosophical approach to suicide from the environmental or political one. On St. Petersburg in Russian literature more generally, see the (reprinted) work of V. N. Toporov, *Peterburgskii tekst russkoi literatury: Izbrannye trudy* (SPb, 2003).

[68] For further discussion, see Julian Graffy, "Demonic Features of Gogol's Petersburg," in Davidson, ed., *Russian Literature and its Demons*. On the religious and folkloric origins of demonism, see Simon Franklin, "Nostalgia for Hell: Russian Literary Demonism and Orthodox Tradition;" and Faith Wigzell, "The Russian Folk Devil and His Literary Reflections," both in Davidson, *Russian Literature and its Demons*.

[69] Gogol, *Sobranie sochinenii*, 39.

Though perhaps an incidental result of a limited source base, the juxtaposition of honor and boredom in suicide notes is highly suggestive. On the one hand, the suicide of honor typically represented an attempt to grapple with social convention – whether to claim moral right or to protest an injustice. Similarly, the official responses illustrate its established place (if contested functions) as a principle regulating social life. Although the condemnation of suicide reworked many long-established moral associations, whether the vices of idleness and luxury or the capitulation to passions and delusions, the very fact that some suicides of honor were deemed partly legitimate points to important shifts in the status of suicide more generally. On the other hand, the suicide of boredom tapped into the poetics of genius, sometimes even constituting an affirmation of the personality against the social order. The official silence meeting such allusions points to a kind of discomfort and confusion regarding these kinds of public claims. Yet Gogol's parody of the romantic suicide, especially its placement into the same world of social artifice and convention, shows how the two paradigms were not mutually exclusive, despite their obvious differences. Indeed, honor and boredom shared many qualities, as another example demonstrates. The great poet of ennui and romantic pessimism, Mikhail Lermontov, was a renowned gambler, who ultimately lost his life in a duel. Similarly, Pechorin, the demonic protagonist of his tale, *A Hero of Our Time*, is disenchanted and bored yet also heroic. In the end, this prototype of the "superfluous man" departs in search of adventure (diversion and meaning?), never to return. Could the pursuit of honor – and the honorable death – also mask a form of hidden ennui?

Part II

Disease of the century

Enlightened century, century of humanism and progress! You amuse the heart of man, lift up his mind, open to him all sorts of miracles in science and art, but you do not see that your weapon is double edged, you do not see that your many-branched tree is burning from one end with a brilliant and bright flame [. . .] but from the other end it is covered in the gloom of despair and death, the groans of terror and screams, the torments of tears and blood. You are life and death, you are heaven and hell.

A. Klitin, *Our Time and Suicide*, 1890

The phenomenon of suicide imposes a moral duty on the representatives of various specializations to labor together and develop preventative measures against this evil which in our days has become the disease of the century.

I. A. Sikorskii, "The Psychic Condition before Suicide," 1896

7   Sciences of suicide

> In the study of the causes of suicide, we would then approach the greatest
> possible ideal when we would know about the entire life of the suicide, his
> character, his nervous system, the hereditary characteristics of his nature, when
> we would have information about his parents and close relatives, [when we
> would] know about his surrounding environment.
>
>   I. O. Zubov, "Suicide in Lifliand Province," 1902

A column on city life in a popular magazine from 1859 opened with the following observation: "By some strange chance, the last month was most abundant in
suicides which are usually rather rare in Petersburg. And there were six cases."
After listing the names and social identities of the victims as well as the methods they used, the report went on to muse about the significance of numbers:
"Statisticians would very likely extract some weighty speculation about the
influence of the month of January on the resolution to take one's life, but statistical conclusions in our skeptical age – being just as hard to believe as official
figures and official phrases – have lost their influence."[1]

Though its conclusion was premature, this mocking commentary foreshadowed important developments. From the late 1860s through the end of the
imperial era, suicide was a standard component in the reporting of city life,
and columns on everyday incidents and crime proved popular among the readers. Equally striking was the irresistible urge to quantify – to compile statistics
based on these new public, rather than bureaucratic sources. Although statisticians had investigated suicide as early as the 1820s and 1830s, strict controls on
education, publishing, and intellectual exchange had hindered the development
of the field. During the second half of the century, in contrast, Russian science
experienced tremendous expansion and creativity – on par with any European
country.[2] Science promised progress, and statistics formed a case in point. This

---

[1] "Gorodskie proisshestviia," *Illustratsiia* no. 58 (Feb. 19, 1859), 123.

[2] For further background, see Alexander Vucinich, *Science in Russian Culture: 1861–1917* (Stanford, 1970), ch. 1; and Elizabeth A. Hachten, "In Service to Science and Society: Scientists and
the Public in Late Nineteenth-Century Russia," Lynn K. Nyhart and Thomas H. Broman, eds.,
Science and Civil Society. Osiris 17 (2002); and David Joravsky, *Russian Psychology: A Critical
History* (Oxford, 1989), chs. 3–6.

respected and popular scientific method could seemingly illuminate any issue, ranging from birth, marriage, and death to the material conditions of the urban working class. With the apparent discovery of autonomous social laws, which were likened to natural laws, society appeared to be self-regulating, governed by objective, mathematical regularities. Not only did this vision implicitly undermine the absolute power of God and the sovereign; it also symbolized the ability of mankind to understand and thereby to change the social environment. Even a solution to the enigma of suicide seemed close at hand. The first step was the compilation of data.

Yet these two innovations – the everyday reporting of suicide along with attempts to calculate rates – had several consequences. Most fundamentally, of course, observers increasingly remarked upon the growing frequency of suicide. Although comparisons with Western Europe suggested that rates in Russia remained among the very lowest in Europe, the fact that the numbers were rising seemed self-evident. Numerous statistical studies, which were now available in Russia and sometimes even translated, had apparently documented massive increases across Europe during the nineteenth century, especially in its most developed areas. With the Great Reforms inaugurating a period of modernization, contemporaries often presumed that Russia would now follow this same pattern, albeit with a time lag. A second consequence – likewise characteristic of Western developments – was the conceptualization of suicide as a social problem, the essential context and cause of which became the socio-hygienic environment of the city, not individual immorality or vice. Though suicide continued to occur in the countryside, specialists and commentators remained focused on the city, the site of progress and peril. The obvious response was social prophylactics, especially changes in milieu, and statistics thereby acquired political overtones. As both newspapers and statistics helped to create society as a rhetorical object, their self-consciously open, public, and scientific gazes would often be contrasted to the allegedly closed and biased perspective of the state.

Yet suicide was not just a social pathology, an exemplar of the intelligentsia's renowned fixation upon the social question. Scholars have tended to underestimate the influence of the bio-medical sciences in Russia, preferring instead to focus upon social thought. Throughout nineteenth-century Europe, however, doctors were diagnosing suicide as the consequence of medical and organic causes and often rejecting its criminal status on this basis.[3] This trend was also apparent in reform-era Russia, though doctors there typically acknowledged linkages to social environment and admired statistical methods. Only in the

[3] The central figures included Forbes Winslow and Etienne Esquirol. On this process, see Barbara Gates, *Victorian Suicide: Mad Crimes and Sad Histories* (Princeton, 1988), ch. 1; and, more generally, Jan Goldstein, *Console and Classify: The French Psychiatric Profession in the Nineteenth Century* (New York, 1987).

1880s and 1890s would the medical study of suicide in Russia become firmly established, and this occurred in tandem with the emergence of psychiatry as a medical specialization and the growing influence of the theory of degeneration.[4] The social did not "engulf" the medical, as Irina Paperno has argued. Instead, the two merged into a distinctive scientific paradigm that both articulated and shaped a deep-seated ambivalence about history and progress, science and society, and the human personality.[5] Not only did this model become a constituent part of public debates about suicide; it also, as Daniel Beer has shown, fundamentally influenced both Russian liberalism and the Bolshevik project.[6] As science re-created suicide as its object, therefore, it developed powerful tools for understanding society, the personality, and the dynamics of social change.

Modern time had been reinaugurated in the 1860s – the serfs had been emancipated, the courts reformed, and the country opened up once again to Western influences. But as the difficulties in modernizing Russia became increasingly apparent in the 1870s and 1880s, the grand expectations about the transformative effects of science and enlightenment began to decline. The peasantry remained backward and isolated, the government seemingly uninterested in further reforms. The question of modernity, of Russia's present and future development, had been raised but never fully answered, and this question would become even more urgent by the 1890s, when thousands of peasants died in a famine and an industrialization drive began to transform Russia's urban centers. At this time, suicide became a symbol of the transformative potential of scientific knowledge and its limits, of civilization and its costs. Even as doctors asserted their own expert knowledge, a cure for the "disease of the century" – a metaphor referring to the incidence of suicide in the social body – was proving elusive. Instead, suicide seemed to be one of a series of diseases produced by modern urban civilization, including drunkenness, depravity, crime, unbridled egoism, mental illness, and nervous disorders. The long-standing nexus between suicide and vice was thus projected upon the modern cityscape.

---

[4] On the influence of degeneration theory in Europe, see Robert A. Nye, *Crime, Madness, and Politics in Modern France: The Medical Concept of National Decline* (Princeton, 1984); and Daniel Pick, *Faces of Degeneration: A European Disorder, c.1848–c.1918* (Cambridge, 1989).

[5] Paperno presumes a general conflict between medical and social models and then reads the nineteenth-century sciences of suicide as an evolution toward Durkheim's statistical sociology. Consequently, she neglects the development of medical and psychiatric approaches after mid-century, especially degeneration theory. See Irina Paperno, *Suicide as a Cultural Institution in Dostoevsky's Russia* (Ithaca, N.Y., 1997), 19–44, 66–73.

[6] As Pick has shown (*Faces of Degeneration*), the interpretation of scientific concepts, such as degeneration, varied among European countries, and Daniel Beer has explored the Russian case. (See his *Renovating Russia: The Human Sciences and the Fate of Liberal Modernity in Russia, 1880–1930*, forthcoming.) Scientific approaches to suicide likewise evidence national particularities, and I thus disagree with Paperno, who dismisses (twice in one footnote) Russian studies of suicide as showing little originality. See her *Suicide*, 230 n. 122.

Suicide as social problem

On the surface, newspapers and statistics approached the phenomenon of suicide from opposing perspectives. Newspapers thus spotlighted individual cases of suicide, and the narration of facts – no matter their accuracy – conferred authenticity upon the report.[7] Short announcements appeared in daily columns on city life or crime, and their numbers rose over the last decades of the century, a trend that could document the growing public interest in suicide as much as any actual growth in incidence. These brief texts typically provided the name and social estate of the person, the method used, and some indication of either the motive or the "secret" taken to the grave. Longer stories reproduced conventional plots about the circumstances leading up to the suicide (poverty, illness, unhappy love affairs), described the discovery of the body, and included excerpts from any notes. Again, these stories became more numerous by the turn of the twentieth century, often with several cases being reported every day. The narratives also became more melodramatic and prurient: suicide had clearly become a popular and increasingly sensationalized topic.[8] In contrast to newspapers, statistics neglected the stories. Their authority depended instead upon the exclusion of individual faces, whether those hidden within the data or those compiling them. The numbers and charts claimed to provide objective access to a social sphere by revealing the laws underpinning it.

Despite these differences, both genres shared an aspiration to realist representation and ultimately shaped one another in an almost circular fashion. Due to the unreliability of governmental statistics, which depended upon the mechanisms of inefficient provincial bureaucracies, statisticians increasingly derived their data from the incident reports published in daily newspapers. Not only did the figures and charts thereby reinforce the facts (and plots) of the original stories; they also replicated their increasing frequency, casting it as a reliable indicator of objective social processes (rather than, for example, the commercialization of crime reports). Newspapers, in turn, reported the statistics as well as general pieces on the phenomenon of suicide. Consequently, the making of suicide into a social problem depended upon a dialogue between the individualizing narratives of newspapers and the universalizing ones of science.

[7] On the techniques of "journalistic realism" and the way newspapers helped to create the impression that the incidence of suicide was rising, see Michael MacDonald and Terence Murphy, *Sleepless Souls: Suicide in Early Modern England* (Oxford, 1990), esp. ch. 9. On the expansion of commercial newspapers, see Louise McReynolds, *News under Russia's Old Regime: The Development of a Mass Circulation Press* (Princeton, 1991), chs. 1–3.

[8] I sampled a wide variety of newspapers – elite and boulevard, progressive and conservative, central and provincial – from each decade since the 1860s. Rather than discuss newspapers as a separate genre, however, I have integrated them thematically into each of the chapters in this and the next section.

In an 1866 article on statistical approaches to suicide, the radical publicist Nikolai Shelgunov made this process explicit. "It is sufficient to open any newspaper and skim the diary of so-called city incidents in order to convince oneself of the irrefutable influence of some fate on human life. Nobody can dispute the unpleasant condition of the man who throws himself into a river or falls head-first from the third floor, and a day does not pass that does not witness such victims. And because the number of suicides repeats with mathematical precision, thinking people can naturally raise the question of suicide as a phenomenon with psychological and social significance."[9] For Shelgunov, as for many of his contemporaries, statistical knowledge held tremendous promise as a new form of cognition, a new way to "see" society as a discrete and autonomous entity. This vision was highly politicized, and debates raged over the relationship between social determinism and free will.[10] Paradoxically, determinism – the idea that man's behavior was not individual and arbitrary but determined by social laws – had voluntarist implications: if suicide (along with other social problems) was the product not of individual will but of social environment, it would be possible to change the environment and thereby to remake the human being. Scientific knowledge was thus intended to improve people's economic and material welfare, to educate and liberate their minds, and to contribute to social progress more generally. As Shelgunov pointedly noted, the causes of suicide could be divided into two categories – those outside of human control (climate, time of year) and those that depend partly or wholly on society (poverty and need, fear of punishment, shame).[11] Not unlike the radical literary critic interpreting his "data," Shelgunov approached newspapers and statistics as objective sources on social reality and extracted from them a vision and agenda of social change. This realist reading soon became a dominant interpretative technique.

Two years later, the first attempt to assess the suicide rate in reform-era Russia appeared in the *Archive of Forensic Medicine and Social Hygiene*, which was an influential journal that published on a broad range of medical and social topics. Choosing the dry subtitle "Data for Moral Statistics," its author, Iu. Giubner, fashioned himself as a scientific expert investigating an empirical problem. He described statistical work as "tedious" and "painstaking" and the method as "outstanding and promising." Like most statisticians, he both laid bare his sources (newspaper reports of suicide in St. Petersburg between 1858 and 1867) and cast doubt on them by asserting that the real rates were indisputably higher. The article consisted of a series of statistical tables on time, place, and method of death, social background, gender, age, cause (where provided), and so forth.

[9] N. Radiukin [N. Shelgunov], "Statistika samoubiistva," *Delo* no. 1 (1866), 312. On the attribution of authorship and for further discussion, see Paperno, *Suicide*, 69.
[10] For further discussion, see Paperno, *Suicide*, 66–70.
[11] Radiukin, "Statistika samoubiistva," 346.

Apparently believing that the numbers spoke for themselves, Giubner effectively excluded himself from the text.[12]

This restraint led to a passionate outburst in the radical journal, *The Deed*. Written under a pseudonym, this polemic illustrates the realist approach to statistical knowledge. Statistics lose their relevance, the author argued, when they exist only "for themselves," without "practical orientation." By limiting themselves to "naked numbers" and "object-less research," Russia's statisticians – and Giubner in particular – were providing more and more data but also confining statistics to a narrow academic relevance. Such statistics possessed the "objectivity of a photograph, which copied a landscape onto paper," for they did not provide the least understanding of their true object. He was interested in far more than mechanical representation: "Only interpreted figures and numerical deductions [*osmyslennye tsifry i chislovye vyvody*] would give [society] the opportunity to see truth, falsehood, salvation, [and] perdition."[13] At issue was positive knowledge about society and social problems, and the language constructed this task as a moral one. Science was to identify the path toward deliverance.[14]

Whereas Giubner had fashioned himself as an expert impartially presenting the facts, his commentator adopted the position of the literary critic, treated Giubner's data as a form of realist description, and sought to extract their true social meanings.[15] First he dismissed the largest rubric of psychological or physical illnesses (almost half of Giubner's ascribed motives) as "transitory conditions." Instead he identified the true "independent causes" as poverty and destitution along with such lesser factors as business difficulties and family relations. "That is," he explained his logic, "someone who has ruined himself or lives in poverty becomes melancholic or pensive, then throws himself in water or smothers himself." While he did not directly analyze Giubner's second largest category of cause, drunkenness (38.3 percent), this too was subsumed into the new causal mechanism based on social milieu: "The principle cause of suicide consists in 'poverty and indigence,' that is, in those very motive forces, which produce the most mortality, drunkenness, crime, and other such abnormal phenomena. The harmful consequences of such motive forces are more noticeable in St. Petersburg than elsewhere thanks to the unusual circumstances of our capital's life: the extreme population density, the high cost of provisions and their poor quality, the humidity of the atmosphere, and the rottenness of the

---

[12] See the reprinted pamphlet, Iu. Giubner, *Samoubiistva v S.-Peterburge. Materialy dlia nravstvennoi statistiki* (SPb, 1868).

[13] Gub, "Vnutrennee obozrenie," *Delo* no. 10 (1868), 83–85.

[14] The moral fervor of the intelligentsia was an oft-cited trait. See Martin Malia, "What is the Russian Intelligentsia?" in Richard Pipes, ed., *The Russian Intelligentsia* (Cambridge, Mass., 1960).

[15] Cf. Joshua Cole, "The Chaos of Particular Facts: Statistics, Medicine, and the Social Body in Early Nineteenth-Century France," *History of the Human Sciences* no. 3 (1994), 3.

soil."[16] Likening Petersburg to a "cesspit" in which social problems festered, the author explained suicide through the environmental metaphor of *pochva*, which can mean both soil and foundation.[17]

This article resolved the tension in pre-reform studies between individual moral responsibility and social context in favor of the latter. While indigence and drunkenness were factors in both periods, they were no longer signs of individual moral failings (lack of foresight, laziness) but social problems. Suicide is "only one sort of those phenomena, which include crime, drunkenness, and mortality rates," Giubner's critic asserted. "Consequently it is necessary to examine them in relation to these other phenomena. Under such an examination, they completely lose their character as 'moral' phenomena and become purely physical ones."[18] Just like other diseases – typhus, cholera, and tuberculosis – suicide was an issue of public health, the consequence of material poverty and filth.

Original scholarly investigations of suicide in Russia appeared only sporadically during the 1860s and 1870s, but a steady stream of translations, compilations, and reviews of Western publications provided an important comparative vantage point. Furthermore, the statistics of suicide were popularized in newspapers, thick journals, and even almanacs.[19] This process of familiarization helped to cast suicide as a social fact. Only statistics, one article in a liberal newspaper asserted in 1872, can illuminate the causes of suicide, all the reasons for the "growth in unhappiness."[20] Indeed, the notion that the suicide rate was growing in Russia, as in Europe, first became a truism in the 1870s. At the center of attention was St. Petersburg, Russia's proverbial window to the West, where European trends always commenced. While the number of annual cases had fluctuated between 41 and 77 in the period 1858–67, the numbers had seemingly jumped to 124 cases in 1870 and 167 in 1872.[21] The problem was also spreading to the provinces. A comparative study of suicide in Odessa (based on newspapers) argued that rates there were even higher than in St. Petersburg or

---

[16] Gub, "Vnutrennee obozrenie," 88. For another article emphasizing the causal role of poverty, see B. Ongirskii, "Statisticheskie itogi samoubiistv," *Delo* no. 11 (1873).

[17] In a penetrating analysis, Paperno (*Suicide*, 67, 86–88) argues that the metaphor of "soil" was a key rhetorical device in this article, allowing its author to deduce suicide's "roots" in Petersburg's "miasmas."

[18] Gub, "Vnutrennee obozrenie," 90.

[19] In discussing statistics, I do not claim that they are accurate, though contemporaries generally treated them as such. See e.g. [S. G. Maksimov], "O samoubiistvakh v S.-Peterburge," *Vedomosti S.-Peterburgskoi gorodskoi politsii* no. 7 (1870), 1; A. S. Suvorin, *Russkii kalendar' na 1873 god* (SPb, 1873), 373–74; and *Vedomosti Sanktpeterburgskoi gorodskoi politsii* nos. 43, 44 (1873).

[20] "Statistika samoubiistva v Peterburge," *Golos* (Dec. 1, 1872), 2.

[21] Numbers vary between sources. See I. Pasternatskii, "Statisticheskoe issledovanie samoubiistv v S.-Peterburge za 1870, 1871, i 1872 gody," *Meditsinskii vestnik* nos. 35–38, 40–41 (1873), here no. 36, 346, and no. 37, 375.

Moscow.[22] In 1882, the first comprehensive statistical study of suicide in Russia seemed to confirm significant increases in the numbers, particularly in the capital cities, but the national rates remained among the very lowest in Europe.[23] Russia's proverbial backwardness was the proffered reason for the comparative lag, for suicide was presumed a disease of civilization – of urban poverty and vices, of secularization and the fragmentation of community. Nevertheless, the definition of suicide as a social problem of growing magnitude had also become an established axiom in Russia, and it was localized into its great urban centers.

Suicide as medical problem

Even before the reform era, parts of Russia's medical community were aware of contemporary European efforts to explain suicide as a form or consequence of disease and insanity. The first Russian doctor to investigate this linkage was probably Ivan Leonov, professor at Kiev's St. Vladimir University. Following the lead of Etienne Esquirol and others, whom he cited, he searched for signs of suicide in the body. Despite the paucity of his data, he claimed to have found changes in the thymus, liver, and skull.[24] Leonov's work was deeply flawed, yet this is also one reason for his historical interest. Appended to his article from 1850 was a comment by the editors of the journal lambasting Leonov's (truly) appalling methodology: he had recounted cases from memory, cited data in support of his argument but not known counter-examples, and contradicted his own typology. With their detailed critique, the editors had not rejected the approach per se but called for a more rigorous scientific method based upon the impartial presentation of facts.[25]

This appeal was a harbinger of the scientific spirit of the reform era, and it would shortly be answered. In a series of articles published in this journal between 1856 and 1858, Ia. Chistovich, adjunct professor at St. Petersburg's Medical Surgical Academy, presented data on several hundred autopsies

---

[22] "Samoubiistva v Odesse (1870–1879)," *Vedomosti Odesskogo Gradonachal'stva* (Oct. 15 and 16, 1881). One article did claim that suicide rates were not increasing in Russia; see "Statisticheskie svedeniia o samoubiistvakh v period 1870–74 godov," *Pravitel'stvennyi vestnik* (May 7, 1876), 2.

[23] Clearly the simple comparison of national suicide rates must be interpreted with skepticism given the major differences in the way suicide was administered and data compiled. Such issues did not especially preoccupy contemporaries though they did presume a major under-reportage in Russia. A. V. Likhachev, *Samoubiistvo v zapadnoi Evrope i evropeiskoi Rossii* (SPb, 1882), esp. 180–83.

[24] See his "Rassuzhdenie o grudnoi zheleze (glandula thymus), v fiziologicheskom, patologicheskom i sudebno-meditsinskom otnoshenii," *Drug zdraviia* nos. 15, 16 (1842); and "O samoubiistve," *Voenno-meditsinskii zhurnal* 55 (Mar. 1850).

[25] Appended to Leonov, "O samoubiistve," 11–16.

conducted by himself and his colleagues since 1838.[26] Organizing his analysis around the causes of death, Chistovich placed suicide under the rubric of "violent and arbitrary death" and combined statistics with brief case studies. In contrast to Leonov but foreshadowing Giubner, he generally avoided making conclusions, instead seeing his primary task in the collection and presentation of scientific data. Others followed this lead, and statistical studies based on forensic records were regularly published in the late 1860s. Though focused on the scientific potential of autopsy, these studies generally presumed a link between individual physiology and social environment, and they thereby made society into an object of science.[27] Implying that diagnosis was the first step toward treatment, one researcher thus wrote: "Is it possible to compile [the many years of data] into *true* tables, which would lead to true conclusions about the character of crime in the given society, which would include the true and sharp characteristics of this society, with its weaknesses like diseased products manufactured by the conditions of social life?"[28] Not only did these specialists freely mix their metaphors; they saw statistical data as a means to define socio-medical problems as spheres of intervention.

Indeed, the environmental approach combined readily with existing medical knowledge. In an article published in the *Medical Bulletin*, Dr. I. R. Pasternatskii compiled statistical data (derived from newspapers) on suicide in St. Petersburg between 1870 and 1872. Framing the charts with the insights of medicine, Pasternatskii described suicide as an "action of our organism" which was inconceivable "without the mental processes that precede it [and] call it forth." To describe the impact of social experience on the mind and body, he extracted a numerically informed case study. One can almost see the hand of the literary critic sketching a "real" social type, only he is not the courageous new man able to rework his world, but rather its helpless victim:

Poverty can lead a man to despair. Material resources, if present at all, are quickly expended down to the last kopeck. The man must pawn his last possessions, search for work. His boots begin to fall apart from the useless running about the city looking for an earned piece of bread; his clothing gives at the seams and turns into rags. [. . .] Having gone blue with cold, his wife and children (which most suicides have), wait with suffering patience for a crust of bread or a hungry death. So the unhappy family

[26] Ia. Chistovich, "Perechen' sudebno-meditsinskikh vskrytii," *Voenno-meditsinskii zhurnal* 67 (Mar. 1856), 70 (Dec. 1857), and 72 (Aug. 1858).

[27] Paperno (*Suicide*, 20–22, 66, and *passim*) further explores the scientific and metaphoric status of autopsy.

[28] Italics in original. See P. Pokryshkin, "Sudebno-meditsinskaia deiatel'nost' v Viatskoi gubernii s 1-go sentiabria 1862 g. po 1-e ianvaria 1865 g.," *ASMOG* no. 3 (1868), 64–65. For similar studies dealing partly with suicide, see P. Pokryshkin, "Sudebno-meditsinskaia deiatel'nost' v Irkutskoi gubernii za 1864–1867 gody," *ASMOG* no. 3 (1869); I. Verevkin, "Perechen' sudebno-meditsinskikh vskrytii," *ASMOG* nos. 3, 4 (1865); and Dr. Surkov, "Sudebno-meditsinskie sluchai v Simbirskoi gubernii v 1860–1864 godakh," *ASMOG* no. 1 (1866).

father returns home (which one would expect to be a room with one window in either a fifth-floor attic or a damp basement), his head is pounding, his wet hands are freezing, and something is happening in his throat and chest that does not augur well; his cheeks are sunken, his eyes express alarm, and a feeling of hopelessness and exasperation is born in his soul. [. . .] What could draw this man to life? What kind of pleasant sensations are conceivable for him? [. . .] Criminal statistics [. . .] show that poverty more than any other [cause] leads to suicide, that a man decides for this crime only when circumstances have blocked the path to honest labor. The man has a choice between suicide and death by starvation.[29]

The role of drunkenness in suicide likewise depended upon a social etiology. Pasternatskii provided a similarly detailed sketch of the process by which alcohol abuse commenced as a way to forget one's material circumstances but then led to mental aberrations and suicide attempts. In his conclusion, he stressed that only a minority of suicides could be considered mentally and physically healthy. While his focus on poverty was characteristic of the period, he introduced a new factor to the study of suicide in Russia and thereby anticipated the next generation of Russian psychiatric thought. Though defining suicide as a social problem, accessible through statistics, he attempted to assess how experience (and social anomalies) can impact the exercise of individual will (*volia*), which he conceived as an organic faculty of mind.

Alongside the definition of suicide as a social problem was thus its conceptualization as a medical problem, and the two paradigms often overlapped. While doctors typically looked to the individual's mind and body in their attempt to explain individual cases and occasionally diagnosed suicide as purely physiological in origin, they often acknowledged the possibility of an underlying environmental or experiential causality.[30] The primary issue for them was simply its physiological mechanism. Although scholarly treatments of the problem were still rare in the 1860s and 1870s, social and medical perspectives would fuse over the next two decades into a disturbing new theory that empowered doctors to diagnose and treat the diseases of civilization but also transformed these diseases into a potential threat to civilization's very survival.

Civilization and the struggle for existence

In 1879, the Italian psychiatrist and statistician Enrico Morselli published a book-length study of suicide that proved immensely influential throughout

---

[29] Pasternatskii, "Statisticheskoe issledovanie," no. 41, 415–16. On Pasternatskii, see Cathy Popkin, "Hysterical Episodes: Case Histories and Silent Subjects," in *Self and Story in Russian History*, ed. Laura Engelstein and Stephanie Sandler (Ithaca, N.Y., 2000), 193.

[30] In 1889, professor of forensic medicine at Kazan University, Ivan Gvozdev, would still insist that all suicides must be preceded by physiological changes in the brain, only at the molecular level. But his insistence on a purely physiological explanation was unusual. See Ivan Gvozdev, *O samoubiistve s sotsial'noi i meditsinskoi tochki zreniia* (Kazan, 1889).

Europe. Though it has since fallen into obscurity, Morselli's study was quickly translated into English and German and extensively reviewed in the Russian press.[31] Influenced by Social Darwinism and neo-Malthusianism, Morselli combined a statistical method with biological models. Arguing that suicide rates increased according to levels of civilization, which he defined as "the idea of progress, similar to that called Darwinian evolution," he asserted that suicide was a result of the struggle for existence and natural selection both within populations and between races. In his conclusion on therapeutics, he noted that a "sad law of necessity" made madness, poverty, crime, and suicide into the outlets for the weak, which was "as inevitable as it [was] advantageous to the material well-being of the surviving." Morselli's only significant remedy for suicide lay in social prophylactics: the proper education of the will, he believed, would "give force and energy to the moral character."[32] While many others had already noted the rising rates of suicide in nineteenth-century Europe and their connection to civilization, Morselli's Darwinist metaphors marked an important shift. Neither nostalgic for traditional worlds nor especially interested in social reform, Morselli argued that human evolution had its unavoidable costs. Suicide was normalized.

Perhaps the greatest compliment to Morselli was paid by the Russian statistician A. V. Likhachev, who, adding data on European Russia, wholeheartedly took over his method, structure, and language in a book published three years later. Yet Likhachev diverged from Morselli's Darwinist argument in one important way. Absent was Morselli's extended conclusion with its praise of Malthus and nonchalant acceptance of natural selection. Instead, Likhachev vaguely affirmed that the "correct understanding of moral statistics gives clear hope for the improvement of human life." The answer lay not in the reinforcement of religious norms or legal punishments, he emphasized, but in the efforts of political economists and jurists to improve social life, especially the economy. His reticence on this point presents a marked contrast to his enthusiasm in paraphrasing other parts of Morselli's text.[33]

Even positive reviews of Morselli suggest that Likhachev's response was not unusual. The Russian reading was initially quite selective. Only his statistics met with almost universal praise. Rejecting Morselli's therapeutics outright, one

---

[31] E. Morselli, *Il Suicidio* (Milan, 1879). For the English translation, see Henry Morselli, *Suicide: An Essay on Comparative Moral Statistics* (London, 1881); I cite the American translation which appeared the following year (New York, 1882) under the same title. On the reception of Morselli in England, see Gates, *Victorian Suicide*, 18–22. In addition to reviews discussed below, see N. Z. "Statistika samoubiistv," *Iuridicheskii vestnik* no. 9 (1880); and "Smes'," *Ogonek* no. 22 (1880).

[32] Morselli, *Suicide*, 115, 367, 374.

[33] While Likhachev's brief conclusion (*Samoubiistvo*, 167–71) differs from Morselli's extended one (*Suicide*, 353–74), their sections on the forward evolution of human civilization are almost identical (Likhachev, 66–69; and Morselli, 115–19).

reviewer argued that his prophylactic focus on moral education was hardly a sufficient measure in light of the unequal chances afforded by the contemporary organization of society. Social reform – particularly with regard to pauperism and the proletariat – would equilibrate the struggle.[34] Another, citing Darwin's own reluctance to apply his theories to human society, criticized Morselli's willingness to dismiss suicides (alongside those suffering from disease, mental illness, and poverty) as the unfit. The therapeutics were again quite different: it was necessary to make a better society, governed not by egoism and antagonism but by mutual aid, solidarity, love, and cooperation.[35] Those who rejected the Darwinist model out of hand generally pointed as well to contemporary economic organization. The problem was not "true civilization" but rather the "contemporary condition of civilization," that is, capitalism, which was causing the disintegration of communal principles and the rise of egoism and "rule of the fist" (*kulachestvo*).[36] In effect, these reviewers understood civilization as the two faces of Janus, with capitalism embodying its costs, science its benefits. Statistics identified the diseases – suicide, poverty, social inequality, crime, drunkenness; the therapeutics lay in social, economic, and (implicitly) political reform.

The initial reception of Morselli in Russia conforms in large part to the reception of Darwinism in the scientific community. As Daniel Todes has shown, Russian scientists were often quite enthusiastic about Darwin's theory of evolution, but his metaphors of struggle and competition as well as his explicit reliance on Malthus inspired criticism and revision. Influenced by Russian political conditions, social thought, and geography, they discounted intra-specific competition in favor of man's struggle with the environment and explored alternative views of social interaction based on such principles as harmony, solidarity, and mutual aid.[37] In the eyes of many conservative and populist thinkers, moreover, the Russian nation (especially the peasantry) embodied communal values – in contrast to Western European egoism, materialism, and rationalism. Since the eighteenth century, suicide, too, had been understood within this framework, and statistics seemed to confirm the truisms. Urban areas and the Western borderlands seemed to possess high suicide rates, and the rural heartlands low rates.

An important shift occurred in the 1880s, however, when a new social-psychiatric model began its rise to prominence in Russia and helped to

[34] E. Likhacheva, "O samoubiistve," *Otechestvennye zapiski* no. 7 (1881), 51–53.
[35] B. S. "O samoubiistve v tsivilizovannykh stranakh," *Russkoe bogatstvo* no. 10 (1885), 48, 51.
[36] See the review of Likhachev in *Otechestvennye zapiski* no. 7 (1882), 129–34. K. Lisin likewise identifies capitalism and the rise of social inequality (rather than poverty or struggle per se) as the chief cause of suicide. See "Samoubiistvo i tsivilizatsiia," *Delo* no. 7 (1882).
[37] See Daniel P. Todes, *Darwin without Malthus: The Struggle for Existence in Russian Evolutionary Thought* (New York, 1989). Alexander Vucinich also points to the weakness of Social Darwinism in Russia. See his *Darwin in Russian Thought* (Berkeley, 1988).

naturalize Morselli's Darwinism. The first effort was published in 1880 by N. V. Ponomarev, who read statistics through the visor of psychiatry. Though he did not paraphrase Morselli, Ponomarev cited him along with other prominent psychiatrists, including Wilhelm Greisinger and Richard von Krafft-Ebing. Having summarized the statistical data in some detail, he posed the crucial question in italics: How does the progress of civilization influence suicide? His exposition was succinct. The rates of both suicide and insanity were rising in civilized societies, he argued, and these two phenomena were connected. "Our era is distinguished by great intellectual and economic upheavals. From this follows the unavoidable intensification of mental activity and the appearance of new, formerly unknown inclinations and passions. In addition, the intensification of commercial and industrial crises, the feverish pursuit of wealth and pleasures, the failures to achieve the latter goals – that's what leads to insanity and suicide." Unlike some earlier proponents of a medical explanation, Ponomarev did not view suicide as a form or product of insanity, nor did he locate its causes within the body, though he did posit a physiological dynamic. Instead, he argued that civilization – industrialization, urbanization, the spread of education – increased the "general irritation of the brain" (obshchee razdrazhenie mozga) which led in turn to extreme affective impulses, mental illnesses, and suicide.[38]

The idea that civilization acts on the brain and nervous system soon became a commonplace in Russia. As Vladimir Mikhnevich observed in a popular study (evocatively entitled The Ulcers of St. Petersburg): "Though the development of civilization brings humanity tremendous benefits, it also excessively stimulates egoistical strivings, the thirst for gain and pleasure, the pursuit of luxury and novelty. All of these factors beget a mass of unsatisfied and unhappy people, with disordered nerves and broken health."[39] By 1901, after a decade of sustained industrialization and urbanization, the statistician E. N. Tarnovskii located the etiology of suicide in the modern economy and urban life more generally, and he emphasized the impact of environment upon the body:

We refer to the economic evolution of contemporary Europe, with the growth of large cities, the extreme development of industrialism and the consequent decline in farming, intense competition and periodic crises, which all lead to nervous overstrain and exhaustion [and] to the development of mental illness. Various kinds of mental illness and suicide are closely related and emerging from one and the same causes. The extremity of a purely urban civilization with its feverish and at the same time not fully regular

---

[38] N. V. Ponomarev, "Samoubiistvo v zapadnoi Evrope i v Rossii v sviazi s razvitiem umopomeshatel'stva," SSSM no. 3 (1880), esp. 107–8, 112–14. Compare the earlier approach of P. M. Ol'khin, who compiled medical case studies out of Western sources. See his O samoubiistve v meditsinskom otnoshenii (SPb, 1859), 5–6. For a second edition: Poslednie dni samoubiits (SPb, 1863).

[39] V. Mikhnevich, Iazvy Peterburga: Opyt istoriko-statisticheskogo issledovaniia nravstevennosti stolichnogo naseleniia (SPb, 1888), 536, 539.

and secure labor, with the mass of the working population's unhealthy life, with the development of individualism, petty, self-loving egoism and vanity – all of this constructs that stifling atmosphere, in which a sick and unbearable condition of the spirit ripens, leading man to take his own life.[40]

As had been the case with Karl Herrmann in the 1830s, several key metaphors provided the link between civilization and suicide: nervous disorders and disease grow out of the "disorder" of modern life, its "extremity," "feverish" character, "unhealthy" living conditions, and "stifling atmosphere." Furthermore, patriarchal traditions still conferred a kind of protection – a view often made explicit in explanations of the lower incidence of suicide among women and peasants. Long-established metaphors were thus expanding to include new meanings.

Concern about fatigue and exhaustion was endemic in nineteenth-century Europe, and they were often constituted as intrinsically modern, the result of economic development and the changing demands of work. This condition debilitated not just the body but also the soul. Fatigue was thought to engender feelings of inertia, apathy, and ennui. In other words, the socio-medical concern build upon earlier associations: the vice of acedia, the malady of melancholy, and the suicide of boredom and *taedium vitae*. Many of these concerns, associations, and metaphors would coalesce into the disease of neurasthenia. First popularized by the New York physician George Beard in the 1860s, the diagnosis became ubiquitous in Western Europe by the 1880s and from there entered Russia as well. Its sudden popularity reflected its capacity to articulate the experiences of modernity, especially its speed, transience, and instability. Indeed, its symptoms included unstable emotions, weakened willpower, and unbridled subjectivism and egoism. By the twentieth century, the diagnosis of neurasthenia in cases of suicide would become extremely common in Russia, but the problem was already identified by the 1890s.[41]

Not just the experience of modern life but also hereditary factors could cause neurasthenia. This apparent paradox lay at the heart of a powerful new theory which was influencing medicine, the social sciences, and criminology. Since the publication of B. A. Morel's *Traité des dégénérescences* in 1857, the theory of degeneration had become increasing influential in Europe. Its explanatory power lay precisely in its conflation of historical, social, and biological processes. According to Morel, adaptation to a pathological environment resulted in pathological changes in an organism, which could in turn be passed on to future generations. Over time, a pathological tendency could consequently

---

[40] E. N. Tarnovskii, "Statistika samoubiistva," *Zhurnal Ministerstva iustitsii* no. 1 (1901), 145–46.

[41] In addition to Nye (*Crime, Madness, and Politics*), see Anson Rabinbach, *The Human Motor: Energy, Fatigue, and the Origins of Modernity* (New York, 1990), esp. 19–44, 153–63. On neurasthenia within Russia's educated classes, see P. G. Rozanov, *O samoubiistve* (Moscow, 1891), 78–79.

lead to physical and nervous disorders within the population. Subsequent theorists, including Morselli, built upon this basic model, with some focusing on the typology of visible pathologies (attempting to measure pathological changes on the body) and others of mental and moral ones, whose symptoms could include insanity, hysteria, suicide, crime, alcoholism, and other forms of deviance. While a handful of theorists, such as Cesare Lombroso, propagandized biological determinism, most continued to allow a prominent role for social influences.[42]

The theory of degeneration typically combined a notion of the inheritance of acquired characteristics (associated with neo-Lamarckian currents) with the Darwinist concepts of struggle, competition, and selection. Indeed, many theorists mixed their metaphors. Morselli's notion of natural selection, for example, defined the struggle for existence in civilized societies as a struggle of intelligence, that is, of the mind. Defeat and suffering could therefore lead to a "perversion of cerebral faculties" and "morbid aberrations" as well as physical infirmity and disease. This process would shape the future of European civilization, though opinion was divided on the primary trend – progress or decline. On the one hand, natural selection could eliminate the unfit and thereby contribute to the improvement of the species. On the other hand, however, the weak and deformed could transmit disadvantageous or useless characteristics and thereby undermine the species.[43] By the 1890s, these premises – with their fundamental ambiguity – informed all scientific treatises on suicide in Russia. As one staff doctor (*ordinator*) in a St. Petersburg military hospital noted in his 1897 study of suicide: "Heredity, psychological instability, degeneration, [all of] which we hardly noticed before, are now universally recognized [*priobreli uzhe prava grazhdanstva*]."[44]

Among the early exponents of degeneration theory in Russia was the Kharkov professor of psychiatry Pavel Kovalevskii, whose textbooks on general and forensic psychopathology were extremely influential. His 1886 exposition of the etiology of psychosis began with the etiology of the psychotic, neurotic, or degenerate personality – the foundation on which psychosis grew. In the beginning, therefore, was heredity: the "neural material" inherited from one's parents. Healthy, honest, and sober people produced offspring with a strong nervous organization in contrast to parents who were psychopaths, drunkards, criminals, or syphilitics. The implications of this process – and Kovalevskii's

---

[42] See Nye, *Crime, Madness, and Politics*; Pick, *Faces of Degeneration*; and Beer, "Renovating Russia."

[43] Morselli, *Suicide*, 358, 361–62.

[44] Il'ia Lebedev, *O samoubiistve s meditsinskoi tochki zreniia* (SPb, 1897), 4. His earlier monograph refers to heredity but does not show the strong influence of degeneration theory. *O samoubiistve v normal'nom i boleznennom sostoianii* (SPb, 1888). For further discussion of degeneration in Russia, see Beer, *Renovating Russia*; and Engelstein, *The Keys to Happiness*, 128–52.

deep-seated fears that psychosis threatened the entire social order – were illustrated by a diagram entitled "The Consanguinity of the First Generation." It showed the progressive decline in a family over five generations, resulting in one suicide, one attempted suicide, as well as cases of hysteria, insanity, and other abnormalities. Kovalevskii was not a biological determinist, however. Even healthy nervous systems – particularly among youth – could be perverted by upbringing, unhealthy influences, and social environment.[45]

Though largely rejected in the late 1870s and early 1880s, the metaphor "struggle for existence" soon became a cliché. At first its use was consistent with earlier approaches. Kovalevskii thus identified a true civilization, which he defined as the "light of knowledge" leading to scientific and material progress that actually reduced the struggle for survival. The existence of pauperism and other "anomalies" meant that civilization was not yet complete.[46] In a statistical study of suicide in Odessa, Dr. I. S. Fal'kner referred to the "abnormal conditions of life, which push man to act in contradiction to the basic attributes of his nature" and likened the "struggle for existence" to the "soil [*pochva*] on which suicide grows." Like Kovalevskii, he underlined the abnormality of struggle. By blaming current living conditions in Odessa, which, by implication, could be influenced, he shared some of the hope of the earlier statisticians who had believed that diagnosis was a sure step toward cure. However, he also gave a passing nod to biology: the struggle either "develops the mind of man" or weakens the nervous system, producing three groups of "victims": suicides, mentally ill, and drunkards.[47]

Just over a decade later, other doctors were using the metaphor in much more radical ways. I. O. Zubov of the Institute of Forensic Medicine at Iurev University opened his extended article on suicide with some general considerations on the nature and course of human life:

It is impossible not to recognize that life in fact has more suffering than pleasure. The wealth of one arises at the expense of the suffering of the masses; each forward step of civilization manufactures new detachments [*otriady*] of neurasthenics, neuropaths, [and] psychopaths [. . .] Even the successes of human thought, its discoveries in all areas of knowledge [. . .] are not for the general good but for the good of the few. And this entire social pathology is created by the struggle for the right to exist. This implacable law is not only the creator [*sozidatel'*] but the destroyer; he does not have mercy on anyone, and only one who for some reason is strong enough for this struggle can live with him on earth. [. . .] And these negative sides of life lead many to physical and mental

[45] P. I. Kovalevskii, *Obshchaia psikhopatologiia* (Kharkov, 1886), esp. 176, 201.

[46] Ibid., 180–82. For a later exposition, which demonstrates much more unease about modern civilization, see his *Sudebnaia psikhopatologiia* (SPb, 1900).

[47] He did not expand on this point. I. S. Fal'kner, *Samoubiistva v Odesse (Statisticheskii ocherk)* (Odessa, 1890), 5–8, 37–39.

degeneration. Finally, the last act in the life drama of these unhappy people sometimes involves the dulling of the strongest stimulus to life – the instinct for self preservation, and they end in suicide.[48]

For Zubov, suicide was pathological from an individual-biological perspective, but normal under the inexorable law of struggle, and he moved easily between medical and statistical models. Both his methods and his equanimity were shared by many colleagues. Analyzing the statistics of suicide in St. Petersburg between 1881 and 1900, Fedor Terekhovko likewise linked the struggle for survival to the exercise and evolution of the mind. Echoing Morselli, he too found it "natural" that the weak and defeated could develop a "diseased functioning of the brain." In his view, this process constituted the motive force of civilization: "It is apparent from all of this that a social illness (nedug) like suicide, just like poverty, prostitution, crime, disease, and insanity, is not an accidental phenomenon; to the contrary, it is a consequence of that law of evolution, to which all living beings are subordinated and the goal of which for people is the achievement of that physical and mental prosperity, for which nature unconsciously works."[49] Though relying more on case studies than statistics, Dr. I. M. Raikher also agreed: "The consequence or physical inevitability of evolution is the victory of the strong over the weak, the survival of the better armed and the extinction of the degenerates [vymiranie vyrozhdaiushchikhsia]."[50]

By combining Darwinist metaphors with the theory of degeneration, these specialists produced a new, more unsettling vision of the social environment. As part of the struggle for survival, social problems (and their human victims) were normalized as the by-product of progress. To be sure, specialists also admitted their concern that the nature of the struggle was itself debased, that sociomedical conditions were also producing victims from among the healthy not just degenerate population. While this concern would grow markedly over the first decade of the twentieth century, the willingness to accept the inevitable costs of progress is striking. A parallel view existed within Russian Marxism of the era. Though no direct influence is apparent, both implicitly allowed a sacrifice of today in the name of a better tomorrow. Believing that the industrialization drive of the 1890s marked the onset of capitalism in Russia and thereby a necessary step of historical development on the path toward socialism, some

---

[48] I. O. Zubov, "Samoubiistvo v Lifliandskoi gubernii (Mediko-statisticheskii ocherk)," *VOGSPM* nos. 5, 6 (1902), no. 5, 692–93. He also explained the lower number of female suicides by women's lesser exposure to the "struggle for existence." (See no. 5, 717)

[49] F. K. Terekhovko, "K voprosu o samoubiistve v S.-Peterburge v dvadtsatiletnyi period (1881–1900)," Dissertation for the degree of Doctor of Medicine (Gatchina, 1903), 270–71.

[50] He was a staff doctor at the Vilnius District Hospital. See I. M. Raikher, "K voprosu o samoubiistve. Mediko-psikhologicheskii ocherk," *Nauchnyi arkhiv Vilenskoi okruzhnoi lechebnitsy* no. 1/2 (1904), 198.

Marxists celebrated the terrible hardships experienced by workers and peasants as evidence of progress, as the precondition for the emergence of revolutionary consciousness among the proletariat. Such faith in the immutable laws of society and history left little room for questions of ethics.[51]

Pathologies of the self

Alongside the new vision of modern society was also a new vision of the person, shaped in a complex interaction by physiology, heredity, upbringing, and environment. Scholarly interest now turned to questions neglected by earlier experts: How does the social inscribe itself upon the biological? Why do some people kill themselves while others do not? One important reason for this new focus was the emergence of psychiatry as a medical specialization in Russia. In the 1880s and 1890s, the number of professional journals, university positions, and private psychiatric clinics grew significantly. Despite the low levels of funding and atmosphere of mistrust with the government, Russia's psychiatrists were asserting their own spheres of competence in diagnostics.[52] In accordance with their professional training, they focused much of their attention on the organic and psychic dimensions of suicide and were well versed in European scholarship. However, they displayed markedly little interest in biological determinism, and their ongoing concern about the social and historical sources of pathology underlined their long-term goals: social prophylactics.

Though accepting that many causes for suicide lay outside the individual, specialists looked for the mechanism of activation within the body. This seemed obvious in those suicides directly linked to mental illness and even drunkenness, but statistics consistently showed that such cases made up no more than half of the total. To explain the other half, they focused on the problem of *affekt*, the psychic impulse (even temporary insanity) associated with strong emotions but possessing a physiological dynamic: it altered mental and nervous reactions, including the "nourishment of the brain" (*pitanie mozga*). This condition, it was believed, provided the basis for most suicides committed for unknown or everyday reasons – unhappiness in love, business failures, shame, fear of punishment, and so forth.[53] This concept built in part on the well-established theory of moral insanity, which distinguished morbid perversions of morality, feelings, and natural inclinations from disorders of the intellect or reason. In his

[51] These and related issues are discussed in Catherine Evtuhov, *The Cross and the Sickle: Sergei Bulgakov and the Fate of Russian Religious Philosophy, 1890–1920* (Ithaca, N.Y., 1997), ch. 2; and Leszek Kolakowski, *Main Currents of Marxism* (Oxford, 1978), vol. 2, chs. 14–15. See also Richard Wortman, *The Crisis of Russian Populism* (Cambridge, 1967).

[52] See Julie Brown, "The Professionalization of Russian Psychiatry: 1857–1922" (Ph.D. Diss., University of Pennsylvania, 1981). See also Martin Miller, *Freud and the Bolsheviks: Psychoanalysis in Imperial Russia and the Soviet Union* (New Haven, 1998), ch. 1.

[53] For a detailed discussion, see Rozanov, *O samoubiistve*, 55–59.

Pathology of Mind (1879), the British specialist Henry Maudsley had argued, for example, that the "disordered state of the nerve element" could lead to "insane impulses, whether mischievous, erotic, homicidal, or suicidal."[54]

As many doctors noted, however, everybody experienced an *affekt* at one time or another, but only a small minority of people tried to kill themselves. The theory of degeneration helped to explain this anomaly. While healthy people did kill themselves, doctors agreed, such cases were rare. Strong and self-possessed enough to counteract an emotional impulse, they only chose death following logical and rational deliberation. In contrast, the weak or the sick could easily succumb. While some exhibited no prior symptoms, the "predispositions" and "tendencies" conferred by heredity, environment, and experience often expressed themselves not just in suicide, but also in nervous disorders, physical infirmities, crime, drunkenness, and vice.[55] This type was given various scientific designations: a neuropathic, psychopathic, or psychopathological constitution. (More colloquial expressions included "defective natures" and "weeds.")[56] These terms were used more or less interchangeably in the study of suicide, for mental (psychopathic) and nervous (neuropathic) disorders were not sharply distinguished. Instead, the convention was to divide suicides into three basic categories: the mentally ill; the degenerates, psychopaths, neuropaths, and pathological natures; and accidental or healthy ones.[57] Scholarly interest in the first category was negligible, for the suicide was simply a symptom of the (more important) psychosis.[58] While so-called healthy suicides received more consideration, the second category became the focal point of attention. Indeed, the metaphor of the late 1860s was reworked. The "auspicious soil" (*blagopriiatnaia pochva*) of suicide, Zubov maintained, was neither socio-material conditions nor the depth of physical suffering; it was now the "unstable psychic constitution."[59]

The point was not, however, to deny the role of social environment but to locate its manifestations within the body. Poverty thus continued to be viewed

---

[54] As quoted in Gates, *Victorian Suicide*, 17.

[55] See Terekhovko, "K voprosu," 27–28, 30, 238, 243; Zubov, "Samoubiistvo v Lifliandskoi gubernii," no. 5, 705, no. 6, 825; N. Mukhin, "Ocherk psikhologii samoubiistva," *Varshavskie universitetskie izvestiia* nos. 2–5 (1903): no. 3, 20–24, no. 5, 59–69.

[56] See N. A. Obolonskii, "Samoubiistvo v g. Kieve," *VNPM* nos. 1, 3 (1902), no. 3, 477; and Zubov, approvingly quoting Oettingen, "Samoubiistvo v Lifliandskoi gubernii," no. 5, 698.

[57] See the case study by A. B. Sobolevskii, "Redki sluchai istericheskikh sudorog ('piaiaska zhivota') s samoubiistvom bol'nogo," *VNPM* no. 4 (1903), 582.

[58] The one significant exception is Lebedev (1897) who presents twenty-six case studies of patients treated in his hospital. Each study was prefaced with a diagnosis (mania, paranoia, melancholy, dementia, etc.)

[59] This metaphor was very common. In addition to Zubov ("Samoubiistvo v Lifliandskoi gubernii," no. 5, 700), see Terekhovko, "K voprosu," 28; and A. N. Ostrogorskii, "Samoubiistva, kak psikhologicheskaia problema," *Pedagogicheskii sbornik* no. 2 (1893), 137. Compare this to the reform era (Paperno, *Suicide*, 86–88), when the metaphoric meaning of *pochva* played on the material environment.

as an important cause of suicide. According to Terekhovko, it provided three main paths toward suicide: poor nutrition and heavy labor could weaken the physical organism, leading to organic disorders in the brain and nervous system; in a psychopathic constitution, the perception or experience of poverty could cause an affective impulse; and, in a few cases, logical deliberation about one's material condition could end in a rational decision to take one's life.[60] The psychiatrist Ivan Sikorskii instead emphasized the conjoined psychological and physiological phenomenon of exhaustion (*utomlenie*), which could be caused by poverty, disease, or difficult moral conditions and which ultimately dulled man's instinct for self-preservation.[61] Given their interest in pathology, it is perhaps reasonable that few of these doctors devoted much attention to the healthy suicide, but most noted that a small number of cases belonged to this category. When they did discuss this phenomenon, moreover, it was often in the context of poverty, and this once again highlights the underlying interest in social prophylactics. Sometimes the language even evoked the reformist rhetoric of earlier years. Calling poverty a "social anomaly," the psychiatrist N. Mukhin argued that it extracted numerous suicides from the healthy and not just the neuropathic population. For him, as for Sikorskii and others, the defining factor in a healthy suicide was its cold, harsh rationality; it was the outcome of logical calculation, not emotional *affekt*, when circumstances had become pathological and allowed no other exit.[62] This concept built on well-established medical opinion that sanity was a function of self-control and will-power. Indeed, the regulation of imagination, emotions, and appetite by the rational mind had long been considered necessary for healthy morals.[63]

The threat to reason and will, doctors agreed, was exemplified most clearly by drunkenness, which, like suicide, was both a social disease and an organic disorder. It weakened the nervous system, affected the functioning of the brain, and formed both a cause and a symptom of degeneration. The role of drunkenness in suicide was thus twofold. It was a parallel phenomenon – both were possible symptoms of a neuropathic condition or degeneration. But it was also a direct cause. As Mukhin argued, drunkenness acted on the moral feeling (*nravstven-noe chuvstvo*), leading to egoism, the neglect of the family, and the decline into

60 Terekhovko, "K voprosu," 236–42.
61 I. A. Sikorskii, "Sostoianie dukha pred samoubiistvom," *Sbornik nauchno-literaturnykh statei po voprosam obshchestvennoi psikhologii, vospitaniia, i nervno-psikhicheskoi gigieny*, 5 vols. (Kiev, 1899–1900), vol. 1, 136–37; and his "Samoubiistvo sredi russkikh vrachei," *VNPM* no. 1/2 (1896).
62 Mukhin, "Ocherk psikhologii," 63–65. Sikorskii, "Sostoianie dukha," 137, 164.
63 Michael J. Clark, "'Morbid Introspection', Unsoundness of Mind, and British Psychological Medicine, c. 1830–c. 1900," *The Anatomy of Madness: Essays in the History of Psychiatry* 3 vols. (London, 1985–88), ed., W. F. Bynum, Roy Porter, and Michael Shepherd, here vol. 3, 74–78.

a life of vice in general.[64] Terekhovko agreed, calling drunkenness the "greatest *porok*," a term which aptly combined vice with disease.[65] Such formulations reflected one of the most influential aspects of the theory of degeneration: it provided an explanation not only for medical pathologies but also for moral ones. Persistent engagement in immoral behavior (including drunkenness) was one of the central signs of a degenerate personality, for morality – the ability to resist temptation – was an expression of will, and willpower one of the first casualties of degeneration.[66] This conflated moral-social-medical problem was most acute in urban centers, as Terekhovko summarized:

Residents of the capital see before themselves a mass of various temptations, and they sooner develop a thirst for all kinds of pleasures, which, with the desire and the means, can be satisfied without hindrance. All of these pleasures usually entail over-indulgences that are physically and morally harmful. In addition, the obsession [for pleasures] can engender laziness, thoughtlessness, a love for luxury, a passion for both carousing and gambling, crime, and, as a consequence, poverty, discontent, disappointment, drunkenness, and suicide.[67]

If drunkenness (leading to the degeneration of will, immorality, and suicide) was thought to be prevalent among the lower classes, the most important factor within educated society was upbringing. Deficiencies at home and school were weakening the younger generation physically, mentally, and morally. Unable "to struggle with life," young people were killing themselves in an *affekt* caused by such trifling setbacks as poor marks at school or disappointment in love. Suicides among young people fascinated the medical community in part because they seemed counter-intuitive: how could someone choose to die before having truly begun to live? Specialists speculated extensively about the natural – and diseased – qualities of childhood and youth. Hereditary degeneration (linked to parental syphilis), an improper upbringing, and "abnormal" conditions of development could all encourage "mental immaturity," "an unsteadiness of emotional mood," and nervous exhaustion. Impressionability, for example, was metaphorically linked to children's still "unformed brains," but it could also take a more extreme, pathological form. "Diseased self-esteem" (*boleznennoe samoliubie*) thus developed when an individual had not learned to assess his own strengths and weaknesses objectively and rationally. Healthy individualism could consequently degenerate into an unhealthy egoism and an exaggerated "feeling of honor," and such individuals could not handle even minor setbacks or failures. The period of sexual maturation was particularly hazardous, for

---

[64] Mukhin, "Ocherk psikhologii," 36–40. Almost every work cited in this section discusses drunkenness.

[65] Terekhovko, "K voprosu," 209–22.   [66] For further discussion, see Beer, *Renovating Russia*.

[67] Terekhovko, "K voprosu," 218.

"early sexual corruption" – even dances and theater – introduced children to emotions and sensations that they could not control.[68] This portrait of childhood and youth was highly unstable, for the "natural" qualities of childhood could easily become diseased, often with tragic results. In casting a range of character traits as pathological, the language of modern medicine thereby rendered them subject to medical intervention.

These issues framed the preoccupation of doctors and psychiatrists with the problem of the will. When Russia's educated society had first confronted this issue in the 1860s and 1870s, a battle had raged between the positivist view of man (as determined by external social laws revealed in statistics) and the Christian view of man (as responsible for his sins before God and hence defined through the exercise of free will).[69] While the debate between science and religion persisted into the early twentieth century, the terms of the medical debate had shifted. With the notable exception of Sikorskii, doctors and psychiatrists continued to downplay the role of free will in suicide, but they now made the will itself into the object of medical investigation. As an organic faculty of mind, it could atrophy, degenerate, and weaken under certain social and biological circumstances.[70]

In discussing causality, therefore, doctors often stressed an involuntary dynamic, with some even describing suicide as a kind of physiological "reflex." While this mechanism had always been associated with cases directly related to illness, this principle (though not the designation of mental illness) could now apply to the neuropathic constitution, "inborn deficiencies," physical ailments, heredity, and even the diseased pursuit of pleasure and vice. Agency lay within the physiological processes of the body (even if it was itself shaped by social factors). One extreme example was Zubov's explanation of the suicide of a peasant who had been suffering from a stomach ulcer: "the cellules [*kletochki*] of the organism call out for liberation from this pain, and this liberation brings forth suicide."[71] By "organism" he meant of course the man.[72]

---

[68] See Ostrogorskii, "Samoubiistvo. Povody k nim," *Pedagogicheskii sbornik* no. 7 (1893), 14–23 and no. 8, 110–16. See also Zubov, "Samoubiistvo v Lifliandskoi gubernii," no. 5, 717–19; Lebedev, *O samoubiistve*, esp. 9–15, 36–39; Terekhovko, "K voprosu," 60–72.

[69] As Paperno has shown (*Suicide*, 67–69, 144–45), this issue informed Dostoevsky's exploration of the individual consequences of positivism and atheism: "a malignant hypertrophy of individual volition" and suicide.

[70] An early example is Pasternatskii ("Statisticheskoe issledovanie") who defines will as the sphere where society and circumstances operate on the person.

[71] Zubov, "Samoubiistvo v Lifliandskoi gubernii," no. 5, 699–700.

[72] An article in a popular weekly newspaper elaborated on this biological process: "In the struggle for survival the organism must constantly fight for its right to exist, and so long as the will is energetic [and] steadfast, the organism easily endures this struggle. But misfortune, should the will weaken. [. . .] Nerve cells end [their] obedience to the central organ of consciousness; the entire mass of atoms, temporarily submitting to the individual organism, attempts to disperse, to flow into the remaining ocean of matter and to return man to that dust from which he sprang to existence." See N. E. "Vrachi-samoubiitsy," *Nedelia* no. 22 (1896), 699.

This repudiation of human agency meant that most case studies of suicide were quite reductive, as Dr. Lebedev's rereading of two famous literary representations illustrates. "What is Werther?" he thus asked. "In our opinion, it is a man with an unstable, neuropathic character, lacking firm principles in life [and] a firmly recognized goal of existence, a man who lives according to the impressions of the moment [and] who is unable to govern his feelings." After analyzing Werther's decline toward suicide, Lebedev turned his attention to modern Russia: "In current times, such a depressing idea is only characteristic of neuropaths with an unstable nervous system and sometimes with degenerate symptoms in the organism. One meets such people as Werther today, they pass as abnormal, unbalanced personalities." As illustration, he recounted the case of an educated young man, who possessed a neuropathic character, a weak physical build, inflated self-esteem, an inability to laugh at himself, and a family history of nervous illness. The fatal act then occurred when he tried to court the wife of a friend but was rejected by her. "The character of the suicide was exactly the same as Werther's," Lebedev concluded, only with a more pronounced neuropathic condition. His second example was Anna Karenina. Her submission to passion followed by her use of opium, which poisoned her nervous system, put her once healthy "organism onto a pathological, neuropathic basis [*pochva*]." Asserting that there were "masses of analogous examples," he recounted the case of a widow with hereditary tendencies toward nervous illness. His literary allusions only underscored his reductive medical discourse, in which suicide became an expression of pathology. Apparently the widow had suffered "inconsequential familial displeasures," including a separation from her family (though apparently no love affair or drug addiction). While Tolstoy had explored the personal and familial dynamics over several hundred pages, Lebedev's case study concentrated solely on her physical symptoms (extreme nervousness, sleeplessness, pulsations, and so forth), that had almost driven her to kill herself. Though mentioning that she had been aware of her illness and sought help independently (she had apparently consulted Father Ioann of Kronstadt), he denied her a voice in describing her own condition.[73] As Cathy Popkin has argued, case studies of hysteria likewise recited symptoms and neglected the story, a technique that affirmed the professional status of the doctor, who alone was qualified to make the diagnosis.[74]

This approach shaped the medical interpretation of suicide notes, which doctors used as windows into hidden mental and physical states.[75] Typically

---

[73] Lebedev, *O samoubiistve*, 3–10. Compare Mukhin, "Ocherk psikhologii," no. 5, 51. For further discussion of how psychiatrists analyzed literary exemplars (and the psychology of writers), see Irina Sirotkina, *Diagnosing Literary Genius: A Cultural History of Psychiatry in Russia* (Baltimore, Md., 2002).

[74] Popkin, "Hysterical Episodes."

[75] Following Likhachev's example in 1882, numerous experts appended suicide notes to their studies, and, unlike him, they quoted extensively from them. See e.g. Likhachev, *Samoubiistvo*,

dismissing the capacity of the victim to possess knowledge of the self, they asserted the primacy of their own diagnoses. Sometimes this perspective was taken to extremes, thereby rendering the professional voice arrogant. The confession of a 35-year-old woman that "it is well known that the life of a governess is so difficult" inspired the Moscow psychiatrist P. G. Rozanov to ruminate about the comparative ease of governesses in comparison to plough-men, stonemasons, and cab drivers. Clearly lacking "an objective assessment of her own condition," the woman had developed false ideas and fallen into melancholy. Rozanov's most impassioned comment occurred in response to a seemingly innocuous note whose author had refused to reveal his motive: "The note of a 28-year-old collegial secretary exudes such dignity and con-ceit that one would sooner attribute it to the head of a department than a notorious psychopath (a drunk and syphilitic to boot). To his credit, one must add by the way, he at least did not mislead suicide experts, [for he] categori-cally maintained that the 'reason for his suicide remains with me.'"[76] In other words, he would not have been able to articulate the true reasons, even had he tried.

A more sympathetic reader of suicide notes was Professor Sikorskii, perhaps because he considered the vast majority of suicides to have been "good people" who had endured a "difficult [life] drama." Nevertheless, he too asserted his professional readings as authoritative and translated the words of the suicide into the language of science. References to personal sorrows, experiences, fam-ily background and especially metaphors became the raw data needing to be reworked so that their true significance could be revealed. In one note from 1886, for example, a private tutor recounted his growing desperation and hunger: his lessons had dried up due to the poor economy, his mother was sick, his father was unemployed, his sister suffered (abuse?) from her husband, and his head hurt, his stomach churned, and his legs were refusing to work. Extracting one phrase, "for three months I have been searching for a quiet apartment but I cannot find one," Sikorskii made his diagnosis: "The letter [. . .] documents psychic exhaustion, called forth by a series of life failures and painful impres-sions." Sikorskii used the man's unfocused need for peace and quiet as evidence for his broader argument that exhaustion formed the primary cause of modern suicide.[77]

231–51; Rozanov, *O samoubiistve*, 143–49; Zubov, "Samoubiistvo v Lifliandskoi gubernii," no. 6, 830–31; and Obolonskii, "Samoubiistvo v g. Kieve," no. 1, 115–21.

[76] Rozanov, *O samoubiistve*, 116–21, 146. For a similar approach using letters as evidence of abnor-mality, see S. N. Iakovlev and P. F. Filatov, "Samoubiistva v Simbirskoi gubernii," *VOGSPM* nos. 1, 2 (1892), no. 1, 12–20.

[77] Sikorskii, "Sostoianie dukha," 136, 139, 143. See also the article published in the *Week* (N. E. "Vrachi-samoubiitsy," 699) which summarized for the mass reader: "The main cause of suicide is exhaustion, which dulls the feeling of self-preservation, weakens the will in its striving to support itself, and draws the organism toward tranquility in the lap of unconsciousness."

Not all case studies were thus as reductive as Lebedev's. Some doctors were beginning to craft fuller narratives of the suicidal subject, drawing upon suicide notes, biographical data, and modern medicine. A good example was Zubov's reading of the life of a teenage suicide. "In [his] letter, as in a mirror," he declared, "the entire pathology of suicide is boldly reflected." The diagnosis was terminal illness. *"The youth turns to suicide not because he does not want to but because he is not able to live any longer."* (Italics in original.) Building on the equation of death with tranquility (*spokoistvie*) used by the youth in his note, Zubov concluded that his nervous system had been so shattered, that the young man now yearned for peace and quiet:

From his relatively short biography it is clear that he was the son of a civil servant, lost his father early in life, and experienced the educational regime of his mother, who was weak of character and unable to direct the unquestionably neuropathic nature of her son onto the necessary path. Already while in primary school, our suicide suffered from strong headaches and extreme mood changes. He learned with difficulty and not satisfactorily, and he turned to the city's amusements at an early age. During his period at gymnasium, he abused sexual delights and finally suffered failure in his final examination. His neuropathic constitution drew him, perhaps irrepressibly drew him into this maelstrom of corrupt pleasure. [. . .] His degenerate brain suffers pain from a serious life, where it is necessary to labor, and consequently searches easy work – only amusement and pleasure. [. . .] In this way [. . .] the need for pleasure becomes a disease, which possesses the entire being of the man, making him its slave.[78]

The story began with the hereditary nature of the boy, continued with the breakdown of paternal rule – symbolized by the death of the father – and culminated in the weak "regime" of the mother, who failed to provide her son the necessary structure and discipline that (presumably) would have shielded him from the vices of the city and prevented his failures at school. The thirst for pleasure and novelty, which had been associated with the rise of civilization already for over a century, was then reworked into a nervous illness. The common metaphors linking death to sleep, a state of rest and peacefulness, were now evidence of neurasthenia, a condition marked by nervous exhaustion and fatigue. Modern psychiatric medicine had provided doctors not just with a new toolbox of diagnostic terms, but a powerful paradigm that could unite them into a coherent narrative.

A cure for suicide proved more difficult. Sikorskii believed that a respite from circumstances would help in many cases, even if this was often impossible for practical reasons, and he, like a handful of other psychiatrists, did consider individual therapy a useful option.[79] For others, however, the therapeutic options seemed more limited. Could hereditary predispositions and

[78] Zubov, "Samoubiistvo v Lifliandskoi gubernii," no. 5, 697–99.
[79] Sikorskii ("Sostoianie dukha," 156–57) recounted a successful case, and Raikher ("K voprosu," 198) likewise cited individual medical intervention.

neuropathic constitutions be treated? Alluding to the lessons of degeneration theory, Rozanov noted that "the suicide of our times is the consequence of the past."[80] Terekhovko agreed, emphasizing that the past – and its living legacy in degenerates – could not be changed: "It is clear that the measures to reduce this social evil must be preventative, not taken when the disease (*nedug*) has already developed in a person, when the idea about peace and self-destruction has already implanted itself into his tired brain."[81] For him, as for others, pro-phylactics referred not to the manifestation of the disease in an individual body but to its incidence in the social body. Consequently, it seemed imperative to make the next generation physically, mentally, and morally fit. In his con-clusion, Terekhovko recommended that measures should be taken "when the subject is not yet prepared for life, when it is still possible to direct the powers of his unformed character and reason into the desired path and to inculcate a healthy understanding, good spirits, love for his neighbors, and recognition of his duty."[82] A healthy family and the proper engagement of both society and the state, Professor N. A. Obolonskii likewise asserted, would produce "healthy fighters" who would be victors in the struggle for existence. This point was cru-cial because "social conditions do not allow for quick change."[83] This focus on moral education provides a striking contrast to the early 1880s when Morselli's reviewers had almost universally dismissed his similar calls to educate the will. Still, Russia's psychiatrists signaled their ongoing concern with suicide not only as a medical phenomenon but also as a social disease caused by such anoma-lies as poverty and drunkenness.[84] As one commentator affirmed, anything that "improves the health of society" (*sodeistvovat' ozdravleniiu obshchestva*) reduces the incidence of suicide.[85] And doctors now claimed the knowledge and the right to lead this mission.

Postscript: Durkheim and the diseases of modernity

In 1897, Emile Durkheim published his seminal work, *Le Suicide*, the founding study of modern statistical sociology.[86] By 1912, when it was translated into Russian, it would enjoy great prestige.[87] Initially, however,

---

[80] Rozanov, *O samoubiistve*, 136.   [81] Terekhovko, "K voprosu," 272.   [82] Ibid.

[83] He also called in passing for popular education as a means to give the people the necessary tools for the struggle. See Obolonskii, "Samoubiistvo v g. Kieve," no. 3, 477–78.

[84] On the social anomaly of poverty, see Mukhin, "Ocherk psikhologii," 63–65. Rozanov (*O samoubiistve*, 136–41) made many specific recommendations, including punitive, educa-tional, and medical measures against drunkenness and the founding of more psychiatric hospitals.

[85] A. N. Ostrogorskii, "Samoubiistva," *Pedagogicheskii sbornik* no. 10 (1893), 291.

[86] I have used the English translation: Emile Durkheim, *Suicide: A Study in Sociology* (New York, 1951).

[87] E. Diurkgeim, *Samoubiistvo: Sotsiologicheskii etiud* (SPb, 1912).

doctors read Durkheim through the visor of their own concerns, simply citing his study alongside many others. In a review of the scholarly literature, Obolonskii approvingly summarized many of Durkheim's specific findings but wholly neglected the core arguments. Like his peers, he blamed suicide on the struggle for survival in modern societies that caused degeneration and neurasthenia and recommended the standard measures to combat these pathologies.[88]

Durkheim did in fact share many of the categories and concepts of his medical colleagues, accepting, for example, that neurasthenia may predispose (though not cause) suicide. Denying any direct causal correlation of suicide with mental illness or alcoholism, however, he insisted that suicide be understood as a social not as a physiological phenomenon and concluded that modern societies suffered from inadequate social integration and solidarity. Yet Durkheim constantly evoked the unleashed appetites, passions, luxuries, and egos of a neurasthenic modernity and thereby included neurasthenia in the domain of sociology as well as psychiatry.[89] The reading of his work by Russia's psychiatrists was selective, therefore, but not wrong. They too merged the medical and social spheres, blurring the boundaries between the individual neurotic personality and the feverish unrest of modern civilization.

When Durkheim's work was reviewed in the Russian press, the critics drew different, if predictable conclusions. They greeted his diagnosis of social pathology with considerable enthusiasm and likewise agreed wholeheartedly on the need for social solidarity, which was a catchphrase within Russian populism and Marxism. Nevertheless, they rejected his therapeutics as wholly inadequate.[90] His references to the potentially integrating function of the social division of labor must have seemed alien to many Russian readers, especially in this period of rapid industrialization, urbanization, and growing social ferment. Indeed, many were beginning to sense the possibility of radical socio-economic and political change. Nevertheless, Durkheim's study helped to reinvigorate sociology, which, as one reviewer pointed out, was not even taught as a separate subject in Russia. What proved most attractive was Durkheim's organic vision of the social collective. Sociology was experiencing unprecedented success, this reviewer claimed, not only because it possessed a precise and exact

---

[88] N. A. Obolonskii, "Sovremennoe polozhenie voprosa o prichinakh samoubiistva," *RAPKMB* no. 1 (1902), 36–53.

[89] Many scholars have explored his reliance on metaphors drawn from medicine and biology as well as concepts of degeneration. On the centrality of neurasthenia to Durkheim's theory, see Nye, *Crime, Madness, and Politics*, 144–54. More generally, see Jack D. Douglas, *The Social Meanings of Suicide* (Princeton, 1967).

[90] See V. B-k, "Samoubiistva vo Frantsii (Pis'mo iz Parizha)," *Nedelia* no. 34 (1897), 1087–88; and N. K. "Samoubiistvo i ego prichiny," *Russkoe bogatstvo* no. 4 (1898), 149. See also A. R. "O samoubiistve," *Obrazovanie* no. 5/6 (1898).

methodology but also because it now "based itself in *biology* and particularly *psychology* – individual and collective."[91] This quality would prove central to Durkheim's resonance in the years following the revolution of 1905, when Durkheim's voice would merge into the broader debate about the threats of degeneration to Russia's modernity.

The transformation of suicide into an object of science occurred as part of a broader process which has been called the "birth of the social" – social problems, social sciences, social conscience, social work. As historians have increasingly turned their attention to the construction of the social and the ensuing technologies of intervention developed by both governments and scientists, they have emphasized the regulative aspects of modernity, especially the administering of social life and individual bodies.[92] By the turn of the twentieth century, a medical model of social pathology was firmly established in Russia as well. With its fusion of history (heredity), society (experience), and biology (human physiology), it provided a powerful tool for understanding a wide variety of pathologies and conditions. Neurasthenia and degeneration could be read just as easily through statistical charts as through case histories, and the smooth transition between populations and individuals was facilitated by both organicist metaphors and the sliding scale between the normal and the pathological.

This revolution in the medical and social sciences reconstituted the entire phenomenon of suicide into a conjoined social phenomenon and physiological event. Its incorporation within a socio-medical framework of explanation thus entailed the repudiation, at least in theory, of its criminal status and hence its legal punishment. Whether with reference to an environmental or to a physiological mechanism, most specialists now denied the role of free will and intention. To echo Zubov's extreme but evocative words, the *cellules* – not the individual – call out for liberation. With this repudiation of the moral choice (potentially) at the heart of suicide, the new paradigms undercut the religious prohibitions, especially the denial of Christian burial. Yet the medical model did not really defuse the defiance within the act, though it did change its valuation. The strange determination to die still violated the sensibilities of modern spectators, just as it had earlier generations.[93]

---

[91] Italics in original. See the untitled review by Osip Lur'e, *Voprosy filosofii i psikhologii* bk. 44, no. 4 (1898), 319.

[92] For an innovative and important study, see David G. Horn, *Social Bodies: Science, Reproduction, and Italian Modernity* (Princeton, 1994).

[93] A different tradition, discussed in Chapter 9, affirmed human freedom in suicide. In his untitled review of Durkheim (319), Osip Lur'e asserted man's right to die, as did the jurist A. F. Koni. See his remarks from November 1892, in "Protokoly zasedanii obshchestva psikhiatrov v S.-Peterburge za 1892 g.," *VKSPN* no. 1 (1893), 44.

Alongside the many changes were important continuities. Since the eighteenth century, suicide had been understood in Russia as a disease of Western civilization that was caused by vices, both old and new – idleness and depravity as well as secularism and free-thinking. Rather than challenging these truisms, modern science supplied statistical evidence and a medical explanation for them. The simpler serial logic of the earlier era was reconfigured into a powerful diagnostic model, one which could successfully integrate an endless variety of vices and disorders. Furthermore, the theory of degeneration gave a new twist to a familiar practice: the ontological primacy of the person – of moral character and patterns of moral behavior – in the medical diagnosis. In many respects, therefore, doctors provided a scientific validation for a moral program: to combat the disease of suicide it was necessary to encourage personal morality, to reduce vice and drunkenness, to inculcate moderation and self-restraint in individual behavior, and to strengthen such social institutions as the family.[94]

One of the by-products of this model was also the proliferation of pathologies, for it claimed to explain not just suicide, but many other phenomena, including crime, drunkenness, sexual deviance, vice, and mental illness. This totalizing vision contained an important paradox. While suicide could evidence Darwinist notions of evolutionary progress ("the elimination of the unfit"), many of these other pathologies instead presaged a process of social degeneration. This very dualism resonated in fin-de-siècle Russia, when signs of both progress and decline were plentiful. During the 1890s, an accelerated industrialization drive was transforming Russia's cities, promising economic (and perhaps political) modernization yet also engendering poverty, overcrowding, exploitation, disease, and crime. To the regret of populists and the delight of Marxists, Russia's path into the (European) future seemed assured.

The prophylactic impulse within this medical-social model further challenged one of the long-standing ideologies of autocracy: the presumption that the state must guide and shape (a passive) society. Most historians agree that the tsarist state was much less interventionalist than its European counterparts, at least until its final decade. Russia's political environment, especially its autocrat unwillingness to cede personal power by vesting authority in independent institutions (whether local government, universities, or professional groups), engendered an increasing political estrangement. While many specialists were now claiming the ability, grounded in science, to diagnose and treat the ills of modern society, they repeatedly stumbled against the restrictions imposed

[94] Note the parallels with a different example discussed in Heidi Rimke and Alan Hunt, "From Sinners to Degenerates: The Medicalization of Morality in the 19th Century," *History of the Human Sciences* no. 1 (2002).

by the state. It is not surprising, perhaps, that Russia's doctors tended to resist strict medical or biological models of deviance, instead according real weight to extra-individual factors, both social and political.[95] Drawing upon their expert knowledge, they were also articulating a new form of paternalism, one which was potentially subversive of a governmental order that allowed social and hygienic problems to fester.

---

[95] In addition to Engelstein, (*Keys to Happiness*), Beer ("Renovating Russia"), and Frieden (*Russia's Physicians*), see Dan Healey, *Homosexual Desire in Revolutionary Russia: The Regulation of Sexual and Gender Dissent* (Chicago, 2001).

8   Crime, disease, sin: disputed judgments

> Sociology justifies suicide, explaining it with economic and social causes; criminal anthropology, psychiatry, and psychology also justify it, denying free will and responsibility in man and encouraging the view of criminals as sick people; in addition, suicide has defenders within contemporary criminal law, who [. . .] seek to remove it from their jurisdiction [. . .].
>
> Father P. Svetlov, "On Suicide," 1890

Perhaps the most ambitious of the Great Reforms was the judicial reform of 1864, the creation of Alexander II's enlightened bureaucrats. Their goal was no less than the establishment of a modern independent judiciary, which would, in turn, perform a crucial role in the modernization of Russian society as a whole. By applying the law fairly, equally, and impartially, the new courts would displace customary law and old patronage systems. Formally autonomous from provincial government within the domain of the justice ministry, they would also limit the arbitrary exercise of administrative power, especially by the governor. Although such ambitious goals were never achieved, the reform partially institutionalized an ideal of the *Rechtsstaat* into the Russian environment and led to a fundamental restructuring of the court system. No longer were verdicts reached in closed sessions and drawing upon written summaries. With public jury trials introduced in criminal cases, the accused now possessed the right to mount a defense, and an oral, adversarial procedure became the norm. Similarly, the weight previously accorded the confession was displaced by a new emphasis on objective standards of evidence. Despite notable shortcomings in the reform and some later attempts to rein in the independence of the judiciary, these changes were significant. Among their side-effects was the rapid expansion of the legal profession, whose members often possessed a keen sense of their important vocation. Furthermore, while Russia's doctors had always been compelled (with little recompense) to perform various duties for the state, including the examination of suspicious deaths, they were now called upon to present and defend their findings to the court.[1]

---

[1] On the legal reform, see Richard Wortman, *The Development of a Russian Legal Consciousness* (Chicago, 1976); and Jörg Baberowski, *Autokratie und Justiz: Zum Verhältnis von*

The judicial reform inaugurated a new era in the legal regulation of suicide. Even before the 1860s, the prosecution of suicide had been declining, which was likely a result of both changing attitudes toward the act as well as the exclusively civil and religious penalties specified in the 1845 penal code. This trend would continue after the 1860s, when the formal prosecution of suicide and attempted suicide became increasingly uncommon. By the end of the century, the official response was generally limited to a police or court investigation, usually in consultation with a doctor. In contrast to the tendency in the first part of the century, judgment was apt to be lenient, and priests were often directed to accord suicides a religious burial. These developments were not accompanied by a decline of public interest. To the contrary, suicide suddenly became highly controversial, as voices from the judiciary, medicine, and the church all combined into a discordant chorus of debate.

As these voices echoed through Russian society, they each offered particular views on suicide and its regulation. The first sphere of discord concerned its legal status. Despite significant disagreement on various points, most jurists agreed that suicide had no place within the criminal justice system. Modernization, they argued, required a purge of religion and morality from the law. In many respects, these jurists were victorious, for suicide was increasingly decriminalized in practice. This trend was encouraged by doctors, who laid claim to suicide as an object of medical knowledge. Given the frequent absence of formal judicial procedure, their assessments of the suicide's state of mind often formed the basis for the certifications provided by investigative authorities. For its part, the church was deeply concerned about both the procedures to be followed in individual cases of suicide and the broader social problem, which it blamed on secularization. During the 1870s, the church struggled – successfully on a formal level – to preserve the criminal status of suicide, seeing the punitive measures of the state as essential in the struggle against secularism. Increasingly dismayed at the judgments of medical authorities, however, the church began to claim a right to autonomous judgment. The regulation of suicide became contentious in the late nineteenth century not because the various authorities – legal, administrative, medical, religious – wanted to relinquish their share of responsibility to others.[2] To the contrary, each of these authorities sought to implement its own distinctive approach to suicide as part of a broader effort to promote the social, mental, and spiritual health of Russian society. This situation

Rechtsstaatlichkeit und Rückständigkeit im ausgehenden Zarenreich 1864–1914 (Frankfurt am Main, 1996). On the relationship between law and administration, see George L. Yaney, *The Systemization of Russian Government: Social Evolution in the Domestic Administration of Imperial Russia, 1711–1905* (Urbana, Ill., 1973), 236–37, 327–28. The best case studies of law and political culture are William Wagner, *Marriage, Property and Law in Late Imperial Russia* (Oxford, 1994); and Laura Engelstein, *The Keys to Happiness: Sex and the Search for Modernity in Fin-de-Siècle Russia* (Ithaca, N.Y., 1992), 17–127.

[2] At most this observation is true for some criminal courts. See Irina Paperno, *Suicide as a Cultural Institution in Dostoevsky's Russia* (Ithaca, N.Y., 1997), 66.

was further complicated by an additional factor: peasant communities were also asserting their own rights of judgment, a right they exercised unilaterally through the desecration of graves. For Russia's educated society, both secular and religious, this "superstition" prompted yet more concern about the progress of civilization and the nature of belief.

Purging superstition from the law

The architects of the judicial reform had always intended to tackle not just the institutions of justice but also its statutory content. However, the revised penal codes of 1866 and 1885 were little different from their predecessors. From the very outset, therefore, the new courts and the new jurists confronted the leftovers of the pre-reform world – the old statutory laws. The five articles on suicide contained in the 1845 code remained unchanged until 1917, but the legal community now subjected them to unprecedented scrutiny. This debate occurred on the pages of legal textbooks as well as legal journals and newspapers, which were all multiplying in response to the demands of a rapidly expanding legal profession. It also occurred in the courtroom, where practical questions of procedure exposed the contradictions within the law. At issue were fundamental principles. On the one hand, most jurists considered the criminal prosecution of suicide to be archaic. On the other hand, they believed in the rule of law. How then were obsolete laws to be applied?

Suicide may be a moral transgression, legal scholars argued, and it may also be a sin, but it was certainly not a crime. In his textbook on criminal law, Aleksandr Lokhvitskii likened the laws regulating suicide to a curious example of the influence of religion on the criminal sphere. In his view, such superstition had no place in a modern system of criminal justice.[3] Other jurists agreed. In his manual, N. A. Nekliudov, professor of law and later procurator general of the Senate's criminal appellate department, wrote: "the theses on the criminality of suicide have already long ago been relegated by the science of criminal law to the sphere of women's prattle [v oblast' bab'ikh razgovorov]." His metaphor clearly associated the criminality of suicide with ignorance and backwardness. That the crime of suicide lacked any criminal penalty provided further evidence of its character as a predominantly religious rather than criminal transgression. Indeed, suicide and attempted suicide were crimes only for individuals of Christian belief, which expressly contradicted the principle of equality under the law. Like his colleague the criminologist and future senator, N. S. Tagantsev, Nekliudov further argued that criminal law regulated social relations and was hence irrelevant to such individual acts as suicide.[4]

[3] Aleksandr Lokhvitskii, *Kurs russkogo ugolovnogo prava* (SPb, 1871), 545–46.
[4] N. A. Nekliudov, *Rukovodstvo k osobennoi chasti russkogo ugolovnogo prava*, vol. 1: *Prestupleniia i postupki protiv lichnosti* (SPb, 1876), esp. 250–52. See also N. S. Tagantsev, *O prestupleniiakh protiv zhizni po russkomu pravu*, 2 vols. (SPb, 1871), esp. vol. 2, 412–16, 423–36.

Thèse legal debates possessed a political subtext. Modernization required not only the eradication of "superstition" from the law but also the defense of human dignity. This principle obliged, in turn, the privatization of faith. As Nekliudov noted, "church penance is a matter of conscience, as elevated and pure as prayer, which is defiled by all coercion and violence."[5] The regulation of belief by criminal law, another jurist agreed, constituted a "crude intrusion of worldly power into the intimate and sacred [*zavetnye*] feelings of a religious person."[6] Yet the evocation of the personality (*lichnost'*) as a new sacred principle potentially shaped new kinds of human rights. Lokhvitskii thus mentioned in passing the right of man to dispose of himself (*pravo cheloveka raspolagat' soboiu*).[7] Most explicit were the oft-cited words of the eminent jurist A. F. Koni: "A very significant number of suicides are committed in sound mind and memory, and the old Latin dictum, '*mori licet cui vivere non placet*', has not lost its meaning for contemporary society. Without reviewing all its tragedy, this dictum is imbued with a respect for the freedom of the human spirit."[8]

Although legal scholars rejected the criminality of suicide as archaic, the new courts were still confronted with existing statutory law. In the aftermath of the judicial reform, questions of process were paramount. In the *Judicial Herald*, the newspaper of the justice ministry, an 1866 article carefully explained the correct procedure in cases of suicide, an effort which suggests that procedures were either not known or not always followed. It posed two questions. Was it necessary to conduct investigations in cases of suicide and attempted suicide? Must the court rule on the evidence presented by the procurator? Both questions were answered in the affirmative. An investigation and decision were essential to establish the fact of a suicide or attempted suicide, the state of mind accompanying the act, and the absence of abetting or instigation. Only if a suicide had been attempted while in sound mind was the case to be sent on to civil or ecclesiastical authorities for further action.[9]

Despite such clear directives, jurisdiction and procedure were hotly disputed. On the one side were those who sought to exclude suicide altogether from the criminal courts. Because the punishments for suicide and attempted suicide were solely civil and religious, it was argued, a police investigation was sufficient. Once the participation of an accomplice or instigator had been ruled out, the case could then be sent directly to the civil and ecclesiastical courts. Indeed, many jurists pointed out, the prosecution of the dead was not allowed under

[5] Nekliudov, *Rukovodstvo*, 252.
[6] A. Kistiakovskii, "O samoubiistve po russkim ugolovnym zakonam," *Zhurnal grazhdanskogo i ugolovnogo prava* no. 3 (1882), 94.
[7] Lokhvitskii, *Kurs*, 546.
[8] See Koni's remarks from November 1892 in "Protokoly zasedanii obshchestva psikhiatrov v S.-Peterburge za 1892 g.," *VKSPN* no. 1 (1893), 44.
[9] "O poriadke proizvodstva del o samoubiitsakh," *Sudebnyi vestnik* no. 41 (1866).

Russian law, and burial necessarily took place long before a court could rule on competence. Based on the premise that suicide was not a criminal act in itself, these arguments quoted selectively from existing law. The opposing side emphasized, in contrast, that the circumstances of each suicide or attempted suicide must be fully investigated to determine whether the suicide was legally culpable for his or her act. Whereas it may seem absurd to place the dead on trial, one court investigator asserted, "it is not the body of the criminal which is being judged but the rights of his personality." The court could return an honorable burial after the fact, should that be necessary.[10]

Individuals on both sides of this dispute often believed that they were acting in the spirit of legality and progress. While some hoped to decriminalize suicide, thereby reducing governmental intervention in an emergent but fragile private sphere, others called for the rule of law. In an 1882 article, the Kiev jurist A. Kistiakovskii admitted his quandaries. Because the denial of Christian burial was too serious a penalty to be left to the possibly arbitrary and rarely impartial decision of administrative authorities, he believed in principle that suicide should be reviewed by the criminal courts. This view reflected a common aspiration that the police be subordinated to the judiciary. At the same time, Kistiakovskii was well aware that the time and expense of ruling on every suicide would overload the court system and distract attention from more serious crimes. While he left open the possibility of appeal should family members be dissatisfied, he came down in favor of a police investigation without formal court participation. He noted in conclusion that such was already the practice throughout Russia.[11]

This outcome was the product of local practices and appellate decisions. In the sphere of criminal law, conflict regularly occurred between courts and procurators.[12] In light of the absence of a defendant (the suicide), procurators

---

[10] See the exchange between P. Makalinskii, "Uchastie politsii v proizvodstve predvaritel'nogo sledstviia," *Sudebnyi vestnik* no. 146 (1870); and P. Lebedev, "K voprosu o proizvodstve del o samoubiistve," *Sudebnyi vestnik* no. 177 (1870), here 1. The debate was continued the next year: P. N. Obninskii, "Ob ugolovnom presledovanii pokusivshikhsia na samoubiistvo," *Iuridicheskii vestnik* no. 6 (1871); P. N. Obninskii, "K voprosu ob ugolovnom presledovanii pokusivshikhsia na samoubiistvo," *Iuridicheskii vestnik* no. 9 (1871); I. N. Shestakov, "Po povodu stat'i P. N. Obninskogo," *Iuridicheskii vestnik* no. 1 (1872); I. N. Shestakov, "Vozrazhenie na ob"iasneniia," *Iuridicheskii vestnik* no. 4/5 (1872).

[11] Kistiakovskii, "O samoubiistve." See also P. A. Arevkov, "Sleduet li proizvodit' predvaritel'nye sledstviia po delam o samoubiistvakh i pokusheniiakh na nikh?" *Iuridicheskii vestnik* nos. 9, 10 (1873).

[12] The problem of inheritance also proved thorny. Whereas civil law specified the invalidation of testaments when the suicide had been judged incompetent, the penal code specified the same procedure as a criminal penalty, that is, for competent suicides. In a series of decisions from the late 1870s, the Senate empowered civil courts to rule on both the fact of suicide as well as the state of mind accompanying it in cases involving civil disputes. For the debate, see A. Kopei, "Dukhovnye zaveshchaniia samoubiits," *Iuridicheskii vestnik* no. 4/6 (1875); P. S. "Eshche po voprosu o dukhovnykh zaveshchaniiakh lits, lishennykh vsekh prav sostoianiia."

asserted their right to close investigations without a formal prosecution. However, some courts insisted upon their obligation to issue a ruling. In an 1866 case, the St. Petersburg appellate court ruled that courts should issue an opinion on the basis of the investigation that would then form the foundation for civil action.[13] In considering a similar conflict of opinion between the Kaluga district court and procurator, Moscow's appellate court ruled in favor of the procurator. The case could be closed. Nevertheless, the courts were to be fully informed about the case and the grounds for closing it.[14] Despite their differences, both decisions held that the key issue in an investigation of suicide was less the suicide itself than the potential involvement of a second party. At issue, therefore, was really whether the suicide had been abetted or instigated.

The legal status of attempted suicide also proved controversial. As its sole penalty was church penance, many police agencies, court investigators, and procurators refused to follow set procedures. Evidence suggests that a lackadaisical response was not uncommon. In December 1866, the peasant Erofei Suprun attempted to hang himself and was saved by a neighbor. The local police informed the court of this fact in January 1867, and the court investigator arrived in January 1868 – a full year later. During his interrogation, Suprun confirmed that he had been told that he had tried to hang himself, but added that he had no actual memory of the incident due to an illness at the time. Without further action, the investigator gave the case to the procurator, who applied to the Kharkov court for a ruling on procedure. The procurator – supported by the young jurist and future senator A. F. Koni – argued that cases of attempted suicide should be removed from his (criminal) jurisdiction and given to ecclesiastical courts, because the only penalty was a religious one (penance). The court disagreed in a split decision. The majority held that an investigation of and ruling on all attempted suicides was necessary, first, to establish the mental competence necessary to transfer the case to an ecclesiastical court, and second, to rule out other, more serious crimes, especially instigation. Hoping to limit the sphere of police intervention, the losing side had argued that the fact of attempted suicide was itself insufficient reason to justify any official investigation.[15]

O zaveshchaniiakh samoubiits," *Zhurnal grazhdanskogo i ugolovnogo prava* no. 6 (1876). For the rulings, see the serial publication of *Resheniia grazhdanskogo kassatsionnogo departamenta Pravitel'stvuiushchego Senata*, decision no. 92 (SPb, 1876), no. 365 (SPb, 1877), and no. 276 (SPb, 1880); see also *Resheniia obshchego sobraniia pervogo i kassatsionnykh departamentov Pravitel'stvuiushchego Senata*, decision no. 19 (SPb, 1877). For a summary, A. L. Borovikovskii, *Ustav grazhdanskogo sudoproizvodstva s ob"iasneniiami po resheniiam grazhdanskogo kassatsionnogo departamenta i obshchego sobraniia kassatsionnogo i I i II departamenta Pravitel'stvuiushchego Senata*, sixth edn (SPb, 1908).

[13] "Po delu o samoubiistve otstavnogo poruchika Petra Abazy," *Sudebnyi vestnik* no. 86 (1866).

[14] "Opredelenie Moskovskoi sudebnoi palaty: Po voprosu o proizvodstve del o samoubiitsakh," *Sudebnyi vestnik* no. 123 (1868), also in *Iuridicheskii vestnik* no. 5 (1867–68).

[15] Materials from the case are located among Koni's personal papers. IRLI, f. 134, op. 4, d. 262.

During the 1870s, the Senate considered three cases of attempted suicide, each time ruling that the criminal courts must establish whether the suicide had been intentional and whether second parties were involved.[16] Until this was accomplished, the church was not required to accept any cases sent to it.[17] That the Senate had to repeat its ruling three times in just seven years underlines the almost absurd proportions of the jurisdictional confusion. In one case of attempted suicide, for example, the police tried to transfer the matter first to the court procurator and then to the diocesan consistory, but both refused to accept it. The procurator and the provincial board then juggled the case between them before appealing to St. Petersburg for direction. The consideration of subsequent cases likewise stumbled on the refusal of the relevant parties to take cases of attempted suicide.[18] Whether the Senate rulings resolved the matter is doubtful, for legal practice varied widely.[19] In 1890, a court investigator refused to intervene in the case of an attempted suicide by a runaway soldier. The matter was again brought before the Senate but only because General P. S. Vannovskii – the Minister of War – personally intervened.[20]

Perhaps the least controversial though most intriguing dimension of this legal debate concerned the status of instigated suicide. Citing the landmark 1854 decision in the case of Ekaterina Leont'eva (who had abused her son), the Senate ruled in 1868 that the statute on instigated suicide should be interpreted with some latitude: by "suicide," one should understand despair resulting in suicide or any other crime.[21] A discretionary judgment in 1854 had now become a substantive precedent. The case involved the minor Ol'ga Umetskaia, a victim of parental abuse, who had not attempted to kill herself but rather to burn

---

[16] As Wagner has shown (*Marriage, Property and Law*), the Senate was now influencing legal practice through judicial revision, though this practice was never formally institutionalized. Its rulings also began to be published as guidance for lower courts not just on procedure but on the application and interpretation of the law.

[17] For an overview of the cases from the perspective of the church, see S. V. Kalashnikov, comp., *Alfavitnyi ukazatel' deistvuiushchikh i rukovodstvennykh kanonicheskikh postanovlenii, ukazov, opredelenii i rasporiazhenii Sviateishego Pravitel'stvuiushchego Sinoda (1721–1895 g. vkliuchitel'no) i grazhdanskikh zakonov, otnosiashchikhsia k dukhovnomu vedomstvu pravoslavnogo ispovedaniia*, 2nd edn (Kharkov, 1896).

[18] The circumstances of these cases are described in the following archival files: RGIA, f. 1354, op. 4, d. 215 (Filipov); d. 323 (Geibovich); and d. 577 (Myznikov). The decisions were published in the serial *Resheniia obshchego sobraniia pervogo i kassatsionnykh departamentov Pravitel'stvuiushchego Senata*, decision no. 15 in the case of Filipov (1872); decision in the case of Geibovich dated Oct. 28, 1874; and decision no. 72 in the case of Myznikov (1879).

[19] In 1887, the Senate investigated how courts handle crimes involving insanity and found some jurisdictions (including Kazan, Ekaterinburg, Viatka) required a formal ruling. Others (including Simbirsk and Perm) simply closed the investigation without a court ruling. See RGIA, f. 1354, op. 6, d. 998, esp. 11. 2, 5–6.

[20] See the case of Mikhail Veremenko, in RGIA, f. 1354, op. 6, d. 1054.

[21] The beginning of the statute reads: "Parents, guardians, and other individuals possessing some sort of power, who, through the manifest abuse of this power combined with cruelty, drive a subordinate or someone entrusted to their guardianship to commit suicide . . ."

down her parents' house. Jurors had agreed that mistreatment had driven her to despair, and Moscow's circuit court had cited the statute on instigated suicide, "indicating the necessity of applying the law by analogy [*po analogii*]."[22] During the next decade, legal scholars scrutinized this rationale, with opinion splitting into two camps. Those critical of the decisions, including Nekliudov and Tagantsev, generally saw them as a well-meaning but misguided deviation from the letter of the law, which they also condemned as rife with contradiction. If the aim was to address the abuse of parental and other patriarchal forms of authority, they argued, it would be preferable to design a new law to do just that. Though recognizing the validity of such criticism, other jurists supported the spirit of the new interpretation, arguing that the Senate had finally focused on the real issue, which was the abuse of authority. While both camps generally backed the revision of family law reducing the power of husbands and parents over wives and children, they forwarded different concepts of legality. Whereas the first argument promoted the rule of law in itself, the second reworked the traditional, instrumentalist view of law as a means to promote justice and the general welfare.[23]

Before 1861, the crime of instigated suicide had evolved within the practices of autocratic paternalism. It had primarily been a means to police and thereby to uphold existing social institutions. Throughout the rest of the century, however, its meanings were very different. Some of its broader resonances were apparent within the more narrow legal debates. According to Nekliudov, the concept of cruelty – despite its inherent and problematic ambiguities – denoted "violence upon the individual" as well as a general pattern of constraint (*stesnenie*) and deprivation.[24] Although the law failed to define cruelty, Tagantsev noted, "it must embrace both physical and also moral tortures [*istiazaniia*] and torments." The jury was faced with determining the precise definition in each case.[25] In contrast to earlier times, jurists now likened the suffering of the victim to a violation of his or her human dignity and right to bodily inviolability. Whereas the goal of intervention had once been to propagate an ethos of paternalism in order to uphold the social system, the dominant intention was now to expose and punish violence as a means to defend individual rights and thereby to transform power relations, especially within the family.

As cases were brought before the new courts, the strategy of procurators was generally to challenge the legitimacy of discipline, which often meant

---

[22] For the full text of the decision, see no. 160 (Po delu Gubernskogo Sekretaria Vladimira i zheny ego Ekateriny Umetskikh), *Resheniia ugolovnogo kassatsionnogo departamenta Pravitel'stvuiushchego Senata* (SPb, 1868), 224–33.

[23] For the first view, see Tagantsev, *O prestupleniiakh*, vol. 2, 442–46; Nekliudov, *Rukovodstvo*, 256–58; Lokhvitskii, *Kurs*, 546–48; and for the second, Kistiakovskii, "O samoubiistve," 89–94.

[24] Nekliudov, *Rukovodstvo*, 256. See also Kistiakovskii, "O samoubiistve," 93.

[25] Tagantsev, *O prestupleniiakh*, vol. 2, 445.

to depict it as violence, a holdover from a pre-modern era. Prosecution was consequently represented as a progressive and modernizing act. However, this strategy also provoked a disconcerting question: are human rights universal? More concretely: do peasants have the same rights as more cultured groups? This problem derived in part from the fact that peasants were largely excluded from the new legal system; matters of civil law and minor crime were to be decided by local *volost'* courts on the basis of customary law. While the formal prosecution of instigated suicide among peasants took place within the regular court system, this notion that peasants should be judged according to custom was quite widespread. In an 1874 case from Poltava province, for example, a jury found the peasant Denisenko guilty of having driven his wife to suicide through his beatings. When the case was appealed to the Senate, the defense attorney adopted two strategies. The first echoed the pre-reform model: he pointed out that the law did not in fact prosecute "light beatings" between spouses; consequently, the beating was not illegal and could not constitute cruelty. The second tactic appealed to customary law: physical discipline could not drive a peasant to suicide because it was a common and accepted practice in peasant families. In its decision, however, the Senate upheld the jury's original verdict. Denisenko received six months' incarceration and church penance.[26] While the defendant lost in this instance, this strategy sometimes worked, for it exploited an ambiguity at the heart of the judicial reform. Law should promote modernization yet also reflect relative levels of culture and understanding.

The countless problems posed by the archaic penal code resulted in a new impetus to revise it by the late 1870s and 1880s. Commission members included such prominent jurists as Nekliudov and Tagantsev, and their goals remained consistent with the spirit of the 1864 reform: the secularization, rationalization, and modernization of criminal law. Although a new code was completed in the 1890s and even approved by the State Council and tsar in 1903, it was never enacted.[27] Nevertheless, the draft text is revealing. The modernizers won on their main point which did not prove controversial within the legal profession: the statutes on suicide and attempted suicide were deleted outright. In contrast, the articles on the abetting and instigation of suicide were retained, and the latter even strengthened. This outcome had long been advocated by local courts, procurators, and investigators.[28] According to the proposed revision, abetting

---

[26] "Po delu krest'ianina Denisenko," no. 222 (Apr. 3, 1875), *Polnyi svod reshenii ugolovnogo kassatsionnogo departamenta Pravitel'stvuiushchego Senata za 1875* (Ekaterinoslav, 1911), 329–30. Scattered evidence suggests that peasants did sometimes recognize the role of physical abuse in suicide. See, for example, EM, f. 7, op. 1, d. 517, 33–34; d. 1854, ll. 5–11.

[27] One reason was timing: the rise of social unrest and the retrenchment of the autocracy. On the commission, see Engelstein, *The Keys to Happiness*, 22–23.

[28] The chairman of the Saratov court argued that the statute on instigation was one of the few in the code that "imposed too weak a punishment," and he recalled a recent "scandalous" case: for

would have a maximum sentence of three years' imprisonment but instigation could result in eight years' penal servitude. The language was also more expansive. Deleting the reference to cruelty, the draft statute used the terms instigation (*podgovor*, also incitement) and assistance (*sodeistvie*). The connotation of oral suasion was made explicit in the text: the crime could occur through "counsel" (*sovet*), "indication or furnishing of means," or "the elimination of obstacles" resulting in a suicide attempt.[29] This concern with instigation – the presumption that individuals had been driven to their desperate acts by moral or physical cruelty – would also permeate the public debates more broadly.

Expert evidence

In light of the judicial reform that was just coming into effect, A. U. Freze, one of Russia's first psychiatrists, published an article on the new role to be played by doctors. In order to avoid unnecessary conflict, he believed it necessary to delineate spheres of competence. While the judge was the representative of jurisprudence in the courtroom, the doctor was the representative of medicine, "answerable not before the judge but before science, before the higher medical instance." Freze reinforced this point repeatedly: "The doctor is not an extraneous figure, collecting material for the verdict of the judge; he is not an assistant, to whom the judge may or may not listen; rather, he is, authorized by his science, an independent judge in particular questions that are not accessible to the representatives of criminal law." Indeed, the view of a judge on questions of medicine, and particularly the state of mind of the accused, constituted nothing more than a "private opinion." Still, he fully accorded jurisprudence its equal status as a science. It was for the judge, not the doctor, to decide whether a disease impaired the defendant's legal responsibility.[30] This eloquent vindication of the doctor as expert was characteristic of the era. Not only did it proclaim science as the ultimate source of truth, it also asserted the status of medicine – including the very new field of forensic psychiatry – as a science. The reform era thus enhanced doctors' ambition for recognition of their status as scientific experts.

With regard to the crime of suicide, doctors had two primary responsibilities. First was the establishment of the physical cause of death, which included a

twelve years, a peasant had been extremely cruel to his wife – he used to tie her upside down to a beam and flog her – until this "gentle and well-behaved woman" had finally hanged herself. He found the maximum penalty of sixteen months imprisonment wholly inadequate. For this and other opinions, see *Materialy dlia peresmotra nashego ugolovnogo zakonodatel'stva* (SPb, 1881), vol. 3, 348–50.

[29] The statute defined the victim as being under 21 or unable either to understand the meaning of or to direct his act. See *Novoe ugolovnoe ulozhenie Vysochaishe utverzhdennoe 22-go Marta 1903 g.* (Moscow, 1903), 148. For an earlier version, *Ugolovnoe ulozhenie. Proekt, izmennyi Ministrom Iustitsii* (SPb, 1898), 116.

[30] A. U. Freze, "O sudebno-psikhiatricheskikh osmotrakh," *ASMOG* no. 1 (1866), 1–4.

determination of suicide as opposed to accident or murder. During the first half of the century, doctors had often limited themselves to this task, and accounts of particularly challenging cases now began to appear in medical journals as well.[31] The second responsibility of doctors was to judge the physical and mental state of the defendant, that is, to assess whether a disease had impaired the mind. Although it is difficult to generalize about the everyday legal role of doctors, which likely varied widely between town and countryside, center and periphery, scattered sources suggest that doctors were exhibiting increasing self-confidence in the diagnosis of the causes of suicide.

Despite Freze's idealism, medical opinion was not always heeded, as in the case of Nikolai Rudin. Arrested for various crimes in 1860, he had cut his throat with a razor en route to prison but failed to kill himself. He subsequently testified that "he had wounded himself in a fit of grief [*v poryve goria*] and delirium [*v bespamiatstve*]." Before the crime, he had felt such a rush [*priliv*] of blood to his head and heart that he had sent several times for the doctor." Though he saw Rudin only after his suicide attempt, Penza city doctor Sherstnevskii not only confirmed the account, but revealed its origins. Despite significant blood loss, Rudin's pulse had been strong, leading Sherstnevskii to conclude that Rudin had experienced a "rush of blood," that he may require an additional blood letting, and finally, that "he was in a state of ecstasy [*ekstaz*] as a consequence of this rush [of blood]." The provincial medical department endorsed this diagnosis, and Rudin then cited it in his legal defense. When the Senate and State Council ruled on this case in 1871, however, the doctor's expert testimony was not heeded. Because derangement (*umootstuplenie*) or complete delirium (*sovershennoe bespamiatstvo*) had not been demonstrated, Rudin was sentenced to penance for the attempted suicide.[32] Though the verdict in this case did not follow the medical argument, such a diagnosis in cases of suicide – a rush of blood to the brain – was not uncommon in this period.[33] The physiological reading of emotions drew upon the writings of German materialists and physiologists, which were not only readily available but also popularized in literature and journals.[34]

---

[31] Though usually crafted as demonstrations of scientific expertise, these case studies did occasionally admit failure. For an unresolved case, see Iulii Shirvind, "Ubiistvo ili samoubiistvo?" *VSMOG* no. 1 (1882). See also K. P. Sulima, "Pokushenie na samoubiistvo posredstvom pererezki shei, vydavaemoe za pokushenie na ubiistvo," *VSMOG* no. 4 (1886).

[32] He also lost his nobility and was sent into exile for his other crimes. See RGIA, f. 1151, op. 7 (1871), d. 33, esp. 8–17.

[33] I. Pasternatskii mentions five such cases. See his "Statisticheskoe issledovanie samoubiistv v S.-Peterburge za 1870, 1871, i 1872 gody," *Meditsinskii vestnik* nos. 35–38, 40–41 (1873), here no. 41, 415.

[34] In an interesting parallel, Irina Paperno shows how Chernyshevskii attempted to measure his emotions by his pulse. On this and the culture of science, see her *Chernyshevsky and the Age of Realism: A Study in the Semiotics of Behavior* (Stanford, 1988), 70–71, and *passim*. She also explores how some suicides authored their deaths within a physiological idiom, even staging them as scientific experiments. See her *Suicide*, 115–18.

Evidence further suggests that doctors increasingly linked women's suicide to emotions, sexual life, and morality, all of which could be subsumed under female physiology and conceptualized in medical terms.[35] This particular logic underpinned the 1876 case of Adelina Kordikh. Though the newspaper report described a plausible context for her suicide (she was estranged from her husband and caring for her children when her infant died), the medical explanation relied upon a physiological dynamic – she killed herself when the excess "breast milk rushed to her brain" causing a mental imbalance.[36] Intense emotional experiences could also drive women insane and thence to suicide. When Elizaveta Skripitsyna hanged herself in 1876, the investigation revealed that her motive was unrequited love. According to her doctor, this experience had so impacted her mental health that she had taken her life in "an attack of insanity" (*v pripadke umoisstupleniia*).[37] Finally, in the 1888 case of Mariia Bershtannova, the diagnosis linked mental illness, physical disease, and sexual deviance. In the days preceding her attempt, she had asked her sister for forgiveness, saying that she felt wretched and wanted to die. After being cut down from the noose and revived, she again described her anguish (*toska*) and alluded to attacks of mental illness. The reason for this behavior, a doctor explained, was in fact a diseased uterus (*beshenstvo matki*), which had heightened her physical desires, causing her to turn to compulsive masturbation and ultimately, it seems, to suicide. Despite this diagnosis, Bershtannova performed church penance for her attempted suicide. The local police had bypassed the courts and sent its report directly to the religious consistory, which had apparently been unconvinced by the doctor's judgment.[38]

As medical theories of suicide grew more refined, the assertion of expert knowledge in the assessment of suicide became increasingly confident.[39] This

---

[35] This trend was pan-European. See Engelstein, *Keys to Happiness*, 101; and Margaret Higonnet, "Speaking Silences: Women's Suicide," in Susan Rubin Suleiman, ed., *The Female Body in Western Culture: Contemporary Perspectives* (Cambridge, Mass., 1986).

[36] *Peterburgskii listok* (Jan. 18, 1876), 3. See also the report linking an attempted suicide to hysteria. *Peterburgskii listok* (May 16, 1887), 3. Pasternatskii listed two cases "caused" by pregnancy under the general rubric of disease. "Statisticheskoe issledovanie," no. 41, 415.

[37] GARF, f. 109, op. 3, d. 3131, l. 3. For a newspaper report that likewise makes unhappiness in love into the cause of her mental illness, see "Vnutrenniaia pochta," *Peterburgskii listok* (Feb. 10, 1876), 4.

[38] GANO, f. 570, op. 559, 1888, d. 50, esp. 2–4. Compare the following medical comment: "The examination of this autopsy involuntarily leads to the thought that the poor girl perished a victim of onanism. [This] quickly and powerfully disturbed the inner sexual organs, still unprepared for activity, leading to a fatal influence on the moral sphere of the organism." See Ia. Chistovich, "Perechen' sudebno-meditsinskikh vskrytii," *Voenno-meditsinskii zhurnal* 72 (Aug. 1858), 79. For a case of a doctor explaining a peasant woman's suicide by a disease of the reproductive organs (and not the concurrent spousal abuse), see EM, f. 7, op. 1, d. 309, ll. 39–40.

[39] See the case study of a peasant man, aged 77, whose suicide was diagnosed as a sudden onset of senile melancholia. His primary evidence was the man's age and the lack of prior symptoms – hence the sudden onset. F. Arkhangel'skii, "Sluchai samoubiistva," *VSMOG* no. 3 (1884), esp. 8–10.

trend was perhaps encouraged by the lack of judicial proceedings: doctors were but rarely called to testify before the court in cases of suicide. By the early twentieth century, therefore, the standard formula found in police records, which often derived from the medical certification, simply stated: "there are no obstacles to burial" (*k pogrebeniiu trupa prepiatstviia ne vstrechaiutsia*). This seemingly innocuous phrase typically functioned as a directive to conduct a Christian service, an interpretation the clergy would passionately attack and sometimes circumvent.

Yet medical knowledge about suicide did not conform easily to legal categories. Most doctors were in fact highly reluctant to define the main causes of suicide – neuropathic constitutions, *affekt* – as forms of insanity per se, though they did consider them pathological.[40] Nevertheless, the theory of degeneration provided a different basis for rejecting legal penalties, as Dr. Rozanov so eloquently advocated: "Really, how exactly is a suicide guilty when he comes from a psychopathic family and is raised in extremely unfavorable circumstances, constantly subjected to the pernicious, debauched influence of a crude, drunken, depraved milieu, and having never received moral support or encouragement? It is time to renounce the antiquated understanding of suicide as a crime."[41] Rather than accepting his limited legal role in the assessment of mental competence, Rozanov instead drew upon his authority as a medical specialist to reject the law itself. Blurring the boundary between medicine and ethics, he judged all suicides as objects, whether of physiology, heredity, or environment. Indeed, almost all studies of suicide published between the late 1880s and the early 1900s explicitly concluded that legal and religious sanctions were both inappropriate and ineffective. Following Rozanov's logic, these specialists viewed their legal role with irony and consequently decided the question "in favor of the accused."[42]

The trial of Varvara Ozerskaia

In 1868, the peasant Stepan Ozerskii was put on trial in Elets (Orel province), charged with having driven his wife Varvara to hang herself.[43] His jurors

---

[40] Only one doctor asserted the inherent insanity of the act. See Ivan Gvozdev, *O samoubiistve s sotsial'noi i meditsinskoi tochki zreniia* (Kazan, 1889), 45.

[41] P. G. Rozanov, *O samoubiistve* (Moscow, 1891), 136.

[42] This is the much-cited formulation of Krafft-Ebing, which was used as an epigraph in S. N. Iakovlev and P. F. Filatov, "Samoubiistva v Simbirskoi gubernii," *VOGSPM* nos. 1, 2 (1892). Professor Ivan Sikorskii, in contrast, affirmed the role of free will in suicide. He thus refused to certify insanity in a suicide he judged as a rational response to pathological circumstances (a young woman who had suffered years of abuse). See IRLI, f. 134, op. 4, d. 264, esp. ll. 6–9.

[43] This entire section is based on transcripts from the trial published as "Sudebnaia zasedaniia. V Eletskom okruzhnom sude (po ugolovnomu otdeleniiu). Po delu o vremenno-obiazannom krest'ianine Stepane Fedoseeve Ozerskom," *Sudebnyi vestnik* no. 143 (1868), 1.

included three members of the gentry, four merchants, and five peasants. This case provides a vivid illustration of how legal and medical issues collided in the phenomenon of suicide. The progressive and modernizing impulse now signified by the prosecution of abuse within the patriarchal family met head on with modern scientific views of suicide as both a social-statistical fact and an expression of individual pathology. Although Stepan was the defendant, the person on trial turned out to be Varvara, *in absentia*.

In the indictment, Stepan, who was 19 years old, was accused of beating and thereby driving Varvara, aged 17, to suicide. In their preliminary testimony (which they largely withdrew at the trial), neighbors stated that they had not witnessed this particular beating but confirmed another instance and mentioned rumors of marital unhappiness. The forensic examination had nonetheless revealed significant signs of prior violence, including numerous bruises and abrasions on her chest, back, arms, and head. The doctor concluded that Varvara had been hit with a blunt object and dragged by her hair. These facts formed the basis for the prosecution, and the procurator focused his questions on the marital relationship. For his part, Stepan admitted beating her "lightly" – not "cruelly" – on the day in question and confirmed that the marriage had not been a happy one. He claimed to have discovered her "dishonor," presumably a previous loss of virginity, on their wedding night. He had consequently beaten her, and she had subsequently repulsed his sexual advances and refused to obey him. Although other witnesses described Varvara as modest and unassuming, her husband considered her evil and obstinate. This information provided the basis for the prosecution. The fact of maltreatment was deemed sufficient documentation of the crime.

In making his case, defense attorney N. I. Kalenius masterfully appealed to customary law, cultural difference, and modern science to dismantle the arguments of the prosecution. He began by undermining the causal relationship between a beating and suicide, a relationship the procurator had taken for granted:

The prosecution is based on the fact that the husband beat the wife, and that the wife hanged herself. There is no connection between these two events: the wife could also have hanged herself when the husband had not beaten her at all; it is also possible that she would not have hanged herself after a beating, as many do not, even those who have been beaten badly. Husbands hang themselves more frequently, although their wives do not beat them; criminal statistics show that the number of suicides among men is three times higher than among women.

Having deconstructed causality with reference to the science of statistics, he then turned to the beating itself and adopted a position of cultural relativism. Quoting both peasant proverbs and the latest legal authorities, he argued that the definition of cruelty depended on the cultural level of the couple. Whereas custom allowed wife beating among peasants, a different standard governed more educated circles. Consequently, cruelty among peasants must be assessed differently than cruelty among elites. "We must examine people and their customs as they are, not as they should be," he asserted. He then evoked a characteristic sentiment that culture was attained through a long-term process of evolution: "With time peasants will probably stop beating their wives, but now, in court, we must only consider what is, not what could be." On this basis, he concluded that cruelty could not be proven. Wife beating was acceptable behavior among peasants. Not only had the blows not been strong enough to cause Varvara's death, they had not even prevented her from eating lunch.

With cruelty thus discounted, Kalenius returned to the problem of causality in order to suggest another explanation for the suicide. In this endeavor, he again referred to modern science. Quoting the forensic report, which described Varvara as having a delicate build, similar to that of a child due to incomplete physical development, he suggested that Varvara was in fact abnormal. Whereas she was already 17 and still not fully grown, the normal age of maturity for Russian women – according to the attorney – was 13 or 14. "I drew this conclusion," Kalenius noted, "with the help of medical authorities, and I believe that my explanation of the natural consequences, which sometimes occur from abnormal [physical] development will be understandable, just as everything which is natural is understandable." Having prepared the jury to hear the natural truth, he proceeded to paraphrase several German scientists, none of whom would have been recognized by members of the jury but who had all written on nervous illnesses arising from abnormal development. In interpreting the scientific jargon for the jury, he found all the described symptoms in Varvara Ozerskaia: an aversion to her husband; an aversion to housework; and irritability when reprimanded. "And for the diseased extravagance [*boleznennoe sumasbrodstvo*] of the wife," he concluded his statement, "the husband has been brought before the court, and for that he languishes in prison! [It is] in your will, gentlemen of the jury, [to] free the accused."

In addressing the issues raised by the defense, the procurator only weakened his case. He argued that the beating had been excessive, because its cause had been so trivial: Varvara had forgotten to feed the hens. In his rebuttal, Kalenius attacked the ignorant condescension of the prosecutor, pointing out the loss of poultry was hardly insignificant for a poor peasant family. Indeed, Stepan Ozerskii was the only working-age man in the household, and his mother and sister had nobody else to support them. Kalenius had constructed a brilliant case. Having cited peasant custom and the newest scientific theories, he appealed to the jury to return the son and brother to his family. In the process, he represented himself as a man of the people, educated at a district school, and equally comfortable with rural life as with the latest scientific advances. The jury was convinced, and the defendant Stepan Ozerskii was quickly found not guilty. The impulse of the judicial reform to modernize social life, in part by sanctifying the principles of human dignity and bodily inviolability, had conflicted with the new sciences which undermined the role of free will in suicide. Patriarchal violence and cruelty were not to blame but rather Varvara's own abnormality – her deviant physiological development.

The church's predicament

Ecclesiastical authorities were faced with a paradox. According to church teachings and canon law, suicide was perhaps the greatest crime, for it was the "fruit of complete unbelief," a rejection of God and the church.[44] Fearing a *de facto* decriminalization of suicide by the 1870s, the church sought to maintain the active role of the judiciary in its prosecution. For this reason, it demanded adherence to the letter of the law when it refused to accept cases of attempted suicide forwarded by the courts and the police without the requisite investigation establishing intent.[45] Reduced state regulation of so-called moral questions (which could include sexuality and marriage as well as suicide) would have diminished the power of the church as well.[46] Despite such efforts, churchmen were also beginning to resent what they considered the intrusion of civil authorities into matters of faith. It was not the fact of police investigation that so bothered them but rather the judgments reached. Jurisdictional conflicts had been rare before the reform era, but the new sciences seemed to undermine fundamental religious principles. The first signs of dismay with the rulings of secular authorities date to the 1870s. By the 1890s, dismay had turned to real anger: too many suicides were being judged ill and hence eligible for a Christian burial.

When suicide emerged as a significant topic in newspapers and journals during the 1870s, it also became a recurring theme in the ecclesiastical press. As religious leaders and commentators began to publish articles and pamphlets on the problem, suicide – both the social problem and the individual act – became one front in a broader campaign waged against the primary moral plague of modern societies: secularism. At stake was the soul of the nation. This engagement parallels broader trends within the Orthodox Church, which grew increasingly assertive in its conservative program, whether in church schools, missionary work, or the regulation of the family.[47] It also parallels the approach

---

[44] S. V. Bulgakov, *Nastol'naia kniga dlia sviashchenno-tserkovnykh sluzhitelei*, 2nd edn (Kharkov, 1900), 1249 n. 3.

[45] In the cases of attempted suicide discussed above, the Senate consistently supported the church on this question.

[46] These issues are discussed extensively in Engelstein, *Keys to Happiness*, chs. 1–3.

[47] The scholarly literature is now extensive. See the important article by Gregory Freeze, "Handmaiden of the State: The Church in Imperial Russia Reconsidered," *Journal of Ecclesiastical History* 36 (1985), 82–102.

of the writer Fedor Dostoevsky, who explored suicide as the logical consequence of a God-less universe.[48]

At issue was first the causal linkage between suicide and secularism, an expansive term that included paganism and atheism as well as the crass egoism and materialism of modern urban civilization. Particularly striking was the scientific basis of argument. Drawing extensively on contemporary social-statistical sources, many religious writers accepted the definition of suicide as a social phenomenon and the accuracy of contemporary statistics. Their particular tale began in antiquity, when, despite isolated voices of opposition (such as Plato), the Greeks and Romans had generally lionized the act of suicide and thereby encouraged it. With the rise of Christianity and its clear prohibition, it was claimed, the number of cases fell drastically until the rediscovery of the classical era during the sixteenth century. Reinforced by Enlightenment thinkers and the relaxation of legal prohibitions, the resurgence of paganism – in the form of secularism and atheism – had finally triumphed during the French Revolution, "when it was attempted to eradicate Christianity and to implant philosophical paganism in its place" and when the "tremendous dimensions of suicide served as a fitting expression of the pagan principles of that time." Finally, during the nineteenth century, the ever-increasing rates of suicide in most "civilized and enlightened countries" continued to document the spread of a pagan, secular, and rationalistic worldview. The explanation for suicide thus depended upon both an ahistorical opposition between Christianity and paganism as well as a historical narrative of secularization. The decline of religious faith deprived modern people of a meaning and goal for life, and neither philosophical materialism (science) nor cultural materialism (the pursuit of money, luxury, personal pleasure) could fill this spiritual hole. Left with nothing beyond petty pride and physical mortality, people experienced life as a burden and were consequently falling into despair and disappointment. Indeed, the social-statistical geography of suicide seemed to support this interpretation. How else should one explain the lower rates of suicide among more religious groups such as peasants and women? To combat the problem, religious commentators called for three measures: to censor publicity around suicide; to apply legal punishments and public forms of shame; and to reinforce religious education.[49]

Throughout the late nineteenth century, clergy writing on the problem of suicide continued to be well versed in the scientific and medical

---

[48] For further discussion of Dostoevsky's views, see Paperno, *Suicide*.

[49] See "Samoubiistvo pred sudom iazychestva i khristianstva," *Tserkovnyi vestnik* no. 26 (1876), 1–3. This theme repeated frequently. See also "Samoubiistvo v iazycheskom i khristianskom mire," *Tserkovnyi vestnik* no. 46 (1880); A. P. "Usilenie manii samoubiistv v novoi Evrope," *Tserkovnyi vestnik* nos. 17, 18 (1882); A. P. "Iz statistiki samoubiistv v Evrope za nyneshnee stoletie," *Tserkovnyi vestnik* no. 18 (1882); and E. Tikhomirov, *Bessmertie dushi i samoubiistvo* (Moscow, 1879).

literature.[50] Moreover, they often used medical metaphors in their diagnosis of the spiritual plagues afflicting society. For their part, many doctors had also become increasingly concerned about secularization, the decline of "traditional" forms of moral governance, and the rising threat posed by vice. Consequently, to view the jurisdictional conflicts about suicide as a straightforward collision of religion with science, tradition with progress, would be simplistic. While the problem was often framed in such polemical language, at issue was more the contested relationship between body and soul. Many clergy feared that the social and medical sciences were claiming jurisdiction over the soul and thereby undermining the concepts of sin and moral responsibility.

"Is it allowed to bring [the body of] a suicide into the church for a funeral service? It is obligatory, if civil authorities have certified that the suicide was committed in an attack of madness or insanity. [. . .] The full Orthodox ritual is to be followed in the burial and prayers." This exchange was published in 1891 as part of a regular column on parish practice in *The Church Herald*, the newspaper of the St. Petersburg Theological Academy.[51] That it was necessary to print this most basic rule suggests that the procedures for the burial of suicides were either not well known or not always followed.[52] The column on parish practice repeatedly returned to the problems arising out of jurisdictional disagreement on questions of burial. Must the priest follow police orders when the circumstances and causes of the suicide had not been provided? When the police did not establish whether the cause of death had been accident or suicide? When the police certified that the suicide had been "a little bit drunk"?[53] Most disturbing for clergy was that Christian burial could be denied to those suicides who had been able to confess and receive the sacrament before dying from their self-inflicted wounds. From the perspective of the law, this was no contradiction, for intention was the sole issue. For the clergy, however, this was a basic assault on their spiritual authority and faith. Many thus believed that a time lapse between a suicide attempt and death was a sign from God; the sinner had been given the chance to repent and receive God's grace. That other suicides, who had died immediately, were accorded Christian burial despite the reservations of the priest and the absence of last rites was deemed a particularly crass injustice. By 1900, this question had been mostly resolved, and the standard guide to parish

[50] For further analysis of this mutual influence, see Daniel Beer, "The Medicalization of Religious Deviance in the Russian Orthodox Church (1880–1905)," *Kritika: Explorations in Russian and Eurasian History* no. 3 (2004).

[51] *Tserkovnyi vestnik* no. 31 (1891), 489. Reprinted in N. Nikol'skii and M. Izvol'skii, eds., *Sistematicheskii sbornik nedoumennykh voprosov i otvetov na nikh vstrechaiushchikhsia v tserkovno-prikhodskoi praktike* (SPb, 1896), 121.

[52] According the complaint of one local police authority in 1873, clergy routinely conducted burials in cases of sudden or accidental death without the permission of secular authorities. See "Iz praktiki tserkovnoi," *Vladimirskie eparkhial'nye vedomosti* no. 10 (May 15, 1873), 302–3.

[53] *Tserkovnyi vestnik* no. 4 (1897), 110; no. 38 (1894), 603; no. 23 (1894), 360.

practice specified that suicides who had confessed and received communion before their deaths should receive a Christian funeral.[54] Priests also emerged victorious on another question: they had a right to know the cause of death and identity of the victim before conducting the burial. Concerned not just about suicide but about heterodoxy, clergy had protested the orders of local police to bury unidentified bodies found drowned in the Volga, which was a religiously heterogeneous region.[55]

Yet clergymen also asserted their right to judge the mental and spiritual state of suicides. The column on parish practice regularly returned to this question. Should the priest follow police directives when he "knows that [the suicide] did not display any signs of insanity beforehand and that no medical examination or autopsy [. . .] took place?" What should he do when "he knows for sure that the certification [of an attack of delirium] cannot be believed?" One column posed the same question but supplied more background information: "A peasant woman who was completely healthy and was only distinguished by extreme irritability, killed herself [. . .] due to an insignificant argument with her husband; a forensic-medical autopsy of the body took place on the basis of which the police provided the certification that no obstacles to a [Christian] burial exist."[56] The problem was clear: "Every [Christian] suicide can be sure that he will be buried with Christian rites; if the spiritual authority poses an obstacle, then it is always possible for the relatives and friends of the suicide to find doctors willing to certify, for a respectable honorarium, that he had taken his life in an attack of insanity."[57] With doctors motivated less by medical ethics than material profit, it was implied, practically all suicides were now accorded Christian burials, and the most effective deterrent to the social problem had been eliminated. Condemning the "abuse of medical certification" in a public lecture, I. Popov called upon the church to fight back. It was time to impose the letter of the law and restore punitive measures. Even in those genuine cases caused by illness, the suicide should receive a funeral lacking majesty (*torzhestvennost'*) and publicity, one which would not serve as temptation to others.[58]

By the 1890s, dissatisfaction with having to obey civil authorities was increasingly translated into demands for increased church autonomy. Throughout the

---

[54] On the controversy, G. Mikhailovskii, "O pogrebenii samoubiits i lits, umershikh neestestven-noiu smertiiu," *Kavkazskie eparkhial'nye vedomosti* no. 7 (Apr. 1, 1878), 254–59; On its resolution, see Bulgakov, *Nastol'naia kniga*, 1249 n. 5, 1251 n. 5.

[55] Mikhailovskii, "O pogrebenii samoubiits," 260–62. See also *Tserkovnyi vestnik* no. 9 (1875), 3; no. 10 (1878), 15; no. 49 (1878), 14.

[56] *Tserkovnyi vestnik* no. 19 (1897), 607; no. 11 (1891), 170; no. 8 (1903), 243.

[57] *Tserkovnyi vestnik* no. 35 (1894), 549.

[58] I. Popov, "O samoubiistve," *Bogoslovskii vestnik* no. 3 (1898), 390–92. This view is confirmed in detail in Bulgakov, *Nastol'naia kniga*, 1250 n. 2. Complaints about doctors recur frequently. See e.g. *Tserkovnyi vestnik* no. 1 (1891), 3; no. 50 (1893), 792–3; no. 35 (1894), 549; and no. 27 (1897), 854.

decade, rumors spread that the church was to be returned its lost rights of
judgment, and the Archbishop of Kharkov even elaborated a specific project.
These hopes proved illusory, however.[59] Nevertheless, some churchmen were
beginning to formulate measures to address the perceived problem. In 1894,
the spiritual consistory in Samara distinguished between the authorization of
police to proceed with burial and the doctor's certification of illness; only the
latter provided any obligation to confer a Christian burial.[60] This was not an
eager submission to medical authority but rather an attempt to identify a loop-
hole by providing a literal interpretation of the standard formula ("there are no
obstacles to burial"). A doctor's explicit certification prevented such a reading,
however. In a circular to his diocese from the following year, Makarii, Bishop
of Tomsk, went even further. Strictly admonishing clergy to obey the law, he
directed them to break it in practice by investigating the circumstances of each
suicide for themselves. In so-called "doubtful cases," when neither competence
nor incompetence could really be established, it was permitted to conduct an
abridged service – the singing of "The Holy God" as the body was carried to
the grave and to perform a short liturgy outside of the church. The location of
the grave was apparently to be determined by the priest, who was likewise to
report the case to his superiors. Should the family members desire additional
prayers or a full service, they were to petition diocesan authorities.[61] While
this was not a formal policy, *The Church Herald* did not criticize it (or note
the contradiction with other directives it published). Furthermore, the guide to
parish practice praised this effort, noting that it was consistent with the original
canon: "rather than relying absolutely on medical certification, priests would
be guided by their personal knowledge of the physical and spiritual condition
of their parishioner." It likewise noted (in bold type) that civil authorities were
not competent to decide the kind of service accorded a suicide.[62] By the turn
of the twentieth century, therefore, the church no longer so feared the decriminalization of suicide but, citing canon law, increasingly asserted its own lost
rights of judgment. Not the doctor but the priest was best able to assess man's
physical and spiritual condition.[63]

Drinking to death revisited

The tension between spiritual and medical knowledge found its most contentious expression in the disputed relationship between vodka and suicide.

---

[59] *Tserkovnyi vestnik* no. 1 (1891), 3; no. 39 (1895), 1238–39; no. 19 (1897), 607; and no. 8 (1903),
243–44.
[60] Summarized in Bulgakov, *Nastol'naia kniga*, 1252 n. 1.
[61] Summarized in *Tserkovnyi vestnik* no. 39 (1895), 1238–39.
[62] Bulgakov, *Nastol'naia kniga*, 1252 n. 2, 1251 n. 2.
[63] I thus disagree with Paperno (*Suicide*, 65–66) who argues that priests eagerly submitted to
medical opinion.

At issue was whether drunkenness should be understood in moral terms, as evidence of sin and culpability, or in medical terms, as evidence of disease and incapacity. A case from Arkhangelsk province illustrates the basic problem. In a series of letters sent to *The Church Herald* in 1879, two residents of the town of Onega disputed the facts and significance of a recent suicide.[64] An ex-soldier named Ivan Stepanov had hanged himself after a prolonged drinking binge. Ordered by the local police to bury Stepanov with Christian rites, the priest had at first refused but then complied after the police protested to the diocesan administration. Still, he allowed himself some latitude in interpreting the police's directives. The body had apparently been buried in the woods, and prayers had been sung after a weekday liturgy.[65]

At the core of the dispute was the relationship between morality and medicine, sin and disease. For the first letter-writer, who was probably a priest, Stepanov's suicide was the logical result of his "tenacious drunkenness," not mental or physical illness: "You see, if drunkenness is categorized as an involuntary disease [. . .] then it could very well happen that all suicides will be judged unaccountable, because police doctors can always name this or that organic or mental disease under the influence of which the suicide took his life. As is well known, there is a theory which denies all free will in man and which sees everything man does as fatal necessity [*rokovaia neobkhodimost'*] and involuntariness [*neproizvol'nost'*]. But why do our church rules remain if we have to consider such opinions and even be guided by them?" For his opponent, however, drunkenness constituted a kind of mitigating circumstance. Quoting an 1848 decree of the Most Holy Synod, he claimed: "those who drink themselves to death have perhaps died an unnatural death but they have not deliberately taken their own lives and thus merit a Christian burial; (it is well known that death from over-drinking is accompanied by the clouding of reason, which does not occur with the consumption of other substances)." He then made a striking comparison: "The excessive consumption of food, nights without sleep, and many other [forms of conduct] often lead our people to an early grave, but are the deceased from such causes [. . .] denied Christian burial?" According to this logic, the fact that the soldier had hanged himself was irrelevant, because the true cause of death was drunkenness, a condition he likened to gluttony. Finally, rising up in indignant self-defense, the first letter-writer rejected this claim. "Sensing the approach of death through the excessive consumption of

---

[64] The following discussion draws on these sources: Odin iz zhitelei g. Onegi, "Zatrudnitel'nyi sluchai iz prikhodskoi praktiki," *Tserkovnyi vestnik* no. 35 (1879), 14; Onezhanin, "Eshche o zatrudnitel'nom sluchae iz prikhodskoi praktiki," *Tserkovnyi vestnik* no. 45 (1879), 15; and Odin iz zhitelei goroda Onego, "Eshche o zatrudnitel'nom sluchae iz pastyrskoi praktiki," *Tserkovnyi vestnik* no. 51/52 (1879), 22–23. For a more detailed analysis, see my "Drinking to Death: Vodka, Suicide, and Religious Burial in Imperial Russia," *Past and Present* 186: 1 (2005).

[65] This solution shows marked parallels to the procedures later outlined by Bishop Makarii. See above.

food," he ironically noted, "someone does not call the priest or the doctor to him, but instead, without saying a word to anyone, goes out to an empty barn and hangs himself there – would the church really condone a Christian burial for such a suicide without a medical examination . . .?" He thus dismissed the Synod's decision on the burial of drunkards as irrelevant to this case. Stepanov may have been drunk, but, in the end, he had chosen the noose. He was not an *opoitsa* but an ordinary suicide. Unfortunately, the exchange ends here, and the resolution of the dispute is unknown.

The distinctive notion of drinking to death as a category of suicide emerged in the seventeenth century, and it reflected the contemporary tendency to conceptualize suicidal intention in terms of moral behavior. This pattern persisted in the eighteenth and early nineteenth centuries, when many suicides were attributed to drunkenness. While actual disputes over burial would only become common in the 1870s, the Synod had issued four relevant decrees between 1839 and 1848.[66] Though intended to clarify procedure, these texts are models of conceptual ambiguity. The Synod initially attempted to define a broad category of "obdurate drunkenness" that would, firstly, permit certain drunken (but accidental) deaths to be categorized as suicide and, secondly, provide evidence of guilt in cases of suicide committed in drunkenness. The editors of the 1845 penal code rejected this formulation, however, arguing in part that "obdurate drunkenness" lacked a medical basis. Consequently, the Synod had been compelled to revise its policies, and it produced the 1848 decree that was later cited in the dispute over Stepanov's suicide in Onega. Even in this last attempt at clarification, the convoluted language only underlined the conviction among church leaders that drinking to death did constitute a form of suicide and that drunkenness was not a mitigating but rather an incriminating factor.[67]

In the 1840s, drunken suicides had generally been found morally and legally culpable, despite these decrees. In the 1870s, however, disputes between priests and police, such as the one in Onega, were appealed to various spiritual consistories, prompting the Senate to order the Synod in 1878 to issue yet another procedural ruling. While the title of the resulting decree referred to the burial of those who have "suddenly died from the superfluous consumption of alcohol," the text simply stated – citing the penal code – that Christian burial may be denied only to "intentional suicides," which did not include "those who had

---

[66] The broader context was legal codification, for drinking to death had never been addressed in either secular or canon law. During the 1830s, the church also reviewed its legal basis and published a corrected version of canon law based on original texts. See *Kniga pravil sviatykh apostolov, sviatykh soborov vselenskikh i pomestnykh i sviatykh ottsov* (SPb, 1839).

[67] The decrees were frequently reprinted in this period. See *Tserkovnyi vestnik* no. 12/13 (1879), 18–19; Mikhailovskii, "O pogrebenii samoubiits," 262–65; and S. V. Kalashnikov, *Alfavitnyi ukazatel'*, 211–12.

perished accidentally from the abuse of alcoholic beverages."[68] (Had Stepanov died "accidentally"?) Guides to church regulations also addressed this issue but they too tended to reinforce the ambiguity.[69] In practice, of course, both perspectives coexisted in this period. When Sergei Makarov, a 19-year-old peasant, attempted suicide, his parents explained that he "was always getting drunk and generally lived immorally." Though he had no motive for or memory of the act, Sergei performed penance.[70] In contrast, a jury in St. Petersburg accepted the notion ("from psychiatry") that drink could cause a "significant moral transformation" in a man leading him to commit a crime without intention.[71]

Conflicts over burial persisted at least into the 1890s, but the medical approach to drunken suicides was gradually gaining authority.[72] In 1900, the standard guide to parish practice was (mostly) unambiguous. Paraphrasing the 1848 decree, it affirmed that those who die from drunkenness cannot be categorized as suicides and must be accorded a full burial. Furthermore, drunken suicides could only be denied burial if it could be proven that the idea of suicide had originated when they were sober and that they drank deliberately to take their lives. Yet even this principle was qualified: due to the clouding of reason produced by alcohol, drunken suicides lost their criminal character. After explaining such nuances, the guide then contradicted them. It cited an 1894 ruling of the Samara diocese supporting a priest who had refused to conduct a funeral service.[73]

The backdrop for these disputes and ambiguities – as the two letter-writers from Onega were well aware – was modern science. By the 1860s and 1870s, drunkenness was construed as a social and medical problem, caused by material deprivation and ignorance and leading to mental disorders and suicide.[74] In the late 1880s, it gained its own medical designation. The etiology of "alcoholic psychosis," according to Pavel Kovalevskii, lay in "insufficient energy in

[68] For the Senate's directive, see RGIA, f. 797, op. 90: 1878, d. 11. The Synod's decree was printed in *Tserkovnyi vestnik* no. 41 (1881), 220.

[69] One effort stated: "An Orthodox funeral is to be denied to all individuals not belonging to the Orthodox Church and to the following members: suicides and those who have died from drunkenness [*umershie ot p'ianstva*], so long that the suicide did not occur when they were insane." Ia. Ivanovskii, comp. *Obozrenie tserkovno-grazhdanskikh uzakonenii po dukhovnomu vedomstvu. Spravochnaia kniga* (SPb, 1883), 204–5.

[70] GANO, f. 570, op. 559, 1888, d. 48, ll. 5–6.

[71] See the report on a certain Cherkasov, who was acquitted of theft and attempted suicide – despite his free confession. The defendant, a previously respectable man, had suddenly acquired an aberrant passion for drink and binged for a week before committing his crimes. His honest testimony, clear remorse, and physical trembling combined with his previously upright conduct convinced the jury that he had indeed been ill. "Interesnoe ugolovnoe delo v S.-Peterburgskom okruzhnom sude," *Nedelia* no. 42 (1866), 667–68.

[72] *Tserkovnyi vestnik* no. 1 (1891); no. 23 (1894).

[73] Bulgakov, *Nastol'naia kniga*, 1250 n. 1.

[74] Pasternatskii, "Statisticheskoe issledovanie," *passim*; and N. V. Ponomarev, "Samoubiistvo v zapadnoi Evrope i v Rossii, v sviazi s razvitiem umopomeshatel'stva," *SSSM* no. 3 (1880), 110–11.

the central nervous system causing insufficient self-possession and resistance to [. . .] alcohol and other intoxicating substances." This could in turn lead to "alcoholic neurasthenia," physical and mental suffering, and ultimately to a suicide attempt.[75] Such ideas became increasingly accepted in the 1890s, as alcohol abuse – like suicide – was linked to degeneration and nervous disorders.[76]

Many voices from the Orthodox Church attacked these developments. Demonstrating his grasp of the medical literature, I. A. Nevzorov nonetheless asserted that most suicides were acts of free will, not insanity. His argument built on the long-standing conception of intention as a function of moral character:

Let there be suicides committed in an abnormal condition; but if a person reached such a condition as a consequence of an improper lifestyle, for example, drunkenness or debauchery, then he can not be considered guiltless, nor unanswerable for his suicide. Can it really be true that we must acquit the inveterate drunkard or libertine, if they – the one as a consequence of unrestrained drunkenness, the other as a consequence of unbridled debauchery – bring about the derangement of their nervous systems and end [their] lives in suicide?[77]

In Nevzorov's view, which was diametrically opposed to Dr. Rozanov's (quoted above), a true Christian must regard suicide as a question of morality, not medicine, and he perceived a fundamental conflict between the two systems. To deny the agency of self-killing was to deny the sinfulness of vice more broadly. This very tendency, he believed, only encouraged the increasing incidence of suicide in Russia.

Condemning both the brutality of Social Darwinism and the scientific denial of free will, the author of another religious pamphlet agreed: "Now people have begun to see themselves as animals that must struggle for life. [. . .] All the weak, the lost [. . .] only improve and advance progress. There can be no talk of responsibility for one's actions for everything occurs according to the insurmountable and autonomous power of external circumstance or under the influence of derangement 'in the reflexes of the thinking brain.' "[78] Likewise dismissing the relevance of the Darwinist struggle, Father P. Svetlov highlighted what he considered the real problem: "Is it possible that the nervousness of the nineteenth century or the physical weakening of man can explain his moral weakening, his loss of determination and steadfastness amidst all the blows and

---

[75] P. I. Kovalevskii, *P'ianstvo, ego prichiny i lechenie* (1889), as quoted in I. Lebedev, *O samoubiistve s meditsinskoi tochki zreniia* (SPb, 1897), 35–6.

[76] For an overview of the extensive literature, see T. Krol', "K voprosu o vliianii alkogolia na zabolevaemost', smertnost', i prestupnost' " (Dissertation for the Degree Doctor of Medicine, Military Medical Academy, 1897); and George E. Snow, "Perceptions of the Link between Alcoholism and Crime in Pre-Revolutionary Russia," *Criminal Justice History* 8 (1987), 37–51.

[77] I. A. Nevzorov, *O samoubiistve* (Kazan, 1891), 10.

[78] This was probably a reference to Sechenev. A. Klitin, *Nashe vremia i samoubiistvo* (Kiev, 1890), 4–5.

adversities [of life]? But to think that would mean to expand the link between soul and body to the full subordination of the soul to the body; it would mean to forget that weak bodies are often greater in spirit than strong or healthy ones."[79] The true origins of suicide thus lay in a disease of the spirit, which was caused by a secular modernity. The priest, not the doctor, possessed the means to its therapy and cure.

Popular belief

One spring day, a woman's body was found in the Volga River: she was in a coffin with two large rocks attached to it. Soon afterwards, the children identified their mother, Anna Baranova, who had died from drink and been buried in the cemetery. According to the police investigation, local peasants had dug up the body and put it into the Volga on the instructions of a village elder. Yet nobody involved claimed to see anything wrong in their action. To the contrary, it had been a kind of "heroic feat" (*podvig*). That spring had witnessed a bad drought, and it was common knowledge that drought and other natural disasters occurred should *opoitsy* or suicides be buried in the village cemetery. At their 1891 trial, the defendants mounted no other defense than their conviction to have acted for the common welfare (*obshchaia pol'za*) in a time of tremendous hardship and threatened famine. They were sentenced to several months' imprisonment – not the Siberian resettlement specified in the penal code.[80] As this case evocatively illustrates, jurisdictional conflict over suicide – particularly the fate of the body – involved yet another party: the peasant community. Acting unilaterally and in the perceived communal interest, Baranova's neighbors had rejected the authority of church and state.

During the late nineteenth century, the national and local press reported many similar cases. These accounts played upon a well-established sense of cultural distance between urban, educated society and rural villagers. Emphasizing the archaic "superstitions" of the "dark masses," they presented peasant beliefs as vestiges of a pre-modern and wholly foreign world. While some articles concluded in a conventional homage to enlightenment expelling the darkness, others made fun of vain efforts to educate the people.[81] Despite such differences in tone, peasant superstition had become an object of curiosity for the modern, urban reader, and newspaper reports typically focused on the sensational aspects of the desecration of graves. This context framed contemporary approaches to peasant beliefs and practices more widely. Just as ethnographic accounts

---

[79] P. Svetlov, "O samoubiistve," *Khristianskoe chtenie* no. 2 (1897), 338–39.

[80] "Sudebnye protsessy: Prestuplenie na pochve sueveriia," *Nedelia* no. 23 (1891), 710–11.

[81] For examples of each conclusion, see Vasilii Perogovskii, "O narodnom obychnom ugolovnom prave na Volyni," *Volynskie gubernskie vedomosti* no. 25 (Apr. 14, 1879), 4; and Tat'iana Sulima, "Proshlym letom," *Step'* no. 25 (June 22, 1888), 379–83.

sometimes presumed a peasant world untainted by modernity and pagan at its core, the church condemned aspects of popular religion as unchristian in a broader effort to assert its own hegemony over matters of faith.[82] For their part, jurists cited crimes of superstition as further evidence of the imperative to modernize society and the law; the first task was to remove suicide from the criminal code.[83] Altogether then, peasants' actions presented a challenge to outsiders. They effectively exposed the subordinate position of the church and tested the visions of modernity and progress held by many within educated society.

Popular religion did often diverge from official church teachings in the nineteenth century.[84] While the exclusion of suicides (and *opoitsy*) from the cemetery was a shared principle, peasants possessed a broader notion of unclean death.[85] As the ethnographer Dmitrii Zelenin comprehensively documented, the rituals of profane burial occurred across the Russian empire, and he identified variable categories of dead bodies, which were considered unclean and potentially dangerous to the living: suicides, *opoitsy*, victims of accidental or violent death, un-baptized infants, strangers, children cursed by their parents, witches, sorcerers and vampires, and members of other faiths.[86] The unnatural dead then belonged to the demonic "unclean force" (*nechistaia sila*). Not only could they wander the earth at night and harm the living, but the devil was known to "ride" suicides and goad them on.[87] Indeed, the linkage between suicide and demonic forces was especially prominent (as it had been in some Muscovite

[82] For a critique of the theory of *dvoeverie*, which shaped religious and ethnographic approaches to peasant belief, see Eve Levin, "*Dvoeverie* and Popular Religion," in Stephen K. Batalden, ed., *Seeking God: The Recovery of Religious Identity in Orthodox Russia, Ukraine, and Georgia* (DeKalb, Ill., 1993).

[83] A. Levenstim, *Sueverie i ugolovnoe pravo* (SPb, 1897); A. Kirpichnikov, "Daleko li ushli my ot mificheskogo mirosozertsaniia?" *Nov'* no. 1 (1885); and L. S. Belogrits-Kotliarevskii, "Mifologicheskoe znachenie nekotorykh prestuplenii, sovershaemykh po sueveriiu," *Istoricheskii vestnik* no. 7 (1888).

[84] For further discussion of peasants and religion, see Chris J. Chulos, *Converging Worlds: Religion and Community in Peasant Russia, 1861–1917* (DeKalb, Ill., 2003); Stephen Frank, *Crime, Cultural Conflict, and Justice in Rural Russia, 1856–1914* (Berkeley, 1999); Vera Shevzov, *Russian Orthodoxy on the Eve of Revolution* (Oxford and New York, 2004); and Christine D. Worobec, *Peasant Russia: Family and Community in the Post-Emancipation Period* (Princeton, 1991).

[85] P. S. Efimenko, "Materialy po etnografii russkogo naseleniia Arkhangel'skoi gubernii," *Izvestiia Imp. Obshchestva liubitelei estestvoznaniia, antropologii i etnografii pri Imp. Moskovskom universitete. Trudy etnograficheskogo otdela* vol. 30. bk. 5, no.1 (1877), 137.

[86] D. K. Zelenin, *Ocherki russkoi mifologii: Umershie neestestvennoiu smert'iu i rusalki* (Petrograd, 1916; reprint: Moscow, 1995), ch. 1. See also Christine D. Worobec, "Death Ritual among Russian and Ukrainian Peasants: Linkages between the Living and the Dead," in *Cultures in Flux: Lower-Class Values, Practices, and Resistance in Late Imperial Russia*, ed. Stephen P. Frank and Mark D. Steinberg (Princeton, 1994).

[87] For further discussion of demonic intervention and the unclean force, see Zelenin, *Ocherki russkoi mifologii*; V. N. Dobrovol'skii, "Nechistaia sila v narodnykh verovaniiakh: Po dannym Smolenskoi gubernii," *Zhivaia starina* no. 1 (1908).

sources). Many peasants apparently believed that the devil could drive someone to kill himself and that suicide was sometimes caused by demonic possession (one symptom of which could be mental alienation and withdrawal).[88] To minimize the dangers, peasants preferred burial at crossroads or forsaken sites; other rituals included driving an aspen stake into the body, decapitating it, or burning it. Nevertheless, fear often remained. According to one ethnographic account, a neighbor of a suicide in Vologda province was afraid of going outside at dusk although the body had been buried about 25 verst from the village.[89] Similarly, many peasants believed that the Christian burial of a suicide or *opoitsa* could result in natural disasters, especially drought. Consequently, peasants would "water" the graves, pray for God's mercy and intervention, and, often as a last resort, desecrate the graves. These cases were common in the late 1880s and early 1890s, when drought, poor harvests, and high taxation contributed to a devastating famine in 1891.[90]

Belief in the immanence of the supernatural and especially the ubiquity of the *nechistaia sila* was uncommon within the church. Nevertheless, ecclesiastical teachings on suicide may have helped to legitimize peasants' actions. Scattered evidence suggests that some priests either actively supported their parishioners or simply closed their eyes to illegal actions. In an 1892 case, for example, a parish priest was sentenced to penance in a monastery for encouraging parishioners to dig up a suicide and throw the body in the woods. In a published decree, the bishop emphasized that some priests still remained indifferent to peasants' superstitions in this regard, neither admonishing nor reporting on their flocks as they should.[91] Popular and ecclesiastical attitudes toward drunkenness also possessed important parallels. Peasants condemned drunkenness as a sin, even the work of the devil, and as a behavior harmful to the family and village. According to one ethnographer, peasants in Vitebsk province distinguished between the obdurate drunkard (*propoitsa*) and the occasional drunkard (*zapoitsa*); the former was perceived as an alien in the community, whose body could be excluded from the cemetery.[92] Such attitudes recall the controversy in Onega as well as the categories of the Synodic decrees from the 1840s.

Despite the strong association of suicide with the unclean force, evidence suggests that peasants did not condemn all suicides out of hand. Their bleak fate

---

[88] See the account in the Tenishev archive: *zadumyvat'sia* was understood as the letting-in of the devil. EM, f. 7, op. 1, d. 552, l. 21. See also d. 837, ll. 6–8. For more discussion and examples, V. Dobrovol'skii, "Narodnye skazaniia o samoubiitsakh," *Zhivaia starina* no. 2 (1894).

[89] A verst is approximately 3,500 feet. See EM, f. 7, op. 1, d. 326.

[90] See e.g. the untitled report in *Podol'skie gubernskie vedomosti* (1890), no. 38, 198; S. B-khin, "Korrespondentsiia," *Kharkov'skie gubernskie vedomosti* no. 132 (1887), 2; and K. "Iz Aleksandrovskogo uezda," *Novorossiiskii telegraf* (June 19, 1887), 3.

[91] *Smolenskii vestnik* (Oct. 2, 1892), 1.

[92] N. Ia. Nikiforovskii, "Ocherki Vitebskoi Belorussii," *Etnograficheskoe obozrenie* no. 4 (1896), 80–81. See also EM, f. 7. op. 1, d. 552, ll. 20–1.

caused families to suffer, and sometimes they prayed for their loved one's soul –
in contradiction to the church's formal prohibition. Occasionally communities
were divided over the location of the grave, with family members wanting a
Christian service.[93] Ethnographic accounts describe peasant families giving
alms – a customary gesture in deaths from natural causes – for the recipients
were supposed to offer prayers in thanks.[94] Similarly, the ringing of bells was
occasionally thought to alleviate the suicide's suffering and even lead to God's
forgiveness.[95] While the church fully recognized the miraculous power of prayer
and bells, suicides were not supposed to be their beneficiaries. Still, in the 1860s,
two priests reported two such cases from their parishes. In both instances, family
members had had visions of the deceased (including a visit to hell), whose
suffering had lessened over time in response to prayers.[96]

The relationship between official church teachings and popular beliefs and
practices was interactive. The church recognized the reality of hell, for example,
as well as the potential intervention of the devil in everyday life, though primarily as a force of temptation. Before disappearing, presumed drowned, Evdokiia
Shcherbakova believed that the devil had possessed her. Though a priest and
several nuns tried to convince her this was not the case, that the devil was only
whispering in her ear, she continued to insist that she no longer possessed a
soul and attempted suicide several times.[97] Another reported case points further
to the interaction of religious and communal beliefs. A young woman died in
childbirth but "woke up" the next day (before her funeral) and claimed that
she had been in the other world (*na tot svet*). Rumors quickly spread that she
must be a great sinner as God had not accepted her. Coming to believe that
she was indeed intended for the devil, she hanged herself – an act that only
confirmed the rumors. Now reputedly convinced that the woman had been a
witch, villagers resolved to render her impotent. Her body was dragged through
the village by the hair before being dumped in a pit which was then filled with
water. Appearing soon afterwards in a vision, however, the woman promised to
leave everyone in peace if only they would fill the pit with holy water and erect
a cross. The villagers collected the money for the cross and had the site blessed
(though it is unclear by whom). As the tale ends there, the young woman presumably remained peacefully in her grave.[98] Peasants believed that they were

---

[93] See the case of a suicide certified as insane and buried in the local cemetery but later dug up and
burned. *Sovremennye izvestiia* (Sept. 24, 1883), 3.

[94] EM, f. 7, op. 1, d. 68, ll. 7–8; d. 517, l. 34; d. 564, l. 1; d. 1435, ll. 6–7; d. 1772, ll. 9–11.

[95] O. P. Semenova, "Smert' i dusha v pover'iakh i v rasskazy krest'ian i meshchan Riazanskogo,
Rannenburgskogo i Dankovskogo uezdov Riazanskoi gubernii," *Zhivaia starina* no. 1 (1898),
232–33.

[96] Sv. Pavel Voinstvenskii, "Zagrobnoe sostoianie samoubiitsy," *Strannik* (Aug. 1866), 74–7; Sv.
Petr Dobrianskii, "Sila molitv sv. Tserkvi po samoubiitse," *Strannik* (Nov. 1866), 76–78.

[97] Blagochinnyi Ierei Matvei Grigor'ev Nikolaevskii, "Chetyre pechal'nykh sobytiia i odno otradnoe," *Pribavlenie k Tambovskim eparkhialnym vedomostiam* no. 7 (Apr. 1, 1866), 197–205.

[98] "Vnutrennie izvestiia," *Khar'kovskie gubernskie vedomosti* no. 219 (Aug. 26, 1883), 3.

good Orthodox Christians, and many of their beliefs were in fact formed within Orthodoxy. When it came to the benefit of their community, however, they also claimed a right to autonomous action. This very autonomy presented a real challenge to the church, which admonished clergy not to remain indifferent to "superstition" but to assert "pastoral influence" and to hinder the commission of actual crimes.[99]

For the police as well, the autonomy of peasant beliefs presented a kind of challenge to their authority. The fate of suicides' bodies, particularly those buried in the local cemetery, even led to overt power struggles with peasants repeatedly watering or moving the body and police posting guards at the gravesite.[100] One 1893 case demonstrates these dynamics particularly well. Not wanting the body buried in the cemetery, some peasants wrote a petition to the local police explaining their views:

During the night of the 24th to the 25th of April the wife of O. B drowned herself. [She had] passed through five doors and very quietly left the house so that her husband and everyone in the house would not hear her – which shows that she was of sound mind and purposely brought herself such a death without confession and Holy Communion. Her husband O. B. stubbornly wants to bury her in the consecrated [ground of the] cemetery, which the parishioners of all three churches do not allow, for they fear various misfortunes [. . .] such has already happened more than once with the burial of such bodies in holy places [. . .].

In response, the police explained the absurdity of the request and the legal consequences of crimes committed out of superstition. A ceremonial burial was explicitly ordered as an example to the "ignorant crowd." Throughout that summer, however, circumstances conspired against the police. A whole series of natural (*cum* supernatural) calamities hit the village – fires and accidental deaths, many caused by lightening bolts – ultimately provoking the peasants to take action by desecrating the body. Unfortunately for the police, the disasters had vindicated peasants' "ignorant" beliefs.[101]

Why did the judgment and burial of suicides become controversial in the late nineteenth century? A simple answer would refer to the secularization of suicide, which, in a regulatory context, provoked conflicts between jurists, doctors, and administrative authorities, on the one hand, and priests and peasants, on the other hand.[102] This explanation comes closest to characterizing the

---

[99] Bulgakov, *Nastol'naia kniga*, 1258–9.
[100] See the account involving the death of a sorcerer (and former church elder) that was rumored to have really been a suicide covered up by the family in B-khin, "Korrespondentsiia," 2. For another case involving overt conflict, see EM, f. 7, op. 1, d. 1854, l. 19.
[101] These events, summarized in a footnote, provided the data for an "ethnographic story." See F. Kudrinskii, "Utoplennitsa," *Kievskaia starina* nos. 4, 5 (1894), here no. 4, 91.
[102] Cf. "Debate: The Secularization of Suicide in England 1660–1800," *Past and Present* 119 (May 1988); and Thomas Kselman, "Funeral Conflicts in Nineteenth-Century France," *Comparative Studies in Society and History* 30 (1988), 314, 319–20, 328–30.

aspirations of jurists. Attacking the conflation of immorality with criminality, reform-minded jurists propounded a secular conception of criminal law and defined its object as the regulation of social relations, not (individual) morality. By attempting to carve a boundary between church and state, they further hoped to transform religion into a private rather than public matter, that is, to place religion into a sphere of private life sanctified by the civil rights of modern citizens, including the freedom of conscience. Although suicide would remain on the statute books until 1917, they largely succeeded in limiting the sphere of criminal jurisdiction, and suicide fell increasingly into an administrative and medical jurisdiction.

The narrative of secularization encounters more resistances when applied to the history of medicine and the church. To be sure, doctors tended increasingly to pronounce suicides (legally) insane, a trend which infuriated many priests and even helped to mobilize the church's vigorous response. At issue, however, was not a simple conflict between science and faith. After all, medical certifications of insanity facilitated the Christian burial of suicides, which highlights two competing visions of the funeral: a means either to provide comfort to the family or to punish the transgression and form a deterrent. Furthermore, doctors and priests shared a fundamental concern about the problem of moral governance in what they both considered an increasingly secular world. If religion no longer provided authoritative precepts for individual behavior and social institutions, how then were morality and social order to be maintained? By investing concepts of immorality and vice with medical and social significance, doctors answered this question by claiming an expanded authority over public health and the social body. Priests, in contrast, sought to reinvigorate the public role of religion and the church, that is, to do battle with the evils of secularism. They were right, of course, that medical approaches subverted the concept of free will and hence sin, but scientific models were also shaping their own ideas, especially of suicide as a social and epidemic phenomenon.

The contested dialogue between representatives of medicine and religion was further heightened by terminological ambiguities. The medical designation for mental illness in Russian is *dushevnaia bolezn'* but the adjective *dushevnyi* derives from the root, *dusha*, or soul. It consequently evokes the spiritual as much as the mental, depending upon the context. In addition to their shared alarm about the mental/spiritual plagues of modern society, therefore, doctors and priests were also extremely concerned about the weakening of the "will," which was thought to play a central role in encouraging vice, immorality, and degeneration. Yet doctors usually conceived volition as a function of physiology, hence in the domain of medicine, whereas priests placed the problem within the sphere of faith and sin. Narratives of displacement – a shift from a religious model of regulation to a medical one – fail to grasp the mutual interplay between religion and science in this period. Both systems were evolving, partly in dialogue, and they possessed conceptual affinities as well as differences.

The conflicts between peasants and external authorities compose an equally complex picture. Many contemporaries understood peasant beliefs as the product of backwardness, a temporal lag in comparison to rational, secularized elites. The endeavors of the police and courts to impose civil authority on questions of burial were not just power struggles, therefore, but acts of cultural modernization. Yet this framework can also obscure the Christian foundations of peasant beliefs, a component often neglected by contemporary ethnographers, as well as the many points of both commonality and conflict between peasants and churchmen. Furthermore, scattered evidence suggests interesting areas of commonality between peasants and urban society. Peasants did not necessarily accept the church's strict prohibition of prayers for suicides, for example, and this parallels opinion in educated society.[103] In sum, the contested regulation of suicide in late nineteenth-century Russia points less to a simple decline in religious sentiment than to changes in its character and aspirations. Attempts to circumscribe religion to a private sphere coexisted with attempts to revitalize the spiritual foundations of Russian society. Russia was indeed in the throes of tremendous social change, but disputes and alliances did not necessarily form along obvious lines, whether secular versus religious, or elite versus popular.

---

[103] See the indignant polemic in *Tserkovnyi vestnik* no. 39 (1895), 1238–39, which was a response to articles in the newspapers *Sovremennoe slovo* and *Novoe vremia* critical of the church's refusal to allow prayers for suicide.

9   A ray of light in the kingdom of darkness

> Where should I go now? Home? No, to go home is the same as going to the grave. Yes, to home, or to the grave . . . It is better in the grave . . . A little grave under a tree . . . How fine! The sun warms it, the rain washes it. In the spring the grass will grow over it, soft grass . . . The birds will fly to the tree, they will sing, raise their young. The flowers will blossom: yellow ones, red, blue . . . all kinds . . . all kinds. How quiet, how nice everything will be. I feel somehow better! I don't even want to think anymore about life. To live again? No, no, I don't want to. It's not worth it.
>
> Aleksandr Ostrovskii, *The Storm*, 1859

> To live in the kingdom of darkness is worse than death.
>
> Nikolai Dobroliubov, "A Ray of Light in the Kingdom of Darkness," 1860

In 1859, the radical literary critic Nikolai Dobroliubov published one of his most influential articles entitled "The Kingdom of Darkness." Applying the principles of real criticism, Dobroliubov interpreted the dramatic corpus of the well-known playwright, Aleksandr Ostrovskii, as an expression of real Russian life. This was a world of petty tyranny (*samodurstvo*), particularly in the family, and its primary consequence was the deformation of the human personality. Not only did it produce "an external submissiveness and a dulled, concentrated grief;" it also encouraged "a slave-like cunning, the most vile deception, and treachery without conscience." At the end of the article, Dobroliubov mused: "True, it is sad, but what is to be done? We must admit it: we did not find an exit from the 'kingdom of darkness' in Ostrovskii's works."[1]

Shortly after the publication of this article, Ostrovskii began writing what would become one of his most famous plays, *The Storm*, which was first performed in November of 1859. The heroine, Katerina, was a young woman from the merchant estate who had been given in marriage to Tikhon Kabanov, a weak man ruled over by his despotic mother. Again Ostrovskii had depicted the "kingdom of darkness" – petty tyranny, warped values and personalities, and boundless suffering. Yet this play ended differently, for Katerina does not

---

[1] "Temnoe tsarstvo" was originally published in *Sovremennik* nos. 7, 9 (1859). See N. A. Dobroliubov, *Sobranie sochinenii*, 9 vols. (Moscow, 1962), vol. 5, 16–135.

Illus. 3 Ostrovskii's *The Storm* was an extremely popular play, and these prints show two of the earliest theatrical images of Katerina: F. K. Snetkova (Aleksandrinskii Theater, 1860) and G. N. Fedotova (Malyi Theater, 1863). Note the traditional merchant dress.

submit. Following her heart, she has an affair, which she is ultimately too honest to hide. Unable to submit to her fate by returning to her husband (who is ready to forgive her), she throws herself into the Volga. (Illus. 3 and 4.) In the final scene, her husband cries over her body, accuses his mother of murder, and mourns his own predicament: Katerina has escaped but he must go on living and suffering.[2]

In the subsequent weeks and months, the play provoked tremendous controversy, and most critics appropriated Dobroliubov's categories. One noted how the play demonstrated the consequences of both the "familial despotism that rules in the kingdom of darkness" and Katerina's emotional and mystical religiosity. These two scourges led to "the loss of will and character, debauchery, and even suicide." Tapping into the long-standing association of suicide with immorality, this critic depicted Katerina as a wholly negative character, who lacked a sense of duty, moral obligation, and human dignity and who consequently ended her life so shamefully. Once again, Ostrovskii had depicted a world "without a single ray of light." Most critics, however, came to Katerina's

[2] See A. N. Ostrovskii, "Groza," in *Sobranie sochinenii v shesti tomakh* (Moscow 1999), vol. 2, 35–90.

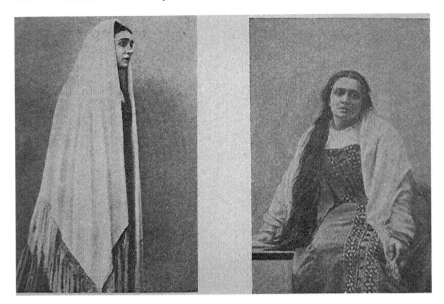

Illus. 4 These representations of Katerina are from later performances of the popular play: P. A. Strepetova (Aleksandrinskii Theater, 1881) and M. G. Savina (Aleksandrinskii Theater, 1907). The changing styles of dress suggest how her image was being adapted into new situations.

defense. To them she seemed the embodiment of pure feeling and instinct, "a pearl of nature," an essentially Russian woman. The tragedy lay in her inevitable victimization, for the kingdom of darkness always destroyed purity and goodness. Despite their veneration of Katerina, they too saw her suicide in conventional terms: she had fallen, a passive victim to external violence.[3]

In the autumn of 1860, Dobroliubov entered the fray with an extended analysis of the play and its critics entitled "A Ray of Light in the Kingdom of Darkness." Katerina was not a victim, he argued, though she did lack a conscious understanding of her predicament. Her suicide was not a defeat but a liberation: she had affirmed the rights of her personality against the pernicious deceit of the kingdom of darkness. "Such a liberation is sad, [even] bitter," he ruminated, "but what is to be done when there is no other exit?" For Dobroliubov, the central fact was Katerina's strength of character – her refusal to submit to slavery – that inexorably led to her suicide. As a heroic protest against the

[3] Most of the reviews were compiled in I. N. Sukhikh, ed., *Russkaia tragediia: P'esa A. N. Ostrovskogo "Groza" v russkoi kritike i literaturovedenii* (SPb, 2002). See in particular the articles of Pal'khovskii (esp. 35–36), Gieroglifov, Panaev, Grigor'ev, and Mel'nikov-Pecherskii. Dostoevsky advanced a slightly different interpretation (esp. 171–74), arguing that Katerina was doomed not because of the despotism but because of the very purity of her nature.

inhuman conditions of life, her death was an assertion of her selfhood. Much more horrifying than her fate, he stressed, were the meaningless and deformed lives of those she had left behind. With this song of freedom in captivity, Ostrovskii had demonstrated the possibility of resistance – an exit from the kingdom of darkness.[4]

Dobroliubov was interested less in suicide, of course, than the character type of Katerina; he lauded her decisiveness as an important sign that the era of "superfluous men" was coming to an end. Just two years later, the publication of Ivan Turgenev's *Fathers and Sons* would confirm the advent of the new man in the character of Bazarov – brashly self-confident, armed with science, and ready to act upon the world. This very development displaced Katerina's heroism, and Dobroliubov's panegyric soon garnered its own critics. The most prominent one on the left would be Dmitrii Pisarev. Rejecting Katerina's emotionality and spontaneity, he described her death as melodramatic and stupid – an impromptu reaction to "petty unpleasantness." Action must be conscious, directed, and social, Pisarev asserted, and the true role models were the tough, thinking rebels – Bazarov and Nikolai Chernyshevskii's Rakhmetov.[5] Yet Bazarov had himself fallen victim to Russia's backwardness in an accident with some parallels to suicide. While performing an autopsy on a peasant who had died from typhus, he cuts himself, fails to seek prompt medical attention, and later dies of the infection. Images of Russia's heroic new people often lingered on their struggles and suffering, and their deaths could possess the motifs of a martyrdom.

Dobroliubov's polemical style, critical methods, and evocative metaphors helped to mold Russian culture in this important transitional period, and his ongoing influence was paradoxically ensured by his premature death in 1861 at the age of 25. His conceptualization of Katerina's heroic feat would also shape the meanings of suicide in late imperial Russia. By likening suicide to protest, Dobroliubov gave the act positive value: it was the ultimate means to defend the individual personality (*lichnost'*) against despotism. Though evoking older traditions of noble suicide, particularly its affirmation of self-sovereignty, Dobroliubov also highlighted the formative role of social environment on the self. His metaphor, the "kingdom of darkness" (*temnoe tsarstvo*), proved influential for it connoted both Russia's social backwardness and the tsarist political system, especially its ethos of custodial care and tutelage. In subsequent decades, autocracy and its patriarchal social institutions were often represented as "kingdoms of darkness" – as sites of arbitrariness and backwardness that obstructed the free development of the personality. Consequently, the problem of suicide came to raise fundamental questions about the self within the social and political order.

[4] Reprinted in *Russkaia tragediia*, esp. 272–78.   [5] Reprinted ibid., esp. 279–309, 324–30.

Despotism in the family

The setting of Ostrovskii's play in a provincial merchant family was not incidental, for the merchant estate was associated with tradition, conservatism, and a
strict adherence to a patriarchal religion. Arranged marriages – as in Katerina's
case – remained common, as did the social seclusion of married women.[6] While
such specific associations and stereotypes underpinned the drama, its cultural
meanings were far broader. Since the advent of sentimentalism in the eighteenth
century, notions of romantic love and affective marriage had begun to challenge
the patriarchal family. This process was multifaceted and often ambiguous. The
"sentimental idyll" of the royal family propagated by Nicholas I, for example,
had combined patriarchal structures of authority with a new emphasis on love
within the family. Literary representations could also be ambivalent. Exhibiting
marked parallels with the conservative outcome of Rousseau's *The New Héloïse*
was Pushkin's tale of Evgenii Onegin and Tat'iana. Despite their love, Tat'iana
rejects Evgenii and remains true to her marriage vow. By the 1840s, however,
and partly due to the influence of George Sand, some elite circles were beginning to envisage – and occasionally enact – radically new forms of family life
that included women's rights to personal development and autonomy and even
sexual freedom. Finally, in the aftermath of the Crimean War, a broad public
debate erupted on the "woman question" (*zhenskii vopros*): their upbringing and
education, their rights and duties, and their potential roles in the public world.[7]

This debate resonated within the broader currents of reform. Just as the abolition of serfdom implicitly challenged the legitimacy of other (patriarchal)
institutions, such as the family, the idealistic aspirations of the era – enlightenment, modernization – transformed women (like peasants) into a symbol
of backwardness and hence a yardstick of progress. By the 1870s, significant
improvements in secondary education for women would culminate in the foundation of university-level courses, which led in turn to the expansion of employment opportunities in teaching and medicine. For conservatives, however, the
emancipation of women came to embody all that was dangerous and degenerate about the reform process. While reform of family law gradually gained
significant support within some official circles and parts of the population,
almost all proposals would be blocked by conservatives as well as the Orthodox
Church, which maintained its jurisdiction over divorce and separation.[8] These

---

[6] For recent scholarship on merchants, see James L. West and Iurii A. Petrov, eds., *Merchant
Moscow: Images of Russia's Vanished Bourgeoisie* (Princeton, 1998).

[7] For an overview of the "woman question," see Richard Stites, *The Women's Liberation Movement
in Russia* (Princeton, 1978), pts. 1–2.

[8] See William Wagner, *Marriage, Property and Law in Late Imperial Russia* (Oxford, 1994). See
also Gregory Freeze, "Bringing Order to the Russian Family: Marriage and Divorce in Imperial
Russia, 1760–1860," *Journal of Modern History* no. 4 (Dec. 1990), 709–46.

developments helped to transform the family into a cultural battleground during the second half of the nineteenth century.

The politicized status of the woman question was both demonstrated and perpetuated by the radical publicist Nikolai Chernyshevskii. In the wake of the controversy over Turgenev's *Fathers and Sons*, he decided to write a positive portrayal of the new generation. Notably, he composed a novel about a young woman named Vera Pavlovna, who is oppressed by her mother until liberated by a student through a fictitious marriage. The young man subsequently claims no rights to her person, and sexual relations only occur much later at Vera Pavlovna's own instigation. The bulk of the novel concerns her personal, social, and professional development, and it concludes with veiled references to a socialist utopia. Passed by the censor in what proved a tremendous blunder, *What Is to Be Done? Stories about the New People* quickly attained cult status, which it maintained almost until the Soviet period, when it – along with Dobroliubov's essays – instead became a staple of the official curriculum. As young people attempted to enact its lessons, such phenomena as fictitious marriages, communal living arrangements, and even sewing cooperatives briefly proliferated, and conservatives bemoaned what they perceived as a new ethos of free love and debauchery that was undermining the social order.[9]

The novel opens with a suicide, or, more accurately, a faked suicide that parodies the genre of a potboiler: Vera Pavlovna's husband pretends to kill himself in order to free her to marry the man she loves.[10] Yet the theme of suicide also provides a backdrop to the plot, which was an implicit rejoinder to Ostrovskii. In contrast to Katerina, who finds no path to liberation other than death, Vera Pavlovna is luckier. Just when all hope of finding an exit from her mother's despotism seemingly disappears, Vera Pavlovna considers suicide in terms once again reminiscent of boulevard literature. She first imagines throwing herself out the window, falling, and hitting the pavement, but is repulsed by the image of her body with her skull split open, her face smashed and bloodied. She then pictures Parisian girls smothering themselves in charcoal fumes and the response of her own family finding her in such a pose.[11] Yet she is saved from this fate precisely because a new kind of man – still non-existent in Katerina's world – has entered the scene and is able to help her. The novel thus evoked two opposing representations of the family. On the one extreme was the old patriarchal unit, in which the exercise of arbitrary power both oppressed the individual (Vera Pavlovna) and warped the personality – hence the greed and

---

[9] For further analysis of the novel, see Irina Paperno, *Chernyshevsky and the Age of Realism: A Study in the Semiotics of Behavior* (Stanford, 1988).

[10] That suicide would be upsetting for his wife is played down; Vera Pavlovna is informed of its fabrication only after the fact. The husband returns later in the novel, marries, and the two couples become close friends.

[11] Nikolai Chernyshevsky, *What Is to Be Done?*, trans. Michael Katz (Ithaca, N.Y., 1989), 139–40.

deceit of her mother who tries to coerce her daughter into a loveless marriage. On the other extreme was the new family, which was based on the principles of equality, dignity, and reason. In effect, only the persistence of mindsets and practices from the past created the circumstances in which a person could take his or her life. With suicide thus situated in the old world of darkness and repression, it had no place in the new, enlightened world of science, progress, and reason.

A rival representation of suicide and family life occurs in the novels of Lev Tolstoy. The causes of Anna Karenina's suicide include both social and personal factors, including her loveless, society marriage, confusion of passion for love, and her mental and emotional deterioration that followed her transgressions. Only at the moment of her death does she understand its meaninglessness and want to live, but it is too late. In contrast, another character, Kitty, finds personal fulfillment in marriage, motherhood, and religion. Yet the fate of Kitty's husband Levin serves as the primary counterpart to Anna's. Though he experiences despair and considers suicide, he ultimately overcomes the temptation with his own surrender to faith and love. Tolstoy certainly did not share Chernyshevskii's politics or solution, but he too mapped a bi-polar world; only God and family served as antidotes to suicide.

Many of Russia's greatest writers would tackle related themes, with the dynamics of the dysfunctional family receiving particular attention. Intrigued by a brief newspaper account of a young woman who had jumped to her death clutching an icon, for example, Fedor Dostoevsky wrote a short story entitled "The Meek One," in which he imagined the life story of a meek suicide, someone who did not grumble but was simply unable to live any longer.[12] The narrative follows the inner monologue of her husband, who vainly attempts to understand his wife's act, in part by considering the many possible causes. Had it been a momentary impulse? Was the trigger within her body – anemia or exhaustion, perhaps? Was he himself to blame? In the end, his thoughts circling upon themselves, he decides on chance: he had come home five minutes too late. According to Irina Paperno, the story is emblematic of the epistemological paradox of suicide, an act which is ultimately "inaccessible" and hence defies rational explanation.[13] The ultimate enigma of suicide is indeed at the heart of this story, but Dostoevsky also explores how the man chooses his own truth, even as he narrates an alternative one. In his attempt to understand the suicide, the narrator tells the story of his marriage. He begins by recalling the circumstances of their meeting, he a pawnbroker and she a young orphaned girl, abused by her aunts, who – predictably enough – are pressuring her into a

---

[12] On the real-life model, see Fyodor Dostoevsky, *A Writer's Diary*, trans. Kenneth Lantz (Evanston, Ill., 1993), 653.

[13] Irina Paperno, *Suicide as a Cultural Institution in Dostoevsky's Russia* (Ithaca, N.Y., 1997), 182–83.

loveless match with an old and violent man. At just this moment, in the midst of the girl's torment, he proposed marriage, convinced of his acceptance though briefly taken aback by her need to think about her answer. Deciding to be "strict" with her, he anticipates future pleasures: " 'I like those proud ones,' I thought. Proud women are especially beautiful when . . . well, when you have no more doubts about your power over them." And further: "There were other ideas I savored as well. For example: I'm forty-one, she's only sixteen. That was alluring, that feeling of inequality; a thing like that is delectable, very delectable." Recollecting their subsequent life together, the narrator-husband describes a pattern of psychological cruelty based around his desire for absolute control, a desire that arose, he ultimately admits, from his own failures and humiliations in life: "I was so much in need of a friend. But I saw clearly that I had to train my friend, that I had to add the final touches to her, even conquer her." Yet he failed. In the end, he suddenly declares his passionate love, and, a short time later, she throws herself out of the window.[14] The parallels to Ostrovskii's Katerina are striking: arbitrary power sought to control them both, and in neither case did their self-willed deaths enact their spiritual deformation.

Finally, in a tradition that includes works by Nikolai Leskov, Mikhail Saltykov-Shchedrin, and Anton Chekhov, attention focused precisely upon this deformation of personality, those characters who are both victims and perpetrators in a system predicated upon arbitrary power.[15] Perhaps the most compelling and ambiguous representation of this type was left to Leskov, whose novella *Lady Macbeth of Mtensk* traced the degeneration of the heroine, Katerina Izmailova, through an extra-marital affair, the murder of her husband (followed by other murders), and ultimately her own self-willed death. With her crimes driven by her absolute amorality, her death is not an affirmation of self but the result of her total moral deformation.[16]

One of the most intriguing dimensions of the literary canon is its gendered character. Just as the image of the serf-abuser had been stereotypically female, these dominant personalities are often (though not always) women, who assume masculine gender roles as the head of the family or even family business, sometimes prefer male attire, and occasionally succumb to illicit passion. Furthermore, many of the men in these tales are figuratively emasculated – weak-willed and controlled by women. Such a pattern suggests the complex theme of female misrule. As in revolutionary France (and later in revolutionary Russia), the feminization of absolutism, especially as represented in the petty tyranny of the

---

[14] F. M. Dostoevskii, "Krotkaia: Fantasticheskii rasskaz," *PSS*, 30 vols. (Leningrad, 1972–90), vol. 24, 5–35. Quotations have been taken from Lantz's translation, in *A Writer's Diary*, 686, 687, 704.

[15] See e.g. Mikhail Saltykov-Shchedrin's *Golovlev Family* and Anton Chekhov's story, "In The Ravine."

[16] Nikolai Leskov, *Lady Macbeth of Mtsensk: A Sketch*, trans. Robert Chandler (London, 2003).

family, could help to undermine the legitimacy of absolutism more broadly.[17] Conversely, the purity of the oppressed, such as Ostrovskii's Katerina or Dostoevsky's "meek one," could symbolize the violence of despotism.[18] Yet more ambiguous readings are also possible. Since the inversion of gender roles also perverted the natural state of men, rendering them passive and cunning, then the solution to the slave mentality could be to define more empowered masculine models. Was this not what Pisarev heralded in his praise of the direct, conscious, rational action of the new man? Furthermore, images of female misrule could also bolster a socially conservative platform. To imply that women were less able to withstand the temptations of power could highlight the dangers of unchecked freedom, especially the liberation of women from their traditional roles.

The multivalent nexus between self-killing and familial despotism resonated not just within literature but within Russian society as a whole, where it melded with the existing legal phenomenon of instigated suicide. Examples from newspapers and courtrooms are numerous. In one case from 1900, a mother was found guilty of driving her two grown daughters to suicide and attempted suicide, and she received a sentence of six months' imprisonment. Witnesses sketched both physical and moral abuse, including the mother's suggestion that her daughters could turn to prostitution if they wished to leave home. Though this case again involved the merchant estate, the newspaper report emphasized the external respectability of the mother, who was educated and received in good society. The journalist's point was to challenge social stereotypes: abuse was a problem not just among the illiterate or backward estates but also within educated society.[19] When a procurator declined to prosecute in another case of alleged instigated suicide, the newspaper instead adopted an indignant voice, implying that the procurator was not interested in justice.[20] Sometimes the "facts" were allowed to speak for themselves. After prolonged resistance, the daughter of a Kazan merchant had been forced into an arranged marriage, and, it was dryly reported in 1885, she killed herself on her wedding night rather than live with the despised man.[21] Many other voices were also contesting the legitimacy of corporal punishment within the family, whether with wives or children. Dostoevsky himself addressed this issue, writing passionately against the acquittal

---

[17] See Lynn Hunt, *The Family Romance of the French Revolution* (Berkeley, 1992); Sarah Maza, *Private Lives and Public Affairs: The Causes Célèbres of Prerevolutionary France* (Berkeley, 1993); and Orlando Figes and Boris Kolonitskii, *Interpreting the Russian Revolution: The Language and Symbols of 1917* (New Haven and London, 1999).

[18] Turgenev and Tolstoy had explored similar motifs within the context of serfdom.

[19] "Sudebnye protsessy: Dovedenie zhestokost'iu do samoubiistva," *Nedelia* no. 14 (1900), 479–81.

[20] "Sudebnye protsessy: Dovedenie zhestokost'iu do samoubiistva," *Nedelia* no. 28 (1899), 912–13.

[21] "Samoubiistvo v brachnuiu noch'," *Nedelia*, no. 5 (1885), 198–99. See also the following cases in *Peterburgskii listok* (Jan. 28, 1876), 2; and *Nedelia* no. 27 (1880), 848.

of a man accused of torturing his 7-year-old daughter.[22] In a similar admission of society's powerlessness, a medical doctor argued that husbands must be told authoritatively – even by their parish priest – that they do not possess the right to beat their wives.[23] Members of the populace at large also appealed to the peace courts for help against domestic violence.[24]

This set of concerns shaped the secret police investigation of the 1880 suicide of Mariia Il'inskaia, who shot herself only moments after having received Holy Communion and was accorded a Christian burial. Shortly after the event, Il'inskaia's father contacted the Third Section, because his wife was claiming that Mariia had fallen in love with an unknown nihilist and learned of an assassination plot. This situation had provided the basis for the medical diagnosis: the conflict between love – the hope that the beloved terrorist would return to the Christian path – and patriotism had unbalanced Mariia, leading her to shoot herself. Given the reality of assassination attempts, the police investigated the circumstances in some detail but failed to uncover a plot.[25] Despite many suggestive details, the lack of hard evidence prompted the gendarme officer to pursue a second, medical-domestic line of inquiry. Speaking to a servant and then to Mariia's favorite aunt, he learned that the mother treated her children badly, especially Mariia. Furthermore, the mother's character was described as "unbalanced, capricious, and half-insane," the product of hereditary disease (*rodovoi nedug*): one of her brothers was also half-insane, the other had shot himself. In the end, the gendarme officer concluded that home life provided the better explanation for Mariia's suicide.[26] As the secret police tended to see conspiracies when none were present, this preference for a domestic scenario is striking. Equally interesting is the conjoined medical-familial diagnosis, which linked abuse, heredity, mental illness, and suicide. Still, the nihilist conspiracy was not wholly displaced. Mariia's experiments with socialist politics – she had cut her hair short in nihilist fashion – now provided evidence of her pathological state.

[22] See his comments on the Kroneberg case in his *A Writer's Diary*, 356–84. A pedagogue likewise described several cases of horrific cruelty, including one involving an 11-year-old boy who had jumped out of a fourth-story window, and he noted the difficulty of removing abused children from their parents' care. See A. N. Ostrogorskii, "Samoubiistva, kak psikhologicheskaia problema," *Pedagogicheskii sbornik* nos. 1, 2 (Jan. 1893), no. 1, 45–46.
[23] He likewise described a case of abuse. See his comments in "Oblastnyi otdel," *Severnyi vestnik* no. 5 (1895), 16–19.
[24] Joan Neuberger mentions that the peace courts did address abuse, sometimes causing some disagreement within families: those sentenced to brief spells in prison for wife or child abuse did not recognize that they had done wrong. See her "Popular Legal Cultures: The St. Petersburg Mirovoi Sud," *Russia's Great Reforms, 1855–1881*, ed. Ben Eklof, John Bushnell, and Larissa Zakharova (Bloomington, Ind., 1994), 240, 242.
[25] Attention focused on one professor, whom Mariia had particularly liked, Sergei Andreevich Muromtsev, who would later become an important liberal activist and the first elected leader of Russia's first parliament in 1906.
[26] GARF, f. 109 III, 1880, d. 794.

As the private conduct of family life was opened to public scrutiny, narratives of familial despotism became a recurring trope. In contrast to the secret police report, journalists and jurists typically evoked the ideals of enlightenment, human dignity, and personal inviolability – in sum, the defense of the personality against external violence.[27] The light conferred by publicity (*glasnost'*) and law would dispel the darkness of corruption and brutality. At the same time, the public spectacle became a form of entertainment. When the merchant's wife Aleksandra Berngardt was tried in 1872 for having driven her 18-year-old daughter Varvara to suicide, the journalist introduced his report with the following observation: "This case has awoken tremendous interest in the city of Smolensk: the courtroom was overflowing with the public, which not only occupied all the seats but also found places in the aisles and windows. Women were predominant. A crowd of people stood by the entryway to the court, and a kind of carnival [*gulian'e*] ensued around the building."[28] Curiosity and the whiff of scandal drew the spectators, and the trial itself surely lived up to their expectations. Numerous witnesses – including the siblings of the deceased – described the day-to-day lives of the Berngardt family, the disposition and character of the main actors, and specific incidents of verbal, moral, and physical abuse.

When the familiar plot of familial despotism entered the courtroom, however, it proved malleable. As the Berngardt case illustrates, the prosecuting and defense attorneys each attempted to fit the evidence into stock narratives and thereby to sway the jury. The case began on December 25, 1870, when Varvara's father reported her death. Having poisoned herself with matches (phosphorus) several days earlier, she had confessed on her deathbed to a liaison with a young man with whom she had conducted a secret correspondence. She feared, it was reported, that he had withdrawn his love. For the siblings of Varvara Berngardt, however, the causes of her suicide were quite different: the cruel treatment she suffered at the hands of their mother. Her two younger sisters described how Varvara had been frequently punished and beaten, often for offenses she had not committed; she had been forced to work beyond her strength and denied necessary clothing, compelling her to take in piece work in the evenings to earn some extra kopecks. Her decision to kill herself had then occurred because her mother had confiscated the box in which she had hidden her suitor's letters, and she feared the punishment that would follow their discovery. Emblematic

[27] And not just in the immediate family. One case involved the brutality and humiliation inflicted upon an officer's servant (a private) by the housekeeper. See "Sudebnye protsessy: Samoubiistvo soldata ot zhestokogo obrashcheniia," *Nedelia* no. 9 (1896), 280.

[28] Reprinted (with a transcript) from *Smolenskie gubernskie vedomosti* as "Sudebnye zasedaniia. Zasedanie Smolenskogo okruzh. suda, 17 i 18 iiunia, s uchastiem prisiazhnykh zasedatelei, po delu o kupchikhe 2 gil'dii Aleksandre Berngardt," *Sudebnyi vestnik* no. 93 (1872), 2; for the continuation, no. 94 (1872).

of their mother's cruelty had been her cold reaction to Varvara's poisoning. She had expressed her hope that Varvara might never rise from her sickbed. Overall, therefore, the position of all three sisters was "extremely constrained" (*kraine stesnitel'no*), a term that implies the restriction of personal freedom.

Their older brother confirmed this account in what was described as "extremely expansive testimony." To escape these "constant and unbearable sufferings," Varvara had appealed to her mother to let her go into service as a governess but had been refused. Moreover, she had once told her brother that if she were not "liberated from her parents' home," she would end her own life. At the very end of his statement, he noted that the cruel treatment continued. On the day his sisters had been called to give their statements, his mother had cut off his 14-year-old sister's hair, apparently "to disfigure her." He also submitted a letter written to him by his sisters in which they praised Varvara's act as the most appropriate exit from a terrible situation and expressed their own fear of falling into a similar despair should they not find another means of escape. These accounts were partly confirmed by other witnesses. One servant had seen Aleksandra Berngardt hit Varvara, and a music teacher had noticed some bruises. Other servants and acquaintances had not seen any incidents, but most cited Varvara's good, quiet, industrious, and modest character, her frequent complaints about her situation, and the strict discipline in the house. Indeed, her mother, whose character was described as bad (*durnoi*), treated Varvara like the most lowly servant.[29]

On the basis of these statements, Aleksandra Berngardt was indicted, and the procurator adopted the evocative language of familial despotism: "the merchant wife Aleksandra Berngardt tormented [*muchila*] her daughters, especially [...] Varvara, by [giving them] excessive work, locking them up inside, and denying them age-appropriate amusements; she beat them more than once, and forced them to bear such moral sufferings that her now deceased daughter had already had thoughts of suicide if only to escape the difficult life which she, given her quiet and meek character, had especially felt." The statements of witnesses, the indictment stressed, had likewise documented Varvara's position "without exit."[30] In sum, the case seemed to follow the well-established plot. Varvara had so suffered under the unjust regime of her mother, that suicide had seemed the only means to preserve her personal dignity and morality.

At the trial, witnesses generally confirmed their statements, though the brother and one of the sisters refused to testify against their mother. For his part, the defense attorney highlighted the lack of direct evidence of cruelty and again suggested that the real reason for the suicide had been Varvara's fears about her suitor's intentions. More fundamentally, he also rewrote the case into

[29] All of the statements were published in *Sudebnyi vestnik* no. 93 (1872), 2.
[30] For the indictment, see *Sudebnyi vestnik* no. 94 (1872), 3.

a different narrative, a "family drama," in which social change had created a conflict of generations. Whereas the parents came from a conservative merchant background, in which hard work and discipline were paramount, the daughters had received a superficial modern education, which had caused them to reject their parents' values and to complain about their harsh lives.

It is impossible to blame anyone for this; masses of people live similarly to the Berngardts. Parents strive to educate their children and – according to their means – give them a cheap education; the daughters learn to chatter in French, dance, play the piano but they fancy themselves educated and despise their parents as uneducated merchants and only dream about how to become the wife of a civil servant in order thus to escape the hated merchant estate.

Having imbibed the superficial rhetoric of personal freedom, the defense attorney asserted, the children lacked the ability to bear even the most minimal of deprivations. The treatment of Varvara had not been cruel, therefore; at most it had been a bit crude at times. Similarly, rather than choosing the path of filial duty and helping his elderly father, the son had refused to take over the family business and instead become a district surveyor. Not the abuse of power, therefore, but the dissolution of the patriarchal family had led to this tragic situation. Varvara's death, he implied, had only demonstrated her own lack of moral fiber. The parents deserved sympathy, the attorney concluded, the children pity; the experience would be a lesson for them both. After a fifteen-minute deliberation, the jury found Aleksandra Berngardt not guilty.[31]

Each case allowed the stock narrative to be recast, sometimes in unexpected ways. When Ol'ga Guseva shot herself in 1888, her husband Fedor was prosecuted though he had not raised a hand against her. No longer was physical violence necessary to a prosecution; this case focused on moral pressure. Fedor had thus rejected Ol'ga on their wedding night, declaring himself unable to remain married to a fallen woman. The trial became the forum for an explicit dissection of sexual behavior and the moral values underpinning the institution of marriage. Due to his concerns about Ol'ga's virginity, Fedor testified, he had interrogated her in the days leading up to their wedding. At this time, she had confessed a sexual past but assured him of its limits, especially her intact virtue. On their wedding night, he again asked her for the truth, and she repeated her oath before they performed the "established act." However, her "softness" and the lack of blood convinced him of her duplicity, and she ultimately confirmed that she had had intercourse with two other men. Attention then focused on his oral suasion and lack of preventive action as well as his callous reaction to her death. Not only had he (reportedly) suggested suicide as a desirable course of action, he had not stopped her from taking his gun as she fled from him and her humiliation. In the end, the jury found Gusev not guilty of instigation, perhaps

[31] Ibid.

because Ol'ga Guseva's own moral fall – ostensibly confirmed by a forensic examination – made it difficult to see her as an innocent victim.

Indeed the representation of her family life, as depicted by both Gusev and another witness, also provided a familiar context for her moral failings. Her condition at home, Gusev testified, had been unbearable, largely due to the injustice of the father who ruled his household in the manner of the harsh medieval manual, the *Domostroi*. Her mother, in turn, he described as sly and malicious (*khitraia i iazvitel'naia*). The other witness, who had known the family for seventeen years, likewise described the severity of the father, resulting in the family superficially conforming to his notions but in reality engendering lies, cunning, and deception (*lozh', khitrost', i pritvorstvo*) rather than love and openness. While he had always considered Ol'ga to be intelligent and moral, she had also possessed a certain slyness (*khitrost'*).[32] This language is almost a direct quotation from Dobroliubov's description of the kingdom of darkness, a parallel that surely was not intentional. Rather, it underlines the resonance of familial despotism as a stock narrative. Though hoping to escape her home life and dreaming of true love, Ol'ga had already been corrupted within its atmosphere of lies and deception. In this sense, she was still a victim, only not of her husband but of her parents.

In 1893, the pedagogue A. N. Ostrogorskii attempted to analyze the psychological basis of suicide among children and youth, and he devoted particular attention to both conditions within the family and the emotional repercussions of punishment. The problem was not just outright "tyranny" (*tiranstvo*) – those relatively rare cases of extreme abuse – but also the more typical conviction held in good faith by many parents that a proper upbringing required severity and punishment. But the times had changed, he suggested, and so had childhood psychology. The experience of punishment did not necessarily provoke feelings of shame, an emotion that some believed could serve as a deterrent against future transgressions. Instead, it increasingly called forth feelings of pride, insult, and the consciousness of injustice, that together constituted a "disrespect toward the personality" (*neuvazhenie k lichnosti*). Though children would not use such a "bookish" term, he stressed, and certainly experienced their feelings in a much more inchoate and immediate manner, their responses to punishment and severity – including suicide – were best understood as attempts to defend their personalities. Ostrogorskii did not postulate reasons for this development beyond a growing tendency in many good families to treat children with understanding and respect, a development that abused children could observe.[33]

---

[32] For the legal papers, see IRLI, f. 134, op. 4, d. 208, esp. ll. 9–16, 18–21; for the press coverage, including the verdict, *Ekaterinburgskaia nedelia* nos. 8 and 50 (1889).

[33] A. N. Ostrogorskii, "Samoubiistva. Povody k nim," *Pedagogicheskii sbornik* nos. 7, 8 (1893), no. 8, 89–94.

Nevertheless, his analysis highlights some fascinating continuities and developments. Like many before him, he placed suicide at the intersection between the old and the new, in this case, the old tyrannical family and the new, more democratic one. Violence now provoked less the cowering fear of a cringing slave than the proud indignation of the insulted individual. This is what gave suicide its veneer of spontaneous protest, Ostrogorskii asserted, for it seemed (to the children) a means to defend their persons against perceived injustice. In his view, however, it remained necessary to find the proper balance between the rights and happiness of individuals and their obligations as members of society. A stronger religious upbringing and the education of the will would help to produce a "sober view of life, moderation and reason of desire."[34] Ostrogorskii was not a liberal, yet his language was deeply political.[35] In criticizing the abuse of absolutist authority, he implicitly challenged its legitimacy and, moreover, acknowledged the rights of the individual. Although Ostrogorskii did not make this connection, his portrait of the proud and dignified new man suggests that older images of noble honor were migrating into new social spheres: a similar indignation at perceived disrespect (dishonor) had underlain many elite suicides in the era of Nicholas I.

According to more conservative commentators, in contrast, the root of the problem lay in the perversion of the natural order in the family, which was caused by secularization. Deficiencies in religious instruction, many argued, had left children unprotected by faith and hence more liable to fall victim to suicidal despair. Equally important was a "soft" and permissive upbringing that was teaching children the wrong lesson – that life consisted of personal pleasure and diversion rather than work, sacrifice, and the overcoming of obstacles. Consequently, modern children possessed inordinate pride and egoism, qualities that made them unable to bear even the most minute setbacks.[36] Condemning the liberal press for putting immoral ideas into children's heads, one article in the arch-conservative *Citizen* stressed that Christianity demands the unquestioning obedience of children, who have no right to judge their father.[37] One religious writer condemned the many egoistical young people who saw family life, especially children, as a burden, and his attention focused on the selfish and pathological desires of those young women, who sought to limit family size, to pursue personal interests, and even to claim equality with their husbands. Such

[34] A. N. Ostrogorskii, "Samoubiistva, kak psikhologicheskaia problema," no. 2, 150, 158.
[35] Director of the military's teaching seminary from 1877 to 1882, Ostrogorskii then became the editor of the journal, *Pedagogicheskii sbornik*, which was published under the auspices of the Ministry of War.
[36] Some proponents of this argument quoted extensively from medicine and science, which shared the concern about moral behavior. See I. A. Nevzorov, *O samoubiistve* (Kazan, 1891), esp. 67–87. For a more scriptural approach, see I. P., *O naklonnosti k samoubiistvu, kak nravstvennoi bolezni nashego vremeni i o spasitel'nykh sredstvakh protiv etoi naklonnosti* (Moscow, 1884).
[37] "Semeinaia neuriaditsa, kak prichina samoubiistva," *Grazhdanin* no. 49 (1873), 1315.

violations of nature, he asserted, deformed the character, causing nervous and other illnesses, as well as suicide. To restore the health of the social body, he called upon men to reassert their natural prerogatives: to reinstate order, authority, and discipline within the family, the building block of society. Only with the restoration of the patriarchal family would the problem of suicide be resolved.[38] Though diverging fundamentally from the arguments of Ostrogorskii and others, these approaches conceived suicide in like terms: the act of self-killing implicated the fundamental norms of political, social, and moral governance in autocratic Russia.

Despotism at school

In May 1870, a pupil at the Larinskaia Gymnasium in St. Petersburg named Nikolenko shot himself. In his note, he described what he considered unfair treatment in his final oral examinations – he had failed to graduate for the second year running – and closed with the following words: "It is the bitter truth, not a drop of lies. Farewell, Papa, Mama, forgive [me] if I was . . . I love you very much and will pray for you, if possible."[39] Whereas the official report blamed Nikolenko's act on his mental instability, the national press pointed instead to systemic problems within secondary education. In an article pointedly entitled, "Suicide from Exam," one commentator declared that "there is no doubt whatsoever" that the accusations must be properly investigated to establish whether the teacher had in fact abused his authority. Indeed, any (alleged) instability was itself the likely product of the exam: "Must not our pedagogues and 'powers that be' shudder to the same degree and bitterly ponder such occurrences?" In conclusion, he advocated a fundamental reorganization of the entire system of examination. Nikolenko's suicide was not the first such case, he asserted, but only the first one to be publicized. Earlier examples remained shrouded in darkness.[40]

Nikolenko's death became a brief *cause célèbre*, and journalists would still cite it years later. Two main issues were at stake: the importance of publicity (*glasnost'*) in illuminating wrongs; and the relationship between suicide and the pedagogical regime of the school. In a striking parallel to the tales of familial despotism, the school would soon resonate as a site and symbol of unchecked arbitrariness, oppression, and the abuse of power. During the 1860s, some progressive voices had already castigated the structure and content of secondary education, especially the deadly grasp of the classical

[38] A. Klitin, *Nashe vremia i samoubiistvo* (Kiev, 1890), 25–37.
[39] See the report in "Dnevnik prikliuchenii," *Vedomosti Sanktpeterburgskoi gorodskoi politsii* (May 31, 1870).
[40] O. Miller, "Samoubiistvo ot ekzamena," *Zaria* no. 6 (1870), 178–80.

gymnasium.[41] By the 1870s, this critique was overlaid with the new concern about suicide. Within school walls, it was feared, children and youth were weakened morally and physically, reduced to nervous exhaustion and desperation, and, sometimes, driven to suicide. The language used to describe this problem was familiar; the secondary school was a kingdom of darkness that must be exposed to the penetrating gaze of the public.

In many respects, the school provided a more explicitly political locus for despotism than the family. Not only were they actually administered within the educational bureaucracy (and hence not answerable to parents and local communities), they were also highly regimented. Following the various student disorders and other signs of political discontent among educated youth, the school became a site of exceptional governmental intervention. Its task was not just to educate youth but to instruct them morally: the curriculum was generally set; the authority of teachers was unequivocal; and, after 1874, pupils' behavior was subject to strict "surveillance" both inside and outside the classroom. This was especially humiliating to pupils and their families, especially given their otherwise privileged social status.[42] The "school regime" consequently became a catchphrase designating the bureaucratic, formalistic, and barren character of official education. In effect, the body of the youthful suicide would become a symbolic site on which Russia's public claimed its right to independence from autocratic tutelage and control.

The erection of actual battle lines between school and public occurred weeks after Nikolenko's death, when a peculiar lawsuit came before one of St. Petersburg's justices of the peace. Building on readers' familiarity with recent events, the *Week* stressed that it was not Nikolenko's teacher who was being prosecuted, as one would certainly expect given the facts of the case. No, it was Nikolenko's mother. The journalist then recounted the following tale. Just three weeks after her son's death, Mrs. Nikolenko had been traveling in a public coach to visit his grave when she noticed a man staring at her. A witness later testified that he too had noticed the man staring at the woman, "with a derisive, sardonic smile," and presumed that they were a married couple in the midst of some sort of argument. But it was in fact the director of her son's gymnasium. "Trembling and pale," yet trying to ignore him, Mrs. Nikolenko had become increasingly agitated and cast many glances at him, but he had maintained his mocking stare. Finally, she threw herself at him, screaming: "Murderer! You killed my son." In an attempt to calm Mrs. Nikolenko (and having learned the context), the other passengers asked the man to leave. Though refusing at first, he did ultimately submit but then filed a lawsuit against Mrs. Nikolenko for public defamation of

---

[41] D. I. Pisarev, "Nasha universitetskaia nauka," in his *Izbrannye pedagogicheskie sochineniia* (Moscow, 1951).

[42] For background, see Patrick Alston, *Education and the State in Tsarist Russia* (Stanford, 1969), chs. 3–4.

character. In her testimony, Mrs. Nikolenko explained her interpretation of the smile. Following her son's death, she recalled, she had lodged an unsuccessful complaint with the gymnasium: "What have you accomplished? said the smile. Nothing. Your son is dead, and you cannot expect anything from me."[43]

What could be a more potent image of injustice: a mother, in mourning for her son, again victimized by a callous and arrogant man? The peace court acquitted Nikolenko, but the spectacle brought the original case back to public attention and raised two important issues: the public function of *glasnost'*, and the school's lack of public accountability. In his testimony, the director had not only claimed that the irregularities in the conduct of the examination were unproven; he also dismissed the investigative reports of journalists as pure "polemic," as unworthy of serious attention. This comment prompted an indignant response on the part of the newspaper, which, it emphasized, had only endeavored to present all the facts. It also reconfirmed the fundamentally arbitrary nature of power in the gymnasium, thereby providing additional evidence that the young Nikolenko really had been driven to his death. If there were no investigations or trials, the article concluded, then the accusations would remain unproven, except in the court of public opinion.[44] The *Week* thus positioned itself as the voice of the public interest, thereby rhetorically evoking a public into being. To fulfill its duty, it then published a series of articles on the Nikolenko case and the broader project of school reform. This publicity spurred the intervention of the curator of the academic district, but, perhaps inevitably, the questions raised by Nikolenko's suicide were never resolved.[45]

Attention returned to the problem of youth suicide the following academic year, when, in January 1871, another controversial case entered the public eye. This time, the young Platon Demert had shot himself while preparing for the examinations in Greek and Latin required for his enrollment in the fifth grade of a gymnasium in Kazan. Prompted in part by the accusations of a relative, who had claimed that the suicide was caused by the study of "dead languages," several newspapers linked the incident to the unpopular system of classical education.[46] Yet the resonance of this case was much broader. With rhetorical bravado, the curator of the academic district, P. D. Shestakov, seems to have promoted the vilification of Latin and Greek as a kind of straw man. In a report to

---

[43] "Sudebnye izvestiia: Delo, vyzvannoe samoubiistvom Nikolenko," *Nedelia* no. 33 (1870), 1080–81.

[44] "Delo, vyzvannoe samoubiistvom Nikolenko," 1080–81.

[45] See e. g. "Smelost' prepodavatelia Sokolova" and "Uchebno-vospitatel'nye proekty," *Nedelia* no. 34 (1870); "Vnutrenniaia khronika," no. 37 (1870); "Vnutrenniaia khronika," no. 39 (1870).

[46] *S.-Peterburgskie vedomosti* (Jan. 16, 1871). As Irina Paperno has pointed out (*Suicide*, 90–92), such accusations built upon a series of associations, including the (platonic) connotations of the teenager's name, the traditions of classical suicide, and the deadness of the languages. Her subtle analysis of these metaphors is very focused, however, and she neglects the broader issues of school suicide.

the minister of education published in the official journal of the ministry – itself a highly unusual occurrence – he lingered on these accusations. How could sober and healthy study motivate a suicide? If the languages themselves were to blame, how had he along with thousands of other pupils ever survived their secondary education? In his view, the problem lay not with dead languages. Instead, suicide must be regarded as an unbalanced act: only a "sick and disturbed imagination" could build an examination into a motive for suicide, and the district curator pointedly referred to the feelings of anguish (*toska*) mentioned by Demert in his suicide note. Furthermore, he countered insinuations that another suicide of a Kazan pupil (in 1870) had been linked to the gymnasium; after all, the young man had completed his examinations satisfactorily. He even mentioned Nikolenko in passing, stressing that he had shot himself after an examination in physics, not Latin or Greek. Finally, and this was his real point, he pointed the finger of blame at newspapers, at the publicity that lends suicide a "halo of martyrdom," casting it as a great and heroic feat and thereby feeding the diseased pride and egoism of youth who long to be heroes.[47]

Although Shestakov tapped into the long-standing associations of suicide with both disease and vice, he failed to shift the categories of public debate. Once again the *Week* picked up on the story. Even before the publication of the official report, it had played down the harmfulness of classical languages per se and proffered what it considered a better explanation for these suicides – the orientation and character of teaching personnel, and the internal administration of schools. It would return to this theme repeatedly over the next months. Dismissing the curator's specific attempt to blame the press, it asserted yet again that the schools themselves must be held responsible and devoted several lead articles to the challenges of school reform. In this way, the causal role of the school regime in the suicide of teenagers became a familiar refrain.[48]

Other commentators likewise mocked the attempt to establish a causal link between youth suicide and either "dead languages" or individual pathologies. They too focused instead upon the heavy hands of the school strangling Russia's youth. In his regular column published in a prominent thick journal, N. A. Demert (the teenager's uncle), lingered on evocative scenes from the educational environment itself. In Kaluga, he reported, pupils were forbidden to gather in groups, even of two or three, whether in private or public arenas. To improve performance in their homework, a school in Kharkov province barred pupils from leaving their houses before 8 p.m. or from playing or running about inside. In one Moscow gymnasium, a pupil was punished for some

[47] This source includes the formal response to the reports in *S.-Peterburgskie vedomosti*. See "Donesenie popechitelia Kazanskogo uchebnogo okruga P. D. Shestakova g. Ministru narodnogo prosveshcheniia," *ZhMNP* (Feb. 1871), 178–83.

[48] See the series of articles in *Nedelia* nos. 5, 12, 13, 15, and 18 (1871). The last one was a report on a suicide in Odessa due, it was summarized, to the school's strict and meaningless rules.

misdemeanor by being told to stand in a corner – for an entire year. After several days, the young man had simply dropped out of school. Evoking the categories popularized by Dobroliubov, Demert categorized youth suicide as a form of "solitary protest" within conditions of "petty tyranny" (*samodurstvo*). Though sad and scandalous, such acts represented "flashes of energy" (*probleski energii*) among an otherwise passive and apathetic youth. Not mentioning his nephew's death but introducing two other cases (from Penza and Odessa) into evidence, he answered Shestakov's accusations. It was not the press that caused suicide or conferred upon it an aura of heroism, but conditions within the school.[49]

As Demert's feuilleton illustrates, isolated cases were now being cited as evidence of a social problem localized within the despotic regime of the school. Both developments were apparent in 1873, when the *Week* began to refer to an "epidemic" of suicide in general and among school children in particular. The term was rhetorically important. In casting suicide as a social disease, it transformed it into an object suitable for scientific study. Noting that specialists were now turning to this difficult but important area, it proceeded to summarize some of the most recent social facts: three teenagers who had recently shot themselves, two in Moscow and one in Ekaterinburg. All had been distinguished as good and industrious students, and one had left a note describing his sense of disappointment in his studies and life more generally. It then quoted extensively from a recent column in another newspaper which had pondered this apparent paradox of young people suffering disappointment and sadness even before their initiation into life. The answer was unambiguous. Youth suffer under a "triple yoke: strenuous academic demands, captious supervision, and insulting suspicion." It continued: "We will not close our eyes [to the fact, that] the majority of our pedagogues, particularly those in our classical gymnasiums, are imbued throughout with the spirit of officialdom and bureaucratic discipline, a slave-like servility to higher authorities and a joyful admonition to those below." Rather than giving youth the necessary freedom and space to grow, the school smothered the youth with paternal supervision (*popechitel'nost'*), making it difficult "to breathe."[50] The logic of this imagery was compelling. The school had already suffocated the soul, the bullet just killed the body.

A week later, the same three cases (and their press coverage) inspired a very different commentary in the conservative *Citizen*. "Yes," it agreed, "an epidemic of suicide among student youth has begun." But it perceived not a victimization of the students but their fundamental cynicism – their disdain for the values of the family and their pleasure in shocking society. "How it is all so stupid,

[49] D. "Nashi obshchestvennye dela," *Otechestvennye zapiski* no. 7 (1872), esp. 83–92. See also his "Vnutrenniaia khronika," *Otechestvennye zapiski* no. 3 (1871), esp. 174–5. On Demert, see Paperno, *Suicide*, 92–94.
[50] "Vnutrenniaia khronika," *Nedelia* no. 22 (1873), 816–18.

vulgar, and empty," the journalist remarked. To save young people, he called upon parents, teachers, and priests to speak to them, and for writers to address the spiritual side of this "terrible phenomenon."[51] Several months later, the magazine attempted to do precisely this. It published a first-person narrative of a gymnasium pupil who had shot himself but been saved in body and soul. The story opened: "I am 17 years old. In a moment of disappointment, I shot myself. [...] But God took pity and saved me." The tale was melodramatic. The narrator was the illegitimate son of a good and religious mother, whose death threw the boy and his beautiful sister upon the mercy of scheming and immoral relatives. Impoverished, trying to persist with his studies and save his sister, he fell into suicidal despair through reading a newspaper report that printed the letter of a young suicide. Luckily, his attempt was unsuccessful. Upon waking up in the hospital, he confessed to a priest, who explained to him that suicide is the result of vice – egoism and pride, and he joyfully experienced God's forgiveness. His tale concludes with two other miracles: his sister marries the teacher who has helped tend him in hospital; and an official in the local educational district offers to become his guardian. With all problems neatly resolved, the narrator observes that he had indeed been a complete egoist.[52] Whether this story was based on actual events is unknown, but its narration certainly drew on well-established motifs: the moral essence of suicide as a product of personal vice; the role of newspapers in "infecting" impressionable readers; and the caring and protective impulses of educational personnel (a teacher, a school director, and a district official). In other words, the story was intended as a rebuttal to the liberal press, a living illustration of how faith and paternalism could save Russia's youth.

As teenage suicide emerged as a generic category in the 1870s, debate often split along political lines. On the left were those who interpreted these cases as evidence in an ongoing indictment of the school regime. Their accounts routinely drew upon the evocative language of despotism: formalism and bureaucracy were suppressing the natural and healthy needs of young people for space, freedom, and autonomy. The role of the press was to illuminate darkness and hence to pave the way for reform. On the right were those who situated suicide into a narrative of decline, a process linked to secularization. The erosion of religious faith, they feared, had undermined the social and the moral order, most evidently in the family but also in the school. Russia's children had become self-centered egoists who neither internalized the precepts of religious duty nor drew strength from religious communion. Not only did they consequently claim the right to question their elders; they also fell easy prey to feelings of loneliness and despair as well as petulance and bravado. In reporting suicides, newspapers

[51] "Tri sluchaia samoubiistv," *Grazhdanin* no. 23 (1873), 671–72.
[52] "Rasskaz zastrelivshegosia gimnazista," *Grazhdanin* nos. 38–40 (1873).

only encouraged these misguided and dangerous urges. This reading construed the act of suicide as a form of disobedience, the product of narcissism and a secularized selfhood. During the 1880s and 1890s, these paradigms would persist but without such clear political distinctions.[53]

For the rest of the century, the annual spate of school suicides in examination season would prompt a ritual chorus of public criticism.[54] The problem thus festered, in part due to the broader dissatisfaction of many parents and pupils with the school system, but it was not yet a major social issue. The ministry of education simply rejected the notion that there was any problem and accused the media of slandering the school system.[55] But concern was present behind the scenes. In November 1882, an official circular ordered local school districts to report all cases of suicide, attempted suicide, and sudden or accidental death.[56]

As youth suicide slowly caught the interest of both pedagogues and doctors, however, they constituted the individual cases as symptoms of a socio-medical problem. Why, asked one pedagogue in 1877, citing statistics, did only a minority of enrolled pupils ever finish the course of study at the gymnasium? Why did so many transfer or drop out? Why had suicide become a recurring phenomenon? In addressing these questions, he discussed physiological life cycles, familial dynamics, and immoral reading materials, but also the norms and structure of the school. What was needed, he asserted, was less bureaucracy and fewer rules and restrictions on pupils' activities. To educate the integral personality, schools must emphasize physical activity and more personalized interaction with teachers, who could then help and guide their pupils through any crises. His vision did not reject paternalism, therefore, but the regimentation of the school that hindered the development of "healthy" and "natural" forms of paternal care.[57] Almost a decade later, V. G. Nesterov, a school doctor, presented a highly critical paper at the Second Congress of the Pirogov Society

[53] Even in the 1870s, the boundaries between these two camps proved porous, as one report from the popular press illustrates. In recounting the circumstances, it implicated problems at school, a harsh father, and the excessive pride of the youth. See "Kto vinovat?" *Peterburgskii listok* (Jan. 27, 1876). See also *Peterburgskii listok* (Mar. 24, 1876).
[54] On the "seasonal" quality of this phenomenon, see "Po povodu samoubiistva detei," *Nedelia* no. 18 (1884), 606–9.
[55] In an official statement from 1880, the ministry argued that most cases were caused by disease and derangement and none involved the study of classical languages. Like the earlier statement, it thereby attempted to deflect attention from the structure of education. See "Oproverzhenie," *Iuridicheskii vestnik* no. 5 (1880), 201–3. According to official sources, the annual number of suicides among secondary-school pupils (male only) averaged around ten in the 1880s and 1890s. See M. Ia. Fenomenov, *Prichiny samoubiistv v russkoi shkole* (Moscow, 1914), 11.
[56] Cited in G. V. Khlopin, "Samoubiistva, pokusheniia na samoubiistva i neschastnye sluchai sredi uchashchikhsia russkikh uchebnykh zavedenii (Sanitarno-statisticheskoe issledovanie)," *ZhMNP* no. 3 (1906), 4.
[57] K. G. Lavrichenko, *Roditeliam i uchiteliam: Voprosy vospitaniia* (SPb, 1894: orig. 1877), esp. 1–5, 15–17, 36–49. See also "Issledovaniia o samoubiistvakh vospitannikov," *Nedelia* no. 14 (1877); and "Po povodu samoubiistva detei," *Nedelia* no. 18 (1884), 606–9.

of Russian Doctors. Not only did the secondary school actually harm pupils'
physical health; it also caused mental and nervous illness, with rates rising in
the more advanced grades. "The incorrect conduct of studies and the extreme
amount of required work burdens mental activity, overstraining it, and as a
consequence leads to a reduction in the general steadiness of the organism of
pupils and a mass of various nervous diseases."[58]

By the 1890s, this interpretation was becoming axiomatic among medical
specialists and progressive pedagogues.[59] Despotism within the school and an
unstable family combined with medical and hygienic factors were endangering
children by weakening their nervous systems and brains.[60] The key to the problem seemed to lie in physiological development, in which school and family
both played crucial roles – either giving children the strength of body, mind, and
will necessary for a life of struggle or, more often, undermining their health and
moral characters. While knowledge could fortify an individual in the struggle
for survival, Professor N. A. Obolonskii argued, its improper acquisition could
undermine the organism: "the importunate and irrational exercise of the mind
can cause its overstrain, weaken mental energy, and thereby call forth spiritual indifference leading without fail to discontent with oneself and all [one's]
surroundings." Though believing this problem to be most pronounced among
neuropathic and psychopathic natures, he argued that the formal emphasis on
abstract learning to the detriment of practical application could increase youth's
unsteadiness, make them unfit for life's struggle, and even lead to suicide. "It
is necessary," he stressed, "that the development of the mind does not occur at
the cost of the physical well-being of the organism and that the nervous system
is not subject prematurely to copious excitement." Not just the school was to
blame. Obolonskii also cited the lack of peace, order, and rational discipline
in the modern family, all of which inexorably led to the inability to regulate
or restrain the self, disappointment, exhaustion, and, ultimately, the conviction
that life was a burden.[61] The pedagogue E. Pokrovskii agreed. "Who hasn't had
the chance," he wrote in 1892, "to see the phenomenon of nervous children at a
very young age when they have not yet had a chance to sample either school or
life?" Irritability and timidity in the earliest years, fed by nursemaids nourishing

[58] V. G. Nesterov, "Sovremennaia shkola i zdorov'e," *Meditsinskoe obozrenie* no. 4 (1887), 399.
See also A. A. Lipskii, "Samoubiistvo detei v S.-Peterburge," *VSMOG* no. 4 (1887), 58–69.

[59] In 1890, two new journals began publishing on matters broadly related to pedagogy, *Russkaia
shkola* and *Vestnik vospitaniia*. Both were progressive and gave readers access to modern theories
of pedagogy.

[60] Such views were also popularized in the non-specialist press. See "Samoubiistvo detei," *Ogonek*
no. 21 (1902); and Grigorii Gordon, "Samoubiistvo sredi detei," *Mir bozhii* no. 4 (1902). See
also the positive review of Zubov's work in a journal intended for teachers and pedagogues:
Pedagogicheskii sbornik no. 12 (1903), 602–5.

[61] N. A. Obolonskii, "Sovremennoe polozhenie voprosa o prichinakh samoubiistva," *RAPKMB*
no. 1 (1902), 46, 53.

their charges with fairy tales and fantasies, evolved into a range of pathological symptoms in youth, including impressionability, headaches, undefined feelings of anguish, and apathy. The root cause was clear: "The law of heredity is blind, mercilessly and inexorably settling accounts with nature for the sins of parents and grandparents." But he also criticized the formalistic structure of the secondary school, especially its emphasis on the acquisition of abstract knowledge to the detriment of physical, emotional, and social development.[62]

With their specialist diagnoses, doctors and pedagogues claimed the knowledge necessary to protect the next generation of youth, and one crucial step was a reform of the school system. Yet the paradigm of degeneration had also radicalized the existing critiques of despotism. A terrible disease, with roots in Russia's despotic and (hence) diseased past, now seemed to be spreading through society, and youth were among its first, most tragic victims. The medical model marked an epistemic shift. In depicting Russia on the brink of a medical disaster, it demanded fundamental changes in social and, implicitly, political life. The sense of urgency was accompanied by disquiet: were prophylactic measures coming too late?

Boredom and the burden of life

On January 6, 1876, Ekaterina Cherkas poisoned herself before going to bed. For the next thirty-two hours, she suffered strong stomach pains but did not reveal their cause to her family and refused to summon a doctor. With her pain steadily increasing, she finally called her sister to her early in the morning of January 8 and told her to look for a note in her writing desk. It read: "January 6, late in the evening. I just drank a phosphorus solution with the goal of taking my life. Life has bored me for a long time [*Zhizn' mne davno nadoelas'*]. Mama, sisters and brothers, forgive me, sinner that I am. Ekaterina Cherkas." Her mother ran for help, but Ekaterina soon died. She was 19 years old, and a reason for her act was never found. The newspaper reporter concluded with a cliché: she took her secret with her to the grave.[63]

During the late imperial era, one broad category of motive both fascinated and puzzled Russia's public more than any other – boredom with life, along with its near relatives, ennui, disappointment, anguish, and despair. The case of Ekaterina Cherkas was emblematic. Her long-suffering silence after drinking the poison demonstrated her clear determination to die, yet her note was mystifying. She was young and healthy, had suffered no abuse, poverty, or unhappiness in love, and lived with a loving family. Why then had she lost interest in life?

[62] E. Pokrovskii, "Iunye zhertvy sovremennogo pessimizma," *Vestnik vospitaniia* no. 7 (1892), esp. 34.
[63] *Peterburgskii listok* (Jan. 10, 1876), 2.

Under Nicholas I, the infrequent allusions to boredom in suicide notes had evoked the meaningless norms of the bureaucracy or elite society, thereby fashioning the self-willed death into an affirmation of the self, even an act of genius. Bemused by such extravagant claims, the official response had been silence. By the 1870s, such allusions were commonplace, and the response was vociferous. The progressive *Week* returned repeatedly to the issue. In 1875, a commentator observed that the suicide without reason, due only to "boredom with life," had become the most characteristic suicide motive of the era, constituting a kind of disease spreading through Russian educated society. Noting once again in 1879 that "disappointment was spreading in an epidemic fashion," it blamed society's apathy, its "crude philistinism," as well as the failure of literature to provide new ideals.[64] Such references continued to function as an almost ritual lament during the next decades, and not just in the liberal press. In 1890, the conservative *Kiev Word* condemned the boredom, "the pathological discontent with life" among educated young people that was "lowering the value of life," "weakening the population's will power," and producing masses of suicide. Claiming that the phenomenon had been unknown during the 1860s and was still unknown amongst the common people, it blamed the "cosmopolitanism" that had displaced the strict but benevolent patriarchy in schools as in society.[65] This new suicide of boredom still implicated the government, though often indirectly, as in the debates about the school regime. More alarming was its implications for Russia's emerging public, precisely that public the progressive media rhetorically invoked as the counterweight to despotism, bureaucracy, and tutelage. Society itself – and not just the tyranny of the patriarchal family and the secondary school – was driving people to their deaths.

In the spring of 1874, the *Week* opened a new series of articles devoted – remarkably enough – to sketching the lives of persons who had chosen suicide, a phenomenon, the editor remarked, that had become unfortunately common in recent times. Though the first article turned out to be the last of the series, it provided a long and detailed account of the life of A. A. Reding, a promising young man who had shot himself "in full consciousness" on January 27, 1874. Well educated with the prospect of a university career, respected and loved by his comrades, and financially secure, Reding had had no apparent reason for his act. The doctor had tried to find a medical cause, some sort of physiological sign of mental disturbance, but he had been forced to conclude that the only reason was the one cited by Reding himself: *Weltschmerz*. "But how could that be?" pondered the journalist. "Could such a feeling form in Russia? Was it

---

[64] References are too numerous to list individually. For these two examples, see "Skuka zhizni," *Nedelia* no. 26 (1875), 837–41; and *Nedelia* no. 32/33 (1879), 957. See also the ironic opening words of a feuilleton that names being bored, anguished, and suicidal as contemporary verbs: N. M., "Literaturnye i zhurnal'nye zametki," *Otechestvennye zapiski* no. 10 (1873), 289.

[65] See the lead article in *Kievskoe slovo* (Jan. 26, 1890), 2.

just repeated out of some book? Was this feeling honest, not affected? Could a Russian actually feel the same as Heine felt?"[66] In answering these rhetorical questions, the anonymous journalist would conclude that yes, *Weltschmerz* had indeed appeared within the Russian lexicon of suicide motives.

The article sketched Reding's biography in unusual detail. By narrating the life story through the prism of its tragic end, it sought to confer meaning upon meaninglessness. Here was a young man, who had showed promise and genius from his earliest youth, who had wished only to serve the causes of truth, science, and social justice. His character had been formed by the reading of Plutarch, Schiller, and other European writers, which had instilled in him both an aspiration toward serious work and an ideal of social welfare. After graduating as the top pupil in his gymnasium, he entered St. Petersburg University in 1868, full of hope for the future and already possessing a matured worldview and critical perspective. This precipitated his first encounter with "real" life. His high standing among his comrades, his authenticity and fraternal solidarity, his readiness to help in word and deed, all compelled him to leave the university after several months and move to the provincial town of Simbirsk. This was a veiled reference to the student protests of that year and his sentence to internal exile. While studying in a state-run institution had always been difficult, the journalist noted, the pursuit of science and his informal study circles had given him hope. In Simbirsk, without friends and torn from all activity, Reding came face to face with the bleakness of reality, and this experience had had an overwhelming influence on his young and receptive nature. The journalist summarized:

At each step he saw the sharp contradictions between his ideals and the apathy of the surrounding society, that bleak, gray everyday life, which lies heavy on the development of our young people. Here [nobody] searches for some glorious goals, everything flows into one full monotony. Then it became clear [to Reding] why so many personalities, full of good inclinations, full of strength, perish without a trace, engulfed by this morass of social life.

Reding was able to return after a year to St. Petersburg, but the experience had impacted his physical and mental health. Refusing to be defeated, Reding prepared for his future scholarly activity, an endeavor that won him a degree and top academic honors in physics. But pure science did not satisfy him, and he continued to seek solutions to the "abnormal phenomena of social life," reading widely in history, philosophy, and literature. His very genius thus made him suffer:

Everyone endures this period when we stop looking at life through the rose-colored prism of youthful eyes, when the dissonances of social life trouble the soul. Each recognizes his powerlessness to battle this evil. But such impressionable natures as Reding feel this

---

[66] G. "Odin iz nedavnikh samoubiits (A. A. Reding)," *Nedelia* no. 13 (1874), 479–81, here 479.

one hundred times stronger. The consciousness of his powerlessness tormented him. Already then did the disease come into being that Heine so accurately characterized with the word *Weltschmerz*.

Finding neither a supportive milieu (*sreda*) – his old comrades were gone – nor a way to enact his ideals into practice, he ended his life with a pistol shot.[67]

This portrait of a superman without a task, a genius in conflict with life, possesses many literary allusions.[68] It evokes the traditions of the superfluous man, the hero who possesses great ideals but cannot act. Yet, as the journalist constantly emphasized with countless references to action and activity (*deiatel'nost'*), Reding did possess the requisite strength, the requisite knowledge and scientific worldview, the requisite ability to transform word into deed. He faltered not because of his own shortcomings or even because of political repression, but because of society's apathy, "the morass of social life." He was perhaps more akin to Turgenev's hero Bazarov, likewise a titanic figure who aspired to conscious activity but fell victim to Russia's backwardness. Accordingly, this "new man" remained a solitary figure, who found inadequate sustenance within society and perished. Yet the suicide potentially destabilized the narrative. Reding's demise almost seems an admission of defeat. Was the task too great? Was Russia's backwardness an insurmountable obstacle? The timing is striking: in 1874, hundreds of youth would flood the countryside in the first great movement "to the people." In retrospect, this collective striving toward action, this attempt to inflame the peasantry into revolution, challenges Reding's solitariness. Such doubts were not articulated, however, for Reding's character was entirely heroic, entirely devoid of any flaw. Consequently, his death functioned as a kind of martyrdom, his existential suffering as an expression of his inner purity and refusal to submit to "reality." In an absolute conflict between inner self and outer world, Reding had rejected the world and thereby remained true to himself. In this sense, parallels can be drawn to Dobroliubov's reading of Ostrovskii – Katerina had likewise refused to let herself be deformed by life. Still, the message of this hagiographic piece is ambiguous. In casting Reding as a positive hero, it conferred upon his death precisely that "halo of martyrdom" so often deplored by conservative voices. Simultaneously, it served as an admonition to the reading public, an appeal to combat apathy with social activity.

The genre of suicide cum martyrdom and its narration as hagiography possessed important parallels with other ways of understanding suicide, especially the critique of petty despotism within the family and school. In both instances, agency is unstable. The individual is somehow driven to his or her death, but the

---

[67] "Odin iz nedavnikh samoubiits," 479–81.
[68] On the monolithic hero, see Aileen M. Kelly, *Toward Another Shore: Russian Thinkers between Necessity and Chance* (New Haven, 1998), ch. 8.

act of self-killing contains elements of conscious protest and genius. Similarly, suicide could connote both individual powerlessness and personal affirmation, a degeneration of will and willpower. Yet an important difference between these genres also existed. Rather than impugning the despotism of the patriarchal family or bureaucratic school, cases involving boredom, despair, or *Weltschmerz* implicated society more generally and even "life" itself.

The referent proved opaque. "Life" sometimes signified the contemporary organization of society, and the narration of a suicide could thereby culminate in revolutionary transcendence. One example of this genre is a poem entitled "The Suicide," published in 1865 by a minor poet, Nikolai Vorms. Calling the suicide a "martyr" (*muchenik*), the narrator laments how "young strength perished" (*pogibla molodaia sila*), extinguished by the relentlessness of life: "He lay pale and silent, / Bloody and exquisite, / He was a victim of a laboring life, / Of struggle dark and vain." The narrator then juxtaposes images of the body, weaving veneration with horror: "The peaceful look of his face, / And his silent beauty, / And the horror of the dark end, / And that fateful wound, / And that blood, the living blood . . ." The ethical condemnation focuses less upon the act of suicide than upon the life that has crushed him: "But you will be pure in your grave / You, the victim of a gloomy fate / You, who battled since youth / With this merciless life." The closing lines of the poem herald an end to suffering on earth when "other days" arrive.[69] Many of these images – especially the final eschatological allusion – would form common tropes in the language of revolutionary struggle. While the images of a "laboring" and "merciless" life could refer to material or spiritual hardship, this poem depicted the suicide as crushed by life yet sanctified in death.

The representation of suicide as a conflict between (inner) purity and (outer) corruption shaped a handful of personal texts. The best example is the case of two friends who killed themselves within two months of each other. While serving in the same regiment, they had been suspected of political disloyalty, held in prison for nine months, and then released when no evidence was found. Both resigned their commissions, and, in April 1882, the first shot himself. Shocked and galvanized by his friend's act, the other, named Shul'tz, wrote of his own impressions in his correspondence that was published posthumously.

The terrible news struck me like a thunder clap. My friend, my very closest comrade, shot himself [. . .]. I still cannot recover from this shock. Now, no misfortune, no grief can agitate me [. . .]. This man, so sensitive toward truth, so morally developed, could not endure the dirt and emptiness of our society, [which] lives basically an animal life. Passionate and ardent, unbelievably fastidious toward everything impure, he constantly suffered, constantly felt himself unhappy. A curse upon this society, whose best people

[69] N. Vorms, "Samoubiitsa," *Sovremennik* no. 8 (1865), 503–4.

must end in suicide! [. . .] My heart is heavy, terribly heavy, and so I yearn to end this nonsense that millions so value and that is called life. If it weren't for my responsibilities, my duty, then I would have ended it all long ago. But the various mediocrities [*shval'*] don't shoot themselves – their name is legion, though the greatest good they could render would be to stop living.

Canonizing his friend as honorable, pure, and moral, "a fighter for eternal truth and light," Shul'tz vowed to endure in the base and hypocritical world. Another letter continued: "I am still alive but don't ask how. [. . .] I am sick of this empty life; I am sick of constantly seeing flagrant lies and horrific ignorance [. . .]. It is bad to live but an animal's life, but it is worse to live intelligently. Having understood our educated society, one needs strong nerves to live in it without extreme repulsion, and instead to regard it with the cold and attentive gaze of the doctor." Shortly after this finishing this letter, Shul'tz shot himself. The reception of his suicide followed the same pattern. In publishing the letters of this "talented personality," the journalist invited readers to contemplate not only Shul'tz's literary genius but his moral purity, his passionate and noble character. Only when confronted with the bloody corpse – the shattered skull and splattered brains – would society finally understand that "these talented natures are perishing in an epidemic fashion." He venerated this martyr to truth as one of many all across the land: Russia was losing her most gifted sons, while the mediocrities, "the scoundrels and fools," were flourishing.[70] As in Reding's case, the suicide became an affirmation of the self, a sign and symbol of inner virtue. But doubt lingered. Was it also a pessimistic admission of defeat?

The narration of suicide as hagiography, as a heroic refusal to debase the self, became a recognizable generic form in the late nineteenth century, a means to read suicide but very rarely to author it. Neither Reding nor Shul'tz had actually made such explicit public claims for their deaths, instead stressing their own sense of *Weltschmerz* and despair. Indeed, these cases also evoked the powerlessness of the individual in the face of social apathy. One note articulated precisely this confusion: "I don't know whether I am dying because I am a coward or because there is strength in me."[71] The stock images, symbolic meanings, and rhetorical strategies of the genre also migrated to less dramatic cases, where its social criticism was often explicit, though not revolutionary in its implications. Suicide was routinely linked to the clichéd "lack of social life" in the provinces, for example, not unlike that which Reding had experienced, for the "musty atmosphere" of apathy and indifference suffocated

---

[70] N. Nikoladze, "Po povodu odnoi smerti," *Ustoi* no. 7 (1882), 40–49. According to another report, the letters possessed "extremely interesting social-psychological material"; see "Iz predsmertnoi perepiski," *Nedelia* no. 33 (1882), 1053–60. See also Paperno's brief discussion in her *Suicide*, 86.
[71] "Maniia samoubiistv," *Nedelia* no. 22 (1884), 734–35.

expressions of real thought, feeling, and activity.[72] In his passionate denunciation of the torments endured by child-apprentices (that sometimes culminated in suicide), one doctor also characterized these young people as "passion-sufferers" (*strasto-terptsy*) in an explicit comparison to Christ.[73] Another familiar plot was the struggle of young people to attain an education despite abject poverty and suffering. One eloquent note of a gymnasium pupil, who aspired to become a professor but fell victim to poverty, generalized his experience into a critique of socio-economic inequality. Even as this note was intended as a public statement, the act of suicide was not heroic: "I die like a dog," the young man lamented.[74] These victims of ill fate were often interpreted as symptoms of social pathologies, especially poverty, and commentators routinely invoked the language of martyrdom, sometimes literally and sometimes ironically.[75]

Such images bothered many observers, as I. A. Nevzorov explained: "What prompted us in particular to take up the pen was that very many [people] not only see no crime in suicide but even relate quite sympathetically to it. Our print organs often eulogize and extol suicides, call them heroes – noble, honorable, exalted persons. They lay wreaths, pronounce eulogies, set them as an example to the young generation." Asserting that this perspective constituted so-called "public opinion." Nevzorov overstated the dominance of this paradigm in part to challenge it from his "religious-moral point of view." Like many others, he was convinced that publicity – whether hagiographic or merely value-neutral – served as a kind of moral contagion. Only a resolute condemnation of the act, including its rigorous punishment, would eradicate the problem.[76]

Despite Nevzorov's assertion, the casting of suicide as martyrdom did not reflect a united public opinion but comprised one strand in a broader debate about the role of the individual in society. Criticism also came from the left. Condemning the idealization of the heroic feat among Russia's youth, the radical publicist Nikolai Shelgunov asserted that the individual had become too extreme, too egoistical and self-centered, and the task was now to forge the social person.[77] Other commentators agreed, stressing that the problem was limited to educated society, that the common people still benefited from social

---

[72] See e.g. "Tri samoubiistva (Pis'mo iz Kazani)," *Nedelia* no. 45 (1874), 1647–48.

[73] Gordon, "Samoubiistvo sredi detei," 106. Some religious writers shared this indignation, though not the metaphor. See *Tserkovnyi vestnik* no. 4 (1897), 107.

[74] For a translation of the note and further discussion of this case, see Paperno, *Suicide*, 107–8.

[75] The note was originally published in the following article, which was driven by this ironic tension. It repeatedly used the word "martyrology" yet regarded many cases with outright disdain. See "Samoubiistvo: Etiud po obshchestvennoi patologii," *Nedelia* nos. 18, 19 (1886).

[76] Nevzorov, *O samoubiistve*, 5–6. See also I. Popov, "O samoubiistve," *Bogoslovskii vestnik* no. 3 (1898).

[77] N. V. Shelgunov, "Ocherki russkoi zhizni," *Russkaia mysl'* no. 1 (1889). For an earlier example of this basic argument, see E. K. "Glasnye dramy intimnoi zhizni," *Nedelia* no. 39 (1873); and E. K. "Urok nekoemu publitsistu 'Dela'," *Nedelia* no. 49 (1873).

integration.[78] The multiplicity of narrative voices also contested the meaning of particular suicides, as in an 1893 case. Whereas the medical student from Kazan described himself as a weed needing to be eradicated (which was a common metaphor in the literature on degeneration), his friends declared him too honorable, too noble to live without a sufficient life's task. The reporter then interpreted the suicide as a contemporary nihilism, and he likened this student to Bazarov. The meaning of life, he concluded, must be found in the conscious and everyday struggle against banality, philistinism, and compromise.[79] These competing explanations highlighted the absence of a hegemonic narrative.

General explanations for the epidemic of boredom and disappointment initially cast the Great Reforms as the central reference point, a moment of rupture in Russian history that presented both opportunity and danger. In the opinion of some observers, the reforms had perhaps been too radical, the changes too sudden, and the result was a breakdown in social order and hence individual well-being.[80] Many others had hoped that the light of science and progress would dispel the darkness of repression and backwardness, but they increasingly feared the ongoing, destructive hold of the past and lamented the incomplete nature of the transformation. By the 1880s, uncertainty became palpable, prompting one commentator to lament in a characteristic fashion, that the "decomposition" of the old order in this period of "transition" had not yet led to the emergence of new ideals.[81] With the reform process incomplete and inadequate, Russian society continued to be backwards and inert, to suffocate under the yoke of arbitrariness, despotism, and custodial surveillance. Among the consequences, it was posited, were the existential feelings of disappointment, despair, and personal inadequacy. In the following decade, Professor Ivan Sikorskii would firmly locate this phenomenon in the domain of pathology. Translating *taedium vitae* as "exhaustion with life," he believed it to be one of the most common causes of modern suicide. The perception of boredom, pessimism, and apathy often assumed an epidemic character in transitional periods, he stressed, "when one worldview was replaced by another." The "extreme exertion of thought" could lead to fatigue, as could the "disappointment" caused by discarding a worldview.[82] As the industrialization drive transformed Russia's cities in the

---

[78] This point was asserted repeatedly in the literature. See e.g. D. Kulikovskii, "Samoubiitsy i nirvana," *Slovo* no. 11 (1880), 184; and B. S. "O samoubiistve v tsivilizovannykh stranakh," *Russkoe bogatstvo* no. 10 (1885).

[79] D. Zh. "Ugroza samoubiistva," *Nedelia* no. 51 (1893), 1650–58.

[80] See the speech of I. P. Merzheevskii, *Trudy pervogo s'ezda otechestvennykh psikhiatrov* (SPb, 1887), 15–37.

[81] *Otechestvennye zapiski* no. 7 (1882), 133. On metaphors of decomposition, see Paperno, *Suicide*, 46, 82–88, 140–43.

[82] He had only three other rubrics: poverty and deprivation; mental and physical illness; and moral causes. See I. A. Sikorskii, "Sostoianie dukha pred samoubiistvom," *Sbornik nauchno-literaturnykh statei po voprosam obshchestvennoi psikhologii, vospitaniia, i nervno-psikhicheskoi gigieny*, 5 vols. (Kiev, 1899–1900), vol. 1, 136, 148–57.

1890s, images of industrial modernity would increasingly displace the reform era as a new narrative reference point. In the new century, a new epidemic of suicide would begin.

The association between suicide and an abuse of power had been well established long before Dobroliubov addressed the issue, but his essays played an important role in transforming its meanings. During the first half of the nineteenth century, the state had sought to regulate the institutions of delegated absolutism, particularly within the context of serfdom, but its goal had been socially conservative. The prosecution of cruelty leading to suicide had enacted a paternalist program, and few officials seriously questioned the need for external forms of social control – supervision, coercion, fear, corporal punishment. Even as some suicides were perceived as victims of abuse, they were not accorded active agency, nor were their acts understood as a kind of protest. During the second half of the century, the relationship between suicide and cruelty changed. A wide range of public figures – jurists, doctors, journalists, writers – began to conceive individual instances of cruelty as expressions of a broader social and political problem that they characterized as despotism. Accordingly, the abuse of power could now be configured as an assault upon the dignity and rights of the personality. The benign paternalism of the *paterfamilias* had been reconfigured into arbitrary rule (*proizvol*). Resentful of the autocracy's ethos of tutelage, a small but growing public was rejecting the ability of the government to lead the difficult process of modernization. Its moralizing paternalism and custodial supervision seemed not only ineffectual but visibly harmful: it hindered the education of the will, stifled individual initiative, and impeded social development. By the turn of the twentieth century, the results seemed clearly evident in the proliferation of social pathologies, including crime, hooliganism, prostitution, alcoholism, poverty, and suicide.

The critique of petty despotism also conferred new meanings upon suicide. Public veneration now competed with public condemnation, but the dominant tone was in fact a deep unease. Because suicide was perceived as "an important index of the health of the social organism, a symptom of diseases eating it away," it was firmly embedded in the social world and thus presumed to possess social meaning.[83] But what was this meaning? The problem in part was that the act itself occupied the intersection between health and pathology. One technique was to read suicide as a heroic affirmation of selfhood, a defense of personal dignity, and a "ray of light within the kingdom of darkness." Yet voices from across the political spectrum also worried that suicide evidenced a new kind of diseased egoism, even pathological levels of pride and narcissism. Young

---

[83] From the review of Durkheim, N. K. "Samoubiistvo i ego prichiny (Pis'mo iz Frantsii)," *Russkoe bogatstvo* no. 4 (1898), 99.

people in particular seemed unable to moderate their desires and passions. At issue was not just whether individuals possessed the right to refuse life, but also whether they possessed the moral and mental capacity to make the decision. Although more suicides were leaving notes, in which they described a range of experiences and motives, few actively authored their deaths as explicitly political statements. The spectators to the private dramas were not so reticent. They scrutinized the bodies and words, inscribing the school regime or familial despotism upon some, pathologies and vice upon others.

Suicide had become firmly embedded within the public domain where it raised questions about the new basis of moral governance. If the individual was no longer to be supervised by external authorities, how were morality and social order to be maintained? How were suicide rates to be lowered, vice and crime to be combated? These questions were all the more pressing given Russia's long autocratic history. Indeed, the contention that the "kingdom of darkness" had deformed the personality and hindered the development of society had acquired a kind of scientific confirmation in the theory of degeneration: Russia's past could now constitute a kind of diseased heredity. Various solutions to the problem of moral governance coexisted, of course. Whereas conservatives typically called for the reimposition of paternal rule and the affirmation of absolute moral codes, radicals emphasized the need for fundamental social and political change. For their part, many specialists were envisaging a system of moral governance based on self-regulation. Rather than rejecting paternalism, they sought to recast it by placing primary emphasis on an integrated and enlightened education that would promote conjoined physical, mental, and moral development. Their exhortation was "a healthy mind in a healthy body," a cliché that illuminates an important aspect of their vision: the proper development of the will required physical strength, sound reason, and the exercise of moral self-control. Society could only become self-regulating when its health had been restored, a task that once again met head on with the many legacies of despotism – the "social morass" of ignorance, apathy, cunning, vice, crime, and so forth. This challenge set the stage for the revolution of 1905–7, which formed the next great rupture, if perhaps more rhetorical than actual, in the history of suicide in Russia.

Part III

Political theology and moral epidemics

Revolutionary epochs – such as Russia is currently experiencing – provide rich materials for the study of social psychology. The influence of the conditions of social life upon the psyche of individuals and entire groups becomes particularly sharp, clear, and prominent.

Natan Vigdorchik, "Political Psychoses and Political Suicides," 1907

Since the time of the Japanese War, we have been living in an atmosphere of death: the mountains of corpses on the field of battle [. . .] were replaced by the hundreds and thousands of executed. Alongside the cadres of death-row inmates appeared the cadres of suicides in the thousands. [The number of] executions has significantly declined, but the number of suicides continues to grow.

S. Arnova, "Suicide in the Past and the Present," 1911

10   Freedom, death, and the sacred

> Somehow I had gotten hold of Ryleev's poem "Nalivaiko," and it became one of my holy relics. [. . .] And I did indeed know Ryleev's fate. Everywhere, heroism, struggle, and revolt were always connected with suffering and death. "There are times, indeed entire epochs, when there can be nothing as beautiful and desirable as a crown of thorns."
>
> Vera Zasulich, quoting the executed Decembrist
poet Kondratii Ryleev, Reminiscences, 1931[1]

> Violent death and self-willed death are closely connected.
>
> L. Prozorov, "Suicides of the Condemned," 1911

In 1879, a young man, identified in the newspaper report only as Somov, killed himself while in prison. Arrested in Odessa for making a revolutionary speech, he had been restrained and placed in solitary confinement due to unspecified disruptive behavior. Using his teeth to maneuver the lamp, he then set his clothes on fire and lay down on his straw mattress. Only the coils of smoke escaping the grate in the door alerted his jailers, who found him engulfed in flames and immediately tried to save him. Despite tremendous physical pain, it was reported, he did not let out a moan, though he survived for several days, his hands and back completely charred away.[2] This silence, noted here in passing, resonated with unspoken significance.

Such events became increasingly common over the next decades, though the strict censorship imposed following the assassination of Alexander II usually prevented their full public exposure.[3] Nevertheless, they entered the unofficial annals of the revolutionary movement, where they were preserved as sacred texts (letters and suicide notes) and the artifacts of collective memory (hagiographical vitas, memoirs, and proclamations). These forms of textual commemoration

---

[1] From the translation in *Five Sisters: Women Against the Tsar*, ed. and trans. Barbara Alpern Engel and Clifford N. Rosenthal (New York, 1975), 69.

[2] "Neobyknovennoe samoubiistvo," *Nedelia* no. 22 (1879), 638–39.

[3] Important cases of self-immolation that I will not be discussing in this chapter involved the revolutionary Mikhail Grachevskii in 1887 (see GARF, f. 98, op. 1, d. 125); and the student Mariia Vetrova in 1897 (see GARF, f. 102, dp. 7 (1897), d. 6T4L. B). Some veiled reporting occurred in the Vetrova case, see "Raznye raznosti," *Nedelia* no. 11 (1897), 350.

elevated specific instances of suicide into heroic feats, universal exemplars of political will and revolutionary virtue.[4] Since the 1860s, of course, suicide had often been represented as an act of self-affirmation against the pernicious claims of arbitrary authority in the "kingdom of darkness," whether in the family, the school, or society more generally. To extend this paradigm to the autocracy was in many respects fully logical and consistent. But these suicides were distinctive in their explicit assertion of political meaning. One memoirist claimed an eminent lineage, comparing populists to the "ancient stoics," who preferred "freedom in death to slavery in life."[5] This analogy aptly evoked the archetype of self-mastery over pain and torment. More common was biblical and religious imagery, especially the narratives of martyrdom. By the early twentieth century, revolutionary suicide would constitute a discrete phenomenon with its own rhetoric and practices, a kind of political theology in which will and fortitude, suffering and sacrifice embodied – quite literally – the truth and justice of the cause.

Precisely these aspects came to the forefront during the revolutionary years of 1904–7, when the unpopular and unsuccessful war against Japan helped to catalyze simmering discontent into organized protest.[6] The year 1905 opened with soldiers shooting upon a peaceful demonstration of workers and their families, many of them carrying icons and portraits of the tsar. The event marked an important break. Though the popular legitimacy of the monarchy had already been declining – despite their language of supplication, the demonstrators had intended to present a petition appealing for wide-ranging socio-economic and political reforms – Bloody Sunday irretrievably undermined the tsar's authority and mobilized broad segments of the urban population. By October 1905, a general strike had paralyzed the country, forcing Nicholas to grant democratic reforms, including some civil liberties and an elected parliament. The tactical retreat worked. With oppositional groups and parties failing to find common ground, the government brutally reasserted its power over the next eighteen months, and conditions approached civil war. As thousands of people were imprisoned and executed, often with but a parody of due process, segments of the revolutionary left turned increasingly to terrorist violence, while many liberals attempted in vain to transform the parliament into a significant political force. The tsarist state would survive the convulsions of these years, but it would never again resacralize its authority, in part because it now competed with a

[4] By the early twentieth century, underground and émigré publications routinely treated individual cases as representative of a general phenomenon. See e.g. the article prompted by the self-immolation of Vladimir Nikiforov, "Novaia drama v tiur'me," *Osvobozhdenie* no. 10/34 (1903), 179–80. These cases also became a standard feature of Soviet-era writings on the tsarist prison. See M. N. Gernet, *Istoriia tsarskoi tiur'my*, 5 vols. (Moscow, 1960–63), esp. vol. 3, *passim*.
[5] O. S. Liubatovich, "Dalekoe i nedavnee. Vospominaniia iz zhizni revoliutsionerov, 1878–81." *Byloe* no. 6 (1906), 142.
[6] For background, see Abraham Ascher, *The Revolution of 1905*, 2 vols. (Stanford, 1988, 1992).

powerful new political force and rhetorical touchstone: the sacred principle of popular sovereignty. One, albeit imperfect site of this emergent new order was the parliament, but another was the ubiquitous image of the injured and suffering body, which came to function as an alternative, if multivalent, locus of the sacred.[7] The history of suicide illuminates this particular transformation in the iconography of the body politic. During these years of bloodshed and violence, suicide – the act, the body, the forms of commemoration – became a site of revolutionary struggle and a symbol of revolutionary transcendence. Its tremendous resonance reflected as well its practical and rhetorical affinities to other forms of violence – most importantly, state execution and revolutionary terrorism, both of which were likewise rendered in a theological key.

The paradoxes are striking. Just as the regulation of suicide was effectively migrating to the experts' domain of medicine, a theological discourse asserted itself, shaping the act and its cultural meanings. The medical and political-theological would uneasily coexist during and after 1905, the one constantly challenging the other. The rise of modern, mass politics in Russia was accompanied, therefore, not only by the emergence of new political institutions and ideologies, but also by the creative adaptation of older traditions. While the religious basis of populist rhetorics has long been recognized, it has generally been cast as an archaic remnant, part of a backwards-looking ideology. The example of political suicide suggests a more productive resonance for theological imagery. As conceived and enacted in the heroic feat of the political martyr, the revolution occupied a moment when the transcendent values of freedom and justice were (potentially) immanent. In other words, the revolution occurred in a kind of sacred time, that some contemporaries even likened to apocalypse. This was neither a secularized restatement of a religious idea nor the veiled resurgence of Christian narratives, for the revolution was understood as a man-made conflagration, not the result of God's intervention, and its sacred principles revolved around the human condition. Though it drew upon Judeo-Christian motifs, this modern form of redemptive politics possessed its own notions of morality, suffering, and transcendence, which, in turn, made specific practices possible, exemplary, and sometimes even obligatory. The dyad of sacred and profane formed an organizing structure that infused the meanings and practices of revolution.[8] Its failure and end would, therefore, often be

---

[7] Visual images of suffering and death dominated the large number of short-lived satirical journals of the period. See David King and Cathy Porter, *Blood and Laughter: Caricatures from the 1905 Revolution* (London, 1983). On how meanings are invested in the injured body more generally, see Elaine Scarry, *The Body in Pain: The Making and Unmaking of the World* (New York, 1985).

[8] Talal Asad argues that this dyad is not equivalent to religious-secular but is a modern construct intrinsic to the secular. The medieval and early-modern dyads were different: divine-satanic (transcendent) and spiritual-temporal (worldly). His analysis of the secular and the sacred has influenced my formulations. See his *Formations of the Secular: Christianity, Islam, Modernity* (Stanford, 2003), ch. 1.

represented as profane time – a return to the imperfections of human history and everyday life. The political theology established in 1905 persisted during the subsequent years, if sometimes in a new guise. As suicide rates would seemingly spiral exponentially, "epidemic" suicide would become paradigmatic of Russia's condition as a nation: revolutionary faith had degenerated into suicidal despair.

The crown of thorns

In his travels through Siberia during the 1880s covertly documenting the abuses of the tsarist system of forced labor and exile, George Kennan, the uncle of the twentieth-century American diplomat and scholar, visited the Kara gold mines, a grim and remote site, where he was able to meet secretly with a group of political prisoners. "When the convicts, with bated breath, began to tell me ghastly stories of cruelty, suffering, insanity, and suicide at the mines, I felt almost as if I had entered the gloomy gate over which Dante saw inscribed the dread warning, 'Leave hope behind.'"[9] The conditions endured by Russia's convicts were indeed hellish. Some suffered years of solitary confinement in such notorious institutions as the Shlisselburg fortress. At times granted the right to correspondence, reading and writing materials, and exercise, at times denied them, they always suffered the arbitrariness of authorities as well as countless physical and psychological indignities. Siberian exile and penal servitude were especially harsh, and not just due to the arctic climate. Convicts often endured numerous man-made hardships, including heavy chains and shackles, appalling hygienic conditions, and numerous restrictions on contact with the external world. Disease was rampant as was mental illness, and prisoners who had lost their minds were often not separated from the others, thereby providing a constant reminder of one's own potential fate. All of these circumstances were then compounded by the knowledge that penal servitude would be followed by exile, that the only way out was escape (often over hundreds of miles of tundra and taiga) or death.[10] While this context in itself can perhaps provide a sufficient motive for suicide, the particular meanings conferred upon the act, by both the actor and the audience, warrant a closer examination. The prison suicide enacted the revolutionary struggle in microcosm.

[9] George Kennan, "Siberia and the Exile System: The 'Free Command' at the Mines of Kara," *The Century: A Popular Quarterly* vol. 38, issue 3 (July 1889), 393. I consulted this on the internet (Feb. 7, 2005). For Kennan's series of articles on Siberia, including this one, see http://cdl.library.cornell.edu/mua/browse.author/k.11.html.
[10] The two classical treatments in the Russian and Soviet canon are Fedor Dostoevsky, *House of the Dead*, trans. David McDuff (New York, 1985); and Alexander Solzhenitsyn, *The Gulag Archipelago, 1918–1956: An Experiment in Literary Investigation*, trans. Thomas P. Whitney, 3 vols. (New York, 1974–78).

As early as the 1870s but especially by the 1880s, Russia's revolutionaries began to produce hagiographic portraits, memoirs, and other texts, including suicide notes, that sought to immortalize in print their valiant resistance to autocracy. Having smuggled some of these out of Russia, George Kennan used excerpts in his two-volume exposé on Siberian exile, which was then translated into Russian.[11] As such publications became increasingly available to interested readers by the early twentieth century (and ubiquitous by 1905), the prison suicide became a symbol for both the extremes of tsarist tyranny and the heroism of Russia's political martyrs, who went freely to their deaths with absolute faith in the victory of light over darkness. The emplotment of these suicides disputed the autocrat's power to make decisions over the lives and deaths of his subjects. This protest constituted an affirmation not just of individual freedom but of a more fundamental kind of self-sovereignty, which depended upon the principle of bodily and spiritual inviolability. By asserting their own bodies as the boundary of absolute power, the revolutionaries transformed themselves into a battleground, a weapon, and a symbol. Disputes about the prison regime often focused upon bodily dignity: clothing; the shaving of the head; the sanctity of the female body (including from the gaze of male jailors); and corporal punishment. Similarly, weapons of opposition ranged from the bodily display of disrespect (not rising at the entrance of an important personage or the demonstrative slapping of officials), to hunger strikes and suicide. This struggle to preserve bodily dignity symbolized a kind of spiritual integrity. The inner person remained intact, shielded from the tentacles of corruption and degradation pervading the autocratic system. Of central importance to both the acts of protest and the texts that framed them was consequently the affirmation of a revolutionary self, a person who was psychologically whole, rigorously virtuous (even ascetic), and internally consistent, and whose identity derived from complete revolutionary dedication.

The prison complex at the Kara mines was the site of numerous suicides, including one of the earliest and prototypical cases, that of Evgenii Semianovskii. The son of a Kiev doctor and himself a trained jurist, Semianovskii had been arrested for revolutionary propaganda in 1875 at the age of 25 and sentenced to twelve years penal servitude. Two years later, he arrived in Kara, which was then just a few years old, and a steady stream of populists soon joined him there. In 1879, many political prisoners were allowed to live in small huts outside the prison itself in what was called a "free command." Though checked twice daily by guards, they enjoyed a modicum of autonomy and fresh air, free from shackles and constant surveillance. In December 1880, however, two decrees arrived from St. Petersburg, the first forbidding all correspondence and

---

[11] Kennan's articles were collected in *Siberia and the Exile System*, 2 vols. (1891) and almost immediately published in a Russian émigré edition.

the second, ten days later, ordering all of the political prisoners back into chains in the prison. The commandant, a humane man who subsequently resigned his post, gave the convicts several days to prepare themselves. Unable to reconcile himself to his fate and already suffering serious stomach and heart problems, Semianovskii resolved not to go "as a sheep to the slaughter." After celebrating the new year with his comrades, he returned to his quarters early on January 1, 1881, where he shot himself.[12] In his long note to his father, that was first published by Kennan and later translated from the English back into the Russian, he explained the general circumstances at the prison and the impossibility of escape before turning to his particular situation:

> I feel that my physical strength is failing day by day. I know that my weakness must soon have its effect upon my mental powers, and that I am threatened with the danger of becoming a complete imbecile – and all this while I have been living outside the prison. My whole life rests on the hope of returning some time to Russia and serving, with all my soul, the cause of right and justice to which I long ago devoted myself; but how can that cause be served by a man who is mentally and physically wrecked? When the hope of rendering such service is taken away from me, what is there left? [. . .] I have therefore come to the conclusion that there is no longer anything to live for – that I have earned the right, at last, to put an end to sufferings that have become aimless and useless. [. . .] I have literally been tortured to death during these last years. [. . .] There is nothing left for me to do but to go insane or die; and the latter alternative is, after all, better than the former.[13]

Having devoted his life to the cause of revolution, Semianovskii argued that his physical incapacity to serve now rendered his suffering meaningless and consequently justified his suicide as a rational expression of self-determination. Though driven to his death by the tortures inflicted by the state, he also sought to make his last act into a meaningful assertion of personal autonomy: "Remember that it is better to die, even as I die, than to live without being able to feel oneself a man of principle and honor." This last reference highlights the creative reinvention of an archaic tradition within the myth-making of the revolutionary movement: the aristocratic suicide of honor. Two particular associations persisted from the earlier period: first, the semiotic linkage between external signs of honor – bodily inviolability, "civilized" conduct – and an inner nobility of character; and second, the active right to defend this (noble) self against both arbitrary political authority and social insult. Semianovskii was

---

[12] Prisoners in a free command occasionally acquired smuggled guns, and exiles living in highly remote locations were sometimes allowed to possess weapons, presumably for hunting and self-protection.

[13] The letter is reproduced in full in George Kennan, "Siberia and the Exile System: State Criminals at the Kara Mines," *The Century: A Popular Quarterly* vol. 38, issue 4 (Aug., 1889), 530. (See n. 9 for further information on this source.) The letter was also published in Russian (based on Kennan's English translation). See "Predsmertnoe pis'mo S. S. Semianovskogo k ottsu," *Byloe* no. 11 (1906), 126–27.

not alone in his resolution; later that year in Kara, one inmate poisoned himself with the phosphorus soaked from matches, and another hanged himself in the bathhouse.[14]

In memoirs published in 1906, a fellow convict and friend argued that Semianovskii's selfless devotion to the liberation movement and moral purity warranted his inclusion in the annals of revolutionary martyrs. His memorial painted a portrait of Semianovskii that drew on religious vitas and an established revolutionary canon.[15] Alongside the ideal of ascetic self-sacrifice was also a more human side of warmth and authenticity. Strict with himself and in the cause of truth and justice, Semianovskii was also modest, delicate, and sincere. In argument, he sought to convince, not to annihilate his opponent. Both the simple folk and the highly educated were at ease with him, feeling free to bare their souls with all their defects and vices. "I do not know [another] man," the memorial concluded, "in whom are united so harmoniously all the qualities of excellence as in Semianovskii." Thus proclaimed a prototype of revolutionary virtue, Semianovskii had lived without error and affirmed in death his personal honor that, in turn, signified the justice of the revolutionary cause.[16] Semianovskii's status as a revolutionary martyr was further ensured by the inclusion of his note as the final entry (for December 31) in the *Calendar of the Russian Revolution* (1907, 1917), a day-by-day chronicle of meaningful events in revolutionary history.[17]

The affirmation of dignity in the face of repression was integral to most prison suicides among populists, who seemed to perceive the act as both a protest against autocratic power and a demonstration of self-will over the impending loss of the self to madness or infirmity. One of the key sources of individual dignity was the collective of political prisoners that provided moral and intellectual sustenance and thereby prevented its members from falling into despair. Numerous memoirs depicted prison life as an ongoing struggle between despotic officials striving to assert absolute authority and prisoners striving to place limits on it. As one famous case illustrates, political suicide also tapped into the principle of group solidarity: it could function as a form of redemptive self-sacrifice, even a gift, for the general welfare of the collective.

---

[14] See the account in Kennan, "State Criminals," 529–32. For a list of inmates at Kara that includes information on background, arrests, sentences, and deaths, see G. F. Osmolovskii, "Kariitsy (Materialy dlia statistiki russkogo revoliutsionnogo dvizheniia)," *Minuvshie gody* no. 7 (1908).

[15] For the most recent analysis of the model of revolutionary asceticism, particularly its gendered aspects, see Sally A. Boniece, "The Spiridonova Case, 1906: Terror, Myth, and Martyrdom," *Kritika: Explorations in Russian and Eurasian History* no. 3 (2003), esp. 581–91. Among the most important inspirations were Nikolai Chernyshevskii's literary portrait of Rakhmetov and Sergei Stepniak-Kravchinskii's profiles of revolutionaries.

[16] S. B. Bogdanov, "Pomoshchnik prisiazhnogo poverennogo E. S. Semianovskii – odin iz pervykh kariitsev," *Byloe* no. 11 (1906), esp. 100, 116–18.

[17] V. L. Burtsev, ed. *Kalendar' russkoi revoliutsii* (reprint of 1907 edn: Petrograd, 1917), 324–26.

Following an incident the previous year in which a female political prisoner
had insulted the visiting governor general, conditions at Kara deteriorated in
1889, and tensions were especially high between the gendarme officer in charge
of political prisoners and the women convicts. A new arrival, Nadezhda Sigida,
decided to provoke an incident in an attempt to get the officer transferred.
Granted permission to see him on August 31, Sigida demonstratively struck
him – a symbolic act reminiscent of the rituals of the duel; the physical assault
was an assertion of her autonomy and a challenge to his authority. Taken immediately afterwards to solitary confinement, she wrote a final letter to her sisters,
which was smuggled out of prison and preserved. Acknowledging her bitter,
if still uncertain fate, Sigida emphasized her unwavering commitment to the
cause, which she, unlike Semianovskii, expressed in religious terms: "Though
you will pity me, though you will cry, take courage and be glad for me, for my
deep faith and devotion to holy truth and good." One memoir suggests that she
regarded her deed as a kind of atonement for an earlier sin. After being sentenced to death, she had allowed her attorney to petition for clemency, thinking
wrongly that this was a formality. In effect, she now seized the possibility of
documenting her commitment (unto death) to the revolutionary cause.[18] The
rituals of (noble) honor coexisted here with the rhetorics of faith.

Over the next weeks, a debate raged between St. Petersburg and Siberia about
Sigida's punishment. Although corporal punishment had recently been certified
as a legal disciplinary measure for political prisoners, it had not yet been generally enforced. This seemed the perfect moment: Sigida's act was (correctly)
viewed not as an individual incident but as a figurative assault on autocratic
power. Desiring a similarly meaningful punishment, Governor General Baron
Korf demanded 100 lashes, and his decision was endorsed by the interior minister despite the reservations of the prison doctor about Sigida's state of health.
Lashed on November 7, Sigida was returned to her cell, where she and her
three cell-mates poisoned themselves.[19] Two died quickly, and two lingered for
several days. They refused to take an antidote and, on doctor's orders, were
consequently denied any drinking water. The news spread through the men's
prison, prompting one convict to shoot himself (though he survived) and sixteen
others to take poison, of whom two died.[20] When later questioned about why
they had attempted suicide, the survivors explained their resolve to endure in
prison "a certain kind of violence upon their persons and even a certain level of
degradation," but to meet threats of corporal punishment with their own deaths.
To them, it constituted "a qualified form of the death penalty."[21]

[18] See the memoir of G. F. Osmolovskii, "Kariiskaia tragediia," *Byloe* no. 6 (1906), 77–79
[19] Their names were Mariia Kovalevskaia, Mariia Kaliuzhnaia, and Nadezhda Smirnitskaia.
[20] These two were Ivan Kaliuzhnyi (Mariia's brother) and Sergei Bobokhov.
[21] See Osmolovskii, "Kariiskaia tragediia," esp. 77–79; and the archival file in GARF, f. 102, dp.
5, op. 127, d. 7961, ll. 2–5, 8, 53, 65, and *passim*. Osmolovskii claims that sixteen male prisoners

In contrast to earlier investigations of discipline and cruelty within the context of serfdom, the authorities explicitly discussed this dynamic. In a telegram dated November 14, Baron Korf noted that the "moral impression" of the punishment, not its physical cruelty, had triggered Sigida's reaction, and it did not move him. He was not a "cruel man," Korf stressed, but he would continue to enforce corporal punishment, even knowing in advance its probable outcome. Such disorders and lack of discipline among these "monsters and regicides" were intolerable, he concluded, criticizing the "soft-heartedness" of some Petersburg bureaucrats who preferred to mollycoddle the convicts. In effect, therefore, Korf was advocating a game of chicken: corporal punishment could be the means to break resistance, even if it turned out to be the functional equivalent of the death penalty.[22]

This episode possessed many layers of symbolic meaning. At its heart was a struggle over the convict's body, and this localized confrontation enacted the broader political and symbolic struggle over Russia's body politic. With her original act, Sigida had sacrificed herself for the welfare of the collective, and the escalation occurred as a dialectic between individual and collective honor: the real violence inflicted upon one body (the slap, the lashing) ultimately produced symbolic – if also very real – acts of solidarity in the mass suicide attempts. Not possessing other means of answering the insult (though hunger strikes did occur in some cases), the prisoners turned to suicide both as the ultimate expression of their own autonomy and as an indictment of the politics of autocracy. In effect, the inscription of power upon the individual body had been converted into the voluntary suffering of the collective – the community of revolutionaries, who claimed, in turn, to act in the name of the long-suffering Russian people. Subsequent hagiographies would celebrate the "martyrs of Kara," who had defended their honor, freedom, and solidarity from tyranny (Illus. 5).

Many of these dynamics were likewise central to our final case study, which is set in the harsh and remote Kolyma region of Eastern Siberia at the turn of the twentieth century. By this time, the revolutionary canon was well established, and the sequence of events unfolded almost inexorably. Once again, voluntary death was constituted as the ultimate means to preserve the integrity of the revolutionary self, for whom personal dignity signified devotion to the cause. In contrast to the events in Kara, however, suicide was not the only perceived response to the violence done to the body of the revolutionary community.

took poison, but the archival record lists seven. It is possible that both are accurate: the poison was perhaps so diluted that only some individuals displayed symptoms requiring treatment.

22 GARF, f. 102, dp. 5, op. 127, d. 7961, l. 20. In an ironic parallel to contemporary public debates about the causes of suicide, another proposed measure was to give the political prisoners more physical labor and fewer books: apparently, too much reading had been the real cause of the incident. See Osmolovskii, "Kariiskaia tragediia," 75; and l. 49 of the archival file cited above.

Надежда Константиновна
СИГИДА.

Марія Павловна
КОВАЛЕВСКАЯ.

Illus. 5 Photos of Nadezhda Sigida and Mariia Kovalevskaia, two of the "martyrs" of Kara.

Born to a poor family, Ivan Kalashnikov had been arrested for conducting revolutionary propaganda among his fellow sailors in the merchant marine, imprisoned for seventeen months, and then exiled to Kolyma where he lived for several years. In the summer of 1900, without cause or provocation, he had been badly beaten up by Cossacks and criminal convicts under the direction of a district police officer. Unable to bear his humiliation and helplessness, he shot himself soon afterwards. In a short note, he asked his comrade, Ludwig Janowicz, to make sure that his young son was properly raised, charged the police officer with responsibility for his "blood," and affirmed his revolutionary spirit, writing: "I die with faith in a better future." The shock was intense for his comrades, as one later recalled: "Until that time we had somehow reconciled ourselves to our condition; they had taken real life from us, but we had built ourselves the illusion of life. [. . .] We struggled relatively successfully with the oppressive feeling of anguish and the consciousness of the pointlessness of our existence, but now that the only thing remaining to us, the only thing we considered inviolable – our personal dignity and honor – had been violated, we felt the entire self-deception in which we had been living until that time." This feeling of helpless desperation persisted for the next month as did the perceived need for protest. At this time, a resolution was found. The political prisoner, A. E. Ergin, assassinated the police officer, thereby avenging the besmirched honor of Kalashnikov and all the other political exiles. He gave himself up without a fight and was taken into custody.[23]

This incident is Janus-faced. On the one hand, it evokes earlier constellations of meaning. The language of honor again alludes to the traditions of the duel, even to the motif of the blood debt. Similarly the figurative opposition of honor to oppressive anguish raises the intertwined images of boredom and *taedium vitae*, thereby setting revolutionary faith and action as the counterpart to despair and inaction. On the other hand, it anticipates developments during and after the revolutionary year of 1905. This conception of the terrorist act placed it alongside the political suicide and corporal (cum capital) punishment. Unlike suicide, however, terror projected violence outwards upon the body of the target-victim conceived as a representative of the state.[24] Despite this difference, suicide and terror were equivalent forms of resistance within the repertoire of revolutionary acts.

The tale from Kolyma did not end with a terrorist finale but with another suicide. Ergin's trial occurred two years later in Iakutsk, and Janowicz was called as a defense witness to testify on the events surrounding Kalashnikov's suicide. In court, however, he suffered a nervous attack and was unable to speak: "these sacred tears" one witness recalled, "agitated and moved everyone present." He later recalled that the sight of the court had prompted memories of his own trial, when four of his comrades had been sentenced to death and he himself to Shlisselburg fortress. Highly cognizant of his own physical and mental deterioration (he had endured eleven years in Shlisselburg and was suffering from tuberculosis), Janowicz applied to remain in Iakutsk, but was medically certified as fit to return to the far north (though the doctor reportedly noted his impending death). Too ill to attempt an escape, he shot himself near the grave of a fellow Polish revolutionary, who had likewise perished in Siberian exile.[25] His first letter was left for the local police:

I ask that nobody be blamed for my death. The reasons for my suicide are nervous disorder and exhaustion resulting from many years of incarceration (18 years in all) in

[23] The quotations are from L. Ergina, "Vospominaniia iz zhizni v ssylke," *Byloe* no. 6/18 (1907), 52–60. See also G. Tsyperovich, *Za poliarnym krugom: Desiat' let ssylki v Kolymske* (SPb, 1907), 148–55.

[24] Indeed, one of the first acts of terror in Russia – Vera Zasulich's attempt in 1878 on the life of Governor General F. F. Trepov – had been provoked by the beating of a political prisoner. On the origins of revolutionary terrorism in Russia, see Claudia Verhoeven, "April 4, 1866: The Karakozov Case and the Making of Revolutionary Terrorism" (Ph.D. Dissertation, University of California, Los Angeles, 2004).

[25] Apparently he shot himself outside of the cemetery for political prisoners but in alignment with their graves. As a Catholic, he anticipated that he could not be buried inside the cemetery but wanted nonetheless to be with his comrades in death. On his last days, see M. Ol'minskii, "Smert' L. F. Ianovicha," *Byloe* no. 12 (1906), 97–100.

extremely difficult circumstances. In essence, the Russian government has killed me, so let it bear the responsibility for my death as for the destruction of countless numbers of my comrades.[26]

Though he had opened with the standard phrase found in numerous suicide notes in Russia, Janowicz played with its ambiguities, ultimately drawing out the same political implications as had the group-suicide in Kara. His death was the functional equivalent of state execution, only implemented by his own hands.[27]

In a second letter, which was addressed to Ergin and his wife, he expanded upon his motives and feelings:

My dear, good friends! Forgive me for my egoistic deed, for my desertion. I know how difficult it is to lose a comrade, I know it because I experienced it myself after the death [by suicide] of Gukovskii.[28] All the same, I cannot find in myself the strength to bear this psychological [dushevnyi] crisis. The thought of resting from the troubles of life has occurred to me before but [. . .] only now have I fully resolved to look for eternal peace. [. . .] Death does not frighten me. [. . .] My nerves are completely shot. Mere trifles cause hysterics in me. I have become an unfit milksop [. . .] and my ability to work is much in doubt. [. . .] Do not grieve too much: in the fifty provinces of European Russia alone, more than three million people die every year (exactly: 3,081,189 in 1896). What does an individual mean? – [It's] but a speck of dust. Of course, it will be difficult for you to live without your true friend, and that grieves me very, very much. But do not pity me. I will happily sleep the eternal slumber. What could be better? However, I do not propagandize this thought for others. I only think that I have fulfilled my duty according to my powers and that I now have the right to rest. I embrace you with all my soul.[29]

In some respects, this letter duplicated Semianovskii's reasoning: only ill health and a consequent inability to contribute further to the revolutionary struggle could justify the act. Yet Janowicz was clearly ambivalent about suicide more generally. It was a form of desertion, which he defined, not as disobedience to a higher authority, but as an anti-social act harmful to the collective. Nevertheless, he did claim the right to die. Having fulfilled his duty, he possessed the right to rest.

Despite his secular, even scientific language and explicit refusal to identify himself as a model, hagiographic portraits of Janowicz were numerous: this "modest martyr of Shlisselburg," this "man tempered by endurance and suffering," had reputedly inspired particular respect from his comrades as someone who "stood higher than the colony of exiles" and possessed that "most noble

---

[26] See Tsyperovich, *Za poliarnym krugom*, 145–46.
[27] This notion of suicide as political murder by the state was common. See the proclamation issued after the 1904 suicide of Comrade Krapivnikov, reprinted in M. V. Il'inskii, *Arkhangel'skaia ssylka* (SPb, 1906), 221.
[28] See below for further discussion.
[29] Ergina, "Vospominaniia," 63–64. Also reprinted in Tsyperovich, *Za poliarnym krugom*, 146–47.

Illus. 6 This photo shows a collage memorializing the "victims of the Kolyma exile" with the hero, Ludwig Janowicz, in the center accompanied by the other two suicides, Ivan Kalashnikov and Grigorii Gukovskii. Among the other photos is one depicting the cemetery, and the caption is from Janowicz's suicide note: "In essence the Russian government has killed me." From: G. Tsyperovich. *Za poliarnym krugom: Desiat' let ssylki v Kolymske.* St. Petersburg, 1907.

virtue" of the revolutionary, the "readiness to sacrifice himself."[30] Indeed, this "remarkable fighter and martyr to the revolutionary movement," had died while "passionately believing in the victory" of the revolution, doubting only his personal strength. With his self-possession thus remaining firm until the end, the suicide note exemplified his "beautiful, exhausted soul."[31] (Illus. 6)

Nervous exhaustion was a common medical explanation for suicide in this period, and the diagnosis here is suggestive. Although Janowicz, like Semianovksii, depicted suicide as an alternative to illness, not as its result, the shadow of madness was growing ever longer. Not all suicides of revolutionaries were venerated as political acts, and a good example is the 1899 death of Grigorii Gukovskii, which Janowicz had mentioned. Although he employed the language of self-sovereignty (reputedly telling his comrades, for example,

[30] Ol'minskii, "Smert' L. F. Ianovicha," 97; and "L. F. Ianovich v ssylke," *Byloe* no. 12 (1906), 85, 94.
[31] Ergina, "Vospominaniia," 41, 63.

"My life belongs to me, and nobody has the right to demand from me that I live when I do not want to live"), his suicide was not lionized by his comrades but instead causally linked to acquired and hereditary psychosis. Before his arrest in 1890, the young Marxist had reputedly possessed all the requisite qualities of a revolutionary: he had been very able, energetic, physically strong, resolute, and decisive. By the end of the decade, however, prison and exile had transformed him into a depressive type, who attempted suicide several times. Yet he also possessed a family history of suicide, including a cousin and a brother.[32] Although the meaningfulness of political suicide presumed a unitary and sovereign self, whose death embodied steadfastness and conviction, the fact of suicide – perhaps inevitably in this period – raised the question of mental health. Revolutionary memoirs often admitted the corrosive effects of state-sponsored violence, especially imprisonment, upon the minds and bodies of revolutionaries, portraying these scars (as Janowicz himself implied in his note) as one of the costs of the struggle. Yet the increasing influence of theories of degeneration also permitted a second possible interpretation. The linkage of Gukovskii's act to a familial medical history raised the possibility that he had been unstable from the outset. Though a secondary trope in this period, this specter would increasingly haunt the image of political suicide. The body of the suicide could potentially signify not just revolutionary heroism but also degenerate instability.

The memoirs that formed one important source for this analysis were published in the few years following 1905, when censorship functionally collapsed. This timing is important. Though the language of revolutionary struggle – especially its imagery of steadfastness, suffering, and self-sacrifice – was well established in underground and exile publications, the fact of mass political struggle provided a new context. One memoir made these linkages explicit: "What does the suffering of a few dozen revolutionaries mean before the heroic suffering of the tens of thousands of anonymous peasants and workers, who spill their blood and dedicate their torments to the difficult path towards freedom?" His answer was clear: "each link" in Russia's revolutionary "martyrology" must be established, so that the historian can piece together the "great and tragic picture of the battle for liberation."[33] In preserving the memory of these solitary fighters, these memoirs did not relegate the revolutionary forefathers to a closed historical past but instead proclaimed them as living exemplars in the

[32] Tsyperovich, *Za poliarnym krugom*, 156–60. A different example is the suicide of Mariia Vetrova, who was portrayed as having been driven to the madness of self-immolation by solitary confinement and a rumored rape. See the illegal pamphlet, *Pamiati Mar'i Fedos'evny Vetrovoi (†12 Fevralia 1897 goda v Petropavlovskoi Kreposti)* (n.p., 1898).

[33] This memoir describes a series of conflicts between convicts and authorities that ended in three executions as well as the deaths of six other prisoners. Janowicz had shot himself next to the grave of one of these victims. See O. S. Minor, "Iakutskaia drama 22-go marta 1889 goda," *Byloe* no. 9 (1906), 129.

mass battles of social revolution. Within the rhetorics and practices of heroic suicide, therefore, was the latent conflation of the individual with the social. Similarly, the new mass campaign against despotism was to leave its imprint not only on individuals but on Russia's body politic as a whole.

Vengeance of the lamb

In a third letter to friends written on the eve of his suicide, Janowicz confessed to having contemplated a different exit from his predicament. "Terrorist acts must be meaningful," he wrote, explaining his rejection of this option. "They must be answers to violence on the part of the administration but not committed only because it is a good moment to take out some scoundrel."[34] The boundary between suicide and terrorism was porous for each could constitute a means to sacrifice the self to the revolutionary cause. Nevertheless, the meaningfulness of terror required particular moral contexts, which were parallel but not identical to the moral contexts of political suicide.[35] Since the late 1870s, the formal theoretical justifications for terror had emphasized, among other factors, the necessity of terror in an authoritarian polity, its function as a limit on unlimited state arbitrariness, and its spectacular, didactic role as a demonstration of the possibility of resistance. Yet terror was not to be random or personal, for its moral right depended upon a series of equivalences: first, the act itself was to be a calculated and deliberate response to specific acts of despotism; second, the sense of fear and personal insecurity experienced by governmental officials was to counterbalance the sufferings of the people; and third, terrorists consciously assumed the moral guilt inherent in the act of violence and often gave up their own lives voluntarily in atonement.[36] Despite evocations of Old Testament notions of vengeance, the morality of terror remained ambiguous. The act of violence sacralized the terrorist in part because it blurred the boundaries between him- (or her-) self and the despotic, god-like tsar. The consequences of this blurring were manifold. In assaulting the embodied sovereignty of the state, the terrorists claimed equivalent self-sovereignty, hence their intense concern with personal dignity and bodily inviolability. But it also obliged their subsequent suffering (and sometimes death), which could thereby acquire a redemptive quality. Finally, the act could be constituted as a gift of the self, whether

---

[34] Ergina, "Vospominaniia," 64; and Tsyperovich, *Za poliarnym krugom*, 147–48.

[35] For a defense of terrorism as a means of struggle for light, freedom, and human rights against the darkness, oppression, and crimes of autocracy, including the suicide of political prisoners, see the underground publication of the SR Party, *Letuchii listok: "Revoliutsionnoi Rossii"* no. 3 (1902), 7.

[36] On terrorism and its formal justifications, see O. V. Budnitskii, *Terrorizm v rossiiskom osvobod-itel'noi dvizhenii* (Moscow, 2000), ch. 1; and Anna Geifman, *Thou Shalt Kill: Revolutionary Terrorism in Russia, 1894–1917* (Princeton, 1993), 11–14.

to the people or to the revolutionary community. That these qualities manifested themselves in the cases of political suicide discussed above is likewise obvious.

Historians largely agree that moral aspirations were central to Russian populist terror of the late nineteenth century, which was a relatively limited and focused phenomenon that enjoyed a significant degree of social acceptance. During the revolutionary era of 1904–7, they argue, a new breed of terrorism and terrorist emerged. By this time, the number and scale of attacks had increased dramatically, with one historian even claiming that a dozen such acts occurred each day.[37] In 1902, the populists' successor organization, the Party of Socialist Revolutionaries (PSR), endorsed the use of terror, and though it formally subordinated its Combat Organization to party discipline, this terrorist wing functioned largely autonomously, and the terrorists themselves enjoyed tremendous prestige within the revolutionary community. Despite their ostensible rejection of terror, Marxists were likewise actively involved in such revolutionary violence as assassinations, bombings, and expropriations. Finally, countless splinter groups also proliferated in the revolutionary years, particularly the SR Maximalists, who proved to be among the most daring, indiscriminate, and violent. The high levels of violence likewise entailed a dramatic rise in civilian casualties. In describing the new forms of political extremism, the historian Anna Geifman contrasts the principled motives and theoretical concerns of nineteenth-century terrorists to the personal motives and intellectual illiteracy of their twentieth-century counterparts. Though not defending the earlier acts of terror, Geifman does chart its degeneration into criminal violence, which she causally links to the welcoming of "base rabble" and "outcast elements" into the fringes of the revolutionary camp as well as the youth, emotional immaturity, psychological instability, and degenerate behavior of the new terrorists. While Geilman does document important shifts in the character and scope of terrorism, she reproduces uncritically the categories of contemporary social and medical discussions, especially as found in records of the secret police. Revolutionary terrorism is thus explained as the product of inner psychological conflicts, irrational drives, and the emotional problems of the terrorists, especially their suicidal urges.[38] The historian V. O. Budnitskii, in contrast, is very reluctant to base historical argument upon such psychological judgments, preferring a nuanced analysis of political, social, and individual factors. Still, he too is struck by the close connections between terrorism and suicide in this period.[39] Such a connection clearly existed, but to base it on tenuous (and tendentious) generalizations about the psychological deficiencies of terrorists removes the

---

[37] Geifman largely conflates terrorist with criminal acts. Though her numbers are perhaps high, the fact that terrorism increased dramatically in these years is undisputed. See ibid., 20–38.
[38] Ibid., 135, 154–80, and *passim*.   [39] Budnitskii, *Terrorizm*, 162–65.

need to take either them or their words seriously. Indeed, patterns of rhetoric and practice provided essential links between suicide, revolutionary terror, and the revolutionary self. These manifestations of political violence framed one another and together gave shape to the revolutionary process.[40]

The first and most obvious point is that the nexus between suicide and revolution was established well before 1905, and that these narratives continued to inform revolutionary experiences. According to the one-time leader of the People's Will, Vera Figner, the modern terrorist most like the heroes of her generation was Egor Sozonov, who assassinated the interior minister V. K. Plehve in 1904.[41] After throwing the bomb that killed Plehve but left himself badly wounded instead of dead, as he had hoped, he tried but failed to reach for his revolver so as not to give himself up alive. In subsequent letters from prison, Sozonov emphasized his indifference to his own individual death: "If we die, then the cause that we love more than anything on earth will live on." Begging his parents not to mourn his fate, he further articulated a Christian vision: "for we are martyrs to our faith, our religion: as they gave their lives for Christ, so we are ready to give ours for our truth, our holy truth, which, in my opinion follows Christ."[42] Another letter holds up the Passion as the primary model: "I think that we, the socialists, continue the work of Christ, who preached brotherly love among the people [. . .] and died for the people as a political criminal. [. . .] When I heard my teacher saying: take up your cross and follow me [. . .] I could not abandon my cross"[43] (Illus. 7). Sozonov would ultimately end his life in a revolutionary act: a prison suicide in 1910 that he intended as a protest against the use of corporal punishment – again a prototypical motive – and thus as an affirmation of collective dignity.[44]

While some terrorists drew upon a Christian notion of suffering, others relied more upon the language of vengeance and sacrifice. A good example is Fruma Frumkina, who had attempted to assassinate a high-ranking police official in Kiev apparently as a prelude to a whole series of similar attempts and who, while in prison, repeatedly attacked her jailors. On the eve of her execution in July 1907, Frumkina asked her friends and family not to mourn her fate, emphasizing the ecstatic willingness of her sacrifice: "I bear the name of the Russian revolutionary and to this name is attributed my steadfastness and

---

[40] I do not seek to provide a comprehensive review of or explanation for terrorism in this period, especially given the huge number of sources. Nor do I deny that other patterns existed or even that some terrorists may have been mentally ill. The point is to take seriously the relationship between rhetoric and practice.

[41] Vera Figner, *PSS*, 6 vols. (Moscow, 1929), vol. 3, 188, 195.

[42] *Eto ia vinovat . . . Evoliutsiia i ispoved' terrorista: Pis'ma Egora Sozonova s kommentariiami* (Moscow, 2001), 120–21.

[43] Quoted in Geifman, *Thou Shalt Kill*, 49.

[44] For his final letters and the general context, see *Eto ia vinovat*, 476–512. See also GARF, f. 29, op. 1, d. 1386.

Illus. 7 This striking image from the satirical art of the revolutionary years 1906–7 illustrates the strong religious imagery: the severed head of the martyr wearing a crown of thorns. From Cover (by Vasilii Beringer), *Payats* no. 2 (1906).

readiness to die joyfully for our cause [. . .]. Russian revolutionaries know how
to live and [how] to die for the happiness of the motherland – and I only follow
their example. [. . .] Farewell!"[45] Contemporaries sometimes remarked upon
the mental derangement of revolutionaries and their acts, including Frumkina,
but the eminent psychiatrist Nikolai Bazhenov testified to her sanity. At issue,
of course, was the moral and political integrity of the terrorist, upon which the
legitimacy of the self-sacrifice depended. The medical model of degeneration
possessed the potential to divest the political suicide of its political significance,
that is, to render it as insane and meaningless violence.

Even as the established narratives persisted in 1905–7, the moral equivalences
underpinning the terrorist act were subverted by both the escalation of terror as
well as its increasingly random and indiscriminate quality. These developments
provoked intense self-scrutiny within the intelligentsia, as liberals and radicals
alike began to ponder whether the act of terror – rather than enacting moral
purity – actually deformed the moral personality or, even more disturbingly,
constituted the expression of an already deformed personality. Increasingly,
therefore, these competing narratives cut into each other and thereby undermined the triumphant eschatology of personal and social revolution. Indeed,
the new "mass" character of revolutionary politics helped to cast the vita of
self-sacrifice onto the level of class and nation, and this rhetorical move would
raise disturbing questions about the ethos of revolutionary transformation and
its impact upon the health and well-being of the population more broadly. These
challenges to the predominant model of self-sacrifice forced a reassessment of
the heroic suicide cum martyrdom.

In the wake of 1905, many liberal commentators began to ponder whether
the revolution itself constituted a kind of metaphysical (and literal) death-wish,
and they developed an alternate vision of regeneration. While this new narrative
of death into life found many expressions, one evocative example illuminates
the dynamics of self-representation and its public reception. The background is
formed by the single most shocking event of terror in these years: the bombing
of Prime Minister P. A. Stolypin's dacha in August 1906, which occurred during
his official office hours and left scores injured and more than two dozen dead.
(Stolypin himself survived, though he would be assassinated five years later.)
More than any other attack this one exemplified the new willingness to kill
innocent by-standers, including children, and it inaugurated the most brutal
phase of governmental repression. Many SR Maximalists were rounded up in
the wake of this event, and several of its organizers were sentenced to death. One
of these individuals was Natal'ia Klimova, whose "Letter before Execution"
was published in 1908 and promptly likened to Oscar Wilde's *De Profundis*.[46]

---

[45] Quoted in D. Merezhkovskii, "Bes ili Bog?" *Obrazovanie* no. 8 (1908), 93, 96. For further
discussion of Frumkina, see Budnitskii, *Terrorizm*, 165.
[46] S. L. Frank, *Slovo* no. 570 (1908), as cited in A. S. Izgoev, "Zamaskirovannoe samoubiistvo,"
Russkaia mysl' no. 10 (1908), 161.

Klimova did not write about the bombing and revolutionary politics, nor did she show any remorse for her actions. Instead she pondered the meaning of her death, both the physical experience, and the spiritual consequences – the dissolution of her individual consciousness. Even as she called herself "the crudest materialist," she confessed to having discovered since her sentencing a new metaphysical joy in life, a boundless and profound love for life in all its great and petty manifestations. And yet, as she noted in conclusion, this pantheistic love did not bind her to life:

Do you know what it means in one instant to feel suddenly the great unity of the entire world – the most exact and beautiful linkage between the most distant star and this microscopic piece of dust that lies on my desk? Between the greatest genius of mankind and the embryonic nervous system of some worm? Between me and the small, white, exact structure and beauty of a snowflake? [. . .] Do you know what it means to feast one's eyes with tender attentiveness upon this great mass [of life?], to love – tremblingly and passionately – every movement, every beat of the pulse of [your] young, newly awakened life? And to know that not one second [of life] has power over you, that you can – without fear, without regret – break it off and end your consciousness for eternity?[47]

Klimova did not rehash the prevailing revolutionary rhetoric, and this absence distinguished her letter from the countless other proclamations of the era.

The "truth" of her words, her "profound soul," her innate "talent" and "sincerity" caught the imagination of Russia's publicists. In an article entitled "Masked Suicide," the prominent liberal commentator A. S. Izgoev argued that Klimova's path toward terrorism was nothing other than a form of suicide by proxy, and he probed the autobiographical narrative that underpinned her letter. Four or five years earlier, he interpreted, quoting her words extensively, she had been cheerful and happy until suddenly, in approximately 1902, she had lost her "joy of life" – which she defined as "the sensation of complete harmony between external conditions and the inner world" – and become melancholic and apathetic. She had first noticed the disjunctions between logic and religion (thereby placing a religious crisis at the origins of the revolutionary *Bildungsroman*). Over time, a series of other disjunctions had also appeared: between critical thought and the stagnation of routine, including the self-confident ignorance of authorities (both pedagogical and parental); and between her conceptions of truth, justice, the necessary and the forms of external life, from social inequalities to political despotism. Consequently, and Izgoev italicized Klimova's words, she lost not only her sense of joy but also "the simple desire to live, and the thought of suicide carefully but powerfully began to possess [her] soul." But Klimova claimed to find an exit from her predicament in total revolutionary dedication. Proclaiming the slogan "all or nothing," total victory or death, she thus sought

---

[47] [N. Klimova], "Pis'mo pered kazn'iu," *Obrazovanie* no. 8 (1908), 65–70.

to enact her truth and right into life and thereby to heal the disjunctions. In actual fact, Izgoev dryly noted, she had joined the Maximalists' group, and "the murder of others became for her a means to kill herself." Because a total victory over all of life's disjunctions is impossible, he emphasized, only "nothing" remains. As Klimova herself recalled in passing, she thought constantly about the psychology of man facing death all the while she herself prepared death for dozens of innocent people. Until this point, Klimova's autobiography was not especially unusual; it seemed to duplicate the experience of countless other young people and even Russia itself. What fascinated Izgoev was her discovery of life whilst awaiting her own execution and its unexpected consequences now that the death sentence had been commuted to hard labor. "You see," he explained, "the pantheistic feeling of universal love serves not only as an impulse for an easy and proud death, not only helps one to die, but also gives one the strength to live." Her new consciousness, he believed, would prevent her from taking another's life, and he confessed deep curiosity about how she would experience the gift of life. Noting that "such profound souls punish and forgive themselves," he even called for a formal pardon so that she would be allowed to develop her personality "under normal circumstances." Finally, he offered her as a role model to Russia's youth, who likewise suffer doubts and disjunctions but could hopefully learn about the meaning of life from her example.[48] In other words, Klimova's redemption provided an alternative to the suicide that was revolutionary violence.

Precisely this issue was an important theme in the controversial *Landmarks* volume that was published the following year and quickly went into several editions. Many of the luminaries of Russian liberalism contributed articles in which they lambasted the traditions of the Russian intelligentsia, especially its ethos of revolutionary self-sacrifice. Rather than knowing how to live, rather than developing an ethic based on life and the cultivation of the individual moral self, Russia's intellectuals only knew how to die for an abstract cause.[49] According to Sergei Bulgakov, Russia's political system laid the foundations of this process, and he reworked the well-known categories: "[A] police regime cripples people [. . .] it helps cultivate a special spiritual arrogance in its victims, a certified heroism, so it speak. [. . .] Subsequently, suffering, resentment at the cruelty of authorities, heavy sacrifices, and losses complete the formation of this heroic type who may possess any trait except doubt about his mission." Religious in its form, if not in its content, this heroism was the defining

[48] Izgoev, "Zamaskirovannoe samoubiistvo," 160–71.
[49] This theme echoes through many of the contributions. See *Landmarks: A Collection of Essays on the Russian Intelligentsia, 1909*, trans. Marian Schwartz (New York, 1977). See also E. Koltonovskaia, "Samotsennost' zhizni," *Obrazovanie* no. 5 (1909). For further analysis, see Aileen M. Kelly, *Toward Another Shore: Russian Thinkers Between Necessity and Chance* (New Haven and London, 1998), ch. 9.

pathology of the Russian intelligentsia. Bulgakov continued: "Heroism preaches the necessity of causing something to happen, accomplishing something beyond one's strength, and, in the process, to give up what is most dear, one's own life. One becomes a hero and, at the same time, a savior of mankind through an heroic act far beyond the bounds of ordinary duty. Although this dream is realizable only for a handful, it lives in every *intelligent*'s heart, and serves as the general standard of judgment. [. . .] Sometimes the desire to escape from life as a result of one's maladjustment to it and the inability to bear life's burdens merge with heroic self-renunciation to the point where they are indistinguishable; so that the question involuntarily arises: is it heroism or suicide?"[50] Bulgakov's formulation here was crucial. Like Izgoev, he sought to de-mythologize revolutionary self-sacrifice by rendering it mundane and not metaphysical; it was a suicide, not a heroic feat and not a martyrdom.

The *Landmarks* collection provoked passionate protests, and its authors were vilified as representatives of political reaction and the emergent bourgeoisie. Nevertheless, the revolutionary left was forced to confront its demons when Boris Savinkov, the one-time leader of the SR Combat Organization, probed the moral essence of terror and suicide in several autobiographical novels. Not so unlike Izgoev and Bulgakov, he too discarded the model of the heroic feat and instead dissected how violence destroys the integrity of the personality. *The Pale Horse* follows a group of terrorists who have targeted a governor but who do not possess the central trait extolled in revolutionary hagiography – absolute faith in the cause. The first to die is Fedor, who is driven to terrorism by an intense hatred for privilege (and the privileged, who, he believes, should all be wiped out). After bombing the governor's carriage, killing the coachman but not the governor, he flees, shoots nine people, and then kills himself. Such is the boundlessness of hate. The next to die is Vania, who, driven by Christian love, knows that "thou shalt not kill" yet nonetheless believes that he must kill. Accepting the burden of his sin and trusting in Christ's mercy, he goes willingly to his execution. By lingering upon Vania's feelings of personal guilt, regret, and moral paradox, the novel challenged the moral certitude within the conventional narrative of terrorist self-sacrifice. The last one to die is the narrator, Zhorzh, who kills without love, hate, or remorse and without faith in revolution. It is simply what he does. After killing the husband of his lover, however, he experiences a sense of emptiness: "I understood: I do not want to live anymore. My words bore me, my thoughts and desires [bore me]. People bore me, their lives [bore me]."[51] Having lived by the sword, he must die by the sword, but neither his assassinations nor his suicide possessed moral value or meaning.

---

[50] S. N. Bulgakov, "Heroism and Asceticism: Reflections on the Religious Nature of the Russian Intelligentsia," *Landmarks*, 36, 39.

[51] One other character, the bomb-maker, also kills herself rather than be arrested, and the last terrorist escapes, but he is a weak and indecisive character. V. Ropshin, [Boris Savinkov], *Kon'*

In contrast to the hagiographies framing the lives of countless revolutionaries, therefore, this text claimed violence itself as its object. Yet the violence of autocracy no longer provides a moral basis for "the vengeance of the lamb." Instead Savinkov shifted the focus from the external foundations legitimizing the terrorist act to both the act of murder itself and its repercussions upon the psyche of the terrorist. Indeed, boredom expressed the crisis of revolutionary faith.

These issues recurred in a dialogue Savinkov initiated with Vera Figner whilst both were in exile in Western Europe. An admirer of Figner, Savinkov even fashioned himself into her "son," and though Figner rejected this characterization, their discussions often returned to the generational divide in Russia's revolutionary movement. In one episode, Savinkov insisted upon the terrible spiritual condition of the man who has decided upon the "cruel deed of taking a human life," and Figner recalled her sense that Savinkov was speaking for effect. Nevertheless, she responded in terms that recollect Klimova's own resolution: "One cannot proceed with a terrorist act with a disjunction in one's soul. The inner struggle is understandable when the question is being decided, but, if decided, then all doubts must be [. . .] left behind. There can be no torment [*terzanie*]."[52] In a later discussion, Figner was struck by Savinkov's passionate contention that the terrorist offers up that which is most valuable to him, his own life. Again Figner claimed not to understand, asserting that her generation had experienced, subjectively seen, neither sacrifice nor struggle in the act of self-sacrifice: "if one takes another's life, [then one can] give up one's own easily and freely." Savinkov responded: "But if you did not value your life, if you did not weigh its value, then you gave the revolution very little; you gave up that which you did not need and committed, it could be said, political suicide."[53] For Savinkov, then, only the gift of the self – that which is most valuable – could confer meaning upon the terrorist act. However, as one liberal commentator perceptively wrote in a review of *The Pale Horse*, the cost to the self was less one's physical life than one's spiritual integrity:

Violence is done to the most valuable part of the personality: that very thing in the name of which the sword was raised is destroyed. Fighting against tyranny in life, the individual creates tyranny in his own soul, crushing one part of his ego with another.

blednyi, 2nd edn., (SPb, 1912), here 124. My reading has been influenced by Daniel Beer, "The Terror of Morality: The Representation of Political Violence in Boris Savinkov's *The Pale Horse* (1909) and *What Never Happened* (1912)," forthcoming; and Kelly, *Toward Another Shore*, 142–47.

52 Figner noted that this issue would recur in one of Savinkov's subsequent novels, *What Never Happened*, in which the focus is kept ruthlessly upon the act of violence, not its "moral" justification: at the moment of the murder, the victim is helpless, no matter his previous crimes. For further discussion, see Beer, "The Terror of Morality."

53 Figner, *PSS*, vol. 3, 179–97. For further discussion of this exchange, see Budnitskii, *Terrorizm*, 159–61.

Within the human personality, there occurs the same horror that takes place in a society morally crushed by tyranny: both oppressor and oppressed are isolated and corrupted. When, sooner or later, there comes a decisive test, a question of life or death for the entire organism, its shattered and maimed components, incapable of united and efficient action, enter into chaotic, suicidal conflicts, and the organism vanishes from the world of the living, in excruciating torments of . . . impotence and despair.[54]

In some senses, Zhorzh's life and death enact a different narrative of revolution, one which Figner and many others failed to grasp. The huge number of victims, the escalation of violence, the failure to transfigure life – had ultimately provoked a doubled crisis of narrative meaning and psychological integrity that Zhorzh articulated as boredom. In the wake of 1905, when Savinkov was writing, a wave of despair and suicide seemed to envelop Russia as a nation.[55] In other words, the crisis concerned not just literary heroes, liberal commentators, and a handful of individuals, but society as a whole. Vania had articulated the problem: "Do you know," he explained to Zhorzh, "it is easy to die for others, to give people one's death. It is harder to give one's life."[56] Had the revolution built upon an ethos of death, of heroic self-sacrifice? Had it subsequently become degenerate and pathological, thereby producing mass despair and suicide?

Vladimir Lenin developed a different exit from this predicament. Throughout 1905 and 1906, he called upon local Social Democrats to organize the active struggle, to throw some bombs, to assassinate the executioners. But he formulated this task in terms not of self-sacrifice, martyrdom, or terror but of training, the tempering of the revolutionary self in active military engagement. In 1906, he published his influential article on revolutionary struggle as "partisan war," in which he called upon small fighting detachments to attack the state and its representatives in preparation for outright class war. Just as the state was using new forms of repression, so must the revolutionary camp develop new forms of struggle. He too rejected the sovereign authority of the state to decide matters of life and death, but his model built upon a military form of equivalence: war knows no morality, only combat, injuring, and – ultimately – victory or defeat.[57]

---

[54] S. A. Adrianov writing on Savinkov's *The Pale Horse*, as quoted in Kelly, *Toward Another Shore*, 145–46.

[55] I will discuss this crisis below and in the next chapter. Another great symbol of it was the exposure of the leading SR terrorist Azef as a police spy. For further discussion, see Anna Geifman, *Entangled in Terror: The Azef Affair and the Russian Revolution* (Wilmington, Del., 2000).

[56] Savinkov, *Kon' blednyi*, 24–25.

[57] See V. I. Lenin, "V Boevoi komitet pri Sankt-Peterburgskom komitete," and "Zadachi otriadov revoliutsionnoi armii," *PSS*, 55 vols. (Moscow, 1958–65), vol. 11, esp. 336, 338, 340–43; "Partizanskie boevye vystypleniia," *PSS*, vol. 12, 228–29; and his "Partizanskaia voina," *PSS*, vol. 14, 1–12. For a penetrating discussion of Lenin's views and their relationship to terror that has influenced my own interpretations, see Verhoeven, "The Karakozov Case," 364–72.

The subterranean kingdom

In the aftermath of the October Manifesto of 1905, when the government granted constitutional reforms and thereby began to split the opposition, pogroms swept through many cities and towns, victimizing Jews, intellectuals, students, workers, and anyone even remotely associated with radicalism. Over the next weeks and months, political reaction gained strength as the government declared martial law in numerous regions and bloodily suppressed the ongoing revolutionary movement – whether labor strikes, union organization, peasant revolts, or the occasional mutiny. In 1906 and 1907, the representation of state-sponsored violence as a kind of war upon the population became very common, for, as the law professor M. P. Chubinskii put it: "the era of military courts and executions" had begun.[58] Although regular courts also passed death sentences, the military tribunals came to symbolize the extremes of violence and arbitrariness, that is, the state's complete disregard for law, justice, or individual rights. Empowered to try, convict, sentence, and execute without right of appeal, the tribunals sent hundreds to their deaths, often on the basis of scanty or no evidence. The death penalty became hugely controversial after 1905, and the facts and figures were widely reported in the commercial press.[59] The issue was raised and the government's policies condemned by the delegates to Russia's first parliament, the Duma, in 1906, and a wide range of public figures also spoke out, including doctors, psychiatrists, jurists, criminologists, priests, philosophers, professors, and writers.[60] While the execution of political prisoners had sporadically occurred in nineteenth-century Russia, it became a mass phenomenon at this time and, as such, an emblem of the new era of mass politics.

"Numbers do not rule the world, but they show how it is ruled." This epigraph framed an article devoted to the "statistics of repression," which included figures not just on death sentences, executions, and other punishments for political offenses, but also on prison suicides. The phenomenon was epidemic, he claimed, an exemplar of illegitimate rule.[61] According to an official statistical review, however, the rising number of prison suicides was proportional to the

[58] M. P. Chubinskii, "Smertnaia kazn' i voennye sudy," in *Protiv smertnoi kazni*, ed. M. N. Gernet, O. B. Gol'dovskii, and I. N. Sakharov, 2nd edn (Moscow, 1907), 112.

[59] Censorship collapsed in 1905–7 and was never completely reinstituted. Furthermore, the commercial press expanded dramatically in this period. A separate rubric was often devoted to reaction and executions. On the press in this period, see Louise McReynolds, *The News under Russia's Old Regime: The Development of a Mass Circulation Press* (Princeton, 1988), chs. 8, 9.

[60] For a cross-section of critical views, see Gernet, Gol'dovskii, and Sakharov, *Protiv smertnoi kazni*. See also (385–423) for a list of 1,397 death sentences pronounced by Russian courts (not including military tribunals) between 1826 and 1906 (not all of which were executed). The last 875 date to 1906 alone, and most of these were carried out.

[61] A. Ventin, "K statistike repressii v Rossii (Iz itogov 1908–1909 g.)," *Sovremennyi mir* no. 4 (1910), esp. 55–57, which lists 78 suicides and 28 attempts in 1909.

parallel growth in the prison population as a whole, which was due to political and agrarian unrest as well as increases in crime. As the author asserted, playing down the extent of the problem, the rates of prison suicide in Belgium in 1907 were seven times higher than in Russia. This fact was apparently intended to demonstrate the relative humanity of the Russian prison in a European context.[62]

Despite such attempts at reassurance, the problem sparked intense public and medical interest, and few accepted its explanation as an incidental by-product of a growing prison population. Many of those who killed themselves in prison had already been condemned to death and were awaiting their execution. Furthermore, many cases, such as the 1910 suicide of Egor Sozonov, were directly intended and understood as a form of political protest. The symbolic meanings were clear at the time, when it inspired a series of student protests.[63] As Figner wrote, the news of the corporal punishment and Sozonov's suicide provoked "revulsion at the executioners who debase the dignity of Russia."[64] Consequently, the meaning of prison suicides depended upon both their immediate environment and their political context, especially the violence of the state upon the population.

The tsarist prison had long been portrayed by radicals and liberals alike as a site of unlimited state arbitrariness, and this representation framed even routine informational articles. When Figner herself had been released in 1904 from "the darkness of her living grave" (that is, two decades in the Shlisselburg fortress), the influential émigré journal *Liberation* reported the event in these terms: "even there, in that subterranean kingdom of unlimited, inhuman arbitrariness, this amazing woman preserved an unwavering courage, a majestic ability to defend her human dignity from the savage tricks of the obtuse and malicious jailers." Not only had her courage and pride supported her comrades; the "halo of her protesting martyrdom" had also inspired the respect of Russia's intelligentsia. Yet Figner did not emerge unscathed, for the prison had left its mark upon the prisoner: she was suffering from emaciation, scurvy, and nervous illness (a fear of open spaces).[65]

Figner's survival with dignity, if broken health, conferred a sacred aura upon her suffering, but the new era of martial law raised the stakes. In the face of mass

---

[62] From an average of 10.5 cases in 1899–1900, the numbers had doubled by 1901–2 (an average of 22), doubled again by 1903–6 (an average of 41.5), and almost tripled by 1907–8 (118 and 103 cases, respectively). E. Tarnovskii, "Pobegi arestantov i drugie proisshestviia v mestakh zakliucheniia za 1899–1908 gg," *Tiuremnyi vestnik* no. 5 (1910), esp. 686, 698–700.

[63] For further discussion, see Susan Morrissey, *Heralds of Revolution: Russian Students and the Mythologies of Radicalism* (New York, 1998), 208.

[64] This was part of her attempt to raise funds in aid of political prisoners. See Figner, *PSS*, vol. 3, 463.

[65] Though published in Paris, the journal attempted to unite the various strands of the "liberation movement" and was smuggled in large quantities into Russia. See "Osvobozhdennye iz Shlissel'burga," *Osvobozhdenie* no. 59 (1904), 160.

executions, it seemed imperative to meet one's death with dignity. According to one eyewitness account, inmates on death row always celebrated when prisoners succeeded in killing themselves, because "that was a victory over the gallows."[66] Yet the prison also functioned as a metaphor: under martial law, the entire country had been converted into one big prison, into a subterranean kingdom of unlimited arbitrariness. Such a portrait of Russia divided into two camps, the executioners and the condemned, was quite common in the period, and the tentacles of violence ravaged both.

One typical revolutionary text recounts scene after scene of execution, in which inhuman cruelties were met by acts of almost superhuman courage – the self-possession, dignity, and occasional revolutionary slogan of the hero.[67] Yet this chronicle of textual witnessing opens with an extended meditation upon an act of suicide, not by one of the condemned but by one of the executioners. The man in question was himself a criminal convict, who, following a lengthy tradition in Russia, had volunteered for the post (after a prolonged search on the part of prison authorities) in exchange for improvements in the conditions of incarceration.[68] On the fateful day, he performed his duties carefully – placing the stool beneath the feet of the condemned, tightening the noose around his neck, kicking away the stool. But when he saw the man in his agony, he threw himself upon the convulsing body, grabbed his legs, and pulled down with all his own weight. The convulsions stopped, and nobody knew what to think. Had his act reflected his "cruel instincts" or his newly awakened conscience? The next morning, the executioner's body was found. There was no note and no witness, just the silent and cold body swinging in the very same noose. Did this murder-suicide somehow affirm humanity in the midst of inhumanity? The potential for redemption? The narrator pondered its broader significance: had not the more high-ranking executioners, such as the judges who passed death sentences, sold their souls and honor no less than had the poor convict? Did they show signs of conscience? In an answer to these questions, he described how a respected local official was progressively corrupted by power, ultimately becoming a depraved and savage force of repression and, as such, the target of a renowned terrorist attempt.[69] The three forms of violent death – execution, suicide, assassination – thereby framed and sustained each other.

---

[66] S. "Smertniki," *Vestnik Evropy* nos. 7, 8 (1910), here no. 8, 129.

[67] Though prison suicides were conceptualized as an honorable alternative to execution, the fact of execution was not shameful. At issue was the conduct of the condemned, especially his (or her) ability to meet death with courage and fortitude. In this respect, Vladimirov's text provides numerous exemplars of honorable death, most notably and famously, Lieutenant Shmidt. See V. Vladimirov [Vladimir E. Popov], "Sovremennye kazni," in *Protiv smertnoi kazni*, 200–4.

[68] The role of the executioner is discussed by Abby M. Schrader, *Languages of the Lash: Corporal Punishment and Identity in Imperial Russia* (De Kalb, Ill., 2002).

[69] I refer to the case of Mariia Spiridonova. See V. Vladimirov, "Sovremennye kazni," 164–70; and Boniece, "The Spiridonova Case."

Not just revolutionary texts generalized the metaphor of the prison onto Russia with all the connotations of violent death. The progressive doctor L. Prozorov also noted: "The question of prison suicides possesses a tremendous meaning due to its connection with the question of political suicides [...] and due to the great affinity of Russian everyday life at large, especially during reaction, to the conditions of existence in prison." Deeply concerned about the "infectiousness" of the prison, Prozorov detailed numerous cases of suicide among prisoners and their family members but also pointed to a parallel phenomenon among the class of executioners – judges, police officers, soldiers, jailors, and their family members. Many of these cases, he suggested, exemplified the sufferings of conscience, and he even characterized them as the "most unfortunate people of Russia."[70] The physician Dmitrii Zhbankov agreed, describing death sentences and executions as "a terrible nightmare for the entire country," a central cause of the growing problem of violence against the self. His articles likewise described case after case of suicide, a line or two devoted to each.[71]

Yet representations of prison suicide as an assertion of sovereign selfhood against political despotism were inherently unstable for the price of imprisonment was often physical and mental damage. Zhbankov was ambiguous on this point. Although he described the prison suicide as a means to escape the executioner and thereby to avenge one's sentence, he characterized the primary motive as the "consciousness of powerlessness and loss of faith in a better future."[72] This description hardly evokes the affirmation in death of either the revolutionary cause or the dignity of the revolutionary self. According to Prozorov, most prison suicides were sane and logical responses to insane conditions rather than acts of insanity, but he too blurred the boundaries. Not only could prisons cause mental illness among completely normal, healthy people (e.g. those without a hereditary predisposition); the psychic state of a person on death row was analogous to a severe depressive condition. He quoted from a psychiatric textbook: "The entire being of the patient is filled with a feeling of grief and horror, a consciousness of powerlessness and hopelessness in the present and an absence of hope for the future and the expectation of the most terrible and horrifying end. This constant feeling of spiritual burden, this eternal condition of fear and horror, this physical and mental powerlessness [. . .] produces an unbearable, hopeless condition of the soul" and often culminates in suicide.[73] In his effort to document the pathogenic role of repression, he potentially undermined the agency of the prison suicide, which, if not insane, was nonetheless a "reflexive act of the exhausted organism."[74] In effect, both Prozorov and Zhbankov

[70] L. Prozorov, "Samoubiistva v tiur'makh i okolo tiurem po dannym 1906 i 1907 goda," *Meditsinskoe obozrenie* no. 12 (1908), 64, 75.

[71] D. N. Zhbankov, "Sovremennye samoubiistva," *Sovremennyi mir* no. 3 (1910), 39.

[72] Ibid., 40.

[73] L. Prozorov, "Samoubiistva prigovorennykh," *Meditsinskoe obozrenie* no. 12 (1911), 80.

[74] Prozorov, "Samoubiistva v tiur'makh," 77.

were making two inconsistent arguments: that political reaction constituted a pathogenic force within the prison (and, by extension, society); and that political suicide nonetheless articulated the steadfast resistance of revolutionary martyrs.

In an attempt to address this contradiction, Dr. Natan Vigdorchik argued that the revolutionary era had in fact witnessed two different forms of suicide, the one exemplifying personal strength and firmness, the other personal weakness and instability. In the first instance, suicide could constitute "the only objectively reasonable exit from a given circumstance," and he cited the politically motivated suicide of an individual facing execution. The second category was more prevalent, Vigdorchik suggested, and at its basis was "a psychic depression, a psychic instability, a decay of the will, a diseased over-impressionability." Between the political causes and the fact of suicide was thus an "intermediary link" in the neuropathic constitution of the individual. Weak forms of instability expressed themselves in the following symptoms that, not incidentally, were often found in suicide notes: a loss of interest in life; a loss of faith in oneself; and a sense that life is boring, pointless, and useless. Vigdorchik also applied this reasoning to the "extremely interesting" problem of suicide masked as political murder. He first distinguished the rational terrorist acts of mature, party-based figures, who were motivated by conviction, from the violent, despairing, and embittered acts of "youth, almost children," who were mentally unstable.[75] At the root of this latter phenomenon was a political psychosis, albeit one that he linked to the suppression of healthy revolutionary instincts: "the thicker the atmosphere of reaction [and] the more terrible the repression, then the more hearts are filled with despair [. . .] and the larger the number of madmen who choose the path of political murder to end their own lives."[76] While Vigdorchik blamed both psychosis and suicide upon the "anxiety and horrors of the revolutionary epoch" and its "atmosphere of fear," he traced a narrative not of revolutionary enthusiasm and ecstasy but of reactionary depression and anguish. Not only had this experience generated psychosis, political suicide, and terrorism; it also lent such familiar suicide motives as boredom new political meanings. This linkage between revolution and despair would become a constituent part of the post-revolutionary crisis.

The epidemic of traumas

In 1906, Zhbankov published the first of a series of articles in the specialized and popular press on the problem of suicide. "Along with the great struggle for liberation," he wrote, "life over the last two years has brought many undesirable

[75] This is, of course, the strand of argument that Geifman (*Thou Shalt Kill*) accepts as empirical fact.
[76] N. Vigdorchik, "Politicheskie psikhozy i politicheskie samoubiistva," *Obrazovanie* no. 12 (1907), 60–64.

phenomena, caused primarily by the fact that the old [order] does not wish to give way to the better, new [order], and, defending itself, resorts to the most dirty, cruel, and loathsome means," including the war against Japan, arbitrary arrests and exiles, the imposition of martial law, and the countless executions, provocations, and mass pogroms. "Consequently, the life of the Russian people has of late, especially since December of last year [1905], been constrained in extremely abnormal conditions that disturb all human relations and make all work for society impossible." The results were clear to see: rising rates of mental illness, violence of all sorts, the declining value of life, unregulated and desperate passions, and suicide. "If the political and socio-economic disorders and bureaucratic arbitrariness continue to exist," he concluded, "then [. . .] the epidemic of bloody traumas will intensify, [then] more and more victims of murder and suicide will be taken from the long-suffering Russian people."[77] Reiterating his thesis in subsequent articles and providing statistics as evidence, Zhbankov claimed that his prediction had come true: the "epidemic of traumas" [*travmaticheskaia epidemiia*] had "stained the entire country with blood."[78]

In his epidemiology of suicide, Zhbankov relied upon a notion of "trauma," in which state-sponsored violence had disrupted the collective mental health of Russian society: the suppression of healthy social activity (i.e. political organization) was producing social pathologies. His approach generalized the image of the "kingdom of darkness" into a broadly social, historical, and medical context. The government's violent assault upon Russian society had created an environment lacking the most basic respect for human dignity and bodily inviolability, and this had consequently produced the massive upturn in cases of rape, murder, and suicide. On the level of individuals, the pervasive fear, both for the self and for the common future, had produced a wide range of pathological conditions, from mental and nervous illness to a kind of sexual bacchanalia, an obsession with living for the moment and hence with private, especially sexual pleasures. Trauma was a relatively new term in the arsenal of psychiatric diagnoses in 1906, and the definition of "traumatic neurosis" in the *Encyclopedic Dictionary (Brokgauz-Efron)* emphasized its origins in a physical trauma that, mediated by the nervous system, led to nervous shock.[79] Zhbankov, however, applied the term in a different way. Rather than presuming

---

[77] D. N. Zhbankov, "O samoubiistvakh v poslednee vremia," *Prakticheskii vrach* nos. 26–29 (1906), here no. 26, 437, and no. 29, 491.

[78] I will discuss the statistics in Chapter 11. See D. N. Zhbankov, "K statistike samoubiistv v 1905–11 godakh," *Prakticheskii vrach* nos. 34–36, 38 (1912), esp. no. 34, 520–22. See also his "O samoubiistvakh v poslednie gody," *Russkoe bogatstvo* no. 4 (1909); and "Sovremennye samoubiistva."

[79] See *BE*, vol 33, 682–83. On the history of trauma, see Mark S. Micale and Paul Lerner, eds., *Traumatic Pasts: History, Psychiatry, and Trauma in the Modern Age, 1870–1930* (Cambridge, 2001).

its somatic origins, he generalized it as a metaphor for the violence of the state upon the social psyche and thereby rendered trauma a fact of both individual and collective psychology. His articles always combined a summary of statistics (to document the social pathology within the population) with numerous brief examples (to illuminate the individual expression).

While Zhbankov's fellow doctors did not always use his specific metaphor of trauma, they did share his causal model with its conflation of individuals with populations. In late 1905, psychiatrists began to report cases of revolutionary psychosis. Increasing numbers of people were seeking psychiatric help for a wide variety of symptoms ranging from sleeplessness, uncontrollable trembling, and nightmares to hallucinations, paranoia, and attempted suicide. What united these cases were the revolutionary themes dominating the psychotic episodes – pogroms, strikes, or political persecution – and psychiatrists initially pondered whether these cases constituted a new form of psychosis. Though this thesis was soon rejected (as the symptoms did conform to existing diagnostic rubrics), many specialists came to insist that the atmosphere of extremity and violence stood outside the range of normal human experience and consequently amounted to a kind of mental shock [*potriasenie*], jolt [*tolchok*], or blow [*udar*]. In his diagnosis of two case studies, one doctor thus generalized: "Fright and fear act sharply and suddenly upon the nervous system and call forth a psychic trauma [*psikhicheskaia travma*] which leads to the development of an hysterical psychosis." Other doctors projected the dynamic unto Russia as a whole, emphasizing the mass dimensions of the current situation and its spread through the entire population. "Those horrors which the population has experienced in recent times and which under no circumstances can be compared to the phenomena of everyday life can undoubtedly play a role as a psychic jolt calling forth a mental illness."[80]

Like Zhbankov, many doctors further posited an antithetical relationship between the pathogenic qualities of governmental repression and the hygienic benefits of democratization. In December 1905, the psychiatrist V. K. Khoroshko published an article, suggestively entitled "The 'Hygiene of the Soul' and Bureaucracy," in which he explicitly blamed the politics of autocracy for causing a wide variety of individual and collective psychoses well before the revolutionary swell of 1905. In his analysis of the psychopathology of contemporary Russian life, he discussed suicide both as a relevant topic in

---

[80] The literature is large, and I have drawn on the following examples: F. E. Rybakov, "Dushevnye rasstroistva v sviazi s sovremennymi politicheskimi sobytiiami," *Russkii vrach* no. 51 (1905) and no. 3, (1906); for the quotations, see the debate reprinted in "Korrespondentsii: Iz Obshchestva Nevropatologov i Psikhiatrov pri Imp. Moskovskom Universitete," *OPNiEP* no. 7 (1906), 120–25; M. Zhukovskii, "O vliianii obshchestvennykh sobytii na razvitii dushevnykh zabolevanii," *VPKAG* no 3 (1907), 142; L. S. Pavlovskaia, "Dva sluchaia dushevnogo zabolevaniia pod vliianiem obshchestvennykh sobytii," *OPNiEP* no. 6 (1906); and her "Neskol'ko sluchaev dushevnogo zabolevaniia pod vliianiem obshchestvennykh sobytii," *OPNiEP* no. 9 (1907).

itself and as a direct consequence of many long-standing autocratic practices, including the persecution of religious sectarians, political repression, prison conditions, corporal and capital punishment, and the bureaucratic regime of the secondary school. Though acknowledging the role of hereditary degeneration in the etiology of psychosis and suicide, Khoroshko privileged the socio-political dynamic behind these psychic wounds, and his point was explicitly political. Indeed, he was writing at a time of guarded optimism during the mass action of the autumn of 1905 but shortly before the bloody suppression of the Moscow Uprising. This optimism framed his analysis of "psychic epidemics," which he defined as "the simultaneous emergence of a single idea among a certain number of people that calls forth identical actions from them." Before turning his attention to psychopathology, Khoroshko pointedly celebrated the "healthy [*normal'naia*] psychic epidemic" that was the revolution. It had infected the entire Russian people with "a striving for light, knowledge, and the validation of human existence," and Khoroshko welcomed its therapeutic benefits: "Let this striving be infectious [. . .] we have nothing to fear from the word [epidemic]!" In his view, the restoration of Russia's collective mental health lay in the revolutionary transformation of the socio-economic and political system.[81] His words proved prescient, though not in the way he had hoped, for the "healthy psychic epidemic" soon seemed to degenerate into a pathological form.[82]

Even doctors supportive of the liberation movement became concerned about its medical and psychiatric impact.[83] The high levels of indiscriminate violence – peasant revolts, hooligan assaults, and terrorist bombings – all seemed to point toward the fall of the revolution from its peak of political consciousness. Yet to dismiss the revolution as a whole was also to dismiss the striving of Russian society for freedom and enlightenment. Zhbankov alluded

[81] Khoroshko appended the resolutions of the Second Congress of National Psychiatrists (from September 1905), which resolved that the etiology of nervous and mental illness lay in "socio-political factors" and condemned the psychic harm inflicted by the government upon both individuals and the population. See V. K. Khoroshko, " 'Gigiena dushi' i biurokratiia," *Russkaia mysl'* no. 12 (1905), 152, 153–56. For the full text, I. A. Sikorskii, ed., *Trudy vtorogo s'ezda Otechestvennykh psikhiatrov proiskhodivshego v g. Kiev s 4go po 11-e sentiabria 1905 goda* (Kiev, 1907), 503–4.

[82] Khoroshko was aware of the parallels between healthy and psychopathological epidemics, as were many of his contemporaries. Lev Sheinis compared the collective suicides of sectarians with the post-revolutionary epidemic. See his "Epidemicheskie samoubiistva," *Vestnik vospitaniia* no. 1 (1909). For further discussion, see Paperno, *Suicide,* 96–99; and Christine D. Worobec, *Possessed: Women, Witches, and Demons in Imperial Russia* (De Kalb, Ill., 2003). On theories of moral contagion that informed the contemporary understanding of epidemic, see Daniel Beer, *Renovating Russia: The Human Sciences and the Fate of Liberal Modernity in Russia, 1880–1930* (forthcoming).

[83] For further discussion, including consideration of more conservative perspectives, see Julie V. Brown, "Revolution and Psychosis: The Mixing of Science and Politics in Russian Psychiatric Medicine, 1905–1913," *Russian Review* 46: 3 (1987); and Laura Engelstein, *The Keys to Happiness: Sex and the Search for Modernity in Fin-de-Siècle Russia* (Ithaca, N. Y., 1992), 255–64.

to this problem with his references to the rising rates of violent crime, sexual licentiousness, and suicide, but he did not dwell upon this dynamic, preferring instead to reiterate the pathogenic agency of the state. Yet a shift in focus was apparent in 1906 when the Moscow Society of Neuropathologists and Psychiatrists set up a commission to study the psychological impact of revolutionary violence and sent a circular to hospitals around the country requesting relevant data. While this circular presumed the causal role of the political situation in the genesis of individual and collective illnesses, it also noted the "strain" (*napriazhenie*) engendered by revolutionary activism, especially in the wake of the preceding period of immobility and stagnation: "It is important to establish whether these events act upon the psychic balance of the masses; whether they call forth a particular condition of enthusiasm [and] ecstasy or, conversely, a condition of intellectual and moral oppression, fear, and fixed ideas or feelings; whether they disrupt the sphere of higher ethical feelings; whether they disrupt in general the nervous-spiritual vitality of the population."[84] Implicit to this language was the comparison of the revolutionary experience to the progression of a disease: the rise, the crisis, the fall. The boundary between the (healthy) revolution and the (pathological) reaction had dissolved.

Suffering and silence

Descriptions of suffering deaths abound in the literature on revolutionary and prison suicide, and many of the accounts were originally published in daily newspapers. Alongside brief designations of methods were often telling details: hanging (with towels, shirts); cutting (with glass, tin cans); poisoning (with home-made extracts derived from tobacco); burning (with the kerosene of a lamp). Some accounts were horrific in their laconic brevity: one prisoner used her hair for a noose; another ripped open an artery with his teeth. Others were more discursive:

In the corner [of the cell] to the right of the entrance was a hook in the wall one *arshin* [about 28 inches] off the floor. True it is hard to hang yourself from such a distance, but his desire to die was so great that he made a plait out of strips from his shirt, stretched himself on the floor, and thrust his head through the noose. The guard noticed him in this position when he had already made himself a cold corpse. One must assume that he took a long time to die and suffered tremendously: his entire face was distorted into terrible convulsions.[85]

The point here is not to titillate the reader with gratuitous violence but to pose some questions: why was such violence done to one's own body? Why was it so

[84] Quoted in Vigdorchik, "Politicheskie psikhozy," 58.
[85] Prozorov, "Samoubiistva v tiur'makh," 72–3, 67. See also Prozorov, "Samoubiistva prigovoren-nykh," and the many articles published by Zhbankov cited above.

often recounted and represented? How were accounts read (and how should we read them)? That individuals facing their own imminent deaths pondered death is perhaps inevitable. Klimova tried to imagine the physical experience of death: "the sensation of the noose around [her] neck, the sensation of the constricting throat, the red and dark circles in [her] eyes."[86] Another eyewitness account emphasized the constant discussions on death row of suicide methods, their pros and cons, the nature and intensity of the agony.[87] However, this preoccupation extended to outside observers – primarily journalists, doctors, and writers, who felt compelled to record the torment of the prison suicide and thereby to inscribe meaning upon it. To contemplate violence was to give it voice, meaning, and history – to serve witness. In other words, the goal of publicity was to break down the prison walls, to transform the hidden dramas into public spectacles. The resultant tangle of images evokes the tangle of revolutionary narratives analyzed in this chapter.

One conventional approach melded almost seamlessly into revolutionary hagiography. For the radical publicist and writer, Vladimir Korolenko, the prison suicide constituted a heroic act of self-will that denied the sovereignty of the despotic state (and he contrasted this heroism to the half-mad illusions of those hoping for a last-minute reprieve). Consequently, the moment of death – and hence suffering – was effaced in its transcendent significance. As illustration, he described one case, quoting a letter from an eyewitness, presumably a cellmate: "The death of comrade Ia-v produced a terrible [i.e. extremely intense] impression upon me – the tremendous power of will, the astounding picture of a hero's death. Before [his] death, he was merry, [he] smoked, talked and laughed. No agitation was noticeable. Then, having felt for his heart [i.e. his ribs], he positioned the knife with one hand, and with the other hit it: once, twice. Then he said: 'Ah, that is good! Take it [the knife] out.' He began to wheeze, then died, without having let out a single loud moan." This portrait represented the complete self-possession of the hero both before and during his death: his suffering does not produce a sound. Yet this suicide was not voiceless, for the man left a note that reiterated the ethos of self-sovereignty as resistance: "I am ending my life in suicide. You sentenced me to death and, perhaps, you think that I am afraid of your sentence. No! Your sentence does not frighten me. But I do not want to have the comedy you intend enacted upon me [. . .]. Death threatens me. I know and accept that. I do not want to await the death that you will effect. I decided to die earlier. Do not think that I am such a coward as you." Finally, Korolenko interpreted: "For this courageous man, death was apparently the final act if not of direct struggle than at least of a polemic with [his] enemies."[88] The meaning ascribed to this death derives from its function as an event within the

[86] [Klimova], "Pis'mo pered kazn'iu," 65–66.   [87] S., "Smertniki," *Vestnik Evropy* no. 8, 128.
[88] Vladimir Korolenko, *Bytovoe iavlenie (Zametki publitsista o smertnoi kazni)* (SPb, 1910),
     25–26.

generic plot of revolutionary struggle and not as a condition of being (torment). The free death of the revolutionary affirms the revolutionary community and the eternal life of the revolution. Indeed, the prison suicide also foreclosed perhaps the ultimate act of state sovereignty – not execution but the imperial gift of clemency.[89]

Madness had long been represented as a potential threat to revolutionary self-possession, one which embodied the ultimate cruelty of tsarist repression. The prototypical acts of political suicide had often been constituted as a kind of victory of the self over madness and thereby over despotism as well. Yet, in the wake of 1905, the shadow of madness fell increasingly over the image of bodily suffering. According to some Western specialists, including the influential Italian psychiatrist, Enrico Morselli, the choice of a painful suicide method constituted evidence of mental illness. Although such explanations were typically rejected by Russian experts, who were quick to point out the limited methods available to prisoners, a sense of doubt and ambivalence remained.[90] A good example is an article published in a medical journal that drew upon both the many revolutionary memoirs published after 1905 and the personal observations of the author, Boris Frommett, whilst in internal exile. Even as Frommett asserted the normality of many prison suicides, especially those who sought to evade the shame of execution, he also acknowledged that a significant number were psychically abnormal. In contrast to Western Europe, he stressed, most prison suicides in Russia occurred not in the initial period after arrest but following a prolonged term of incarceration: "[One's] psychological balance is destroyed, and one's own suffering is the only consolation; then, a view of suicide as a particular form of protest develops. In this case, exclusively terrible methods are chosen, such as self-immolation." Even as he heralded the heroism of Semianovskii, Sigida, Janowicz, and others, the author also stressed the inevitable madness caused by incarceration. His final example was drawn from his own experience:

The former terrorist [Meshcheriakov], a person with extremely over-strained nerves, not fully normal, [who] often laughed inopportunely and sometimes talked nonsense, was transferred upon doctor's orders to Vologda for treatment in a psychiatric hospital. Before his departure, I encountered him as joyful and animated. Later [. . .], I received a letter from a comrade in which he informed me that [Meshcheriakov had been transferred back into exile]. He returned, I was told, sad and depressed. Soon afterwards, the unfortunate, mentally ill, cut himself with a dull kitchen knife; he had the patience to saw his throat for twenty minutes. The housekeeper found Meshcheriakov lying on his bed cutting his throat with slight moans.[91]

---

[89] I would like to thank Daniel Beer for pointing this out.
[90] Although Prozorov cites and rejects Morselli's argument, his article is likewise an excellent example of this ambiguity. See his "Samoubiistva prigovorennykh," 93.
[91] Boris Frommett, "Samoubiistva v politicheskikh tiur'makh i ssylke," *Vrachebnaia gazeta* no. 51 (1910), 1612.

The central image of this account is Meshcheriakov's silence and patience, yet it provides a stark contrast to Korolenko's text. Was it illness that allowed him to saw silently at his neck for twenty minutes? Or, conversely, did this act embody a final attempt to affirm his self-sovereignty and human dignity? Was selfhood only to be found in death? Frommett did not comment directly, though he did ruminate upon the long-term influence of prison and exile upon the psyche: "The old connections are lost, you are derailed, spiritually and physically maimed."[92] Dr. Prozorov echoed this ambivalence. Though he, like Frommett, lauded the courageous resistance of his heroes, particularly those facing execution, he repeatedly emphasized the "trauma" of imprisonment, how its "poison" remained for a long time in the organism, wounding and weakening it.[93]

Precisely such connections between the maimed mind and the maiming of the body fascinated the psychiatrist Nikolai Bazhenov, who saw in them an explanation for death-row suicides. He distinguished the physical violence of execution from the more cruel psychological torture of the death sentence, which he described as "the taking of hope from man, the ravaging of his soul with dark and desperate despair." He continued: "Each of us is sentenced to death but with an indeterminate limit. If this limit is defined, if we know the exact day and hour of our death, then living becomes impossible, and people begin to turn to suicide, and thereby to escape the tormentingly obsessive, all-encompassing and all-eclipsing thought [*mysl'*] about the fateful day, about the inexorable limit."[94] Only this violence upon the soul makes the violence upon the body comprehensible. Or, to reverse the order, the bloody body of the suicide reveals the spiritual torments of the soul. By transforming suffering into an existential, spiritual condition, rather than an event, Bazhenov called upon his readers to contemplate it, and he provided for this purpose extended excerpts from Dostoevsky and Victor Hugo. An opponent of the death penalty, Bazhenov argued that governmental violence was illegitimate precisely because it ravaged the soul. Rather than a sign of selfhood affirmed, the bloodied body displayed the spiritual torture inflicted by the state.

Intrigued by the sacred foundations of modern politics, the decadent writer Dmitrii Merezhkovskii took the opposite approach. For him, "physical violence" seemed "a prologue to some kind of metaphysical affirmation." Moved yet also profoundly troubled by the figure of the terrorist-martyr, he pondered the meaning and psychology of revolutionary death. In an article from 1908 entitled "Demon or God," he explored the self-representations of Fruma Frumkina

---

[92] Ibid.   [93] Prozorov, "Samoubiistva v tiur'makh," 75.

[94] Bazhenov focused his discussion upon ordinary criminals rather than political prisoners, asserting that if the inhumanity of the death penalty could be proven for those genuinely guilty of horrific crimes, it would make an even stronger case against its use in political cases. He likewise acknowledged the particular condition – the "heroic elevation of spiritual vitality" – among many political prisoners facing execution. See N. Bazhenov, "Psikhologiia kaznimykh," *Protiv smertnoi kazni*, 255, 275.

and Maksim Berdiagin, who had gone willingly to their fates whilst proclaiming the truth and ultimate victory of their cause. Berdiagin's suicide on the eve of his execution particularly fascinated Merezhkovskii. Whereas "Frumkina had died in order to speak, Berdiagin [had died] in order to be silent, and this silence was stronger than any words." He boycotted the trial, which was typically – as in Frumkina's case – used as a tribune of revolutionary speech. And further, in his effort "to die free," as Berdiagin himself had put it, he had boycotted the scaffold. Merezhkovskii lingered on the most gruesome details of Berdiagin's physical death, thereby reading (Christian) metaphysics into the torment and mutilation of the suffering body. On the eve of his execution, Berdiagin had first taken a large dose of morphine but had lost his battle with nausea. He then tried repeatedly to pierce his cerebellum with a needle. Next, he broke off the handle from a spoon and tried to stick it into his heart. Again he failed, leaving some ten gashes on his chest. Finally, he covered himself with his blanket and lay down, chest first, upon a nail in an effort to puncture his lungs and heart. According to a subsequent autopsy, he would only have been able to live for another 30 to 40 minutes with this wound, yet he then removed the nail, returned it to its hiding place, and cut his carotid artery in two places with the handle of the spoon. "What is this?" Merezhkovskii wrote. "How can we condemn or absolve this? Our blood freezes in our veins, our tongues are speechless." Such a death – a Passion? – must possess meaning, yet its enormity transcended speech itself. In his conclusion, Merezhkovskii intertwined his voice with the voices of Berdiagin and Frumkina, whose revolutionary faith they had articulated in a moral idiom: love, brotherhood, justice, paradise, the holy ideal. Was this the apocalypse, he wondered. Or were they the possessed? His closing lines evoked Dostoevsky's well-known novel but, in its ultimate fading away into a wordless question, it silently recalled the second category of his title: God.

"My demon and your demon," Frumkina wrote to Berdiagin, "will calm down when Russia is free and happy. Not before. Do you understand now? The struggle is difficult and therefore one wants to assume the heaviest burden." The heaviest burden is the burden of the sword, the burden of blood, the burden of hating love. There's such a "demon," such a "devil" in these "possessed"; – a "demon". . . .?[95]

Representations of the suffering body repeatedly evoked silence, wordlessness, speechlessness. This quality did possess a practical dimension: silence was often critical to the success of a prison suicide, for watchful jailors were charged with preventing precisely such a victory over the scaffold. Yet, this silence also resonated with meaning. For the community of the elect, it enacted the fortitude and self-possession of the hero, who was able to maintain control throughout his torment. The spectacle of the suicide thereby enacts revolutionary

[95] Merezhkovskii, "Bes ili Bog?" 91–96.

Illus. 8 An image of a hanged woman – a suicide? – within the context of revolutionary violence. The smoke in the background, the rope, and the blood flowing from her mouth are all red. The title of the journal is "Land of Dreams," from Cover, *Strana mechti* no. 1 (1906).

transcendence. Unlike the most spectacular of executions, however, this pain was self-inflicted, and that very fact confounded some observers, who sometimes denied agency to the act. Did not self-willed suffering evidence madness? Was it not the loss of mental self-possession that allowed such a physical mutilation? For Merezhkovskii, in contrast, to witness the horror, even if only textually, was to be rendered speechless before a higher, metaphysical truth, which was beyond words, beyond even his comprehension. Yet his reaction raises a further potential. Had the violence become meaningless? To paraphrase one of the reviews of Savinkov's novel: perhaps the shattered and maimed organism had simply vanished from the world of the living in excruciating torments of impotence and despair.

In early twentieth-century Russia, suicide joined the repertoire of revolutionary acts.[96] Heroic suicide had certainly been discussed in the late nineteenth century, and cases had been narrated as martyrdoms, but the deliberate authorship of suicide as a political gesture had been rare. The new narratives and practices evolved out of public view – behind prison walls and in Siberian exile – where they had enacted the revolutionary struggle in microcosm. One model, as the epigraph suggests, was found in the Decembrists, who had likewise suffered and died with stoic dignity. Yet only one of the Decembrists' suicides had been explicitly configured as a political act of self-affirmation: that of the non-noble, Ivan Sukhinov, who had wished to avoid the humiliation of a commoner's execution. But the difference was not just one of magnitude – the scores of people now choosing death. The new forms of heroic suicide also contained inner tensions. Devotion to the revolution was often cited as a means to heal the disjunctions between inner self and outer world, but revolutionary death could then enact not only self-sovereignty against the autocracy but also self-subordination to the cause and the collective. That is, it could affirm either the I or the we. The years of revolution had also transformed political death – pogroms, terrorist attacks, state executions, political suicides – into a mass phenomenon, and these were all reported in the mass media. Although the prolific images of the injured and martyred body came to confer substance upon the revolutionary experience, they did not possess a stable meaning, either for the individual or for Russia as whole (Illus. 8).[97]

---

[96] Another such moment occurred in revolutionary France. See Dorinda Outram, *The Body and the French Revolution: Sex, Class and Political Culture* (New Haven, 1989), ch. 6.

[97] Following Scarry (*The Body in Pain*, esp. 111–39), I agree that the injured body possesses no inherent meaning but can substantiate external issues. But the injured body can also become over-determined when the available narratives and ideological interpretations provide too much signification.

11   Children of the twentieth century

> We, people of the twentieth century, without faith, without hope, without the
> desire to live. Neither Christ, nor socialism, nor man exists for us. Nothing
> exists except for thought [*mysl'*], and thought leads to suicide.
>
> Suicide note, 1911

Time seemed to quicken in early twentieth-century Russia, propelling with it
the transformation of space and the human being. As the psychiatrist P. Ia.
Rozenbakh wrote for a popular magazine in 1909: the "mind-whirling speed"
of technical innovation had spurred unprecedented economic development –
large-scale factories, the growing distinctions between capital and labor, the cult
of money, the market of consumer goods – and this, in turn, had transformed
the city into a site of seduction, danger, and agitation. "Along the streets of
our Babylons from morning till evening rush the electric trams, automobiles,
carriages; all of these weapons of accelerated movement threaten one another
and pedestrians with the danger of collisions and fill the air with warning sig-
nals thereby lending street life the character of constant anxiety." Not only
had the new economic and commercial landscape awakened appetites, fatigued
the body, and strained the nervous system. The recent political struggles in
Russia had also produced an "eternal anxiety" within the population. While
some individuals may live "as if outside historical influences," Rozenbakh
noted, the technical, economic, cultural, and political conditions of contemporary Russia had left their imprint upon the majority, producing epidemic levels
of neurasthenia, hereditary degeneration, and suicide.[1]

This complex montage – time accelerating, space compressing, desires multiplying, values crumbling, individuals disintegrating – comprises a central feature of the modern predicament and sensibility more generally. Just as it seemed
that the individual was to be liberated – whether through scientific knowledge,
technical innovations, or the world-historical agency of the proletariat – slavery
adapted its forms to the rhythms of the machine, the crowds of mass politics,
the lures of consumption, the drives of the unconscious. The new configuration

---

[1] P. Ia. Rozenbakh, "O prichinakh sovremennoi nervnosti i samoubiistv," *Novoe slovo* no. 11
(1909), 41–47.

of time and space was displayed in the marketplace of the boulevard, whose primary mouthpiece was the mass-circulation newspaper. In some respects a consummate modernist text, the newspaper juxtaposed the multiple and multiplying perspectives of the modern city within an ever-shrinking world and thereby helped to fragment its readers, to deny them an Archimedean point from which they could grasp the whole.[2] Yet even as absolute meaning slipped away, as the world lost its stability and unity, the quest did not end. Instead, the faith in the hidden reality of meaning proved to be a defining element of the modern.[3]

Though it too shared in this montage, Russia's experience of modernity was nonetheless particular. Not just a political event, the 1905 revolution had been propelled by a complex mixture of eschatological visions that had conferred narrative structures upon history, political action, and autobiography.[4] When the expected transfiguration of life did not occur, these narratives began to unravel, a process that de-sacralized revolutionary time, historicized the past, and rendered present, everyday life profane. Consequently, the loss of absolute meaning intrinsic to the modern condition overlapped with the political event and, for many, the self-destruction of the revolutionary ideal. But the desire for lost unity would persist.

The period between 1907 and 1914 was full of contradictions. The government had turned back the revolutionary tide, but its legitimacy had been irretrievably damaged. The new parliament provided a forum for political debate, but it failed either to build the foundations for a new democratic order or to overcome deepening social and political divisions.[5] Yet despite the political stalemate, Russian society was extremely lively and creative. Urbanization, especially the increasing educational levels and cultural aspirations of city populations, had combined with the temporary collapse of censorship in 1905–6 to encourage a massive expansion in the world of print and entertainment, which, in turn, shaped anxieties about sex, crime, and public

[2] Peter Fritsche, *Reading Berlin, 1900* (Cambridge, Mass., 1996).

[3] The literature on modernity is huge. Important works include Marshall Berman, *All That is Solid Melts into Air: The Experience of Modernity* (New York, 1982); Reinhart Koselleck, *The Practice of Conceptual History: Timing History, Spacing Concepts*, trans. Todd Samuel Presner (Stanford, 2002); and Anthony Giddens, *Modernity and Self-Identity: Self and Society in the Late Modern Age* (Stanford, 1991); for a popular overview, see Terry Eagleton, "Newsreel History," *London Review of Books* (Nov. 12, 1998).

[4] On the narratives underpinning the revolution, see my *Heralds of Revolution: Russian Students and the Mythologies of Radicalism* (New York 1998); Igal Halfin, *From Darkness to Light: Class, Consciousness, and Salvation in Revolutionary Russia* (Pittsburgh, 2000); and Frederick C. Corney, *Telling October: Memory and the Making of the October Revolution* (Ithaca, N. Y., 2004).

[5] See Richard Wortman, *Scenarios of Power: Myth and Ceremony in Russian Monarchy*, 2 vols. (Princeton, 1995, 2000), vol. 2, pt. 3; and Geoffrey Hosking, *The Russian Constitutional Experiment: Government and Duma, 1907–1914* (Cambridge, 1973).

morality.[6] As many intellectuals and liberals rejected the path of revolutionary violence, they reworked evolutionary models in the hope that these could underpin a new ethos of personal and socio-political development. But doubts persisted. Was progress even possible in Russia given its long history of autocratic repression? As one commentator put it, Russia was young in culture but old in diseases.[7]

In the decade before the outbreak of World War I, epidemic suicide became a paradigmatic phenomenon of Russia's modernity. The resonance of suicide was partly a result of its commercialization. Incident reports filled daily newspapers, not just one or two but often ten or twenty. They were accompanied by lurid and sensational exposés, woodblock prints, scholarly analyses, updates on the latest figures, regular columns, readers' letters, and even satirical humor. Specialist journals and popular magazines likewise devoted considerable attention to the phenomenon, as did writers and film makers. Its resonance also reflected its contested political and scientific status. After the bloody years of conflict, narratives of revolutionary suicide remained very influential. Most striking was their migration from the prison to the secondary school, which, among other consequences, now rendered the "school regime" an explicit site of both political struggle and medical intervention.[8] Alongside the vitality of revolutionary narratives was also their decomposition, and tales of decline, disintegration, and fall likewise proliferated. Mass political violence, it was feared, had reduced the value of life more generally and thereby produced nihilism and neurasthenia, especially among Russia's youth, who seemed to be living and dying for the sake of the moment. These concerns formed the mirror images of revolutionary transcendence, and the cultural meanings of suicide consequently fluctuated between a series of binary oppositions: hero–degenerate; faith–despair; strength–weakness; purity–corruption; political–personal; sacred–profane. These representations facilitated new forms and practices of subjectivity. Suicide became a recognized, if not necessarily accepted, means to act upon the environment, even an attempt to re-establish the value and meaning of life. Simultaneously, it also became an expression of life's profanity and meaninglessness, an admission of personal and political defeat. The spectacle of suicide – with this dichotomous essence – transfixed Russia's public through the waning years of the Romanov dynasty.

---

[6] Important works on this topic include Laura Engelstein, *The Keys to Happiness: Sex and the Search for Modernity in Fin-de-Siècle Russia* (Ithaca, N. Y., 1992); Joan Neuberger, *Hooliganism: Crime, Culture, and Power in St. Petersburg, 1900–1914* (Berkeley, 1993); Mark Steinberg, *Proletarian Imagination: Self, Modernity, and the Sacred in Russia, 1910–1925* (Ithaca, N. Y., 2002); Louise McReynolds, *Russia at Play: Leisure Activities at the End of the Tsarist Era* (Ithaca, N. Y., 2003); and her *News under Russia's Old Regime: The Development of a Mass Circulation Press* (Princeton, 1991), ch. 11.

[7] I. O. Zubov, "O samoubiistve," *Vrachebnaia gazeta* nos. 44, 45 (1912), 1574.

[8] Laura Engelstein has discussed the metaphor of the school regime in both a political and a sexual-disciplinary context. See her *The Keys to Happiness*, 232–36, 240–48.

The power in numbers

The suicide rate seemed to explode after 1905, and the numbers themselves exemplified the new sense of mind-whirling speed. As one doctor explained: "The process of people's psychological adaptation to the conditions of life occurs with a known friction [*trenie*] and demands a certain number of victims. When this process begins to occur faster, the friction increases and with it the number of people who are unable to adapt in time to the new conditions, and they are compelled to exit this life."[9] Pathologies were proliferating not in a slow, incremental process but in a rushed, exponential leap.

According to official statistics, Russia remained in fact among the least suicidal of European nations, with roughly 32 annual cases per million population in the late 1890s (in comparison to first-place Saxony with 319).[10] Yet bureaucratic sources were deeply suspect to such independent specialists as Dmitrii Zhbankov, who sought less to establish the real suicide rate than to transform it into a political issue, a symptom of the deep-seated political pathology spreading within Russia's social body. On the basis of newspaper accounts collected from June 1905 through 1911, he found a massive rise in suicides and attempted suicides, from 557 in 1906 to a peak of 3,975 in 1910 followed by a modest decline to 3,248 in 1911.[11] By 1914, an independent specialist had finally assessed the long-term development of the suicide rate according to official statistics, which he used for reasons of consistency and despite their known shortcomings. His results suggested that rates in European Russia had almost doubled between 1803 and 1905 (from 16 per million population to 31), which was a modest increase by European standards, but that the pace of growth had then markedly accelerated, with 49 cases per million registered by 1910, a 58 percent increase in just five years. This constituted a completely new trend, he concluded.[12]

The spiraling problem in Russia's major cities was especially disturbing. Even official statistics revealed a rate of increase of at least twofold in the years after 1904–5, placing St. Petersburg among the suicide capitals of Europe.[13]

---

[9] N. Vigdorchik, "Politicheskie psikhozy i politicheskie samoubiistva," *Obrazovanie* no. 12 (1907), 51–52. The pathological speeding up of time was a frequent motif. See also O. B. Fel'tsman, "K voprosu o samoubiistve," *Psikhoterapiia* no. 6 (1910), 227.

[10] It is striking that his comparative figures are for the years 1895–99, in other words, before the upsurge in the early twentieth century. See S. A. Novosel'skii, "Ocherk statistiki samoubiistv," *Gigiena i sanitariia* nos. 8–10 (1910), here no. 8, 552.

[11] He examined newspapers from several cities (including St. Petersburg, Moscow, and Odessa) and explained the decline by the fact that he had not consulted Odessa's newspapers in 1911, and Odessa possessed one of the highest suicide rates in the Russian empire. He did not discuss the possibility that newspapers were also publishing more on suicide due to interest in the topic. See Dmitrii Zhbankov, "K statistike samoubiistv v 1905–11 godakh," *Prakticheskii vrach* nos. 34–36, 38 (1912), here no. 34, 520–21.

[12] Rates in most parts of Europe at least doubled in the nineteenth century and sometimes increased by 300–400 percent. M. Fenomenov, *Prichiny samoubiistv v russkoi shkole* (Moscow, 1914), 13–28.

[13] Ibid., 34–36, 38.

316 Political theology and moral epidemics

According to an independent statistician, however, official statistics significantly underestimated the dimensions of the epidemic. His analysis suggested that the number of cases in St. Petersburg had risen from 903 in 1906 to a high of 3,196 in 1910 only to fall slightly to 2,962 in 1911. When calculated in relation to population, the rate had increased from 500 cases per million residents to a massive 1,640 in 1910 (and 1,550 in 1911), easily the highest rate in Europe.[14] Also noteworthy was the upsurge in the southern port city of Odessa, where the rate proportional to population had approximately doubled in just five years.[15] The epidemic in the cites raised disturbing new issues about gender, for the number of suicides among urban women was apparently rising much faster than among men. In contrast to the ratios typical for Europe and nineteenth-century Russia (of roughly 3–5:1, male to female suicides), Russia seemed to be approaching a 2:1 proportion. In some cites, including Odessa and Warsaw, more actual cases were being registered among women than men.[16] Although the accuracy of these statistics is impossible to establish, the fact that suicide rates were rising after 1905 was both commonly accepted and – at least to some extent – probably accurate.[17]

While suicide clearly occurred in both rural and urban environments, public and specialist attention focused almost exclusively upon the city, the laboratory of the modern[18] and, apparently, of modern suicide. Since the 1890s, Darwinist metaphors had become commonplaces, and most specialists now

[14] N. I. Grigor'ev published frequent updates on the suicide rate in both newspapers and specialized journals. For a summary of his data, see his "Samoubiistva i pokusheniia na samoubiistvo v Peterburge v 1911 g.," *Russkii vrach* no. 6 (1913), 187–88. See also G. Gordon, "Sovremennye samoubiistva," *Russkaia mysl'* no. 5 (1912), 75. On the situation in Moscow, see I. Syrkov, "Samoubiistva v Moskve v 1908 i 1909 gg," *Izvestiia Moskovskoi gorodskoi dumy* no. 5 (1910).

[15] A series of studies was published by I. P. Ostrovskii, a doctor at the emergency medical service in Odessa, which was probably the best in the country. See his *K voprosu o samoubiistve v Odesse za piatiletie 1903–1908* (Odessa, 1908); and his "Samoubiistva i pokusheniia na samoubiistvo v g. Odesse za 1908 god," in *Trudy vrachei stantsii skoroi meditsinskoi pomoshchi v Odesse*, vol. 3 (Odessa, 1909). Compare also Fenomenov, *Prichiny samoubiistv*, 34, 36.

[16] See Ostrovskii, *K voprosu*, 13–21; and his "Samoubiistva," 18–19. On Warsaw, see S. Arnova, "Samoubiistvo v proshlom i nastoiashchem," *Zhizn' dlia vsekh* no. 3/4 (1911), 477. One factor was the inclusion of attempted suicides into the statistics, for women generally have a higher rate of attempt but a lower rate of success.

[17] Two main factors account for both the discrepancies and the increases. First, official statistics generally excluded cases of attempted suicide, whereas independent studies almost universally included them. Second, official sources depended upon the bureaucratic registration of suicides, which was often irregular; in contrast, independent studies (such as Zhbankov's) were often based on newspaper reports, but his numbers were likely influenced by the market-driven dynamics in the reporting of suicide. The probability that rates were actually increasing is supported by the studies of Fenomenov, Grigor'ev, and Ostrovskii in particular. Fenomenov used official sources; Grigor'ev used both official police registrations and the press bureau of the newspaper of the Petersburg police chief; and Ostrovskii used the records of the emergency medical station. While it is possible that improved methods of collecting data influenced the rising rates, the increases occurred quite dramatically over a very short time period.

[18] The term is taken from Karl Schlögel, *Petersburg: Das Laboratorium der Moderne 1909–1921* (rev. edn: Munich, 2002).

contended that the struggle for survival had become even more fierce after 1905, producing still more casualties. Female suicide was a case in point. It was explained less by reference to gendered physiological peculiarities – a common tactic during the nineteenth century – than by reference to economic dynamics.[19] No longer was the protective embrace of the patriarchal family shielding women from the vagaries of the economy. Instead, their rapidly increasing socio-economic independence was drawing them into the brutal struggle for survival, and this new equality had its price. The commodification of female labor inevitably raised the issue of state-regulated prostitution, with one specialist thus suggesting a link between the high rates of female suicide in the commercial center of Odessa with its renowned trade in "living female goods."[20] As Darwinist metaphors entered into everyday parlance, however, the tremendous scope of the problem posed a quandary: did progress really require so many victims? According to one professor, who expressed his scholarly opinion in a daily newspaper, the answer was an unambiguous yes. The suicide of the weak, the "poorly adapted," facilitated social progress, and they should be thanked for their service. He described the phenomenon as society's "self-purging" (*samoochishchenie obshchestva*): eliminated were those with "little value," people with poor heredity, psychic instability or some other deficiency.[21] In contrast to the relative equanimity with which such views had earlier been expressed, the response was now heated and critical. As Zhbankov curtly noted, if a healthy fish perishes due to polluted water, then the problem lies in the water, not in the qualities of the fish.[22]

The ever-expanding dimensions of the crisis thus compelled specialists to turn their attention to practical measures of socio-economic and political hygiene. Precisely these interests underpinned the concern about the growing incidence of suicide among workers and the urban under-classes. Arguing (not altogether accurately) that this constituted a wholly new phenomenon, they spotlighted the interconnected roles of the socio-economic order, revolutionary activism,

---

[19] Conversely, one doctor argued that women's ongoing economic dependence on male breadwinners provided the context for most suicides, and she likewise stressed women's innate impressionability and neuroticism. See Dr. Sofiia Bogatina, "Samoubiistva sredi zhenshchin," *Zhenskii vestnik* no. 11 (1910), 219–22.

[20] See Dmitrii Zhbankov, "O samoubiistvakh v poslednie gody," *Russkoe bogatstvo* no. 4 (1909), 30; Zubov, "O samoubiistve," 1630; and G. I. Gordon, "Prostitutki i samoubiistvo," *Rech'* (Apr. 23, 1910).

[21] Prof. G. Kozhevnikov, "Liudi durnoi nasledstvennosti," *Utro Rossii* (Aug. 28, 1911). For a similar view, see M. Men'shikov, "Otsokhshie list'ia," *Pis'ma k blizhnim* no. 4 (1910).

[22] Zhbankov, "K statistike," 569–70. Zubov moderated his earlier language, acknowledging that poor conditions could drive people to their deaths who might otherwise have survived. See his "O samoubiistve," 1574. See also anon., *"Nevedomyi krai" (O samoubiistvakh. Tsifry i chelovecheskie dokumenty* (n.p., n.d.,) 13–14. A moral perspective with a focus on unjust suffering also characterized suicide notes and the writings of workers; see Steinberg, *Proletarian Imagination*, 79–82 and *passim*.

and governmental policies.[23] As one doctor interpreted: the relatively low number of suicides among workers before 1905 had reflected their lagging cultural and political development in relation to their Western European, especially German counterparts, but the revolution had marked their accelerated rise to (modern) political consciousness. Suicide rates had then remained low in 1906, despite the growth in unemployment, precisely because workers still possessed many of the political and economic institutions established during the revolutionary year. Subsequently, however, the economic downturn had led to high levels of unemployment and financial insecurity, and the politics of reaction had denied workers their safety net. The state had suppressed those organizations – unions and mutual-aid societies – that could unify workers and defend their interests; it had trampled on newly won legal rights; and it had obstructed the establishment of a fair and just system for the distribution of labor.[24] In other words, the focus on the economic environment of suicide facilitated calls for socio-political intervention. The only means to address the epidemic was a concerted struggle against material need, unemployment, and prostitution as well as political oppression and arbitrariness. This tendency to conflate the socio-economic with the political even found expression in the categories of suicide statistics; some independent statisticians grouped everything from unemployment and poverty to political repression under the single rubric of "social and political causes."[25] Furthermore, the efforts of the government to address the problem were often lampooned. When access to the popular poison, essence of vinegar, was restricted, for example, one satirical journal fantasized a bureaucratic utopia, where all suicide methods would be banned – not just knives and weapons but also trains, trees, rivers, and tall buildings.[26] The point, of course, was that the government was unwilling to address the root causes of the epidemic.

Critiques of the state's role in the economy were quite common in this period, but their use as an explanatory paradigm for suicide reflected as well a newly prominent Durkheimian view of the social body. The repression of self-initiative (*samodeiatel'nost'*) *cum* revolution, many argued, was fragmenting society into a conglomeration of isolated, alienated individuals and preventing the emergence of new forms of social integration, especially in the work

[23] For an overview that emphasizes the shift from medical-psychological to socio-economic frameworks of causality, see Fenomenov, *Prichiny samoubiistv*, 69–72.

[24] See the conference paper presented by V. N. Tsederbaum and the subsequent discussion, especially the comments of Dr. Karapetov, "Samoubiistva i obshchestvennye sobytiia v Rossii," *Trudy XI Pirogovskogo s"ezda*, ed. P. N. Bulatov, vol. 3 (SPb, 1913), 189–95.

[25] See e.g. Zhbankov, "Sovremennye samoubiistva," *Sovremennyi mir* no. 3 (1910), 28–29; and Statistik, "Samoubiistva v Moskve za 1910 god," *Russkie vedomosti* (Apr. 14, 1911).

[26] "Protiv samoubiistva (Utopiia)," *Satirikon* no. 42 (1909), 6. Medical journals did take the problem of poison more seriously. See the articles by L. I. Serbilat'ev and B. V. Vladykin, both in *Russkii vrach*, no. 46 (1910); and no. 38 (1912).

force.[27] The fact that life had lost its "value" [*tsennost'*] was reiterated countless times, and this metaphor possessed both a political dimension (the tit-for-tat violence of state executions and terrorist attacks) and economic ones (the commodification of man and his labor). As one doctor summarized: "There – where social apathy rules, where social initiative and solidarity are lacking, where the personality is suppressed and humiliated, where isolation, estrangement, and alienation rule, where the material existence of numerous classes borders poverty and destitution – there the poison of suicide will mercilessly claim more and more victims, who have become, alas, the 'superfluous people' of this dull and vacant era of stagnation [*bezvremen'e*]."[28] This final term – literally a time "without time" in the Russian – likewise recurred frequently. Sometimes it evoked the modernist notion of cyclical time and sometimes the sense of historical time obstructed. Implicit in this context was the role of the autocratic state in hindering modernization.

The harm wrought by the disjunctions between socio-economic and political development affected not just workers and the urban poor but also educated youth. The disproportionate number of young victims was a real peculiarity in Russia's post-revolutionary experience of suicide. In a significant divergence from the Western European pattern, statistics showed that suicide rates were highest not among the old but among the young, and the trend was strengthening. According to Zhbankov's data (1905–11), 75.1 percent of suicides were aged 30 or under. Other specialists found similar patterns: 71.62 percent in Odessa (1904–8); and 76.72 percent in St. Petersburg (1910–11). In all these samples, moreover, the highest number of cases fell into the age group of 15 to 25 years, which constituted well over half of the total number of cases.[29] Both public and specialist attention dwelled almost exclusively upon this aspect of the epidemic, making Russia's youth into the emblem of the post-revolutionary crisis. This reflects in part the long-standing association of youth – its vitality, its narratives of becoming – with modernity.[30] Yet the concern also reflected an ongoing confrontation with recent history. As in the case of workers, the explanations often linked political with socio-economic factors. The parallel lines of

---

[27] The two most eloquent expositions of a Durkheimian view are Vladimir Vol'skii, "Traurnyi progress," *Sovremennyi mir* no. 6 (1912); and V. Bazarov, "Samoubiistvo, kak sotsial'noe iavlenie," *Zaprosy zhizni* no. 19 (1912).

[28] I. P. Ostrovskii, "Voprosy sravnitel'noi psikhologii samoubiistva u vzroslykh i detei," *VPKAG* no. 3 (1911), 66.

[29] See Zhbankov, "K statistike," no. 35, 534; Ostrovskii, "Samoubiistva," 20; and Grigor'ev, "Samoubiistva," 188. One partial explanation would be the high proportion of younger people in the migrant city, but this alone can not explain the strikingly atypical pattern. Compare the very different statistics for Western Europe as listed in Fenomenov, *Prichiny samoubiistv*, 86.

[30] Franco Moretti, *The Way of the World: The Bildungsroman in European Culture* (London, 1987). See also Giovanni Levi and Jean-Claude Schmitt, eds., *A History of Young People in the West*, vol. 2: *Stormy Evolution to Modern Times* (Cambridge, Mass., 1997).

narrative causality for university students were especially prominent. Students' rise to political consciousness in 1905 had helped to democratize education and to transform the universities into key sites for the revolutionary movement. These accomplishments had been followed, however, by the government's suppression of student organizations (both political and economic), which had, in turn, fragmented the student collective, leaving its members alienated, disappointed, and impoverished, both materially and spiritually.[31] For secondary-school pupils, in contrast, the explanation tended to emphasize a pathological speeding-up of the life cycle. Not only had they attempted to emulate their elders by bringing revolution into the classroom, a small number had also engaged in such violent activities as terrorism and expropriations.[32] In the subsequent years, moreover, they seemed to be falling victim to two different Molochs: the repressions of the state-run school and the seductive pleasures of mass culture. By the eve of World War I, public discussions increasingly linked youth suicide to the crass materialism, careerist ambitions, and narcissistic self-indulgence of Russia's emergent bourgeoisie.

The government also began to recognize the power of numbers in this context. Since the 1880s, the education ministry had generally monitored suicides among its pupils, but concern mounted early in the twentieth century. A circular from May 1905 drew the attention of district curators to the problem and proposed a religion-based prophylactic. Not only were schools to ensure that its pupils fulfilled all the rules of Christian morality; they were also to conduct morally edifying discussions with the appropriate pastoral admonitions following any actual incident.[33] Alongside this time-honored attempt to mobilize religion and custodial supervision in the struggle against suicide was a more modernizing impulse: the collection of data. Circulars directed schools to report every case of suicide, attempted suicide, or accidental death, and a new form was developed to standardize the information.[34] Though the process was irregular, paper flooded into the archive of the ministry's Medical-Sanitary Division – literally thousands of documents, including school records, doctors' reports, suicide notes, and other materials, as well as hundreds of folios filled with clippings from newspapers and journals.[35]

Some of this information was worked up into annual statistical reports that were published between 1906 and 1916. The first effort provided both a critical

---

[31] For further discussion, see my *Heralds of Revolution*, ch. 7.

[32] On the reputedly unruly and disorderly engagement of secondary-school pupils in revolutionary activities, see Engelstein, *The Keys to Happiness*, ch. 6.

[33] RGIA, f. 733, op. 199, d. 33, ll. 8, 43–44.

[34] School districts were occasionally reminded, and the ministry requested the cooperation of the judiciary. See RGIA, f. 733, op. 199, d. 107, l. 1; and d. 175, ll. 126–27.

[35] These are collected in RGIA, f. 733, op. 199. Henceforth all archival citations in this chapter will be to this collection unless otherwise specified.

discussion of the problem in the European scholarly literature and an analysis of statistics for Russia from 1880 to 1904. Dismissing the two extreme tendencies either to vilify the school or to shift all the blame onto the family, society, or the mental state of the victim, its author stressed the need for dispassionate, scientific analysis. His conclusions balanced delicately between these poles, pointing to four interconnected factors: society, which produces neurotic and unbalanced children unfit for education; the school, which follows an overly standardized pedagogical model, overtaxes the pupils, and neglects their physical well-being; the family, which often treats children strictly and unjustly; and more general conditions, including the physiology of youth and the pressures of civilization. Although the volume did not specify prophylactic measures beyond the need to strengthen the medical-sanitary supervision of pupils (that is, to empower doctors within the school environment, a proposal that was also emanating from regime critics), it extensively reviewed the conclusions of the German pedagogue Gustav Siebert, who, in addition to socio-hygienic measures designed to counter the spread of degeneration, called for improved physical education, legal measures against the physical abuse of children, and the complete reorganization of the school.[36] In sum, this report was textually driven; its statistics were interpreted, blame was apportioned, and substantive prophylactic measures were implicitly set out. Subsequent volumes presented a stark contrast: written texts – whether introductions or conclusions – soon disappeared only to be temporarily replaced by appendices filled with dozens of suicide notes (edited to prevent the identification of their authors).[37] The public response was predictable. On the one hand, reviewers condemned the ministry's dry formalism, thereby transforming the statistical charts into a symbol of bureaucracy, of the state's failure to employ any substantive measures to halt the epidemic. On the other hand, they lingered on the words of the suicides themselves, "human documents" as they were often called, which provided a stark contrast to the anonymous inhumanity of statistics.[38] In light of the negative publicity, the suicide notes for the 1909 edition were censored and in subsequent years left out altogether.[39] All that remained was page

[36] See G. V. Khlopin, "Samoubiistva, pokusheniia na samoubiistva i neschastnye sluchai sredi uchashchikhsia russkikh uchebnykh zavedenii (Sanitarno-statisticheskoe issledovanie)," *ZhMNP* no. 3 (1906), 1–4, 38–49, 58–65.

[37] See the series edited first by G.V. Khlopin, then N. G. Ushinskii, and finally E. A. Neznamov, *Samoubiistva, pokusheniia na samoubiistva i neschastnye sluchai sredi uchashchikhsia uchebnykh zavedenii Ministerstva Narodnogo Prosveshcheniia* (SPb, 1907–16)

[38] Critical reviews appeared annually in all major newspapers. See e.g. "Zhizn' i kazennaia statistika," *Peterburgskii listok* (Apr. 23, 1908); and N. Dneprov, "Strashnaia statistika," *Gazeta kopeika* (Aug. 11, 1909). See also the comments in journals, for example, R. G., "Iz zhizni srednei shkoly," *Vestnik vospitaniia* no. 8 (1909), 116–17. Many articles were collected in the ministry's archive. See d. 145, ll. 216–41, *passim*.

[39] For the texts of unpublished notes, several of which contained explicit accusations against schools, see d. 147, ll. 1–4.

after page of statistical charts. The drive to compile information about suicide within the school-age population had stumbled against the state's inability to use it.

Independent specialists, led by Dr. Grigorii Gordon, conducted an open campaign against the state school, and statistics provided one of his lines of attack. In countless articles for the specialized and mass press, Gordon repeatedly emphasized the under-reportage of official statistics, which signified the state's failure to acknowledge the dimensions of the problem or to enforce proper prophylactic measures. According to his collection of newspaper reports, the number of suicides among pupils and students was skyrocketing. While the official figures for the entire period from 1882 to 1909 totaled 995 cases, he had compiled 1,358 cases for just eight years (1902–9), of which 683 involved secondary-school students. Whichever statistical source one used, however, the rapid tempo of growth seemed indisputable: a three-to-five fold increase between 1905 and 1910. Though anxiety about the problem was spreading throughout Europe, Russia's experience was unique. The number of annual cases (proportional to the school population) was three to four times higher in Russia than in Prussia, and the trend was upwards.[40] Predictably, such patterns were understood as products of Russia's particular political situation, especially its reproduction in the world of the secondary school.

This situation spurred Russia's medical community into action. In 1910, the Society for the Preservation of the People's Health, a progressive organization, formed a special commission "for the struggle against school suicides." Its tasks included both the scientific study of the problem and the development of prophylactic measures. With its members including not just doctors but luminaries of Russia's educated society, the commission met regularly over the next years to discuss papers and various projects, including the compilation of data, statistical surveys, school reform, and the founding of an organization to help needy students.[41] Many of these projects would end in failure. In light of its long-standing fear of social activism and student radicalism, both of which were on the rise again by 1911 and 1912, the government frequently obstructed these and related activities.[42] The lack of concrete achievements was acknowledged at the seventeenth session of the commission in October 1912, which resolved

---

[40] His figures vary slightly, and I have taken most from G. Gordon, "Sovremennye samoubiistva," *Russkaia mysl'* no. 5 (1912), 83–84. Official statistics reveal a similar proportional pattern; see Fenomenov, *Prichiny samoubiistv*, 54, 81.

[41] For the published protocols, see *ZhROONZ* no. 3 (1911), 44–60; and no. 3–4 (1912), 115–48.

[42] On events in higher education after 1910, see my *Heralds of Revolution*, ch. 8. In addition, the Lena Goldfields massacre of 1912 heralded the revival of working-class activism, which would reach a peak in July 1914. On the labor movement in this period, see Victoria Bonnell, *Roots of Revolution: Workers' Politics and Organizations in St. Petersburg and Moscow, 1900–1914* (Berkeley, 1983).

that more engagement within society was necessary to mobilize pressure for reform.[43]

To understand Russia's predicament in the years after 1905, many contemporaries repeatedly turned to the comparison with (a sometimes idealized) Western Europe. England, the birthplace of capitalism, possessed a comparatively low suicide rate (within a European context), which was often explained by the advanced level of political life and social organization. This stability, in turn, was thought to be promoted by an educational system focused on the individual pupil, his harmonic physical and mental development.[44] Furthermore, the contention that the number of suicides had risen in the wake of the 1848 revolution and Paris Commune was often repeated in the Russian press, and though the epidemic was perhaps stronger in Russia, it was – in this sense – "normal."[45] Finally, some studies were beginning to indicate that suicide rates had stabilized after a century of growth and were even falling in some parts of Europe; this suggested that the causes were to be found not in modernity itself but in the period of transition.[46] The prognosis was at least partly encouraging: once the transition had been made in Russia, then rates would stabilize there as well. Yet there were several qualifications. First was the strength of political reaction: until the transition from autocratic past to democratic future could be accomplished, the brutalities of capitalism could not be alleviated. Second was a fundamental ambivalence regarding capitalism itself: images of both the free market – whether in labor or goods – as well as liberal individualism were often negative, typically countered by ideals of equality, solidarity, and justice. Third was the political challenge of medical degeneration: few doubted that the population was suffering from advanced forms of degeneration, caused by both heredity and current economic and political conditions and that the solution lay in "healthification" (*ozdorovlenie*). But the necessary prophylactic and therapeutic measures were obstructed by the state.[47] This circular predicament does much to explain the enthusiasm with which many doctors and other specialists would ultimately decide to participate in the Bolshevik project to "improve" the population. But it also illuminates the close nexus between politics and

---

[43] "Protokol 17 zasedaniia Kommissii po bor'be s shkol'nymi samoubiistvami," *ZhROONZ* no. 12 (1912), 32.

[44] For a panegyric on the English educational system, see Fel'tsman, "K voprosu," 239–40; and L. Slonimskii, "Samoubiistvo s obshchestvennoi i nravstvennoi tochek zreniia," *Vestnik Evropy* nos. 1, 2 (1914), esp. no. 2.

[45] For a summary of the statistics, see Fenomenov, *Prichiny samoubiistv*, 48–49. See also Augustin Cabanès, *La Névrose révolutionaire* (Paris, 1906).

[46] This point was stressed by Vol'skii, "Traurnyi progress," 284–86; Fenomenov, *Prichiny samoubiistv*, 13–23; and D. Cherepanov, "K voprosu o samoubiistvakh," *Russkie vedomosti* (Feb. 1, 1913).

[47] For an detailed discussion of "healthification," see the article by the founder of St. Petersburg's Psycho-Neurological Institute, V. M. Bekhterev, "O prichinakh samoubiistva i o vozmozhnoi bor'be s nim," *Vestnik znanii* nos. 2, 3 (1912), here no. 3, 259–62.

economy – which increasingly went under the label of capitalism – that was perceived to be obstructing the emergence of a new kind of social bond. The epidemic of suicide suggested that Russia was experiencing an incomplete or even a deformed modernity, in which the persistence of the "old" was polluting the "new," and in which "human life was profaned at every step."[48]

The school regime

"You see," explained a well-known educator in the liberal journal, *Herald of Europe*, "our school, if we regard it seriously, is not far removed from a prison." At issue was the growing number of suicides linked to the secondary school. Noting that five years had passed since the "days of freedom," he scornfully dismissed the contention made by some conservatives that the problem was caused by the revolutionary events or the malevolent presence of agitators manipulating "unbalanced, youthful natures." Instead, he built upon the resonant analogy with the prison: "Are not our schools punitive institutions, where knowledge is instilled in pupils with the help of bad marks and the periodic purge, where the education of children is based exclusively in repression, where educators, in a pathetic unity with police officials, 'spy' on pupils and 'inform' upon their behavior to higher authorities?" Such oppression had infected the family and society at large, he contended, thereby transmitting the suicidal impulse.[49] Another commentator agreed, describing how school directors were now employing methods of supervision and punishment previously associated with the prison, including peep holes and solitary confinement in darkened cells (with pupils even placed on a month-long waiting list for the latter).[50]

   The association of suicide with the bureaucratic regime of the secondary school had been established long before 1905. In earlier decades, pupils had also taken their own lives, sometimes leaving notes in which they cited problems at school or their feelings of anguish, but they had not generally authored their deaths as public statements, much less as deliberate accusations or protests. The debate in the press had then retold these incidents within the narrative of despotism, casting these young people as victims of arbitrary power (though the specters of vice and disease had always hovered nearby as well). After 1905, the dynamics of school suicide changed. The explicit analogy between the school and the prison, which had become an open site of revolutionary struggle, politicized the school to an unprecedented degree. The analogy both reflected and encouraged a new phenomenon: young people were themselves adapting the heroic, political suicide into the school environment and insisting upon the

[48] G. I. Gordon, "Pessimizm i samoubiistva sredi uchashcheisia molodezhi," *Zavety* no. 3 (1912), 166.

[49] Arkadii Velskii, "Shkol'nyi gipnoz (Iz zapisok pedagoga)," *Vestnik Evropy* no. 5 (1910), 277–78.

[50] V. Portugalov, "Melkii bes i ego zhertvy," *Novyi zhurnal dlia vsekh* no. 17 (1910), esp. 101–2.

revolutionary status of their acts. This process occurred in an intense media spotlight. Even as their audiences – whether journalists, public, or parents – did not typically endorse the act of suicide, they understood the political allusions and often perpetuated them.

An oft-cited case was that of the Kiev pupil, Vasilii Babienko, aged 15, who had shot himself in the autumn of 1909 in an explicit protest against the school regime. An orphan without significant financial support, Babienko had been living with a caring, local family and doing well at school. That autumn, however, he had received some failing marks, and though these were only provisional, he felt victimized and used his suicide to communicate with the public. The letter opened in a dialogue with prospective readers, thereby demonstrating his (altogether reasonable) presumption that it would be publicized. It then turned to his motives:

I personally shot myself not from despair, not from a fear of life, for there is no reason to despair as it is only the first quarter [of the academic year], and I do not fear life . . . I know it. But everything I have seen and heard has compelled me to raise my head, to express my protest. Before, I was so insignificant, a "voice calling out in the wilderness," but now, as each of my words resounds from the depths of the coffin [. . .] my voice penetrates the soul, for "the dead do not lie."

In his note, Babienko dwelled upon the mind-numbing burden of the secondary school, the irrelevance of real learning and the primary concern with the diploma, all of which deformed pupils and teachers alike. Closing with a call to arms, he admonished his readers for their indifference: "Yes, you are used to it, but let my death compel you to see with new, cleared eyes [. . .]. Remember that my blood flows into the sea of blood, spilled due to societal negligence. Let my drop of blood fall so that the moment will draw nearer when the sea floods its banks [. . .] and compels you to come to your senses."[51]

Babienko had deliberately designed his death as a public and political act, and it was received as such. His funeral was attended by a large crowd, and the subsequent press commentary encouraged the interpretative cycle. "Yet another death. Yet another letter from there, beyond the fateful boundary," proclaimed a Kiev newspaper. "The death of the pupil Babienko has progressed from a personal to a social act. It was the result not of personal despair, not of Babienko's personal needs . . . [It was instead] a method of struggle. Anarchists kill others, frighten [them] with physical torments and death; the noble youth kills himself, frightens [us] with life, with life based on the blood of others, frightens [us] with such dreadful torments of conscience." The journalist then ruminated upon the

---

[51] The letter was frequently reprinted in newspapers and subsequent articles. For the full version, see *Na pomoshch' molodezhi: Sbornik statei, pisem, i zametok o studencheskikh nuzhdakh i samoubiistvakh uchashchikhsia* (Kiev, 1910), 25–27. For its discussion, see also G. Gordon, "Samoubiitsy i ikh pis'ma," *Novyi zhurnal dlia vsekh* no. 2 (1911), 109–10.

failed methods of political struggle – the word had proved powerless, the sword had defiled its bearer – and described Babienko's tactic as "the boycott of life." (Given the fact that he had shot himself, this description is paradoxical.) Yet the commentator's sympathy masked his confusion and perhaps condescension. He concluded that the youth had erred, if not in his words, then in his action.[52] Even as Babienko's political claim was acknowledged, therefore, the gulf between cause and effect – school and suicide – was still too great, and the act thus remained fundamentally unintelligible. "To what level of despair must one progress and how much faith in human justice and solidarity must one lose," another observer mused, "in order to chose suicide as a means to attract the public's attention?"[53] He left this question unanswered.

Babienko was not alone. Young people repeatedly used their suicides to cast blame on individuals, especially teachers. Among the most direct was the note of one 16-year-old youth: "In my death I ask that you blame the teacher of mathematics, [name], in the Simakov gymnasium."[54] Another pupil ironically thanked a teacher for a poor grade and the school's director for not exempting him from fees.[55] The note of one young man, Semen Slonim, who poisoned himself while at school but survived, played upon many conventional motifs of political suicides. Asking that his poetry and portrait be distributed to his comrades as a keepsake, he portrayed his death both as a murder and as a sacrifice to the collective, albeit of classmates rather than political prisoners. He even concluded with a reference to his task accomplished: "The one who is guilty in this is the villain, pedant, and formalist [teacher of mathematics] Pepke, the scoundrel, who has now become a murderer. Over the course of three years he systematically drove me to what has happened. [. . .] My death will function as a service to the entire class. I bequeath vengeance to you my comrades. [. . .] I think that I have fulfilled my duty to the class, and I die with a serene heart."[56]

Such attempts to transform the act of suicide into an accusatory gesture, even a revolutionary act, were so common that they spilled out of the school. In May 1908, a 14-year-old tailor's apprentice threw himself under a train and left the following note: "I decided to end my life in suicide. I die for a better future for all boy-pupils." A day later, another apprentice, aged 16, also threw himself under a train, writing: "I die for the edification of all artisans. The death of two boys, I am sure, will have a positive influence upon all master-artisans." For their part, journalists made the transition from the particular to the general.

---

[52] E. Kuz'min, "Iz moego okna," reprinted in *Na pomoshch' molodezhi*, 28–31.
[53] Velskii, "Shkol'nyi gipnoz," 277.
[54] See d. 215, l. 192. See also a similar case in d. 141, ll. 28–31.
[55] See d. 147, l. 2. Compare the similar note in another case reprinted in anon., *"Nevedomyi krai,"* 9.
[56] See d. 217, l. 363.

Having drawn the obvious connection between the workshop and the school, they lamented how all young people were being raised in an atmosphere of mistrust, fear, malice, and hatred.[57] Precisely this concentration on the school over the workshop angered one young suicide, an 18-year-old seamstress named Anna Kraizman. Condemning both the unequal opportunities within society as well as the unequal press coverage of suicides, she wrote: "But does not a worker also possess a soul?" For her, death was an equalizer: "I depart for that place where there are neither rich nor poor, educated nor illiterate."[58] Yet despite her impassioned appeal, Kraizman's note did not attract sustained public attention.

With the school, not the workshop, garnering the most attention, the resonance of these many tales depended less on their novelty than on their recognition value. The reader knew what had happened before perusing the story; only the details varied. Not only had the school long been blamed for youth suicides, but the image of the sadistic pedagogue had become a literary commonplace. Newspapers often compared real people and cases to the anti-heroes of Anton Chekhov's short story, "The Man in the Case" and Fedor Sologub's novel, *The Petty Demon*. After 1905, however, the scale of the problem increased dramatically as literally hundreds of suicides clamored for the public's attention on the pages of newspapers, magazines, and journals. Most young people neither blamed specific people nor broadened their grievance to the "school regime" but rather cited a specific incident at school or left no explanation at all. Nevertheless, the question of generalized responsibility was at the forefront of public attention. When a 15-year-old girl poisoned herself at her Tagenrog school during her religion lesson, headlines proclaimed "Gymnasium or Torture Chamber," "Provincial Pictures," "Dreadful Fact." A month before her suicide, it was reported, she had stolen a book and sold it to pay off a debt but had then voluntarily confessed her misdeed. Rather than informing the parents, the head of the gymnasium had systematically harassed the girl, calling her a thief in front of her friends.[59] In Vitebsk, a 16-year-old boy had been caught reading a book secretly during a lesson he had found boring; he had been sentenced to twelve hours incarceration and threatened with a poor grade in behavior.[60] Believing that his chances for university had been ruined, he poisoned himself. Following critical reports in the capitals' newspapers, the gymnasium's director wrote a letter to Russia's most prominent liberal newspaper demanding its publication

---

[57] These events caused a large outcry in the press. For some clippings, see d. 124, ll. 42–43, 63, and *passim*.

[58] Reprinted in anon., *"Nevedomyi krai,"* 21–23.

[59] For the official form on her suicide, see d. 125, l. 39. For some of the press coverage, see P. Surozhskii, "Gimnaziia ili zastenok," *Sovremennoe slovo* (Nov. 5, 1908); "Provintsial'nye kartinki," *Birzhevye vedomosti* (Nov. 7, 1908); "Strashnyi fakt," *Taganrogskii vestnik* (Oct. 30, 1908). These and others are clipped in d. 124, ll. 123–31.

[60] For the official form on his suicide, see d. 125, l. 8.

with a citation from the censorship and press statute. Denying any wrongdoing, he stressed that the causes of the suicide remained unknown, that the incident at school was a mere coincidence. This letter only provoked a cutting editorial commentary: "Does not the fate of children lie in good hands? . . . The man in the case has not lost his cold-bloodedness and self-possession. For him, the lock-up and the suicide are simply the 'chronological comparison of two facts' (!) Not only does he not see a connection between the two of them, but claims that 'it is impossible to establish any connection.'"[61] As another newspaper noted in conclusion to its report on this "1001st story" of pedagogical violence, "commentary is superfluous."[62]

In fact, of course, commentary was the business of the press, and the school regime proved to be a powerful metaphor for the heavy hand of the state in the maintenance of order. In the emotional words of one critic, school suicides enacted "the drama of a child's soul, profaned with crude violence, tormented with inhuman fanatic formalism, driven to despair and [. . .] a terrible death."[63] As in previous decades, moreover, journalists vigorously resisted the accusation that they were causing the problem by conferring sanctity upon the victims. Rather, as one indignantly wrote, publicity constituted a civic duty, a necessary measure in the struggle against any epidemic, because it helped to identify the general causes and the necessary prophylactic measures: "During the cholera [epidemic], we cried: Don't drink the water! [. . .] We made the courtyards, bazaars and streets healthy and thereby tried to limit the growth of the epidemic, achieving generally successful results." If the epidemic of suicide was akin to any other epidemic, therefore, it was necessary to identify the "poison of mental contagion" and to clean up its environment. The source seemed clear: "Everywhere the school, its ghastly bureaucratism, its callous, soulless pedagogues who find nothing more reasonable than [. . .] to offend [pupils'] pride [. . .] and to abase their dignity. For the fact of the matter is [that] this is the diseased water, the deliberately constructed, favorable conditions of infection."[64] In this way, the moderate and liberal press mobilized a campaign against the bureaucratic school under the banner of public health.

The constant repetition of this theme helped to shape new forms and spaces for political action. Even when explicit accusations were not made in suicide

[61] "K samoubiistvu gimnazista (Pis'ma direktora gimnazii)," *Rech'* (Dec. 20, 1908); Skeptik, "Chelovek v futliare," *Rech'* (Dec. 22, 1908); see also "Prostaia istoriia," *Birzhevye vedomosti* (Dec. 18, 1908). (See d. 124.) See also the comment in the pedagogy journal, R. G., "Iz zhizni srednei shkoly," *Vestnik vospitaniia* no. 2 (1909), 121–23.

[62] *Vecher* (Dec. 24, 1908) in d. 124, l. 173. An extended article in a progressive pedagogy journal also discussed these and other suicides from the autumn of 1908, describing the list as a "sad martyrology." See Al'f, "Bezmiatezhnoe zhit'e (Ocherki russkoi zhizni)," *Obrazovanie* no. 9/10a (1908), 1–15.

[63] A. Gurevich, "Zametki iz tekushchei zhizni," *Russkaia shkola* no. 4 (1907), 77–78.

[64] A. Poliatskii, "Pisat' li?" reprinted in *Na pomoshch' molodezhi*, 32–36.

notes, the family often cast the suicide as a victim. As a result, a struggle would ensue over the attribution of motive: whereas the school administration typically cited the pupil's mental instability, parents blamed the school. The most common tactic was the deliberate cultivation of publicity. The mother of a 15-year-old pupil sent a letter to a local newspaper claiming that "the sensitive, nervous girl could no longer endure the unfair treatment" at school and, for this reason, had poisoned herself.[65] In another case, a father wrote an impassioned letter blaming the new director and inspector of the school for his son's death. Aware of the dangers of exam-related suicides, the family had always downplayed the importance of marks, and the father concluded that the unfair intervention of the director in the examination process had pushed the youth over the edge. Tapping into the language of liberalism, he wrote: his son's "youthful self-esteem had already been too wounded, his human dignity too long offended."[66] Other parents instead attempted to invoke the criminal statute on instigated suicide; one mother thus submitted a legal declaration charging a religion teacher with driving her daughter to suicide with "unjust and prejudicial treatment."[67] Finally, cases of suicide also mobilized parents to act collectively. In one instance, a dossier was assembled against an unpopular religion teacher after he had reputedly driven a pupil to suicide by giving her an intentionally humiliating grade of F+. Another confrontation, this time with the academic district, occurred when parents tried to get a school director fired. She had constantly reprimanded a star pupil for unruly hair – itself the result of having had her head shaved due to typhus – ultimately driving the girl to poison herself.[68]

The resonance of suicide as a public act also politicized the funeral and memorial. Though school directors and local police usually forbade any form of display, friends and fellow pupils often attended burials in large numbers, sometimes bringing wreathes, distributing leaflets, or making speeches. Such commemorations possessed a long history in Russian radical culture, and they had also formed important ritualized events during the revolutionary years of 1904–7. Consequently, commemoration – even just the collective singing of "Eternal Memory" – was understood by all parties concerned as a political act.[69] It sacralized the death, transforming the suicide into a kind of martyr.

---

[65] *Peterburgskaia gazeta* (Oct. 29, 1908). She died over a month later; see V. Pataleev, "Pamiati ugasshego tsevtka," *Peterburgskii listok* (Dec. 14, 1908). See d. 124, esp. l. 161.

[66] See d. 238, ll. 125–28.

[67] See d. 106, ll. 127–28. This motif recurs regularly. In another example, two young women in Penza explained their attempted suicide as an effort to provoke a judicial prosecution of the school's director. See d. 237, ll. 86–91.

[68] These two cases are discussed along with others in D. Zaslavskii, "Dni nashei zhizni," *Novaia zhizn'* no. 11 (1911), 240–44.

[69] For further discussion and other examples, see my *Heralds of Revolution, passim.*

These dynamics were well exemplified in the 1912 death of Nikolai Sergeev, a pupil at one of the capital's elite gymnasiums. Though he had not left an explanatory note and the school cited his mental derangement, his friends produced a series of proclamations that ascribed his motive to the "school-prison," especially its culture of spying and oppression. More specifically, Sergeev had been the driving force behind a secret study circle that a school inspector had discovered. As a result, he had been threatened with expulsion in his final year of study. Unable to give up the "living cause" of the circle or, for familial reasons, to leave school, the youth had perceived but two options – to lose himself in reckless debauchery (by renouncing his principles), or to end it all.[70] One student wrote an allegory about the secondary school, which was dedicated to Sergeev's memory:

In the exultant light of the bright summer sun, an eagle was born. Happily he looked upon the radiant world [. . .]. He grew strong, felt a tremendous power in himself, stretched his sturdy wings, ready to shoot like an arrow into the deep blue sky . . . But at that moment crude hands grasped him, clipped his wings, and put him into an iron cage. [. . .] And the eagle dashed about, tried with his beak, his talons, to break out of the cage [. . .] He then looked around and saw many other small cages also filled with young eagles. They too raged, they too broke their beaks, spattered blood upon their breasts.

Having been told that he must stay caged for eight years before being allowed to fly, "the young eagle said: 'Very well, I will sit for eight years and then whirl into the limitless heights of the blue sky, higher than the mountains, higher than the clouds.' 'No,' said his comrades, 'you will receive the right to fly only below the mountains, below the clouds.' And the heart of the young eagle bled." Resolving to avenge himself upon his "executioners," he decided to endure his sentence, sustained by solidarity with his fellow prisoners. The prohibition of this contact – a reference to the forbidden study circle – provided the impetus for suicide. "The last joy was taken from the young eagle," the proclamation concluded, and he pierced his "fervent young heart" only months before his liberation.[71]

The eagle formed a common motif in revolutionary rhetoric, and yet it was also, in its double-headed form, a symbol of autocracy. This blurring of images embodies the explicitly political challenge. The suffering of the young eagles acquires a sacred aura, and the violent death possesses a potentially redemptive quality. Proclamations drew out the political ramifications of suffering: "The school is inextricably linked to the government. All the humiliation inflicted upon us there is necessary for the maintenance of despotism." Similarly, they emphasized that the path to redemption was to be found in commemoration.

---

[70] "O 'Vitmerovtsakh' (Arkhivnaia spravka)," *Revoliutsionnoe iunoshestvo 1905–1017: Peterburg* (Leningrad, 1924), 145.

[71] Ibid., 150–51.

Pupils were called upon to protest against the "school-prison" by gathering at Sergeev's gravesite: "You died, comrade, you fell victim to the scholastic pedantry of our secondary school, but your spirit lives on. [...] We will continue your cause, we will take vengeance for you." Only the presence of local police prevented the demonstration.[72]

Just like the prison that left its mark upon the body and psyche of the prisoner, however, the school also injured its pupils, and this fact likewise cut into the narrative of heroic (school) suicide. Did these deaths constitute heroic feats of resistance? Or were they the result of moral, physical, and mental pathology? If the latter, was it hereditary or acquired? The proclamations issued following Sergeev's death admitted this paradox. After all, the wings of the healthy, young eagles had been clipped, their beaks broken and breasts spattered with blood. Another proclamation lamented: "We are maimed there [in the school], from which only cripples exit with shattered nerves and a poisoned soul or else brazen careerists."[73] Similarly, in his suicide note, Babienko had tapped into the logic of the kingdom of darkness. "Are we guilty," he asked, "because the school has deformed us? Where is the man who is used to consciously lying? Where is the man who makes himself vindictively cruel? Where does he meet with a cruelty that is purely savage? In school, school, school!"[74] Following the pattern first popularized by Dobroliubov, he did not distinguish between the perpetrators and their victims, the teachers and their pupils: all had been mutilated and disfigured by the violence of arbitrary rule.

Most doctors and pedagogues likewise combined the political with the medical. On the one hand, they agreed that the school constituted the single most important factor in the epidemic, and Dr. Gordon cited it as a direct cause in 35 percent of cases.[75] More specifically, he condemned its "arbitrariness" (especially in the system of assessment and examination that pupils often justifiably experienced as unjust) and its general "regime," which was formalistic and punitive rather than supportive and encouraging. On the other hand, the influence of the school was also more pernicious. Its focus on grades rather than learning, its emphasis upon the mind rather than the body and soul, its reliance on fear rather than love – all of these qualities overstrained the mental, emotional, and physical health of pupils, leading to neurasthenia and cases of affective suicide superficially unrelated to the school.[76] Not surprisingly, the archives of the education ministry contain scores of doctors'

[72] Ibid., 145, 147, 148, 150, 151.   [73] Ibid., 145.

[74] *Na pomoshch' molodezhi*, 27. See also the letter a boy wrote to Maksim Gorky about the school. "K psikhologii sovremennoi russkoi shkoly," *Zaprosy zhizni* no. 2 (1912), 85–86.

[75] G. Gordon: "Samoubiistva uchashcheisia molodezhi," *Novoe slovo* no. 9 (1911), 29–30. In contrast, one commentator asserted that 83.3 percent of cases possessed school-related causes; see B. Shvetsov, "Samoubiistva v srednei shkole," *Russkaia shkola* no. 10 (1906), 127.

[76] Fenomenov, *Prichiny samoubiistv*, 83–84. These concerns also influenced the discussions at the tenth session of the Commission for the Struggle against School Suicides (1911) and the student

reports that attribute particular suicides to neurasthenia, degeneration, and so forth.[77]

As the revolutionary events of 1904–7 faded into the past, this alternate narrative of deformation gained in prominence. Even Gordon increasingly emphasized the pre-existing socio-medical pathology within the student population. In an article from 1912, he described the growing "nervous-psychic unsteadiness" of youth, which formed a "menacing symptom of the degeneration of society."[78] In some respects, this shift from the political to the medical marked a return to the more holistic approach that had dominated the specialist literature before 1905, when not just the school but also the family and society had shared the blame. But it also occurred in reaction to the extreme politicization of suicide: the language of despotism had become so common and expansive that it was losing its explanatory power. Was there perhaps a difference between the prison and the school? Between the revolutionary awaiting execution and the pupil who received a poor mark? Into this gap of unintelligibility stepped the language of pathology.

Equally significant, therefore, was the explicit diagnosis of psychic deformity among teaching personnel. One remarkable case study published in a psychiatric journal described K., aged 48, a school inspector who was credited with having personally driven eighteen pupils to suicide. Empowered in his official function to attend final examinations – and to intervene at will – he would deliberately humiliate the children, in part by asking them questions even their teachers could not answer. While parents and the local press had campaigned against him, they had failed to get the powerful bureaucrat fired. What the psychiatric evaluation claimed to reveal was a hidden psychosis: the man was in fact a sexual sadist, who could only experience sexual arousal and satisfaction at the sight of cowering and fearful students. Rather than being arrested or committed to a psychiatric institution, however, this man had been promoted into positions where he was able to pursue "his pernicious vice," strewing his path with youthful victims. The author of the study concluded by calling upon psychiatrists and pedagogues to be vigilant, for this was not an isolated case; the current system of education provided an optimal environment that attracted and rewarded such predators.[79] The very fact of this case study – with its final warning – documents the extreme resonance of the school regime as a dual site of political repression and medical pathology.

questionnaire presented at the eleventh session (1912); for the protocols, see *ZhROONZ* no. 3/4 (1912), 120–29.

[77] For published examples, see N. M. Popov, *Sovremennaia epidemiia shkol'nykh samoubiistv v Rossii: Klinicheskie materialy* (Kazan, 1911).

[78] G. Gordon, "Samoubiistva molodezhi i ee nervno-psikhicheskaia neustoichivost'," *Novyi zhurnal dlia vsekh* no. 9 (1912), 105.

[79] Dr. N. V. Krainskii, "Pedagogicheskii sadizm," *Sovremennaia psikhiatriia* (Sept. 1912).

The politicization of youth suicide around the issue of the school regime involved various perspectives that loosely conformed to conventional political divisions. On the one side were the supporters of order – the school administration, some parents, and conservative commentators. In their view, the causes of the epidemic lay primarily in a modern, secular society that had lost its moral ballast combined with the political disorder engendered by 1905. On the other side were those who blamed the atmosphere of political reaction, in the school as in the country as a whole. Yet many parents, pedagogues, and doctors were critical less of intervention itself than of the custodial and despotic intervention of the tsarist state. In other words, they asserted their own enlightened authority over school and family, an authority they based upon the rhetoric of both liberalism and science. In the final years before the outbreak of war in 1914, public engagement grew significantly, and the pages of Russia's journals and newspapers were filled with articles critiquing the current system of education, especially its harmful effects upon the bodies and psyches of youth, and proposing a wide range of specific pedagogical and hygienic measures.[80] The ongoing spate of youth suicides combined with the highly visible failure of the state to enact school reform had politicized public opinion as well as the medical and teaching professions.

Heroes of emptiness

In November 1909, Sarra Sheliubskaia, aged 16, drank a large dose of carbolic acid (phenol) while at her Odessa school and died soon afterwards. The case sparked tremendous interest because it dramatized the contradictory faces of youth suicide. The day after having received a failing grade on a written physics test and being admonished for her complete lack of knowledge, Sheliubskaia had been called upon by her physics teacher to answer a question for oral assessment. Perceiving this as a deliberate attempt to humiliate her before her peers, she refused, reportedly saying, "I will not answer because my knowledge will hardly have increased over the course of one night." As such audacity could harm the prestige of the gymnasium, the teacher reported Sheliubskaia's misbehavior to school authorities, who gave her the choice of apologizing or being expelled. Sheliubskaia refused to apologize, however, saying that she did not believe herself at fault, and the argument continued between her parents at home. She poisoned herself the next day at school, having left the following note for her teacher: "They demanded that I apologize to you, but I do not belong to that

[80] See e.g. N. Krupskaia, "Samoubiistva sredi uchashchikhsia i svobodnaia trudovaia shkola," *Svobodnoe vospitanie* no. 10 (1910–11); and N. Oettli, "K voprosu o samoubiistvakh nashei molodezhi i reforme nashei shkoly," *Svobodnoe vospitanie* no. 4 (1912–13). Many other articles were published in this left-wing journal; see no. 8 (1909–10); no. 8 (1911–12); no. 1 (1912–13); no. 4 (1914–15); no. 9 (1914–15).

[category of persons] who apologizes. You knew me as the idler Sheliubskaia. Know as well that I was raised on the principles of Hedda Gabler. My father told me to apologize, so 'I apologize.' After all this, I do not advise you to boast about your knowledge of pupils' psychology."[81] Huge crowds (numbering in the thousands, according to one local newspaper) gathered several days later to make their farewells; they were accompanied by foot patrols and mounted police. The flower-strewn coffin was carried by hand in an orderly procession to the synagogue, and many people showed up afterwards at the cemetery, though speeches were not allowed there. One wreathe from her classmates read, "to our glorious friend Sheliubskaia, who perished tragically."[82]

On the surface, this was a school-related case, and the press coverage focused upon the events leading up to the suicide, especially the intentions of the physics teacher. One newspaper explicitly blamed him, depicting his actions as a deliberate attempt to humiliate the girl. Lamenting that the tragedy would never end, it likened the school to the machines of modernity: "the wheels of our pedagogical mechanism turn just like the wheels of the soulless steel automobile, neither reckoning with living people. If the wheel accidentally catches you – farewell! Only a corpse returns." In response, an open letter signed by twenty-five parents and published in another local newspaper affirmed that this particular teacher was not the typical "automaton" found in many schools but in fact a fair man.[83] True to form, the school's director also attempted to deflect attention from the school by writing a rambling, rumor-filled report to his superiors linking her suicide to circumstances at home (involving Sarra's supposedly crude and uneducated father, a trader),[84] an (unconfirmed) pregnancy, and her reading of [Otto Weininger's] book, *Sex and Character*.[85]

Yet Sheliubskaia's own reference to Henrik Ibsen's suicidal heroine set this case apart, as one prominent columnist recognized. Though expressing pity for the agitated and unbalanced soul, he rejected the widespread idealization of Sheliubskaia – her apotheosis, he termed it – for other girls now envied her this death, this heroic refusal to reconcile herself to the surrounding "vulgarity and lies." Instead, he argued, the incident was a product of the endemic "neuroticism and diseased susceptibility" of contemporary youth. "A beautiful and proud

[81] For the initial reports of the school on the circumstances of her death, see d. 144, ll. 178–86.
[82] For the press reports on the funeral, see "Pokhorony Sarry Sheliubskoi," *Odesskoe obozrenie* (Nov. 6, 1909); and "K samoubiistvu Sarry Sheliubskoi: Pokhorony," *Odesskie novosti* (Nov. 7, 1909); both in d. 146, ll. 107, 145.
[83] See *Odesskii listok* (Nov. 6, 1909), and *Odesskie novosti* (Nov. 7, 1909). All Odessa newspapers were filled with articles on this case. For clippings, see d. 146, ll. 93, 95, 102, 105, 141–44, 146, 149.
[84] This possessed, of course, anti-Semitic overtones. For further discussion of Odessa and the image of the market, see Roshanna Sylvester, "City of Thieves: Moldavanka, Criminality, and Respectability in Pre-Revolutionary Odessa," *Journal of Urban History* 27: 2 (2001).
[85] A Russian edition was published in Moscow in 1909. For the reports, see d. 175, ll. 132–35.

death in the manner of Hedda Gabler is a lie; what is not a lie is a beautiful life, full of self-sacrifice and heroic feats. [. . .] Real, true heroism consists not in dying beautifully but in filling your surrounding life, as much as possible, with beauty, content, and the beauty of high ideals."[86] Though recognizing the symbolic importance of the literary allusion (and Sheliubskaia's desire for the heroic), this columnist dismissed the suicide as a mere symptom of sick nerves in a sick era.

The allusion deserves further consideration, however, for both the fictional act and its real-life imitation posed a set of problems integral to modern suicide. *Hedda Gabler* was one of Ibsen's most controversial plays, in part because its generic form – and, consequently, its representation of suicide – were highly ambiguous (which allowed the columnist to accuse Sarra of misinterpreting its true meaning). At issue was whether it was a tragedy or a melodrama. If the first, then Hedda Gabler's suicide possesses transcendent meaning – it enacts her heroic resistance, her freedom from the webs of social conformity that envelop modern man (and woman) and prevent true self-fulfillment. If but a melodrama, however, then her death is rendered meaningless, even absurd. This ambivalence is further played out upon the level of aesthetics: tragic death must be beautiful to be meaningful. In the play, Hedda Gabler is at first inspired by another character's suicide, but is then repulsed upon hearing of its physical ugliness – he had accidentally shot himself in his bowels rather than his heart. She herself would not make the same mistake. Yet the aestheticism of the tragic act can also call its content into question. If the meaning lies in the beauty of the pose and gesture, then is the act not deprived of substantive content? In Sarra Sheliubskaia's case, the beauty was found in the majesty of the funeral, not in the manner of death – carbolic acid poisoning causes excessive sweating, yellow eyes and skin, convulsions, and vomiting, details which were absent from press accounts. But the question remained: was it a proud and heroic form of defiance, an affirmation of her personal dignity against the teacher's insult, or a childish expression of petulance, of what her contemporaries called "diseased self-esteem"?

Tragedy or melodrama? The same quandary preoccupied the popular writer, Leonid Andreev, who had himself attempted suicide as a youth and later written two influential short stories on the topic.[87] In a brief opinion piece, he first asserted man's "sacred right" to a free death as the only "true guarantor of freedom," thereby upholding the long-established tradition associated with Cato's

---

[86] Loengrin, "Zigzagi: Po povodu samoubiistv sredi molodezhi," *Odesskie novosti* (Nov. 6, 1909). Also in d. 146, l. 106.

[87] On his suicide attempt, see L. N. Andreev, *S.O.S.: Dnevnik (1914–1919); Pis'ma (1917–1919); Stat'i i interv'iu (1919); Vospominaniia sovremennikov (1918–1919)*, ed. R. Devis and B. Khellman (Moscow and SPb, 1994), 62–64. For the two stories, "Rasskaz o Sergee Petroviche," and "V tumane," in his *Sobranie sochinenii*, 14 vols. (SPb, 1911–13), vols. 2, 4.

feat. He then stressed, however, that two distinct forms of suicide coexisted: the one inspired by man's reason, will, and strength; the other by un-reason, an absence of will, and weakness. Though difficult to distinguish in individual cases, he admitted, their difference was as great as between tragedy and melodrama. "In the first instance, the hero perishes and his death is his affirmation and completion of struggle; but in the drama – man is simply crushed, life drives over him and there is no 'self' in his [self-killing]." The distinction reflected the dependence of death upon life: "In order that a death from one's own hands becomes heroic, it is necessary that the life that is lost has value." Otherwise, man does not kill himself, but is killed by life, by "an agonizing, wretched, and incoherent life." Though he did not draw out the implications, Andreev implied that the contemporary epidemic was a product of weakness not strength, of melodrama not tragedy.[88] In this framework, the oft-lamented devaluation of life after 1905 had also devalued death, and Andreev's argument is reminiscent of Boris Savinkov's, who had claimed that the self-sacrifice of the terrorist act is only meaningful if the life given up has value. Yet Andreev was nonetheless indicting current conditions in Russia and thereby creating a space for social and political hygiene. The hundreds of youthful deaths may not be heroic protests, but they were the passive victims of an empty and devalued life. He, along with Mikhail Artsybashev, another popular writer who wrote frequently about suicide, thus affirmed the legitimacy of the principled suicide yet effectively relegated this act to the sidelines, at least for the moment.[89]

For Maksim Gorky, in contrast, the era of heroic feats had not passed into history. This influential and extremely popular writer had become the primary spokesman in Russia for the realist tradition of a socially engaged literature, and he roundly condemned what he considered the diseased pessimism, nihilism, and mysticism of modern writers, who were now failing to provide young people with positive role models. While youth had always formed the heroic vanguard of revolutionary politics in Russia, he stressed, they had fallen into despair after 1905 primarily because they were living "in a sick atmosphere, poisoned by all sorts of doubts, saturated by the smells of death, corrupting and rotting."[90] Indeed the harmful affects of reading upon the young generation became a frequent refrain in public and scholarly debates, just as it had in the late eighteenth century. Many observers lamented the dearth of social and political

---

[88] "Samoubiistvo (Nasha anketa)," *Novoe slovo* no. 6 (1912), 4–5.

[89] For Artsybashev's comments, see "Samoubiistvo (Nasha anketa)," 5–8. Of interest are also the comments of I. E. Repin who passionately condemned the act. For a different perspective, see L. N. Tolstoi and Grigorii Petrov, *O samoubiistve* (Moscow, 1910).

[90] Maksim Gorkii, "Izdaleka," *Zaprosy zhizni* no. 7 (1912), 387. Parenthetically, Gorky's belief in the heroic would find its ultimate expression under Stalin, when he co-wrote perhaps the most notorious literary work extolling the moral and political benefits of forced labor. See the translation of his co-authored work, *Belomor: An Account of the Construction of the New Canal between the White Sea and the Baltic Sea* (New York, 1935).

ideals as well as the decadent preoccupation with sex and death. Yet Gorky's images of disease and poison were not just metaphors. Instead, as a prominent psychiatrist, F. E. Rybakov, emphasized, modern literature constituted a real threat to public health. Many contemporary writers were mentally ill, he argued, and their illness – especially their unsteadiness, their diseased and exalted hyper-subjectivity – expressed itself within the very fabric of their works, corrupting the language, the characters, and the plots. These texts then spread the infection into society as whole. Nobody, not even the healthy, can evade this "mental contagion," he warned, especially in light of "the atmosphere of general nervous agitation and spiritual ferment" in Russia.[91] Just like the revolutionary idea had once spread its contagion in 1905, now the bacilli of suicide had invaded Russian literature and society.

Gorky nevertheless asserted that a renewed political engagement was possible. To begin, it was necessary to attack the "internal enemies," who artfully sowed the seeds of doubt. Then writers must once again provide the guiding lights.[92] Yet some commentators remained skeptical about Gorky's response, seeing it more as an homage to the past rather than as a real vision of the future. In their view, the doubts and pessimism engendered by both the failure of 1905 and the emptiness of commercial culture could not be countered solely by a reaffirmation of faith.[93] This depute recalls the categories of the Odessa columnist who had rejected Sheliubskaia's model of death in favor of a "beautiful life full of self-sacrifice and heroic feats." The problem was how to re-establish a transcendent meaning – a heroic narrative that would displace the profane banalities of everyday life.

Precisely this challenge preoccupied many young suicides and framed their final words. In an oft-cited note, one young woman imagined the two possible paths her life might have taken: the heroic engagement that inexorably culminated in prison, Siberian exile, and her slow physical and mental disintegration there; or the submission to everyday life that led to marriage, the vulgar "animality" of procreation, and the death of meaning. Neither seemed to be worth the trouble. "I am still pure," she emphasized. "Be glad that I depart without having succeeded in bathing myself in dirt. I do not understand the goal of human life. The fact is, we all must die. The difference is only that some do it sooner, some later."[94] Others, in contrast, identified themselves as anti-heroes, as degenerates whose very existence was harmful to the general

[91] F. E. Rybakov, *Sovremennye pisateli i bol'nye nervy* (Moscow, 1908), esp. 4–5, 43–44. On moral and mental contagion more generally, see Daniel Beer, *Renovating Russia: The Human Sciences and the Fate of Liberal Modernity in Russia, 1880–1930* (forthcoming).

[92] Gorkii, "Izdaleka," 387.

[93] Vladimir Vagner, "Samoubiistvo i filosofskii pessimizm," *Zaprosy zhizni* no. 49 (1912), 2811–16.

[94] Khlopin, *Samoubiistva*, v 1907, 53. Further discussed in Mariia Raikh, "Iunye samoubiitsy i ikh pis'ma," *Zhenskoe delo* no. 8 (1910), 7.

welfare. One young woman, only 18 years old, employed a metaphor commonly used by degeneration theorists. Before drowning herself, she curtly observed: "a weed must be pulled from the ground." (The doctor subsequently diagnosed acute neurasthenia.)[95] A young man explained his decision to shoot himself in terms likewise reminiscent of the public discussions of youthful unsteadiness and weakness: "I believe that my primary failing is a lack of will. It would have been necessary, as much as possible, to correct this evil. [. . .] But this proved impossible. Everybody is weak now, everybody needs support, and I only increase the number of powerless people."[96]

Countless suicide notes protested the profanity of existence and lamented their own powerlessness to change it. Such motifs had already been associated with suicide during the second half of the nineteenth century, but they were now reworked into the contemporary setting. When two friends shot themselves in 1907, they left notes exploring this theme. "The deformed conditions of life in general are responsible [for my death]," wrote one of these young women. "There is already too much dirt, vulgarity, and baseness. Every manifestation of thought, [every] honest expression of feeling, every protest against injustice is stifled by life. [. . .] There is no place to move, no strength to breathe. And how much use can one be within contemporary conditions of life? I don't want to be a half-animal, a half-corpse like the vast majority. What is the point of living?"[97] Her friend provided a slightly different explanation, and her autobiographical narrative recalls the letter of Natal'ia Klimova, the woman who had resolved the disjunctions of life in her dedication to revolutionary terrorism. In contrast to Klimova, who was both content with her choice and joyous in her pantheistic celebration of life, this young woman translated the end of the revolution into her own personal failure:

I came to the thought of suicide after a prolonged meditation on life and what nature provided me for this life. Contemplating life I saw an abyss of evil, I saw that life is terribly mutilated, deformed, perverted. Already a few years ago all these negative sides of life took away my desire to live. But then I did not choose suicide but began to search for another exit. And I found one. I remained alive solely in order to fight against evil in all its manifestations and to sow seeds of good upon the hard-won territory. In this struggle and consequent work, I set myself the goal of striving for the higher principles of truth, good, and beauty, to strive for freedom, justice, and light . . . in a word, for all that is the best, the beautiful, the exalted in the world. [. . .] Thus I lived the last three years, but then I began, somehow involuntarily, to turn my attention upon that which I had accomplished. I discovered that it was too little, a kind of microscopic size. [. . .] I came to the sad conclusion, that nature had given me too little for the kind of life that

---

[95] The letter was reprinted in Khlopin, *Samoubiistva*, v 1907, 50. For the report on its author, Alexandra Polezhaeva, see d. 106, l. 185

[96] Khlopin, *Samoubiistva*, v 1908, 63. This was the case of Vladislav Shchepanovskii, who shot himself.

[97] Khlopin, *Samoubiistva*, v 1907, 54.

justifies staying alive. When I understood this, not the smallest desire to live remained. I do not want to live and to bring society only that amount of use of which I am capable [. . .] Such people are many in our society.[98]

Readers of such notes were most troubled by the age of their authors. These two women in particular were only 16 and 17 years old. How could they be so despairing whilst so young? Alongside this constant refrain, however, was an underlying comprehension. At least their ideals – truth, freedom, justice, good, beauty – made sense. After all, these were the goals of a heroic narrative: the search for the absolute and transcendent, the elimination of the unclean and profane.

Still more disturbing, therefore, was the possibility that these ideals had themselves lost meaning. Also at issue for many observers – parents, journalists, doctors – was whether Russia's youth had now acquired a false view of the heroic. Were youthful suicides "heroes of emptiness" in an "epoch of decline"?[99] Had political protest degenerated into the trivial dramas of personal and sexual life? Was the school not a prison but really just a school? This point returns full circle to Hedda Gabler and her imitator Sarra Sheliubskaia. The problem, as they saw it, was that modern literature was not just infecting young people with pessimism and a sense of powerlessness; it was also providing false heroes, especially those Nietzschean supermen who based their claim to heroism not on political models but on their rejection of social and especially sexual conventions. Within the Russian literary canon, Artsybashev's controversial hero Sanin was the primary exemplar of this new kind of hero. Completely uninterested in political and social issues, he scorned all limits placed upon his individual freedom and self-expression, including – with his lust for his sister – the ultimate prohibition of incest. Sanin does not kill himself, though he does encourage another character to do so.[100] The novel was blamed, however, for inspiring young people to reject social activism in favor of extreme individualism. In the wake of their political disappointment, it was widely alleged, young people were turning inwards, losing themselves in personal concerns and sexual debauchery. Symbolic of this decadence were the notorious (if poorly documented) "leagues of free love," in which young people were supposedly initiated into the mysteries of carnal pleasure. Zhbankov wrote extensively about what he termed the sexual bacchanalia of these years, and he causally linked it to the epidemic of suicide.[101] He was not alone. Others, too, perceived a decline from political consciousness into private pleasures, and

[98] Ibid., 54–55.
[99] Unicus, *O samoubiitsakh nashego vremeni* (Nizhnii Novgorod, 1910), 2–3.
[100] See the new translation with a useful introduction by Otto Boele, Mikhail Artsybashev, *Sanin: A Novel*, trans. Michael R. Katz (Ithaca, N. Y., 2001).
[101] See D. Zhbankov, "Polovaia vakkhanaliia i polovye nasiliia: Pir vo vremia chumy," *Prakticheskii vrach* nos. 17–19 (1908); and "Polovaia prestupnost'," *Sovremennyi mir*

they pondered the many implications. Whereas young people had once lived in and for the future, sustained by a vision of freedom, justice, and equality, they were now condemned to an endless, meaningless, and profane present, the only exit from which was death.[102] Conservatives perceived the same pattern, though they formulated it in a different language: "It is, of course, but one step from Sanin to suicide. When a person turns himself into a beast [*oskotinivat'sia*], when he destroys everything in himself that distinguishes him from an animal, then there is no other path."[103]

The new refrain was "to live for the moment," but such a vision of an eternal present seemed to lead only to death. And young people were dying for no apparent reason, simply for the moment. Two teenagers had fallen in love and met every day for three years. One afternoon they brought fruit, sweets, and a revolver to a grassy field and shot themselves there, having left the following note: "We decided to die because we love each other. We request that nobody be blamed for our deaths. We die cheerfully." From the perspective of the journalist, the act reflected their desire to die amidst the poetry of love, before its decline into the prose of everyday life.[104] Other people were motivated by the desire to die beautifully. One young man saw his death as a grandiose and meaningful gesture. He left the following note of explanation: "In my death I ask that nobody be blamed. I make my farewells to the sons of the earth and depart to the children of the sun. I say to the entire world: Humanity – fight for aristocratic individualism. Long live H. Ibsen and F. Nietzsche."[105] In other instances, meaning was attached to the specific rituals and aesthetics of the act. Before drinking cyanide together, three teenage girls put on white dresses, played Chopin's funeral march on the piano, danced, and arranged their bodies artfully around the room. Newspapers then published wood-block prints claiming to depict the arrangement of the bodies upon their discovery[106] (Illus. 9). This suicide was fashioned as a *tableau mort*, an attempt to confer a purely aesthetic order upon the empty profanity of life, and the massive funeral procession through St. Petersburg provided the appropriate finale. For two other teenage girls, in contrast, the beauty of suicide lay less in the act than in the burial. Rather than discuss their motives or ritualize their final moments, they

no. 7 (1909). See also A. Gladkii, "Vzgliad khudozhnikov na zhizn' i samoubiistvo," *Vestnik vospitaniia* no. 6 (1913).

[102] For a good example of this perspective, see the letter to the editor excerpted in the column of K. Slavnin, "K bor'be s samoubiistvom," *Novaia Rus'* (Aug. 17, 1909); clipped in d. 145, l. 256.

[103] L. M., "Druz'ia smerti," *Zemshchina* (Feb. 16, 1912); clipped in GARF, f. 102, DP IV, 1912, d. 151, l. 7. For other examples, see Stefan Kedrovich, "Gde prichiny?" *Kolokol* (Oct. 15, 1909); and "Bolezn' nashikh dnei," *Volga* (Oct. 25, 1909). Clipped in d. 146, ll. 60, 76.

[104] See Skitalets, "Umiraem veselo," *Gazeta kopeika* (Oct. 10, 1909); clipped in d. 146, l. 49.

[105] Printed in *Tambovskii krai* (Aug. 17, 1908); clipped in d. 124, l. 79.

[106] For further discussion of this case, see my "Suicide and Civilization in Late Imperial Russia," *Jahrbücher für Geschichte Osteuropas* no. 2 (1995).

Illus. 9 The boulevard press published many prints depicting suicides, especially, as in this case, the discovery of the body. This sensationalism was an integral part of the newspaper coverage of the epidemic. From "Triple Suicide Pact," *Peterburgskii listok* (March 4, 1910).

used their notes to direct the organization of their funerals – their dresses and hair styles, the flowers, the pall bearers, and so forth.[107] Despite their endless variation, these cases had one quality in common: the authorship of the self in self-willed death. Whereas the revolutionary suicide had embodied a politics of redemption and transcendence, these deaths were self-referential. The meaning of the act was the act itself.

The large number of such cases fed the persistent rumors about mysterious suicide clubs that periodically broke out in these years, usually propelled by titillating reports in the media. A parallel phenomenon to the purported leagues of free love, these groups were not unique to Russia but a (reputed) phenomenon throughout the Western world and more recently in Japan.[108] Their structure generally followed the same basic pattern. Members of the club would meet regularly at secret meetings during which a kind of lottery would occur. The person who "won" would then be obligated to kill him or herself within a specified period of time. Occasionally, as in Robert Louis Stevenson's famous story, a double lottery would select both the suicide victim and the agent of death, thereby removing the burden of self-killing.[109] Almost all accounts, Western

---

[107] See d. 147, ll. 2–3.

[108] See the examples listed in G. I. Gordon, "Kluby samoubiits," *Sovremennoe slovo* (Jan. 25, 1911).

[109] Robert Louis Stevenson, *The Suicide Club* (reprint: 2000). Numerous films have been based upon this work, starting with a four minute short film from 1909 directed by D. W. Griffith,

and Russian, emphasized the youth of members, their generally high level of education, and their commitment to the principle of suicide, that is, their rejection of life upon philosophical grounds. Within the Russian context, this last point was especially prominent, and descriptions of these groups evoked the image of the underground study circle (*kruzhok*), an archetypical institution of revolutionary education. Common to both were the ritualized secrecy, formal charters, the notion of members as a privileged "elect," and even the goal of propagandizing a worldview (albeit in the latter instance around the ideal of suicide). Indeed, accounts almost universally described not decadent drinking and maudlin conversation, but rather the vigor of a circle with animated discussions, the presentation of learned papers, and the leadership of a charismatic figure. Their professed goal was social: to liberate humanity from suffering through voluntary self-destruction.[110] Interest in the suicide club was so great that Russia's elite political police conducted several investigations between 1912 and 1915.[111] Conclusive evidence either way was never found, though Dr. Gordon was convinced that they really did exist, in Europe as in Russia. Precisely in periods of decline, alienation, and repression, when freedom and progress are suppressed, he contended, "then unification becomes possible upon the basis of death, upon the basis of suicide."[112]

In important respects, the suicide club became an emblem of the epidemic. Its form and ethos were obvious counterparts, even a parody, of revolutionary institutions. Not only did it provide a kind of banner under which individuals united in solidarity, but it even constituted a means to overcome the proverbial anonymity and alienation of life in the modern city.[113] Yet its ethos of liberation promised not redemption, not transcendence, but only death. That the governing motif was chance provided in turn a potent symbol of this meaninglessness. These suicides really did not possess any motive or cause but were determined only by fate – the draw of the cards, the fall of the roulette ball, the throw of the dice. Many fictional and eyewitness accounts emphasized the pleasure of the risk-taking, the almost unbearable and hence electrifying suspense, details reminiscent of high-stakes gambling. This parallel is apt for another reason. As

through *The Suicide Club*, dir. Maurice Elvey, 1914; and *Robert Louis Stevenson's The Suicide Club*, dir. Rachel Samuels, 2000. For more information on these and other adaptations, see www.dinamico.unibg.it/rls/films.htm#suicide (consulted July 4, 2005). For a modern Japanese film on the topic, see *Suicide Club*, dir. Sion Sono, 2002.

[110] For accounts, see N. Pruzhanskii, *Zhizn' ili smert': O samoubiitsakh* (SPb, 1908), 5–9; the letter to the editor signed N. Fon-Guk, "Liga samoubiits v Peterburge," *Birzhevye vedomosti* (Feb. 6, 1912), clipped in GARF, f. 102, DP IV, 1912, d. 151, l. 1; and the purloined letter of S. Ogloblin (dated Apr. 5, 1915) in GARF, f. 102, DP OO, 1914, op. 244, d. 226, l. 3.

[111] Newspaper clippings and investigative reports were collected in GARF, f. 102, DP IV, 1912, d. 151; and f. 102, DP OO, 1914, op. 244, d. 226.

[112] See Gordon, "Kluby samoubiits."

[113] Another kind of group was founded for the same reason, to unite the lonely, but it sought to prevent suicide. See M. Liberson, *Stradanie odinochestva* (SPb, 1909).

in early nineteenth-century narratives of gambling, suicide became an obligation of personal honor; membership and participation in the club constituted a kind of commitment to bow to fate.[114]

Despite their repetition, these tales did not lose their ability to shock, and observers were divided. In 1908 and 1912, a rash of such rumors prompted intense public debates, including exchanges between feuilleton writers and their readers, who sent dozens of letters to newspapers. One of these exchanges was even reprinted as a pamphlet (Illus. 10). According to the journalist, these were "small, insignificant little people with monstrous self-esteem, who terribly wanted to distinguish themselves somehow from the crowd, to display their insignificant I, but they are [really] so ordinary that they have no other means to do so than to commit suicide." Others perceived more heroic natures, suggesting that the rejection of life was really a rejection of slavery and submission. One reader further noted that the great writers Andreev and Gorky had each attempted suicide, and he conjectured that the Romantic poet Mikhail Lermontov would have himself joined such a club had one existed at that time.[115] The controversy over the suicide club thus replicated the broader debates about revolution, freedom, and violence. The search for meaning had seemingly culminated in a heroic, yet empty death.

A term that frequently recurred in both the specialist and popular discussions of epidemic suicide was unsteadiness (*neustoichivost'*), and it connoted an entire range of undesirable and pathological traits of character.[116] As one specialist summarized:

It is necessary to recognize the extreme nervousness of our youth as the principal, fundamental cause [of suicide], and united with this nervousness is a staggering weakness of will, an inertia, a flabbiness, a want of habit in overcoming obstacles, an absence of hardiness, a tendency to drop ones hands quickly and fall into despair, a total inability to struggle with the unpleasantness met in the lives of every person. Therefore, we need not waste our energy in searching for motives for each individual suicide [. . .] but must concentrate our attention upon studying the causes of this nervousness [. . .] and finding the means to give our youth what it now lacks: physical and moral strength, a fortified will, tenacity, firmness and determination, fearlessness in the struggle with the adversities of life, the ability to work for the achievement of set goals.[117]

These desirable traits recall the positive hero, whose exceptional qualities had long been extolled within both the (radical) literary canon and revolutionary

[114] See GARF, f. 102, DP IV, 1912, d. 151, l. 1; and the letter to the editor likening both life and death to a game of chance, reprinted in Pruzhanskii, *Zhizn' ili smert'*, 19.
[115] Pruzhanskii, *Zhizn' ili smert'*, 8, 17, 21–22, and *passim*.
[116] I am indebted to my discussions with Daniel Beer on this point, as on others.
[117] N. Vysotskii, "Zadachi shkoly v bor'be s samoubiistvami uchashchikhsia," *Russkaia shkola* nos. 4, 5/6 (1910), no. 4, 54.

Illus. 10 A newspaper column that led to a lively debate between readers and
the columnist on the meaning of suicide clubs was published in book form with
this sensational cover. The title reads: "Life or Death: About Suicides," from
N. Pruzhanskii, *Zhizn' ili smert': O samoubiitsakh* (St. Petersburg, 1908).

hagiography. The heroes of the revolution, those martyrs to the violence of autocracy, had reputedly possessed personal strength and fearlessness in struggle, fortitude and determination – in a word, *stoikost'*, the steadfastness that embodied and promised the final victory. This convergence between the political and the medical was not causal, for these discourses possessed their own developmental traditions. But it did facilitate a creative process of conversion: the shadow companion of the revolutionary hero was the weak and diseased degenerate. Many young suicides drew their inspiration from both sets of images and, in turn, transformed their own words and bodies into public spectacles. Death seemed to provide them a way to resolve the disjunctions of life, either by affirming their selfhood or by destroying it. The preservation of life was less important than its embodiment in a principle, whether dignity, purity, or what can perhaps be termed social utility (the elimination of the self as weak or unfit). In this sense, they did not aspire to a liberal ideal of the individual, that is, one who authors the self through determination, resilience, hard work, and overcoming adversity. Indeed, this was the real point of the passage above – not to glorify the hero in the act of self-sacrifice but to laud perseverance and steadfastness in everyday life.

The resonance of epidemic suicide played precisely upon these conversions. Were suicides heroes or degenerates? Perhaps the best answer is that they were both and neither. The very conceptualization of the suicidal act in Russia had long contained this inherent duality, rendering all suicides potentially heroic and degenerate, sacred and profane. Despite the frequent accusations heaped upon the government for its reactionary policies and obstruction of prophylactic measures, epidemic suicide was primarily understood as a symptom of a disease within the social body. The failure of the 1905 revolution had been a failure of Russian society, which had proven too weak and flabby to overcome obstacles and achieve its goal: the reconstitution of the body politic. The binary categories of the epidemic referred simultaneously to the individual suicides and to Russian society as a whole. After all, Babienko may have condemned the burden of the state school, but he had directed his protest to society, its inertia, apathy, and torpor in the face of blood and suffering. In rejecting the profane, everyday life of a stagnant present, he conceived his voluntary death as a means to achieve Russia's redemption. With his "drop of blood," as he called it, he sought to re-inaugurate the sacred, eschatological time of revolution.

Epilogue

> But then I understood that there was an exit and that I would only see happiness
> and joy there, ahead, on the edge of death.
>
> Natal'ia Klimova, "Letter before Execution," 1907

> And we are not only, in Foucault's words, animals whose life as living beings
> is at issue in their politics, but also – inversely – citizens whose very politics
> is at issue in their natural body.
>
> Giorgio Agamben, *Homo Sacer: Sovereign Power and Bare Life*, 1998

People have taken their own lives throughout human history. Suicide has consequently been regarded as an anthropological or social constant, even a defining component of our humanity. Yet this perspective represents a particularly modern approach to the phenomenon. The very notion of a common humanity (and hence universal human rights) is itself a modern one, for being has historically been qualified by a wide range of criteria: citizenship, caste, gender, estate, class, race, religion, and so forth. This propensity to universalize the human element within suicide obscures in turn both its historically distinctive meanings as well as the striking repetitions over time. Indeed, its valuation has fluctuated widely, not just its positive or negative judgment but also its relative importance. Suicide was an issue during the Enlightenment, for example, but only a marginal one; it was certainly not considered, as Albert Camus famously claimed, the one truly serious philosophical question. In charting how suicide became an iconic act in late imperial Russia, this book has argued for a particular relationship between suicide and modernity, but one that was contingent and historical, not universal in nature.

Modernity thus has its own traditions. Yet because the modern is often defined against the traditional (and thereby invents it), these two categories have usually been cast as opposites – the one dynamic and productive, the other stable and unchanging. As such they can represent sequential stages of historical development.[1] This normative framework can produce the concept of an "incomplete" or "deformed" modernity, a problem which preoccupied many Russians in the

---

[1] On tradition and modernity, see Talal Asad, *Formations of the Secular: Christianity, Islam, Modernity* (Stanford, 2003), esp. 12–16; and his *Genealogies of Religion: Discipline and Reasons*

late imperial period. It continued to plague the Bolsheviks, who feared the contamination of their project with the remnants of the past and who themselves were accused of rushing history, thereby perverting the true nature of socialism. The problem has also been projected upon the map of Europe, sometimes to Russia's intended advantage but more often to its detriment. Whereas tradition was typically "Russian," modernity was a European import. These categories have likewise shaped the historical interpretation of the Soviet experiment, with Stalinism in particular described as a resurgence of such "native" Russian traditions as authoritarianism, peasant mentalities, and so forth.[2]

More recently, modernity has itself become an important category in the historiography of Russia. Many historians now view the early Soviet era as a particular incarnation of a pan-European modernist project that built upon a set of scientific and political technologies developed in late nineteenth-century Europe. The Bolsheviks' self-assigned task was thus to reconstitute, administer, and rationalize the social (in part by eliminating "tradition" – superstition, ignorance, peasant agriculture).[3] A second strand of historiography has instead focused on the other modernity, not the emergence of the "all-seeing" or "garden" state, but the making and unmaking of identities, the fragmentation of truth and reason. Its locus was the late-imperial metropolis, with its new technologies, glass palaces, and poetics of estrangement.[4] Despite their many achievements and considerable merits, these approaches have inadvertently flattened our reading of Russia's modernity. They often perpetuate the old divisions

of Power in Christianity and Islam (Baltimore, 1993). See also Eric Hobsbawm and Terence Ranger, eds., The Invention of Tradition (Cambridge, 1992).

[2] See especially Robert Tucker, "Stalinism as Revolution from Above," in Tucker, ed., Stalinism: Essays in Historical Interpretation (New York, 1977); Moshe Lewin, The Making of the Soviet System: Essays in the Social History of Interwar Russia (New York, 1985); and Nicholas Timasheff, The Great Retreat: The Growth and Decline of Communism in Russia (New York, 1946).

[3] The literature is too extensive to cite here. Of particular importance in setting the terms of debate was Stephen Kotkin, Magnetic Mountain: Stalinism as Civilization (Berkeley, 1995). In historicizing the political-scientific technologies and practices of the Bolsheviks, Peter Holquist has moved progressively back in time, initially focusing upon World War I but more recently upon the colonial heritage. See especially his "To Count, to Extract, and to Exterminate: Population Statistics and Population Politics in Late Imperial and Soviet Russia," in Ronald Gregor Suny and Terry Martin, eds., A State of Nations: Empire and Nation-Making in the Age of Lenin and Stalin (New York, 2001). The comparative perspective is central. See also Amir Weiner, ed., Landscaping the Human Garden: Twentieth-Century Population Management in a Comparative Framework (Stanford, 2003).

[4] The best examples, both of which focus upon issues of self-fashioning, are Louise McReynolds, Russia at Play: Leisure Activities at the End of the Tsarist Era (Ithaca, N.Y., 2003); and Mark Steinberg, Proletarian Imagination: Self, Modernity, and the Sacred in Russia, 1910–25 (Ithaca, N.Y., 2002), esp. 5–9 for a useful definition of the term. In contrast, both Laura Engelstein and Daniel Beer examine issues of discipline within late-imperial Russian liberalism, though with contrasting arguments. See Engelstein's The Keys to Happiness: Sex and the Search for Modernity in Fin-de-Siècle Russia (Ithaca, N.Y., 1992); and Beer, Renovating Russia: The Human Sciences and the Fate of Liberal Modernity in Russia, 1880–1930 (forthcoming).

between political and social history, with the one privileging the mechanisms of disciplinary and state power, the other social life and self-fashioning. Only occasionally do the two interact.[5] With their almost exclusive emphasis on the period after 1861 – or, more typically, 1900 and 1917 – they have also created a modernity without traditions or, perhaps more accurately, without Russian traditions.[6]

The early twentieth century marks the end, not the beginning of this book. The shift in temporal perspective helps to destabilize conventional narratives. The point is not to reveal the invention of modernity, though the concept was certainly invented, but rather to explore its inventiveness. Russia's modernity was a kaleidoscope of multiple traditions and influences, Russian and Western, a kaleidoscope that combined both faces, the regulatory project and the politics of identity. Suicide is an ideal, if disturbing, topic for this kind of investigation; it is a conjoined phenomenon and act, an object of regulation and a form of self-fashioning. Its history in Russia – as elsewhere – was marked not by a progression from tradition to modernity, but a complex interplay of regulatory and objectifying forces (religious, legal, administrative, scientific, social) with individual, subjectifying interventions, enduring cultural tropes with specific historical appropriations. Even as patterns persisted over time, they were recast and reshaped, whether grafted onto other practices or displaced into new contexts. These echoes, repetitions, and affinities were creative, constitutive in turn of new meanings and practices even as they evoked prior ones. This study has taken the words and actions of individuals seriously, not to reveal either the true, underlying cause of suicide or its inherent meaning, but rather to restore politics and contingency to its cultural history.

Why did suicide become such a highly political act in twentieth-century Russia? The answer in part is that it had always been political. In Muscovy, it had been configured as a form of disobedience against God and his representatives on earth, as an act associated with demonic forces as well as worldly

---

[5] For two studies which explore individuation within the categories of Soviet modernity, see Igal Halfin, *Terror in My Soul: Communist Autobiographies on Trial* (Cambridge, Mass., 2003); and Jochen Hellbeck, *Revolution on My Mind: Writing a Diary Under Stalin* (Cambridge, Mass., 2006). Another study focuses on regulation but also seeks to integrate individuals, primarily within the parameters of dissent (or resistance). See Dan Healey, *Homosexual Desire in Revolutionary Russia: The Regulation of Sexual and Gender Dissent* (Chicago, 2001).

[6] The so-called neo-traditionalists emphasize the persistence of Russian traditions after 1917 (such as the practice of petition writing). Many excellent studies have been published, but the conceptualization of the traditional and the modern remains an unresolved issue. For a general discussion, see Terry Martin, "Modernization or Neo-Traditionalism? Ascribed Nationality and Soviet Primordialism," in David Hoffman and Yanni Kotsonis, eds., *Russian Modernity: Politics, Knowledge, Practices* (London, 2000). In an otherwise interesting study, Oleg Kharkhordin has situated Soviet surveillance in a Russian tradition, but his linkage of the medieval to the modern is not convincing. See his *The Collective and the Individual in Russia* (Berkeley, 1999).

immorality and self-will. Martyrdom, in contrast, was a virtuous submission to God's plan. The late seventeenth century marked a period of crisis and transition. The spectacle of mass self-immolation occurred within a transcendent idiom: whereas the dissenters craved eternal salvation, believing their fiery sacrifice to be divinely consecrated, their opponents construed their deaths as demonic, leading only to eternal perdition. Yet the branding of these self-styled martyr-doms as suicides also superimposed a worldly idiom, a conversion that was reinforced by governmental intervention, both in the repression of Old Belief and in the criminalization of suicide. Henceforth, suicide was also framed within the ideology of absolutism and the service state. The techniques developed by the government to regulate suicide displayed the personal basis of autocratic power, its ethos of tutelage, and its self-representation as a well-ordered polity. Yet tutelage itself should not be understood as particularly Russian or archaic (especially given its important place in most European welfare states). The tute-lary practices of governance in imperial Russia formed one part of the state-led project of modernization until the mid-nineteenth century. One result was the politicization of suicide, usually implicit, as a violation of the socio-political order. This occurred partly as a by-product of its reception by officials and, at times, a critical public. However, the processes of cultural Westernization had also provided educated individuals with a new array of images, narratives, and ideals with which to author their lives, including sometimes their deaths.

By the mid-nineteenth century, the meanings of self-killing, especially its nexus with paternal authority, were shifting. Not just an outcome of violence, as on the manor estate, it could be an answer to it – an accusation, a form of protest. Fundamental to this conversion were also new understandings of suicide. Just as the idiom of sentimentalism was encouraging a view of the act tinged with pity and compassion, making the perpetrator into a kind of victim, new scientific paradigms were likewise undermining its criminal and moral agency. Yet a crucial factor was also the elaboration of a new symbol and source of transcendent meaning: the human being, the sacred and inviolable dignity of the personality. Paradoxically, perhaps, suicide became a perceived (if contested) means to affirm and defend the sanctity of life – not life in itself, but life infused with justice, truth, and value. At the same time, however, the languages of science translated the phenomenon into a sign and symptom of pathology, of diseases spreading within the social body. When these two configurations meshed, in turn, with the symbols, narratives, and practices of revolutionary politics, they produced new potentialities of meaning and action. Alongside new programs of intervention into the social body (to treat its ills, to excise its sores, to increase its vitality and productivity) were also new forums for death, both suicide and mass political violence.

These issues echoed across the 1917 divide. Indeed, the revolution produced new inflections upon familiar themes. The history of suicide in the 1920s can be first understood within the parameters of the modernist state.[7] By the time suicide began to emerge as a significant issue in 1921–22, the old criminal statutes on suicide and attempted suicide had been eliminated, and the new government was promoting a scientific approach to the problem that resonated with many doctors, psychiatrists and social scientists, despite some ideological differences. The revolution seemed to promise the radical socio-economic and political transformation they had long thought necessary to combat suicide and other social problems. The ultimate achievement of socialism – its collectivism, social solidarity, and rational economic order – would then herald the end of suicide, for individuals would no longer have reason to take their own lives. Its persistence in the meantime continued to be read as a by-product of modernization, but also as an archaic remnant of the old, pre-revolutionary world, a result of petty-bourgeois influences and mentalities. Alongside the regulatory framework, however, NEP-era suicide also raised challenging issues of identity and symbolic meaning. Many individuals continued to author their deaths as a means to act politically, whether to criticize the shortcomings of the new regime or to eliminate the self as unfit.[8]

Yet revolutionary politics raised the stakes in the dispute over sovereignty, over the right to determine life and death. By the late 1920s, suicide had become an anti-Soviet act. For Communists, it represented a failure to subordinate personal life to the interests of the party and revolution, a degenerate unsteadiness (*neustoichivost'*) indicative of the absence of political consciousness, an absence that could be caused by medical factors (pathology) or political will (treason).[9] Indeed, suicide and consciousness were explicitly construed as

---

[7] For the history of suicide in the 1920s, on which this discussion draws, see Kenneth Pinnow, "Making Suicide Soviet: Medicine, Moral Statistics, and the Politics of Social Science in Bolshevik Russia, 1920–1930" (Ph.D. Dissertation, Columbia University, 1998); and his "Violence Against the Collective Self and the Problem of Social Integration in Early Bolshevik Russia," *Kritika* 4: 3 (Summer 2003); and "Cutting and Counting: Forensic Medicine as a Science of Society in Bolshevik Russia, 1920–29," in David Hoffman and Yanni Kotsonis, eds., *Russian Modernity: Politics, Knowledge, Practices* (London, 2000).

[8] Although they are interpreted purely within the context of early Soviet history, examples are cited and discussed in the following works: Anne E. Gorsuch, *Youth in Revolutionary Russia: Enthusiasts, Bohemians, Delinquents* (Bloomington, Ind., 2000), 177–79; Vladimir Brovkin, *Russia After Lenin: Politics, Culture, and Society 1921–29* (London, 1998), 53–54, 128–29; Gábor T. Rittersporn, "Between Revolution and Daily Routine: Youth and Violence in the Soviet Union in the Interwar Period," in Corinna Kuhr-Korolev, Stefan Plaggenborg, and Monica Wellman, eds., *Sowjetjugend 1917–1941: Generation zwischen Revolution und Resignation* (Essen, 2001), 72–78; Sergei Zhuravlev, "Sowjetjugend im Spannungsfeld unterschiedlicher Gewaltformen," in Kuhr-Korolev et al., *Sowjetjugend*, 91–92; and Vera Spiertz, "Geheime Berichte über den Freitod junger Rotarmisten (1923–1927)," in Kuhr-Korolev et al., *Sowjetjugend*.

[9] In 1927, Trotsky's ally Adolf Ioffe shot himself, citing his own poor health and political difficulties but also rendering his act a protest. At the Fifteenth Party Congress, Emelian Iaroslavskii mounted a combined medical-political attack, denouncing Ioffe as mentally ill but also as decadent and morally rotten, suffering from a Karamozov-like degradation. See the discussion in Halfin, *Terror in My Soul:* 275–76; and Adam Ulam, *Stalin: The Man and his Era* (Boston, 1973), 285–86.

opposites, as one commentator explained: "He who is a conscious Communist or a conscious worker cannot become a suicide because he does not belong to himself and is not his private property. Rather he belongs to his Party and his class."[10] Within the heroic context of building socialism, moreover, the rendition of suicide as a social problem – an index of collective ills – had become politically unviable, and suicide statistics disappeared.[11] A century after Nicholas I's minister of education had first demanded it, therefore, this negative phenomenon was finally plunged into oblivion.

Nevertheless, the individual act found two significant expressions in the political rhetoric and practices of Stalinism. The first configuration built upon the well-established phenomenon of instigated suicide.[12] During the 1930s, cases of suicides were investigated in some detail with attention focusing on whether the act had been provoked by an abuse of authority on the part of local officials or some other kind of cruelty or maltreatment. The premise of investigations was that some suicides were attempting to send a message to the state, which was often apparently the case.[13] The act had now become a calculated dialogue on both sides: some people actively authored their deaths as "victimization" or accusation; and the state actively read suicides in search of such meanings. The second configuration evoked the traditions of heroic death. As tensions mounted towards the bacchanalia of violence in 1937–38, suicide was sometimes chosen as the ultimate proof of innocence, of being a good and honorable Communist. In response, however, such acts were categorized as "anti-party weapons" and plots, a means, in Stalin's words, to "spit at and deceive the Party."[14] Suicide was again configured as an act of illegitimate self-will, a refusal to submit to constituted authority (the Party). In this political dispute over sovereignty, the suicide was an enemy of the people to be ritually excised from the Soviet body politic.

[10] As quoted in Pinnow, "Making Suicide Soviet," 61. Following the suicide of the poet Vladimir Maiakovskii in 1930, Gorky defended a highly limited right to suicide, which prompted a heated polemic by a physician, who rejected all justifications, arguing that a person belongs to his society, not to himself. Discussed in Pinnow, "Making Suicide Soviet," 62–63.
[11] This absence largely continued until the 1990s. See Gábor T. Rittersporn, "Le Message des données introuvables: L'Etat et les statistiques du suicide en Russie et en URSS," *Cahiers du monde russe* 38: 4 (1997).
[12] Despite the decriminalization of suicide, criminal statutes on instigation had been retained, and one police source from 1924 estimated that it occurred in 5–10 percent of cases. On the legal aspects, see Pinnow, "Making Suicide Soviet," 85 n.10. For the estimate on its incidence, see A. Uchebatov, "Samoubiistva i organy doznaniia," *Raboche-Krest'ianskaia militsiia*, no. 7/8 (1924), 21–23.
[13] Sheila Fitzpatrick, *Everyday Stalinism: Ordinary Life in Extraordinary Times: Soviet Russia in the 1930s* (New York, 1999), 172–75.
[14] J. Arch Getty and Oleg V. Naumov, *The Road to Terror: Stalin and the Self-Destruction of the Bolsheviks, 1932–1939* (New Haven, 1999), 321–22, and *passim*. Fitzpatrick (*Everyday Stalinism,* 175) also notes this motif. Most important is the discussion of Communist death in Halfin, *Terror in My Soul,* 274–83.

Yet some Communists now accepted the necessity of submerging the self into the historical movement, a necessity that could also frame a voluntary death. The most famous example is Nikolai Bukharin, whose decision to participate in his trial and execution was immortalized in Arthur Koestler's novel, *Darkness at Noon*. In explaining his decision to "repent" during his final speech before the court, Bukharin described the meaninglessness of a death – its "black vacuity" – outside the Soviet project. Only repentance, going down upon his knees before the Party, would end his inhuman isolation from that which constituted "the essence of life." Later, not long before his execution, Bukharin recounted in a personal letter how he was filled with "enormous, limitless love."[15]

His words recall those of Natal'ia Klimova, the young terrorist who had celebrated her pantheistic joy in the plenitude of life while awaiting her death sentence. Though divided by some three decades, their words merit comparison. "This [feeling of] limitless universal love," she wrote, "brings the very fact of individual death down to a level not of a terrible but of a simple and inconsequential if very interesting phenomenon." Her dedication to the revolutionary ideal (and its requisite violence) had allowed her to conquer the ultimate fear: "Death – strict, secret, terrible – always burdens man, his will, his truth. Death turns the heart to ice, fetters desire, binds the will, and only those who have been able to throw the burden [of death] from their shoulders can joyfully proclaim: 'Oh, yes, now I am free, because there is no power on earth before which I must bow my desire.' And I did it, and I am free." Even as Klimova found her "I" on the edge of death, she did not expect immortality; she instead imagined her body converted into the spring grass of 1907, her life energy into electricity.[16] Bukharin, in contrast, bowed his "I" to the Party, rendering his death an act of reconciliation. He thus hoped for posthumous rehabilitation, that is, for his political immortality. These two particular, not universal cases illuminate the politics of subjectivity within modern forms of voluntary, political death. They do not conform to the more straightforward paradigms, especially the opposing images of active "individualism" (the affirmation of personal freedom or autonomy) and passive "victimization" (the loss of self through external violence, medical pathology, social anomie). Instead, selfhood could be affirmed – and freely sacrificed – within an idiom of loving submission (to History and the Party) and joyful dissolution (into natural life).

In many respects, suicide became an exemplary act and phenomenon of the modern era, integral to the emergence of the modern disciplines of sociology and

---

[15] For the transcripts, Robert C. Tucker and Stephen F. Cohen, eds., *The Great Purge Trial* (New York, 1965), 666–67. Bukharin again refers to repentance in his prison correspondence, as quoted in Halfin, *Terror in My Soul*, 280. I draw in general on Halfin (280–83), who suggestively describes entrance to the party as a form of suicide: the death of the autonomous individual in a fusion with the movement, that is, with History.

[16] "Pis'mo pered kazn'iu," *Obrazovanie* no. 8 (1908), 65–70.

psychiatry but also to modern dilemmas about the self, freedom and obligation, redemption and transcendence. Although Russia's experiences were historically specific, many of the same issues have resonated throughout the West, if sometimes in other guises. In the twentieth century, suicide was configured at the intersection between human sovereignty and the iron cages of constraint, active resistance and passive victimization, the affirmation of the self and its erasure. Suicide is not – to contradict Camus – the one truly serious philosophical problem, but it did become possible to conceive it as such. The "problem" was less a reflection of an eternal and universal human condition than one field of its discursive composition. Modernity – its politics, its inventive traditions, its (dis)enchantments – was inscribed upon the body of the suicide.

Selected bibliography

ARCHIVAL SOURCES

I. ROSSIISKII GOSUDARSTVENNYI ISTORICHESKII ARKHIV (RGIA), ST. PETERSBURG

> Fond 733: Ministerstvo narodnogo prosveshcheniia
> Fond 796: Kantseliariia Sinoda
> Fond 797: Kantseliariia Ober-Prokurora Sinoda
> Fond 1149: Departament zakonov Gosudarstvennogo Soveta
> Fond 1150: Departament voennykh del Gosudarstvennogo Soveta
> Fond 1151: Departament grazhdanskikh i dukhovnykh del Gosudarstvennogo Soveta
> Fond 1167: Komitet 6-ogo Dekabria 1826 g.
> Fond 1263: Komitet Ministrov
> Fond 1290: Tsentral'nyi statisticheskii komitet, MVD
> Fond 1345: Senat (Ugolovnyi departament)
> Fond 1354: Senat (Obshchoe sobranie)

2. ETNOGRAFICHESKII MUZEI (EM), ST. PETERSBURG

> Fond 7: Etnograficheskoe biuro Kn. Tenisheva

3. INSTITUT RUSSKOI LITERATURY (PUSHKINSKII DOM) (IRLI), ST. PETERSBURG

> Fond 100: F. M. Dostoevskii
> Fond 134: A. F. Koni
> R. III: Sobranie istoriko-literaturnykh materialov

4. ROSSIISKII GOSUDARSTVENNYI ARKHIV DREVNYKH AKTOV (RGADA), MOSCOW

> Fond 16: Vnutrennee upravlenie

5. ROSSIISKAIA GOSUDARSTVENNAIA BIBLIOTEKA, OTDEL RUKOPISEI (RGB), MOSCOW

Fond 297: N. V. Sushkov
Fond 323: A. V. and M. V. Khrapovitskii

6. GOSUDARSTVENNYI ARKHIV ROSSIISKOI FEDERATSII (GARF), MOSCOW

Fond 29: Kantseliariia Nerchinskoi katorgi Zabaikal'skogo oblastnogo pravleniia i voennogo gubernatora Zabaikal'skoi oblasti
Fond 98: Shlissel'burgskaia tsentral'naia katorzhnaia tiur'ma
Fond 102 (DP OO): Departament politsii, Osobii otdel
Fond 102 (DP IV): Departament politsii, IV deloproizvodstvo
Fond 102 (DP V): Departament politsii, V deloproizvodstvo
Fond 102 (DP VII): Departament politsii, VII deloproizvodstvo
Fond 109: Tret'e otdelenie
Fond 109 III: Tret'e otdelenie, III ekspeditsiia
Fond 109 IV: Tret'e otdelenie, IV ekspeditsiia

7. GOSUDARSTVENNYI ARKHIV NIZHEGORODSKOI OBLASTI (GANO), NIZHNII NOVGOROD

Fond 5: Nizhegorodskoe gubernskoe pravlenie
Fond 101: Arzamasskie uezdnye striapchie
Fond 133: Nizhegorodskii sovestnyi sud
Fond 176: Nizhegorodskaia gubernskaia palata ugolovnogo suda
Fond 180: Nizhegorodskii gubernskii prokuror
Fond 570: Nizhegorodskaia dukhovnaia konsistoriia

PRINTED PRIMARY SOURCES

A. D. "Samoubiistvo detei." *Nasha shkola*, nos. 1–4 (1910).
A. P. "Iz statistiki samoubiistv v Evrope za nyneshnee stoletie." *Tserkovnyi vestnik*, no. 18 (1882).
    "Usilenie manii samoubiist v novoi Evrope." *Tserkovnyi vestnik*, nos. 17, 18 (1882).
A. R. "O samoubiistve." *Obrazovanie*, no. 5/6 (1898).
Adamovich, L. *Bolezn' veka.* Kovno, 1912.
Akty sobrannye v bibliotekakh i arkhivakh Rossiiskoi imperii Arkheograficheskoiu ekspeditsieiu Imp. Akademii Nauk. 4 vols. SPb, 1836.
Al'f. "Bezmiatezhnoe zhit'e (Ocherki russkoi zhizni)." *Obrazovanie*, no. 9/10a (1908).
Andreev, L. N. *Sobranie sochinenii.* 14 vols. SPb, 1911–13.
    S.O.S.: Dnevnik (1914–1919); Pis'ma (1917–1919); Stat'i i interv'iu (1919); Vospominaniia sovremennikov (1918–1919), ed. R. Devis and B. Khellman. Moscow and SPb, 1994.
Andreev, Nikolai. *"Son Zorina." (Problema samoubiistv).* Kazan, 1910.
Androssov, V. *Statisticheskaia zapiska o Moskve.* Moscow, 1832.

Ar. "K epidemii samoubiistv." *Novaia Rus'* (Mar. 20, 1910).

"Samoubiistva v Peterburge po dannym statisticheskogo komiteta." *Novaia Rus'* (Mar. 24, 1910).

Arevkov, P. A. "Sleduet li proizvodit' predvaritel'nye sledstviia po delam o samoubiist-vakh i pokusheniiakh na nikh?" *Iuridicheskii vestnik*, nos. 9, 10 (1873).

Arkhangel'skii, F. "Sluchai samoubiistva." *VSMOG*, no. 3 (1884).

Arnova, S. "Samoubiistvo v proshlom i nastoiashchem." *Zhizn' dlia vsekh*, no. 3/4 (1911).

Artsybashev, M. *Sobranie sochinenii v trekh tomakh*. Moscow, 1994.

fon Attengofer, G. L. *Mediko-topograficheskoe opisanie S.-Peterburga*. SPb, 1820.

B. S. "O samoubiistve v tsivilizovannykh stranakh." *Russkoe bogatstvo*, no. 10 (1885).

Bakhtin, N. "Psikhologiia samoubiistva." *Pedagogicheskii sbornik*, no. 9 (1913).

Bantysh-Kamenskii, N. N. "Moskovskie pis'ma v poslednie gody Ekaterinskogo tsarstvovaniia. Ot N. N. Bantysha-Kamenskogo k kniaziu Aleksandru Borisovichu Kurakinu (1791 i 1792 gody)." *Russkii arkhiv*, no. 11 (1876).

Barsukov, Nikolai, ed. *Dnevnik A. V. Khrapovitskogo*. Moscow, 1901.

Bashutskii, Aleksandr. *Panorama Sanktpeterburga*. SPb, 1834.

Bazarov, V. "Samoubiistvo, kak sotsial'noe iavlenie." *Zaprosy zhizni*, no. 19 (1912).

Bekhterev, V. M. "O prichinakh samoubiistva i o vozmozhnoi bor'be s nim." *Vestnik znaniia*, nos. 2, 3 (1912).

Beliakov, S. A. "O samoubiistve i neschastnykh sluchaiakh v psikhiatricheskikh zave-deniiakh." *VKSPN*, no. 3 (1893).

Belogrits-Kotliarevskii, L. S. "Mifologicheskoe znachenie nekotorykh prestuplenii, sovershaemykh po sueveriiu." *Istoricheskii vestnik*, no. 7 (1888).

Berdiaev, N. *O samoubiistve*. Paris, 1931.

Bernatskii, V. *Samoubiistva sredi vospitannikov voenno-uchebnykh zavedenii*. SPb, 1911.

Bogatina, Sofiia. "Samoubiistva sredi zhenshchin." *Zhenskii vestnik*, no. 11 (1910).

Bogdanov, S. B. "Pomoshchnik prisiazhnogo poverennogo E. S. Semianovskii – odin iz pervykh kariitsev." *Byloe*, no. 11 (1906).

[Bolotov, A. T.] "Iz neizdannogo literaturnogo naslediia Bolotova. Opyt nravouchitel'nym sochineniiam: 1. O neznanii nashego podlogo naroda." *Literaturnoe nasledstvo*, no. 9/10 (1933).

Bondarenko, V. "Ocherki Kirsanovskogo uezda Tambovskoi gub." *Etnograficheskoe obozrenie*, no. 3 (1890).

Borodin, D. N. *Alkogolizm i samoubiistvo*. SPb, 1910.

Borovikovskii, A. L. *Ustav grazhdanskogo sudoproizvodstva s ob"iasneniiami po resheniiam grazhdanskogo kassatsionnogo departamenta i obshchego sobraniia kassatsionnogo i I i II departamenta Pravitel'stvuiushchego Senata*. 6th edn. SPb, 1908.

Brazilevich, G. *Student-samoubiitsa: Sbornik*. SPb, 1910.

Broide, S. "O samoubiitsakh." *Sud idet*, no. 13/14 (1925).

Bronzov, A. A. "Khristianskoe samoliubie." *Khristianskoe chtenie*, no. 8 (1897).

"Samoubiistva." *Tserkovnyi vestnik*, no. 5 (1912).

Brukhanskii, N. P. *Samoubiitsy*. Leningrad, 1927.

Budishchev, A. *Strashno zhit'*. Moscow, 1913.

Bulatov, P. N., ed. *Trudy XI Pirogovskogo s"ezda*. SPb, 1913.

Bulatsel', L. F. *Issledovaniia o samovol'noi smerti*. Revel, 1894.

Bulgakov, S. V. *Nastol'naia kniga dlia sviashchenno-tserkovnykh sluzhitelei*. 2nd edn. Kharkov, 1900.

Bul'mering, M. "O samoubiistve." *Iuridicheskii vestnik*, no. 5 (1860).

Burtsev, V. L., ed. *Kalendar' russkoi revoliutsii*. SPb, 1907. Reprint: Petrograd, 1917.

Chekhov, A. P. *Polnoe sobranie sochinenii i pisem*. Moscow, 1975.

Cherepanov, D. "K voprosu o samoubiistvakh." *Russkie vedomosti* (Feb. 1, 1913).

Chernyshevsky, Nikolai. *What Is to Be Done?* Trans. Michael Katz. Ithaca, N.Y., 1989.

Chistovich, Ia. "Perechen' sudebno-meditsinskikh vskryti." *Voenno-meditsinskii zhurnal*, vol. 67 (Mar. 1856); vol. 70 (Dec. 1957); vol. 72 (Aug. 1858).

D. "Nashi obshchestvennye dela." *Otechestvennye zapiski*, no. 7 (1872).

"Vnutrenniaia khronika." *Otechestvennye zapiski*, no. 3 (1871).

D. K. "Tendentsioznoe samoubiistvo." *Russkoe bogatstvo*, no. 12 (1880).

D. Zh. "Ugroza samoubiistva." *Nedelia*, no. 51 (1893).

Demidovich, P. P. "Iz oblasti verovanii i skazanii Belorussov." *Etnograficheskoe obozrenie*, no. 2/3 (1896).

Dobrianskii, Sv. Petr. "Sila molitv sv. Tserkvi po samoubiitse." *Strannik*, (Nov. 1866).

Dobroliubov, N. A. *Sobranie sochinenii*. 9 vols. Moscow, 1962.

Dobrovol'skii, V. N. "Dannye dlia narodnogo kalendaria Smolenskoi gubernii v sviazi s narodnymi verovaniiami." *Zhivaia starina*, no. 3/4 (1898).

"Narodnye skazaniia o samoubiitsakh." *Zhivaia starina*, no. 2 (1894).

"Nechistaia sila v narodnykh verovaniiakh: Po dannym Smolenskoi gubernii," *Zhivaia starina*, no. 1 (1908).

Dobryi, R. *Pochemu molodezh' konchaet samoubiistvom*. SPb, 1911.

Dostoevskii, Fedor. *PSS*. 30 vols. SPb, 1972–90.

A Writer's Diary. Trans. Kenneth Lantz. Evanston, Ill., 1993.

[Druzhinin, A. V.]. "Samoubiistvo." *Sovremennik*, no. 12 (1848).

Durkheim, E. *Le Suicide*. Paris, 1897.

"Dusha po smerti." *Pokoiashchiisia trudoliubets*, pt. 4. 1785.

Dymov, Osip. "Samoubiitsa." *Novoe slovo*, no. 5 (1912).

E. K. "Glasnye dramy intimnoi zhizni." *Nedelia*, no. 39 (1873).

"Urok nekoemu publitsistu 'Dela'." *Nedelia*, no. 49 (1873).

Efimenko, P. S. "Materialy po etnografii russkogo naseleniia Arkhangel'skoi gubernii." *Izvestiia Imp. Obshchestva liubitelei estestvoznaniia, antropologii i etnografii pri Imp. Moskovskom Universitete. Trudy etnograficheskogo otdela*, vol. 30, bk. 5, no. 1 (1877).

"Sud nad ved'mami." *Kievskaia starina*, no. 11 (1883).

"Epigrama na smert' Lukretsii." *Novye ezhemesiachnye sochineniia*, pt. 2 (Aug. 1786).

Ergina, L. V. "Vospominaniia iz zhizni v ssylke." *Byloe*, no. 6/18 (1907).

Esquirol, J. E. D. *Des maladies mentales*. Paris, 1838.

Eto ia vinovat ... Evoliutsiia i ispoved' terrorista: Pis'ma Egora Sozonova s kommentariiami. Moscow, 2001.

Ettinger, Evg. "K sovremennym nastroeniiam." *Zaprosy zhizni*, no. 11 (Mar. 14, 1910).

F. K. "Skuka." *S.-Peterburgskii vestnik*, no. 6 (Sept. 1780).

F. P. "Psikhologiia shkol'nykh samoubiistv." *Volkhovskoi listok*, nos. 415, 419, 421 (1905).

F. S. Sh. "Koe-chto o sueveriiakh." *Saratovskie gubernskie vedomosti*, no. 11 (1885).

Fal'kner, I. S. *Samoubiistva v Odesse (Statisticheskii ocherk)*. Odessa, 1890.

"Fedor Sologub o samoubiistvakh." *Novaia Rus'* (Mar. 16, 1910).

Fedorov, V. P. *Roditeli i deti ikh – samoubiitsy*. Saratov, 1911.

Fel'tsman, O. B. "K voprosu o samoubiistve." *Psikhoterapiia*, no. 6 (1910).

Fenomenov, M. *Prichiny samoubiistv v russkoi shkole*. Moscow, 1914.

Figner, Vera. *PSS*. 6 vols. Moscow, 1929.

Freze, Doktor. "O sudebno-psikhiatricheskikh osmotrakh." *ASMOG*, no. 1 (1866).

Fride, A. Ia. "Samoubiistvo." *Novoe slovo*, no. 1 (1909).

Frommett, B. "Samoubiistva v politicheskikh tiur'makh i ssylke." *Vrachebnaia gazeta*, no. 51 (1910).

G. "Odin iz nedavnikh samoubiits (A. A. Reding)." *Nedelia*, no. 13 (1874).

G. R. "O nedugakh sovremennoi molodezhi." *Vestnik vospitaniia*, no. 1 (1907); no. 1 (1908); nos. 2, 8 (1909).

Gailin, Ia. "O samoubiistvakh." *Novyi zhurnal dlia vsekh*, no. 19 (1910).

Galagants, D. A. *Doloi samoubiistvo – Zhizn' khorosha*. Baku, 1909.

Gekker, N. L. "Politicheskaia katorga na Kare." *Byloe*, no. 9 (1906).

Generozov, Ia. *Russkie narodnye predstavleniia o zagrobnoi zhizni na osnovanii zaplachek, prichitanii, dukhovnykh stikhov*. Saratov, 1883.

Georgievskii, Grigorii. "Zelenye Sviatki: Semik i Semitskaia nedelia." *Moskovskie vedomosti* (June 1, 1894).

Gernet, M. *Moral'naia statistika*. 2 vols. Moscow, 1922–27.

   Prestupnost' i samoubiistva vo vremia voiny i posle nee. Moscow, 1927.

   O. B. Gol'dovskii, and I. N. Sakharov, eds., *Protiv smertnoi kazni*. Moscow, 1906. (2nd edn. Moscow, 1907).

Gessen, Sergei. *Zagovor dekabrista Sukhinova*. Moscow, 1930.

Gippius, G. "Lunnye murav'i." *Chertova kukla*. Moscow, 1991.

Giubner, Iu. *Samoubiistva v S.-Peterburge. Materialy dlia nravstvennoi statistiki*. SPb, 1868.

Gladkii, A. "Vzgliad khudozhnikov na zhizn' i samoubiistvo." *Vestnik vospitaniia*, no. 6 (1913).

Glinka, S. N. *Zapiski Sergeia Nikolaevicha Glinki*. SPb, 1895.

Gogol', Nikolai. *Sobranie sochinenii*. 7 vols. Moscow, 1976–79.

Gorchakov, D. P. "Plamir i Raida. Rossiiskaia povest'." *Sochineniia Kniazia D. P. Gorchakova*. Moscow, 1890.

Gordon, G. I. "Ekzameny i samoubiistva uchashchikhsia." *Rech'* (May 25, 1908).

   Preface. *Samoubiistvo: Sotsiologicheskii etiud*, by E. Diurkgeim, ed. V. Bazarov. SPb, 1912.

   "Golodnye samoubiistva." *Zhizn' dlia vsekh*, no. 4 (1912).

   "Kluby samoubiits." *Sovremennoe slovo* (Jan. 25, 1911).

   "Nabolevshii vopros." *Rech'* (Apr. 4, 1908).

   "Otchego nasha molodezh' konchaet tak chasto samoubiistvom." *Svobodnoe vospitanie*, no. 1 (1912–13).

   "Pessimizm i samoubiistva sredi uchashcheisia molodezhi." *Zavety*, no. 3 (1912).

   "Prostitutki i samoubiistvo." *Rech'* (Apr. 23, 1910).

   "Samoubiistva molodezhi i ee nervno-psikhicheskaia neustoichivost'." *Novyi zhurnal dlia vsekh*, no. 9 (1912).

   "Samoubiistva v Rossii." *Bodroe slovo*, no. 15 (1909).

"Samoubiistva v srednei shkole." *Obrazovanie*, nos. 3, 4a (1909).
"Samoubiistva uchashcheisia molodezhi." *Novoe slovo*, no. 9 (1911).
"Samoubiistva uchashchikhsia v 1908 i 1909 gg." *Rech'* (Sept. 21, 1910).
"Samoubiistva v vysshikh uchebnykh zavedeniiakh v 1908 g." *Sovremennoe slovo* (Apr. 19, 1909).
"Samoubiistvo sredi detei." *Mir bozhii*, no. 4 (1902).
"Samoubiitsy i ikh pis'ma." *Novyi zhurnal dlia vsekh*, no. 2 (1911).
"Shkola i samoubiistva." *Nasha zhizn'*, no. 246 (1905).
"Sovremennye samoubiistva." *Russkaia mysl'*, no. 5 (1912).
"Vospitanie i samoubiistvo." *Sovremennoe slovo* (Apr. 7, 1911).
Gorkii, Maksim. "Izdaleka." *Zaprosy zhizni*, no. 7 (1912).
Grigor'ev, N. I. "Alkogolizm kak obshchestvennoe zlo." *Izvestiia S.-Peterburgskoi gorodskoi dumy*. Bezplatnoe prilozhenie, 1908.
"Samoubiistva i pokusheniia na samoubiistvo v Peterburge v 1911 g." *Russkii vrach*, no. 6 (1913).
"Samoubiistvo v S.-Peterburge za pervuiu polovinu 1909 g." *Rech'* (Aug. 22, 1909).
"Samoubiistvo v S.-Peterburge za pervuiu polovinu 1910 g." *Vrachebnaia gazeta*, no. 36 (1910).
Gub. "Vnutrennee obozrenie." *Delo*, no. 10 (1868).
Gurevich, A. "Zametki iz tekushchei zhizni." *Russkaia shkola*, no. 4 (1907).
Gvozdev, I. *O samoubiistve s sotsial'noi i meditsinskoi tochki zreniia*. Kazan, 1889.
Herrmann, Ch.-Th [Karl] "Recherches sur le nombre des suicides et des homicides commis en Russie pendant les années 1819 et 1820." *Mémoires de l'Académie Impériale des Sciences de St.-Petersbourg*. Series 6, vol. 1 (1832).
"Recherches sur le nombre des suicides et des homicides commis en Russie pendant les années 1821 et 1822." *Mémoires de l'Académie Impériale des Sciences de St.-Petersbourg*. Series 6, vol. 2 (1834).
I-. Mar-., trans. [Rech' Katona]. *S.-Peterburgskii Merkurii*, pt. 3 (1793).
I. P. *O naklonnosti k samoubiistvu, kak nravstvennoi bolezni nashego vremeni i o spasitel'nykh sredstvakh protiv etoi naklonnosti*. Moscow, 1884.
I. Z. "Pis'mo samoubiitsy." *Novye ezhemesiachnye sochineniia*, pts. 101, 102 (1794).
Iakovlev, S. N. and P. F. Filatov. "Samoubiistva v Simbirskoi gubernii." *VOGSPM*, nos. 1, 2 (1892).
Iakunin, Ivan. "Samoubiitsa." *Delo*, no. 11 (1875).
Ianson, Iu. "Neschastnye sluchai s liud'mi v 1880 g." *Izvestiia S.-Peterburgskoi gorodskoi dumy*, no. 6 (1881).
Ignat'ev, M. "Issledovanie o dushevnobol'nykh po otchetam russkikh psikhiatricheskikh zavedenii." Dissertation for the degree of Doctor of Medicine, Military Medical Academy, 1902.
Il'inskii, M. V. *Arkhangel'skaia ssylka*. SPb, 1906.
Iurlov, V. "Simbirskaia zapis' o kladakh (Materialy dlia etnograficheskikh zametok)." *Simbirskie gubernskie vedomosti* (Mar. 4, 1867).
Ivanov, A. I. "Verovaniia krest'ian Orlovskoi gubernii." *Etnograficheskoe obozrenie*, no. 4 (1900).
Ivanov, F. "Poslanie Katona k Iuliiu Kesariu." *Trudy obshchestva liubitelei rossiiskoi slovesnosti*, pt. 3 (1812).

Ivanov, P. "Narodnye rasskazy o domovykh, leshikh, vodianykh i rusalkakh." *Sbornik Khar'kovskogo istoriko-filologicheskogo obshchestva*. Vol. 5, no. 1 (Kharkov, 1893).

"Ocherk vozzrenii krest'ianskogo naseleniia Kupianskogo uezda na dushu i na zagrobnuiu zhizn'." *Sbornik Khar'kovskogo istoriko-filologicheskogo obshchestva*. Vol. 18 (Kharkov, 1909).

Ivanovskii, Ia., comp. *Obozrenie tserkovno-grazhdanskikh uzakonenii po dukhovnomu vedomstvu. Spravochnaia kniga* SPb, 1883.

"Iz IX knigi Farsalii Marka Anneia Lukana: 1. Katonovo uveshchanie. 2. Rech' Labiena pri khrame iupitera Ammona k Katonu; i otvet sego na onuiu." *Trudoliubivaia pchela* (Nov., 1759).

"Iz zapisok grafa E. F. Komarovskogo." *Osmnadtsatyi vek. Istoricheskii sbornik*. Vol. 1. Moscow, 1868.

"Iz zhizni srednoi shkoly: O samoubiistvakh sredi uchashchikhsia." *Vestnik vospitaniia*, no. 1 (1908).

"Iz zhizni srednoi shkoly." *Vestnik vospitaniia*, no. 9 (1908).

Izgoev, A. S. "Zamaskirovannoe samoubiistvo." *Russkaia mysl'*, no. 10 (1908).

Izmailov, V. "Rostovskoe ozero." *Priiatnoe i poleznoe preprovozhdenie vremeni*, pt. 5 (1795).

K. "Iz Aleksandrovskogo uezda." *Novorossiiskii telegraf* (June 19, 1887).

K. "Rasskaz zastrelivshegosia gimnazista." *Grazhdanin*, nos. 38, 39, 40 (1873).

"K psikhologii sovremennoi russkoi shkoly." *Zaprosy zhizni*, no. 2 (1912).

"K zhizni." *Priiatnoe i poleznoe preprovozhdenie vremeni*, pt. 2 (1794).

Kaiser, Daniel H., ed. & trans. *The Laws of Rus': Tenth to Fifteenth Century*. Salt Lake City, Ut., 1992.

Kalashnikov, S. V., comp. *Alfavitnyi ukazatel' deistvuiushchikh i rukovodstvennykh kanonicheskikh postanovlenii, ukazov, opredelenii i rasporiazhenii Sviateishego Pravitel'stvuiushchego Sinoda (1721–1895 g. vkliuchitel'no) i grazhdanskikh zakonov, ot nosiashchikhsia k dukhovnomu vedomstvu pravoslavnogo ispovedaniia*, 2nd edn. Kharkov, 1896.

Kamenev, G. "Ramier ili samoubiitsa." *Ippokrena ili utekhi liubosloviia*, pt. 6 (1800).

"Sof'ia." *Muza*, pt. 1 (Mar. 1796).

Kannabikh, Iu. V. "Istero-tsiklotimiia i neskol'ko slov o samoubiistve." *Psikhoterapiia*, no. 1 (1912).

Karamzin, N. M. "Bednaia Liza." *Moskovskii zhurnal*, pt. 6, 2nd edn. (1802).

"Novogo roda samoubiistvo v Anglii." *Vestnik Evropy*, pt. 2, no. 8 (1802).

"O samoubiistve." *Vestnik Evropy*, pt. 5, no. 19 (1802).

Pis'ma N. M. Karamzina k I. I. Dmitrievu. Ia. Grot and P. Pekarskii, eds. Vol 1. SPb, 1866.

"Samoubiitsa. Anekdot." *Moskovskii zhurnal*, pt. 1, 2nd edn. (1803).

Kardinalovskii, P. M. *Poval'noe samoubiistvo*. Odessa, 1910.

Karnovich, E. *Sanktpeterburg v statisticheskom otnoshenii*. SPb, 1860.

Katon, tragediia Adissonom [sic]. Trans. Aleksei Kolmakov. SPb, 1804.

"Katon v Livii." *Panteon inostrannoi slovesnosti*, pt. 1 (1789), reprint: 1818.

Kedrovich, S. "Gde prichiny?" *Kolokol* (Oct. 15, 1909).

Kennan, George. *Siberia and the Exile System*. 2 vols. (1891).

Kheifets, Z. E. *Samoubiistvo po evreiskomu zakonodatel'stvu*. Vilna, 1909.

Khlopin, G. V. "Samoubiistva, pokusheniia na samoubiistva i neschastnye sluchai sredi uchashchikhsia russkikh uchebnykh zavedenii (Sanitarno-statisticheskoe issledovanie)." *ZhMNP*, no. 3 (1906).

Khlopin, G. V., N. G. Ushinskii, and E. A. Neznamov, eds. *Samoubiistva, pokusheniia na samoubiistva i neschastnye sluchai sredi uchashchikhsia uchebnykh zavedenii Ministerstva Narodnogo Prosveshcheniia*. Series. SPb, 1906–16.

Khoroshko, V. " 'Gigiena dushi' i biurokratiia." *Russkaia mysl'*, no. 12 (1905). *Samoubiistvo detei*. Moscow, 1909.

Khovanskov, Grigorii. *Zhertva muzam ili sobranie raznykh sochinenii, podrazhenii i perevodov v stikhakh*. Moscow, 1795.

Kirpichnikov, A. "Daleko li ushli my ot mificheskogo mirosozertsaniia?" *Nov'*, no. 1 (1885).

Kisin, M. "Samoubiitsa." *Novaia zhizn'*, no. 7 (1911).

Kistiakovskii, A. "O samoubiistve po russkim ugolovnym zakonam." *Zhurnal grazhdanskogo i ugolovnogo prava*, no. 3 (1882).

[Klimova, N.] "Pis'mo pered kazn'iu." *Obrazovanie*, no. 8 (1908).

Klitin, A. *Nashe vremia i samoubiistvo*. Kiev, 1890.

Klushin, A. "Epitafiia G. P. M. A." *S.-Peterburgskii Merkurii*, pt. 3 (1793). "Neschastnyi M-v. Povest'." *S.- Peterburgskii Merkurii*, pt. 1 (1793).

Kniazhnin, Ia. *Vadim Novgorodskii. Tragediia Ia. Kniazhnina s predisloviem V. Savodnika*. Moscow, 1914.

Koltonovskaia, E. "Samotsennost' zhizni." *Obrazovanie*, no. 5 (1909).

"Kommissiia po bor'be so shkol'nymi samoubiistvami. Protokoly." *ZhROONZ*, no. 3 (1911); no. 3/4 (1912).

Koni, A. F. *Samoubiistvo v zakone i zhizni*. Moscow, 1923.

Kopei, A. "Dukhovnye zaveshchaniia samoubiits." *Iuridicheskii vestnik*, no. 4/6 (1875).

Korolenko, V. G. *Bytovoe iavlenie (Zametki publitsista o smertnoi kazni)*. SPb, 1910.

Korovin, V. I., ed. *Landshaft moikh voobrazhenii: Stranitsy prozy russkogo sentimentalizma*. Moscow, 1990.

Kostomarov, Nikolai. *Ocherk domashnei zhizni i nravov velikorusskogo naroda v XVI i XVII stoletiiakh*. SPb, 1887.

Kotliarevskii, A. *O pogrebal'nykh obychaiakh iazycheskikh Slavian*. Moscow, 1868.

Kovalenko, I. Z. *Opyt izucheniia pokushenii i zakonchennykh samoubiistv sredi gorodskogo naseleniia*. Kharkov, 1926.

Kovalevskii, P. *Obshchaia psikhopatologiia*. 1886. *Sudebnaia psikhiatriia*. SPb, 1902. *Sudebnaia psikhopatologiia*. SPb, 1900.

Kozhevnikov, G. "Liudi durnoi nasledstvennosti." *Utro Rossii* (Aug. 28, 1911).

Kraevskii, B. *Po povodu samoubiistv sredi uchashchikhsia*. Kharkov, 1910.

Krainskii, N. "Pedagogicheskii sadizm." *Sovremennaia psikhiatriia* (Sept. 1912).

Krestovskii, V. *Peterburgskie trushchoby*. 1864–1867. Reprint: SPb, 1993.

Krol', T. "K voprosu o vliianii alkogolia na zabolevaemost', smertnost' i prestupnost'." Dissertation for the Degree of Doctor of Medicine, Military Medical Academy. SPb, 1897.

Krupskaia, N. "Samoubiistva sredi uchashchikhsia i svobodnaia trudovaia shkola." *Svobodnoe vospitanie*, no. 10 (1910–11).

Kudrinskii, F. "Utoplennitsa." *Kievskaia starina*, nos. 4, 5 (1894).

Kulikovskii, D. "Samoubiitsy i nirvana." *Slovo*, no. 11 (1880).
Kutuzov, S. "Lishnie slezy." *Svobodnoe vospitanie*, no. 9 (1914–15).
Lavrichenko, K. G. *Roditeliam i uchiteliam: Voprosy vospitaniia*. SPb, 1894.
Lebedev, I. *O samoubiistve s meditsinskoi tochki zreniia*. SPb, 1897.
    O samoubiistve v normal'nom i boleznennom sostoianii. SPb, 1888.
Lebedev, Nikolai. *Samoubiistvo kak sotsial'no-eticheskoe zlo*. Moscow, 1913.
Lebedev, P. "K voprosu o proizvodstve del o samoubiistve." *Sudebnyi vestnik*, no. 177
    (1870).
Lebedintsev, K. "Nasha molodezh' i voprosy polovoi etiki." *Vestnik vospitaniia*, no. 8
    (1907).
Leibovich, Ia. *1000 sovremennykh samoubiistv*. Moscow, 1923.
    "Zhenskie samoubiistva." *Rabochii sud*, nos. 8, 9 (1926).
Lenchevskii, L. "Pokhoronnye obriady i pover'ia v Starokonstantinovskom u., Volynskoi
    gub." *Kievskaia starina*, no. 7 (1899).
Lenin, V. I. *PSS* 55 vols. Moscow, 1958–65.
Leonov, Ivan. "O samoubiistve." *Voenno-meditsinskii zhurnal*, vol. 55 (Mar. 1850).
    "Rassuzhdenie o grudnoi zheleze (glandula thymus), v fiziologicheskom, pato-
    logicheskom i sudebno-meditsinskom otnoshenii." *Drug zdraviia*, nos. 15, 16
    (1842).
Leskov, Nikolai. *Lady Macbeth of Mtsensk: A Sketch*. Trans. Robert Chandler. London,
    2003.
Levenstim, A. *Sueverie i ugolovnoe pravo*. SPb, 1897.
Levitskii, I. I. *Bor'ba s samoubiistvami uchashchikhsia*. Irkutsk, 1911.
Levitskii, O. I. "Starinnye vozzreniia na samoubiistvo i otgolosok ikh v narodnykh
    obychaiakh iuzhnoi-Rusi." *Kievskaia starina*, no. 12 (1891).
Liberson, M. *Stradanie odinochestva*. SPb, 1909.
Likhachev, A. V. *Samoubiistvo v zapadnoi Evrope i evropeiskoi Rossii*. SPb, 1882.
Likhacheva, E. "O samoubiistve." *Otechestvennye zapiski*, no. 7 (1881).
Lipskii, A. A. "Samoubiistvo detei v S.-Peterburge." *VSMOG*, no. 4 (1887).
Lisin, K. "Samoubiistvo i tsivilizatsiia." *Delo*, no. 7 (1882).
Liubatovich, O. S. "Dalekoe i nedavnee. Vospominaniia iz zhizni revoliutsionerov, 1878–
    81." *Byloe*, no. 6 (1906).
Lokhvitskii, Aleksandr. *Kurs russkogo ugolovnogo prava*. SPb, 1871.
Loparev, Kh., ed. "Otrazitel'noe pisanie o novoizobretennom puti samoubiistvennykh
    smertei: Vnov' naidennyi staroobriadcheskii traktat protiv samosozhzheniia, 1691
    goda." *Pamiatniki drevnei pis'mennosti*. Vol. 108. SPb, 1895.
L'vov, Pavel. "Sofiia. Russkaia povest'." *Priiatnoe i poleznoe preprovozhdenie vremeni*,
    pt. 2 (1794).
Maizel', I. "O samoubiistvakh sredi uchashchikhsia." *Vestnik vospitaniia*, no. 8 (1908).
Makalinskii, P. "Uchastie politsii v proizvodstve predvaritel'nogo sledstviia." *Sudebnyi
    vestnik*, no. 146 (1870).
Makarov, N. V. "Samoubiistva v russkoi armii." *Voenno-meditsinskii zhurnal* (July
    1902).
Maksimov, S. V. "Narodnye prestupleniia i neschastiia." *Otechestvennye zapiski*, no. 1
    (1869).
    Nechistaia, nevedomaia i krestnaia sila. SPb, 1903.
    Sibir' i katorga. SPb, 1871.

[Maksimov, S.] "O samoubiistvakh v S.-Peterburge." *Vedomosti S.-Peterburgskoi gorod-skoi politsii*, no. 7 (1870).

"Maniia samoubiistv." *Nedelia*, no. 22 (1884).

Martovskii, L. *Tri tipa samoubiistv*. Kovno, 1910.

Materialy dlia peresmotra nashego ugolovnogo zakonodatel'stva. Vol. 3. SPb, 1881.

Mediko-statisticheskie svedeniia po gorodu S.-Peterburga i S.-Peterburgskoi gubernii za 1836 god. SPb, 1837.

Merezhkovskii, D. "Bes ili Bog?" *Obrazovanie*, no. 8 (1908).

Mikhail B. *Epidemiia samoubiistv i zaraza adskoi mysl'iu*. Tver, 1913.

Mikhailovskii, G. "O pogrebenii samoubiits i lits, umershikh neestestvennoiu smertiiu." *Kavkazskie eparkhial'nye vedomosti*, no. 7 (1878).

Mikhailovskii, N. K. "Zhiteiskie i khudozhestvennye dramy." *Sochineniia N. K. Mikhailovskogo*. Vol. 4. SPb, 1897.

Mikhnevich, V. *Iazvy Peterburga: Opyt istoriko-statisticheskogo issledovaniia nravstvennosti stolichnogo naseleniia*. SPb, 1886.

Miller, O. "Samoubiistvo ot ekzamena." *Zaria*, no. 6 (1870).

Minkh, A. N. "Narodnye obychai, obriady, sueveriia i predrassudki krest'ian Saratovskoi gubernii." *Zapiski imp. Russkogo geograficheskogo obshchestva po otdeleniiu etno-grafii*, no. 2 (1890).

Minor, O. S. "Iakutskaia drama 22-go marta 1889 goda." *Byloe*, no. 9 (1906).

M-ko, D. *O samoubiistve*. Odessa, 1912.

"Monolog. Iz tragedii Katon, sochinennoi g. Adissonom [*sic*]." *Novye ezhemesiachnye sochineniia*, pt. 25 (July 1788).

Morselli, Henry. *Suicide: An Essay on Comparative Moral Statistics*. New York, 1882.

Mukhin, N. "Ocherk psikhologii samoubiistva." *Varshavskie universitetskie izvestiia*, nos. 2, 4, 5 (1903).

Mumortsev, A. N. *O sovremennom pessimizme i samoubiistvakh*. Moscow, 1914.

N. "O samoubiistvakh." *Grazhdanin*, nos. 11, 12 (1874).

N. E. "Vrachi-samoubiitsy." *Nedelia*, no. 22 (1896).

N. K. "Samoubiistvo i ego prichiny (Pis'mo iz Frantsii)." *Russkoe bogatstvo*, no. 4 (1898).

N. K. "Samoubiistva uchashcheisia molodezhi i uchitel'skaia korporatsiia." *Svobodnoe vospitanie*, no. 8 (1911–12).

N. Kh. "Neschastie." *Priiatnoe i poleznoe preprovozhdenie vremeni*, pt. 2 (1794).

N. M. "Literaturnye i zhurnal'nye zametki." *Otechestvennye zapiski*, no. 10 (1873).

N. Z. "Statistika samoubiistv." *Iuridicheskii vestnik*, no. 9 (1880).

Na pomoshch' molodezhi: Sbornik statei, pisem, i zametok o studencheskikh nuzhdakh i samoubiistvakh uchashchikhsia. Kiev, 1910.

Naumov, F. A. "Stremlenie k samoubiistvu u slaboumnogo paranoika." *OPNiEP*, no. 7 (1907).

Nekliudov, N. A. *Rukovodstvo k osobennoi chasti russkogo ugolovnogo prava*. Vol. 1: *Prestupleniia i postupki protiv lichnosti*. SPb, 1876.

Nesterov, V. G. "Sovremennaia shkola i zdorov'e." *Meditsinskoe obozrenie*, no. 4 (1887).

"Nevedomyi krai" (O samoubiistvakh. Tsifry i chelovecheskie dokumenty). [n.p., n.d.]

Nevzorov, I. A. *O samoubiistve*. Kazan, 1891.

Neznamov. "Ekho dnia." *Novoe vremia* (July 16, 1910).

Nikiforovskii, N. Ia. "Nechistiki. Svod prostonarodnykh v Vitebskoi Belorussii skazanii o nechistoi sile." *Vilenskii vremennik 2*. Vilnius, 1907.

"Ocherki Vitebskoi Belorussii." *Etnograficheskoe obozrenie*, no. 4 (1896).

Nikoladze, N. "Po povodu odnoi smerti." *Ustoi*, no. 7 (1882).

Nikolaevskii, Blagochinnyi Ierei Matvei Grigor'ev. "Chetyre pechal'nykh sobytiia i odno otradnoe." *Pribavlenie k Tambovskim eparkhial'nym vedomostiam*, no. 7 (Apr. 1, 1899).

Nikol'skii, D. "O shkol'nykh samoubiistvakh. Pis'mo v redaktsiiu." *Svobodnoe vospitanie*, no. 11 (1910–11).

Samoubiistva sredi uchashchikhsia. 1915.

Nikol'skii N. and M. Izvol'skii, eds. *Sistematicheskii sbornik nedoumennykh voprosov i otvetov na nikh vstrechaiushchikhsia v tserkovno-prikhodskoi praktike*. SPb, 1896.

Nikol'skii, Pavel. *Samoubiistvo*. Tambov, 1910.

Nizhegorodtsev, M. N. "O vliianii meteorologicheskikh uslovii na dushevnoe rasstroistvo s neskol'kimi dannymi o raspredelenii v godu samoubiistv, prestuplenii, i smertnosti." *Trudy V s"ezda Obshchestva russkikh vrachei v pamiat' N. I. Pirogova*. Vol. 1. SPb, 1894.

"Novaia drama v tiur'me." *Osvobozhdenie*, no. 10/34 (1903).

Novoe ugolovnoe ulozhenie Vysochaishe utverzhdennoe 22–go Marta 1903 g. Moscow, 1903.

Novosel'skii, S. "Ocherk statistiki samoubiistv." *Gigiena i sanitariia*, nos. 8–10 (1910).

Statistika samoubiistv. SPb, 1910.

"O melankholii i melankholikakh." *Sovremennik*, no. 8 (1848).

O naklonnosti k samoubiistvu, kak nravstvennoi bolezni. Moscow, 1881.

"O poriadke proizvodstva del o samoubiitsakh." *Sudebnyi vestnik*, no. 41 (1866).

"O samoubiistvakh." *Gigiena i sanitariia*, no. 7 (1910).

"O samoubiistve: Iz sochinenii Zh. Zh. Russo." *Priiatnoe i poleznoe preprovozhdenie vremeni*, pt. 2 (1794).

"O smerti Sokratovoi." *Sochineniia i perevody, k pol'ze i uveseleniiu sluzhashchiia* (Apr. 1760).

"O Sokratovoi smerti." *Novye ezhemesiachnye sochineniia*, pt. 71 (1792).

"O sueveriiakh, obychaiakh, poveriiakh i primetakh zhitelei s. Stavuchan, Khotinsk. uezda." *Kishinevskie eparkhial'nye vedomosti*, no. 18 (Sept. 15–30, 1873).

"O 'Vitmerovtsakh' (Arkhivnaia spravka)." *Revoliutsionnoe iunoshestvo 1905–1917: Peterburg*. Leningrad, 1924.

Obninskii, P. N. "Ob ugolovnom presledovanii pokusivshikhsia na samoubiistvo." *Iuridicheskii vestnik*, no. 6 (1871).

"K voprosu ob ugolovnom presledovanii pokusivshikhsia na samoubiistvo." *Iuridicheskii vestnik*, no. 9 (1871).

Obolonskii, N. A. "Samoubiistvo v g. Kieve." *VNPM*, nos. 1, 3 (1902).

"Sovremennoe polozhenie voprosa o prichinakh samoubiistva." *RAPKMB*, no. 1 (1902).

Obozrenie gosudarstvennogo upravleniia po chasti obshchestvennogo blagoustroistva v 1831 godu. SPb, 1834.

Oettli, N. "K voprosu o samoubiistvakh nashei molodezhi i reformy nashei shkoly." *Svobodnoe vospitanie*, no. 4 (1912–13).

Ogloblin, N. "Ocherki iz byta Ukrainy kontsa XVIIIv. (I. Sozhzhenie ved'my.)" *Kievskaia starina*, no. 5 (1887).

Ogronovich, V. N. "K voprosu o samoubiistve." *VPKAG*, no. 2 (1912).

Ol'khin, P. M. *O samoubiistve v meditsinskom otnoshenii.* SPb, 1859.

Poslednie dni samoubiits. SPb, 1863.

Ol'minskii, M. S. "Smert' L. F. Ianovicha." *Byloe*, no. 12 (1906).

Ongirskii, B. "Statisticheskie itogy samoubiistv." *Delo*, no. 11 (1873).

"Opredelenie Moskovskoi sudebnoi palaty. Po voprosu o proizvodstve del o samoubii-tsakh." *Sudebnyi vestnik*, no. 123 (1868).

Orlov, P. A., ed. *Russkaia sentimental'naia povest'.* Moscow, 1979.

Osmolovskii, G. F. "Kariiskaia tragediia." *Byloe*, no. 6 (1907).

"Kariitsy (Materialy dlia statistiki russkogo revoliutsionnogo dvizheniia)." *Minuvshie gody*, no. 7 (1908).

Ostrovskii, A. N. *Sobranie sochinenii v shesti tomakh.* Moscow, 1999.

Ostrovskii, I. P. *K voprosu o samoubiistve v Odesse za piatiletie 1903–1908.* Odessa, 1908.

"K voprosu o vvedenii odnoobraznoi registratsii sluchaev samovol'noi smerti v Rossii." *Trudy vrachei stantsii skoroi meditsinskoi pomoshchi v Odesse.* Vol. 5. Odessa, 1911.

"Samoubiistva i pokusheniia na samoubiistvo v g. Odesse za 1908 god." *Trudy vrachei stantsii skoroi meditsinskoi pomoshchi v Odesse.* Vol. 3. Odessa, 1909.

"Voprosy sravnitel'noi psikhologii samoubiistva u vzroslykh i detei." *VPKAG*, no. 3 (1911).

Ostrogorskii, A. N. "Samoubiistvo, kak psikhologicheskaia problema." *Pedagogicheskii sbornik*, nos. 1, 2 (1893).

"Samoubiistva. Povody k nim." *Pedagogicheskii sbornik*, nos. 7, 8 (1893).

"Samoubiistva." *Pedagogicheskii sbornik*, no. 10 (1893).

Ostrogorskii, N. "Pedagogicheskie ekskursii v oblasti literatury." *Russkaia shkola*, no. 3 (1908).

Otchet Ministerstva iustitsii. Series: 1834–68.

Ozolin, V. *"Doloi samoubiistvo!"* Riga [n.d.].

P. S. "Iuridicheskaia khronika." *Zhurnal grazhdanskogo i ugolovnogo prava*, no. 6 (1876).

Pamiati Mar'i Fedos'evny Vetrovoi (†12 Fevralia 1897 goda v Petropavlovskoi kreposti). n. p., 1898.

Pamiatniki drevne-russkogo kanonicheskogo prava. In *Russkaia istoricheskaia bib-lioteka.* Vol. 6. SPb, 1908.

Pamiatniki literatury drevnei Rusi. Series. Moscow, 1978–94.

Pasternatskii, I. "Statisticheskoe issledovanie samoubiistv v S.-Peterburge za 1870, 1871, i 1872 gody." *Meditsinskii vestnik*, nos. 35, 36, 37, 38, 40, 41 (1873).

Pavlov, A., ed. *Nomokanon pri Bol'shom trebnike.* Odessa, 1872.

Pavlovskaia, L. S. "Dva sluchaia dushevnogo zabolevaniia pod vliianiem obshchestven-nykh sobytii." *OPNiEP*, no. 6 (1906).

Perogovskii, Vasilii. "O narodnom obychnom ugolovnom prave na Volyni." *Volynskie gubernskie vedomosti*, no. 25 (Apr. 14, 1879).

Petrov, S. "Detskie samoubiistva i bor'ba s nim." *Vestnik sem'i i shkoly*, nos. 2, 3, 4 (1910).

Petukhov, Evgenii. *Serapion Vladimirskii, russkii propovednik XIII veka.* SPb, 1888.

Pisateli-dekabristy v vospominaniiakh sovremennikov. 2 vols. Moscow, 1980.

Pis'ma russkikh pisatelei XVIII veka. Leningrad, 1980.

"Pis'mo Katona k Iuliiu Tsesariu." *Sobesednik liubitelei rossiiskogo slova*, pt. 8 (1783).

"Po delu o samoubiistve otstavnogo poruchika Petra Abazy." *Sudebnyi vestnik*, no. 86 (1866).

Po povodu chastykh ubiistv i samoubiistv: Razmyshlenie o putiakh k blazhenstvu i schast'iu. SPb, 1888.

"Po povodu samoubiistva detei." *Nedelia*, no. 18 (1884).

Pokrovskii, E. "Iunye zhertvy sovremennogo pessimizma." *Vestnik vospitaniia*, no. 7 (1892).

Pokryshkin, P. "Sudebno-meditsinskaia deiatel'nost' v Viatskoi gubernii s 1-go sentiabria 1862 g. po 1-oe ianvaria 1865 g." *ASMOG*, no. 3 (1868).

"Sudebno-meditsinskaia deiatel'nost' v Irkutskoi gubernii za 1864–1867 gody." *ASMOG*, no. 3 (1869).

Polnoe sobranie postanovlenii i rasporiazhenii po vedomstvu pravoslavnogo ispovedaniia Rossiiskoi Imperii. Series.

Polnoe sobranie russkikh letopisei. Series.

Polnoe sobranie zakonov Rossiiskoi Imperii. Sobranie 1 (1649–1825). 45 vols. SPb, 1830.

Polnoe sobranie zakonov Rossiiskoi Imperii. Sobranie 2 (1830–81). 55 vols. SPb, 1830–81.

Ponomarev, N. V. "Samoubiistvo v zapadnoi Evrope i v Rossii v sviazi s razvitiem umopomeshatel'stva." *SSSM*, no. 3 (1880).

Popov, Ardalion. *Sud i nakazaniia za prestupleniia protiv very i nravstvennosti po russkomu pravu.* Kazan, 1904.

Popov, I. V. "O samoubiistve." *Bogoslovskii vestnik*, no. 3 (1898).

Popov, N. M. *Sovremennaia epidemiia shkol'nykh samoubiistv v Rossii: Klinicheskie materialy.* Kazan, 1911.

Portugalov, V. "Melkii bes i ego zhertvy." *Novyi zhurnal dlia vsekh*, no. 17 (1910).

"Poslanie Katona k Iuliiu Kesariu." *Trudy obshchestva liubitelei rossiiskoi slovestnosti*, pt. 3 (Moscow, 1812).

Posse, V. *Na teme zhizni.* SPb, 1909.

Vyrozhdenie i vozrozhdenie. SPb, 1912.

Pouncy, Carolyn Johnston, ed. and trans. *The Domostroi: Rules for Russian Households in the Time of Ivan the Terrible.* Ithaca, N.Y., 1994.

Povalishin, A. *Riazanskie pomeshchiki i ikh krepostnye.* Riazan, 1903.

Pravila Pravoslavnoi tserkvi s tolkovaniiami Nikodima, episkopa Dalmatinsko-istriiskogo. 2 vols. SPb, 1911–1912.

"Predsmertnoe pis'mo S. S. Semianovskogo k ottsu." *Byloe*, no. 11 (1906).

"Prestuplenie na pochve sueveriia." *Nedelia*, no. 23 (1891).

Proekt ugolovnogo ulozheniia Rossiiskoi Imperii. Pt. 3: "O nakazaniiakh za chastnye prestupleniia." [SPb, 1813]. In *Arkhiv Gosudarstvennogo Soveta.* Vol. 4. SPb, 1874.

Proekt ulozheniia o nakazaniiakh ugolovnykh i ispravitel'nykh, vnesennyi v 1844 godu v Gosudarstvennyi Sovet, s podrobnym oznacheniem osnovanii kazhdogo iz vnesennykh v sei proekt postanovlenii. SPb, 1871.

"Protiv samoubiistva (Utopiia)." *Satirikon*, no. 42 (1909).

Protiv upadochnichestva, protiv "Eseninshchiny". Moscow, 1926.

"Protokoly zasedanii obshchestva psikhiatrov v S.-Peterburge za 1892g." *VKSPN*, no. 1 (1893).

Prozorov, L. "Samoubiistva dushevno-bol'nykh v bol'nitsakh." *Sovremennaia psikhiatriia*, nos. 7, 8 (1911).

"Samoubiistva prigovorennykh." *Meditsinskoe obozrenie*, no. 12 (1911).

"Samoubiistva v tiur'makh i okolo tiurem po dannym 1906 i 1907 goda." *Meditsinskoe obozrenie*, no. 12 (1908).

"Samoubiistva voennykh." *Meditsinskoe obozrenie*, no. 10 (1914).

Pruzhanskii, N. *Zhizn' ili smert': O samoubiitsakh.* SPb, 1908.

R. G. "Iz zhizni srednei shkoly." *Vestnik vospitaniia*, no. 1 (1908), nos. 2, 8 (1909).

R. L. "Bor'ba s samoubiistvami." *Zaprosy zhizni*, no. 17 (1910).

R-uk. "Kratkoe opisanie sela Dankouts, Khotinskogo uezda." *Kishinevskie eparkhial'nye vedomosti*, no. 17 (Sept. 1, 1889).

Radin, E. P. *Dushevnoe nastroenie sovremennoi uchashcheisia molodezhi po dannym Peterburgskoi obshchestudencheskoi ankety 1912 goda.* SPb, 1913.

Radishchev, A. *PSS.* Moscow and Leningrad, 1938–41.

Radiukin, N. "Statistika samoubiistva." *Delo*, no. 1 (1866).

Raikh, M. "Iunye samoubiitsy i ikh pis'ma." *Zhenskoe delo*, no. 8 (Feb. 28, 1910).

Raikher, I. "K voprosu o samoubiistve. Mediko-psikhologicheskii ocherk." *Nauchnyi arkhiv Vilenskoi okruzhnoi lechebnitsy*, no. 1/2 (1904).

"Rasskaz zastrelivshegosia gimnazista." *Grazhdanin*, nos. 38–40 (1873).

Resheniia grazhdanskogo kassatsionnogo departamenta Pravitel'stvuiushchego Senata. Series.

Resheniia obshchego sobraniia pervogo i kassatsionnykh departamentov Pravitel'stvuiushchego Senata. Series.

Resheniia ugolovnogo kassatsionnogo departamenta Pravitel'stvuiushchego Senata. Series.

Rodin, D. "Dvizhenie samoubiistv po razlichnym stranam za gody voiny i posle nee." *Vestnik statistiki*, no. 7/9 (1924).

Rossiiskii Verter, pospravedlivaia povest', original'noe sochinenie M. S. molodogo, chuvstvitel'nogo cheloveka, neschastnym obrazom samoizvol'no prekrativshego svoiu zhizn'iu. SPb, 1801.

Rossiiskoe zakonodatel'stvo X–XX vekov. 9 vols. Moscow, 1984.

Rostopchin, F. V. "Vesti iz Rossii v Angliiu 1796 goda. Pis'ma grafa F. V. Rostopchina k grafu S. R. Vorontsovu." *Russkii arkhiv*, no. 4 (1876).

Rostov, N. "Samoubiistvo M. F. Vetrovoi i studencheskie bezporiadki 1897 g." *Katorga i ssylka*, no. 23 (1926).

Rousseau, J. J. *Julie ou la nouvelle Héloïse.* 1761.

Rozanov, P. G. *O samoubiistve.* Moscow, 1891.

"Statisticheskii ocherk samoubiistv i popytok k samoubiistvu v Moskve za 1870–1885 gg." *VOGSPM*, no. 11 (1891).

Rozenbakh, P. Ia. "O prichinakh sovremennoi nervnosti i samoubiistv." *Novoe slovo*, no. 11 (1909).

Rybakov, F. E. "Dushevnye rasstroistva v sviazi s sovremennymi politicheskimi sobytiiami." *Russkii vrach*, no. 51 (1905); nos. 3, 8 (1906).

Sovremennye pisateli i bol'nye nervy. Moscow, 1908.

S. "Smertniki." *Vestnik Evropy*, nos. 7, 8 (1910).

S. D. "Nashi samoubiitsy." *Nedelia*, no. 12 (1901).

"Samoubiistva: Etiud po obshchestvennoi patologii." *Nedelia*, nos. 18, 19 (1886).

"Samoubiistva sredi uchashchikhsia." *Diskussii Venskogo psikhoanaliticheskogo fereina*. Odessa, 1912.

"Samoubiistva v Peterburge." In *Russkii kalendar' A. Suvorina na 1875 g.* SPb, 1875.

Samoubiistva v SSSR v 1922–1925 gg. Moscow, 1927.

Samoubiistva v SSSR v 1925–1926 gg. Moscow, 1929.

"Samoubiistvo." *Chto nibud' ot bezdel'ia na dosuge* (1800).

"Samoubiistvo." *Delo ot bezdel'ia ili priiatnaia zabava*, pt. 3 (1792).

"Samoubiistvo bogootstupnika." *Vladimirskie eparkhial'nye vedomosti*, no. 15 (1873).

"Samoubiistvo detei." *Ogonek*, no. 21 (1902).

"Samoubiistvo (Nasha anketa)." *Novoe slovo*, no. 6 (1912).

"Samoubiistvo pred sudom iazychestva i khristianstva." *Tserkovnyi vestnik*, no. 26 (1876).

Samoubiistvo: Sbornik statei. Moscow, 1910.

"Samoubiistvo v Odesse (1870–79)." *Vedomosti Odesskogo gradonachal'stva*, nos. 223, 224 (Oct. 15, 16, 1881).

"Samoubivstvo [sic]." *Pokoiashchiisia trudoliubets*, pt. 4 (1785).

Savinkov, Boris [V. Ropshin]. *Kon' blednyi*. 2nd edn. SPb, 1912.

Semenova, O. P. "Smert' i dusha v pover'iakh i v rasskazy krest'ian i meshchan Riazanskogo, Rannenburgskogo i Dankovskogo uezdov Riazanskoi gubernii." *Zhivaia starina*, no. 2 (1898).

Serbilat'ev, L. I. "Otravleniia uksusnoi essentsiei za posledniia 7 1/2 let (s 1-go ianvaria 1903 g. po 30-oe iiunia 1910 g. vkliuchitel'no) po dannym gorodskoi muzhskoi Obukhovskoi bol'nitsy v Peterburge." *Russkii vrach*, no. 46 (1910).

Shein, P. V. "Materialy dlia izucheniia byta i iazyka russkogo naseleniia severozapadnogo kraia." *Sbornik otdelenii russkogo iazyka i slovesnosti imp. Akademii nauk*. Vol. 51. SPb, 1851.

Sheinis, L. "Epidemicheskie samoubiistva." *Vestnik vospitaniia*, no. 1 (1909).

"K istorii samoubiistva." *Russkaia vysshaia shkola obshchestvennykh nauk v Parizhe*. SPb, 1905.

Shelgunov, N. "Ocherki russkoi zhizni." *Russkaia mysl'*, no. 1 (1889).

fon Shel', G. *Samoubiistvo i sovremennaia tsivilizatsiia*. Odessa, 1893.

Shestakov, I. N. "Po povodu stat'i P. N. Obninskogo." *Iuridicheskii vestnik*, no. 1 (1872).

"Vozrazhenie na ob"iasneniia." *Iuridicheskii vestnik*, no. 4/5 (1872).

Shigaleev, N. "Epidemiia." *Slovo* (Feb. 26, 1908).

Shirvind, Iulii. "Ubiistvo ili samoubiistvo?" *VSMOG*, no. 1 (1882).

"Shkol'nye samoubiistva. Bor'ba s nim." *Vrachebnaia gazeta*, no. 36 (1905).

Shvetsov, B. "Samoubiistva v srednei shkole." *Russkaia shkola*, no. 10 (1906).

Sidamon-Eristova, E. A. *O samoubiistve*. Moscow, 1910.

Sikorskii, I. A. *Psikhologicheskaia bor'ba s samoubiistvom v iunye gody*. Kiev, 1913.

"Samoubiistvo sredi russkikh vrachei." *VNPM*, no. 1/2 (1896).

"Sostoianie dukha pred samoubiistvom." *Sbornik nauchno-literaturnykh statei po voprosam obshchestvennoi psikhologii, vospitaniia, i nervno-psikhicheskoi gigieny*. 5 vols. Kiev, 1899–1900. Vol. 1. Kiev, 1900.

"Skuka zhizni." *Nedelia*, no. 26 (1875).

Skvortsov, Ivan "Oshibochnost' pessimisticheskogo vozzreniia na zhizn' i vrednye posledstviia ego." *Khristianskoe chtenie*, no. 1/2 (1880).

Slavnin, K. "K bor'be s samoubiistvom." *Novaia Rus'*. Series, 1909–10.

Slonimskii, L. "Samoubiistvo s obshchestvennoi i nravstvennoi tochek zreniia." *Vestnik Evropy*, nos. 1, 2 (1914).

"Smert' Katona ili rozhdenie rimskogo edinonachaliia." *Ippokrena*, pt. 8 (1801).

"Smert' Sokrata." *Rastushchii vinograd* (July 1786).

Smidovich, V. "O nasil'stvennykh i sluchainykh smertiakh v Tul'skoi gubernii za 1879–84 goda, sravnitel'no s drugimi guberniiami eropeiskoi Rossii." *VSMOG*, no. 1 (1887).

Snarskii, Mikhail. "Deti-samoubiitsy." *Peterburgskaia gazeta* (Dec. 18, 1909).

Snegirev, I. M. *Pokrovskii monastyr': chto na ubogikh domakh v Moskve*. Moscow, 1872.

Sobolevskii, A. V. "Redkii sluchai istericheskikh sudorog ('piaiaska zhivota') s samoubiistvom bol'nogo." *VNPM*, no. 4 (1903).

Sobolov, A. "Prichitan'ia nad umershimi Vladimirskoi gubernii." *Etnograficheskoe obozrenie*, no. 3/4 (1911).

"Sobstvennoruchnye zapiski o zhizni akademika A. V. Stupina." *Shchukinskii sbornik*. Vol. 3. Moscow, 1904.

"Sokrat." *Panteon inostrannoi slovesnosti*, bk. 2 (1792), reprint: 1818.

Sologub, F. *Melkii bes*. 1907.

Solovtsova, A. "Samoubiistva detei." *Vospitanie i obozrenie*, no. 7/8 (1910).

Sorokin, P. A. *Samoubiistvo, kak obshchestvennoe iavlenie*. Riga, [n.d.].

Speranskii, V. N. *Publichnaia lektsiia na temu "Samoubiistvo pered sudom filosofii i literatury."* Moscow, 1912.

Stalinskii, E. "O samoubiistvakh na Kavkaze i za Kavkazom." *Sbornik svedenii o Kavkaze*. Vol. 1. Tbilisi, 1871.

"Statisticheskie svedeniia o samoubiistvakh v period 1870–74 godov." *Pravitel'stvennyi vestnik*, no. 100 (May 7, 1876).

Statisticheskie svedeniia o Sanktpeterburge. SPb, 1836.

Statisticheskii vremennik Rossiiskoi Imperii. SPb, 1866.

Statistik. *Samoubiistvo kak sotsial'noe iavlenie*. [n.p., n.d.].

"Samoubiistva v Moskve za 1910 god." *Russkie vedomosti* (Apr. 14, 1911).

"Statistiki samoubiistv v Peterburge." *Golos* (Dec. 1, 1872).

Steblin-Kamenskii, R. A. "Grigorii Anfimofich Popko (12 aprelia 1852–20 marta 1885 g.) (Opyt biografii)." *Byloe*, no. 5 (1907).

Sto odin. "Ded moi pomeshchik Serbin. Iz zapisok cheloveka." *Russkii vestnik*, no. 11 (1875).

Strahan, S. A. K. *Suicide and Insanity*. London, 1893.

Strakhov, Nikolai. *Moi peterburgskie sumerki*. SPb, 1810.

Struiskii, D. "Samoubiitsa." *Sovremennik*, no. 7 (1837).

"Sudebnye zasedaniia. V Eletskom okruzhnom sude (po ugolovnomu otdeleniiu). Po delu o vremenno-obiazannom krest'ianine Stepane Fedoseeve Ozerskom." *Sudebnyi vestnik*, no. 143 (1868).

"Sudebnye zasedaniia. Zasedanie Smolenskogo okruzh. suda, 17 i 18 iiunia, s uchastiem prisiazhnykh zasedatelei, po delu o kupchikhe 2 gil'dii Aleksandre Berngardt." *Sudebnyi vestnik*, nos. 93, 94 (1872).

Sukhikh, I. N., ed. *Russkaia tragediia: p'esa A. N. Ostrovskogo "Groza" v russkoi kritike i literaturovedenii*. SPb, 2002.

Sulima, K. P. "Pokushenie na samoubiistvo posredstvom pererezki shei, vydavaemoe za pokushenie na ubiistvo." *VSMOG*, no. 4 (1886).

Sulima, Tat'iana. "Proshlym letom." *Step'*, no. 25 (June 22, 1886).

Surkov, []. "Sudebno-meditsinskie sluchai v Simbirskoi gubernii v 1860–1864 godakh." *ASMOG*, no. 1 (1866).

[Sushkov, Mikhail]. *Pamiat' bratu, ili sobranie sochinenii i perevodov Mikhaila Sushkova, naidennykh posle ego smerti.* Moscow, 1803.

Rossiiskii Verter, poluspravedlivaia povest'. SPb, 1801.

Suvorin, A. S. *Ocherki i kartinki.* Vol. 2. SPb, 1875.

Suvorov, N. *O tserkovnykh nakazaniiakh. Opyt issledovaniia po tserkovnomu pravu.* SPb, 1876.

Svetlov, P. "O samoubiistve." *Khristianskoe chtenie*, no. 2 (1897).

Vernoe lekarstvo ot samoubiistva. Kiev, 1913.

Svod Zakonov Rossiiskoi Imperii. 15 vols. SPb, 1835.

Syrkov, I. "Samoubiistva v Moskve v 1908 i 1909 gg." *Izvestiia Moskovskoi gorodskoi dumy*, no. 5 (1910).

Tagantsev, N. S. *O prestupleniiakh protiv zhizni po russkomu pravu.* 2 vols. SPb, 1871.

Tarnovskii, E. "Pobegi arestantov i drugie proisshestviia v mestakh zakliucheniia za 1899–1908 gg." *Tiuremnyi vestnik*, no. 5 (1910).

"Statistika samoubiistva." *Zhurnal Ministerstva iustitsii*, no. 1 (1901).

"Svedeniia o samoubiistvakh v zapadnoi Evrope i v RSFSR za poslednee desiatiletie." *Problemy prestupnosti.* Vol. 1. Moscow and Leningrad, 1926.

Temnyi, Vasilii. *Prichiny samoubiistv.* Moscow, 1910.

Teodorovich, K. *Tragediia detskoi dushi.* Lodz, 1911.

Terekhovko, F. K. "K voprosu o samoubiistve v S.-Peterburge v dvadtsatiletnyi period (1881–1900)." Dissertation for the degree of Doctor of Medicine. Gatchina, 1903.

Tikhomirov, E. *Bessmertie dushi i samoubiistvo.* Moscow, 1879.

Tolstoi, L. N. and Grigorii Petrov. *O samoubiistve.* Moscow, 1910.

Toluzakov, S. "Oni i my." *Pedagogicheskii sbornik*, no. 6 (1908).

Trakhtenberg, A. "O samoubiistvakh sredi uchashchikhsia." *Russkaia shkola*, no. 11 (1908).

"Zarazitel'nost' samoubiistva." *Birzhevye vedomosti* (May 6, 1908).

Trefolev, L. N., ed. "Predsmertnoe zaveshchanie russkogo ateista." *Istoricheskii vestnik*, no. 1 (1883).

"Tri sluchaia samoubiistv." *Grazhdanin*, no. 23 (1873).

Troitskii, A. "Narodnoe verovanie v rusalok." *Penzenskie eparkhial'nye vedomosti*, no. 19 (1892).

Trudy komissii sostavleniia zakonov: Proekt ugolovnogo ustava. Vol. 3. SPb, 1822.

Trudy pervogo s"ezda otechestvennykh psikhiatrov. SPb, 1887.

Tsederbaum, V. N. "Samoubiistva i obshchestvennye sobytiia v Rossii." *Trudy XI Pirogovskogo s"ezda*, P. N. Bulatov, ed. Vol. 3. SPb, 1913.

[Tsyperovich, G. V.] "L. F. Ianovich v ssylke." *Byloe*, no. 12 (1906).

Tsyperovich, G. V. *Za poliarnym krugom. Desiat' let ssylki v Kolymske.* SPb, 1907.

Turnov, A. N. "Poniatiia krest'ian Orlovskoi gubernii o prirode fizicheskoi i dukhovnoi." *Zapiski imp. Russkogo geograficheskogo obshchestva po otdeleniiu etnografiia.* Vol. 2. SPb, 1869.

Uchebatov, A. "Samoubiistva i organy doznaniia." *Raboche-krest'ianskaia militsiia*, no. 7/8 (1924).

"Uedinenie." *Pokoiashchiisia trudoliubets*, pt. 4 (1785).

Ugolovnoe ulozhenie. Proekt, izmennyi Ministrom Iustitsii po soglasheniiu s Predse-datelem Vysochaishe uchrezhdennoi Redaktsionnoi kommissii. SPb, 1898.

Ul'ianova, A. "Samoubiistva detei." *Svobodnoe vospitanie*, nos. 8, 9 (1909–10).

Ulozhenie o nakazaniiakh ugolovnykh i ispravitel'nykh. SPb, 1845 (revised edn: 1866, 1913).

"Umershie nasil'stvenno i vnezapno v Rossiiskoi Imperii v 1888–1893 gg." *Vremennik Tsentral'nogo statisticheskogo komiteta MVD*, vol. 41 (1897).

Unicus. *O samoubiitsakh nashego vremeni.* Nizhnii Novgorod, 1910.

Uspenskii, D. I. "Pokhoronnye prichitaniia." *Etnograficheskoe obozrenie*, no. 2/3 (1892).

V. B-k. "Samoubiistva vo Frantsii (Pis'mo iz Parizha)." *Nedelia*, no. 34 (1897).

Vagner, V. "Samoubiistvo i filosofskii pessimizm." *Zaprosy zhizni*, no. 49 (1912).

Velskii, Arkadii. "Shkol'nyi gipnoz (Iz zapisok pedagoga)." *Vestnik Evropy*, no. 5 (1910).

Ventin, A. "K statistike repressii v Rossii (Iz itogov 1908–1909 g)." *Sovremennyi mir*, no. 4 (1910).

Vekhi: Sbornik statei o russkoi intelligentsii. Moscow, 1909.

Veselovskii, K. S. *Opyty nravstvennoi statistiki Rossii.* SPb, 1847.

Vigdorchik, N. "Politicheskie psikhozy i politicheskie samoubiistva." *Obrazovanie*, no. 12 (1907).

Vladykin, B. V. "Otravleniia uksusnoi essentsiei po dannym gorodskoi Petropavlovskoi bol'nitsy za vremia c 1904-go po 1910-yi god (vkliuchitel'no)." *Russkii vrach*, no. 38 (1912).

Voinstvenskii, Sv. Pavel. "Zagrobnoe sostoianie samoubiitsy." *Strannik*, (Aug., 1866).

Vol'skii, V. "Traurnyi progress." *Sovremennyi mir*, no. 6 (1912).

Vorms, N. "Samoubiitsa." *Sovremennik*, no. 8 (1865).

Vostokov, A. A., ed. *Proekty ugolovnogo ulozheniia 1754–1766 godov.* SPb, 1882.

Vremennik Tsentral'nogo statisticheskogo komiteta MVD. Series.

Vysotskii, N. "Zadachi shkoly v bor'be s samoubiistvami uchashchikhsia." *Russkaia shkola*, nos. 4, 5/6 (1910).

Z. "Nel'zia ne govorit' eshche i eshche (Po povodu ekzamenov)." *Svobodnoe vospitanie*, no. 4 (1914–15).

Zagorskii, P. "Smertnost' v S.-Peterburge v 1878." *SSSM*, no. 2 (1880).

Zaitsev, I. K. "Vospominaniia starogo uchitelia I. K. Zaitseva." *Russkaia starina* (June 1887).

Zaslavskii, D. "Dni nashei zhizni." *Novaia zhizn'*, no. 11 (1911).

Zavadskii-Krasnopol'skii, V. A. *Smert' i samoubiistvo.* Petrograd, 1915.

Zelenin, D. K. *Izbrannye trudy. Stat'i po dukhovnoi kul'ture, 1901–1913.* Moscow, 1994.

Ocherki russkoi mifologii: Umershie neestestvennoiu smert'iu i rusalki. Petrograd, 1916. Reprint: Moscow, 1995.

Zhbankov, D. "K statistike samoubiistv v 1905–11 godakh." *Prakticheskii vrach*, nos. 34–36, 38 (1912).

"O samoubiistvakh v poslednie gody." *Russkoe bogatstvo*, no. 4 (1909).

"O samoubiistvakh v poslednee vremia." *Prakticheskii vrach*, nos. 26–29 (1906).

"Polovaia prestupnost'." *Sovremennyi mir*, no. 7 (1909).

"Polovaia vakkhanaliia i polovye nasiliia: Pir vo vremia chumy." *Prakticheskii vrach*, nos. 17–19 (1908).

"Sovremennye samoubiistva." *Sovremennyi mir*, no. 3 (1910).

Zhebunev, Sergei. "Otryvki iz vospominanii." *Byloe*, no. 5 (1907).

Zhertva razlada: Prichiny samoubiistv po V. S. Solov'evu i Tiutchevu. SPb, 1908.

Zhukovskii, M. "O vliianii obshchestvennykh sobytii na razvitii dushevnykh zabole-vanii." *VPKAG*, no. 3 (1907).

"Znamenitel'naia mogil'naia nadpis'." *Grazhdanin*, no. 19 (1873).

Zolotarev, S. "Deti revoliutsii." *Russkaia shkola*, no. 3 (1907).

Zubov, I. O., "O samoubiistve." *Vrachebnaia gazeta*, nos. 44, 45 (1912).

"Samoubiistvo v Lifliandskoi gubernii (Mediko-statisticheskii ocherk)." *VOGSPM*, nos. 5, 6 (1902).

"Samoubiistvo vo flote." *Meditsinskie pribavleniia k morskomu sborniku*, no. 3 (1906).

Index

2056448R00214

Printed in Great Britain
by Amazon.co.uk, Ltd.,
Marston Gate.